Frances Sanger Mossiker was born in Dallas in 1906. She attended the Hockaday School and went on to study French and Romance languages at Smith College, Barnard College and the Sorbonne. Her first book, *The Queen's Necklace*, was published in 1961. She was also the author of *Napoleon and Josephine* (1964), *The Affair of the Poisons* (1969), *More Than a Queen: The Life of Josephine Bonaparte* (1971), *Pocahontas: The Life and Legend* (1976), and *Madame de Sévigné: A Life and Letters* (1983). The *New York Times* said on her death on 9 May 1975: 'She wrote in a way that combined painstaking attention to detail with a lively style that made her a bestselling author on both sides of the Atlantic.'

The Queen's Necklace

by Frances Mossiker

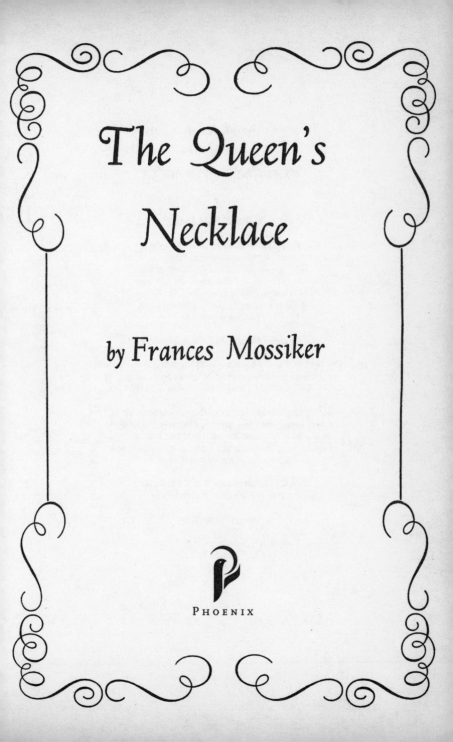

PHOENIX

To my husband, Jacob Mossiker,
and
my mother, Evelyn Sanger

A PHOENIX PAPERBACK

First published in Great Britain in 1961
by Victor Gollancz Ltd
This paperback edition published in 2004
by Phoenix,
an imprint of Orion Books Ltd,
Orion House, 5 Upper St Martin's Lane,
London WC2H 9EA

A CIP catalogue record for this book
is available from the British Library.

ISBN 1 84212 614 8

Printed and bound in Great Britain by
Clays Ltd, St Ives plc

Acknowledgments

I here express my gratitude to those who gave so generously of their time and services in my behalf: to His Excellency, Wiley T. Buchanan, Chief of Protocol of the State Department, for his good offices in providing entrée to the United States Information Service of the American Embassy in Paris, where I enjoyed the co-operation and assistance of Mr. Harold Kaplan, serving in 1957 as cultural attaché, and of Mme. Anne-Marie Degory, special assistant to the attaché, who facilitated and expedited my research in the French libraries, archives and museums. My special thanks to M. Bernard Mahieu of the Archives de France; to Mme. Janine Roncato, Mlle. Nicole Villa, Mlle. Chabrier and M. Jacques Lethève of the Bibliothèque Nationale; to the staff of the Bibliothèque Mazarine; to the staff of the curators' offices of the palaces of Versailles and Trianon; to Mme. Bonnefous, conférencière, Monuments Historiques (Ministère de l'Éducation). My warmest thanks to Miss Hibernia Turbeville, law librarian, Southwestern Legal Foundation of Dallas, Texas, for her resourcefulness and untiring exertions in scouring the libraries of the United States for hard-to-find books requisite to the preliminary study of l'Affaire du Collier; to Mr. Alan Bromberg, professor of law, Southern Methodist University, Dallas, for sympathetic critique as well as for assistance in interpretation of ancien-régime legal procedure; to Miss Dorothy Dignam of N. W. Ayer and Son for gemmological expertise; above all, to my editor, Mr. Robert Gottlieb, for invaluable directives and ineffable understanding.

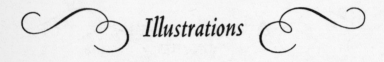

Illustrations

The Count and Countess de La Motte

The Count and Countess Cagliostro

Cardinal Prince Louis de Rohan

Marie Antoinette

Louis XVI

Mademoiselle Leguay d'Oliva

Mademoiselle d'Oliva with Count de La Motte at the Palais Royal

The Queen's Necklace, composed of 647 diamonds weighing a total of 2,800 carats

Countess de La Motte escapes from the Salpêtrière prison: crossing the Seine near the Bastille

The Countess and her maid, disguised as peasants, continuing their journey on foot

Marie Antoinette, surrounded by an admiring entourage, shortly after the birth of her son on October 22, 1781

A scandalous little vignette, showing Marie Antoinette and the Duchess de Polignac in deep embrace

A cartoon: Marie Antoinette is represented as a harpy, tearing up *The Rights of Man* with her claws

A cartoon: 'The holy family steps across from the Tuileries to Montmidy'

The Palace of Versailles by Jacques Rigaud

The Bastille by Jacques Rigaud

Contents

CONTENTS

Introduction

THE DIAMOND NECKLACE AFFAIR? The Queen's necklace? L'Affaire du Collier? Nearly everyone remembers vaguely, remembers something, sometime heard, somewhere read . . . Was it Dumas? Carlyle? A biography of Marie Antoinette? A film? A textbook on European history?

No history of France ever fails to mention it—it is a chapter unto itself in many—the incident that set off, sparked the French Revolution, giving definition and direction to the new world trend toward democracy and republicanism.

Napoleon's eagle eye fastened upon it almost as soon as it happened —"The Queen's death must be dated from the Diamond Necklace Trial." And Talleyrand, with statesman's acuity: "Watch out for this diamond necklace business. It may well rock the throne of France."

Not the cause. The causes, deep down, rumbling, had been already present for generations. The only question was, in Carlyle's words, "Through what crack . . . what crevice, what crater will the French explosion carry itself?" That of the diamond necklace affair, as contemporaries analyzed and subsequent historians endorsed—the diamond necklace affair, to the French Revolution what the Boston Tea Party was to our own.

To judge the impact in its day, it must be translated into terms of twentieth-century personalities: such headlines, say, as "THE QUEEN IN

SECRET MIDNIGHT RENDEZVOUS IN BUCKINGHAM PALACE GARDENS WITH
ARCHBISHOP OF CANTERBURY"; "MILLION-DOLLAR NECKLACE DISAPPEARS—
CHURCH HEAD CLAIMS HE GIFTED QUEEN—PALACE SOURCES DENY"; "MYS-
TERY MAN JAILED IN NECKLACE SCANDAL—CHURCHMAN DEFENDS ASSOCI-
ATE, MASTER-MAGICIAN HOUDINI." And for love interest, as if anything
more were needed: "GLAMOROUS COUNTESS ACCUSED AS ARCHADVEN-
TURESS."

There was a cast of characters exaggerated to the point of grotesquerie
—utterly preposterous, unlifelike, except for the incontrovertible fact
that they lived; lived, breathed, moved, had their being, played out their
incredible roles and shed warm, wet blood in violently dying.

The plot, like the characters, is farfetched, contrived, with an ama-
teurish overabundance of coincidence in violation of all acceptable
dramatic formulas. No self-respecting playwright would risk a critical
drubbing for such a concoction of unlikely story—improbable, impossible, except that it happened. Dumas refused to concede himself out-
Dumased and tried to squeeze the Necklace Case characters into his
sure-fire melodramatic novel form; with The Queen's Necklace he failed
miserably for once, paled by reality. Goethe, in Faust, could make the
characterization of Mephistopheles dramatically credible, but he could
not do as much in his Der Gross-Cophta for Count Cagliostro, a flesh-
and-blood hero—whose flesh was not yet dust at the time of publication.

Carlyle had better luck with the essay form, with his "Diamond Necklace" in 1833. Where his friend Goethe had been emotionally distressed by the recondite implications of the case, Carlyle was simply outraged: "That unutterable business of the diamond necklace," that
"mud-volcano of a Cardinal," that "mass of delirious incoherences," that
"Great Quack-Face of Cagliostro" and "that fair irrational [Countess]
. . . untamable as a fly." That an antic such as theirs should have
affected the orderly processes of world history so distressed Carlyle's
nice sense of the historical proprieties that he rejected every word of
their firsthand accounts, particularly the leading lady's several autobiographies, which he dismissed en masse with a disdainful "Strange volumes!
Cheerfully admitting them all to be lies . . ." He refused to recognize
what present-day criminologists hold to be accepted fact: Let a man talk
lengthily enough about himself, and he cannot keep from telling some
part of the truth; even a simile can be as revealing as a Rorschach test.

Sainte-Beuve saw such things realistically: "The original documents
are all there, available, such as they are. They reveal or they conceal, but

they are convincing. Whatever we accept today as historical fact we have had to accept on those terms." For the necklace scandal can count dozens of reporters. Every one of the five defendants in the great Necklace Case Trial left his own "True Story of My Life," or a bosom friend or a counselor at law to write it for him. (If it appears from the instance of the diamond necklace story that almost everyone in the eighteenth century wrote his memoirs, it was, happily, a century of graceful, witty, felicitous self-expression in both the spoken and the written word—in conversation, in correspondence, in journals, in memoirs.)

First came the stories of the five principals as told by them to their lawyers, the defense pleas drawn up by legal counsel in refutation of the Crown's charges: trial briefs for the Countess de La Motte-Valois, Cardinal Prince de Rohan, Count Cagliostro, Rétaux de Villette and Mademoiselle Le Guay d'Oliva.

Secondly there are the memoirs and other publications personally authored by four of the notorious defendants: the Countess, Villette, Cagliostro and the Count de La Motte.

And lastly there is extant a purple patch of souvenirs by three supernumeraries, published posthumously by their heirs, executors or editors, and running into numerous editions to satisfy a public curiosity whetted keener still, rather than diminishing, with the passing decades: by Count Beugnot, the Countess de La Motte's first and perhaps most serious romantic interest, by the Abbé Georgel, secretary and vicar general to Prince Louis de Rohan, and by Madame Campan, first lady in waiting to the Queen.

In other men's novels and dramas, the star performers and the supporting players of the necklace drama act out their real-life roles unconvincingly, like automatons twitched on a string through a series of fantastic motions by an eccentric hand. In their own memoirs, life stories, diaries, souvenirs, in their own words on police blotters, on lawcourt documents above their own signatures, they suck in the breath of life again, protest their innocence, shrill out claims for justice, vindication or just plain sympathy. Once invoked, they are not easily exorcised. Impassioned, passionate, theirs are no pale shades, their fires are not quenched. They are importunate, clamorous: "Let me tell it! I was there, wasn't I?"

They tell it here. For the first time since they originally told or wrote it, they give their own versions, in their own words, with the original inflections.

I relinquish the telling to them gladly, standing by only to serve as moderator when they turn upon one another—accusing, damning, denouncing, betraying—or to comment on glaring discrepancies in the various accounts and on the contradictions which abound (the Countess de La Motte-Valois being apt, in the second edition of her memoirs, to contradict herself in the first, while Count Beugnot and Rétaux de Villette, both credited with having enjoyed the lady's favors, start off by making a controversial point of "the perfections of her snowy bosom"); and to serve also in the capacity of cicerone* through that maze of print and manuscript which has been called "the greatest lie of the eighteenth century."

For not only are there extant these piquant firsthand accounts by the cast proper, there is as well a mass of reportage by contemporary gossipmongers, in both the professional and the nonprofessional categories. All the newspapers of Europe carried reports of the case throughout the dozen-odd sensation-packed months of the trial's progress. Additionally, there were the semiprofessional journalists, bringing out pamphlets, handbills and broadsheets off fly-by-night hand presses—the racy, spicy feuilles volantes hawked along the Champs Élysées and under the arcades of the Palais-Royal.

Most amazing of all, however, is the fact that, with only three exceptions, all the official records and documents of the trial, hundreds of painstakingly handwritten pages, are still there (the bulk of them in the Archives de France): the dossiers of the prosecutor general for the Crown and the president of the Parliament of Paris, the highest judicial body of the ancien régime; the notebooks and memoranda (scribbles, jottings, doodles) of the various defense attorneys; the entire series of formal interrogations, confrontations and depositions, each properly signed by defendants and witnesses and sealed and attested by the court officials; the minutes of the trial proper; the verdict, vote by vote. The collection even includes the Bastille records on the Diamond Necklace Case prisoners (somehow saved from the rioters on that first and most spontaneously celebrated of Bastille Days, the one of 1789). What is amazing is that this accumulation of material should have survived the revolutionary looting and government-office chaos as Citizens' Commit-

* And interpreter, translating all of the documentation from the original French (for the first time in extenso).

tees succeeded Kings, as Emperors succeeded Consuls and Directors, and Presidents took over from these.

Not only are all the original documents of the necklace drama still there for the researcher to examine, but so are all the places save only the Bastille, and where the stage sets are not yet struck he can ponder them too and attempt to reconstruct the action as it took place thereon: the palaces of Versailles and Trianon for backdrops unparalleled in splendor and glamour; in Paris, the Palais de Justice, central seat of justice to the capital today as it was in the days of the Necklace Trial, on the Left Bank the grim hulk of the Salpêtrière lowering over the Seine and the Botanical Gardens, and across the river the imposing Hôtel de Rohan, a veritable palace, the Paris residence of the Rohan princes. While close by, at Number 10 Rue St. Gilles, there stands the Countess de La Motte's handsome town house, the gates of the carriage entrance gone but the wheel ruts of her elaborate equipages still visible, cut deep into the cobblestones of the spacious courtyard. From the Rue St. Gilles it is only another hundred steps farther to the corner of the Boulevard Beaumarchais, to the site of the once elegant mansion of the Man of Mystery, Count Cagliostro, third member of that select, suspect, sinister coterie. It may be a product of the imagination, but there is a hangover of mystery, something baroque and disquieting about the place, with its deep, dark courtyards, its walled-up secret staircase, with its green-and-gold tracery of a serpent barely discernible under the flaking whitewash below the cornice.

Given such a treasure trove of source material and documentation surviving from the Necklace Trial (there is no testimony so striking as that at firsthand), the obvious question that comes to mind is why the spate of previous historians has not seized upon so apt a narrative form. The memoirs of the persons directly involved in the necklace affair have been frequently quoted, but fragmentarily, in brief excerpts only, brief excerpts meticulously extracted to support the particular version of the case to which the particular author subscribed—the biographers, like the characters they describe, having all been (or having all become) obsessed: their obsession, to impose their personal interpretation, their own solution of the puzzle upon history.

The treacherous, trompe l'œil landscape upon which the plot unfolds is the Court of Versailles, with its intrigues and counterintrigues, its cabals and camarillas. On its throne, at the time of the necklace intrigue, sat Louis XVI, whose ancestors had "bequeathed him a revolution," in the words of Mignet, an avant-garde revolutionary politico.

The original bequest from Louis XIV, le Roi Soleil, was glory—in arms, in politics, in the arts—and, to enshrine it, the Palace of Versailles, the thousand-windowed, the gilded. But everything about the Sun King, the Grand Monarque, was on the grand scale, excessive, even his life span; his reign from 1643 to 1715 was overlong, overexposure for France to "sun" and glory. The first symptoms of national economic decline appeared in the years of that monarch's most popular successes. "France was ruined long before she had ceased to be victorious," is the way Alexis de Tocqueville put it.

The glories of the Sun King's reign shone on well into that of his successor, great-grandson Louis XV, le Bien-Aimé, who seemed well content to bask in the afterglow—a Louis so well-beloved by his people that when he fell dangerously ill in 1744, campaigning with his troops at Metz, six thousand masses were paid for and intoned at Notre Dame alone for the recovery of that young Apollo-Mars of a monarch. Later, however (later by thirty years of self-indulgence in inglorious military and amorous exploits, in a record squander of personal and national resources), Louis's people grew manifestly less fond, so that when he died of smallpox in 1774 only three paid masses for his soul were recorded at Notre Dame, and very little mourning. His blackened, putrefying body was carted off hastily, unceremoniously, to the royal vaults at St.-Denis, and a grandson, the Dauphin Louis, and Marie Antoinette, the radiant young Dauphine, were proclaimed King and Queen.

Louis XVI: neither a Sun King nor a Well-Beloved; no sobriquet inspired by awe, no nickname redolent of affection ever softened the edges of his Roman numerals. Louis XVI was doubly ill-starred in that, unlike his two immediate predecessors, he could neither play the King nor look it, whereas either talent might have served to hold Marie Antoinette, essentially a very feminine creature.

Louis XVI's ancestors had bequeathed him, in addition to the Palace of Versailles and what was left of the glory, a crushing national debt, the feudal caste system with its privileges and impositions dating back to the Middle Ages, an outmoded, ramshackle, stalling machinery of government and, along with these, the aforementioned Revolution.

The monarchy slapped at the gadflies, exiling Voltaire, imprisoning Beaumarchais, while Louis, in a curious and feeble expression of royal pique against Benjamin Franklin, commissioned the Royal Sèvres Manufactory to reproduce the popular engraving of the popular ambassador in the bottom of a pastel porcelain chamber pot!*

Louis could no more cope with a Franklin (or a Voltaire, a Rousseau or a Beaumarchais) than he could expunge the image of liberty which had suddenly taken shape in the mind's eye of eighteenth-century man—although where this inept sovereign failed it is unlikely that even a Grand Monarque could have succeeded. France was in a ferment of unrest, with every Frenchman muttering at his lot and railing against the past and all the institutions of the past. It now seems clear, however, that the defection of the nobility carried the gravest threat to throne and Church. How strange a spectacle, how striking a phenomenon, that of the nation's greatest noblemen renouncing their splendorous birthrights by repudiation of their fundamental fealties.

The aristocrat-intellectuals of the eighteenth century, their raison d'être—the administrative function—pulled out from beneath their feet by a jealous monarchy in the preceding century, were everywhere to be seen flirting with the dangers of democracy and republicanism, just as the capitalist-democrat-intellectuals of the twentieth century would be seen flirting with the perils of Communism.

With revolution imminent in France, the diamond necklace scandal, breaking in 1785, served to spark and set it off. The incident was not only an incitement but an allegory epitomizing the state of the nation, the abuses of Church and State responsible for the riot. The diamond necklace, the great jewel itself, might be said to have been the blazing, shimmering symbol of the exquisite, the extravagant, the prodigal era, while the characters of the necklace drama, as in the cast of a morality play, personified the virtues and vices of the ancien régime.

If previous recitals of the necklace story are subject to criticism for their prejudices and passions, this one is pledged to editorial objectivity. Whatever conclusions may have been reached out of extensive research by this editor, they shall not be imposed upon the reader. It is my proposition, rather, to do him the courtesy of allowing him the exercise of his own wits upon the puzzle.

Provided he be provided with suitable introductions to all the personalities involved and with the pith of the evidence compiled for the judges on the benches of Parliament—then the reader has as good a

---

* The chamber-pot (vase de nuit) story is a "little-known anecdote" related by Madame Campan in her memoirs.

chance and as clear a right as any man before or after him to resolve the problem, to draw up his own indictment, to nominate his own candidates for victim and for victimizer, to distinguish between guile and candor, to descry the wolf in sheep's clothing and to pick him (or her) out from among the flock of lambs all bleating innocence.

As one of them, the Countess de La Motte, puts it:

The philosophical reader, the moralist, will find here ample material for reflection on the depravity of human nature; the political scientist will be gratified by discovery of the clues to obscure political intrigues on the carpet at the time of the international negotiations described herein; the superficial reader—he who reads purely for pleasure —will be rewarded with the solution to a mystery which, as I am generally assured, continues to excite the greatest curiosity.

PART ONE

The Luminaries

The Countess de La Motte-Valois

(1756-1770)

STORY OF MY LIFE*
BY THE COUNTESS DE LA MOTTE-VALOIS

I HAVE DREAD REVELATIONS to make here; I must rip away the veil shrouding the past, name names so exalted I dared not breathe them until I had, by a miracle, reached the shores of this land of liberty. But now continued silence on my part can only accredit the charges hurled against me; Honor ever more imperiously commands me speak. Still, sensitive feminine creature that I am, I shrink from picking up the pen to expose the intimate details, the innermost secrets of my life. How many times the pen has slipped from trembling fingers, tears blotting out the words faster than I could write! Far easier it would have been to sing out my sorrows to the remotest echoes, like the lonely nightingale. But this too is part of my cruel destiny, to be denied even the privilege of privacy and seclusion. Notoriety and slander pursue me across the seas; I must await the hours of darkness and of night to venture out, to avoid the stares of the curious.

What else could I expect—I whose name was disastrously linked with

---

* Vie de Jeanne de Saint-Rémy de Valois *is the title of the Countess's autobiography, which was published in French* (London, 1791, *and* Paris, 1792), *but the book will be referred to informally herein as the* Story of My Life.

that of a great queen and of a prince clad in the Roman purple, I who was caught up in an extraordinary chain of circumstances, its mainspring a diamond necklace, its culmination a celebrated trial, and over all such mystery as to provoke endless conjecture? No wonder the eyes of Europe and the world fasten upon me! Thus far, the guilty have triumphed; bribery, treachery, secret political intrigues have made a scapegoat of the Countess de La Motte-Valois.

This is the reader's introduction to Jeanne de Saint-Rémy de Valois, Countess de La Motte—Countess, that is, until the dawn of the more democratic days of the French Revolution, when, politic as ever, she discarded the aristocratic title in favor of a simple "Citizeness" or "Madame," signing her numerous volumes as "Çi-Devant Comtesse," erstwhile Countess.

Historians and biographers are prompt to make the charge of "congenital, accomplished liar" against the Countess, but the truly amazing story of her illustrious origins in combination with the humblest beginnings, as she tells it here, is incontestably true—fact, not fiction, and verified by the authorities on the genealogy and quarterings of the French nobility. If, in other sections of her Story of My Life, she lapses into the "romantic," she would have stood ready—resourceful as she always was—with the justification that such embellishment has always been accepted practice among good storytellers, in which company she indubitably belonged.

So it does not seem sporting, here in the opening chapters, to issue the customary warnings to the reader to beware of her highly colored, egocentric version of the sequence of events; there will be time enough later to point out discrepancies and contradictions. Why not, here, hear her out on both her origins and her early history, which go unchallenged in the main by both contemporary and subsequent biographers? Here, where she puts her best foot forward (a "tiny, exquisite foot," in the hyperbole of one of her panegyrists), writing her heart out to win over her audience; all elegance here, all prunes-and-prisms, capitalizing the virtues (Injured Innocence and Honor, Imperious Pride), Clarissa Harloweish, possibly patterning her dulcet tones after those of Richardson's mawkish heroine.

But the Countess de La Motte is consistently inconsistent, even in matters of literary style: on this page the grande dame, the noble soul, mellifluous; on the next page the fishwife, the vixen, vituperative, forget-

ting to mince her oaths in roundly damning her enemies, or, reverting to
the genre of her illustrious ancestress Marguerite de Navarre, earthy,
ribald, telling racy stories, patois anecdotes about "good peasants" on
her ancestral acres in the province of Champagne, slapping her delicately
rounded thigh and laughing to split her sides (or "dampen her dress," as
she twice relates, obviously to her own great merriment).

Irresistible, irrepressible, she was an extraordinary woman even for her
own extraordinary age, and recognized as such: the villainess if not the
heroine, the chief protagonist if not the villainess, of the most celebrated cause célèbre of the eighteenth century; by all odds, the archetype
of the archadventuress and the femme fatale, exerting a fatal fascination
upon the men with whom she came in contact, from adolescence on—
beginning with her foster father and the bishop of her diocese.

She moved in an aura of beauty, "a certain piquancy, an air which
men call radiance," to hear her tell it, and to hear the legion of her
memoir-writing admirers tell it in their catalogue of her attractions, head
to toe—even her archenemy and nemesis, the Jesuit Georgel, conceding
the point by his recurrent references to her as "that Circe."

An enchantress, the Countess, in person and in personality, with
charms enough to charm the very birds out of the trees—a brilliant
cardinal out of the highest hierarchical branches, and all the cocks of the
walk of her day—to eat tamely out of her hand alongside her cuckoo
(some said cuckold)of a husband; a flock of gulls and pigeons, plus an
occasional bird of prey, a raven of her own feather. Beguiling, bewitch-
ing, the Countess de La Motte-Valois, fascinating to the drab female of
the species as well as to the male, when and if and as it served her purpose to exert her charms to coax them to her hand. A femme fatale in the
literal sense of the word, "born under an evil star, a strange fatality at-
taching itself to my life (the curse of the Valois), and not to mine alone,
but touching the lives of all connected with me."

So she writes about herself in her Story of My Life:

Now friends and strangers, just and unprejudiced judges, press about
me, urging me to give my version and the forthright story of my life, in
justification of my conduct, in vindication of my tarnished reputation.
Not that I have ever been indifferent to public opinion; I care deeply
for, and pray hereby to regain, the precious esteem not only of this generous English nation which gives me refuge but of my own beloved native land as well.

At last the time has come; I can hesitate no longer, torn between the yearning to prove my innocence and the reluctance to bring shame upon the illustrious personages to whom I was once attached by bonds of loyalty and reverence.

It was not that Her Most Christian Majesty Marie Antoinette, Queen of France, and His Eminence Cardinal Prince de Rohan willfully worked my destruction, but rather it happened that in the terrible clash of their terrible personal intrigues, I was caught up between and, like an atom, smashed.* There, then, at last I have named them, those celebrated figures once so dear to me: the generous Prince to whom I vowed eternal gratitude, the enchanting Queen whom I can say I literally worshiped and the image of whose lovely face I must force, even now, from my memory if I am to find the courage to go on.

But I make no apology for the revelations that are to follow; they contain the defense of my Injured Innocence and Honor, which is justification enough for publication. They contain, as well, a confession of my indiscretions and my follies, as I have confessed them daily, on my knees, before Him who reads in the depths of souls. I hasten to avow them to the public, for, having dared use the word "Honor," I can already see the smirks and smiles of the malicious. Well, then, here is admission of mistakes and weaknesses enough to satisfy my enemies. Is it not, however, a monstrous self-righteousness which condemns the weak for the very reason that they were not born strong? Candidly, such was my lot, and that of countless others like me. Rumor has painted me the heroine of many a gallant episode. If I have been too susceptible to love, may the reader be not too impervious to condonation. Alas! Nourished on humiliation, with tears' salt to season it, I will make no vain display of pride here; all I reclaim of Honor is that small portion to which the lowliest clings when convinced of his good intentions.

Yes, I have been guilty of mistakes; the most serious was that I became the accomplice—and pawn—of persons in such high places that I had no

___

* These are literally the Countess's words—"un atome écrasé," an eighteenth-century term of reference to the pre-Socratic doctrine of atomism. Throughout I have avoided taking liberties in translation of the French texts and have been scrupulous in using only the actual words of the author quoted, or the words attributed by an author to another. The one liberty I have taken with the texts of the copious literary works of the Countess de La Motte is that of treating them as one, so long as they are authenticated publications originating with her, drawing now from the first or second edition of her memoirs, now from her two-volume Story of My Life, or again from her trial briefs, defense pleas, petitions, pamphlets, brochures and holograph letters, as well as from her signed statements, depositions and interrogations, in the official records of the Diamond Necklace Trial.

chance to survive in the rarefied air of their lofty spheres. These powerful interests, with tentacles and agents reaching across frontiers and seas,
have, the reader may be sure, made every effort to keep this exposé out
of print. Threats have succeeded bribes. With what scorn I have disdained both, the reader may also surmise. One last vain attempt—more
offers of gold from the French court—held up the presses until this very
moment. But if I do not spare others, neither shall I spare myself. I shall
tell it all, relentlessly flick a scalpel across that period of my life which is
an anguish to reopen and remember. I shall proceed to the dissection of
my own soul.

My autobiographical task is the more difficult in that I am not a professional writer. I make no pretense to literary achievement here; it is
only the outpouring of an outraged heart. No matter. Innocence has its
own eloquence, sorrow its own accents, despair its own compelling disorder.* With that my story should be readable. So I will write, and I dare
to hope that the world—and posterity—will weigh the evidence impartially before they judge me: either acquit me with honor or condemn
me for eternity.

I was born thirty-four years ago in Fontette in the French province of
Champagne, and of illustrious origin, fatal origin perhaps, but one my
enemies cannot disprove—nor I deny, even were it to my greater happiness. Blood royal flows in my veins. Retrace five generations on my family tree, and you come upon a king.

In the official register of French peerage, there stands the record of my
genealogy, certified by that final authority, Monsieur d'Hozier de
Sérigny, judge-at-arms of the nobility of France. It verifies my direct descent from King Henri II of the house of Valois, which, as I need remind no student of French history, gave the nation its most valorous
rulers. By his mistress, Lady Nicole de Savigny, Baroness de Saint-Rémy,
King Henri had a son, the founder of our line, whom he recognized and
legitimized by a single official act encompassing both, as was then legal
custom, granting him the title of Henri de Valois, Baron de Saint-
Rémy, along with high places in the court, knight of the King's Order,

---

* There is justification for the Countess's use here of the word "disorder" to describe
her narrative form and elsewhere of the adjective "slapdash" in reference to her literary style, but the implication that her book is simply the "outpouring" of an amateur is not strictly accurate. She herself acknowledges enjoying editorial supervision
by her current "protector" and coexpatriate in London, Count de Calonne (like his
mistress, an inveterate enemy of the Queen), and she says, furthermore, "Former Finance Minister Calonne recommended a literary man to assist me with the proper
format for my memoirs, to annotate and edit the outpourings of my outraged heart."

gentleman of the King's bedchamber, colonel of regiments of cavalry and foot, governor of Châteauvilain. As was likewise the royal custom, a marriage was arranged for the Lady Nicole with a gentleman of suitable rank, one of the King's knights; whereupon she retired to the estates the King had provided for her and their son, to the rich properties of Fontette, St.-Rémy, Châtellier, Essoyes, Noez and Beauvoir in northeastern France. These, in 1590, she bequeathed to their son along with a handsome monetary endowment which, as she stated in her will, "the late King bestowed on me in 1558 as patrimony for Henri Monsieur, our son."

In 1559, only a year after assuring this legal patrimony to his son, King Henri II, famed as a valiant warrior, fell accidentally but mortally wounded by one of his own knights in a tournament in the courtyard of his Paris palace. It seemed a curse had fallen on the house of Valois, for, of Henri's three sons, each reigning briefly, not one had issue; so that when the last of these, King Henri III, was struck down by the fanatic blade of an assassin monk, the line of the Valois came to an end. And the way to the throne was opened to a cousin, King Henri IV, of the Bourbon family (with incontestably the clearest claim after the Valois).

In the years that followed, my ancestors, generation after generation, held posts of prominence and distinction in the court of their kings and highest rank in their nation's armies. They deemed it tactful, however, to drop their Valois title, contenting themselves with that of Baron de Saint-Rémy instead, lest they give offense by a reminder, even in name, of a historically older, though superseded, royal-family branch.

If I have lengthily described my lineage (and if I further include in print the supporting genealogical charts in this autobiography), the reader may be sure that it is no boastful gesture by which I invite him to inspect it, but because I honestly believe that it is an indispensable factor in the story of my life; it is the justification of the earliest stirrings of my innate ambition, the motivation for my every act from childhood on. Without it, there can be no understanding of the real Jeanne de Saint-Rémy de Valois.

If it is vanity on my part to point to my father's lineage, is it not humility to point out that my mother, Marie Jossel, was the concierge's daughter, herself a servant maid in the Château de Fontette? Her uncommon beauty attracted my father's eye; her quick peasant wit informed her that he might be in a highly susceptible state in the aftermath of a blighted romance, a broken engagement to the daughter of a neighboring countess. With feminine wiles, Mademoiselle Jossel made the advances, and my father found consolation in the arms of the pretty serving wench. Their romance soon reached a degree of intimacy which obliged my father, by marriage, to repair his mistress' honor and legitimize their coming child. His father, however, an inflexible and proud old man, seeing only dishonor to an illustrious name, refused permission for six full years. My father, at the age of thirty-six, despairing of parental assent, married Marie Jossel in the church at Langres, a nearby town where they had been living, and by a second ceremony legitimized the son of their union, my brother Jacques.

A year later, upon my grandfather's death, my parents could return to the ancestral château at Fontette, where I was born on July 22, 1756.

The very day upon which she saw my grandfather into his tomb and my father in possession of his inheritance, my mother, breaking out after years of inhibition, revealed herself in her true colors: without morals as without education, with low and vicious instincts, vulgar tastes, disreputable passions. To cap the climax, her disastrous fecundity assured tne honors of paternity to her husband the Baron at least once a year. Several of the children died; a girl, Marianne, who lived, evoked in my mother only resentment at further sacrifices in her personal pleasures and adornment.

Unfortunately my father now broke the centuries-old family tradition whereby almost every male member had taken up the noble profession of arms in the service of king and country. May my tongue cleave to my palate, my hand be paralyzed by Supreme Justice if I show disrespect to the man whom I called father and dearly loved, but I am committed to the truth and must admit that nature, while endowing my father with a sensitive soul and a kindly heart, denied him the strength of character necessary to meet the vicissitudes of life. He was weak, indolent and a slave to his passion for his wife, and he was enticed by her into carousal and debauch in company with her peasant relatives and vulgar friends.

What a glaring example my mother was of a person elevated to a sphere too far above her own without compensation for lowly origin! In truth, though, she benefited little from what she had envisaged as a lofty sphere. She had hoped to move through the Château de Fontette now as chatelaine instead of concierge, but the four round towers were crumbling into the moat, and the upper stories, roofless and open to the rain, soon became uninhabitable.

Admittedly, preceding generations had made gradual inroads into the

vast original land grants made by King Henri II to his son, the founder
of our line, the estates of Noez, Beauvoir, Essoyes, Gros Bois, Châtellier
having been sold or hypothecated. Even so, at this juncture wise administration and economies might have preserved the rest of the great ancestral domains. Instead my father, to satisfy his wife's incessant extravagances, began dissipating, acre by acre, the remaining Fontette estate a
few miles from the town of Bar-sur-Aube; the farm, the granary for
storage of crops and produce, the vineyards and several sections of forest
and pasture—these slipped through his fingers one by one as needed to
meet some urgency. Well-to-do farmers of the region were only too ready
to open their purses to my father on usurers' terms to acquire the long-
coveted fields of Fontette, which my father, with no business acumen,
disposed of, though not by legal transfer—he simply yielded or ceded
them, often without signature or written instrument. Ah, let me pass in
silence over the years and the deprivations which consummated the ruin
of the fortunes of a family founded by the son of a king and say only
that, in time, we were reduced to actual want.

Will the reader grant me indulgence here to sketch the portrait of the
woman who wielded such fatal influence over my father? She was tall,
with elegance in her bearing and an intriguingly enigmatic expression
in her long-lashed blue eyes; lustrous dark-brown hair, falling in ringlets
to her shoulders, enhanced the alabaster of her skin. Add a mind un-
schooled but quick to comprehension, a gift for lively if not brilliant
repartee, and you have a catalogue of charms so potent that even a man
older and wiser than my father might have been unable to resist. Such
was my mother, such were her attractions. Is it any wonder she was vain
and, with her capricious nature and violent moods, soon dragged her
husband into the maddest enterprise of all?

She persuaded herself that she was a fool to waste her young life
in this dull provincial village where creditors pressed and neighbors
mocked at her discreditable beginnings. Why, with her beauty and her
husband's titles, it was to Paris they should go! To my father she represented it as the one hope for repairing the breach in the family fortunes,
the one hope for restoring the ancient splendor of the family name.
Where but in the capital could they remind the nation of its responsibility to the last descendants of its most glorious line of kings? Where but
at the Court and Palace of Versailles remind the Bourbon monarch of his
obligations to his Valois cousins?

This was the chimera that enticed my father to his destruction.

Stripped now of the last of his regal patrimony, or believing himself to be (in his mental confusion), he was to abandon Fontette, the cradle and the grave of his forefathers. He would carry with him, as his only treasure, the papers describing the properties that had once been his—a box of crumpled, crumbling parchments instead of fertile soil. He would renounce the tranquil rustic life to plunge without friends or sponsors, without influence as without resources, into the maelstrom of the wicked, cruel city.

It was on a dark and terrifying night that we left Fontette, my parents, my brother Jacques and I. For—can I bring the reader to believe an act at which nature shudders?—our unnatural mother had abandoned our sister Marianne, a babe in arms, to the tender mercies of a mercenary farmer, one Durand. How it distresses me, even now, to recall the perils to which that innocent little creature was exposed—tucked into a reed basket, like a female Moses, and with scarcely enough cover to protect her from freezing in the bitter cold! My mother tiptoed up at midnight to Durand's house and hung the basket on a window, then darted back into the shadows where my father, my brother and I stood watching helplessly. . . .

And what had I to expect from such a mother, except to be her second victim? Only four at the time, I still adored her, followed at her every step when she showed me a mood of affection. Worst of all to me seemed the capriciousness of her behavior. I have always wondered if hers was a considered cruelty, if she could have taken a perverse pleasure in a child's uncertainty whether to expect a blow or a caress.

All I know is that these experiences of mental shock and emotional anguish left indelible traces, never to be alleviated by the passage of all the years.

Only the four of us, then, set out on the long road to Paris, our parents dragging my brother and me by the hand when our footsteps lagged. Our resources being insufficient for more than an occasional fare on the public coaches, most of the journey* was made in short day's stages, afoot. Even so, by the time we came to the outskirts of Paris our funds were very nearly exhausted.

The next day my mother introduced me to a procedure I found exceeding strange. Leading me into a local cabaret, she instructed me to go around among the tables, hold out my hand and speak these words: "Kind lady, kind gentleman, take pity on a little orphan child who de-

* Bar-sur-Aube is approximately 150 miles from Paris.

scends in a direct line from Henri the Second, one of your country's greatest kings."

This extraordinary beggar's patter could not but excite curiosity. Some people questioned me sympathetically and rewarded me with coins; others shoved me roughly aside with a curse or threat which sent me flying back to my mother—only to be thrust back to my frightening rounds.

In the days that followed she devised other techniques. Selecting a busy street, she would walk along holding my hand while I spoke my beggar's plea. Seeing the tears streaming down her cheeks, too young to know she could summon them at will, I broke into accompanying sobs. When a passer-by showed interest, she would display the charts of our genealogy, the sole possession of value remaining to us, and unroll, as prize exhibit, the parchment scroll with a sketch of our family coat of arms (to a child's eyes a thing of beauty, the sole such in our drab existence): the silver shield crossed by azure bars, and three golden fleur-de-lis, royal lilies of France, all surmounted by a crown. The lettering beneath comprised the Valois motto or device, proud words I had learned proudly to recite: "From my ancestor, the King, I derive my name, the lilies and my blood."

It is notable, however, that never in my father's presence did my mother put me through these beggar's paces.

The original purpose of our expedition to the capital had been to recover the family legacies, but my father was never the one to have achieved it. In six months' time he had sunk into apathy and melancholia, and his intellectual capacities had deteriorated to the point where his wife treated and governed him like a child. It was her decision to go to Versailles, for, if ever a chance should come to present his petitions and his claims, it would be at the King's palace, at his court. But unfortunately we had to move on after three months; the royal Versailles police were stricter in the matter of public morals than any other in the Paris region, and they made it impossible for my mother to pursue, on the royal city's streets, that most shameful of all professions—which she had, by now, embraced.

We made the rounds of the Paris suburbs: from Versailles to Boulogne, from Boulogne to St.-Cloud, and then back to Boulogne again, settling there because of kind Father Enoch, the parish priest, our good and only friend, a compassionate man who ministered to our needs. To him my father entrusted the box of precious family papers, in order that he might verify what he called "this curious story" of ours. The good father also promised to sort out the great mass of documents—birth, marriage and death certificates, land deeds, titles and liens—for these, he explained, must be put in order before he could present them to the prominent parishioners, influential noblemen and government officials whom he hoped to interest in our case.

We had only this good priest to whom to turn on the day my father, innocently walking in the forest park of St.-Cloud, was arrested by a mounted policeman, who confiscated his credentials and violated the respect due a man of noble birth by throwing him into a common prison for common criminals. Not until weeks later could Father Enoch ascertain the charges against him: suspicion of imposture, unlawful appropriation of the Valois name and titles.

Father Enoch's petition showing the legitimacy of these claims finally reached the hands of the King's Minister of Justice; but six weeks' imprisonment had mortally impaired my father's health, and the order for his release had to be accompanied by another order—for his transportation and admittance to the public hospital, the grim Hôtel-Dieu of Paris. A carriage was provided to deliver him from the arms of the law into the arms of charity, in which tender embrace he would expire. I do not know whether my father was properly grateful for this great concession on the part of the nation which his ancestors had served so gloriously, this signal distinction which could be attributed solely, mind you, to his royal lineage!

My mother took my brother and me to Paris to see him. Ah, the poignant sadness of that last meeting with our fond and contrite father! It is ineradicably engraved into my heart, for although I was only five years old I was deeply affected. Despite his weakness he held out his arms to me, and I flew into them. He spoke to me in tones so low I could hardly hear: "Poor child . . . if only I could live long enough to watch over you while you are so young . . . but I must abandon you to your mother . . . oh, God! What a mother! . . ." Gasps or sobs cut off his words; then: "Remember one thing, child, remember always, remember every day of your life—*you are a Valois!* Never dishonor the name!"

Those were the last words I heard him speak. I was snatched from his side; the next day he was dead. His death was an irreparable loss. In defense of me, against my mother, he had made the one stand of firmness in his life. Now I was without friend or defender.

The very day of my father's death my mother was delivered of another child, a girl, Marguerite. And not much more than three months later she took up with a dashing soldier named Raimond, a native of Sardinia.

Whether at the instance of the landlord or because of the remonstrance of the priest, the pair soon moved on to the village of Chaillot, where no one would know or bother them, and to lodgings befitting our abject poverty: one miserable room with a single poor bed for Raimond and my mother, a heap of straw as pallet for the children—upon which, I might add, I considered myself fortunate to lie when I could find a place beside the other two.

My brother, with a small stool and brushes, bootblack equipment, was sent out to practice his trade on the streets, and I to beg again. With a quota set hopelessly high at ten sols for weekdays, twenty sols—one franc—for Sundays and holidays. To rally pity more effectively, my mother loaded my sister Marguerite upon my back; she was a tiny baby, but heavy for the shoulders of a girl of six. My father's words were still ringing in my ears, but my mother's threats were louder still, and so, with shame written on my face and a tremor in my voice, I solicited public charity.

When passers-by accused me of barefaced lies or of reciting the lesson of some clever professional mendicant, I tearfully protested that I had the story from my father on his deathbed. That if they didn't believe me, they could go ask Father Enoch in Boulogne; he would tell them I spoke the truth. Child that I was, already I seemed to have an awareness, an understanding of what it meant to have Valois blood in my veins; already, certainly, I felt the first stirrings of Valois pride in my soul. What would my illustrious ancestors have said could they have foreseen that a daughter of their race would one day be reduced to such indignity, their glorious name prostituted, their honor tarnished? Only extreme fear of my mother kept me at the loathsome calling.

Even so, I could seldom manage to collect the sum she had set me; often I took shelter under a doorway or in a stable, preferring the night and the cold to her punishment. But I could seldom escape. Raimond would search the alleys and lead me home, trembling like a lamb that meekly bends its neck to the slaughter. My mother would close our door, strip off my few miserable rags and fall upon me so furiously with her rod as to rip off pieces of my skin. Nor was that the end of the punishment. Raimond used to tie me to the foot of the bed, and if I dared cry out in pain during the night my mother would return even more viciously to her beating, until the rod broke in her hand. Thus I was assigned early lessons in the school of Adversity; Patience became my familiar Virtue.

By this time, Raimond had appropriated my father's title, along with his widow. Calling himself Baron de Valois and flourishing the family credentials, he had the effrontery to station himself for public begging in so prominent a spot as the Place Louis XV* in Paris. To give the devil his due, Raimond, as I remember him, carried off with a flourish the role he had so impudently assumed. He had the physical endowments for it. His bearing was noble, his face interesting, and he looked more aristocratic than most aristocrats. It was easy to believe that here was a gentleman of noble birth whom fortune had brought low.

The police were less easily taken in; twice they arrested and jailed him for public begging and imposture, the third offense involving consequences more serious than Raimond had bargained for. He was condemned to the pillory—twenty-four hours of it—with head and arms pinioned through the apertures of the wooden frame, to which was affixed a sign bearing a list of the titles he had fraudulently appropriated. In addition, the sentence carried a five-year banishment from France.

The scene of his exposure and public shame was the scene of his impostures, the Place Louis XV. What reason impelled my mother to take young children to witness that horrid spectacle, I do not know. She must have been passionately in love with Raimond, and she showed her anguish, being especially bitter in her reproaches to me for having refused to acknowledge her paramour as my father (and Baron de Valois) in the police questionings, as my brother had been persuaded to do.

The police had granted Raimond one week to recover from his ordeal and make ready for departure. My mother decided to accompany him into exile, telling us and the landlord that she would return shortly. With her lover, she closed the door on the room and her three small children,† leaving one sack of chestnuts as sole provision. Three weeks went by without a word from her, and we owed our subsistence to the charity of neighbors and the few coins I could collect on the streets.

It must have been about a month after our mother deserted us that I went one day, with little Marguerite on my shoulders, to the Passy road, where there was always busy traffic of carriages en route to the country houses and châteaux just outside the gates of Paris. This was the day of

* Now the Place de la Concorde.
† When their mother left them, in 1764, Jacques was nine, Jeanne eight and Marguerite two.

my fateful encounter with the Marquis and Marquise de Boulainvilliers —whether to my fortune or misfortune the reader must himself decide, since I have never been able to.

As I stationed myself at the edge of the broad king's highway, I saw a splendid coach-and-four approaching: the horses with silver-and-blue cockades nodding and silver-and-blue ribbons plaited in their manes; on the box a coachman in a silver hat, beside him two pages, and behind, four grooms riding—all in silver-and-blue liveries, the Boulainvilliers colors; within the carriage, on satin seats, a magnificently clad lady and gentleman. The horses happened to be walking slowly enough for me to hop up on the doorstep, a bouquet of wild flowers in my hand and Marguerite's face visible over my shoulder, her pretty face which I had found to be invariably appealing. The beautiful lady ordered the coachman to halt and regarded us with examining but kindly eye.

"We are poor orphans, madame," I hurried to say, "who lost our father long ago, and our mother a month past, when she deserted us." Then, seeing that the Marquise was listening with interest, I went on quickly to give her a full account of our family history. The Marquis, lolling against the cushions, showed his impatience and reproached his wife for stopping the horses to listen to such nonsense, such tales concocted to work on people's sympathy. But the Marquise, ignoring his ill humor, leaned toward us through the window, patently moved by my recital, and I took courage to answer that it was truth I spoke and that it could be verified by sending a servant to Chaillot to ask our landlord, Monsieur Dufresne.

"It's a fantastic tale," the Marquise conceded, "but I promise you, child, that if your story does prove true, I will replace the mother you have lost. I warn you, on the other hand, if you are lying to me you will be sorry. My husband is Lord High Provost of the city of Paris, and he will see that you are punished if you try to deceive us."

"Oh, no!" I cried. "I would never deceive a lady so kind as you, who takes pity on orphan children!"

Breathless with excitement, I watched the carriage out of sight, then ran all the way home to tell Dufresne and my brother of the adventure —and could prove it all by the gift of the gold piece in my hand.

The very next morning, there, asking questions of the landlord, was one of the Boulainvilliers grooms I had seen the day before; and the landlord confirmed all that I had said. Whereupon the messenger announced that we children were to pack immediately—"Which should not take long, from the looks of this room of yours! Then you are to come on to Passy, this very afternoon. Anyone around there will point out the Boulainvilliers château."

Following his orders, we said goodbye to Dufresne and to the neighbors who had befriended us; then we set off down the road, my brother with our few possessions in his arms, I with the baby, Marguerite, in mine.

When we came to Passy, the first thing we saw was the château on the hill above the Seine, and we presented ourselves at the gatekeeper's lodge. The gatekeeper opened the great gilded iron gates and directed us up the drive, while a servant in blue-and-silver livery ran ahead to advise the Marquise of our arrival.

We were shown into a great hall in the center of which rose a magnificent stairway, all curving marble steps, banisters all trimmed in gold, so splendid that we children stood gaping. At the top of the stairs, a number of fine ladies and gentlemen had come out of the salon to look at us.

The Marquise came down and asked if I remembered her, to which I could breathe a fervent "Yes!" She sent us off in charge of her maids, who were to bathe and properly clothe us, while our brother was turned over to the menservants to undergo a similar metamorphosis.

While we were being scrubbed and bathed, the three Boulainvilliers daughters came in to see us.

"Oh, Maman says you are to be our new little sisters!" the youngest, Mademoiselle de Passy, just my age, exclaimed, and, hugging us, she told us we were to be loved as such. I still remember how I beamed with joy at this blissful turn of fate. What happiness I foresaw in this new life of ours!

For the next two weeks, however, we were confined to our room, for it developed that we were in need of treatment to heal the skin sores of malnutrition, to extirpate the vermin of filth, those horrid concomitants of poverty. As soon as we were pronounced cured the Marquise decided to send my sister and me to a boarding school in Passy kept by a Madame Leclerc, while our brother would attend the husband's academy for boys.

My progress in general over the next two years was so rapid that Madame Leclerc could give my benefactress a flattering report on my intelli-

THE QUEEN'S NECKLACE

gence and application, commenting that it was a pity I had been denied earlier training. (I enjoyed the exercise of my excellent memory, and I had been yearning to learn to write.)

Our schoolmistress sent an equally glowing report on my sister Marguerite, who was only four but showed great promise. Shortly after this occasion, the adorable little creature, a favorite with all who knew her, fell suddenly ill and died of smallpox. The Marquise, in Paris at the time and unaware of the sad event, happened to be starting for a visit to Passy, but just as she left the city gates she heard news of the epidemic raging in the vicinity and, terrified of the disease, ordered the carriage turned back to the city instantly.

This was the first of a series of events that deprived me of seeing the Marquise over a long period of years. At one stroke of cruel fortune, I had lost a beloved sister and a no less beloved foster mother.

During the next five years I was entirely delivered over to the tender mercies of Madame Leclerc, my miserly schoolmistress, who, although my tuition and board were regularly paid, took advantage of the fact that I was, after all, only a poor protégée of the Boulainvilliers' and so set me to the household chores. Thus I became all at once chore girl, cook, laundress, waitress—all things, indeed, save happy or cherished. My schoolmates jeered at a scullery maid with Valois pretensions. I had not one friend or confidante with whom to share my tribulations.

How such menial tasks offended my indomitable pride the reader may readily imagine. I tried to console myself by remembering that at least I now enjoyed good health and a roof over my head and no longer slept in alleyways to escape physical punishment. Yet my periods of calm were brief; resentment at injustice soon flooded back again, engulfing me in my customary melancholy.

I came to reproach my benefactress for inconstancy and caprice. Alas, I did her an injustice. Actually, she never wavered in the devotion she had pledged. If for a long time she seemed to forget me, it was her husband's doing. His heart a stranger to the generosity of hers, he had, from the first encounter, opposed what he termed her "rash gesture"— adoption of three waifs of doubtful origin from off the streets.

But all these are things a child of my age at that time could not know or understand, and so she would consider herself forgotten. Had I but realized, any woman with a soul less noble than that of the Marquise might well have renounced a ward whose protection cost her so dear in marital harmony—now for the reason of avarice, later for another reason *still more evil.*

Not until the time of my First Communion* did I decide, in desperation, to try to reach the Marquise by letter. This bold stroke of mine proved successful; the deceitful Madame Leclerc shortly received orders to bring me to the Boulainvilliers' town house in Paris. A few days later, arrangements were made to apprentice me for a three-year period to a Mademoiselle Lamarche, the Marquise's dressmaker, the most popular in the capital.

It was my moody and restless nature, I suppose, which prevented me from applying myself assiduously enough to training in this profession. At any rate, I fear I showed little talent for it.

Talent enough and assiduity went into her unceasing efforts to establish her Valois claims, prodding Father Enoch at Boulogne into continuing his already extensive correspondence with the Fontette authorities, which at length produced important documents, records of the original deeds and titles to the ancestral properties in that region, all of which, at the Marquise's instructions, were promptly forwarded to her.

And shortly thereafter Jeanne was summoned to the Boulainvilliers' to "meet with a number of their prominent government and political friends," who accorded her "a most flattering reception," she says.

My curious family history and bright prospects were the main topics of conversation. Questioned exhaustively as to my family and my father, I gave them every detail memory could supply. Expressing their interest and sympathy in my cause, they yet recommended patience, since such matters were necessarily subject to delay and complications. Still, enough encouraging words were spoken to lead me to hope that my affairs would now at last be brought to the attention of those ministers of the King empowered to deal with restitution of the Valois claims and titles.

But when dinner was announced and I was dismissed, it struck me as ironical that I should be obliged to leave the salon to return to a seamstress' bench—to turn up the hem of a dress that might be worn tomorrow by one of the great ladies who had received me so graciously today.

If Mademoiselle Lamarche was one of the most fashionable couturières

* *This was in 1770, when Jeanne was fourteen.*

in Paris, she was also one of the busiest, and the heavy work was hardly appropriate for a person with a constitution as delicate as mine. The long wearying hours, added to my other problems and concerns, induced a fever, diagnosed as virulent; whereupon I was installed in a spacious apartment at the Boulainvilliers' residence. My illness lasted six weeks, and I had only just entered upon a state of convalescence when I was sent back to work, to another modiste, a Madame de Boussol, at the stupendous salary of two hundred francs a year.*

The new situation being even more disagreeable than the last, I suffered a relapse which brought on convulsions so severe that two women were required to nurse me. These soon perceived, from words escaping me in my delirium, that it was the wounds of the soul which expressed themselves in symptoms of pain that racked the body. The end of four months found me still not completely recovered, a walking skeleton, but the Marquise, inexorably determined, sent me back to Madame de Boussol's, still so weak that I fainted away over the worktable.

Now does the reader at length begin to find mystifying this course of action on the part of the Marquise for whom I have claimed nobility of soul? Inconsistency between her supposed benevolence and the apparent disregard for my well-being? If I have postponed giving the key to the enigma, it is because of my reluctance to expose the true character of my benefactress's husband, a man who should have served as father to me but who assumed the title only to disguise his sinister motives.

I was only a girl of fourteen when I left the school in Passy, but my early budding figure had already flowered into full and perfect womanhood. It would be unbecoming in me, surely, to enumerate my personal attractions. Indeed, it is difficult for a woman to gauge her charms who has been much exposed to masculine adulation, to whom men pay insidious compliments. So I will keep silence on that score and confine myself to the observation that my appearance, be it as it may have been,

---

* Approximately forty-five dollars. The term "francs" used here and throughout refers to the ancien régime franc d'or, or gold franc, which had a value different from that of the modern republican silver franc. It is of course impossible to express that value accurately in terms of the American dollar, which did not exist before 1794, but an approximation can be made based on the rate of exchange in use shortly after the dollar was established. On that basis, the pre-1786 gold franc had a value of approximately 22.75 cents—slightly less than four and a half to the dollar.

In many of the French documents and other sources I used for this book, the monetary amounts were expressed in livres. Inasmuch as the livre, a money of account, had the value of the old franc d'or and was commonly referred to by that name, I have chosen for the sake of uniformity to use the term "franc" or "gold franc" throughout.

sufficiently impressed the Marquis de Boulainvilliers as to inspire his formulating designs upon me.

From the first day he looked at me in Paris, in my white Communion dress, he began to shower me with compliments and gifts of a nature calculated to delight, yet not startle, a heart upon which he planned a surprise attack. At that tender age, susceptible to flattery and attentions, unworldly, unaware of the extent of man's depravity, how could I read a reprobate's soul? In my own naïve one, only gradually were suspicions awakened; in the beginning he so skillfully disguised his motives that even the Marquise was taken in.

And therewith begins a classic story of seduction. Almost one waits for her to say, "And the Villain still pursued me"—and, shortly, she will! Reports of gifts of "silks and satins, gold pieces in ever larger denominations," reaching the Marquise's ear by the backstairs grapevine, won Jeanne the sharpest reproof she had heard to date from those gentle lips, as well as "advice for future conduct." In view of her ward's constantly recurrent "seizures," "fevers," "relapses," the Marquise found herself constantly discomfited, "upon the horns of a dilemma—whether to abandon her ailing ward to a public hospital or to expose her youth and innocence to the wiles of a crafty seducer." In choosing the latter course, she determined "to be on her guard to foil his every maneuver," her ward tells us. "But how can Virtue foresee the trickery of Vice?" Or how forestall the Marquis, slipping to the invalid's bedside—

. . . clasping my wrist ostensibly to check the pulse, touching my brow to test the fever, or even my breast, with the inquiry as to whether I felt any congestion in the region of the lung—all in so fatherly a tone of voice, and even those liberties with my person so perfunctorily performed, as to evoke in me a strange embarrassment at making protest.

At this point, the Marquis, yielding wholly to his guilty passion, transgressed the limits of his erstwhile prudence. Trusting to his last magnificent gift [of a diamond-encircled repeater watch], he chose the midnight hour to consummate my ruin, tiptoeing up the steps and down the hall to the room where I lay sleeping the sleep of the innocent. Gently though he turned the knob, still some sound awakened me, and, startled, I pulled aside the curtains about my bed.

Heavens, what a sight awaited me! The Marquis de Boulainvilliers in robe and slippers, his face barely discernible in the flicker of the hooded lantern he was just preparing to extinguish. Trembling seized my every limb, although the shock of disillusionment exceeded terror. The blindfolds ripped at last from my eyes, I saw no longer a man to be revered as father and protector, but an enemy intent on my downfall! Loathing every benefit hitherto accepted from his hand, indignation expelling former trust, it required no great exertion of virtue to repel his advances.

I spurned his entreaties, promises and menaces alike, and when he moved toward my bed I threatened to awaken the whole house with my screams if he did not leave my room on the instant. At this threat he departed, but not before he had cursed what he termed my "ridiculous obstinacy" and had sworn that I should be made to regret a rebuff for which he would have his vengeance.

From that night on, he was to be my implacable enemy, seeking every occasion to do me harm. Secretly, that is; outwardly, he feigned indifference. . . .

At that juncture, it was back to the weary grind, from Modiste de Boussol to a Madame Coulon, lingerie maker:

Thimble and needle may well be the most suitable practice for my sex, but not for me, and certainly not at a wage of twelve sous a day!

Leaving Madame Coulon's employ, I went to another—only to experience grim proof of the old adage that we never know when we are well off. At Madame Coulon's I had wished myself back at Madame de Boussol's. At Madame de Boussol's I had wished myself back at Mademoiselle Lamarche's. How ardently I now wished myself back at Madame Coulon's when I discovered that I had been sent to work as servant to a servant—a woman who had formerly served in a noble household. In comparison, how enviable the dressmaker's art now seemed to me!

Her new duties included not only the usual household drudgery but the chore of carrying buckets of water up four steep flights of stairs for this "eccentric" . . . who had the habit of daily cold baths!

The supreme indignity! Descended as I was from the First Family of France, a princess of the blood, nature had endowed me at birth with an indomitable pride, but no spirit of resignation. Nor did my foster mother ever seek to inculcate that latter virtue in me; instead, she encouraged in me every manifestation of ambition, which she termed "the inevitable defect of all great souls," and had further stimulated my pride with constant promises of action at court in furtherance of my claims, and with predictions of dazzling prospects and a brilliant future.

I opened my heart to her in these words: "I am sensible of the honor you do me by your patronage, but I was not born to endure the abject state to which I am reduced. I can never forget that my forefathers occupied the highest positions in the court of their King, some of them ruling as governors over the French nation. Why, to them it must have seemed only a brief hour since their family had occupied the throne itself. This is the blood royal that flows in my veins!"

`My benefactress, touched by my outburst, embraced me, her tears of charity and compassion wetting my cheek . . .

And then hastened to explain that efforts at court were not being neglected, but that a formidable stumbling block had been encountered in the person of His Highness the Duke d'Orléans, to whom the Valois title and apanage had been awarded years ago, the Valois line having been thought to be extinct with the disappearance of Jeanne's ancestors from court and capital so long ago.

But efforts in Jeanne's behalf were going forward nevertheless, the Marquise insisted, and, as soon as the papers were in order and incontestable, a petition would be presented by influential Boulainvilliers friends close to the monarch.

Meanwhile, she implored me, "Be patient! You must realize why I cannot keep you here at home. I only regret that it is beyond my power to provide you with the education and maintain you in the station suitable to your illustrious birth and rank—to which, let us hope, the King will one day soon restore you."

The Marquise dismissed me on this encouraging note, but I could not long sustain it, back at my degrading domestic service; my ever smoldering resentments seethed out of control. I compared what I was with what I should have been by virtue of my heritage. I rebelled at a world that denied me my birthright. The injustice of fate became my innermost conviction. How else explain a young Jeanne de Saint-Rémy de Valois, only just struggling up from misery and obscurity, already aspiring to the glory and rank of her ancient, illustrious Valois name?

Physical privations and brutality for childhood trauma, insecurity and frustration for adolescent experience, psychosomatic illness and obsession for maturity: thus might Jeanne de Valois have put it had she been writing in the post-Freudian era. If "soul searching" was an eighteenth-century term for it, as such she dredged up enough to satisfy any competent practitioner of the twentieth-century Freudian art. For what more profound revelation could a psychoanalyst hope?

And if, as she said, "product of a corrupt society, brought up on too lenient an interpretation of the moral code," she clawed, cajoled, connived, scrambled, scrounged her way to the top of the ancien-régime heap, clutching at straws and at coattails, how else to recover her "rightful Valois rank and station"?

Another Becky Sharp. Or, rather, it is Becky Sharp who is another Countess de La Motte-Valois. So many parallels exist between the characters and stories of the two as to give cause to wonder whether Thackeray (writing half a century after the Countess's death and fifteen years after Carlyle's smashing sketch of her in the "Diamond Necklace" essay) may have, consciously or unconsciously, modeled Becky after her.

No Valois, to be sure, Becky yet gave herself what airs she could with mysterious hints at descent from petty Gascon nobility; for both Becky and the Countess de La Motte there was the same drear background of underprivileged youth and slavey school days, breeding the same resentments, the same yearnings after the fleshpots into which they both pried with the same dainty, greedy little fingers; both married great boobies of military husbands; Jeanne snared the premier peer of France, and Becky's Marquis of Steyne was his British counterpart.

The Countess's name, like Becky's, has become a synonym for a fascinating female, engaging, ingratiating; an intriguing intrigante; a bold, tough-fibered, tenacious individualist; a shifty, unscrupulous, conniving woman with her way to make in the great world.

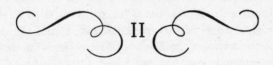

II

Marie Antoinette
and Prince de Rohan

(1770)

IN TYPICAL JEANNE DE VALOIS style, preoccupied, obsessed with herself and her own affairs, that authoress nowhere in her several autobiographies makes mention of the year 1770's most memorable occasion in Paris, in all of France.

One might expect at least some moan of complaint against the extra hours and the heavy duties that spring of 1770 when Jeanne was fourteen and an apprentice to Modiste Lamarche, who must have been swamped with orders for the most sumptuous gowns of many a season for the state functions, balls, receptions, galas and theatricals in honor of the approaching nuptials of the Dauphin Louis-Auguste, Heir Apparent, future King of France, and the Austrian Archduchess Marie Antoinette.

Paris might effervesce with excitement, but Jeanne de Valois's reaction was, predictably, resentful, petulant: If Mademoiselle Lamarche's noble clientele could anticipate a splendid round of revel and ritual, and Mademoiselle herself the clink of gold in the cashbox, what had Jeanne and the other seamstresses to expect but needle-sore fingers, aching backs and eyestrain? They might consider themselves fortunate to obtain so much as half an hour off to catch a fleeting glimpse of the royal procession, which was scheduled to skirt the city of Paris en route to Versailles.

If, however, Jeanne had visited her guardians recently, she could have regaled her co-workers with inside information on the pompous spectacle, since the Marquis de Boulainvilliers, as Provost of Paris, headed the capital's welcoming committee; and if Jeanne had won an invitation to Passy for the great day of May 15, she could have turned the workroom green with envy, for from the Boulainvilliers château on the edge of the Bois de Boulogne (less than half a mile from the King's Château de la Muette, where the royal wedding party was to stop on the last lap of the journey) one would be close enough to hear the violins of the King's orchestra, to see the night sky flare with fireworks; and from the terrace on its heights above the Seine and the Passy road, spectators would have a front-row seat for the whole magnificent procession; might even glimpse the bride herself, that girl of fifteen, born only a year before Jeanne de Valois, but, as Jeanne may have reflected bitterly, to how different a destiny.

All the world loves a lover, a royal lover above all—the twentieth century being no exception, as witness the international hullaballoo over the Windsor idyl, the Princess Margaret romances, the Monaco wedding extravaganza. There was a deeper significance, to be sure, in the curiosity and interest of the French nation in this royal bride and groom. In an absolute monarchy, where the sovereign held power of life and death over his subjects, the character of the new rulers was of vital concern to the populace.

Those who had occasionally seen their Crown Prince, Louis-Auguste, had seen a great hulk of a boy nearly sixteen, heavy of body, blinking out of myopic eyes, a dullard to the casual observer. The people knew little about the Dauphin except that he and his two brothers and two sisters, orphaned early, had been raised by the Countess de Marsan, to whom they had been entrusted by their grandfather, Louis XV, himself too preoccupied with the ministers in his Cabinet and the mistresses in his boudoir to concern himself with his successor—this unpromising, sullen adolescent. No one, least of all the King, bothered to penetrate the unprepossessing exterior to discern the qualities of heart and mind. The King dismissed his grandson with the comment "He's not a normal boy," and an occasional reprimand about his queer tastes for manual labor and lockmaking, or the way he stuffed himself at table.

At the dinner party the night of the wedding at Versailles, the night the union was to be officially consummated, the King, at the head of the royal board, noticed the bridegroom on his right, shoveling in his food, and leaned over to whisper, "Don't overload your stomach tonight."

"Why not?" exclaimed the young husband, loud enough for all to hear. "I always sleep better on a full stomach."

The King glanced at the radiant young creature on his left—a glance of sympathy. If her consort fell short of fairy tale standards for princes, she was the personification of a Princess Charming; on that point practically every contemporary witness is agreed. Whether hers was a valid beauty depended upon the beholder's eye; opinions varied. Apparently she had something better than mere beauty: animation, charm and grace—the illusion of beauty. Her French tutor, Abbé Vermond, a priest given to few enthusiasms, had written enthusiastically to France about his pupil, "You might find faces more classically beautiful, but I doubt if you could find one more attractive." She seemed to "walk in beauty"— she was all grace in motion and, perhaps sensing it as her element, was rarely still: she danced, ran, rode or drove her horses or her sleigh, moved across the stages of her private theaters in utter grace. If opposites attract, here between Marie Antoinette and Louis-Auguste should have been the perfect match: she all animation where her mate was lethargy, all grace to his ungainliness, all sparkle to his lackluster; volatile, mercurial to his stolidity; all fire to his ice.

That ranking connoisseur of female flesh, King Louis XV, pronounced his granddaughter-in-law "enchanting." He sent a messenger galloping off to Vienna the moment she arrived, to tell her mother, the Empress Maria Theresa, "The whole royal family is infatuated with Marie Antoinette." At fifteen, hers was still a budding beauty, and appropriately enough the rose was chosen as her symbol; the artist who had portrayed her face emerging from the heart of unfurling petals was awarded a competition prize by the grandfather-King.

The Empress, negligent heretofore about this child's formal education, had undertaken, immediately before the girl's departure for France, an eleventh-hour study course. The subject: procreation. No birds-and-bees nonsense; this girl's prime function was the succession, the dynasty. When six portraits of the groom arrived in Vienna as gifts for his fiancée, they revealed no face to titillate a bride, but the Empress scolded that romance had nothing to do with international alliances. "Passionate love soon disappears," she warned. "Domestic happiness consists of mutual trust and kindness." But what glowing moonstruck young thing ever heeded such, even if she were being groomed for queenship?

Maria Theresa was aware that Marie Antoinette was "frivolous, *thoughtless, headstrong,"* as she phrased it, but, of the sixteen royal children, the girl was her mother's "delight," her spoiled darling, her fairhaired child for whom the most splendid role had been reserved.

The wedding by proxy took place in Vienna on April 19 amidst pomp and splendor; the procession, 132 persons strong, set out for the French border. At Strasbourg, Marie Antoinette stepped onto French soil. As an eyewitness, a young woman of approximately the same age as the Princess, described it:

The Princess' entry into Strasbourg was a triumph! Oh, if I lived a hundred years I could never forget that day, the fetes, the shouts of acclamation! Her procession from the bridge was sheer magnificence. That night there was a fireworks display to make you think the end of the world had come: a parade of mythological creatures, gods and goddesses of the sea, the Hapsburg and Bourbon coats of arms, the intertwined initials M.A.-L.A.—jewelers' designs in the sky. There was lavish distribution of food to the populace; I saw whole oxen roasting on giant spits, fountains running wine, and loaves of bread so thick on the streets that even the poor did not bother to stoop to pick them up. The whole city was illuminated, the cathedral strung with lanterns from foundation stone to the tip of the cross on the highest spire.

I had the honor of being presented to her, in company with several other young ladies of high rank in the region.

This is the Baroness d'Oberkirch, dashing off an entry in her daily journal, which her grandson would publish fifty years later as a treasure trove to historians. Her sixth sense for the telling trivia, her chitchat as inconsequential and diverting as this morning's Elsa Maxwell column make the Baroness beyond any other the historian's darling. With her little feather duster of a pen, she flicks the dust off dry-as-dust historical personages to reach the persons beneath—a service she performed for most of the crowned heads of Europe in her day, beginning with this blond one of Marie Antoinette's in her diary entry of May 7, 1770.

The Princess received us with a simplicity and graciousness which promptly made devoted subjects of us all. She had a gracious, friendly word and a bouquet for each of us. I still have a spray of lily of the valley from it, pressed in my floral memory book.

The Dauphine was, at fifteen, already quite tall and with a beautiful figure, even if still somewhat on the slim side. Her face, an elongated oval; her features regular, nose aquiline, eyes vivid blue and keen. On her very small mouth was what some might term a slightly disdainful expression. She had the Hapsburg lip, a pronounced version of it. There are simply no words to give an idea of her dazzling complexion, literally a blend of lilies and roses. In her ash-blond hair, swept up from a high forehead, there was only the lightest sprinkling of powder. And, oh, the way she had of holding her head, her queenly carriage, the elegance and grace of her whole person! Irresistible, she won all hearts!

Her Highness was lodged overnight at the Episcopal Palace of Saverne, where the venerable Bishop-Cardinal Prince de Rohan had the honor to welcome his exalted guest.

The next morning his nephew, Prince Louis de Rohan, bishop coadjutor of Strasbourg, received the Princess on the steps of the cathedral. He, instead of his uncle, was to celebrate a special mass and deliver the sermon. Beneath the towering façade he stood awaiting her arrival.

Louis de Rohan's was a splendid and imposing figure—as a man, a prince, a prelate. Handsome, tall, with fine aristocratic features, prematurely gray at thirty-six, in his long scarlet moiré robes, a golden jeweled miter on his brow, he came down to the Princess' carriage and a princess could recognize in him the first nobleman of the realm. The Rohans had been sovereign princes of Brittany; they ranked immediately behind the royal Bourbon family, their cousins, taking precedence over all the other French nobility. Prince Louis, witty, polished, charming, an intellectual, a patron of the arts, the flower of the Rohan clan, was their candidate for even higher honors. "One of those select mortals born to honors —as the sparks fly upward," Carlyle said of him. Already successor-designate to his uncle's bishopric, the richest in all Christendom, he would in all probability be successor to the cardinalate as well (in those prereform days of the Church when bishoprics and cardinalates were considered appanages of the great lords temporal); thence why not the Prime Minister's post, in the tradition of Cardinals Richelieu, Mazarin, Fleury?

Prince Louis knew that he represented his powerful family's hopes in this direction; his blue eyes fastened on the young Princess whose favor would be of utmost importance to his successes. This was an auspicious beginning. Marie Antoinette must always remember that he had given her the official ecclesiastical welcome to her new land. He was not too much older to be friend and companion to this couple who would be

France's next rulers, just enough older to claim respect and confidence.

He saluted Marie Antoinette with the grace and dignity for which he was renowned. From the open doors of the cathedral behind him the mighty organs swelled in full diapason to drown the shouts of acclamation. All fell silent as Prince Louis began his speech, as gallant and affecting a one as might be expected from a man so brilliant that he had been elected while still in his twenties to the French Academy, to the company of the Forty Immortals.

"You will be for us the living image of the beloved Empress whom Europe has so long admired and whom posterity will continue to venerate. The spirit of Maria Theresa is about to unite with the spirit of the Bourbons," he said, and Marie Antoinette's tears evidenced her responsiveness to the caressing voice in its graceful tribute.

Prince-Bishop Louis led her to the high altar. She knelt on the red velvet prie-dieu at the altar's base. Prince Louis lifted the monstrance for the benediction. While silvery notes of harp strings tinkled down from the lofty choir, these two were joined in sacred and intimate communion. His fine hand, with its jeweled bishop's ring, upraised to bestow God's blessing, her head bowed to receive it, they shared the sacrament of benediction—these two who were to destroy each other.

(Baroness d'Oberkirch, who was in the cathedral that day, would be struck by it later. She was to write in her journal, "What strange coincidences there are in life!")

During the next seven days' journey, Marie Antoinette's thoughts may have strayed back to the handsome Alsatian prince-prelate. He could not but have made an impression. Any queries on her part, on his account, would have elicited sidelong glances, little moues, smirks, an air of reluctance to gossipmongery, from her French entourage—before they plunged straightway into gossipmongery: If Her Highness really wanted to know, the Rohans were unbearably overbearing. The French nobility had made recent, if vain, protest to the King about the Rohans' prestige and privileges, outranking them all, walking directly behind the royal family and the princes of the blood.

If Marie Antoinette had not noticed the Rohan motto on the gates of their Strasbourg palaces, her traveling companions would have called it to her attention: "Roy ne puis, prince ne daigne, Rohan je suis . . ." (If I cannot be a king, I disdain to be a prince, the name of Rohan shall suffice . . .)

The Rohans, as was their wont, had monopolized all the highest places at the court. The Countess de Marsan, who had been placed in charge of the upbringing of the Dauphin, the bridegroom himself, and his brothers and sisters, was a Rohan by birth. The Rohans could count three cardinals on the family tree—this one, Prince Louis, confidently expecting to be the fourth.

Whoever took it upon himself to enlighten Marie Antoinette on the subject of Prince Louis was not so naïve as to expect a churchman of great family to be necessarily devout. But this one! No moderation whatsoever! Galloping across the countryside on the hunt from dawn to dusk (a world's record of 1,328 shots in one day, more than two shots a minute for ten straight hours). And the parties in his château at Saverne after the chase, with Tokay flowing, and the gayest women of the province—or still gayer ones imported from the capital! Probably even Vienna had heard the stories about Prince de Rohan and the beauteous Marquise de Marigny, sister-in-law of the dear, dead Pompadour? For a year now the little Marquise had been riding around Europe in the bishop's carriage in the flimsy masquerade of a too pretty choir boy.

But to give the devilish bishop his due, what he lacked in morals he made up in manners. "Charming as charming could be, gallant, magnificent, nobility written on his face, grace in his manner, it was impossible not to enjoy his company even if one was shocked by his frivolousness," was the evaluation of Madame de Genlis, tutor to the Duke d'Orléans' children and mistress to the Duke. "Prince de Rohan was none of the things a man in his exalted position should have been, but no one in any position could be so winning as he. Behind this attractive façade there was overwhelming ambition and ardent passion—with no principles whatsoever to hold them in check."

Marie Antoinette may have been surprised at the gossip about Prince-Bishop Rohan, and yet not too surprised. At the cathedral in Strasbourg he had looked at her with the respect of a subject for his sovereign, but there was always something else in that tender blue gaze of Rohan's, an expression less easily definable, one that gave a desirable woman to know that she was being clearly seen—as a desirable woman.

If Marie Antoinette suspected that her noble informants in the carriage were envious of the almighty Rohan tribe, it was too bad that she repeated their gossip to her mother when, shortly thereafter, Prince Louis was named French ambassador to the straitlaced Vienna court.

But Marie Antoinette must have had a thousand other questions to ask of her French retinue as they neared Versailles, that "thousand-windowed palace": Was it true that a thousand nobles resided there, three thousand liveried servants, that there were two thousand horses in the stables? Her home palace of Schönbrunn was a copy; copies had gone up in every capital of Europe, paltry things compared to the original Versailles was a Seventh Wonder, the most grandiose, most vainglorious gesture of man in his own glorification, acres and acres of marble and stone in terms more pretentious than the Parthenon, St. Peter's, the temples of the Nile or any other to the glory of God.

Under hundreds of triumphal arches, the bridal procession continued its flower-strewn way to Compiègne, where the King, in his impatience, had had the idea to "go out to meet my granddaughter," with the reluctant bridegroom in tow. Marie Antoinette should have been prepared by her mother's warning and the six portraits: hers was no Prince Charming.

The next day, May 15, the gorgeous cavalcade bypassed Paris and went along the Passy road, past the Boulainvilliers' terrace, where Jeanne de Valois may have stood watching with the three Boulainvilliers girls—their father, the Marquis, waving to them from his carriage in the procession as it moved on toward the Château de la Muette. There Marie Antoinette met the royal family: the aunts (the King's three old-maid daughters) and the Count de Provence and the Count d'Artois, her husband's young brothers.

She joyfully spied one familiar face from home—Count Mercy d'Argentau, her mother's trusted friend and ablest diplomat. The Empress had just assigned him as ambassador to France, a tower of strength to stand watch over her daughter. Count Mercy had been in a turmoil all day at a rumor that the King had invited Countess du Barry, his flashy mistress, to join the royal party; and there she was, ablaze with diamonds, the lush blue-eyed blonde, with her superb, experienced body, and Zamor, her four-foot blackamoor page boy in plumed turban, to carry her train while she bowed to the Dauphine.

The next day, May 16—Versailles, and the second wedding in the palace chapel. Six thousand bluebloods had secured admission cards for the privilege of gazing upon twenty-two members of royalty while they dined.

The last act was also public.

The whole court thronged after the royal family to watch the young couple put to bed, the King of France handing his heir the royal nightshirt, the Duchess d'Orléans helping a blushing bride into her gown.

The Archbishop had come from Reims to bless the matrimonial bed and sprinkle it with holy water. All present bowed low and followed the King out the door.

The newlyweds were alone and the royal bed curtains closed about them. They were alone, but it can be known today—as it was to all the lords and ladies of the court some two hundred years ago—exactly what happened. The bridegroom himself wrote it in his diary under the dateline May 17, 1770, in his own handwriting: one word, "Nothing."

A strange situation, it must be regarded now as then. Temporarily explicable in terms of timidity, awkwardness, inexperience, "infantilism," faulty "glandular development." Very possibly so, in the adolescent described consistently as "heavy," "sluggish of mind and body"—and senses.

But when the status quo persisted? A flood of letters from the Austrian Empress to her daughter began to arrive: "Toinette must not be in too great a hurry, for that, by increasing her husband's timidity, will only make matters worse." "Caresses and cajoleries! If you show yourself impatient, you may spoil the whole thing!" "Above all, none of your wicked temper!" The voluminous correspondence between mother and daughter stacked up over ten years, the letters signed "Toinette" in the Vienna State Archives, the mother's in the Paris vaults, box upon box of them, strapped in cardboard cartons, the paper sheets moldery and crumbling, the anguish and concern fresh as a fresh wound.

By the end of the year the Empress had called in her doctors in despair. "If a girl as pretty as Marie Antoinette cannot stir the Dauphin," she wrote to Count Mercy, "then every remedy will be useless."

French court physician Dr. Lassonne thought otherwise. He diagnosed the Dauphin's impotence not as psychogenic but the result of a trifling physical defect, phimosis; the remedy, correction by minor surgery, minor as a circumcision. But the Dauphin, shuddering at the sight of the scalpel to be used without benefit of anesthesia, vacillated, procrastinated, seized on the alternative prescription of "diet and exercise—and time," seven years of it!

If anything could be worse for a sensitive young bride, it was the fact that all this was public knowledge. The succession to the French throne came under the heading of affairs of state; every ambassador at Versailles rushed off daily bulletins to his home capital. In less serious vein, it became a prime topic for persiflage, jingle, caricature to that curious, gossiping court. The Gallic attitude toward sex was then what it is now, and the most popular quiz game of the day called for the answer to "Who will supplant the Dauphin in the Dauphine's bed?"—serious and early damage to a woman's reputation.

What far-reaching effects, even on world history, Dr. Lassonne's scalpel might have had if wielded earlier! Had the future King Louis XVI felt himself man and master in his own bedroom and with his own wife, he might have felt himself man and master in his council chamber, capable of portentous decisions when portentous crises came.

As for the effects on this woman who would be Queen, "according to our present lights and in view of our present social habits, we cannot regard it as physiologically unnatural for a girl to remain virgin until she is two-and-twenty," Stefan Zweig, the first of her myriad biographers to dare to touch upon the delicate problem, wrote in 1933. "But the case was peculiar in this way, in a way that makes uncanny nervous reactions easily explicable. Again and again, for the space of two thousand nights, the husband to whose embraces she was assigned, awkwardly and fruitlessly endeavored to take possession of her youthful body."

Her mother anguished over the situation primarily because an heir was needed to consolidate the alliance, but she never showed the slightest understanding—much less, sympathy—for the obviously neurotic phenomena her child was displaying. No such word as "neurosis" existed, but the pitiful symptoms should have been recognizable under some eighteenth-century term. The strained, high-pitched gaiety, the frantic pursuit after pleasure, the follies of extravagance, the headstrong flouting of etiquette, the cutting edge of the sarcastic mocking tone, the noticeable blushes and tremors at the touch of a gallant's hand! Count Mercy caught the dangerous overtones when Marie Antoinette "went into a few details of the distress of her situation as a married woman." "My dear mother should understand that mine is a difficult situation." "I must have some distraction and I can find it only in more and more amusements." Or, as again to Mercy: "I am terrified of being bored!"

If the "Impasse of the Alcove" was the first topic of conversation at Versailles in 1771, the second was the Marie Antoinette-Du Barry "War over a Word." The word in question: just one civil one, one courteous recognition on the part of the Princess, for which the King's favorite had been waiting tremulously for over a year. By the rigid Versailles code of etiquette, a lady of lower rank must wait until the lady of higher rank addressed her, and First Lady Marie Antoinette let her wait—until the whole ridiculous affair assumed the proportions of an international incident. Empress Maria Theresa must write her child to be gracious to a woman who, in Vienna, would have been shipped off to a reformatory! But Prussia and Russia were pushing Austria into the partition of Poland, and, of all times, now Maria Theresa needed the French King's support.

On January 1, 1772, Marie Antoinette surrendered. As the ladies of the court filed past in the exchange of New Year's greetings, Marie Antoinette allowed her glance to meet the Du Barry's and pronounced nine momentous words: "There is quite a large crowd at Versailles today."

"But that is as far as I shall go," she informed Count Mercy. "Never again shall that creature hear the sound of my voice."

"That creature" never did—and never complained about it, either. Indeed, she seemed somewhat nervous about a victory over a princess who would one day be her Queen. Du Barry's reign would end with her lover's, and he was sixty-two now in 1774 and showing it, the signs of excess and debauch. Message after conciliatory message from the favorite to Marie Antoinette went unacknowledged, but one day inspiration came to Du Barry—in the persons of her jewelers.

Her jewelers were Böhmer and Bassenge, a remarkable pair of young Germans. Bassenge, the aesthete, was the designer, Böhmer, bland, blond, the practical businessman and salesman of the team. "A most amiable man, Böhmer," according to the Paris correspondent of the Imperial Court of St. Petersburg, "and held in high regard for his exquisite taste and a polished manner rarely found among men of his class and trade." Böhmer and Bassenge's glittering creations had made them the rage of fashionable Paris and had won them appointment as court jewelers to the King of Poland.

But the King of Poland was a nothing compared to a Madame du Barry, who was many things to many people, but in truth, as a customer, was a jeweler's dream come true. Entrée to her boudoir such as they enjoyed was a privilege for which peers of the realm and Cabinet ministers vied.

There is reason to suppose that they had come to show her the working sketch for "THE DIAMOND NECKLACE"—all in capital letters, from Böhmer's very intonation—although Böhmer may have professed himself reluctant to show it to her on the drawing board lest Madame la Comtesse become impatient waiting for the reality. And it would take months, he warned, to comb the world markets for gems such as these, huge and flawless; cousins in Istanbul, in Brazil, were on the lookout for him for the diamond necklace stones (most of the jewelers of the day were Jews, as were Böhmer and Bassenge). Böhmer was to go to Hamburg to see a rare stone, a fifteen-carat button stone for the cluster center, and to Amsterdam for the best diamond cutters.

For this was to be the jewel of jewels that Böhmer and Bassenge were confecting, to dazzle the eyes of sultans and kings, even His Most Christian Majesty of France. That the latter would purchase the creation was taken for granted by the jewelers and their patroness alike; Louis XV had lavished the equivalent of over half a million dollars on his Countess in the last sixteen months, and her predilection for diamonds was as certain as death and taxes, the latter being steadily raised to provide the diamonds. If the Du Barry was Louis's foible, her jewel box was her forte.

Böhmer had taken the King's purchase of the jewel for granted in his grand-scale borrowing—the equivalent of some quarter of a million dollars for uncut stones alone, 2,800 carats of them. He was a genius at high finance; not everyone could have arranged for the necessary credit. He had his dreams (or his obsessions), and the diamond necklace was to be the opus magnum, his most ambitious project, a very monument to the jeweler's art. Only the loveliest throat in the world (their patroness's) should wear it.

Proximity to that loveliest throat appears to have overwhelmed all men, so Bassenge may have found difficulty in getting out his words in description of his design: that it was a conceit of his that the necklace, like a great ship or palace or estate, should bear a name, "the Necklace of the Slave"—heavy jeweled chains to fetter a beauteous captive, a Slave of Love, a Queen of Diamonds.

But by then, in all likelihood, the Queen of Diamonds, the Slave of Love, had turned away to try on a pair of girandoles, dripping great pear-shaped gems. (The necklace was still on the drawing board, in the talking stage; the chandelier earrings, reposing on velvet in a leather case, were ready to be fastened to pearly ears, the wire through the lobes, the pendants dangling to the shoulders.)

But Madame du Barry must have quickly laid them back in their case at Böhmer's mention of the fact that he had had the honor of showing these very earrings to the Dauphiness, who had lavishly admired them and, in regretfully refusing purchase, had explained that it was only for reasons of economy.

This was the remark that must have given the Du Barry her inspiration to send a message to the Dauphiness that she, the Countess, would gladly suggest to the King that he present the girandoles as a gift to his granddaughter, if the granddaughter so pleased.

If she so pleased? How dared "that creature" imagine the Dauphine would be beholden to her? The answer was disdain—and silence. Marie Antoinette might have a passion for jewels, but she could afford to wait: all the crown jewels of France would one day fall into her lap.

But would they? There were persons in high places who said that she might well be back in Austria before that prize should fall to her. Madame Campan, who had the sharpest eyes and keenest ears in high places in Versailles at the time, writes in her memoirs that there was talk of annulment of the unconsummated marriage: "Persons in the most important positions at court assured me of the possibility of divorce, and many indications served to confirm the rumor. There was a strong anti-Austrian faction which had opposed the marriage from the beginning . . ." (including the aunts, the King's three daughters, to whose suite Madame Campan was attached as reader). "The Chancellor [Maupeou], who was Madame du Barry's friend, and the powerful Rohan family had not abandoned their opposition even after the wedding, but merely changed tactics. The Dauphin's conduct toward his wife was providing grounds for hope—hope of disrupting the Austrian alliance."

One member of the Du Barry-Rohan clique was Prince-Bishop Louis de Rohan's aunt, the Countess de Marsan. Ill will flared up openly between Marie Antoinette and this "Governess of the Children of France," as was her official title. It began with a careless criticism by Marie Antoinette on the subject of the education of the Dauphin's little sister Madame Elisabeth. "As always in a court," notes Madame Campan, "by nightfall everyone knows what everyone else has said that morning." Countess de Marsan must have bridled. Such impertinence, coming from a chit of a girl whose own education was glaringly defective, whose French was far from fluent, was still sprinkled with Germanicisms! Madame Campan continues:

From that moment on, Countess de Marsan's salon became a hotbed of intrigue—or, rather, slander—against Marie Antoinette; her most inconsequential remarks and actions were misinterpreted, Countess de Marsan making a crime of Marie Antoinette's girlish gaiety and of her innocent, if exuberant, amusements, such as a romping game in the privacy of her own apartments with some of her youngest maids of honor, or the children of her serving women.*

Marie Antoinette might shrug off Countess de Marsan's opinions, but when reprimands on the very same inconsequential misdemeanors came also from her mother, that was something else again.

What she could not understand at first was how reports of such innocent, if exuberant, pranks traveled all the way to Vienna. First she suspected the Austrian ambassador to Versailles, Count Mercy, but his denials convinced her. Moreover, he could point out the talebearer: Prince Louis de Rohan, the new ambassador of France to Austria—that same Adonis of a bishop ("la Belle Éminence") who had made the official speech of welcome to her in Strasbourg Cathedral and impressed her with his melting glance and high-flown phrases about "the spirit of Maria Theresa whom Europe has so long admired." And all the while he had been anti-Austrian, part of the Du Barry clique, to whom he owed his ambassadorial appointment! The hypocrite—he had even come to see her at Versailles just before he left for Vienna, had kissed her hand and asked what messages he might carry "from the noble daughter to the noble mother."

Marie Antoinette could understand that her mother had been taken in too, showing Prince de Rohan high honor in the reception at her Palace of Schönbrunn. The man made a wonderful first impression. But now Marie Antoinette would promptly brief the Empress upon the latest scandalous rumors circulating about him. "It is said," she wrote in a letter to Maria Theresa, "that the bishop coadjutor of Strasbourg will be named to the ambassadorial post in Vienna, replacing Baron de Breteuil. He comes from a mighty house, to be sure, but the life he leads more closely resembles that of a roistering military man than an ecclesiastic . . ."

Prince de Rohan was later to claim, in self-justification, that it was the Empress herself who had insisted on his making reports to her on her daughter, but Madame Campan claims that "he far exceeded the call of duty, was overzealous in his mission, echoing his aunt's unjust criticisms and launching into a series of sneaky denunciations. He constantly

---

* One of the youngest, most rompish maids of honor to Marie Antoinette was Jeanne de Valois's foster sister, the youngest daughter of the Boulainvilliers', Mademoiselle de Passy. A horrified account of one of her most publicized "misdemeanors" appears in a passage from Madame Campan's memoirs in the Appendix.

pictured the young Dauphine as turning all hearts against her by indiscretions offensive to the dignity of the French court. Marie Antoinette could not long remain in doubt as to the source of the slander, and from this period dates the dislike and coolness which she ever afterward manifested to Prince de Rohan."

The Empress sent Baron Neni, her trusted secretary, to Versailles to double-check on her trusted ambassador, Count Mercy, and her daughter. Baron Neni, after making a careful survey of the situation, writes Madame Campan, "advised the Empress that it was an outright case of libel by a hostile faction." Whereupon Maria Theresa instructed Neni to go to the French Foreign Affairs Ministry and request the recall of Ambassador Rohan. Only evasive answers were forthcoming; the almighty Rohans had stepped in to protect the flower of the family.

Marie Antoinette knew they must bide their time, but to her mother the French ambassador became a veritable thorn in her side. What airs these Rohans gave themselves! Parading into her capital like a visiting potentate, with two gilded, lacquered carriages worth forty thousand francs apiece, in a cloud of outriders, in a fanfare of music from his scarlet-clad band, with his stable of fifty horses and his pair of ferocious Heyduc Guards, professional Hungarian strong-arms with plumed bonnets and wicked swords. Shameful French ostentation. Shameful French morals, too, for her straitlaced city. "Frankly, I am nervous about my Vienna ladies," the Empress wrote Mercy. "Young and old, pretty, ugly, all alike are bewitched by the man!" Nervous, too, about her son, Emperor Joseph II, who "loves to chat with Rohan even if it's only to hear his indiscreet gossip, his amusing small talk; he sat beside him at a recent dinner party chattering away for over two hours, about what heaven only knows—except that shortly after my son showed marked interest in making a visit to Paris!"

Likewise horrifying to a pious Empress, a centaur-Nimrod of a bishop, in loud green-and-gold hunting jacket, galloping through a religious procession on a holyday so that he and his fellow sports might get across the street in a hurry to join the chase. Next came the "Case of the Silk Stockings": a wave of contraband French luxury imports smuggled into Vienna under cover of diplomatic pouch, not by Prince de Rohan but by members of his undisciplined embassy staff. There were more Paris-made silk stockings sold in Vienna than in Paris during Rohan's first year there, as Madame Campan heard Marie Antoinette tell it. And when Maria Theresa had to rescind the traditional diplomatic customs immunity she brought down on her head the wrath of the entire diplomatic corps.

Next came the "Dinner Party Incident," a startling innovation in seating arrangements doing away with the traditional one long table to seat one hundred to one hundred fifty guests, frozen in staid formality; instead, a galaxy of small tables for four or six or eight, in gay and intimate circle. Even Count Mercy must have had to smile as he relayed this complaint of her mother's to Marie Antoinette. The success of the novel entertainment, the distinguished and delighted guests lingering on late into the night—therein lay the Empress's grievance; partly piety, partly pique.

"I will not have that man corrupting my nobility!" the Empress roared by courier, a letter doubtlessly amusing to her daughter in Versailles. "That man" was giving her mother a difficult time, turning Viennese society topsy-turvy, although there were grounds for suspicion that Viennese society was heartily enjoying every minute of it.

As Marie Antoinette herself might enjoy it, for to look at the matter in another light, she and Prince de Rohan were making common cause, mutiny against etiquette—she in his native court, he in hers; he harried by her mother, she by his aunt. Actually, this dashing Rohan prince gave every evidence of being a superb host, a gay and diverting companion, and it may well have occurred to the Dauphiness that when he returned to Versailles (where they could do with a few more blithe spirits) he would be a welcome addition to that society—provided, of course, that he gave up that horrid Du Barry clique.

But then Marie Antoinette heard about The Letter, the letter Ambassador Rohan had written to "that creature"—and then it was no longer a laughing matter, not even to Marie Antoinette's blithe spirit.

The first news of the letter reached her the very morning after the Du Barry supper party; for one of the guests present (no one has ever discovered which), it was simply too good a story to keep. Countess du Barry, the story ran, had taken a letter from her purse and read it aloud to the whole hilarious company around her table: Prince de Rohan's top-secret report on the imminent partition of Poland at the hands of Russia, Prussia and Austria, the latter loudly protesting conscientious moral scruples at the rape of a defenseless neighbor.

"I have just come from an audience with the Empress of Austria," Prince de Rohan's letter ran, "and I found her weeping for the woes of persecuted Poland. In one hand she clutched a handkerchief to stanch her tears, in the other a sword to hack out Austria's slice of poor butchered Poland."

Prince de Rohan would later insist that it was not to the Du Barry that his famous sword-and-handkerchief letter had been sent; that, quite properly, this communiqué had been addressed to the French King and the Foreign Affairs Ministry.

Primarily, it was Rohan's bad luck to have composed an epigram witty enough to make the Versailles rounds. Marie Antoinette had been touched to the quick. It was viciousness and insolence, on Rohan's part, to have served up her mother's honor with the dessert at a Du Barry orgy. Damnable insolence and viciousness. Unforgettable, unforgivble.

Her mother pressed her to take action with her husband, the Dauphin, and her grandfather-in-law, the King: "Without bringing formal complaints through regular channels, I shall expect the King to satisfy my honor by ridding me of this reprehensible representative!" But Marie Antoinette must continue to bide her time; she had no influence to do anything about it.

Not only no influence; she was caught up in crosscurrents of intrigue and hostility, astray in a maze of protocol, during those first years at Versailles—even her husband unfriendly, if not hostile, keeping her company only for the miserable, silent public dinners and masses.

So it was good to find one friend, almost her own age, Mademoiselle Genêt (the future Madame Campan), the reader in the old-maid aunts' apartments. The two girls sang duets together, Mademoiselle Genêt playing skillful accompaniment on harp or piano. Mademoiselle Genêt had made a reputation with her "dramatic readings," delighting the Dauphine, whose sole literary taste was for the theater. She made the request that Mademoiselle Genêt be transferred to her retinue as lady in waiting. Even the Countess de Marsan could not disapprove; the erudite Mademoiselle Genêt was of good family, if lesser nobility. Her father, in the diplomatic corps, had hesitated about allowing his daughter to accept the appointment with the elderly princesses. He feared the pitfalls of court life for a young girl, the enmities, the intrigues. "But, oh, the glamour of it!" as the fifteen-year-old exclaims in her memoirs.

A formal court dress of rose silk, pleated down the back, with a train and great panniers—even a little rouge. What a thrill, after a drab schoolgirl's uniform! And the magic aura of grandeur that surrounds royalty, overwhelming to the senses of ordinary mortals! That first day in Mesdames' presence, my heart pounded, my voice trembled, my eyes failed me. What kind of reader must they have thought me—unable to get out a word!

Not long after her assignment to Marie Antoinette's household, an excellent match was arranged for Mademoiselle Genêt, as she explains, with a gentleman by the name of Campan, himself in the Dauphine's provisioning department; his father was official secretary. (This scant line is the first of her two succinct references to her husband in all three volumes of her memoirs.) Louis XVI later provided a handsome dowry, five thousand francs revenue yearly, in addition to Madame Campan's fifty thousand francs yearly stipend for her duties as supervisor of the domestic staff, custodian of accounts, of privy purse and jewel box, and glorified appointment secretary and receptionist who granted or refused admittance to the royal presence and presented visitors to Her Majesty (this was after Marie Antoinette became Queen).

Having drawn this prize plum of a position, Madame Campan might cheerfully depreciate her "superior education and learning," which were not at all to the Queen's taste (she quotes Marie Antoinette as saying, "Deliver me from the intelligentsia!" and "No intellectual could ever be friend of mine" and "Too much wit and learning depress me"). So Madame Campan carefully kept her erudition, like her petticoats, from showing, and consistently turned her lighter side, with no trace of Napoleon's future official pedagogue. If Her Majesty preferred sprightly chatter, a helping hand with the Mercure de France puzzle, Madame Campan could oblige. When it came to small talk, pungent critique on the comedy of morals and manners, she must have been, in person, infinitely diverting; in literature she is, incontestably, a gifted gossip.

Another thing in common was their extravagances, Madame Campan's debts twice involving her in difficulties from which a royally generous hand extracted her. Young matrons, they enjoyed a cozy, easy informality, if not an intimacy—against which old courtier Campan cautioned his daughter-in-law: "The confidante of royalty can hope for, at best, a brief and, inevitably, a dangerous favor."

In any case, theirs proved a successful relation for over twenty years, one of the rare examples of Marie Antoinette's constancy in friendship, a still rarer example of good judgment in her choice of a friend. She could count on Madame Campan to the end—although later, in her memoirs, Madame Campan would protest (too much?) that she had not failed in the "ultimate loyalty." If there were those who claimed otherwise, the counterclaim was based on the theory that had she been loyal she would not have been alive to tell the tale.

Mere quibbling in the backwash of the centuries. We can be content that the rouged and panniered Boswell ("Charmian" Campan) survived to leave a reasonably reliable delineation of Marie Antoinette as a woman rather than a queen ("I shall open the door, so to speak, to the sovereign's private apartments"), in the off-stage, off-throne moments of her life.

One such moment as the scene described in Madame Campan's entry of May 10, 1774, "in a small room in Marie Antoinette's private apartments, where the Dauphin had come to join her, the two of them waiting together there for news of King Louis XV's death." Smallpox had stricken the monarch ten days previously at his hideaway house of Trianon, across the park from Versailles. There was a rule of etiquette for death—as for every occasion—decreeing that a King of France must die in his bed of state, so the sufferer had to be transported back to the palace, where he now lay dying. But the Dauphin, the heir, could not be subjected to contagion.

Madame Campan continues:

Throngs of curiosity seekers milled through the corridors of Versailles, and hundreds of noblemen had jammed into the Oeil-de-Boeuf,* off the dying King's suite . . . Suddenly Marie Antoinette and the Dauphin heard a terrible rumble, as of thunder. It was the stampede of the lords and ladies of the court deserting the old King's apartments, rushing, running to hail the new! Hundreds of footsteps reverberated across the Hall of Mirrors. And it was by this weird sound that Marie Antoinette and the Dauphin learned that their reign had begun.

* The reception room adjoining the King's state apartments and reserved as a waiting room for high-ranking court dignitaries. It took its name from the two distinctive oval, or bull's-eye (oeil-de-boeuf), windows in the domed ceiling.

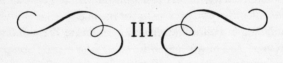

III

Count Beugnot, Monsieur de La Motte and Rétaux de Villette

(1774-1783)

THE HOPES OF FRANCE rose high with the accession of a new, young King and Queen. There is innocence intrinsic in youth. The old King's reign of corruption was over, his wars, mistresses, profligacy no longer to deplete the national treasury or to overwhelm the people, who alone bore the brunt of taxation.

This was a "virtuous young King," clean-living, modest, earnest. Youth's inclination is to liberality, to reform; liberal thought and reform were in the air, in the mind, in the heart; with the new school of French philosopher-Encyclopedists, with Voltaire's explosive thinking and writing, with Rousseau and his daring concept of a "social contract"; with the startling example of the British people's constitution, with the American Revolution brewing.

Reform was indicated for France and her creaking, outmoded, inefficient feudal system. Originally under that system privilege (rank, land, exemption from taxation) had been awarded the nobility in return for services rendered to their vassals: military protection, administration of justice and economic processes, all of them functions of government and considered by the people in the Middle Ages, as government is today, worthy of support. But these services were no longer rendered by the nobles, who were absentee landlords now, having removed from their demesnes to Versailles (and simultaneously, during the reign of Louis XIV, been stripped of their original powers and functions, making them court satellites, national parasites). Thereby they had voided the medieval feudal contract between liege lord and liegeman, but the feudal privileges, obnoxious now to the subject populace, would never be voluntarily yielded from out of the nobility's rigor-mortis clutch.

With the accession of the new King, prospects brightened for Jeanne de Valois, as is reflected in her Story of My Life.

At this point [in 1774], a most interesting development took place in our affairs.

The Marquis de Chabert, my brother's commanding officer in the Navy, had become my foster mother's valued ally in the struggle for restitution of our family rights. Chabert, struck both by my brother Jacques's devotion to duty and by his illustrious lineage, enlisted the aid of his cousin, Monsieur d'Hozier de Sérigny, judge-at-arms of the French nobility, who produced a certificate supporting our claims to the full honors of the house of Valois and delivered it to Chérin, the King's official genealogist. Thereupon things took a sudden turn for the better, and the Marquise hastened to complete final preparations for that long-awaited event, my brother's formal presentation to the King, under his rightful title, Baron de Valois.

My benefactress made a happy surprise of the great occasion. Invited to a dinner party at her house (my first such invitation to dine in company there, a dream come true), I noticed a stranger in the salon, a young man in an old, worn greatcoat, a red kerchief knotted as cravat about his throat, and I wondered what this singular personage could be doing in that society—when suddenly something familiar in his smile, in the sound of his voice, set me trembling. He reminded me of Jacques, only he was handsomer than I remembered him, more polished.

When he cried, "It is your brother who takes you in his arms!" I embraced him, laughing, crying, both at once. He was as stirred by emotion as I.

My heart bounded with joy, and despite my ill humor at being sent back to the dressmaker's I slept not a wink, but spent all the night in breathless anticipation, building castles in Spain!

By May 1, 1775, Jacques was attired "as befitted his high station" and was ready for his introduction to Louis XVI's Prime Minister, the Count de Maurepas, and the Cabinet, the traditional preliminary to presentation at Versailles. And "on that great day the Marquis de Boulainvilliers (our foster father serving as sponsor), the Marquis de Chabert, the Count de Vergennes, the Prime Minister and Finance Minister Necker performed the honors of my brother's presentation to King Louis XVI."

On the subject of the Versailles ritual, Baroness d'Oberkirch from Strasbourg is more informative than Jeanne de Valois:

What a red-letter day it was for me, the day of my presentation to Louis XVI and Marie Antoinette! A flattering ceremony, to be sure, but strenuous and exhausting, involving several days' activity from morn to night without a moment's repose, what with all the preliminary functions and excitements, the required preliminary visits to the King's ministers and court officials.

The indispensable formality of verification of my titles had taken a whole year's time: submission of written proof of nobility patents, which must date back in an unbroken line to 1399, an epoch preceding all so-called "recent ennoblements." Chérin, head of the King's Bureau, verifies the documents, then pronounces as to their authenticity. Anyone who gets past Chérin the Incorruptible, as he is called, has proven his claims beyond the shadow of a doubt.

It was five-thirty in the afternoon when I was introduced into the throne room of Their Majesties. How solemn a moment, with everyone staring at you! How frightening the thought of making a mistake, a clumsy move; you struggle to remember all the lessons in walking backward, the deft kick to your train to avoid catching a heel and tumbling over—the very thought is worse than a nightmare! I made my required obeisances, one at the entrance door, one in the center of the hall, the third before the throne of the Queen, who rose to greet me. Leaving the hall, walking backward, three more obeisances in farewell. Marie Antoinette spoke most graciously to me; the King merely smiled. It is said that His Majesty seldom speaks to those presented to him.

His Majesty did speak, however, to the Baron de Valois, as the latter's sister reports it:

The sovereign thus, at last, acknowledged my brother as scion of a family which had once worn the crown of France, one bearing a name which doubtless this Bourbon monarch would have liked to bring to

46

honorable extinction rather than revive it to public notice. For he recommended that my brother take the vows and join the Church, commenting that it was perhaps "nobler to serve one's God than one's monarch"; whereupon Jacques (who had no taste for an ecclesiastical career) dared make reply that in serving his King he could not fail to serve his God as well. The sovereign of the French, sensible to the wit and justice of the response, then deigned to promise his protection to my brother in the naval career he had chosen.

By a government certificate of May 6, 1775, the title of Baron de Valois was awarded to my brother, that of Mademoiselle de Valois to me, that of Mademoiselle de Saint-Rémy to our sister Marianne. As of the same date, each of us was awarded a brevet specifying a pension of eight hundred francs per annum, payable quarterly and subject to no deduction, the payments to begin December 9, 1775.*

While assuring my foster mother of my eternal gratitude for her endeavors, I could not resist expressing my surprise and disappointment that all her endless solicitations at court in our behalf had resulted in so niggardly a pension from the Crown.† There was, however, some consolation in the Finance Minister's explanation that the important thing was to have obtained recognition of our claims from the King, and that thus we might hope for improvement in our financial status commensurate with improvement in that of the national exchequer, so seriously depleted by the preceding reign.

A court debut so extraordinary as my brother's piqued general curiosity and interest, the newspapers carrying accounts of the event. How directly the vicissitudes of fortune influence public opinion! If fortune smiles upon you, friends surround you, smiling too; if fortune deserts you, your friends do likewise. My life offers proof of this sad fact. No sooner were we recognized as descendants of the Valois than all the

---

* "On record as of December 9, 1775; 800 francs a year as subsistence from the King's Privy Purse accorded to the two ladies of Saint-Rémy de Valois whose origin derives from Henri II." (From Documents de France, Vol. 1382, on file in the Archives de France.)

† Was it so niggardly a gesture on Louis XVI's part, as Mlle. de Valois deems—his pension allotment of 2,400 francs (some $550) yearly to the three Valois scions? Kings are as dismayed as the next man (more so, more being expected of them) at the appearance of poor relations, at several generations' remove. To draw a parallel to the Valois' application to the Bourbons at the Court of Versailles, one might postulate the appearance at the Court of St. James's of a sixth- or seventh-generation descendant of some Hanoverian by-blow. What favors might such a one expect of his distant Windsor cousins on the British throne beyond, perhaps, a "grace and favor house" in Windsor Park and a modest allowance?

world rushed round to cultivate our acquaintance. My pride had always been at a level loftier than my actual station in life, so I was far from overwhelmed at the compliments lavished upon me in this new situation. Rather it seemed to me that such homage had ever been my due, was no more than that to which I had always been entitled.

It was gratifying to hear that our story had caused a stir at Versailles, and the Marquise pressed the advantage, making the rounds of the government bureaus with my brother just before he left for Brest to join his ship; inducing Monsieur Necker to make Jacques an additional grant of five thousand francs toward the purchase of his ensign's commission and other expenses incumbent on a naval officer.

With dazzling new promises to the Marquise by the Cabinet ministers, our hopes soared high, only to be dashed by the strangest of catastrophes . . .

Strange, indeed: "a horrid stench and sickening vapors rising from the basement of the Boulainvilliers' Paris residence, pouring up through every room, out into the streets." The something rotten, in this case, being the Marquis's distillery, "operating clandestinely in an evasion of taxation on the sale of spirituous liquors." The still had exploded, "publishing his shameful subterranean secret to the world!"

An accident resulting in an exile order from the hand of the King, banishing the Boulainvilliers' for many months to their Montgeron estates. The nobility, says the Countess,

. . . taking its cue from the monarch, hurriedly broke off relations; my innocent foster mother, in disgrace through the vile mercantile speculations of her husband (to whom she was so superior in rank and character), found herself abandoned by even her most intimate friends. . . .

My expenses constantly exceeding my income, financial embarrassment soon forced me to accept the Marquis's offer of advances on my pension. By the end of the year, though I had denied myself the barest essentials of living, I found that I had no choice but to anticipate the first two quarters of the following year. There came to me the crushing realization that my elevation had been an empty honor, a chimera of favor and fortune. The congratulations now rang hollow in my ears, as so many taunts and jeers.

If I have seldom mentioned my sister Marianne, it is not that she was ever forgotten, although we had not seen each other since the midnight my mother left her in a basket, hanging on Farmer Durand's window, on our Fontette estate near Bar-sur-Aube. The Marquise de Boulainvilliers had from time to time held out to me the hope of reunion with this long-lost sister, and as soon as the King granted us our pensions she wrote to Durand to instruct that Marianne be brought to Paris.

Finally it came, that longed-for day! Marianne and I had a thousand things to tell each other, a thousand questions to ask, although our hearts were so overflowing that our lips could not shape the words. We were united in transports of delight.

Happy hours that only one sorrow could penetrate! The Marquis de Boulainvilliers had not renounced his plans for my seduction, my resistance served only to inflame his criminal passion. He still pursued me and made openly insulting propositions—such as marrying me to one of his toadies, an arrangement whereby I would be able to stay on in his household without offense to the conventions or damage to my reputation.

Thus things came at last to the point where, to escape his importunities, I had no alternative but to retire to a convent, there to continue my education, and Marianne was disposed to follow me. I had suffered to think that I should be the cause of trouble in a family so dear to me, and I was rewarded by expressions of gratitude from the Boulainvilliers' daughters for my consideration in this matter.

And so, on the thirtieth of March, 1778, Marianne and I entered the Abbey of Longchamps (for young ladies of quality) in the Bois de Boulogne, near Paris. Convent life offered the charm of novelty. I experienced a peace of mind I had not hitherto known—free from worldly delusions which, while promising pleasure, yield only pain, free from the importunities of a man who had become the torment of my life.

I joined the postulants of the convent in their vigils, fasts and prayers, and at the end of seven or eight hours I resolved to take the veil. The Marquise, however, exacted the promise that I wait until I had reached the age of twenty-five before taking the eternal vows. (Oh, would to heaven I had persevered against all opposition!)

It was toward the end of that same year, in December of 1778, that Marianne and I were invited to the Boulainvilliers' Paris town house as guests for the round of festivities attendant on the wedding of their youngest daughter, Mademoiselle de Passy, to the Count de Tonnerre. . . .

The Marquise, regarding us as adopted daughters, treating us as members of the family, included us in all the brilliant social round. Lavishly and elegantly gowned, we were always at the Marquise's side, the object of her attentions, and everyone wanted to know who we were. Not unnaturally, public opinion had it that we enjoyed a fortune commensurate with our rank. We became the center of attraction.

Another, even more prominent guest at the Passy-Tonnerre nuptials stole the show, although Jeanne de Valois fails so much as to mention his name (another example of the puzzling, tantalizing lacunae in her Story of My life). He was Dr. Benjamin Franklin, the Boulainvilliers' neighbor at Passy for most of his seven-year residence in France as ambassador of the new United States.

His marked predilection for the pretty, pert little bride provided subject for banter about the "Sage's" pangs of regret at losing his favorite young female companion—subject for the bon mot of the social season: "How is it, Dr. Franklin," one waggish guest inquired of the popular American, "that as inventor of the famous lightning rod you could not keep thunder [tonnerre] from striking your dear little Mademoiselle de Passy?"

After the wedding and the thrilling Paris visit, the convent at Longchamps had lost its charms for me. Everything seemed depressing, insipid, after Paris, where a brilliant social pageant had unfolded before my eyes, where I had reveled in the pleasures opulence can provide. I cannot express in words how keenly I felt the change. My heart longed for the diversions of the great world. I lived in memory of the capital's delights. I forgot that I had ever sighed for a recluse's life. Not for me to bury myself alive behind convent walls!

Marianne and I, however, had come to realize how impossible it was, on our meager pension, to maintain ourselves in the style befitting the lofty social sphere into which we had been introduced. In our dilemma, we knew we must find some expedient by which to live within our narrow budget, but a proper one at which we need not blush.

It was at this juncture that my sister suggested our going to Bar-sur-Aube; in a small provincial town instead of the opulent capital, perhaps our income would suffice to provide us a decent way of life.

There was another, more compelling motive for the trip to Bar-sur-Aube: to be at the site of our family's ancestral acres, the great domain of Fontette—cradle and grave of every member of our Valois branch, with the sole exception of our father, who, having mortgaged away acre after acre, lay buried in his pauper's grave in Paris. It was an accepted fact that he had not received a tenth part of the real value of the property. Everyone was always telling me that there were legal loopholes, that in many instances the present property holders lacked any record of title or transfer; their only evidence of ownership was a twenty-five-year tenure. I heard it on every side—that with just the slightest influence it should prove feasible to recover the usurped Fontette estate. The Marquise de Boulainvilliers, after preliminary research, counseled us to make on-the-spot investigation and determine once and for all what hope there was for recovery.

Knowing everyone of distinction in the Champagne region, the Marquise had provided us with letters of introduction to her noble friends, recommending us as her protégées and adopted daughters to their attention and patronage.

Thus it was not only with her approval but on her express advice—and with high hope of restoring to its former ancient glory our proud Valois name—that we set out, in 1779,* for Bar-sur-Aube.

Bar-sur-Aube—the town of Bar on the River Aube, in northeast France—toward which Mademoiselle de Valois was heading, could boast a long and interesting history extending back to ancient Gaul. Its encircling walls were more recent, dating from medieval times. Caesar had bivouacked here and so had Charlemagne, rooting about among the toppling columns for souvenirs of his hero.

Centuries-old walls, even in a state of perfect preservation, and assorted Roman ruins and relics were attractions less likely to appeal to a lively young Mademoiselle de Valois than the more vibrant ones of a young man about Bar, dapper, debonair, a lady's man and a handsome one—Jacques Claude Beugnot.

At the time of Mademoiselle de Valois's arrival in Bar-sur-Aube, Beugnot was twenty-one, Paris-educated in the law, a precedent set by his father, the crown representative for legal and tax affairs for the province.

* The Countess de La Motte-Valois, in her own words under oath to the Parliament of Paris in 1786, clears up any confusion that may exist as to time and dates in her early years: "Six years at the pension of Madame Leclerc in Passy; three years with Paris couturières; two years at the home of the Boulainvilliers' subsequent to the award [1775] of pensions from the Crown; two months at the Abbey of Yerres; twenty-one months at the Abbey of Longchamps . . . thence to Bar-sur-Aube [1779-80] . . ."

Well-to-do, of eminently respectable and respected bourgeois stock but not aristocracy—a class distinction a man was never allowed to forget for a single hour of a single class-conscious day—Beugnot was a member, as he writes, of the "young liberal" society of the town. Naturally.

Eager, able, ambitious, he was already set, on the mark, ready to embark on what would prove a brilliant political career, and he would never, never have believed anyone who told him then that it was on his youthful dalliance with the Valois girl that he must rest his hopes for enduring fame.

Entering the political arena in 1789 as home-town delegate to the first National Assembly, Beugnot proved himself an agile political acrobat by being one of the few to come through the guillotine orgy with his head upon his shoulders. The "liberal" of one generation becomes the "conservative" of the next in ordinary times, but the timing of the adage needed acceleration to meet the accelerated ideological transitions of the French Revolution; this year's or this month's "liberal" was next year's, next month's "reactionary" (and traitor) in the eyes of the Jacobin party radicals, who arrested Beugnot along with hundreds of other fellow delegates whose fervor had not kept frantic pace with their own in recent months. A second nimble stunt by Beugnot was landing on his feet, on the very top of the shifting political heap, as a member of Napoleon's administration* and with a fine new Empire title of "Count." But the neatest trick of all must have been his back flip after the restoration of the Bourbon monarchy, into the Council of State under kings Louis XVIII and Charles X—hereditary peer Count Beugnot, with one ministerial portfolio after the other: Interior, Treasury, Marine, Police, Postmaster General.

Having survived the Old Regime, the Revolution, the Directory, the Consulate, the Empire, the Restoration, having run the full spectrum of political coloring from revolutionary blood red to imperial purple, durable Count Beugnot died in his château at Bagneux near Paris, at the azimuth of age and honor, with the Archbishop of Paris in person to administer the last sacraments.

By then everyone, including the Archbishop, had forgotten that the venerable Count Beugnot's name had once been linked with the sensational diamond necklace scandal—until Beugnot's grandson, in 1866,

* Napoleon, from St. Helena, in a letter: "When Beugnot served me as prefect, he could always be relied upon for the truth."

published the grandsire's memoirs. Most of the several volumes devoted to accounts of his turbulent epoch, though wittily and expertly written and interesting to researchers, were seldom off the shelf. Count Beugnot's liaison with the notorious Valois woman was described in Volume One; steadily circulating, this one, reprinted, quoted, gathering no dust:

As a young man in Paris, I met with an adventure which was to cost me the sharpest anxieties and greatest difficulties of a career beset with difficulties and anxieties. This adventure began with the arrival in Paris of a lady later to achieve notoriety under the name of the Countess de La Motte.

To explain how I first made her acquaintance, I must go back to an earlier period of my life, in Bar-sur-Aube, when I was member of a group of young liberals who frequented the society and salon of Madame de Surmont, wife of the Provost General of the city.

One autumn day in 1782,* the whole town was agog about a rumor that two runaway princesses had turned up at—of all places—the Red Head Inn, the most disreputable tavern in a town where the best was none too good. The thought of princesses ensconced in such a spot set us all into gales of laughter. Information forthcoming the next day shed light on the mystery which had shrouded the arrival of the young ladies: The eldest bore the resounding title of Mademoiselle de Valois, her sister that of Mademoiselle de Saint-Rémy. They had run away, we learned, from the Convent of Longchamps and made a beeline for Bar-sur-Aube, where they would make a concerted effort to regain possession of the vast properties which had formed their ancient patrimony. These properties in the region consisted of the great estates of Essoyes and Verpilliers and the domain of Fontette.

When I repeated the story that evening to my family at dinner, it rang a bell in my father's memory. He told us that fifteen or twenty years before, when he used to make yearly trips to Fontette on tax assessment business, the parish priest there never failed to touch my father for his pet charity—"those poor Valois children, a disgrace to the parish." There were three of them, abandoned by their parents, in a tumbledown shack; the neighbors used to shove food scraps in to them through a hole in the wall. "I saw it with my own eyes," my father exclaimed, "although the priest would never open the door wide, wanting to spare

* Beugnot's error. It was 1779.

me the sight of those pitiful tots, half naked, gnawing on bones and crusts like little savages. He assured me my donations would help put clothes on their backs."

My father's account was no exaggeration. He had seen the head of this miserable clan, described him as a man of athletic proportions whose sole means of livelihood had been wild game, stag or deer or boar, which he hunted—or, more accurately, poached—in the forests, and wild fruits and nuts from these forests or, whenever possible, the more cultivated varieties from out his neighbors' fields and orchards. For the last two or three generations, this had been the family's epic way of life—tolerated by the neighbors out of fear, by the authorities out of some old inherent respect for the long-famed Valois name. Only one treasure had been preserved from out of the ruins of the once great Valois fortunes: their genealogy. The Fontette priest forwarded it to Chérin, official genealogist of the King, who proceeded to the examination of the titles and certified their direct descent, in the male line, from the founder of their house, Baron de Valois, natural son of King Henri II.

A certificate from Chérin, that highest authority in the kingdom, was conclusive. And at that point the government took action: King Louis XVI accorded pensions to the three heirs, an appointment to the Royal Naval Academy to the boy and free board and tuition at the Convent of Longchamps for the girls.

At this time, the childhood guardians joined forces with the King's ministers in a common project: to induce the young Valois to take the vows of the Church. It was hoped that the Baron would raise no objection to celibacy in the noble Order of the Knights of Malta, and that his sisters could be persuaded to the veil.

In short, the idea was to propel them gently but firmly into the religious life, in the embrace of which their family and name would be brought to honorable extinction—a family and a name that it would cost the King a fortune to restore to its former estate and glory. The legitimate Valois line was already run out, extinct, back in the misty past. What earthly purpose would it serve to revive this bastard branch? And now, of all times, with the national treasury empty, and the King in need of money for a host of other more important things! This was a practical and sensible solution from the King's point of view, and it might well have succeeded had not Mademoiselle de Valois been endowed by nature with resourcefulness equal to frustrating the maneuver.

The brother in the Navy had attained the rank of ship's lieutenant and the sisters had spent six years at the Convent of Longchamps, when one fine morning the two young ladies, with the lightest of bundles under arm and the slenderest of purses in pocket, climbed over the convent wall to try their fortunes in the great world outside.

Mademoiselle de Valois has since told me how she came to decide on this sudden move. The abbess of Longchamps, hitherto obsequious in her manner, had suddenly in recent days shown herself importunate, insisting that the girl come to a decision—a decision, that is, to take the veil.

Now, convent life held not the faintest attraction for Mademoiselle de Valois, who concluded, at this point, that powerful influences were at work to insure that she be immured behind convent walls; for, as she reasoned, these powerful interests were fearful of the claims she would inevitably make for restoration of her Valois rights. From the very day she departed the tumble-down Fontette shack, she had begun to formulate grandiose plans for pursuance of those claims, and these ideas had been stimulated by the recent government action of recognition and awards.

The timing of the flight had been unfortunate—at a moment when she was short on funds—but, as she explained it to me later, the abbess, in their final interview, had gone so far as to threaten her. Mademoiselle de Valois had to choose between yielding and flying and had decided on the latter course, come what may. She had encountered little difficulty in influencing her sister to the same course, because for quite some time she had become the one to make decisions for the two.

So here she was safely come to port (if the Red Head Inn at Bar-sur-Aube may so be euphemized) and with only six gold francs left to clink together after travel expenses. She had sent off letters to all the prominent nobility of the region, whose favor and patronage she besought, but until she heard from these possible sponsors she had nothing to live on but credit: such credit as she might secure on the collateral of her winning ways and repeated mention of high-sounding names of local celebrities with whom she could rightly claim to be "in correspondence."

It was at this juncture that she received a visit from Madame de Surmont. We had gone to great pains to determine the lady on this course. Madame de Surmont had at first resisted our urgings, but we had finally persuaded her that her position as First Citizeness of Bar-sur-Aube imposed on her the obligation to act as protectress to young ladies of quality in flight from one knew not what—possibly persecution—and shamefully neglected by the nobility. We had finally struck on the responsive chord; Madame de Surmont had herself announced to the ladies at the Red Head Inn, who expressed their pleasure, nay, their impatience, to meet her.

From that visit Madame de Surmont returned enchanted. She had been utterly captivated by Mademoiselle de Valois, who has since proven that she knew how to captivate many another. Madame de Surmont expressed indignation at the local gentry's indifference, in such a crisis, to ladies of title, cousins of the King's, no less! Madame de Surmont further expressed her willingness to offer the young ladies the hospitality of her home, provided she could win her husband's consent. This gentleman, town provost and First Citizen, head of the police, judge of civil and criminal court, member of king's council for the province, yielded reluctantly—reluctantly being the way he always yielded when confronted by the instances of his wife. Thereupon the Mesdemoiselles de Valois were installed in the Surmont residence—the very result we had set out to accomplish!

Mademoiselle de Valois was not a valid beauty in the strict sense of the word. She was of medium height, but svelte and exquisitely proportioned. She had the most expressive blue eyes imaginable under dark, high-arched brows. Her face was slightly elongated and though her mouth was somewhat wide, her teeth were magnificent and, as is often the case with that type, her smile enchanting. She had lovely hands, a tiny foot. Her complexion was extraordinarily fair. In the matter of her bosom, nature had proven capricious, setting out on a superb design, only to stint on material in the execution, leaving the beholder wishful that the artist had been more expansive.

Mademoiselle de Valois was devoid of formal education, but she had native wit, a keen and penetrating variety. In a contest since birth with the social order, she flouted its laws and showed little more respect for those of morality. It was evident that she played fast and loose with both, as nonchalantly as if she had never suspected their existence. All of this added up to a combination enough to dismay an analytical observer, but utterly beguiling to the average male who did not examine so closely.

Her sister, Mademoiselle de Saint-Rémy, was a big buxom blonde, quite pretty, very dull, exceedingly stupid. Their brother, the Baron de

Valois, presented no distinguishing features of personal appearance or intellect, but he was a well-behaved man and a meticulous officer. He loved his profession and devoted himself wholeheartedly to it, never allowing himself to be distracted by memories of ancient family glory and delusions of grandeur such as obsessed his sister.

This, then, was the Valois family, which found its end in notoriety and shame instead of in anonymity and honor, as some effort had been exerted to arrange.

The Mesdemoiselles de Valois brought new life and zest into the Surmonts' society. The young men who were received there were not slow to perceive that these noble ladies (like the princesses in story books) would not be so haughty as to scorn the suit of some romantic (and rich) young commoner, were any so bold as to aspire to their proud hearts and hands. Their prospects were brilliant, to be sure, but the recovery of their vast family fortunes was subject to unpredictable delay, and in the meanwhile a girl had to live on eight hundred francs a year. Now, a girl simply couldn't live on a pension such as that—and it was furthermore to be feared that Madame de Surmont might weary of the daily sacrifices to which her impulsive gesture of hospitality had committed her.

The very day after their arrival, Madame de Surmont had loaned her guests two white dresses, with little hope, however, of their being able to wear them, in view of the fact that Madame de Surmont was prodigiously fat. Imagine her astonishment next morning when the girls appeared in dresses fitting to perfection, snug at waist and bosom; they had sat up all night cutting and altering the gowns to their dimensions. In all matters the Valois ladies proceeded with similar liberties, and Madame de Surmont began to find the tactics of princesses rather too highhanded for comfort.

When Madame de Surmont had invited them to her home, it had been for a week at most. A year later, they were still there.

Time passed, in much the same way it always does in small provincial towns, but Mademoiselle de Valois, even on so narrow a stage, gave early evidence of her budding genius, treating the natives of Bar-sur-Aube to a dress rehearsal while waiting to make her debut on the world stage. She insinuated herself into the affections of Monsieur de Surmont, pulling the wool over his eyes so successfully that he was blind to the tricks she played on all the rest of the household, including Madame de Surmont herself. That good lady has often told me since that the most miserable year of her life was the one she spent in the society of that little demon.

Although I saw her not too often after her arrival in Bar-sur-Aube, still it was time enough for me to fall under her spell like all the rest. I admired (without recognizing the danger) that daring spirit of hers, which nothing daunted and which was in striking contrast to that of the conventional, timid local belles. Not that Mademoiselle de Valois couldn't, when it served her purpose, affect the demureness or even the gentle weakness so becoming to her sex. She had youth, glorious eyes and a smile that went straight to your heart—more than enough to make me her devoted slave.

At home I must have sung her praises from morn till night, for it was in the year that the Mesdemoiselles de Valois came to town that my father urged me (the first such instance I can remember) toward immediate departure for Paris. The fact was that he stood in deathly fear of the signal honor that might be done his house: the possible mingling of his red bourgeois blood with the blue of the Valois'!

In Paris, letters from home kept me in touch with the daily activities of the young ladies, with all their girlish pranks and escapades. Then came the startling news that Mademoiselle de Valois had wound up singling out for favor a Monsieur de La Motte, nephew of Monsieur de Surmont. My correspondents told me that that haughty heart had finally found its master—though I was somewhat astonished at the social milieu in which the "master" had been located.

Monsieur de La Motte, a gentleman by birth, was homely but a man of splendid physique, dexterous in all sports. Despite his homeliness, his face had a pleasant and gentle expression. He was not entirely lacking in wit, but what little he possessed was directed toward shady dealings and enterprises of questionable nature. Devoid of fortune of any kind, he exhibited great skill at wangling credit, could point to a state of indebtedness normally attainable only by a man of far greater means, and got by, thanks only to his financial legerdemain and an allowance of three hundred francs a year paid out by his uncle, Monsieur de Surmont, to keep him in his regiment.

His father's military service had been rewarded by the King with the Cross of St. Louis and the rank of quartermaster in the Gendarmerie before his hero's death at the Battle of Minden. The Gendarmerie, as the first cavalry regiment of France, was unique in that it afforded officer's rank to every mounted man and thus had become the refuge not only of the impoverished nobility but also of the bourgeoisie, who could not aspire to rank above captaincy in any other branch of the service. Thus, as the third of his name in the corps, Monsieur de La Motte might well have hoped—with good behavior—for rapid advancement; but good behavior was precisely that of which he was least capable.

That very same month, word reached me that the romance between Monsieur de La Motte and Mademoiselle de Valois had progressed so rapidly that marriage was now considered a distinct possibility.

To this point, Mademoiselle de Valois tells much the same story as Count Beugnot, though the accounts may vary later. As heroine of her own romance, she reveals its tender progress in infinite detail:

When we came to Bar-sur-Aube, my sister Marianne and I, we were promptly included in the town's round of social activities. Assembly balls were popular and frequent diversions, but the favorite by all odds was play-acting.

Monsieur de La Motte, on furlough from his regiment, played a leading role opposite mine of soubrette in a most piquant comedy which we gave to loud applause and audience acclaim. Monsieur de La Motte displayed a talent which promptly prejudiced me in his favor. On his side, he had shown me marked attention from our first meeting. At every occasion he sought to inspire in me the sentiment which I had inspired in him, and there was nothing banal about his compliments. Of handsome build, he cut a dashing figure in his scarlet uniform, his silver-brimmed hat and his swaggering red cape across broad shoulders. His manner elegant, he was a persuasive conversationalist. With attractions of mind as well as of person, he could not fail to be agreeable to me, as to many another of my sex. I was the envy of many. Given a woman so favorably impressed (if her heart be free and occasion for meeting frequent), love is seldom slow to follow!

Madame de Surmont, remarking her nephew's passion, did everything in her power to forward the match, often leaving us alone together on the pretext of Monsieur de La Motte's coaching me in my role. Nor were these moments lost to love. The reader may observe that there was imprudence in allowing such tête-à-têtes, but, young and inexperienced as I was, how was I to guess the danger? I admit ingenuously that I loved Monsieur de La Motte from the moment I came to know him. He had a candor rare and refreshing in a man of the world, yet he combined it with the polish and suavity of a courtier. His deportment gave me every reason to suppose his intentions honorable.

Though neither birth, rank nor fortune gave him the right to speak to me of marriage, still I listened. Even more he was made a happy man. He implored me to go at once to Paris to ask the consent of my foster mother. His aunt, Madame de Surmont, wrote to her also describing Monsieur de La Motte as a gentleman of quality with bright prospects for future advancement; and the bishop of Langres, who had shown me great courtesy since my return to his diocese, undertook to act as mediator with the Marquise de Boulainvilliers in Paris and to present personally, on the part of Monsieur de La Motte's mother, the formal request for my hand.

In Paris, the Marquise readily agreed to the visit of the bishop of Langres; she had always wanted to meet this worthy prelate, whose opinions, talents and merits she had long admired from afar. With inexpressible impatience I awaited the outcome of their conference. The next morning, the bishop himself deigned to give me the word I longed to hear— the consent of my benefactress to the fulfillment of my fondest hopes.

The Marquise's permission granted, Monsieur de La Motte and I could busy ourselves with final preparations to hasten the happy day, setting it for June 6, 1780.

The wedding banns had been posted at the church of Fontette, and my sister and I went there on Sunday for High Mass. When we made our entry, all the peasants rose to pay their respects to the children of their former seigneur. We were ushered to the seat of honor, the pew which the lords of Fontette had always occupied, and the curate stepped down from the altar to bring the holy water and sacramental bread to us at our seats, as tradition decreed. After Mass, the church bells were rung in our honor and all our good villagers flocked round to express, in their own humble way, their pleasure at seeing us. We gave them six francs apiece (as was also the custom), with which they purchased wine to drink toast after toast to our health and happiness. Then they escorted us to the old Château de Fontette, showing us over the lands which had originally constituted the family estates. All this, I could not help thinking, should have been my own. If only my poor father had been more prudent, less credulous, in maintaining the dignity of his ancestors, his children might have maintained the position to which birth entitled them. Oh, vain regret!

The nuptial ceremony took place at midnight, the traditional hour in our province, and the church was filled with spectators attracted by interest or by curiosity. The Marquis de Boulainvilliers having pettishly refused to sign my marriage contract, a distant relative, the Squire of Bonchemin, was named and signed as my guardian.*

The next day Madame de Surmont gave a great dinner party, to which a prodigious number of guests had been invited. There were two tables, one in the antechamber, one in the dining room; every apartment was open and soon crowded. Profusion of food and drink in every variety was the keynote of the entertainment. The dinner was followed by a ball at which we danced far into the night. The health of the bride was an excuse for drinking wine as though it were water.

Bar-sur-Aube had been surprised at the suddenness of our marriage, the final preparations having been concluded in secrecy. There had been no secret, to be sure, about Monsieur de La Motte's attentions; there had been talk of marriage, but only conjecture—none had dreamed it would be consummated so soon.

The conjectures had reached Beugnot's ears in Paris, family and friends writing him by every post to keep him informed of the rapid-fire developments:

All in the same month they wrote me, first, that there seemed possibility of an engagement; in the next letter, that the engagement had been announced (with the blessing, what's more, of the bishop of Langres) and then, in almost no time at all, that the marriage had been celebrated. Each of these communiqués, one following upon the other, doubled the astonishment caused me by the previous one—an astonishment that was at its peak when I heard, the very month thereafter, that Madame de La Motte had been happily delivered of twins.†

---

* The civil register at Bar-sur-Aube gives the full list of witnesses to the marriage contract and the ceremony in the parish church of St. Mary Magdalene. The principals sign as:

Jeanne de Saint-Rémy de Valois, age 24
Nicolas Marc-Antoine de La Motte, Esquire, age 26
Marianne de Saint-Rémy de Valois, sister of the bride
Madame de Latour, sister of the groom
Monsieur de Surmont, President of King's Council, Provost of Bar-sur-Aube, Judge of Civil and Criminal Court, Lieutenant General of Police
Jean Durand, Farmer, Resident of Fontette (former foster father of Marianne)

† The register of the parish church of St. Mary Magdalene at Bar-sur-Aube, under the date of July 6, 1780, notes the baptism of "Jean Baptiste and Nicolas Marc, twin

If I had been up to now wonder-struck and amarvel at so strange an alliance, it was, by this latest development, transported from out of the realm of the wondrous and marvelous into that of the commonplace. Here, then, was the explanation for everything—including the bishop's blessing, evidently under duress. Madame de Surmont had been deceived to the very end by Mademoiselle de Valois and her nephew. When she learned of the dishonor they had done her house, she sent the former packing and forbade the latter her door.

They went seeking refuge to the house of Madame de Latour, the bridegroom's sister, who, herself having slightly less than enough to live on, could hardly be expected long to feed two extra mouths.

Madame de La Motte raised a thousand francs by mortgaging her crown pension for the next two years, to pay her share of the inevitable expenses of trousseau and nuptials. As his contribution, Monsieur de La Motte sold his horse and carriage for six hundred francs cash—no large sum, but clear profit, in view of the fact that both had been purchased on credit in his garrison town of Lunéville. In this fashion, merrily as a wedding bell, the newlyweds set up housekeeping.

Although this first chapter of Beugnot's memoirs is entitled "The Countess de La Motte," he has not a word to say as to how she acquired the title of Countess. The lady herself touches on it, but lightly, in later chapters of her own.

Now, the marriage register at Bar-sur-Aube, as noted, shows the groom's signature as simply "Nicolas Marc-Antoine de La Motte, Esquire"—no more; and his family in the region never pretended to anything but a simple "Monsieur." Yet in no time at all, the La Mottes turned up signing "Count" and "Countess" to everything (particularly to the tradesmen's bills and loan applications) and proceeded so smoothly to the annexation that their biographers ever after accepted the designation; their contemporaries, Paris friends, neighbors, newspaper reporters, police and law-court clerks, were all equally misled. The fact that there were two La Motte families in the province was helpful: one, the hero's, non-noble (military gentlemen mostly, except for one shopkeeping uncle in Bar-sur-Aube), the other family of La Mottes of

---

sons born to Nicolas de La Motte, King's Cavalryman, and Jeanne de Valois, his wife." The register shows, moreover, that none of the family were present to serve as godparents, but only the maids and valets of the Surmont household. The twins survived the ceremony by only a day or two.

ancient nobility and high standing; a confusion which redounded to the benefit of a clever pair.

So now it is the "Count" de La Motte who writes her a letter, as the "Countess" recounts in her memoirs,

. . . to ask me to join him at his Lunéville garrison. The stir I created in Lunéville might have gone to the head of many women, but never was one less vain of her looks than I. A certain piquancy of face, an air of health and youth (which men call radiance) and an extraordinarily vivacious personality—these, by some magic, made up for any want of beauty in my case, to such an extent that I was forever the object of the importunities of presumptuous men. At Lunéville I was besieged by all the Lovelaces of the Army.

Primarily by a scoundrel who, having failed in an attack on my virtue, sought to buy my favors by first reducing my husband and me to desperate straits. This scoundrel was the Marquis d'Autichamps, my husband's commander and the man whom I have to thank for my lifelong distrust of his sex! Expressing his interest in our situation, he offered to serve as our "patron and protector" and kept telling us that we would get nowhere here in godforsaken Lunéville, that Paris was the place for us if we hoped to get ahead. In the capital, he insisted, we could count on him and his influential friends, whose aid he would enlist in securing an honorable and lucrative Army position for my husband. To this course of action it was not difficult to persuade us, and Monsieur de La Motte and I made ready for the journey. A day or two before the date set for departure, however, it developed, to our amazement, that the Marquis had never expected Monsieur de La Motte to go at all—it had been his intention to escort me alone! Claiming that my husband had had two leaves recently, the commander point-blank refused him a third, leaving Monsieur de La Motte no choice but to hand in his resignation from the corps. Here, then, were the first fruits of "protection and patronage," a lesson in what to expect from the friendship of the powerful and mighty of this world, from the lavish promises of ardent males!

Of all the "Lovelaces of the Army," the red-caped cavaliers in Lunéville among whom the bride admits "creating such a stir," the most cavalier of all was one comrade-at-arms and boyhood chum of her husband's upon whom she made an indelible impression: Rétaux de Villette, a tall, handsome young buck, blue-eyed and fair-haired, with that look of distinction inevitably conferred by "touches of premature gray at the temples." Having early run through a modest inheritance, Athos Villette had followed Porthos La Motte in the line of least resistance—into the cavalry.

With rather better education than most for his class and time, Villette could count many more accomplishments: a pleasing voice in song, to his own almost professional mandolin accompaniment, and a versatile pen turned to a variety of uses—to journalism (his articles appearing in the Gazette of Leyden and other European newspapers), to poetry (dedicated to his dear friend's wife), to memoirs (of course) and later (it was suspected) to a spot of forgery. Talented Villette would hitch his wagon to the rising La Motte star, to form a triple (ménage à trois) constellation.

His memoirs, a slim volume somewhat pretentiously entitled Mémoires historiques des intrigues de la cour, purport to be a record of "what actually happened between the Queen, the Count d'Artois, Cardinal Rohan, Madame de Polignac, Madame de La Motte, Cagliostro . . . by the Sieur Rétaux de Villette."

And they begin:

My readers will be mistaken if they accuse me of showing partiality to Madame de La Motte in this volume. That fire, which long blazed so hot, scorching my soul, has by now burned itself out, down to embers.

I have depicted her as she was: pretty, infinitely pleasing, but too obliging, too good-natured not to have been weak; too ardent not to have been libertine. Such, nevertheless, was the woman whom I loved to distraction, who showered me with loving kindness—whom I yet brought myself to betray.

Fortuneless myself, born at Bar-sur-Aube of poor but honest parents, born with an irresistible penchant for pleasuring, I surrendered unreservedly to Madame de La Motte, who, subject to the same penchant, intoxicated me with her favors.

As a young girl, unfortunately, Mademoiselle de Valois had been subject to no early training, no discipline such as might have taught her self-control; hotheaded, and with that little head full of delusions of grandeur, reacting impulsively to every prompting of a runaway imagination, to every flare of passion, she had allowed herself to be seduced by the bishop of Langres.

Her pregnancy was the result of that seduction, and the prelate, to cover his traces, persuaded the Marquise de Boulainvilliers to consent to the marriage of the young lady to Monsieur de La Motte, who himself had ample reason to suppose the child his own.*

In Lunéville, the Marquis d'Autichamps, the corps commander, no sooner laid eyes on Madame de La Motte than he fell madly in love with her. Drunk with passion, he made no effort to conceal it from the world; and with Madame de La Motte hardly more discreet, her husband had little choice but to snatch her from the arms of his commander and turn in his resignation from the corps.

This much Madame de La Motte confirms:

My husband's request for honorable discharge entered, we went flying to Strasbourg, where my foster mother had gone to consult the famous Count Cagliostro about her illness. Just missing the Marquise, who had gone the day before to the château of Prince de Rohan at Saverne, we took to the road again the next morning to follow her there.

It was at Saverne that I saw that great lord for the first time. Flattered and enchanted by the cordial reception given me by the premier prince of the Church and the realm, I read only the happiest presages for the future.

Little did I dream, when the Marquise presented me to His Highness Prince de Rohan, how fatal would be the outcome. Human wisdom cannot pierce the veil that shrouds our destiny!

And Carlyle: "Thus, then, has destiny at last brought it about. Thus, after long wanderings, on paths so far separate, has the time come, in this late year 1783, when, of all the nine hundred millions of the earth's denizens, these preappointed two behold each other."

* The Countess de La Motte herself never hints at the existence of such a relation with the bishop despite her detailed account of "that worthy prelate's many kindnesses and attentions to me throughout my girlhood," in her Story of My Life. But if she did not tell the story of seduction to Villette, it seems inconceivable that he would have manufactured it out of whole (ecclesiastical) cloth, unless he bore the "worthy prelate" some grudge (for which no evidence exists)—an early example of the startling discrepancies that crop up throughout the accounts of the principal character-narrators. At the risk of belaboring the point of the mystery of the twins' paternity, it is irresistible to wonder whether Beugnot did not secretly and smugly attribute it to himself—bringing to a total of three the candidates for that honor.

IV

Abbé Georgel

(1774-1777)

THE FIRST QUESTION that comes to mind is, Whatever was Prince-Ambassador de Rohan doing rusticating in provincial Strasbourg, instead of peacocking it in his Vienna embassy or at the Court of Versailles?

To deprive him of that embassy had been Marie Antoinette's first exhilarating test of power over her new king of a husband, the first example of her meddling in affairs of state. Later, when the epithet "Austrian woman" was hurled at her as the angriest charge of the Revolution, she may have remembered this first instance of her service, as French Queen, to the interests of Austria. Immediately upon the accession of Louis XVI, the very first order of business had been a new set of Cabinet ministers and the exile of "that creature," the Du Barry (not too far, not too long, actually; just a few months at a pleasant convent, better treatment than she had dared hope for from her new sovereigns, with a quite decent pension and confirmation of title to her very nicest château, Louveciennes). And within two months after mounting the throne, Marie Antoinette had proceeded to the business of ridding her mother of Ambassador Rohan. ("Every day more indiscreet, more insolent, more unbearable!" Maria Theresa was still railing at him, although she did seem to sense some danger to her child from "the Rohan family, so large and mighty that some people here in Vienna fear they will find means to be revenged upon my daughter for the part she played in the ambassador's recall.")

What a pleasure now for a young Queen to deliver this message to Rohan through his aunt, the Countess de Marsan, her own old critic and enemy: Let her tell her nephew (back in France for the coronation) to spare himself the embarrassment of making plans to return to Vienna; changes were shortly to be announced by the Ministry of Foreign Affairs. To Rohan in his suspenseful state an audience with the King brought only a chill "I will advise you later what is to be my pleasure in this matter." And when Rohan sought audience of the Queen to present a letter he had carried from Vienna for her from her mother, she crushed hope with the word that he should hand the letter to his niece, Princess de Guéménée, one of the Queen's new circle of gay young intimates.

This niece, then, seemed the very one to intercede for him, but watch-dog Count Mercy warned the Queen to beware of Rohan's maneuvers.

"I did my best to persuade the Queen to say a straight-out No to Prince de Rohan," Mercy reported to Vienna, "but she took a less definite course, pretexting now a promenade, now a party, some one or other previous commitment preventing the granting of an audience to the Prince"—so that eventually, in high dudgeon, Rohan had to leave for his Strasbourg diocese without ever seeing his sovereign.

Why was the Austrian Empress so nervous about Rohan's winning over the Queen? "Knowing him as I do," Maria Theresa wrote Count Mercy, "a flatterer, flexible, ingratiating, amusing, I believe him fully capable of insinuating himself into my daughter's favor." The very type to appeal to Marie Antoinette, and her mother knew it. "Although my daughter holds Prince de Rohan at a distance, I think her quite capable of changing her mind, out of either her heedless, reckless manner of thinking or her habit of yielding to the whim of her favorites of both sexes."

While Prince de Rohan sat, suspenseful, in Strasbourg, waiting to learn the King's pleasure, the Vienna embassy had been left in the capable hands of Rohan's own personal secretary and vicar general, the Abbé Georgel, acting as interim chargé d'affaires.

Georgel, a Jesuit alumnus, becomes in the eyes and the book of Madame Campan "the wily, crafty Jesuit, the man who knew more about the Diamond Necklace Case than anyone in the world!"—so it can come as no surprise that he wrote his memoirs. Carlyle agrees that "Georgel passes for the grand authority on the necklace business," but, he adds, "he is vague as may be, writing in what may be called the 'soaped pig' fashion, yet sometimes you do catch and hold him. It is to be remembered that poor Abbé Georgel wrote in exile and with cause enough for prepossession and hostilities."

Georgel states his position in his memoirs:

Though I wish that this affair could have been forever buried under a shroud of oblivion, such notoriety has it received, such masses of memoirs have been published about it pro and con, confusing or misleading public opinion, that I feel someone should attempt to bring order out of the chaos of conjecture. And since it was I alone, during those dark days, who held in my hands the thread of daily communication between government authorities, judges, lawyers, the Cardinal and his family, I who directed the far-flung investigations which finally unmasked the principal agents and unwound the web of the infernal intrigue, perhaps I am the one best qualified to do it. I have no ulterior motives of my own, no passions, no hatreds; my sole motive here is to reveal the truth. I shall merely lay the facts before the reader—place him, as Horace phrased it, at center stage, where he can clearly hear the voices of the actors and judge them for himself.

"None was more loyal to the Cardinal," the editor of Madame Campan's memoirs says of Georgel, "none more ingenious in evolving defenses for the prelate." Georgel was all of that: Rohan's man Friday, his right hand—in diocese and personal affairs—his major-domo, his alter ego. Or, to go all the way with Carlyle: "Our vulpine Abbé Georgel, Rohan's nursing-mother, through fair court weather and through foul, shall triumphantly bear him. . . . In Vienna, above all things, his Jesuit familiar is with him. For so everywhere they must manage: Eminence Rohan is the cloak, Jesuit Georgel the man or automaton within it."

In Vienna, Georgel had just played hero in a midnight cloak-and-dagger episode on dark city ramparts, where, actually wrapped to the ears in a cloak, he had kept a rendezvous with a masked man, a spy who was to continue meeting him there over a period of months to sell him Austria's and all Europe's top-secret secrets. As a result, Ambassador Rohan could proudly dispatch important inside information such as news of the planned partition of Poland long before it came to public notice. Rohan was justified in bewailing the ingratitude of kings for what was, on the whole, an ambassadorial job well done. That he had been a highly popular representative for his nation in Austria not even the Empress could deny: "Rohan's partisans, men and women, all ages, are numerous here, including Chancellor von Kaunitz and the Emperor Joseph himself."

With Georgel on the ramparts and himself on the qui vive, Rohan could point to a creditably executed mission in Vienna. Even the Count de Vergennes, the new French Minister of Foreign Affairs, had stated it as his opinion, in a letter to the Austrian Empress, that Ambassador Rohan was possessed of "keen wit and a singular knowledge in the fields of diplomacy and politics."

Then "the exasperating Why, wherefore, how came it?" of this royal displeasure fallen on his head. What could it be but that damned epigrammatic partition-of-Poland letter read aloud at Madame du Barry's supper table?

That Ambassador Rohan wrote "the letter with the 'handkerchief in one hand, sword in the other' line cannot be denied," Georgel confesses, "but it was never intended for Madame du Barry. This constituted the misrepresentation in the matter." This was the fact that must be explained to the Queen.

It was a letter so private as to be sent separate from the diplomatic pouch, destined only for the eyes of the Duke d'Aiguillon [at that time the Foreign Minister] and King Louis XV. Prince de Rohan, after two months of perplexity and uncertainty, and believing his honor to be at stake in this matter of his return to Austria, wrote a letter to Louis XVI presenting his side of the case. To this there was no reply; the King confined himself to advising the Countess de Marsan that the Vienna embassy was destined for a man approved by Queen Marie Antoinette and the Empress of Austria. Shortly afterward it became known that the man was Baron de Breteuil.

Presumably to Rohan's acute distress; for, oddly enough (though oddities and coincidences are the rule, not the exception, in this history), it was this same Baron de Breteuil whom Rohan had supplanted upon his own arrival at the Vienna embassy a brief two years previously; Breteuil, still in the midst of unpacking and settling himself into the ambassador's seat and suite, had been summarily recalled and replaced by Rohan in 1772. Now, in 1774, Rohan was out, Breteuil back in. A game of musical chairs full of ominous discord, to a tune of pro-and-anti-

Rohan, pro-and-anti-Austria caballing in the French Foreign Ministry.

"Breteuil may well encounter embarrassment at his debut here in Austria—" the Austrian Empress could sense it—"with everyone in Vienna prejudiced in favor of his predecessor, Prince de Rohan."

And she was right. The Viennese promptly criticized Breteuil's manners, his dress, even his wig; they were nettled when he (nettled likewise) issued the statement that he was "neither a gambler nor a party giver like the previous French ambassador." "Certainly a rustic in comparison to the gallant Rohan," Maria Theresa wrote, in 1775, of Breteuil; "worst of all, my son the Emperor sets the example for all the odious comparisons, and was even seen to make a mocking gesture over Breteuil's shoulder to the Abbé Georgel."

To Georgel, of all people—whom Breteuil accused of inheriting his master's animosity, perpetuating his master's spitefulness. Georgel, having refused to bequeathe to Breteuil the name of his masked secret informant, quotes the Baron as saying, "I will be chief minister of France one day, and will make you and Rohan feel the weight of my authority!" An accurate prophecy; exactly eleven years later, Minister Breteuil, one of the most powerful figures in France (the head of two important ministries—the King's Household and the Government of Paris), would bark out the arrest order for Cardinal Prince de Rohan.

Rohan had requested permission for a short, face-saving farewell expedition to Vienna to bid goodbye to his wide circle of friends. But at Maria Theresa's "I would take it as a personal insult," Louis XVI refused, and Rohan was obliged to content himself with mailing farewell tokens instead: miniatures of his classic profile etched on slim discs of ivory which Viennese admirers promptly encircled with precious stones and had mounted into rings. Even Chancellor von Kaunitz wore a Rohan memento on his third finger, to the amazement of the Empress: "I wouldn't have believed it if I hadn't seen it with my own eyes."

Georgel, back from Vienna, entered the lists wearing Rohan colors and, as the abbé tells it in his memoirs, won the next several tilts for Rohan from the Queen,

. . . his openly declared adversary, who had done everything in her power to keep the Prince from those high places and dignities of the court to which he might reasonably aspire.

We will see the Prince then, in constant combat with the Queen, attain, against her wishes, that highest of all positions, the Grand Almonership*—head of episcopate and clergy in a joint charge with the King, independent of all other Cabinet ministers, disburser of endowments for colleges and hospitals, celebrant of Mass in the royal chapels on all holy days and commander of the Order of the Holy Ghost.

The promise of this post for Prince de Rohan, made to his aunt, the Countess de Marsan, by Louis XV, had been put in writing by that monarch, and the document bore his signature. After the coronation of Louis XVI, the Countess de Marsan presented the former monarch's pledge to the new one, who agreed to ratify it upon the death of the aged incumbent, Grand Almoner de La Roche-Aymon. But Marie Antoinette, whose aim was to force Prince de Rohan from the court, succeeded in turning the King against him and cunningly proposed a stratagem to deprive Prince de Rohan of the promised office, yet satisfy the Rohan family—by giving the Grand Almonership to his brother instead, and consoling Prince Louis with a cardinalate. When I got wind of this, I advised the Countess de Marsan of the intrigue afoot, but she refused to believe that a Queen of France would stoop to such deception.

The morning after the death of the Grand Almoner de La Roche-Aymon, Countess de Marsan sought the first audience with the King after his levee. Their interview may serve to reveal the character of a monarch who was to be of interest to all posterity. To the King's offer to make Prince de Rohan a cardinal instead of Grand Almoner, Countess de Marsan replied, "There can be no favor to compensate for the one promised on Your Majesty's sacred word of honor. It is the only reward I ask or will accept in return for the services and care I lavished upon your childhood."

THE KING: "I cannot fulfill the promise. I have given my word to the Queen."

COUNTESS DE MARSAN: "Your Majesty cannot have two words of honor. If the word of a gentleman is sacred, what then the word of a king? Having made public your word to me, I must of necessity make public that the King has failed in his word of honor—merely to please the Queen."

THE KING: "But would you have me take into my royal household a man who is distasteful to me and supremely distasteful to the Queen?"

* The Grand Almoner of France, literally disburser of the King's alms, the national charity fund, had at his discretion the granting of all pensions and donations and was also titular head of the French Church hierarchy.

COUNTESS DE MARSAN: "I pledge myself and all the Rohans to this: that if in two years my cousin has not had the good fortune to redeem himself in your eyes and favor, he will hand in his resignation from the Grand Almonership."

The Queen manifested her displeasure to the King and made a point of letting Prince de Rohan feel it as well. When the new Grand Almoner came to render thanks for his appointment, as was customary, she received him with so chill an air that all present could see that he had incurred her extreme disfavor. Thus she continued inflexible and inaccessible to him. In vain he wrote three letters protesting his innocence of offense; his letters were never read, never opened. In vain he sought the mediation of persons close to the Queen, appealed to her brother, Emperor Joseph, during his visit to France, to request that he be allowed to present his side of the case, make his apologies. The Queen's responses proved that her mind was made up; there was no possible hope for reconciliation.

The Queen, in a letter to her mother dated March 4, 1777, announced Rohan's appointment to the office of Grand Almoner:

My opinion of Prince Louis coincides with that of my dear mother. I consider him not only an unprincipled man but even a dangerous one . . . with all his intrigues; and had the decision been left to me, he would never have had a place here at court. Still, that of Grand Almoner brings him into no contact whatsoever with me—and little more, actually, with the King, whom he will see only at the levee and at Mass.

While the Abbé Georgel, of course, never saw this particular letter of Marie Antoinette's, he was nevertheless extraordinarily well advised of all the enemy camp's activities:

Having suffered defeat in the first contest, the Queen now hastened to prevent Prince de Rohan's attaining the cardinalate to which, traditionally, the King nominated his Grand Almoner; she induced the King to promise it to the Archbishop of Rouen instead, at the death of the incumbent, Cardinal Noyon. The house of Rohan, which could number several cardinals, was deeply resentful, and I undertook to secure the nomination from the King of Poland, to whom Prince de Rohan had rendered important services during his Vienna embassy. The King of

Poland agreed to nominate Prince de Rohan if the French King did not object. When Cardinal Noyon died, at one in the morning, the courier I had stationed at his house rushed the news to me before sunrise; I was at Versailles at the pillow of Prime Minister Maurepas before six; and he, before seven, had secured the King's signature; my courier had set out for Warsaw before nine. The Queen went to the King at ten, only to learn that the Grand Almoner had been ahead of her.

Another rankling defeat, and more to come. Her disfavor could not prevent Prince de Rohan from acquiring two more coveted titles: administrator general of the Sorbonne (an honor for which cardinals vied) and abbot of St. Waast of Arras, with 500,000 francs revenue, most welcome at this particular time to amortize the exorbitant debts contracted in expenses at the Vienna embassy and for the rebuilding of the château at Saverne after a disastrous fire.

Even Prince de Rohan's great personal income plus his 100,000 francs annual revenue from the diocese of Strasbourg could not have covered all this, in addition to the enormous expense of maintaining standards of living befitting his rank and position.*

Why should I not reveal here how I managed all these things for him? In a report of the successful march of an army is not credit given to the advance guard, the scout, the sentry? Nor is it inappropriate to call attention briefly to the intrigues to which one needed to resort in the courts of kings.

But "no longer, not now," as Georgel writes in the opening lines of his memoirs:

I am today a free agent; no bonds of dependency or loyalty restrict my freedom of expression. Yet, lest the parts herein played by prominent personages rouse slumbering passions and resentments, I shall not allow these memoirs to be published until after my death; thus shall I avoid wounding any of the personages involved, or even their descendants, and also preserve my own few remaining years untroubled by recriminations.

I have described the brilliant situation in which Cardinal Rohan found himself despite opposition from a powerful Queen. Having soared so high, he must needs soar higher still, and thus he opened up the

* Prince de Rohan's total annual income is estimated to have been in excess of 1,200,000 francs (some $273,000).

abyss into which we shall see him plunge. His fall from court favor was the unending torment of his life.

By eighteenth-century consensus, no crueler blow could befall a nobleman than banishment to his estates, away from "the perpetual house party" of Versailles Palace. ("The provinces were unthinkable!") Jeanne de Valois has described the banishment that crushed the Boulainvilliers' —their "disgrace" (as was the word for it) over the basement distillery explosion—as "the Marquise's affliction, abandoned by even her most intimate friends." Eighteenth-century memoirs were full of such dramatic incidents: "On hearing of his disgrace, the Duke, who is religious, behaved with Christian submission; when they went to tell the Duchess, she thought, from their faces, that her son must have died."

> Alas! at court, our emotion is the delicatest, unsurest . . . [Carlyle again.] A moment ago, Eminence Rohan seemed waltzing with the best . . . now looking upwards, he can eye, from his burning marl, the azure realms, once his; and Cousin Countess de Marsan and so many Richelieus, Polignacs, and other happy angels, male and female, gyrating there; while he . . . ! Nevertheless, hope, in the human breast . . . springs eternal. . . . The outcast Rohan bends all his thoughts, faculties, prayers, purposes, to one object; one object he will attain, or go to Bedlam. How many ways he tries; what days and nights of conjecture, consultation; what written, unpublished reams of correspondence, protestation, backstairs diplomacy of every rubric! How many suppers has he eaten; how many given—in vain! It is his morning song, and his evening prayer.

Those happy court "angels, male and female," had recently and blissfully gyrated, according to Madame Campan, "at a novel gala given at the Little Trianon Palace by the Queen in honor of the visiting Russian party, the Grand Duke [son of Catherine the Great—the future Czar Paul I] and his Grand Duchess . . ." * Madame Campan tells the story in her memoirs:

The illumination of the new English Gardens added an exciting and delightful touch: lanterns, burning in large flowerpots concealed

* For Baroness d'Oberkirch's description of that gala, see the Appendix.

among the shrubbery and flowers, brought out every exquisite color variation. But the highlight of the scene was the Temple of Love, on its hillock, ingeniously and brilliantly illuminated by cords of firewood burning bright through the night in a ditch behind the small marble edifice.

Cardinal Rohan, most indiscreetly, took the liberty of coming to Trianon that night without an invitation, without even the knowledge of the Queen. Now, Cardinal Rohan, consistently treated with great coolness since his return from Vienna, had not dared apply directly to Her Majesty for permission to witness the illuminations. Instead he had bribed the concierge of Trianon Palace to admit him, promising to remain hidden in the gatekeeper's lodge until after the carriages of the Queen and the royal party had departed. Breaking his promise, His Eminence had taken advantage of a moment when the caretaker was busy elsewhere to go out into the gardens, and was seen there mysteriously lurking in the shrubbery, his red cardinal's hose showing beneath his greatcoat.

Her Majesty was infuriated at such effrontery and the next day ordered the concierge dismissed. Everyone expressed indignation at the Cardinal's treachery toward the poor concierge and sympathized with him at losing his position.

Touched by the misfortune of this father of a large family, I besought and obtained the Queen's pardon for him, although I have since reproached myself for the impulse which motivated my action. Had the concierge of Trianon been promptly dismissed, and the dismissal publicized, with the Queen's disfavor toward Cardinal Rohan even more emphatically marked, this might, perhaps, have prevented the shameful and all too famous intrigue of the diamond necklace. Except for the underhanded maneuver by which the Cardinal succeeded in gaining entry to Trianon, except for the air of mystery he affected when the Queen encountered him there, he could never have claimed later that he had been deceived by an intermediary between himself and the Queen.

At this point, the Abbé Georgel (as well as Carlyle) is censorious of Prince de Rohan:

With all his lofty places and titles, with his high rank, his handsome person and noble bearing, his intellect and gift of speech—what more could a mortal ask, what was missing that he could not enjoy his great privileges and high esteem?

The fact was that he could enjoy nothing; the gall of the Queen's enmity rose bitter in his throat, and his every hour of every day was poisoned by it. This was the obsession that led him to clutch at the celebrated diamond necklace as the sure means back into royal favor, this was the obsession that led him into such fatal liaisons.

Of these, the first was with the Countess de La Motte, who will play the leading role in the lamentable scenes to follow. She was born in abject poverty and under a thatched roof; it was a case either of fortune making sport or of an outright curse. As hapless victim of unjust fate, hers was a curious case well calculated to appeal to a compassionate and benevolent man like Prince de Rohan, to spur him to personal generosity and to promotion of her cause at court; it would have given him great satisfaction to have played a part in restoring her to the original high estate of her ancestors.

The Countess de La Motte, while not a great beauty, was strikingly attractive, with all the graces of femininity and youth. Her eyes sparkled to the play of her sparkling wit; her mobile face lighted up when she spoke, and she spoke exceeding well. An air of good faith in what she said gave her lips the gift of persuasion. But behind that seductive façade of hers lay the soul and the sorcery of a Circe.

Cagliostro

(1780-1783)

MEMOIRS
OF THE ABBÉ GEORGEL

AT THIS same period, by malevolent coincidence, another, even stronger, stranger influence came to bear upon the Cardinal's mind, seducing him into the treacherous bypaths of the occult and the supernatural. I do not know what monster of evil, what archenemy of mankind vomited upon these shores this scintillating new genus of charlatanry, this new apostle of the "universal religion" who wielded despotic power over his proselytes, subjugating them utterly to his will.

This man Cagliostro, whose origin remains a mystery to this day, had traveled, under various aliases, through all the countries of Europe, had been chased out of St. Petersburg, Warsaw and Vienna. In the hope that the land of France would prove more fertile ground for the seeds of his esoteric theories, he suddenly appeared in Strasbourg.

Count Cagliostro, careering, careening across Europe with his Countess in his black japanned coach emblazoned with brilliant cabalistic and Masonic symbols, appeared on September 19, 1780, to keep his historically appointed date of arrival in the Alsatian capital.

His fame had preceded him, had reached Strasbourg ahead of his liveried outriders, his six brilliantly caparisoned coal-black horses. Crowds lined the banks of the Rhine as the wheels of his gaudy equipage clattered across the boards of the Pont de Koehl, the bridge by which Marie Antoinette had crossed from Germany into France and which was now laden with throngs almost as thick to witness the grand entry of the Man of Mystery, Man of Miracles, the alchemist, prophet, adept, seer, friend of mankind—what you will. There were a score of titles for him who was reputed to travel from capital to capital upon what some called his "sacred mission"—the healing of the sick, the comforting of the poor—while others, such as the jealous Swiss celebrity, theologian-physiognomist Lavater, pronounced him "a supernatural being sent into the world on a diabolic mission."

Speculation was rife, imagination ran riot, fantasy flourished on the subject of the mystagogue enveloped in clouds of Oriental incense and splendor (and a full-length blue-fox greatcoat), the figure of the man being further obscured by the pall of time, the smokescreen of prejudice. There was no tale too fantastic to be told about him, to be credited, repeated, printed: that his was the secret of immortality, that he could summon up the spirits of the dead, foretell the future, recall the past; that he had witnessed the launching of Noah's Ark upon the floodwaters, as he had the Crucifixion at Golgotha ("Did I not warn Him against Judas?"—and the valet's reply, "You forget, Master, I have been in your service only a thousand years"); that he had been initiated into the mysteries of Eleusis as into those of the Temple of Solomon; that he was grandmaster of the Illuminati (or the Rosicrucians), the company of German mysticist elite.

For some months, years, periods of his life, even rumor lost track of him, but on September 19, 1780, Count Cagliostro, in a flourish of trumpets, drove into Strasbourg. This much is established fact (a rarity in any history of his life) and supported by the official record of the man's own testimony under oath to his judges in the Parliament of Paris, that "he had journeyed across all Europe with his wife and upon their return from Russia had entered France in the year 1780 . . ."

An enigma to his contemporaries, Cagliostro has baffled his biographers, who, springing up legion in his own century, have continued to write, rant and conjecture about him ever since.

Thomas Carlyle, writing his "Cagliostro" essay in the early 1800s, made no honest effort (though claiming that his hand "itched") to "draw aside [the] curtain" of malice, rumor and superstition already veiling the figure of the man, not yet dead so much as half a century at the time when Carlyle wrote.

Although Carlyle's delineation is the one most familiar to English readers, it is invalidated by its very passion; it is a view of Carlyle in one of the finest tantrums in English prose, but hardly enlightening. With such livid rage and anger does he lash out at Cagliostro that one re-checks to make sure there could have been no face-to-face encounter, no personal animosity to account for so violent a reaction. But no, at Carlyle's birth date in 1795 Cagliostro was already rotting in his papal dungeon, and the phenomenon can be accounted for only by the fact that Carlyle's two literary idols, Schiller and Goethe, contemporaries of Cagliostro's, admitted freely to having been seriously prepossessed (obsessed?) by the recondite implications surrounding the Man of Mystery. Carlyle writhed with resentment at the thought that his so-termed "Great Quack-Face"—"Count Front-of-Brass," "King of Liars," "Prince of Scoundrels"—could have exercised so strong an influence over the minds of the two German intellectual giants whose works he reverently translated.

> The great Schiller, for example [Carlyle writes], struck both with the poetic and scientific phases of the [Cagliostro] matter, admitted the influence of the former to shape themselves anew within him; and strove with his usual impetuosity to burst (since unlocking was impossible) the secrets of the latter; and so his unfinished novel, The Geisterseher [the medium or spiritualist] saw the light.

> Still more renowned is Goethe's drama of the Gross-Cophta [the Grand Cophta of Masonry, that is] which, as he himself informs us, delivered him from a state of mind that had become alarming to his friends; so deep was the hold this business had taken of him.

So deep the hold, that Goethe would make a pilgrimage to Sicily, supposed birthplace of Cagliostro, to investigate his origins.

Alexandre Dumas, later in the same century, would publish a magnificat to the Cagliostro legend: a quartet of novels with the Count for

D

hero, in his subversive role as grandmaster of the French lodges and alleged architect of the French Revolution.*

Cagliostro was already a legend in his own time (a time that seemed made expressly for him, or he for it). Extravagant figures were offered as to the number of the miracle healings performed by him. Estimates of the number of patients treated by him in Strasbourg alone ranged all the way from fifteen hundred to fifteen thousand; on some days, it was said, upwards of five hundred poor cripples besieged the Man of Miracles. It was as if all the lame and the halt of Alsace and Lorraine had come limping, stumbling, shuffling, hobbling to converge upon his door and, in token of the miracle, hung up their crutches, braces, canes upon the walls of his dwelling, as pilgrims do at the shrines of Lourdes or Fatima or St. Anne de Beaupré.

"They say that the great man is married to a sylph," the archaeologist Labarthe rhapsodized, "one of those beneficent sprites the Rosicrucians consider to inhabit the upper air." The Countess Cagliostro, a conversation piece in her own right, was high priestess of the female Lodge of Isis; a Roman noblewoman, by her own account; a svelte, blond, beautiful "sylph," by all accounts—though whether blue- or black-eyed was a burning question of the day.

> Duels were fought on the subject of the color of the Countess Cagliostro's eyes [another rhapsodic reporter wrote], or whether the dimple was in her left cheek or her right! When she rode out on her black stallion, Djérid, her ardent admirers rushed to see her pass . . . her riding costume accentuating her hour glass form, minimizing the narrow waist, maximizing the curve of her salient breasts . . .
>
> Though she looked not a day older than twenty, she dropped discreet hints of an eldest son who was a captain in the Army of the Netherlands . . .†

---

* The novels are Joseph Balsamo, Memoirs of a Physician, The Queen's Necklace and The Storming of the Bastille. The Masonic mission in France (in Dumas's version and authentically so) was more overtly revolutionary than in America, where the founding-father Masons went to pains to conceal the connection, although all the leading American revolutionaries were by now co-operating with their French fellow Masons (Franklin and Payne in France itself) in forwarding the joint republican-Masonic aims.
† Théodore Gosselin Lenotre, Vieilles Maisons, Vieux Papiers.

The Abbé Georgel is a contemporary less inclined to rhapsody. He leaves the impression that, given the choice of centuries to live in, he would have chosen another, Cagliostroless one:

That empiric's whole way of life and behavior was shrewdly calculated to attract attention. Although he lived in greatest opulence, making a grand gesture of his largesse, the source of his revenues remained unknown. What banker or what letter of credit he used was impossible to discover.

He refused to cater to the rich and mighty. If such personages sought him out, he drew himself up so haughtily that they had difficulty gaining access to his presence, with the result that when he later condescended to receive them they were flattered by the condescension. In this manner, he stimulated the adulation necessary to the purposes he had in mind.

Further to add to the aura of mystery surrounding him, he claimed to be an Egyptian, an initiate into the secrets of nature, with all of nature's resources, the healthful properties of the animal, vegetable and mineral kingdoms, at his command for the healing of disease and the prolongation of human life. His most famous potions were a "wine of Egypt" and an "*elixir vitae*" a single drop of which caused such sensational results as to win him thousands of ardent followers and spread his reputation across the Continent. Overnight cures wrought by Cagliostro in Switzerland and Strasbourg, of diseases hitherto pronounced incurable, were termed miraculous. His name was on every lip.

Beyond the shadow of a doubt, thick folds of the curtain of mystery that surrounded Cagliostro were draped by his own hand: his very alias of "Count Cagliostro," obviously chosen for the sinister, cryptic ring to it; his trappings, those of charlatanry and mysticism—the exotic garb, décor and paraphernalia, the ritual robes encrusted with jeweled zodiacal and numerological insignia, with emblems of minor- and hither-Asian cults (Thoth, Apis, Astarte, Hermes Trismegistus); the famous candle-lit séances with child mediums, and crystal balls for gazing, and swords unsheathed upon the altar with the rose cross burning bright—all, indisputably, denoting a marked talent for showmanship in his special occult métier. Even so, a great part of the aura of mystery about him was the product of the minds of that scientifically ignorant, superstitious eighteenth-century audience to which he so brilliantly played;

and it does not necessarily follow that his miracle cures should be dismissed as mere quackery.

One of the charges made against him is that he dabbled in alchemy, yet it was from such dabblings in the ancient pseudo science that the modern science of chemistry evolved; and many of the alchemists' brews—Paracelsus' opium, mercury, sulphur, iron, arsenic—linger on in the modern pharmacopoeia. In his séances he used techniques of applied psychology and of religious and optimistic autosuggestion whose principles, unformulated in his day, would be developed by psychiatry, by Mary Baker Eddy and by Coué and become eminently acceptable to the twentieth-century mind. And the "magic passes" of "animal magnetism," or mesmerism, that he resorted to in his healings would, thanks to Charcot and Freud, be defined and applied as hypnotism, a method valued today in several areas of medical science.

In his treatment of the sick Cagliostro applied these principles with a creditable admixture of common sense, as Baron de Gleichen's Souvenirs suggest:

The graver the malady, the more resourceful Cagliostro became. A woman [in Strasbourg] about to be confined, and having been given up by the midwives, who doubted their ability to save her child, sent for Cagliostro in her extremity. He answered the summons immediately, as was his custom, and, after an examination, guaranteed her a successful accouchement. What is more to the point, he kept his word.

He afterward confessed to me that his promise was rash, but, convinced that the child was alive by the pulse of the umbilical cord, and perceiving that the mother lacked only the strength, spirits and confidence to bring her babe into the world, he had relied on the virtues of a singularly invigorating and soothing potion with which he was acquainted. The result, he considered, had been due to luck rather than skill . . .

Cagliostro was doubtlessly endowed with psychic powers which he was able to call into play in his healings and séances but which in all probability were imperfectly understood by the man himself as well as by his audience, in that age preceding the definition of psychic research, parapsychology, extrasensory perception, clairvoyance, clairaudience, telepathy, prescience, when all the supernormal, preternatural phenomena were yet to be dissociated from the supernatural.

In Cagliostro's day, such phenomena still lay within the realm of superstition, of the occult, the mystic, even the diabolic, within the category of witchcraft and sorcery; and Cagliostro was considered (may even have considered himself) a necromancer, soothsayer, exorcist, Geisterseher (Schiller's word for him—literally, ghost see-er).

With his mysterious, mystifying gifts of second sight, mind reading, augury, with his "magnetic" gaze, mesmerizing his subjects into a state of trance ("somnambulism" was the popular word for it at the time) —with these uncanny, paranormal faculties incomprehensible to him, Cagliostro may have practiced them indiscriminately, exploited them, even prostituted them in tawdry magic shows, with a flourish of the prestidigitator's arts along with the conjurer's: transformations of "hemp into silk, pearls out of pebbles, roses out of powder . . . materializations of the devil," side shows offering sylphs in satin-lined glass cases, homunculi in bottles, even (pièce de résistance) a mandragore, one of those "little earthly creatures who cry at night out of the earth at the foot of trees . . . born of the 'voluptuous and ambiguous tears' of a hanged man . . ." *

But there was no such mumbo-jumbo evident in Cagliostro's revelations of his "philosophy." There even Georgel, a hostile witness, fails to make a case against him, hard as he tries:

Cagliostro's religious theories held fatal appeal to mens' imaginations; his followers revered him as the oracle of god. It was his teaching that men could live by the one great commandment alone: Do unto others as you would have others do unto you.

Cagliostro made no criticism of any of the religions of the world; he even insisted on respect for the established religions of the day and the land in which he found himself. "Although the Divinity," he said, "may prefer the simpler, purer, natural worship of the original, the natural philosophy, as it was formulated by the Old Testament patriarchs and prophets, He is not offended by whatever form men have given it in different ages and different climes."

This may seem a tolerant, respectful and respectable statement of a man's articles of faith, yet it was disquieting to a doctrinal Abbé Georgel. The real shocker to the Jesuit, however, came in "Cagliostro's insolent pretension that the secrets of the prophets and the patriarchs—the way

* William Bolitho, Twelve against the Gods.

to direct and conscious communion with the Divinity—were within the reach of men of good will in every age to seek and find if they would attain to such communion, a communion to which Cagliostro implied he himself could attain." Clearly to the abbé this is heresy, despite the fact that Georgel's own patron saint, Ignatius of Loyola, in his famed handbook of disciplined Christian mysticism, Spiritual Exercises, indites a not dissimilar passage: "I can find God at all times, whenever I wish, and any man of good will can do the same."

And then there was Cagliostro's reply to the oft-repeated question of "Who are you?"—his widely quoted, widely derided "I am he Who is" (which finds an echo in Aldous Huxley's "Any theocentric saint, sage or prophet is a human being who knows Who he is").

Twice on trial with his life at stake, first before the grave judges of the Parliament of Paris and later before the terrible ones of the Inquisition, Cagliostro twice refused to reveal his origins; he carried that secret to his grave—if it was his grave in the papal fortress-prison of San Leo (as has been disputed), and if he stayed in it (as has been disputed too).

Those who consult the encyclopedias will find it stated as categorical fact that Count Alessandro di Cagliostro was "Giuseppe Balsamo, of Palermo." It is enough to shake one's faith in reference books, in view of the fact that the basis for such identification must rest for eternity upon the evidence of an anonymous letter to the Paris police and on Cagliostro's "confession" to the Inquisition, whose verdicts were suspect the world over. (What value can attach to a confession, followed by retractions, then more confessions, in the apostolic courtroom where "the rack was displayed at every session of Cagliostro's trial," according to the Rome correspondent of the Paris Moniteur?)

The anonymous letter came to the desk of Paris Police Commissaire Fontaine in December 1786, at the very moment when it was most obviously to the government's interest to discredit and defame Count Cagliostro, as a Diamond Necklace Case witness considered inimical to the Queen. Dated November 2 and "postmarked" Palermo, the letter (now in the Paris police files in the Archives de France), states that Anonymous had had the story from a fellow Palermitan, one Antonio Braconiere, to the effect that Braconiere's wayward nephew Beppo Balsamo and the world-famous, self-styled Count di Cagliostro were one and the same.

" 'I am positive of my facts,' this Braconiere told me," wrote Anonymous, " 'since I speak of my own sister's son . . . born to her in 1743, christened Giuseppe [Joseph] Balsamo . . .'" Thus, simple peasant stock on the distaff side; on the sword side, a humble Jewish peddler father.

Braconiere told Anonymous that he had positively identified this nephew as the notorious Cagliostro by the popular engravings of the latter, which, at the height of the Necklace Case publicity, had reached even that remote Mediterranean isle. Beppo's family, in the uncle's chronicle, had not been loath to see him depart those shores, with the island police already on his traces after a juvenile-delinquency record including petty larceny, a spot of forgery and a touch of pandering.

When Anonymous expressed his astonishment at the identification of the peasant lout with the high priest of the rococo, his informant, he wrote, "further convinced me by pointing out that the title "Cagliostro" had not been snatched out of thin air, but had been borrowed from a maternal uncle, one Joseph Cagliostro of nearby Messina." Beppo had furthermore written home a description of his picaresque adventures across the face of Europe with his Roman-beauty bride, on a confidence game of a pilgrimage.

Italy, Spain, Portugal had all known the Balsamos. They were known to that other adventurous Italian, Casanova (although he never saw, knew, recognized or identified the Cagliostros), who ran across the Balsamos in southern France, "dressed in penitential garb and soliciting alms to make their pilgrimage to the shrine of Santiago de Compostela."

According to Casanova's memoirs, "The female mendicant, interesting by reason of her youth, beauty and aristocratic air, sat in the inn [at Aix-en-Provence] . . . holding a crucifix of yellow metal six inches long, while her mate arranged shells on his black baize coat"—unmistakably the shell game, that eternal favorite of eternal rascaldom.

Honeymooning in all the European capitals, the Balsamos departed most of them at the instance of the constabulary, as they did London in 1771. Elusive though he generally was, Balsamo presented himself the following year at the Paris police station to make official, signed request for a gendarme to be assigned to assist him in recovery of his beauteous bride from the arms of a more affluent, if not more ardent, Parisian admirer.

The anonymous Palermitan correspondent in his November 2, 1786, letter now invited the Paris police to look up their Balsamo file of 1772 for a comparison of the description and handwriting of the two couples, Balsamo and Cagliostro. The authorities of a hostile regime needed little urging, and their handwriting experts shortly declared the signature in the Balsamo dossier to correspond to that in the Cagliostro file.

Considering the circumstances of the well-timed anonymous letter, suspicion must attach to the whole experiment, including the possibility of outright forgery as concerned the Balsamo documents, turned up at so opportune a moment by the Paris police.

Undeniably, some cogent arguments for identification of the Balsamos with the Cagliostros do obtain—the fact, for example, that both Signora Balsamo and Countess Cagliostro were Romans, that both were beauties, and that neither could write, not so much as her name.* But there is nowhere positive confirmation of the identification; not a single person who had known Balsamo in the 1770s ever came forward to recognize or identify him as Cagliostro in the 1780s. And even the court of the Inquisition had to admit that it had "failed to produce a single witness against Cagliostro who had actually known Balsamo." The apostolic court's explanation that "all those who had known Balsamo were dead" cannot but be considered an improbability—a scant fifteen years having elapsed since the Balsamos' frequent brushes with the police across the entire continent of Europe and in the British Isles.

The controversy raged at the time; rages on.†

Moreover, how to reconcile the metamorphosis of a loutish Beppo Balsamo with that exquisite of a Count Cagliostro, along with Franklin and Mesmer one of the three most prominent, most sought-after foreigners in Paris, lionized by the high society of the capital—that exalted, cultivated, sophisticated, finicking, precious eighteenth-century audience which he held enthralled—occult high priest to a congregation of noble atheists, grandmaster to a Masonic lodge whose membership roster read like the Almanach de Gotha? To win an audience as critical as that of a first-night opera, Cagliostro's performance must necessarily have exceeded that of a mountebank of a Balsamo.

---

* In explanation of this deficiency on the part of Countess Cagliostro, the Count offered the interesting theory that it was traditional among the great and ancient families of Rome that their young daughters be not taught that art, lest they engage in clandestine romantic correspondence.

† If the centuries-old controversy seems clearly to suggest resolution by modern-day handwriting expertise applied to the Balsamo-Cagliostro signatures, this research failed in that endeavor only because M. Mahieu, incumbent archivist of Paris' Archives de France, with the best will in the world failed to locate the Balsamo dossier, although Second Empire archivist Émile Campardon reported it in those files as late as mid-nineteenth century.

Encyclopedias to the contrary, the veil of mystery over the who and whence as relate to Cagliostro has never been rent, not by all the police force of France nor all the secret service of the Holy See, at the time or since.

He was "apostle," "prophet," "adept" to the occultists and theosophists; "Grand Cophta" to the Masons; "Great Quack-Face of the eighteenth century" to Carlyle; to William Bolitho, in the twentieth century, "adventurer," one of the all-time great, categorized with eleven others including Alexander the Great, Mohammed, Columbus and Napoleon to comprise Bolitho's title Twelve against the Gods, possibly the most apt, certainly the most dispassionate, appraisal to date—adventurer in esoterica, as Casanova, another one of the twelve, was in erotica.

"Of the major euphorias," Bolitho thinks, "the queerest and oldest is the side-path of Magic"; Cagliostro's

> profession of magician [was] one of the most perilous and arduous specializations of the imagination . . . the hostility of God and the police to be guarded against . . . as difficult as music, as nervous as the manufacture of high explosives . . . Technically, in the upper atmospheres where [Cagliostro] flew, it is social. For it aims to satisfy the deepest wishes of the human heart, which are rarely individual; and its tools are secret societies. The fear of death, cryptosexual longings for supernatural terrors and beauties and all the rest of the complex motive that sends men to Mahomet, Beethoven or Cagliostro, cannot be satisfied adequately except by a church, an orchestra, or a free-masonry. In occultism, this apparatus must be secret, for it is not a salvation, but an escape; an escape from the prison of reality, into another world, without birth or death, outside the organic flux . . . The inscription over the little side door, where Cagliostro dangled the key, is

Oser
Vouloir
Se taire

DARE! WILL! KEEP SILENCE!

87

D*

This, then, is the man who in 1780 first met the Prince de Rohan. In Abbé Georgel's words:

Prince de Rohan happened to be in residence at his château at Saverne at the very time Count Cagliostro, having dazzled Switzerland, burst upon an astonished Strasbourg.

The newcomer's assiduities to the poor, his disdain of the rich, enhanced his reputation as a superior being, aroused universal excitement and fanaticism. Those honored by his friendship left his presence singing delirious praise.

Curious to meet so extraordinary a man, His Eminence Prince de Rohan went to Strasbourg to seek him out.

Again, the instance of "a preappointed two behold each other." Carlyle's reference was to the meeting of the Countess de La Motte and the Cardinal, but it applies equally to the Cardinal's meeting with Cagliostro; equally, to Cagliostro's meeting with the Countess de La Motte.

She had thus far only glimpsed the celebrated mystagogue when, as she tells it in her Story of My Life, she "went flying to Strasbourg," on the traces of the Marquise de Boulainvilliers, who "had gone to consult the famous Count Cagliostro"—whether upon the ills of the flesh or upon those of the spirit the Countess de La Motte does not distinguish: whether for a dram of his "wine of Egypt" or for one of his candle-lit séances, where, among the spirits of the dead he purportedly could summon up, that of high-spirited Mademoiselle de Passy might frolic up for a mother desolate over her youngest daughter's recent untimely death. (The Marquise de Boulainvilliers was apparently more than desolate, she was perhaps even deranged, if her husband, the villainous Marquis, is to be trusted in his allusion to his wife's "caprices, her bizarre moods, her goings on with Cagliostro in Strasbourg"—or, rather, if the Countess de La Motte is to be trusted in this her quotation of the Marquis's allusion.)

At any rate, the Countess de La Motte's Story of My Life makes only passing reference to her passing through Strasbourg with her husband en route from Lunéville, "stopping by Cagliostro's house to inquire the Boulainvilliers' whereabouts"—elbowing her way, presumably, haughtily and impatiently, through the press of poor and invalid encamped upon his doorstep—only to learn that the Marquise had gone on, that very day, to Saverne.

The Countess de La Motte and Cagliostro would meet again and come to know (if not like) one another better.

As would the Countess and Cardinal Prince de Rohan. Their first brief meeting at Saverne was a mere formality—the presentation of the Boulainvilliers' winsome protégée to Monseigneur, her deep obeisance to kiss his bishop's ring—but an encounter that would establish a rapport between them, to blossom later, in Georgelian idiom, into a fleur-du-mal, a flower-of-evil liaison. At that first encounter, the Cardinal's tender blue gaze, his roving eye, would be attracted by the Countess's self-evident attractions; her own "glorious, expressive blue eyes" would be dancing or soulful, as the recital of her "curious and interesting history" required—a tale she told, and told well, at the Marquise's prompting.

But that first day in his château at Saverne, with both her guardians as well as her hulking cavalier of a husband present, the Cardinal's mind would have registered at most a pleasing, hardly a lasting, impression.

As for the impression made by la Belle Éminence upon the Countess de La Motte, the young bride of twenty-seven may have categorized even a handsome prince-prelate of forty-nine as middle-aged, if not downright elderly, although she providently filed away his name for possible future reference in her memory book of imposing figures; and she would unerringly riffle back through the pages to flip up his when the time came for her to search out influential patrons, exalted sponsors at court and in the capital.

But in the year 1783, the three, the Countess de La Motte-Valois, Cardinal Prince de Rohan and Count Alessandro di Cagliostro, had met only fleetingly.

If the character sketches of these three appear grotesquely exaggerated, blown up to larger-than-life proportion, cast in the epic mold, each was a unique, a nonpareil personality. Each, in his own right, had a stellar magnitude; and if their trajectories crossed (at the city of Strasbourg in the 1780s), they three, hurtling toward one another through time and space, would collide with a crash to resound through the centuries.

As to Her Most Christian Majesty Marie Antoinette, Queen of France, her luminous comet train had crossed Prince-Bishop de Rohan's at the high altar of Strasbourg Cathedral as early as 1770, and again, as recently as 1781, at the Versailles chapel, when Grand Almoner de Rohan had officiated at the baptism of the first Dauphin although the royal mother, across the font, did not vouchsafe him so much as a glance, so much as a word—claiming later that she never would, that she never did, neither to him nor to either of the other two luminaries of the diamond necklace affair, insistent to the end that the course of her (tragic) star, the brightest in the eighteenth-century firmament, never impinged upon the courses of theirs.

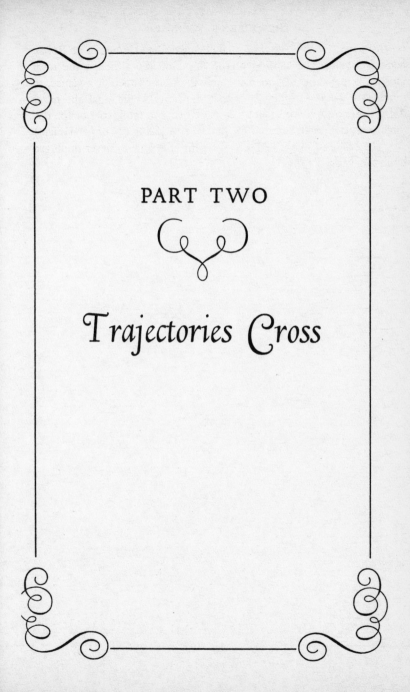

PART TWO

Trajectories Cross

VI

The Cardinal Meets Cagliostro
and the Countess
(1780-1783)

WITH ASTROLOGY AMONG CAGLIOSTRO'S ARTS, as among every alchemist's, the casting of a horoscope should have warned him that his and
Prince de Rohan's was an ill-starred friendship.

Perhaps it did, since he exhibited some reluctance at entering into the
association. It was Prince de Rohan who was insistent (at once skeptical
and credulous, cynical and gullible, typical of his age, the Cardinal had
always been irresistibly attracted to the supernatural); or so the Abbé
Georgel tells it in his memoirs.

Prince de Rohan went to Strasbourg to seek out Cagliostro, but access
to that renowned figure was not so easily obtained.

"If His Eminence Cardinal Rohan is ill," came back word from Cagliostro, "let him come to me, and I will heal him. If he is in good
health, he has no need of me, nor I of him."

Such an arrogant message, far from offending the Cardinal, created
exactly the opposite effect, that of whetting his curiosity. Admitted at
last into the sanctuary of the new Aesculapius,* he saw in the face of
that uncommunicative man, as he told me afterward, a dignity so impressive that he felt himself in the grip of an awesome religious experience.

* On plea of an asthmatic attack.

This first encounter, a rather brief one, served only to intensify the Cardinal's desire for closer acquaintance. In this he finally succeeded. Or, rather, it was the wily charlatan who gradually insinuated himself into the confidence of the Cardinal, into control over his mind and will —and all so smoothly, so imperceptibly that the Cardinal credited himself with having effected the intimacy.

"Your soul," Cagliostro said one day to Prince de Rohan, "is worthy of my own. You deserve to be the confidant of all my secrets"—an accolade from the Master to overwhelm the Cardinal, who had delved all of his life into the secrets of alchemy and botany.*

From this time forward, the intimacy between the Cardinal and the Count Cagliostro advanced apace and became a matter of public gossip. The Count (and the woman who passed as his wife) took up residence in the Cardinal's château at Saverne, where day after day, night after night, the two men were closeted in secret confabulation. When the Cardinal made occasional trips to Paris, he left the Baron da Planta, his equerry, in Alsace to see to it that Cagliostro should want for nothing at Saverne.

This same Baron da Planta, with whom Cardinal Rohan at this period shared his innermost thoughts and affections, also became the Cardinal's trusted agent in the complicated dealings which were about to begin with the Countess de La Motte and Cagliostro. A Swiss of noble family and a Protestant, he was a silent sort of man, sparing of speech in an effort to stimulate the impression that he was greatly given to cerebration. Having been cashiered out of both the French and Prussian armies for his obstinacy (as I ascertained in an inquiry into his background), the ex-officer was vegetating despondently in Vienna when Ambassador Rohan came across him, and he accepted with alacrity the Prince's offer of a place in his retinue. His several disgraces and his financial embarrassment had made him less opinionated and less difficult to control. Despite his somber and disapproving air, I always saw him curb his will before that of the Cardinal, to whom he appeared unreservedly devoted.

I remember having learned from a reliable source that Baron da Planta was in the habit of arranging costly and extravagant entertainments for the Cagliostros in the Cardinal's palace, orgies where the Prince's rarest Tokay wine flowed like water. But when I warned the

* In Vienna the Cardinal had conducted a series of successful experiments on the derivation of saltpeter from sea water, and he was still engaged in attempts to interest the King and the government in undertaking grand-scale production of the chemical, from which he predicted a fortune could be made.

Cardinal, as I thought my duty, that these new friends were taking advantage of his hospitality, he merely replied, "I know all about it. What is more, I have given them the privilege of abusing my hospitality if they so choose."

This attitude could leave me in no further doubt as to the Prince's enthusiasm for Count Cagliostro, but, even so, I was far from believing that the man had become his oracle, his guide, his compass. . . . Everyone was talking about this intimacy between a Cardinal and a charlatan.

It was the first thing the Baroness d'Oberkirch heard when she reached Strasbourg.

Curiosity aroused, the Baroness suggested to her husband that they go "pay their respects," as she phrases it, "to the Bishop-Prince of Strasbourg." The Oberkirchs were Protestants, but, like all the rest of the regional nobility, they went to pay him court, although it is doubtful that they would have gone so soon had the Baroness not been so curious. In this instance it was a rewarding haste, for she arrived at Saverne just in time to witness the fateful, incongruous entanglement in its very origins and to write it up in her daily journal, from which her memoirs were compiled—with the adventure still fresh in her mind, with such verve and incisiveness as to render the account as vivid as if written yesterday.

Just as soon as we returned from our trip to Germany, we went immediately to Saverne, where His Eminence had built and decorated a palace fit for a sovereign, which he maintained on a regal, ruinously extravagant scale—a staff, for example, of fourteen maîtres d'hôtel and twenty-five footmen. Imagine!

It was three o'clock in the afternoon when we arrived, and His Eminence was just coming from his chapel, wearing a scarlet moiré soutane and an absolutely priceless rochet of English lace. For High Mass at Versailles, he had a petit-point alb, so magnificent one dared not touch it—a floral design interspersed with medallions bearing the Rohan crest and device, and valued at more than 100,000 francs—but that day at Saverne we had to content ourselves with sight of only the English lace model (good enough for us provincials?), one of the least outstanding of his collection, as the Abbé Georgel, his secretary, hastened to assure us.

The Prince came forward, in his hand a rare and magnificent illuminated book of devotions, a family heirloom of great antiquity (he considered it beneath his dignity to use a printed missal when he celebrated Mass), and greeted us with a gallantry, a courtesy, a great-lord manner such as I have rarely met with in any of the courts of Europe, and with polite inquiries on the subject of our health and family such as to make our news appear his major concern.

Exceedingly well informed, Cardinal Rohan was a pleasing, fascinating conversationalist. He was describing a recent trip to his diocese across the Rhine when he was suddenly interrupted by a footman, who, flinging wide not one but both of the double doors—the highest mark of honor—announced, "His Excellency, Count Cagliostro."

I whirled round in my chair. I had heard talk of this adventurer, of course, ever since my return to Strasbourg, but I had not yet seen him. I was absolutely stunned to see him make this kind of entrance into the Cardinal's salon, to hear him announced with such pomp and ceremony; still more amazed when I witnessed the welcome the Cardinal gave him.

Count Cagliostro, in Strasbourg since September, had created a positive sensation with his claims of miraculous cures and healings, despite the fact that his so-called cure-all cured far from all; actually, he made well only those who already enjoyed good health or those whose imagination was as potent as his elixir. All kinds of tales were spread about him. It was said he was an Arab, but his accent sounded Italian or Piedmontese to me. I have since learned that he was actually born in Naples. At this period in his career, to attract attention, he affected all manner of bizarreries, such as sleeping in a chair instead of a bed, eating no meat, living on vegetables and cheese.

While not actually handsome, his face was the most remarkable I have ever seen. His eyes, above all. They were indescribable, with supernatural depths—all fire and yet all ice. It seemed to me that if any two artists sketched him, the two portraits, while having some slight resemblance, might yet well be totally dissimilar. Ambivalent, he at once attracted and repulsed you; he frightened you and at the same time inspired you with insurmountable curiosity.

Diamonds of magnificent size and brilliance sparkled on his shirt, his watch chain and his fingers. If they weren't paste, they were worth a king's ransom, and he claimed to fabricate them himself. Trappings like these reeked of the charlatan a league away.

No sooner had the Cardinal caught sight of the man than he went running toward him and, greeting him at the door, spoke briefly in a low tone of voice—words which I made no effort to overhear. Both men then started across the room toward my husband and me.

I had risen from my chair at the instant the Cardinal had stood up, but I hastened to sit down again lest this adventurer think that I was taking notice of him. Very shortly, however, I found I had no choice but to do just that, and I must admit today that I have never regretted doing so, for the supernatural and the extraordinary have always fascinated me.

Despite my husband's resistance and my own, the Cardinal, after a few moments, found a way to bring us all into the same general conversation. He had the tact not to introduce the man to me or to use my name directly to him—else I would immediately have left the room— but he did succeed in bringing the conversation round to such a point as to make us all participate.

Cagliostro had fixed his eyes upon me from the moment he had entered. My husband must have been making signs to me to suggest our leaving, but I never noticed at the time. I was conscious of only one thing: Cagliostro's eyes boring into my brain like a drill. I can find no other expression to fit the sensation.

Suddenly Cagliostro interrupted the Cardinal, and spoke abruptly:

"You lost your mother long ago. You hardly remember her. You were an only child. You have one daughter—and *she* will be an only child. You will have no more children."

I started in surprise and looked over my shoulder to see who it was to whom he was talking, for I simply could not believe that he had had the audacity to address me, a woman of quality, directly (a surprise I have not got over to this day). Needless to say, I made no answer.

"Oh, madame, do please answer," said the Cardinal in a tone of entreaty.

"Upon such matters, Monseigneur," said my husband, "the Baroness d'Oberkirch does not reply to those whom she has not the honor to know." His tone was close to impertinence, and I was afraid that he had shown himself disrespectful to the Bishop-Cardinal.

My husband rose from his chair and bowed, but in a rather aloof and haughty manner. I bowed also. The Cardinal, accustomed to the truckling subservience of courtiers everywhere, seemed embarrassed, as if uncertain at first what attitude to assume.

And all the while, Cagliostro's eyes were still fastened upon mine.

Finally the Prince went up to Baron d'Oberkirch and spoke words so conciliatory and so courteous that my husband could not resent them: "Monsieur de Cagliostro is a savant, an exceptional personage, and so an exception to the rule applying to ordinary men. Do stay a moment longer, my dear Baron, and permit the Baroness to answer. There can be no sin in it, no impropriety—and besides, if there were, does not a cardinal have a private stock of special dispensations and absolutions for just such special occasions?"

"I do not have the honor of being a member of your flock, Monseigneur," Baron d'Oberkirch broke in with a lingering trace of ill humor.

"I know that only too well, dear Baron," the Cardinal said, smiling. "And I never cease to regret the fact. You would do honor to our Church. But, Madame Baroness, will you not tell us whether Monsieur de Cagliostro was mistaken in his pronouncement about your family? I beg of you that you will inform us."

"He was not mistaken on any count as to that which concerns the past," I answered, unable to resist the amazing truth.

"Nor am I ever mistaken in that which concerns the future,"* Count Cagliostro's voice blared out, brassy as a trumpet veiled in crepe.

I cannot deny here, I must admit it: I was overwhelmed at that instant by an almost irresistible desire to seek the man's predictions on my destiny. Only fear of antagonizing my husband, who disdained such mummery, restrained me.

The Cardinal stood by, wide-eyed, clearly under the spell of the talented magician. (Has he not since proven it?) Cagliostro was cavalier in his treatment of the Prince—as with all his titled disciples, as if they were under infinite obligation to him, rather than he to them.

That day will remain indelibly imprinted upon my memory. I had difficulty tearing myself away from Cagliostro's gaze, from a fascination which I will not today deny, although I find it even more difficult today to explain.

As we stood at the door in leave-taking that afternoon, he made another prediction, and in the most positive of terms: that of the imminent death of Empress Maria Theresa of Austria. At that very hour, he said, she was drawing her last breath. (The official report of the Austrian Empress's death did not reach Strasbourg until five days later!)

* Nor was Cagliostro mistaken in this instance. The Oberkirchs had only the one daughter, who married Count de Montbrison and whose son published the Baroness's memoirs after her death, dedicating them to his grandmother's dear friend, Czar Nicholas I of Russia.

But I had not heard the last of Cagliostro, and the rest of the story is, if anything, stranger and more inexplicable than anything that has gone before.

Later that month, a letter marked with the great Rohan seal brought us an invitation from the Cardinal to a dinner party at Saverne. Unaccustomed to the honor of such attentions from the Prince, we were at a loss to account for this one.

"I'll wager," said my husband, "that he wants to seat us across the table from that damned sorcerer of his. If so, I'll make him a very disagreeable dinner partner."

"Cagliostro is in Paris," I replied.

"Oh, no, he came back a month ago with a dozen silly women on his trail. To be healed by Cagliostro has become the rage. An epidemic of madness."

"I thought I heard that he had gone to Paris, that he cured Prince de Soubise, the Cardinal's uncle, after the Paris doctors had given up hope."

"Perhaps, but he's been back here long enough to perform a new miracle. This time it's the Marquis de La Salle, commandant of Strasbourg, who claims Cagliostro cured him of a violent fever—an imaginary one, no doubt. No telling who will consult him next. I will admit, however, he does things in the grand manner. A philanthropist, in the true sense of the new word, if I understand it correctly." My husband's adventuresome use of this word "philanthropist," recently coined by the Encyclopedists, amused me as much as the rest of the things he had to say.

We hesitated about replying to the Cardinal's invitation. Baron d'Oberkirch really wanted to refuse, but not I—for I was still possessed by that incomprehensible urge to see the "sorcerer" again, to use my husband's word for him. Fear of offending His Eminence, however, was what decided us to accept.

I confess that my heart was pounding away as I entered the château at Saverne. I was struck by some indefinable emotion. Fear was in it, but excitement too, and a sense of anticipation.

We had not been mistaken. Cagliostro was present.

One simply cannot imagine the passion with which people were flinging themselves at his feet. It had to be seen to be believed. People flocked round, besieged him, vying for a word, a glance. An infatuation little short of idolatry; indeed, people had begun actually deifying him.

Baron d'Oberkirch had not exaggerated. Two stars from the Comédie Italienne and a dozen ladies of quality had come running after him from Paris to Strasbourg.

I had resolved not to make myself conspicuous in that company by any dissenting comment, but, rather, to accept him—or at least pretend to—like all the rest, as an adept, as the prophet of a divine science. But I had likewise promised myself not to give him an opportunity to show off before me in his fatuous, pedantic way; nor to become involved with him; above all, never to invite him to cross our threshold.

As soon as he saw me, he greeted me respectfully; I returned his greeting with no affectation of hauteur but with no cordiality either.

I could not imagine why the Cardinal had singled me out to win me over to his way of thinking. We were fifteen at dinner, but it was to me that he gave all his attention, and he was almost coquettish in his efforts to bring me around to his point of view. Seating me at his right, he conversed almost exclusively with me and employed every possible argument to sway me. I resisted gently but firmly. By the time we were ready to leave the table, he was becoming impatient and got down to confidences. If I hadn't heard it with my own ears, I wouldn't have believed it possible that a prince of the Roman Catholic Church, a Rohan, a man of intellect and honor in so many fields, could have allowed himself to be utterly dominated by a mountebank.

"Indeed, Madame Baroness, you are a difficult woman to convince if all the things you have heard yourself, all the things I have just told you, have failed to do so. Well, then, I see I must take you into my confidence. Remember, please, that this is absolutely secret."

Having no desire to share his secrets, I found this new tack embarrassing. His Eminence's notorious indiscretions (of which he had just given me proof) made me fearful of sharing the honor of his confidence with so many others, the majority of whom were beneath his dignity. I was about to refuse, and he sensed it.

"Now, don't say No," he insisted. "Please listen to me. Do you see this?" "This" was a huge solitaire he was wearing on his little finger; on the broad facet of the stone was engraved the Rohan crest. It was a ring worth twenty thousand francs at least.

"It is a magnificent stone, Monseigneur. I have been admiring it."

"Well, then. It was Count Cagliostro who made it. Created it, do you understand, out of thin air. I saw him do it—never took my eyes off the crucible, watched the whole operation. Does this come under the heading of any of the known sciences? What do you think now, Madame Baroness? How can people say he's hoodwinking me, exploiting my friendship, when jewelers have estimated this diamond at twenty-five thousand francs? You'll have to admit that it's an unusual swindler who makes presents such as this."

I was stunned, I admit. The Cardinal could see it, and he pressed his advantage, sure now of a victory.

"And that's not all. He makes gold as well as diamonds—made five or six thousand francs' worth, before my very eyes, up above there in the palace attics. And he'll make more, much more, make me the richest prince in Europe. These are no dreams, madame; he transmutes base metals into gold, a proven established fact. And think of his predictions of the future, all fulfilled, and the miraculous cures he has wrought. I tell you he's the most amazing man in the world—and the most sublime. If his mind has no equal in the world, neither does his heart. What charity he bestows, what good deeds he performs! It surpasses all imagination."

"Do you mean to tell me, Your Excellency, that you have given him nothing in return for all this? Not even a small advance, no promise of any kind, no commitment binding you in some way to anything? Pardon my curiosity, but since it is you who have chosen to make these revelations . . ."

"You are correct, madame, and I can assure you it is a fact: He has asked nothing of me, he has received nothing from me."

"Ah, but, Monseigneur," I exclaimed, "to pay so dearly to win your confidence, the man must expect to exact some great, some dangerous concession from you! If I were you, I would be on my guard. He will lead you far afield."

The Cardinal answered me only with an incredulous smile, but I am sure that later on, in the midst of the necklace affair, when Cagliostro and the Countess de La Motte had dashed him into the abyss, he must have remembered what I said to him that night of the dinner party at Saverne.

Our conversation continued along the same lines for the rest of the evening, but I think I finally discovered the purpose of his persuasions. The poor Prince was serving another's purposes. Cagliostro knew of my girlhood friendship and close association with the Grand Duchess of Russia, and he had probably persuaded Prince de Rohan to work on me. Had I been convinced of Cagliostro's occult powers, I might well have acted as his spokesman, gained him entrée to Her Imperial Highness. There was merit in the plan; it failed only because to resist I summoned up my last ounce of will power (not my power of reasoning—that had failed me; not my convictions—they had been shaken).

It is certain that had I not made this supreme effort of will to control my natural tendency toward the supernatural, I too might have become the dupe of that man of many intrigues. The supernatural is so alluring, the unknown—the sciences of alchemy and astrology—so thrilling! I cannot today pretend otherwise: Cagliostro was possessed of a demonic power; he enthralled the mind, paralyzed the will. I will here only relate the phenomenon, will make no attempt at explanation of it, leaving that to those wiser than myself.

Cardinal Rohan was later to lose a fortune in his entanglements with this "altruistic" individual. But I hear that, to this day, none of the things that have happened have disillusioned him, and that when he speaks of Cagliostro tears come to his eyes. What a mentality, that Cardinal Rohan! What a brilliant career he threw away, what harm he wrought by his weaknesses and indiscretions! It is true that he is still paying dear—but then, he had many a sin to expiate.

The Cardinal, however, considered himself to have been the innocent victim of a perverse fate which had arranged that he should be driving "one September day of 1783 along the high road from Saverne to Strasbourg when the carriage of the Marquise de Boulainvilliers happened to come around the bend"; and he related it in this light, stating it under oath, three years later, to the Parliament of Paris:

Our carriages halting, I went to greet the Marquise, who introduced me to a young lady seated beside her, whose name, she said, was a famous one—Valois!

"The name is one to which Madame has legitimate claim," the Marquise explained, "although unfortunately she lacks the fortune which should accompany the glorious title."

And on this point the Countess's own deposition to Parliament coincides with the Cardinal's—for the first and last time.

It was at Saverne that I saw Cardinal Rohan for the first time . . . Such interest and sympathy as he displayed in listening to my story could not but raise my hopes for the favor of his patronage at court. . . .

She continues the narrative in her Story of My Life.

When the Marquise left Saverne to return to Paris a few days later, she invited Monsieur de La Motte and me to take an apartment in her town house in the capital. I accepted this invitation with alacrity and accompanied her there, although my husband was obliged to part from us to go to Lunéville to arrange for his honorable discharge.

Monsieur de La Motte was to have joined me in Paris later, but, alas, by November my beloved foster mother was no more. Smallpox, which she had always so dreaded, had struck, depriving me of my guardian angel. My sole comfort was always to be that it was I who kept constant vigil at her bed for seventeen days and nights, clinging even to her lifeless remains. I had to be carried away by force, and it was not until four days later that I regained consciousness, and then only to fall into fearful convulsions at the realization that I was orphaned for a second time.

If the Marquis had just lost a wife, then, by happy happenstance, here was another woman in his household—a most convenient arrangement for him. He soon came directly to the point, offering to make me his mistress and share his fortune with me, offers calculated to appeal to a woman's vanity and ambitions. My having a husband, he explained, constituted an added convenience, an added protection to my reputation as well as his.

"I will arrange a commission for Monsieur de La Motte in a regiment where he will not be near enough Paris to bother us. Nor need you worry about what my daughters will have to say—I know how to silence them. Frankly, can you expect me to regret my wife? Haven't you witnessed a thousand times her capricious moods, her scenes of jealousy? And her bizarre behavior ever since our daughter's death, her goings on with Cagliostro!" (Alas, I had to say to myself a second time in my young life, so this is what men are like!)

Vain, touchy about the difference in our ages, the Marquis would never have heeded my indignant reproaches, so I resolved upon disdainful silence as the best means of smothering the adulterous fires in the old reprobate.

Yet what a performance the Marquis gave to impress the world with his sorrowing: his elaborate mourning costume and melancholy air, the salons draped in black crepe, tall mourning candles everywhere, though these were not allowed to flame unseen, but were snuffed out promptly upon the exit of each visitor—a mélange of miserliness and pride that resulted in a tragicomic scene. An equerry of the Prince de Conti, arriving to present his master's condolences and ushered prematurely into the salon, surprised the widower in the act, in his indecorously hasty relighting process. Breathless from these exertions, slowing down to a funeral-march tempo, rolling his eyes heavenward and unfolding a large handkerchief to catch his tears, the old hypocrite delivered himself of this hilarious line:

"Ah, monsieur, you can see that I shall not long survive my dear Marquise!"

At these words I could no longer control myself. Rushing out, I burst into such gales of laughter that I had to run to my room to repair the damage I had done the costume I was wearing.

As my health improved, I began to enjoy going out again and receiving visitors at home, but every male caller aroused the suspicions of the Marquis. The doctor who had attended me in my illness; the Marquis's own sons-in-law, Baron de Crussol and Viscount de Fodoas, who came to inquire as to my health or take me driving in their carriages; my husband's young Surmont cousin—any and all who showed me the slightest attention were promptly transformed, in the eyes of the jealous Marquis, into so many lovers. Not even that worthy prelate, the bishop of Langres, was safe from the Marquis's suspicions.*

In the midst of this constant wrangling, Monsieur de La Motte's arrival was doubly welcome to me. The Marquis's first move was to try to turn my husband against me, to convince him of the indiscretion of my conduct, complaining that I treated his home like a hotel, entertaining men, some of whom he had never seen before. "Your wife is pleasure-mad," he told my husband. "She disappeared on a weekend jaunt with your own cousin from Bar-sur-Aube. But one conquest does not suffice her; even my sons-in-law are on terms of intimacy. You can take my word for it: I have studied her character from childhood. I do not think she should stay on in my house—people will talk. After all, there are certain social conventions, proprieties, which cannot be openly flouted."

My husband was too sensible to pay attention to such stories, one more scandalous than the next, but he pretended to listen attentively in order to ascertain the Marquis's real sentiments.

Once the Marquis was convinced of the futility of his lecherous advances, his former courtesies turned into persecutions of so petty a na-

* Evidently the Marquis, as well as Villette, was privy to that old affinity.

ture that I blush to cite examples. Not daring to come out openly to ask us to leave the house, he resorted to the device of making our life there gradually intolerable, withdrawing day by day another article of decent living, retrenching on the table service, substituting candle ends for tapers. There was nothing for it but for Monsieur de La Motte and me to separate ourselves from his household.

My marriage to Monsieur de La Motte proved to have been a union of drought with famine. He was as devoid of fortune as I. On his marriage contract he had listed his estate at six thousand francs, but apparently this was a figure hypothecated on the mists of the River Marne, for neither he nor I ever saw a centime of it, neither in capital nor in interest.

With no resources to meet current needs, with great anxiety as to the future, I remembered words spoken on my father's deathbed and indelibly engraved upon my youthful mind: *"Never forget you are the descendant of Henri the Second, a king!"*

The problem of the La Motte finances is thoroughly examined also by Count Beugnot in his memoirs.

The La Mottes had time to assess their situation, coming to the self-evident conclusion that it was desperate. There was no alternative but for Madame de La Motte to try her luck with another trip to Paris.

Cash was lacking and credit scarce, when my father came to their rescue with a loan of a thousand francs—my father apparently retaining a soft spot in his heart for the "little lass of Fontette" to whose welfare he had in the past so often made contribution. Or perhaps he prided himself on an occasional recklessness of generosity, of which this gesture was undoubtedly an example. As a matter of fact, he had become exceeding fond of Mademoiselle de Valois from the very moment he had made sure that she would never become his daughter-in-law. He had been so delighted to see her married off that he would gladly have defrayed all the wedding expenses.

I have already spoken ill of Madame de La Motte and will be obliged to speak more later, but I want to do her justice on this point: Her gratitude to my father was unfailing; she never spoke of him or of the kindness he rendered her without genuine affection and tenderness. In her brief moments of prosperity, she not only returned the amount of the loan but made every effort to pay him interest as well. Twice my father sent back to her a box of gold she had left with him—the interest money, she called it, although it was a sum very nearly equal to the principal.

My father's thousand-franc loan the couple divided equally: Monsieur de La Motte setting out with five hundred francs for Fontette, where he was to get down to the business of recovering the Valois properties; Madame de La Motte, with a like amount, taking off for Paris, there to turn to advantage whatever information her husband's on-the-spot investigations might bring to light.

She took lodging on the Rue de la Verrerie, at the Hotel de Reims (although the term "hotel" seems flattery for that dingy, dirty little tavern, which was about on a par with the Red Head Inn at Bar-sur-Aube). It was from this hostelry that there came to me, one morning, a note from Madame de La Motte announcing her arrival in Paris; a postscript pointed out that she had brought with her a letter from my father, which she would be pleased to deliver to me personally that very day.

On my side, there was more than one reason to account for an eagerness to see Madame de La Motte. That very day was none too soon, and I set out for the Hotel de Reims without delay.

She gave me leave to open the letter from my father, who expressed therein his genuine interest in the bearer. He urged me to examine her claims carefully, establish whether they were legally sound, and, if so, assist her to the limit of my capabilities. He added that he found the lady irresistible, a discovery I had made for myself far earlier. My father noted that she was well aware of the complications in her affairs and that it would be inhuman to abandon her, though he failed to make any mention whatsoever of the humanitarian impulse which had prompted him to make her a substantial loan.

I gave the matter my serious attention, just as my father had requested. I instituted an investigation of the titles in the public records of the regions where the Valois properties were located; and I personally undertook the research in the Archives Office in Paris, where I had no difficulty locating the letters patent signed by Henry II in 1558, by which he had made grant to his natural son, the Baron de Saint-Rémy, of all the lands we were trying to recover. I could not so readily trace the sequence of the deeds and transfers by which these estates had passed out of the hands of the Saint-Rémys into those of subsequent owners. The last person in possession proved to have been a Monsieur Orceau of Fontette, who had just recently turned over these lands to the King in a property-exchange transaction—a circumstance which might be regarded as highly favorable to our claims, since all that was needed now was for the King to open up his hands in a generous gesture to restore to the Saint-Rémys the domain of their ancestors. And who knows whether this very thing might not have been brought about if the claims of my client had been presented to the King under more favorable auspices? If we could have managed to interest some powerful, influential parties close to the King or in government in our reclamation suit, and if success had crowned these efforts, how different a story this might have been.

My efforts, however, proved fruitless. Monsieur de La Motte showed not the slightest comprehension of what I had outlined for him to work on. His idea of a good first move had been to make a triumphal entry into Fontette, the scene of his wife's miserable beginnings. For some unfathomable reason of his own (certainly premature, if a celebration) he had deemed it appropriate to have a Te Deum sung in the village church, after which he was seen tossing out handfuls of coins to the assembled villagers—all this in serious depletion of his modest five-hundred-franc stake, barely sufficient for expenses of travel and investigation, much less for any such lordly gesture of largesse.

In Paris, his wife displayed little more logic. When I sought to explain what I had thus far accomplished and what I planned next to do, presenting a résumé of the obstacles and difficulties in our path, she tossed her head and shrugged impatience at such a stilted, conventional approach to her affairs—such as might have been expected, she implied, from some timorous legal novice, not from a seasoned barrister of my ingenuity and imagination.

To hear her tell it, it was all so simple, this affair of hers. Had we not in hand the original land grants to the estates of Fontette, Essoyes, Verpillières—definite proof of her ancestors' ownership? Well, then, these same lands were today reported in possession of the King; what difference to her whether she retrieved her property from the King or from another, just so she got it back, and got it in a hurry! It was merely a matter, now, of stepping in to take possession, and all I had to do was indicate to Monsieur de La Motte the legal move to make. If I lacked the enterprise and imagination, then she would take over and send him instructions to proceed forthwith. Words to set me trembling, knowing her as capable of recommending follies as he of perpetrating them.

When Monsieur de La Motte had exhausted his capital (even sooner

than expected), he retired to his sister's house in Bar-sur-Aube, his affairs
no further advanced than when he had set out, the sole data he had supplied me being a list of names of Fontette attorneys to whom I might
apply for legal trivia beneath the dignity of a man of his rank and station. Therewith all local investigations came to an end.

In Paris we made better progress. I had drawn up a petition, not without merit, wherein I represented my client's case as "The final insult of
cruel fortune to the Valois line—the sad lot of a side branch of that
ancient family tree which for so long cast its royal shadow across France
and the other nations of Europe." My composition well larded with
philosophical reflections (which were literarily stylish at the time), I
apostrophized the Bourbons, beseeching them to "pay their natural
debt to the Valois who had bequeathed them so magnificent a heritage."

This composition I submitted to Élie de Beaumont (a literary as well
as legal arbiter, and as such frequently consulted on matters of jurisprudence which veered off the beaten path), who was so gracious as to
praise my opus with the remark, "What a shame that a case of this kind
cannot be brought before the Parliament of Paris! It would be enough to
make your reputation."

Instead, as it developed, I was not even to attain to the honor of publication, for all my labors. For, by consensus of legal opinion, the case
came into the domain of royal favor; and in that light, to have printed
anything on the subject would have constituted disrespect to the King—
any sort of publicity would be construed as an affront to His Majesty.

If nothing else, this petition of mine did serve to raise me to new
heights in the esteem of Madame de La Motte; she considered the battle
won although her lawyer did not share his client's optimism. To have
brought the case to a successful issue, there were, as I had realized from
the beginning, three requirements: first, influence; second, champions
of the cause in high places at court; last, though not least, financial back-
ing. Precisely those which were lacking to us!

Even so, I composed a second petition to the Crown, condensed into
the briefest form possible to assure its being read through by the persons
who would undertake to present it to the King, and one day, God willing, by the King himself.

These labors kept me very busy during the summer of 1783. Madame
de La Motte was still living at that horrid little Hotel de Reims, and for
the best of reasons: she was behind in her rent and owed the proprietor
a great deal of money. Two small loans of ten louis each which I had

made her over a period of months made hardly a dent in her indebtedness.

I could not invite her to meals at my apartments, since I maintained no regular household establishment, but once or twice a week she did me the honor of accepting my invitation to dine at the popular Cadran Bleu restaurant on the Champs Élysées, and there she astonished my youthful eyes by the zest of her appetite. On other days she took my arm for promenades which invariably wound up at a café. She had a distinct fondness for what she called a "really good glass of beer," although I remember no instance of her having come across any she rejected as inferior. While she sipped her glass of beer she nibbled at two or three dozen hot canapés, and this nibbling was so frequent that I could not but conclude that she must have dined very lightly that day, if, indeed, she had dined at all.

Then, one morning, she showed up at my door, her face alight with excitement. She had just received notice of an audience granted her by Cardinal Rohan, the Grand Almoner of France. The audience had been set for the following day at noon, and she had come running to me to ask the loan of three items: my carriage to ride in, my lackey to walk behind the carriage and my arm to serve as escort.

"You simply can't say No," she exclaimed, "for I must make a good impression on His Eminence! And to quote you your own theory, in Paris there are only two effective methods for soliciting financial assistance—humbly, barefoot on the church steps, or in the grand manner, riding in a fine carriage, elegantly."

I concurred, raising no objection to the first two items on her list, demurring only at the loan of my arm, and that for reasons of protocol: I would not be admitted to the presence of the Cardinal except in my capacity as her legal representative, and then only if he had expressly granted permission.

My objection having been found valid, I suggested as compromise that I ride with her as far as the Palais-Cardinal gardens and wait for her there, outside. That, then, was how it was decided.

The first interview between Madame de La Motte and Cardinal Rohan lasted half an hour. She came out radiant with hope. His Eminence had promised personally to intervene in her behalf at the court and to exert every influence to back up her claims. He had twice read through my petition to the Crown, exclaiming that he simply couldn't get over the fact that descendants of Henri II should be thus neglected by the present King. He had touched upon the possibility of a grant from the national charity funds, of which he was treasurer, but had approached the subject with delicacy and tact, and Madame de La Motte assured me she had followed my advice: she had not risked spoiling a good first impression by painting too dismal a picture of her situation and had avoided giving the impression of entering His Eminence's presence with her hand out.

Several days went by. I had retired to my study, begging off from even my customary daily promenades with Madame de La Motte on the plea of readying a brief for a very important lawsuit shortly to come to trial before Parliament. It is my nature to become wholly engrossed in whatever I undertake and bitterly resentful of interruption.

I was deep in concentration one morning in my study when Madame de La Motte breezed in on a fresh gale of enthusiasm over a note from His Eminence inviting her to a second visit to the Palais-Cardinal. The tone of the note was affectionate, but not without a measure of dignity. She had come running to request of me the same three favors as before, but this time I was not in the mood to grant them to her. I suppose I must have been rather discouraged about the outcome of the case on which I was working, but primarily I was in bad humor at being interrupted and, as was my wont, took it out on the guilty party.

Several days went by without my seeing Madame de La Motte. Meanwhile, apparently, she had taken her complaints to a mutual friend of ours, a Madame de Crozat, to whom she described me as a fantastic individual who was all on fire about her one day and cold as ice the next, citing the example of my having forcibly ejected her from my study upon the occasion of her recent visit.

In recent months now it had been to Madame de Crozat to whom she had turned for the occasional small loans without which she could not get along—if not enough to pay up her hotel bill in full, at least enough to keep her from being evicted. Madame de Crozat could not deny Madame de La Motte's numerous shortcomings and was as dismayed as I by the symptoms of her character weakness. But Madame de Crozat always ended up on the same refrain: "Poor little thing, she's had such a bad time of it! Who knows whether in her plight you or I would show up any better?"

It was agreed that I should come to Madame de Crozat's for Sunday dinner and that Madame de La Motte should be invited too; there, under the auspices of the hostess, peace was to be restored between her two guests.

At the dinner party on Sunday, Madame de La Motte displayed cordiality to the rest of the company, a chill civility to me. I thought that in her expression, in her manner, I could detect a new composure, a lessening of tension; there was evidence too, for the first time, of a trace of hauteur, a hint of condescension. And instead of waiting for me to drive her home from Madame de Crozat's, as had been our custom, she called for a carriage upon the stroke of seven and made her departure alone.

What I deduced from all this was that her second visit to the Cardinal must have resulted in considerable advancement of her affairs. I was foolish enough to come close to being jealous, but, first and foremost, I was burning with curiosity. The very first thing, next morning, I was waiting beside her pillow when she woke . . .

On the other hand: "She told me everything"—thus Rétaux de Villette, last seen among her red-caped cavaliers in Lunéville but now in Paris, after resigning, like friend La Motte, from the cavalry. Villette, whose reach would never exceed his grasp, would have been well satisfied with "a commission in the Paris mounted police," but, as he reveals in his memoirs, he found himself instead promoted to the post of Madame de La Motte's confidential secretary—

. . . eyewitness to every event that transpired from the day of her arrival in the capital, repository of her confidences, privy to the ins and outs of all her intrigues, in on the secrets of her liaison with Cardinal Rohan from the very beginning. She told me everything, including details so intimate that she was reticent about them even in the presence of her husband.

The death of her benefactress had struck Madame de La Motte like a thunderbolt. The Marquis de Boulainvilliers, smitten by her charms, had offered refuge beneath his roof, where, under the guise of protector to her and her sister, he had seduced them both. He wound up quarreling with both and running them out of his Paris residence.*

* As in the case of the Countess's seduction by the bishop of Langres, she makes no mention of this in either her Story of My Life or her memoirs, leaving unresolved the question of whether Villette concocted the story or whether the Countess thought it inappropriate to the characterization she chose to present of herself.

E

Thus the La Mottes found themselves without shelter and without benefactor, a pension of eight hundred francs (against which they had borrowed the next several years' revenue) comprising their sole worldly possession.

But Madame de La Motte could count other treasure: native wit, a fair and radiant complexion, eyes that were bright and keen. As for her bosom, in that category she had every attribute that men most ardently admire: snow-whiteness, firmness, separation—peaks of perfection! * Rich in feminine graces, what more did she require to compensate her for the injustices of fortune? What more, as a matter of fact, to repair these injustices, make a fortune on her own?

Neglected, so to speak, by her husband, who carried his burnt offerings to the altars of other goddesses of love, Madame de La Motte had to calculate carefully to balance her romantic inclinations with her budget: yield to one man out of necessity so that she could afford to yield to another out of choice. Whether temperamentally so inclined or whether influenced by economic pressures, she had launched upon a career of dazzling men, calling into play every one of her thousand charms to enslave them by. In her selection of lovers, she tried, of course, to combine pleasure with profit whenever possible.

When a man and a woman fall upon hard times, it is only natural that they should rack their brains for an expedient whereby to extricate themselves. To this end, Monsieur and Madame de La Motte were engaged in conference when suddenly the same bright thought flashed upon them both: that benevolent Monseigneur Cardinal Rohan! Surely the Grand Almoner of France, with all the national charity funds at his disposal, would not deny them some slight relief in their desperate straits.

Acting upon this inspiration, Madame de La Motte presented herself before His Eminence and pulled out all the stops to play upon his sympathy, to stir compassion in any soul not impervious to the tenderer sentiments. The Cardinal's soul being far from an impervious one, he was visibly affected. He lamented the fact that she had neglected coming to him sooner, took out a purse filled with gold and gave it to her, urging her to return to visit him soon again. In addition, he promised to seize the first opportunity to forward her affairs at court, adding that, with

* What, then, to think of Beugnot's criticism? (See page 56, supra.) A mere caviling at perfection? Or a striking example of the persistent conflict of testimony in these various accounts? Here are two competent eyewitnesses making a controversial point even of Madame de La Motte's "snowy bosom."

this in mind, he would expect her to give him her entire confidence. He could foresee no great difficulty in effecting the restitution of her properties; it should be very simple, really, what with her Valois name and her infinite charms . . .

Startled into an involuntary movement of surprise, Madame de La Motte had risen from her chair. The Cardinal, disconcerted, broke off in mid-sentence. He bowed and stammered out some conventional phrases of farewell, and Madame de La Motte took her leave.

She could not fail to note the vivid impression she had made upon the Cardinal and his nervousness and agitation at their parting. Back home, with her purse full of gold, she gave me her observations on his reactions, and we agreed that here was a lover not to be neglected.

Only a few days had gone by when a messenger appeared with a note from the Cardinal appointing a rendezvous for that evening. At this Madame de La Motte dropped everything, to devote the day to preparation of the costume for that night. All that feminine coquetry could devise, that Parisian modistes and perfumers could purvey, in alluring frills and furbelows, in ornaments, sachets and scents, all these Madame de La Motte appropriated to the elaborate ritual of her toilette. Then, with that imposing air of hers—imposing and yet seductive—with that noble manner she could so well assume upon occasion, she betook herself to the Palais-Cardinal at the appointed hour.

There was not a courtesan in Paris with such a boudoir, so elegant a setting for voluptuous intimacy, as the one into which Madame de La Motte was shown. The Cardinal, all eagerness, visibly impatient, made inquiry as to her health, then seated her beside him on the couch and, in a most affectionate tone, urged her to give him a detailed account of her situation, the status of her finances and her prospects. When Madame de La Motte had satisfied these sympathetic queries, the Cardinal gave warm assurance that he would immediately request his cousin, Marshal de Soubise, to arrange an Army commission for her husband—a husband whose neglect, he was grieved to learn, should give her cause for dissatisfaction. How could the Count neglect a wife, His Eminence wondered aloud, in whom were combined such great attractions, such youthful radiance, such infinite charms? A woman indeed fashioned expressly by nature for the conquest of men's hearts! While the Cardinal talked, he pressed her hands in his; his eyes glinted with desire. And Madame de La Motte, gazing at him tenderly, gave him to understand that there was no favor of hers to which he might not aspire.

His Illustrious Eminence that night could consider himself a happy man. The two exchanged pledges of fidelity and devotion, and they parted each with good reason for satisfaction with the other.

The seductive "boudoir" to which Villette refers was referred to then —as it is referred to now by the guides in the Palais-Cardinal—as the Salon des Singes, the Monkey Salon (now open to the public, eliminating the necessity of any "rendezvous appointed by His Eminence"). As setting for what Villette termed "voluptuous intimacy," the great reaches of the formal salons and reception rooms would never do as well as this delicately proportioned, diminutive room, its French windows overlooking the inner gardens—a room, as Madame de La Motte described it to her secretary, in which to "know the man" (now as then) and his exquisite if decadent and perverse tastes.

Today the couch for cozy twosome is gone, with all the other furnishings. The Salon des Singes is down to bare walls, which yet are not bare: on the ornately carved and gilded white paneling, artist Huet's colors are as brilliant and exotic as the day he completed his series of chinoiseries, ladies and gentlemen of the French court in Oriental garb and pastime against an Oriental landscape. Delightful, charming, irreproachable, these central scenes, although as much cannot be said for the minor motif of the smaller panels below; "grotesqueries" is the word for this series of monkey movements, monkeyshines: sinuous little beasts disporting themselves in a variety of poses, mostly ribald or obscene. One particularly amuses the palace guides: splendid, scarlet-clad, ever so daintily he holds aside his tail, to lower himself and thus extinguish a bright-burning candle flame—Huet's queer conceit of a simian-sphinctero snuffer, though Madame de La Motte may have described it to Villette in less elegant terminology. Another prankish little beast adorned a hinged panel which concealed an altar where a prankish Cardinal chose to celebrate the Mass. Panel, monkey, sacramental paraphernalia are vanished, gone; only the metal hinges, the recess and gossip pages by the Cardinal's contemporaries attest to the former sacred and profane state.

The room has still another secret: a door cut by sleight-of-hand incision into Huet's paneling, on the wall opposite the altar, and leading into the master bedroom, as every good boudoir should. And from the master bedroom there was (and still is) a secret staircase, spiraling darkly down to the garden to spare a feminine visitor (like Madame de

La Motte) the embarrassment of parading past the guardroom to the main stairs that sweep down to the marble entrance hall—the Palais-Cardinal's famed stairway of honor, an architectural trick of pitch and proportion to accommodate a choir of Michelangelesque wing-spread angels—which might intimidate a solitary midnight visitor (like Madame de La Motte) in a silken susurrus of skirts.

But back to Count Beugnot, "close to being jealous" and "burning with curiosity," waiting beside her pillow when she woke the morning after Madame de Crozat's dinner party, "to demand certain explanations which I considered due me," as he tells us.

I wanted to know whether Madame de La Motte had delivered the unabridged version of my petition to the Cardinal, whether His Eminence had agreed personally to present it to Monsieur des Forges, the administrator of the royal domain, whether Cardinal Rohan would sponsor our petition for a relief grant on the national exchequer. To which questions Madame de La Motte answered me only in the vaguest generalities: that Monseigneur the Cardinal simply couldn't be kinder, that he was positively perfect to her and would do anything he was asked to do. When I insisted that there were certain specific procedures, certain commissions which she must request him to perform, I was told that one simply didn't handle matters with a cardinal "as one might with a petty solicitor"! I was told to stop worrying, that everything was going very, very well.

There seemed hardly any place in her new life for a young barrister with his reputation yet to make. I was forced to the conclusion that, as far as I was concerned, the signal for retreat had been sounded. However, to determine once and for all exactly where I stood with her, I proposed dinner at the Cadran Bleu for the following Wednesday, and this invitation was accepted.

On Wednesday across the table at the Cadran Bleu Madame de La Motte was in high spirits, which bubbled over, venting themselves in sarcasm and malice at the expense of our mutual friends and at mine as well. I made vain effort to steer the conversation into more serious channels. It was soon evident that, in accepting my invitation, her strategy had been to eat the dinner but mystify the host. This little game I found intensely annoying, and I threatened to abandon her to her follies. To which she made reply, quite debonairly, that she could now afford to dispense with my services. My face tensed; she could see that I was about to lose my temper. Thereupon she went to the pains of assuring me that I had been extremely helpful to her in untangling the legal technicalities of her case, in composing her petitions—in all things, indeed, which came within a lawyer's scope—but that at the point which she had now reached she needed counselors of an entirely different caliber. What she needed now were those who could show her how to reach the ear of the Finance Minister—how to get to the Queen! Those who could advise her what to do as well as merely what not to do—the latter, she insisted, being my forte. Advisers, in sum, who were capable of devising a clever intrigue and carrying it through. Next I had to hear, and from her own pretty lips, that when it came to matters such as these I was the most inept of men.

She had already taken her first steps without me, as she now explained. She had arranged, through the good offices of her good friend Baron de Crussol, for an honorary commission for her husband in the Count d'Artois's Royal Bodyguards—only a steppingstone to future advancement, but a distinct improvement over that ridiculous provincial cavalry regiment where he had made a laughingstock of himself and her. With her husband's duties taking him to Versailles now, she would go there too. Certainly it was the best place for her if she was ever to call herself to the attention and the favor of the Queen.

This was the first time Madame de La Motte ever mentioned, in my hearing, the name of her sovereign.

I had to admit that there was some logic in what she said. Above all, I applauded her decision to leave that horrid little Hotel de Reims in favor of Versailles, although I implored her to be on her guard against the sharpers she would run into on every street corner in Versailles, professional intrigants always on the verge of making a fortune, always glib with dangerous advice to others on how to go about similar fantastic schemes. As for me, I would no longer importune her with my advice and "moralizing," but would reserve my good will and zeal to serve her until such time as she would have an important case to take before a court of law. (Words of mine which Madame de La Motte apparently never forgot, for two years later, from the depths of the Bastille, she would write to remind me of that promise and hold me to it, asking me to defend her when she went on trial for her life.)

From the day of our Cadran Bleu dinner, then, I discontinued the prudent, practical advice which I had heretofore lavished upon Madame de La Motte and took no further action in her affairs. This did not mean, however, that I renounced the pleasure of her company. That very same evening I escorted her to the Comédie Italienne, to a performance of *Richard the Lionhearted*, and we parted one from the other reluctantly and tenderly that night. If there were some areas in which we found ourselves at cross-purposes, there were others in which we moved in harmony and mutual delight. . . .

The next news I had of her came several days later, from the man who rented carriages to us both (to Madame de La Motte only upon my guarantee, and therefore reporting regularly on her transactions). He could tell me only that she had left Paris for Versailles, which left me dying of curiosity, wondering who had paid her hotel bill. The last loan made her by Madame de Crozat dated back some six weeks. For quite a while now, Madame de La Motte had been considerate enough to make no further inroads upon my slim reserves. I came to find out, by sheer accident, that a relief grant of 2,400 francs had been awarded her from the funds of the Grand Almonership by the Grand Almoner. This seemed a proper application, in unexceptionable amount, of the national charity fund annually designated by the King for relief among impoverished nobility.

I turned things over in my mind and came to the soberer conclusion that Cardinal Rohan and Madame de La Motte were really poles apart, and that I must have been very frivolous and evil-minded to have suspected any closer liaison between the two.

But Villette had heard it differently:

Encouraged by the Cardinal's liberality, Madame de La Motte saw no reason for economizing, but spent his money as fast as he handed it over, launching on a lavish round of expenditure. Lacking in judgment and discernment as in discretion, she went around publicly congratulating herself on having acquired the handsomest member of the whole College of Cardinals as her lover!

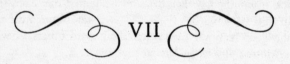

VII

The Countess at Court

(1783-1784)

MEMOIRS
OF COUNT BEUGNOT

So NOW WE SEE Madame de La Motte upon her arrival in Versailles, starving to death, ambitious and utterly unprincipled, a woman who would stop at nothing to achieve her ends and would feel entirely justified in defiance of a social order which had denied her her birthright. Thrown now into contact with a crowd of court hangers-on, elegant toadies, scalawags, schemers, she proved herself no novice but a star pupil in the Versailles school of vice.

It was at Versailles that she took up with an old crony of her husband's from cavalry days, one Rétaux de Villette. No fool like his former comrade-at-arms, Villette was, in fact, a cut above all the rest of the company, a dilettante in the fine arts, with special talent in music and literature. The debts which he ran up everywhere prevented his settling in any one spot; he commuted between Paris and Versailles, with no visible means of support in either. His personality ingratiating, he was excessively suggestible; his character metal had been tested, so to speak, but not transmuted, in the crucible of harsh experience. He was, by this time, ready to consider (more than consider—to employ) the most desperate measures, the most sordid expedients anyone might suggest to forward his career, although, it should be noted, he would have expressed such readiness, as was his wont, in a well-modulated, cultivated voice, in polished, gracefully turned phrase. For Villette was the gentleman thief personified. (He was likewise the scamp who produced a reasonably good facsimile of the Queen's handwriting whenever Madame de La Motte called upon him for such service.)

It was during her first Versailles visit that Madame de La Motte promoted Villette to the rank of private secretary, and it should be noted that the letters and billets-doux which they composed between them were lacking in neither wit nor grace of style.

With grace of style, Villette can speak for himself:

It is certainly true that I loved Madame de La Motte to distraction, but I will not deny that I could discern distinct personal advantages to me in our relation. I knew that, thanks to her wide and lofty acquaintance, she might be in a position to place me with some great lord or prince, assuring me a brilliant future. I leave to the reader to imagine what benefits I might have derived had I been other than I am. But, lacking in drive and energy, in will and determination, I was weak enough to allow myself to become the tool of Madame de La Motte and the Cardinal. It is human nature to be weak, so how could I resist a woman whom I adored, a prince of whom I stood in awe, both holding out such promise of happiness for my future?

The Countess describes this period of her life quite differently:

I need not remind the reader how—and at what price—Cardinal Rohan showered me with his benefactions when, in my hour of distress, I turned to him. This prince assured me that he regarded my restoration to high estate as his personal mission. He had petitions drawn up, he corrected and edited them himself, himself undertook circulating them among the King's ministers and in the offices of the royal-domain agencies.

It was at this period, then, that I launched on the ill-starred venture of seeking out sponsors and patrons, influential people in government circles to whom the Marquise de Boulainvilliers had recommended me in the hope that they would present and press my claims at court. I knew a great many important people, some even who might have been described as friends by anyone still naïve enough to believe in friendship.

The hope of persuading these prominent personages to act in my behalf drew me to Versailles, where I was to waste years of my life in petitions and solicitations during the administrations of a rapid succession of finance ministers between 1781 and 1784: Messieurs de Fleury and d'Ormesson, who passed like fleeting shadows across the Versailles scene; then Monsieur de Calonne, whose term of office, conversely, seemed interminably long to an embittered and impoverished French populace.

Anyone familiar with that gushing, effusive individual will be well able to imagine the fine promises he made me. I was even, one day, to hear him propose that I share the treasure of his affections—his heart and handsome self—with his current official mistress, Madame d'Arveley!

But the net result of countless conferences was the announcement that, the Fontette property in question being presently in possession of the Duke de Vrillières (a Cabinet minister), further action was precluded for the time; that, instead, the King had agreed to augment my pension.

No longer on good terms today with literature, I have forgotten the name of the poet who sang of the travail of the mountain in bringing forth the mouse, but, be that as it may, all of Monsieur de Calonne's labor pains in my behalf served only to produce a meager seven hundred francs additional to the niggardly eight hundred originally granted at the time of the King's recognition of our family status—a grand total, that is, of fifteen hundred francs a year on which I was expected to maintain myself in the "glorious Valois tradition."

Indignant at the indignities to which she was subjected at the hands of ministers and underlings—sneers, slights and more "outright propositions" (declarations en forme) such as Calonne's—she once resorted to a technique not yet labeled "sit-down strike": Telling Calonne, "I'll just sit down here and make your office my residence until the King affords me the means to maintain one of my own," she "found a chair, and sat for three hours . . . attendants peering in from time to time to discover whether I intended to carry out my threat." The undersecretary finally enticed her to vacate the seat by the promise of a 2,400-franc cash award, although, as she bitterly complained, "I was weary of accepting royal dole when what I asked was restitution of my rightful heritage and family domains."

Oh, how cruel [her *Story of My Life* continues] is the indifference of ministers, the insolence of petty officialdom! The student of human nature will understand the heartbreak, the disappointments to be experienced by the man or woman who must curry favor with those in power. Heaven help the little man, the nobody! Heaven *must* help him, for the bureaucrat will not. He will find no sympathy, no comfort, not even the customary graciousness which is one of the most winning characteristics of the French. Instead, sad to relate, the bureaucrat, after lending a distracted ear to the poor petitioner's plea, hurriedly shows him out of the office with an "I'm terribly sorry, but I'm simply swamped today—can't you come back such-and-such a day," etc., etc. That day comes; one makes the journey to Versailles or Fontainebleau; one returns to the bureau—only to find the Minister is absent. Then, after having petitioned, entreated, implored, having been put off time and time again, one finds oneself right back where one started, with only a resentment at having wasted one's time and money to be so duped. Of promises and compliments, in my rounds of government offices, I heard aplenty, but as to actual assistance, none was forthcoming.

Once action on my claims was initiated, frequent trips from Paris to Versailles, Versailles to Paris, Paris to Fontainebleau were necessitated; there was assiduous attendance to be paid on Cabinet ministers and government functionaries, there were appointments for audiences to be made (sometimes accorded, more frequently denied or postponed), and, in consequence, heavy expenditures were entailed.

During those years, nourished on false hope, the dupe of broken promises, I became involved in expenses which far exceeded my income. To pay the debts incurred in spending months at a time at Versailles, following the court to be within beck and call of government ministers, I was forced to borrow considerable sums. If my patroness, Her Highness Madame Elisabeth, had not secured a safe-conduct certificate from the police to protect my husband and me from arrest and lawsuit by our creditors, we would have been in dire straits indeed.

MEMOIRS
OF COUNT BEUGNOT

From the day of her arrival in Versailles, Madame de La Motte ran straight into the very snares against which I had sought to warn her. She handed out copies of her petition to every rascal who claimed to have an inside track in government circles, and she succeeded in record time in discrediting both herself and her cause. She was soon surrounded by those professional court parasites, a species common to every court and capital, who make a living, such as it is, by promoting schemes of their own or by exploiting other people's.

To sit in on this game of intrigue, Madame de La Motte held trump cards in her famous name and curious history; the onlookers tried to show her how to play her hand. She was encouraged (if, indeed, much encouragement was needed) to make the most fantastic moves, often in the worst of taste. To cite only one: She pretended, one day, to fall in a faint in the antechamber of Madame Elisabeth. . . .

Madame Pothey, lady in waiting to Madame Elisabeth, the King's sister, remembered the incident much the same, in testimony she gave three years later during the diamond necklace investigation:

Madame Elisabeth, informed that a lady of quality had fainted away from starvation in Her Highness's own antechamber, read the petition clutched in the hand of the unconscious woman and ordered litter bearers to carry the victim back to her lodgings in the town. Madame's doctors attended the young woman, and the Princess sent her a gift of two hundred francs. Madame's chaplain, Abbé Malet, took up a collection amounting to three hundred francs, destined for the invalid's benefit.

"If ever there was a time in my life for hope, it was then," the "invalid" Countess de La Motte insists in her memoirs.

My history and my name had become the talk of the court.

It was public knowledge that I was under the special patronage of Madame; and it was to her ardent solicitations that I owed the King's brevet of 1784 by which my pension was raised to 1,500 francs. Madame personally presented my petition to the Finance Minister and to Monsieur des Forges, administrator of the royal domains. Monsieur des Forges, however, urged me to pay my court to the Queen, admitting that it was practically impossible to render me any service without Her Majesty's approval, that Madame wielded little influence—all favors were at the disposition of the Queen.

All I ever really needed for success in recovering my family fortunes was a truly powerful patron or sponsor to press my claims. One such appeared, but unfortunately I could not take advantage of the opportunity when it presented itself; if the reader understands the nature of my relations with Cardinal Rohan, he will understand why not.

I refer to the King's own brother, the Count d'Artois, who, having seen me at the chapel of Versailles, honored me with attentions of a nature I had not foreseen or sought to arouse. The steps taken by the Prince to inform me of his admiration, and his overtures in my direction, came to the ears of his wife, who, gratified by my discreet conduct in such an embarrassing situation, deigned to grant me a reception and honored me henceforward with her favor.

Villette heard (from the Countess or from others?) a somewhat different version and reported it differently in his memoirs:

His Royal Highness the Count d'Artois saw her and desired her. Prince de Hénin, his equerry, delegated to take steps necessary to procure her for his master, arranged matters easily. Madame de La Motte was neither rich enough nor morally rigorous enough to resist the tender advances of a Royal Highness.

Madame Elisabeth and the Countess d'Artois, advised of the frailties of their protégée, withdrew the favor they had formerly shown her. After that Madame de La Motte vegetated dejectedly in Versailles for a while, and later she was forced to abandon her projects and return to Paris.

"This period in the life of the Countess de La Motte is shadowy, obscure . . . difficult to trace," according to Counselor-at-law Target, dean of the French bar and chief counsel to Cardinal Rohan in the trial days ahead, who should have known whereof he spoke, having unleashed his full pack of private investigators upon her trail to trace her from her dilapidated cradle on through every phase of her past:

The Countess's seems, at times, to have been a precarious existence, a strange conglomeration of opulence and destitution: a valet, three lady's maids, a blackamoor messenger boy, a hired carriage—signs of affluence. But at the same time, rented furniture, unpaid hotel bills, quarrels with innkeepers—signs of pauperism.

When the La Mottes were evicted from the Hotel de Reims in Paris, they left owing 1,580 francs to Brussaut, the landlord, who up to the very end had gone on advancing them board as well as lodging. In November of 1782 a quarrel broke out over an alleged theft of napkins by one of the Countess's maids. Brussaut charged the Countess with having struck his wife and having pushed her down the stairs; Madame de La Motte counterclaimed that Madame Brussaut had tried to strangle her. This altercation gave rise to a lawsuit still pending in this year of 1786 in the Court of the Châtelet.

To escape the lawsuits and arrest threats of other creditors, the Count de La Motte abandoned the city for refuge in the suburb of Brie-Comte-Robert, at the Good Hope Inn. The Countess lived for a while at Versailles, then returned to Paris to an attic room in the Hotel d'Artois, where she was provided board and lodging by a Madame Briffault, the mother of Rosalie Briffault, who served the Countess then, as now, in the capacity of premier lady's maid.

In October of 1783, the La Mottes borrowed enough money to follow the court to Fontainebleau, taking lodgings on the Rue Avon. A procession of eminent and elegant gentlemen came, one by one, to visit the Countess. The La Motte apartment consisting of one room only, the Count—in order to keep warm—went to spend the days in the public reception rooms of the Fontainebleau Château, while high-ranking military officers and judges vied for the honor of calling on the Countess and leaving material tokens of their esteem.

Considering that a more representative residence was essential to the success of her court solicitations, the Countess signed a lease for spacious and handsome quarters in a house at No. 13 Rue Neuve St. Gilles.* These, however, could not be furnished until May of 1783, and even then only by means of a 5,000-franc loan from Isaac Beer, moneylender, upon the endorsement of Cardinal Rohan—who was obliged to pay the note off for her in 1785. Not until Easter of 1784 could the La Mottes move into their new quarters. The yearly rental of 1,200 francs and the simplest furnishings were still far beyond their means. All they had to count on were occasional loans from friends, some modest gifts from Cardinal Rohan and the Countess's yearly pension of eight hundred francs, which, toward the end of 1783, was raised by the King to fifteen hundred.

Thus, signs of better times to the contrary, the apparent prosperity of the house on the Rue Neuve St. Gilles was only a cover-up for a continu-

* The house number in present-day Paris street listings is No. 10 Rue St. Gilles.

ing state of indigence. The couple managed to get by there only through the deftest financial jugglery: speculations in merchandise, goods obtained on credit, then pawned for ready cash; an occasional few hundred francs sponged from an unwary neighbor or even Madame Briffault, mother of their maid; a hundred écus here to pay off a valet shouting for back wages, a hundred écus there to meet the next installment of the rent; the house lavishly furnished one day, empty to the rafters the next—mirrors, pictures snatched off the walls, loaded onto the lackey's shoulders and rushed out the back door to escape seizure by creditors knocking at the front. Not until the next windfall, a contribution from an admirer of the Countess's or a lucky night at the gaming table for the Count, was there a chair to sit in, a bed in which to sleep. At such times as there was a table in the house, the service was of common pewter; silver place settings seen there were on loan, for state occasions, from their co-tenant, Baron de Vieuvillers.

And always, over and over again, the journeys to Versailles and Fontainebleau, the never ending stream of petitions to government bureaus. Penniless but haughty, greedy but prodigal, piling up debt, intriguing, besieging court officialdom, demanding assistance with all the importunity of desperation, with all the temerity of overweening pride, caught up between the temptations of poverty and the grandiose projects of ambition, the Countess de La Motte exhibited the basest characteristics of the poor, obsequiousness and servility, and at the same time the basest qualities of the rich, extravagance and arrogance. This depraved and contradictory character explains the great-lady airs she gave herself at Versailles and the cases of assault and battery in which she was involved in Paris. Liveried lackeys to wait at table, but no food on the platters which they passed. Silks and satins for her gowns, but no chemise to wear underneath. A tasteless ostentation, a shameless pauperism.

Finally, in the month of April 1784, her situation proved so desperate that she was reduced to the expedient of requesting permission from the King to sell her crown pension and that of her brother; hers, consisting of fifteen hundred francs annual revenue, brought the sum of six thousand francs cash in hand; her brother's, of eight hundred francs, went for three thousand in ready money.

And Villette, as well as Target, had unsympathetic comment to make on this particular phase of the Countess's life:

Madame de La Motte's liaisons with the court had so stimulated her vanity that she talked of them incessantly, possibly to enhance her prestige.

She might, at this particular period, have made her fortune, had she only known how to take advantage of her opportunities; but, utterly impractical, improvident, unstable, giddy and, to do her justice, generous to a fault, unable to refuse any solicitation for favors or patronage, wed to a corrupt, libertine gambler of a husband as undisciplined as she, what chance was there of her making anything of her life?

Given this strange mélange of pride, acute sensibility and reckless generosity, stir in abandon and inconstancy (an unending succession of lovers), and you can guess what is to come.

There is extant, in a private collection, a holograph letter of this period, dated October 6, 1782, addressed by the Countess de La Motte to her foster sister, the Baroness de Crussol: "Most of my furniture is in the pawnshop. The few pieces remaining to me, and even my personal effects, have been seized by creditors. If I can't get hold of six hundred francs by Thursday, I will be reduced to sleeping in the streets!"

And surviving in the files of the Paris police in the Archives de France is a second letter from the Countess, dated May 16, 1783, and addressed simply "Monsieur" (probably Finance Minister d'Ormesson, in archivist Campardon's opinion). "Monsieur" must have forwarded it to Lenoir, the lieutenant general of police, for at the top is the notation, "Lenoir: Impossible to grant the favor requested. Can we do something else for her?"

The letter reads:

MONSIEUR:

You will have to admit that fate is indeed cruel to me. I know that Monsieur des Forges as administrator of the royal domains is opposed to granting me the estate of Fontette, for which I have instituted claim as rightful owner. I don't understand what difference it can make to him whether I or another becomes the King's tenant there.

You are too just a man, monsieur, not to see the matter in this light, having already agreed that I may well hope to

better my fortunes. Thus I throw myself upon your mercy. If
you cannot help me with one project, perhaps you can with
another.

It is certainly not my intention to threaten anyone, but if
some relief is not soon forthcoming, I will have no choice but
to go over the heads of the officials, throw myself at the feet
of the King and take my grievances directly to him.

My furniture in pawn, threatened with arrest for debt,
with all the attendant scandal which could seriously damage
my reputation—what else can I do? I must find a way to live,
to take care of my family. Heaven has not yet decided on my
fate, but if Providence does not soon take pity on me, I am
afraid of what may become of me!

I am no longer ashamed of admitting that I go about
the world begging charity. I had to borrow three hundred
francs from Baron de Clugny at the Ministry of Marine to
save myself from starving—a sum which, counting on your
generosity, I promised to pay within two weeks.

Surely no one, monsieur, is more to be pitied than I—my
husband without a position, my ailing sister on our hands,
an extra burden and expense.

No matter what becomes of me, I think it shocking that a
blood cousin of the King's, one he has himself acknowledged,
should be abandoned to such a plight. You may think I exaggerate the situation, but I insist that I am denied even the
smallest favor. I am not surprised that there is so much crime
in the world, and I assure you that only my religion has preserved me from temptation; if I should succumb, and end
up badly, I do not believe that it would be I who would be to
blame, but the authorities, who had the power to help me
and refused.

> I am, monsieur, your very humble, very
> obedient servant,
> COUNTESS DE LA MOTTE-VALOIS

And in her memoirs:

In utter desperation, in the early hours of the morning I decided to
end my life. I took two loaded pistols from the desk, slipped unseen out

of the silent, sleeping house and, holding the hood of my cape across my face, made my way to a forest a league outside Versailles. The steel of the lethal weapon cold against my brow, I sank to my knees to send up one last prayer to my Creator. But my lips could not form the words; a voice within me cried, "How dare you pray to a God whose law you are about to transgress? Stop!"

My whole body shook; cold sweat trickled down my cheeks. The homicidal weapon slipped from my hand—and then I could pray.

Comforted by prayer, I felt hope returning to my heart and my natural love of life reviving; these two sentiments imbued me with enough strength to regain my dwelling.

And then, according to chief counsel Target, the climax to this period of despair:

After Madame de La Motte had sold her pension and that of her brother, she realized that she had forever forfeited the sole resource which might have provided lifetime security. It was at this point, seemingly, that she first conceived the idea for her grandiose imposture, her supremely insolent and daring hoax.

To spread abroad a false rumor of one's power and influence, to collect money by inspiring hopes that can never be fulfilled—this is a stratagem to which intrigants have so long resorted, it is a ruse so hoary and overworked, that it might seem that no more dupes could be taken in by it. Yet it continues an effective trick, and Madame de La Motte carried the criminal temerity to unparalleled lengths.

It was not to Cardinal Rohan alone that she made her deceitful confidences: she told it to the four winds; all with whom she came into contact heard the fable. Her house buzzed with it; the secret was whispered in one's ear the moment one came in the door. And people believed the story; the poor man and the speculator addressed themselves to her, the former to seek help out of his distress, the latter to seek help in forwarding his schemes.

And what were these tales the Countess spun, these fables she concocted? One shudders to speak them aloud, for they violate the profound respect due majesty: Her Valois name and her misfortunes, she said, had stirred the Queen to sympathy and opened the way into the royal presence. She was received by the Queen in secret; privately honored by Her Majesty's interest and friendship, she would soon publicly enjoy the royal bounty—her family properties were shortly to be restored to her. While waiting to reap so rich a harvest, she went about peddling her supposed influence as royal favorite; her greatest satisfaction, she implied, came from her power to render aid to others who were unfortunate, as she once had been. As the height of audacity, she dared show—though with an air of mystery—letters addressed to her, purportedly, by the Queen. She pointed out the expressions of affectionate sentiments and the superscription "To my cousin, the Countess de Valois."

To buttress the crime of fraud, she would commit the crime of forgery.

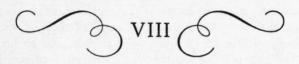

VIII

The Countess and the Queen

(1784)

STORY OF MY LIFE
BY THE COUNTESS DE LA MOTTE-VALOIS

DESPONDENT over the indifference of the King's ministers and the insolence of petty government officials, all these years I kept hearing the same refrain: "Try to reach the ear of the Queen. The only hope for success is through the Queen."

Finance Minister d'Ormesson, to whom I had presented Madame Elisabeth's letter of recommendation, explained to me that she had little influence with her brother, the King, and thus little influence in government circles. He urged me to seek the favor of the Queen, who had all benefits at her disposal. Madame Elisabeth herself admitted her lack of power and counseled me to direct all my efforts toward interesting the Queen in my cause. Everyone versed in court intrigue advised me that without the Queen's approval no government favor was forthcoming. "Try to get to the Queen, from whose hand all blessings flow," they kept saying.

As Austrian Ambassador Count Mercy said it, in a letter to Vienna, "The Queen's influence is so great that most of the Cabinet ministers have no choice but to obey her; they dare not even remonstrate."

As Madame Campan said it, in her memoirs, "Within the charmed and narrow circle of the Queen's intimates lay the earthly Paradise. There were ambassadors created, there all favor and privilege bestowed."

STORY OF MY LIFE
BY THE COUNTESS DE LA MOTTE-VALOIS

It was just about this time that, suffering a second miscarriage and seized with convulsions, as it happened, just below the windows of the Queen's apartments, I found sweet consolation in the knowledge that my indisposition had aroused Her Majesty's concern and sympathy. Her distress was so evident as to cause the King to inquire the source, and he was told that she had just witnessed the sad spectacle of a young woman in a dreadful seizure. "She is a Valois," the Queen continued, "the wife of the Count de La Motte. They are a young couple, and I pity them with all my heart."

Everyone advised me to follow up promptly on this expression of interest manifested by the Queen. In the great world, in the court of kings, there is a maxim to the effect that one cannot allow oneself to be forgotten for even a moment; so, as soon as I had recovered, I took to stationing myself at a spot where I could not fail to be noticed, in the Hall of Trophies leading to the palace chapel, at the hour when the royal family passed on the way to Mass.

The first time, the Queen turned toward me and fastened me with a steady and attentive gaze; thereafter, whenever she saw me she deigned to smile. All the court soon remarked that I had captured Her Majesty's attention, and it became known that she had spoken of me with cordial sympathy. In view of this flattering distinction, all my friends—above all, the Cardinal—urged me to make the most of the Queen's evidently favorable disposition.

Above all, Cardinal Rohan—a man who never lost sight of his own personal interests. If I had no secrets from him, he had none from me. Reading deep in each other's soul, each of us knew the other's consuming ambition. His, indeed, was known to all the world: to become, at any price, Prime Minister of France. Mine was more modest; all I asked of life was to become mistress of Fontette. Mighty obstacles, stemming from the same cause, lack of the Queen's favor, blocked both our paths.

Both of us obsessed by ambition, small wonder that we were drawn together and that we combined forces to achieve our heart's desire.

This was how matters stood, then, when the first feeble rays of royal favor fell upon my head, revitalizing the Cardinal's ambition, rekindling his hopes.

Witness to an especially dazzling smile with which the Queen, in passing, honored me one day, the Cardinal hailed me with the words which, astonishing me then, have never faded from my memory. "Do you realize, Countess," he inquired, "that my fate as well as your own rests entirely in your hands?"

Recovering from my first shock of surprise, I asked the Prince whether he was joking or speaking seriously.

"I could not be more serious," he replied. "Sit down and listen attentively. First of all, remember this: Fortune wanders through the world, like justice, blindfolded and extends her hand at hazard to whomever she happens to encounter upon her rapid, erratic path. But if that person fails to seize hold quickly, he has forever lost his chance; such a moment never recurs. Your moment, your chance, has come. I am not the only person to have noticed this, although I am the most interested observer. I have established as a certainty the fact that the Queen has taken a fancy to you."

"A fancy to me!" I exclaimed. "You must mean that Her Majesty has taken pity on me—that her tender heart has been stirred to compassion by my misfortunes."

"You may give whatever name you choose to the sentiment you have aroused within her breast," said Cardinal Rohan. "All you need know is that your looks appeal to her, and that you must not allow the warm prepossession she has manifested in your favor to cool off. You can see that the key to all grace and privilege dangles from her chatelaine, that there is no hope elsewhere in this court. Put all your faith, then, in the Queen, and remember that my fate, along with yours, rests in your hands."

The Cardinal concluded by advising me to write to the Duchess de Polignac; as counsel, he could not have given me worse.

It was true, to be sure, that one could hope for presentation to the Queen only through the Polignac clique, but the Duchess, jealous and fearful of losing the royal favor she monopolized, disdainfully repulsed any outsider who sought so much as a smile or a glance from the Queen.

I was not a Polignac protégée; the Duchess could see no advantage, but only risk, in helping me; so, after keeping me waiting for hours in her antechamber, she rejected my request for an audience.

"Is it possible," I asked the valet who delivered the message, "that Madame de Polignac dares write me in such a tone?"

I was outraged by the attitude of this haughty and imperious woman. Well could I remember the Polignacs in Paris when they were impoverished nonentities; when my employer, Madame Boussol, sent me to try to collect her bills and Madame de Polignac could pay only in promises for the modiste and in compliments for me! Why, before enjoying this recent favor of the Queen's, Madame de Polignac could not obtain credit from a single merchant in Paris and had not a decent dress to her name—so the story goes—when the opportunity arose for presentation at court. Did the Duchess fear my revealing to the Queen what I knew about her past? Did she fear the advantage of my name and rank over hers?

At any rate, my every attempt having been frustrated by the Polignacs, who stood athwart all avenues of approach to the Queen, I told the Cardinal bitterly that I wanted to hear no more about the matter.

"You are too easily discouraged," was his reply. "You give up at the first hard blow. The wind is favorable; you must set sail. So it is a bold stroke I now propose: You must seize your opportunity at the Cordon Bleu investiture ceremony, which is scheduled for the second of February. Throw yourself at the feet of the Queen as she passes down the Hall of Mirrors at the head of the procession."

Being in the habit of allowing myself to be entirely governed by Cardinal Rohan, I promised to follow his advice.

The solemn occasion, the great day, at hand, I went to the palace in full court regalia and, armed with detailed instructions from the Cardinal, took my place in one of the state reception rooms through which the Cordon Bleu procession would pass on its return from the chapel. An hour, two hours passed; at long last the Queen appeared, and, my heart pounding with fear and hope, I threw myself at her feet.

Her Majesty most graciously raised me up, accepted my petition and, with that wondrous graciousness of hers, promised to read it—encouraging me to hope.

Knees trembling, I withdrew from the royal presence. I was barely inside my door when I received a visit from His Eminence. After rendering him a detailed account of all that had happened, I wrote—again upon his suggestion—to Madame de Misery, the Queen's lady in waiting, begging her to deliver to Her Majesty the letter I enclosed.

That very evening came the reply: an invitation to be at her apartments at seven-thirty!

With her first word, Madame de Misery gave me to understand that the honor about to be done me, that of presentation to the Queen, was one which must be kept secret from all the world; the slightest indiscretion on my part would be my complete undoing. It is appropriate that I stress for the reader and that the reader not forget the advice given me by Madame de Misery upon this occasion, for it will serve to clarify many important developments in my story which might otherwise seem obscure.

I waited until eleven o'clock, when the Queen was to leave her card party. At last she appeared. Oh, God, how beautiful she was! How utterly irresistible her smile! I was always to see her thus, although on this first meeting her kindness and graciousness outshone even the charms of her person. Awe and respect so overwhelmed me that I could not at first articulate a word; but the sovereign's graciousness soon restored my presence of mind and some portion of my natural vivacity, enabling me to explain my motives in seeking her protection after years of vain solicitation of the ministers.

Her Majesty told me she had read my petition and appreciated my desire to recover my Valois heritage. "Although I shall forward your claims," she informed me, "I shall have to do so through your brother. It will seem only natural that he, as Baron de Valois, official head of the family, be the one to come to Versailles to solicit restitution of the Valois properties, and I promise you to support those claims energetically. There are, however, personal and private reasons why I cannot at this time openly sponsor your cause."

The Queen was at this period surrounded by persons set to spy upon her every move. She was known to have complained of her position in that it necessitated her treading delicately with those imperious Polignacs, who, as has been claimed, had in their possession papers and letters in the Queen's handwriting which constituted a constant menace to the peace of mind and reputation of the sovereign. "Those leeches"— the Queen's word for them—had so deeply insinuated themselves into her confidence that she could never free herself. Arrogantly confident of their hold over the sovereign, the Polignacs displayed such impudence in affairs of state that the Queen found her situation well-nigh intolerable.*

My first meeting with the Queen ended with Her Majesty's presenting me a purse of gold and enjoining upon me the strictest secrecy with regard to our rendezvous. (A comic-opera secret, if you will, in a loud stage whisper. For despite my discretion, such an interesting state of affairs as my budding intimacy with the Queen could not long be concealed—not in a place like the Palace of Versailles. Every day someone else approached me, whispering mysteriously, claiming to be in on the delicious secret, until I could count self-appointed confidantes by the dozen. I could never figure out how so many people had all managed to become so well informed so quickly! Everyone wanted to advise me; I had as many counselors as the King.)

That first day, the Queen left me with an embrace and with the words, "Au revoir. We shall meet soon again."

A few days later I received a message instructing me to present myself between eleven and midnight at the Little Trianon. There the Queen received me in the most flattering manner. Enchanted by her condescension, I received fresh proof of her generosity: a purse containing bank notes totaling some ten thousand francs.

I am reluctant to weary my reader with a detailed account of my subsequent rendezvous with the Queen. Suffice it to say that I received frequent and unmistakable proof of her favor and her bounty. But heaven had decreed that I fall victim to intrigue, and every step I took was a step toward catastrophe.

From the revelations made here, the reader will find it clear that it was the overweening ambition of the unfortunate Prince-Cardinal which originally led me (shoved me, so to speak) into the private apartments of the Queen. As I have already explained, I had no secrets from Cardinal Rohan, so he could now congratulate himself upon the success of the daring stratagem he had recommended to me to gain entrée to the Queen; he could also exact of me the promise to seize upon the very first propitious moment to recall him to Her Majesty.

---

* This curious statement concerning the Queen's relations with the Polignacs cannot be dismissed as another La Motte fantasy; Madame Campan confirms the situation in a passage in her memoirs (see the Appendix).

MEMOIRS
OF THE ABBÉ GEORGEL

When Cardinal Rohan advised the Countess de La Motte to address herself directly to the Queen, it was upon the assumption that a generous sovereign would be struck, as he had been, by the incongruity between the Countess's illustrious name and her state of poverty.

In the admission, however, that he himself was unable to assist the Countess to secure an audience with the Queen, the Cardinal made the fatal error of carrying his confidences to excess, going so far as to describe his consuming grief at having incurred the enmity of his sovereign. He further confided in the Countess that the Queen's hostility was the perpetual torment that darkened his brightest hours.

STORY OF MY LIFE
BY THE COUNTESS DE LA MOTTE-VALOIS

Cardinal Rohan confided to me that he had been languishing in exile ever since the accession of Marie Antoinette. Only once, and briefly—as he told it—had there appeared a glimmer of hope: when, as Archduchess, she had passed through Strasbourg and he had been delegated to receive the royal bride; when, the Prince having thrown himself at her feet to kiss the hem of her robe, she had bidden him rise and had blushingly extended her hand for him to kiss. He had kissed it with transports of delight. "Those," Cardinal Rohan concluded with a sigh, "were the last kindly looks or words the Queen has ever bestowed on me."

MEMOIRS
OF THE ABBÉ GEORGEL

This injudicious burst of confidence to Madame de La Motte by the Cardinal served as the infernal spark to set off the most devastating explosion. This reckless confidence inspired a scheme of deception unparalleled in the annals of human folly.

Here is the outline of that scheme: Madame de La Motte undertook to convince the Cardinal that she had succeeded in establishing herself on a familiar footing with the Queen; that, imbued with appreciation of the generosity and nobility of the Cardinal's soul, she had spoken of him so glowingly as to have dispelled the Queen's prejudices one by one, persuading Her Majesty to permit him to write her a letter in justification of his conduct which in the past had been considered offensive; that whereas the Queen must await the propitious moment to restore her favor to him publicly, she meanwhile appointed their mutual friend, the Countess de La Motte, as intermediary in a correspondence which, though necessarily secret for the time, must eventually lead the Cardinal to the very heights of national prominence and power.

That a woman in her twenties should conceive of such an intricate ruse; that a cardinal, a prince in his fifties, should be taken in by it, should trip and fall headlong into the snares successively set out for him —here is a phenomenon to tax the credulity of posterity. An imagination capable of hatching such an intrigue is inevitably an imagination stirred by the fiercest cupidity; furthermore, the Countess de La Motte could discern, in her benefactor's excessive credulity, a gold mine in which she could delve at will, heaping up treasure enough to assure her lifetime security.

Here, then, came to be forged the first links of that chain which would coil about him fatally to entangle him and drag him to his doom.

"How grateful I am to you, my Prince," this artful and designing woman said one day to the Cardinal, "for your advice to go directly to the Queen with the story of my misfortunes! A first visit giving rise to a second, a second to a third, I am now privileged to come and go informally—the rules of etiquette having been suspended in my case—to the private chambers of Her Majesty's apartments. I have been fortunate enough to win her affection and her confidence."

This opening gambit produced the calculated effect: The Cardinal's interest in Madame de La Motte redoubled; the hope was born to him that through her intercession he could at last overcome the Queen's prejudices against him. From that moment on, Madame de La Motte's progress reports were so artfully graduated that the Cardinal was utterly convinced; from that moment on, this mistress of the art of intrigue became, in his eyes, the intermediary who was preparing the way for his reconciliation with the Queen, the reconciliation for which he had been sighing out his heart for years.

His Eminence coached the Countess's every step: how to go about introducing his name, casually, into her conversations with the Queen; how to grasp every opportunity for expatiating on his anguish at her disfavor, at her refusal to give him so much as a chance at self-justification. . . .

STORY OF MY LIFE
BY THE COUNTESS DE LA MOTTE-VALOIS

The Cardinal suggested expedients for bringing his name into our conversations, proposed the very words I was to speak, coached me in my role as an actor rehearses with his leading lady.

But so deep-rooted was the Queen's prejudice against the Cardinal that to rush matters would have been to bungle them. Only after long months could I report that I had managed to break the ice—describing the Cardinal as a noble soul who had fallen victim to the calumny of his enemies. Of course, I had to tread delicately, avoiding above all any hint of the nature of my relations with His Eminence.

MEMOIRS
OF THE ABBÉ GEORGEL

"Happily, I have at last succeeded in introducing your name into my conversation with the Queen," said the Countess to the Cardinal one day. "Her Majesty questioning me upon my past, I described my visit to Saverne with the Boulainvilliers' and your sympathy and generosity toward me in my misfortunes. But above all, I spoke of your good works in your diocese, of your grateful parishioners daily singing your praise and blessing you for your benefactions."

MEMOIRS
OF THE COUNTESS DE LA MOTTE-VALOIS

"I am gratified, of course, to hear such a glowing report on Cardinal Rohan," Her Majesty replied, "although I must admit it takes me completely by surprise. I never dreamed Monseigneur capable of such nobility of action; he does not generally enjoy so good a reputation as you give him. Other versions have led me to think of him in quite another light."

MEMOIRS
OF THE ABBÉ GEORGEL

"The Queen being thus far apparently not bored by my account," the Countess de La Motte reported to the Cardinal, "I ventured to add that the distress of your disgrace had afflicted you to such a point as to affect your health, but that your keenest anguish resulted from your vain struggle to be permitted to plead your cause before a sovereign idolized by all of France!

" 'But how can Prince de Rohan ever hope to clear himself of the shame of his misconduct?' the Queen exclaimed.

" 'The graver the charge, the more it behooves Your Majesty's justice to permit that his case be stated.'

"My pleas bore fruit: I am authorized to ask you for your self-justification, to be written in your own hand and delivered by me to the Queen!"

STORY OF MY LIFE
BY THE COUNTESS DE LA MOTTE-VALOIS

The Cardinal convinced me that if it was not within my power to fulfill all his fondest hopes, then at least I might succeed in diminishing to some extent Her Majesty's aversion to him. Thus I again took courage and advised the Cardinal to venture to address a letter to the Queen which I would endeavor to present to her at a propitious moment. Yes, I admit, it was I who gave him this advice. But how could I dream that the imprudent Prince, knowing the Queen's attitude, would forthwith proceed to further indiscretions?

MEMOIRS
OF THE ABBÉ GEORGEL

This authorization from the Queen for a letter of self-justification—a figment of the Countess's imagination, but a reality to the Cardinal—

signified to him the radiant dawn of a glorious new day. Very soon his apology, written in his own hand, and designed to dissipate any last unfavorable impression lingering in the mind of the Queen, was entrusted to the hands of Madame de La Motte.

A few days later she brought back to the Cardinal a dainty sheet of the finest gilt-edged notepaper, upon which Marie Antoinette, whose handwriting a clever forger sought to imitate, had written in reply: "I have read your letter and am happy that I need no longer consider you guilty. I cannot yet grant you the audience you seek; as soon as circumstances permit, I shall advise you. In the meanwhile, remember, be discreet."

These few words plunged the Cardinal into inexpressible ecstasies. From that moment on, in his eyes, the Countess de La Motte appeared a tutelary angel, opening up the paths to happiness. From that moment on, she could have asked anything in the world of him and had it for the asking. From that moment on, her enchantress's hand across his eyes shut out every ray of light which might have penetrated a mind not so utterly obsessed.

In order to inaugurate a correspondence which would serve to nourish the vanity and ambition of the blindfolded Prince, the Countess de La Motte encouraged him to write another letter to the Queen to express his joy and gratitude at her message. Thus it was that letter and reply, letter and reply rapidly succeeded one another. In this copious correspondence (of which, fortunately, not so much as a scrap of notepaper ever came to light) the sequence of the letters supposedly from the Queen was so artfully graduated, so subtly nuanced as to give the Cardinal reason to believe that he had succeeded in inspiring the implicit trust and the liveliest interest of the Queen.

The Countess deemed the Prince's state of ecstasy sufficiently pronounced to risk, in a letter purportedly from the Queen, a request which should have aroused suspicion: Marie Antoinette, according to this letter, desirous of making a charitable donation in secrecy to a proud but indigent family, found herself short of funds, and so she commissioned her Grand Almoner to borrow for her the sum of sixty thousand francs and send them to her by Madame de La Motte.

Monseigneur the Cardinal has since admitted that even so obviously baited a snare failed to arouse suspicion in his mind. How could he have believed that the Queen, with the Minister of Finance and the royal treasury at her command, and for an act of charity, above all, would have ever resorted to such a clandestine borrowing arrangement?

But the Prince was so unsuspecting that to speed the loan transaction he did not hesitate to take the Jew Cerf-Beer into his confidence, presenting such a service to the Queen as a rare opportunity for the money-lender to gain her royal good will and protection for himself and all his race. Cerf-Beer did not hesitate to lend the sum. Cardinal Rohan endorsed the note and delivered the money to Madame de La Motte, who lost no time in bringing the Cardinal a letter of thanks written upon the Queen's dainty gilt-edged notepaper.

From that moment on, signs of greater prosperity were evident in that conniving woman's household. Lest the Cardinal be struck by the sudden change in her standard of living, he was told that the lavish bounty of the Queen had wrought the happy metamorphosis.

The Countess de La Motte, self-appointed messenger in a correspondence which was the product of her own imagination, artistically injected and developed hints of a growing interest and a confidence on the part of the Queen which, presaging grandiose plans for the Cardinal's political future, were designed to engross his thoughts and stimulate his affection. He was drunk with joy; this exchange of letters with the Queen became his constant and most cherished preoccupation. In the throes of an illusion so powerful as to paralyze his reason and impel his every action, his entire being was subordinated to a single thought: The Queen has restored me to her favor; she honors me with confidential missions through her appointed intermediary, the Countess de La Motte. I thus abide by every command relayed to me and am prepared for any sacrifice to prove myself worthy of Marie Antoinette's choice of me as her agent.

Let the reader imagine dispassionately what hold such a delusion might come to exert upon the mind of a man long obsessed with the desire to please his sovereign. From this time forward, the overcredulous Prince staggers blindfolded and unquestioning in the tortuous corridors of a labyrinth of deception.

Among her repertoire of stratagems, Madame de La Motte struck upon one to create the impression that she was summoned frequently by her intimate friend, the Queen, to secret rendezvous at the Little Trianon. To surround herself with an air of mystery, to effect entrance and exit at Trianon as required for her devious purposes, she had managed to strike up an acquaintance with the concierge of that palace. Often she would notify the Cardinal in advance of the date of her supposed appointments with the Queen and of the hour at which she expected to make her departure. The Prince, who delighted to let his thoughts feed on anything that might nourish his sweet illusions, often stationed himself at a vantage point where he might witness these comings and goings of the Countess.

One night when she knew the Grand Almoner was awaiting her exit, she arranged for Villette, the principal accessory to her crimes, to escort her out through the palace gates and some distance beyond. It was a brilliantly moonlit night. Cardinal Rohan, in disguise, met Madame de La Motte at a spot previously appointed and asked her the name of the man, who had by now turned back and re-entered the palace grounds. She told him that it was Desclaux, the Queen's confidential messenger at Trianon.

At this stage of the game the diamond necklace transaction had not yet been initiated, but this foresighted female magician was already busily setting the scene with all the stage properties requisite to her most ambitious feat of legerdemain, skillfully laying out, at all the strategic positions, the foundation stones upon which to erect the structure of her grandiose swindle. Villette had been promised a share in the golden harvest when it was ripe for reaping; Villette's contribution was the criminal talent of imitating the handwriting of the Queen; he was the secretary, writing at Madame de La Motte's dictation the little letters on gilt-edged notepaper purportedly from the Queen.

Madame de La Motte's protracted stays at Versailles can be dated as beginning sometime after the delivery of the sixty thousand francs of which she had bilked the Cardinal. Her installation in commodious quarters there, by her account, was at the expense of the Queen, who wanted her dear friend close by. . . .

Meanwhile . . . her fertile imagination produced yet another proof to confirm the Cardinal in his delusion, to still any lingering doubt.

It so happened that the Queen was given to a certain mannerism: Her Majesty, upon issuing from her apartments and continuing through the Hall of Mirrors on her way to chapel, had a habit of turning her head—of nodding, as it were—as she passed the doorway of the Oeil-de-Boeuf. Madame de La Motte, keenly observant, made mental note thereof.

. . . She sought out the Cardinal and told him, "I have just left Her Majesty, who requests me to deliver to you this message: Station yourself tomorrow, as if by accident, in the Oeil-de-Boeuf, at the hour when she passes down the Hall of Mirrors to High Mass. If you are there, she will nod to you as she goes by, as a signal of her approbation and satisfaction. Her Majesty has asked me to tell you that she will be looking for you there. . . ."

A rose-colored glass held before the eyes renders all objects seen through it as bathed in a rosy light, and the next day . . . the Grand Almoner, taking his place in the Oeil-de-Boeuf, was convinced that he had distinctly perceived the predetermined signal. Thus does the art of illusion achieve its effects.*

The illusion had still not lost its dazzle a year or more later when the Cardinal, under interrogation, gave his version of the incident:†

Concerned at receiving no sign of recognition from the Queen in public, I complained to Madame de La Motte that my affairs did not seem to be progressing in that I had had, as yet, no outward proof of the Queen's restoration of her favor.

Madame de La Motte answered me with the words, "Go tomorrow to pay her your court, and you shall see."

On the day indicated, as I walked down the Hall of Mirrors, the Queen passed by. She turned toward me with a glance so markedly friendly that Monsieur de Belsunce, who happened to be there with me, remarked, "I cannot understand why people think you on bad terms with Her Majesty. Surely just now she seemed to look upon you with distinct cordiality."

Indeed, whether by happenstance or by the machinations of that La Motte woman, I had good reason to hope for restoration of the Queen's favor.

* Regarding the date of this Oeil-de-Boeuf incident, Georgel's memoirs and Cardinal Rohan's statement (see footnote below) are at variance. Georgel ascribes it to early 1785, immediately following the theft of the necklace, whereas the Cardinal gives the year as 1784, before the theft. Like the historian Funck-Brentano, I feel that the Cardinal's date is preferable to that of the abbé—who was not an eyewitness and who wrote his account many years later—and, further, that logic favors the dating of the incident not only before the theft but also before the Grove of Venus scene described in Chapter VIII. (Georgel also dates it before the Grove of Venus scene, but he puts them both in 1785.) In the interest of presenting the story in the most likely chronological sequence, I have placed this section of the abbé's memoirs here.
† In a statement to a commission of three Cabinet ministers sent by the King in August 1785 to question him in the Bastille. One of the three, Marine Minister de Castries, recorded the statement in his journal (unpublished), which in turn is quoted by Louis Hastier in his La Vérité sur l'affaire du collier. It should be noted that Carlyle, who accepted Georgel's dating of the Oeil-de-Boeuf incident in 1785, did not have access to the Castries-Rohan material, in which the year is given as 1784.

MEMOIRS
OF THE ABBÉ GEORGEL

It was to Count Cagliostro and to the Baron da Planta that the Cardinal confided all his hopes for the happy future which was to result from his correspondence with the Queen.

The Cardinal's secretary, young Ramon de Carbonnières, was to become the third member of this select, small coterie. Carbonnières was a highly talented young man; his field of knowledge was extensive, his mind quick and keen, his literary style forceful as well as graceful. He had won the Cardinal's implicit confidence and would have merited the honor had he not, following His Eminence's example, succumbed completely to Cagliostro's dangerous ideologies. Assuredly that charlatan must have possessed some potent charm to have acquired such influence over the will and imagination of his disciples. It was difficult to reconcile such blind devotion to Cagliostro with a superior intellect.

Madame de La Motte soon joined this exclusive little committee of the Cardinal's confidants, by whom the letters to and from the Queen were read aloud and commented on, and who decided the line of action for that glorious day on which the Cardinal's most grandiose hopes were to be realized.

Madame de La Motte played them all for fools.

Cagliostro, called constantly into consultation, directed the Cardinal's every step throughout the whole miserable affair. This modern-day soothsayer must doubtless have misread the omens as revealed in the entrails of the sacrificial victims, for, upon emerging from the state of trance in which he communed with the Bright Angel of Light and the Dark Angel of the Shadows, Cagliostro predicted that the secret correspondence with the Queen would result in the manifestation of the ultimate royal favor to the Cardinal, that he would thereby attain supreme power in government and that he would use this power to forward the noblest ideals of mankind, to the glory of the Supreme Being and to the welfare and happiness of the French nation.

If, at this moment, the Cardinal's fate hung in the balance, the weight of Cagliostro's oracle tipped the scales against him.

The Cardinal would not make a move without a pronouncement from Cagliostro. When the *soi-disant* Egyptian took refuge in Switzerland (constrained to quit Strasbourg by the authorities, who had come to consider his mysterious ideology subversive), the Cardinal sent his secretary Carbonnières along to cater to the creature comforts of the seer and also to ensure prompt transmission of his prognostications, in secret cipher and by special courier, whenever the Cardinal had need of consultation.

Not finding the Swiss refuge to his tastes, Cagliostro, with Carbonnières still in attendance, moved on to Lyons, where he made new proselytes who further swelled his fortunes.

If not the philosopher's stone (the discovery of which was generally attributed to him), the charlatan could claim an even richer treasure trove in the boundless enthusiasm of his converts. I know of men who, for his sake, impoverished—nay, even ruined—themselves without so much as a regret. So complete was Cagliostro's mastery over men's minds that his disciples considered themselves enriched by enriching him.

The secret source of Cagliostro's inexhaustible wealth was the Masonic organization—the Egyptian lodges he founded wherever he was allowed to proselytize. Thanks to this extraordinary and mysterious source of income, Cagliostro could well afford to appear altruistic and sublimely disinterested; to offer him money for his medical services or healings was to insult him.

It was during Cagliostro's sojourn in Lyons that the Grand Almoner left Paris to return to Alsace. The Baron da Planta was appointed to stay on in Paris for the purpose of handling the secret correspondence, to relay the little letters on gilt-edged stationery to the Prince in Saverne by post express or special messenger whenever Madame de La Motte deemed it necessary. This rather extraordinary journey of the Cardinal's to Alsace came as a result of orders in one of the little letters purportedly from the Queen: the Cardinal was advised that his recall from Strasbourg to Versailles would be timed to coincide with the moment selected for his public restoration to royal favor.

During the Prince's absence from Paris, a little letter supposedly written by the royal hand brought a request for a second loan of sixty thousand francs for the same philanthropic purposes as the first and set the date for reimbursement of the total sum borrowed. It was again Cerf-Beer who was expected to do the financing, upon the same terms and guarantees as on the previous occasion. The Baron da Planta, who made delivery of the gold to Madame de La Motte, was at the same time authorized to draw on the Cardinal's private funds, even to sell off the personal effects or properties of His Eminence in the event that she should require further loans.

This order was transmitted to His Eminence's treasurer with instructions not to mention it to me. The latter, however, felt constrained to advise me, in view of the fact that such withdrawals would affect certain prior commitments and regular disbursements of which I, as vicar general and comptroller of the estate, stood, in a sense, guarantor.

Needless to say, the 120,000 francs delivered in two payments to Madame de La Motte for transmittal to the Queen, as it was thought, never reached her hands. Indeed, the Queen never had any knowledge of the transaction. The money went to enrich the coffers of Madame de La Motte.

She dared not make too flagrant a display of luxury in her Paris establishment, lest she expose herself to embarrassing inquiry. She had her reasons for sending the Cardinal off to Alsace; she herself was yearning to be off, with all her brilliant equipage, for her birthplace at Bar-sur-Aube, there now at last to show herself in a style befitting a descendant of the Valois.

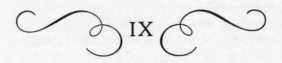

The Countess in the Provinces

(1784)

MEMOIRS
OF COUNT BEUGNOT

I HAD LEFT Paris to spend the holidays in Champagne without seeing
Madame de La Motte again, and without—I think I may truthfully add
—too poignantly pining for her. I had had conclusive proof that it was
impossible to keep her to the paths of reason and discretion, and I gave
up in despair when I learned of the company she was keeping in Versailles and her debuts there.

When I reached Bar-sur-Aube, everyone lay in wait to question me on
the subject of Madame de La Motte, but I maintained reserve in my
replies. I went into detail only with my father, to whom I made it clear
that it was no longer possible for any self-respecting man to be involved
in the affairs of his protégée.

The vacation months were passing pleasantly enough. Every year I
returned to the city of my birth with increased gravity and dignity. I no
longer limited myself to Madame de Surmont's social circle, but agreed
occasionally to subject myself to boredom at the assembly balls, and I
had even reached some sense of appreciation of the demure and modest
feminine charms there on display when a letter came to me from Madame de La Motte—a cordial letter in which she announced that, hav-

ing a few days free, she was coming to spend them with her friends at Bar-sur-Aube.

In an offhand manner, as if, indeed, it were the most natural thing in the world, she mentioned that she had sent her household furnishings and saddle horses on ahead; she herself was to be expected two days later. A similar letter to her sister-in-law contained, in addition, instructions on accommodations to be prepared for herself and retinue.

Madame de Latour came running, reeling with astonishment, to ask me what it was all about. I told her that I knew no more than she. Comparing letters, we agreed that there was a definite intent to mystify, by which we refused to be taken in; that Madame de Latour would make no advance preparations for the "Princess and her entourage"; that neither of us would make any mention whatsoever of the letters we had received.

Imagine our astonishment, then, when, on the appointed day, we saw a heavy-laden wagon pull into town, drawn by a handsome team of horses and followed by a pair of unmistakably valuable saddle horses.

There was no reason further to doubt, nor to hold back. To provide accommodations for the household staff already in evidence, not to mention that part due to arrive shortly after, a large house had to be rented, the proprietor bundled out in a hurry, the apartments readied at top speed. A maître d'hôtel who had arrived with the wagon proceeded to the ordering of provisions that would have constituted a six-months supply for the best-stocked larder in Bar-sur-Aube. People were stopping one another along the streets, exclaiming over the latest developments—as fantastic as some tale out of *The Arabian Nights*—when in drove Monsieur and Madame de La Motte themselves, in an elegant English carriage, preceded by two outriders.

My father, wise as he was, allowed himself to be carried away by appearances and enjoyed a secret satisfaction at being able to charge me with miscalculation.

"My son," he said, "you have developed a deplorable habit of making snap judgments. Just because Madame de La Motte did not show proper appreciation of your briefs and petitions, you treated her—by your own admission—harshly. Your behavior was unjustified. I think that I am perhaps as well versed as you on the subject of royal-domain affairs, and I have never considered it impossible for Madame de La Motte to recover possession of her family properties. In fact, matters must be far advanced; I have had confidential information to the effect that the Queen is taking a personal interest in the case. The trouble with you is that you are seeing too much of that Latour fellow. I refuse to have anything more to do with him; that wicked tongue of his would find ill to speak of even our Lord Savior were He to return to walk the earth today. I do hope that you will not allow yourself to be influenced by Latour on this occasion, and that, in regard to Madame de La Motte, you will show yourself what you should never have ceased to be, her respectful and devoted friend. That poor child!" exclaimed my father, in a sentimental mood. "When I think of the handful of coins I used to give the curate of Fontette from time to time to help clothe the little creature!"

Monsieur de Latour (whom my father had stopped seeing because, given occasion, he would, indeed, have spoken ill of the Heavenly Father) was the scourge of the countryside with his bons mots and scoffery. He was a witty man, a stimulating conversationalist, endowed with all the social graces when he chose to exert them, but he had a singular knack of pointing up the element of the ridiculous in situations innocent thereof to any other. Admittedly, he stopped at nothing to achieve his effects. Otherwise he was a man of honor, as incapable of committing a vicious action as of resisting a malicious word (the latter, however, was perhaps little less reprehensible than the former). The pattern of his life had somehow worked out to confine him to Bar-sur-Aube. I never knew why, unless it was through the accident of a garrison-town romance, a youthfully impetuous marriage to the sister of Monsieur de La Motte. He was out of place in Bar-sur-Aube; Paris would have been his true domain. A man such as he would have been the most cordially detested in the capital—and the most sought after.

I found myself alone with Latour at Madame de La Motte's the day of her arrival. He greeted me shaking with laughter and bent on my joining in the hilarity.

"By heaven!" he exclaimed. "How right I am in my theory that your sophisticated Parisians are the most gullible folk on earth! Where else but in Paris, I ask you, could this little hussy and her great gawk of a husband have succeeded in rooking the citizenry out of such treasures as they flourish today before our eyes? With the lady you are familiar— no pun intended! A half hour in her company suffices as introduction to her impertinence and her contempt for truth. As for the husband, he is a cavalryman, who can be counted on to scrounge an extra bale of hay from the commissary and to sling it over his shoulder into the stall; but expect no more than that of him. Why, the 'Princess' with all her charms, the 'Prince' with all his genius could not have found a living soul in Bar-sur-Aube, with the exception of your good father, to lend them a sou, yet here in the last hour they have unloaded a collection of silverware more extensive than the whole town put together can boast, including the chalice and the Holy Sacrament on the cathedral altar. O Paris, holy Mecca of fools and rascals, I salute you for yet one more marvel!"

"Have done!" I replied. "You carry the jest to extremes. In the last analysis, they are your relatives, and you have today accepted their invitation to dine."

"Irrefutably, they are my relatives; it is that very fact which gives me grave concern. For after I shall have enjoyed hearty laughter over this phantasmagoria, I shall in all probability be doomed to bitter weeping over it, and you know my aversion to that grimace. As for eating their dinner, no matter how splendid, we do them honor by sitting at their table. As to Madame de La Motte's relations with the Queen, I make no comment. Just between you and me, I suspect that the wife of our Lord and Sovereign King is not the most prudent of women, but, merciful heavens, she can't be mad enough to be involved with specimens such as these! Be that as it may, let us try to enjoy our dinner—all the while remembering our resolve not to appear impressed by anything, no matter how impressive. There's no surer method of annoying this pair."

There were eight of us at table, including the host and hostess, and a dinner was served which would have been pronounced superb by any company in Paris. Although Bar-sur-Aube is one of the most ancient of Gallic cities, never before had it witnessed such a display of splendor, not even when it was honored by the visit of Julius Caesar, who, as legend has it, stopped by for the purpose of hanging the mayor and magistrates of the period. Faithful to our resolve, Latour and I ate with hearty appetite but without a word of comment, as if such banquets were our daily fare, and we maneuvered the conversation along lines precluding any opportunity to the others for eulogizing on the feast spread out before us. Monsieur de La Motte, clearly disgruntled, determined to make us admire the table silver, the last word in style and craftsmanship; at which Latour contended that the design was an old one which had been discarded as impractical. He and I did not deviate from the *nil mirari* as order of the day.

After dinner Madame de La Motte invited me to follow her into the study, where she complained of the insolence of her husband's brother-in-law. She made a point of telling me that a great change had been effected in her fortunes, that she now found herself in a situation highly auspicious for herself and her family, and that all her friends and relatives would be well advised to adopt a new tone with her. She dropped a few hints on the subject of her lofty connections at Versailles and concluded by saying that she only regretted that she could not be sure of allowing us the two weeks' visit she had promised. Whereupon I gave her a first example of the "new tone" she had recommended by permitting myself not so much as a single question on any of the topics which she had covered. I did undertake to advocate to her brother-in-law that he approach her in the future more respectfully, though I hardly dared flatter myself on the success of my intervention.

The following day Madame de La Motte set out on a round of formal visits, dressed in a style as lavish as might be expected from the prevailing tone of the establishment. She was already aglitter with diamonds. She went to ridiculous lengths in her advances and her air of familiarity with the local nobility. Great and small, however, they were one and all enchanted with her. Everyone whom she visited returned the call, although when she wanted to pursue it further with a series of small parties, the respectable ladies of the town sent their regrets under a diversity of pretexts, and Madame de La Motte's social circle was limited to the young people and women of her husband's family—so strict, at that period, was the moral code in a small provincial town.

"Madame de La Motte is charming," these good ladies told me, "and we love her with all our hearts, but would you have us expose our daughters to dangerous ideas, encourage ambitions they could never satisfy?"

I faithfully observed the rules of respect and discretion Madame de La Motte had prescribed. She appeared completely to have forgotten our former relations, and I followed her lead. Indeed, it would seem I had been somehow suddenly metamorphosed, in her eyes, into the decorous gentleman, the family friend with whom a pretty married woman could talk freely about her problems. Accordingly she revealed to me the secret disappointments of her Bar-sur-Aube sojourn, her embarrassment at the social standing of her husband's family.

I consoled her as best I could and pointed out that for a woman in her position a small provincial town was simply not the place for residence, that what she should have was a town house in Paris and a château in the provinces. She told me that she did not want to buy property

at the present because she expected momentarily to recover possession
of her family domains, and that it was on the ancestral acres that she
proposed to build. The Paris town house was a foregone conclusion, but
she wanted another in Bar-sur-Aube to spend the summer season in
while waiting for her château to be erected. I took the liberty of pointing out that it was considered quite chic to live in a thatch-roofed peasant's cot while awaiting completion of one's château alongside. But no,
Madame de La Motte, apparently, had had her fill of "living under
thatch" and was not to be diverted from parading her newly acquired
opulence in the region which had witnessed her early destitution. Despite my advice, she bought the house in Bar-sur-Aube, paying twice what
it was worth, and turned it over to architects who perpetrated every
structural folly the size of the lot would permit and a few more besides.

I noted with some astonishment that in her social contacts Madame
de La Motte was scrupulously proper, that she fulfilled her obligations
punctiliously while asking little in return. She distributed her philanthropies throughout the neighborhood and paid her bills promptly.

One morning she made a friendly visit to my father and returned, as
I have previously mentioned, the thousand francs he had loaned her a
year and a half before; when she departed, she left a handsome gold to-
bacco box on the mantel. Why my father construed this token of appreciation as an insult I never knew, but he sent it back to her. Madame
de La Motte, who might with some justification have taken offense at
the return of the gift, did not, but asked me to urge my father to keep
it. Knowing his attitude, I declined the commission. In despair, she
begged me to keep the blasted thing for myself, which I again refused,
certain that my father would not condone the indelicacy of my accepting a present he had seen fit to reject.

Madame de La Motte's Bar-sur-Aube visit was drawing to a close, and
before it was over those who had not been bold enough to frequent her
salon had come to rue their decision. Monsieur de Latour alone continued to hold out against her. I urged him to give credit where credit
was due; here, in the case of Monsieur and Madame de La Motte, affluence, suddenly and mysteriously as it had come, had wrought a decided
improvement in manner and deportment.

"I'll go along with you part of the way," he answered. "The wife is a
little minx who has matured, but the husband has deteriorated—he
left a fool and returns a fop. I persist in my poor opinion of them and
shall voice it until they reveal by what legitimate endeavor they have

amassed, in four months' time, such a fortune as they have flaunted in our faces here. Even you who champion her, can you really bring yourself to believe that the King, the Queen, the Count d'Artois, the Minister of Finance or any one of the powers that be would have showered gold over the heads of this pair who came asking no more than a mere loaf of daily bread? Ours is an extravagant age, I grant you, but this is going entirely too far! I have heard the whisper everywhere that Madame de La Motte enjoys the favor of the Queen, but though I have listened attentively the last two weeks, neither one of them has had the impudence to mention a word about it in my presence. I would be ashamed to be taken in so easily. Believe it yourself, if you like, but I won't go for it; I'll stand on what I know to be the facts. Now, I do know, for instance—and know it through you—that a liaison exists between Madame and Cardinal Rohan. I know that she was driven to the palace of His Eminence five or six times in a coach at your expense, and that she probably returned there as many times thereafter on her own light foot. Among all the lady's acquaintances, Cardinal Rohan is the only one to whom such prodigality is not improbable. That leaves me with two alternatives from which to choose: Either His Eminence voluntarily provided all the treasure we have seen here displayed or he was cheated out of it. I will spare you the second alternative on the condition that you grant me the first; and even then I find it difficult to understand how a little provincial coquette could have seduced a prince, a prelate, a good-for-nothing of such prominence."

I could not deny the logic in Monsieur de Latour's rude deductions, but I clung to a course of moderation: "I intend to wait before pronouncing judgment. If I have heretofore been quick to criticize what I considered criticizable, why should I not now readily praise what I consider praiseworthy?"

Already at this period, Madame de La Motte possessed a magnificent diamond parure—pin, sautoir, bracelet, earrings, rings—and another such in topazes. Her dresses of embroidered and brocaded Lyons silks she had obviously brought along expressly to model for us, and they were well worth the effort; her silver service was complete, and in the latest style. Cardinal Rohan's lawyer, Target, was mistaken when he claimed that the display of all this magnificence began after—and as a result of—the necklace theft; Madame de La Motte was dazzling the eyes of Bar-sur-Aube a full nine months earlier. The source of it all must surely have been the two relief grants of sixty thousand francs each awarded to her by the Grand Almoner of France on the treasury of the Grand Almonership, and a third sum of thirty thousand francs out of the Cardinal's private purse. By credit manipulation of the 150,000 francs, she could easily have purchased household and personal effects worth twice that amount, an expedient which doubtless occurred to her. In the beginning it had been mostly for the personal satisfaction of showing off at Bar-sur-Aube; but having once discovered (and on my advice) that the best way to go about asking charity is to drive up in a fine carriage, she was committed to that course, and the impression of prosperity became a necessity for her if she was to convince the world that she basked in the royal favor and disposed of influence in lofty quarters.

I saw Madame de La Motte the day she left for Paris; she seemed highly pleased at the "cordial reception" that had been accorded her in Bar-sur-Aube, as pleased as if such had actually been the case.

She pretended suddenly to remember that she owed me money; I had forgotten about it myself, never dreaming she would bother her pretty head with such a trifle. Nonchalantly, she handed me a roll of twelve hundred francs, at which I protested that although I could not remember the exact amount it certainly had not been so much as that.

"Take it, anyhow," she said. "If it's too much, give the excess to your mother for her favorite charities."

My computations made, I presented twenty louis to my mother, who was overjoyed and who in the years to come never ceased to champion Madame de La Motte's innocence, even after the verdict rendered by the court.

Madame de La Motte went back to Paris toward the end of November. I stayed on in Bar-sur-Aube until January of the following year. For the first time, I was giving consideration to the idea of a permanent return to the provinces. Accordingly I took a greater interest in regional affairs, and this did not go unnoticed; a distinctly warmer welcome was accorded me everywhere. My fellow citizens indicated clearly that I was a man with whom they would be pleased to work in the community interests. My attitude in regard to Madame de La Motte—the fact that I had joined in neither the absurd adulation of some nor the disdain of others —won me general approval. Considered opinion coincided with mine, that judgment should be withheld while awaiting future developments and that in the meanwhile the lady was entitled to the benefit of the doubt.

Upon my return to Paris, I was confirmed in my opinion that Madame de La Motte's prosperity stemmed from her intimate liaison with Cardinal Rohan, and I regulated my conduct with her upon that premise, showing discretion in presenting myself at her door, waiting to go there to dine until honored with a formal invitation. I allowed her to set the terms of our relations; I manifested appropriate respect.

She did, however, let herself go in my company on the subject of her hopes and plans, and with that casual air which presupposes success; it was in her scheme of things, she told me, for her brother to retire from the Navy, an unrewarding and boring service in peacetime. She had the promise of a regiment for him, and she had bought a captain's commission for her husband, after which a colonelcy should not be too difficult to wangle. As for her sister, Marianne was assured the position of abbess at either the Abbey of Douxières or that of Poulangy, whichever was preferred; in any case, Marianne was to be saved from her sister's folly, a rash and inconsidered marriage.

"If only I had married a man of title and position at court, as I so easily could have done," she exclaimed, "how much more rapid progress I would have made! My husband is a hindrance to me instead of a help; in order to get anywhere I must use my name above his, and that in itself is in violation of the conventions."

From the refrain of her remarks, I gathered that she was making rapid ascent into the rarefied atmosphere of the Cardinal's lofty social stratum; she had already achieved fluency in the jargon of courtier expertise spoken there.

She invited me several times to dinner, and I was always careful to make my appearance in formal dress of black and with my hair worn long, signs of respect which patently pleased her, for she never failed to introduce me as a "promising young magistrate" and to seat me at table immediately below her titled guests. The company to be found in her salon, at least at that particular period, was composed of the very best of Paris society. At her house I usually encountered the Marquis de Saisseval, a man of wealth, a big gambler and prominent at court; the Abbé de Cabres, councilor of Parliament; the Count d'Estaing, a gentleman of the King's household retinue; Rouillé d'Orfeuil, governor of Champagne; and such financiers as Darcy and Lecoulteux de La Noraye, the two of them competing hotly for the privilege of serving her as business manager.

I recall these details because they correct one of the most glaring er-

rors made by the Cardinal's lawyers: they tried to make out Madame de
La Motte as a common adventuress, without stopping to think that in
so doing they made the Cardinal out a complete imbecile (which he assuredly was not).

Here is the version that comes closer to the truth: Madame de La
Motte, as I have already said, had natural wit, a rare talent for intrigue,
and physical attractions more than enough to justify any man's predilection. From the day the Cardinal first met her, he showed her the kind of
attention which no man of his rank could refuse to the last descendant
of an illustrious house. After serving her apprenticeship at Versailles,
this lady of many intrigues began to concoct her romantic scenario for
the Cardinal and played it out with consummate artistry. She wove
about herself a cloak of whispers concerning her mysterious relations
with the Queen, whispers which the Cardinal was all the more disposed
to credit since, to his knowledge, the Queen's past offered precedent
for just such secret liaisons. Madame de La Motte heightened the illusion by an apparently discreet code of behavior, by occasional mysterious disappearances from her Paris haunts into retreat ostensibly at Versailles or Trianon. At this stage of the game, I—and others like me—
were kept at a distance, and those to whom the rule of respect proved
burdensome were banished altogether.

The sentiments aroused in the Cardinal's breast by his first encounter
with Madame de La Motte now took on even deeper significance. Since
it was so patently to his interest that her stories should be true, he
wound up believing them implicitly.

One must pause to recollect the Cardinal's position at court. While
ambassador to Vienna, he had committed the irreparable sin, in the
eyes of Marie Antoinette, of drawing too realistic a picture of the Archduchess who was destined for the throne of France; this honest appraisal
brought about his disgrace. The King, as was his wont with churchmen
of notorious immorality, criticized Cardinal Rohan openly, yet tolerated
him in his high position.

It so happened that of all the courtiers under royal disfavor Prince de
Rohan was the one who suffered the most acutely from it; the royal displeasure caused him unending torment. Now, it was the Countess de
La Motte to whom he looked for reconciliation with his sovereign, for
all the benefits of royal favor so sorely needed by a man who without it
could lay claim to being only a prince of the house of Rohan, a cardinal,
Grand Almoner of France, commander of the Order of the Holy Ghost,

Bishop of Strasbourg, sovereign Prince of Hildesheim, abbot of Nou-
moutier and of St. Waast, director general of the Sorbonne, member of
all the academies of France, darling of all the great ladies of Paris; with
an annual income of seven or eight hundred thousand francs—and so,
of course, head over heels in debt.

At the time his relations with Madame de La Motte deepened into intimacy, ambition, a passion fiercer than love, was already blazing in his
heart, the flame of one serving to kindle higher that of the other until
the poor man was overcome by a kind of delirium. Under circumstances
which I will later recount, I had occasion to glance through some of the
Cardinal's letters written at this epoch to Madame de La Motte. They
were all afire; two such emotions in combustion were terrifying. The
destruction of these love letters was fortunate for the memory of the
Prince, but constituted a distinct loss to the study of the human heart,
the remotest corners of which dark cavern they illuminated.

At the period of which I write, the Cardinal had as yet accorded to
Madame de La Motte only one or two grants from the Grand Almonership, along with various others from his personal funds. She could have
asked much more; the time was still far off in the distant future when
he would be able to refuse her anything. But soon now the magnificent
hoax of the necklace was to be essayed; every steppingstone leading up
to it was so carefully aligned that success was assured, despite the most
glaring discrepancies, the most transparent deceptions. Cardinal Rohan
would believe it all; he was no longer capable of judgment.

This is the background material without which one cannot hope ever
to come close to the truth of that strange affair. Instead, it seems that
for some reason word went out to picture Madame de La Motte as a
common adventuress who dreamed up one day the theft she would
commit the next. From that point of view the Necklace Case became an
insoluble mystery to which every man sought the clue in the light of his
own personal prejudices or from out of the mass of conflicting testimony
and comment, while the most audacious accusations—and the most absurd—were leveled as high as the throne itself.

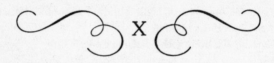

X

The Key to the Enigma

"THE QUEEN'S REPUTATION, sad to say," as Count Beugnot sadly said it, "provided the key to the whole diamond necklace enigma, the explanation of the web of intrigue the Countess de La Motte was able to weave to enmesh the Cardinal," so that neither he nor any of his contemporaries would have had a moment's hesitation in believing that the Queen had taken a sudden fancy to the Countess de La Motte, that the Countess had attained to a sudden, secret intimacy with her sovereign.

"At this point we must pause to make a rather sad commentary," Beugnot writes in his memoirs,

. . . one which cannot be omitted, however, since it supplies a vital clue to the mystery of Madame de La Motte and the diamond necklace affair.

The Queen had, at that time, a reputation for frivolity and indiscretion which, doubtless, she never deserved. It was said generally that she was always in financial difficulties as a result of her follies and extravagances. People quoted remarks of hers, cited traits which made her seem less a reigning Queen of France than a reigning belle, an alluring and desirable woman. People began to think and speak of her in just those terms.

The lords and ladies of the court went even further and thus stimulated a startling new disrespect among the other classes of society. The Queen was no longer considered the Great Lady of Versailles to whom one hardly dared raise one's eyes, above suspicion as above the glance of common men. Maria Leszczyńska, her predecessor, although elevated to that high rank by a sort of miracle, had nonetheless maintained the dignity thereof; in dying, it would seem, she had broken the mold.

Of a Maria Leszczyńska, Queen of France, of a Victoria or an Elizabeth II of England no such rumors could ever have gained circulation. The very first whisper would have been repudiated; their names could never have become involved in a scandal such as that of the diamond necklace.

But a Marie Antoinette of France . . . "Her Majesty has utterly forgotten her dignity," Austrian Ambassador Mercy sighed by letter to the Empress-mother of the French Queen. And Maria Theresa, moaning in reply: "You can imagine how distressed I am about my daughter, who is rushing full speed to her doom . . ." Then, directly to her child: "The newspapers, the leaflets which used to delight me because they had so much to say about my daughter's magnanimity and kindness of heart, have suddenly changed their tune. I read in them nothing now except accounts of horse racing, gambling, the turning of night into day, so that I can no longer bear to look at them and often shut myself away from society lest I even hear such matters spoken of. I, who love my little Queen and watch over her every footstep, cannot fail to warn her of her frivolousness. . . ."

By the time Marie Antoinette came to the throne in 1774, after four years of sharing the marriage bed with Louis XVI, she was not yet a mother, not yet, actually, a wife. After becoming Queen, she was to endure three more years of technical virginity—unchaste, tormented.

Not until 1777 did her brother, Emperor Joseph of Austria, on a visit to Versailles, succeed in persuading his brother-in-law to submit to the minor surgery long indicated by the medical staff for correction of the—in Ambassador Mercy's term of reference—"fatal object." In justice to Louis XVI, it must be said that his procrastination had been due less to fear of the scalpel than to profound religious convictions. Believing firmly (who, if not he?) in the divine right of kings, he feared to counter the divine will which had denied him the potency to beget heirs. Only Austrian brother-in-law Joseph's dialectics could convince him that a circumcision did not constitute a circumvention of divine au-

thority. Louis's may have been a stubborn and limited mentality, but his superstition that a scalpel should not tamper with destiny seems justified by historical developments: no heir of his was ever to ascend the throne of France.

MEMOIRS
OF MADAME CAMPAN

When, in 1777, the son of the Count d'Artois was born, the market women and fishwives who, asserting their prerogative, crowded the palace at times of royal births followed the Queen to the very door of her apartments, shouting in the coarsest and most vulgar terms that it was up to her, not to her sister-in-law, to provide heirs to the French crown. The Queen hurried to close the door upon these licentious harridans and closeted herself in her room with me to weep over her plight.

I have often had occasion to admire the way the Queen rose to meet the great crises in her life; she was so touching in her hours of adversity. At this time she still had no hope of becoming a mother, and there was much whispered talk in France about the obstacle which had so long prevented the King's availing himself of a husband's privileges.

Finally, one day toward the end of the year 1777, the Queen, alone in her private apartments, sent for my father-in-law and me and, smilingly extending her hand to us to kiss, told us that knowing us to be her true friends she was sure we would rejoice with her in the good news that she was, at long last and in the true sense of the word, Queen of France and could now hope to provide heirs to the throne. She told us that though she had managed all these years to conceal her sorrows in public, she had in secret shed many a tear. Monsieur Campan and I computed that she gave birth to the Princess Marie Thérèse Charlotte exactly a year after this confidence.

And from this joyous moment on, the King gave every evidence of a man deeply in love. Good Lassonne, the royal couple's doctor, had often spoken to me of his distress at an estrangement the cause of which had taken him so long to cure; from this time on, however, his only concern seemed to me to be on the very opposite score.

On August 25 of that year, the Spanish ambassador at Versailles, by diplomatic pouch to Madrid: "The King mentioned the matter with ut-

most frankness to one of his maiden aunts: 'I find the pleasure very great and only regret that so long a time has passed without my being able to enjoy it.'"

But "two thousand nights" of frustration and humiliation upon the marriage bed had taken their toll, and it is not too surprising that Marie Antoinette subconsciously should shun it, as her brother Joseph's letter would reproach: "Do you not show impatience when your husband speaks to you, shrink away from his touch when he caresses you?" And Marie Antoinette would admit to one of her associates, "I should neither be grieved nor very annoyed if the King were to develop a passing fancy, a temporary attachment, as he might thereby acquire vitality and experience."

The dynasty was her destiny, and she would ensure the succession: four "Children of France," as the royal children were designated—two sons and two daughters (all to be baptized by Cardinal Rohan, though she would still refuse to address a word to him even across the font). In the first flush of pride at her achievement she would tell Madame Campan, "I am now experiencing the most important happiness of my life." But only three months later Madame Campan notes: "The King was very set in his habits and allowed nothing to upset his routine; he retired promptly at eleven o'clock. Up to this time he had never failed to share the nuptial bed, but the noise made by the Queen when she came in late from parties appeared to disturb the King, and it was agreed, with no ill will on either side, that the Queen should in future advise him on the nights she would stay out late; and at this period the King began to spend the night in his own apartments, a thing which had never happened since their wedding."

"My tastes do not accord with the King's," Marie Antoinette wrote to a Viennese friend, Count von Rosenberg. "He is interested only in hunting and machinery. . . . I know you will agree that I should look out of place beside a forge; the role of Vulcan would not suit me, and I fancy the role of Venus would be more uncongenial to him than my tastes—of which, indeed, he does not disapprove . . ."

"Dares not disapprove" was what she meant, what Madame Campan said outright: "Who would have dared criticize the diversions of a young, gay, pretty queen? Only a mother or a husband would have had the right; and the King offered no opposition to Marie Antoinette's will or whim. His long indifference had been succeeded by admiration and love; he had become a slave to the every desire, every fancy of the Queen; and

she, delighted by the happy change wrought in the King's heart and at-
titude, made no effort to conceal the satisfaction it gave her to have
come to exert such a hold over him."

"This indulgence of the King's, which covers everything," Count
Mercy complained, "makes it impossible to divert the Queen from things
which cannot be for her own good"—things such as horse racing and
gambling, gambling above all, the all-night sessions of Faro at towering
high stakes. "It is the one subject," according to Mercy, "on which the
Queen will admit no protest." And the extravagances of her wardrobe!
"Marie Antoinette preferred the title of Queen of Fashion to that of
Queen of France," observed Madame de Boigne, another contemporary
memoirist. "Always more of a woman than a queen," in politician
Rivarol's diagnosis. And Madame Campan, admitting Marie Antoinette's
craze for Rose Bertin, the Chanel of her day,* remarked, "The Queen,
who now began to make clothes her principal interest, was naturally
imitated by all the other women, and it was widely said that, as a result,
she would bankrupt the ladies of France."

But the passion more costly than gambling or clothes was the passion
for diamonds. Who, if not the Queen of France, should possess the
world's most magnificent? Madame Campan writes:

Very shortly after Marie Antoinette became Queen, the jeweler Böhmer, highly recommended by many of her friends at court, came to show
her his lavish and elaborate creations—among them, a pair of girandole
earrings, originally designed for Madame du Barry and priced at 400,000
francs, each earring composed of six enormous, perfectly matched, flawless white diamonds. Marie Antoinette could not resist her desire to
own them, but proposed that Böhmer replace the two round stones at
the apex of the chandelier with two round gems of her own. To this
Böhmer agreed, at a reduction of forty thousand francs. Although the
King had just doubled her allowance, Marie Antoinette asked Böhmer
for terms, installment payments extending over a period of four or five
years.

I have omitted none of the details relative to this first of the Queen's
dealings with Böhmer, thinking them appropriate and of value in throwing light on the all too famous necklace affair. For it was this same Böh-

* "The airs that Bertin woman gave herself" exceedingly annoyed the Baroness
d'Oberkirch, kept waiting endlessly in the showroom of that first famed exponent of
haute couture '(I'll show you a little model I worked out recently with Her Majesty . . .").

mer whose stupidity and cupidity were, in a sense, responsible later in bringing about that accursed event which constituted such a fatal blow to the happiness and reputation of Marie Antoinette.

Count Mercy reported to Vienna on the Queen's passion for jewels: "Although the King, during the past year, has given the Queen on various occasions more than 100,000 écus' worth of diamonds, and although Her Majesty already had a prodigious collection, nevertheless she was determined to acquire these chandelier earrings from Böhmer. I did not conceal from Her Majesty the fact that, under present economic conditions, it would have been wiser to avoid such a tremendous expenditure, but she could not resist—although she handled it carefully, keeping her purchase a secret from the King."

She kept likewise "secret from the King" her next purchase, bracelets more costly still than the chandelier earrings—diamond bracelets, in the purchase of which Her Majesty worked out an arrangement with Böhmer whereby the jeweler agreed to accept some of her own stones as an exchange and partial down payment. Even on this basis, "Her Majesty was obliged to analyze her personal accounts," wrote Mercy, "and discovered that she was in dire straits financially" (in debt to the tune of a half-million francs). "Most reluctantly she was obliged to ask the King to pay her debts" (including the greatest part of the Böhmer and Bassenge earring account), "which he agreed to do, remarking that he was not surprised at her financial difficulties in view of her passion for diamonds."

This report of Mercy's to Vienna brought a letter from the Empress in October 1776. "I hear that you have been buying diamond bracelets at a cost of a quarter of a million francs—" ("Now, how on earth have my bracelets reached Vienna so soon?" exclaimed Marie Antoinette, never suspecting Mercy) "with the result that you have thrown your finances into such disorder, accumulated such a burden of debt that to find a way out of the difficulties with your jewelers you have sold some of your own diamonds very cheap. You make light of the bracelets, and the rumors may be exaggerated, but it is more serious than you think. A sovereign is demeaned by decking herself out so lavishly, at such vast expenditure, and especially at a time like this. Loving you as I do, and for your own good, I cannot keep silence. Don't risk losing, by such frivolities, the esteem you won in the beginning. The King has a reputation for moderation and economy, so it will be upon you that all the blame will fall. I hope I do not live to see such a change effect itself in the opinion of your people . . ."

She did not live to see it. Dying four years later, in 1780, Empress Maria Theresa was spared the sight of her daughter's name and reputation sullied by the diamond necklace scandal, spared the sight of her daughter before the Revolutionary Tribunal when admission of her profligacy was wrung from her by Public Prosecutor Fouqier-Tinville:

FOUQUIER-TINVILLE: It must have cost immense sums to build and furnish the Little Trianon, where you gave those parties at which you played the goddess.

MARIE ANTOINETTE: It is likely enough that the Little Trianon cost huge sums of money, and perhaps more than I intended; I became gradually involved in more and more expense. . . .

And a letter from the Countess de La Marck to King Gustavus III of Sweden: "The Queen goes deeper and deeper into debt, meddles in legal and political affairs, spends all her time at the Paris Opéra or the Comédie, drips with plumes and pompoms, makes fun of everybody . . ."

Not only her extravagances, but also her indiscretions! It is from her mother and her brother that the most telling indictments come (these family letters were released from the Austrian archives in mid-nineteenth century). Here is brother Joseph in one letter out of dozens:

Have you ever stopped to think what effect your ill-chosen friendships and intimacies may have upon the public? Don't you see that by choosing associates of dubious reputation you appear to be participating in and condoning vice? Did you ever stop to reflect upon the disastrous consequences of your gambling, the bad atmosphere and bad company around the gaming tables? Bear in mind that the King never gambles, making it all the more scandalous for you alone in the family to support the evil custom.

In like manner, think for a moment of the questionable incidents in which you have been involved at the Paris Opéra balls—escapades I have learned from your own lips. I will not conceal from you my opinion that of all your amusements these Opéra balls are the most unseemly. As for your going in disguise, incognito, do you honestly believe that you are not recognized? Really, now, everyone knows who you are. Your mask simply gives people the privilege of saying things unsuitable for you to hear, things said to titillate your ear, make you think they are said innocently. The place has, in fact, a very wicked reputation. Why these escapades, this unbecoming behavior? Why do you rub shoulders with a crowd of libertines, loose women and strangers, listening to improprieties, perhaps uttering them yourself? Really, this sort of thing does not become you and shocks respectable people who have your interest at heart. The King is left alone all night at Versailles while you cheapen yourself mingling with the riffraff of Paris! In truth, I tremble for your welfare, seeing that in the long run things cannot go on like this. . . . The revolution will be a cruel one, and perhaps of your own making. . . .

The sense in which Joseph used the word "revolution" is not the political one meaning the overthrow of a system, but a more personal one: an upset or fall for which his sister was headed. But, though not a prophecy of the French Revolution on the Austrian Emperor's part, his words reflect a dim sense of foreboding which he himself may not have fully understood.

And Madame Campan added:

Rumors of the Queen's flirtations once started, there was simply no limit to the foolish conceit among the young gallants of the day, no end to the scandalous stories circulated about the Queen in Paris. If at a hunting party or a gaming table she so much as spoke to a Monsieur Dillon or Lambertye, to any one of a number of young coxcombs whose names I can no longer even remember, they promptly were characterized as her "favored lovers." If at the theater she so much as asked some young gentleman when the next act would begin, the young fop was so presumptuous as to think he had attracted the Queen's interest. Lulled into a sense of security by her own innocence, the Queen scorned such rumors . . .

What but "foolish conceit" could have been expected of such "young gallants"—a Monsieur Dillon or Lambertye, a Duke de Lauzun or de Guines, a Count von Fersen—in the society of a voluptuously handsome,* a vigorous and healthy young woman of normal tenderness and passions, in a marital status so anomalous as to provide subject matter for public ribaldry, cartoon, verse? What could be expected of this young woman herself, continually playing with fire? Count Mercy fills in the clinical picture with his report to Vienna that the Queen was suffering from "sudden nervous attacks," the vapors, in eighteenth-century parlance, signs of an "amorous irritability—pale and red by turns, trembling."

From the Swedish ambassador's account to King Gustavus III:

I have to report to Your Majesty that young Count von Fersen is so much in the Queen's good graces as to have aroused suspicion in certain quarters. I must admit that I myself believe she has a fondness for him; the signs I have seen are all too plain to leave any doubt. In such circumstances, Count von Fersen has behaved in the most exemplary fashion, not only in respect to his modesty and reserve but also in his decision to go to America. He has put an end to all danger by his departure, and it cannot but be admitted that to have withstood such a temptation signifies him to be endowed with a resolution hardly to be expected at his age. During the last few days before he left for America, the Queen could hardly keep her eyes off him, and when she looked at him they filled with tears. . . .

In response to Count Mercy's rapid succession of urgent dispatches ("Her Majesty has utterly forgotten her dignity!" "It seems impossible to show her the error of her ways!"), brother Joseph set out on his visit to Versailles in 1777—only to be won over by the sister he called "the pretty featherhead . . . so good-natured and charming that I have spent hour after hour with her without noticing the passing of time . . . not quite grown up yet, little inclined to give matters serious thought, but with a ready wit and an insight which has frequently surprised me. . . . Her virtue is unassailed and, indeed, she is austere by nature rather than by reasoning" (possibly Emperor Joseph's way of saying that a Hapsburg archduchess, a Queen of France, had been born and bred to a deep inner belief—like her husband—in the divine right of kings, a royal credo transcending and supplanting a lesser mortal's code of ethics).

---

* Voluptuous by actual measurement (in centimeters, here translated into inches): waist 23½, bust 43½, according to the meticulous entries in the notebook of the Queen's dressmaker, Madame Eloff.

That pride in her destiny she expressed in her letter to her mother upon her accession to the throne: "Although God decreed that I should be born in the rank I occupy, I cannot but marvel at the dispensation of Providence thanks to which I, the youngest of your children, have been chosen to be Queen over the finest realm in Europe." Unlikely that she would have risked bringing down upon her head the divine wrath sure to be invoked by a queen's transgression of that Eleventh Commandment unto royalty, more stringent than all the other ten upon lesser mortals: The dynasty is sacred. Do not betray it. Marie Antoinette would never have risked the "sin of lèse-dynasté," as French author Pierre Audiat termed it. Audiat's, likewise, was the term "limited lovers" as applicable to Marie Antoinette's most ardent, most warmly encouraged admirers during the years she fulfilled her proud and sacred duty of ensuring the Bourbon succession.

The Versailles courtier, the sophisticate, in accepting the theory of the Queen's "limitation on lovers," attached significance to her constantly changing, flamboyant feminine friendships and intimacies. "There have been very generally ascribed to me two tastes," Marie Antoinette wrote her mother, "that for women, and that for lovers." (On this subject there was no answering blast from Vienna. Tacit condonation of the lesser of two evils?)

Count Mercy deplored the Queen's "vagaries of affection"; Madame Campan resented the necessity of so much as touching upon the Sapphic slur: "I find it repugnant to enter into any detail in defense of the Queen with regard to the infamous accusation with which poison pens have dared attack her—the ugly interpretation of the Queen's tender friendship for the Princess de Lamballe and the Duchess de Polignac."

Was there any foundation in fact for the rumor adding the name of the Countess de La Motte to the list of "Queen's favorites" enjoying just such a "tender friendship" with Marie Antoinette? The rumor gained currency, the Countess de La Motte herself being one of the many to foster it.

Cardinal Rohan gave it credence; the Queen's past, in Count Beugnot's words, "offered precedent for just such illicit liaisons"; the Abbé Georgel's memoirs cite ample reasons why His Eminence so readily accepted the story as fact:

Cardinal Rohan, as he came to know Madame de La Motte, recognized in her a sharp and sparkling wit that promised great talent for intrigue; he recognized that she was precisely the type to interest and appeal to the Queen. He found nothing extraordinary whatsoever in the idea that Her Majesty would have welcomed into her intimate circle a woman who was the most delightful and diverting of companions, a useful and skillful intrigante.

If the Countess ran with a fast and rakish set, if she had acquired a rather dubious reputation around Paris and Versailles in recent months, what of ·that? Did not the Abbé Vermond, Marie Antoinette's own secretary and father confessor, write his royal mistress, "A tarnished or a lost reputation, immorality, misconduct of all kinds seem to constitute title for admission to your society"?

And Madame Campan, in a sketch of that intimate society of the Queen's, listed other qualifications:

The newest songs from the Comédie, the most timely joke or pun or quip, the bon mot of the day, the latest and choicest titbit of scandal or gossip—these comprised the sole topics of conversation in the intimate group about the Queen; discussion on a serious plane was banished from her court. The Queen found intellectuals overpowering to her taste. "Deliver me from the intelligentsia," she remarked. No pedant could ever have expected to be included in her circle of intimates.

On all counts, the Cardinal not unnaturally thought, the Countess de La Motte fulfilled the requirements for entrée to the vive la bagatelle society of Madame Campan's description—that sophisticated little friend of his, with her resounding Valois name, her piquant face and graceful figure, her spontaneous humor and rippling, infectious laughter, gay, vivacious, ingratiating, a virtuoso at the harp or at the gaming table, a superb raconteuse—the very best company imaginable. Fit for a queen, especially a pleasure-loving and frivolous one.

The Cardinal—and his contemporaries—would have had not a moment's hesitation in crediting the Countess de La Motte's claim to sudden, secret intimacy with her sovereign; no hesitation in crediting the Countess's claim that her sovereign, in financial difficulties, sought relief from the Cardinal's Grand Almonership funds with the Countess de La Motte as intermediary.

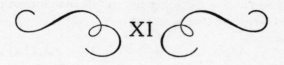

XI

The Grove of Venus

(Midsummer 1784)

MEMOIRS
OF THE ABBÉ GEORGEL

THROUGHOUT THESE MONTHS, Madame de La Motte continued to work upon the imagination of the Cardinal, building up his hopes by means of the purported correspondence with the Queen; the little letters on gilt-edged notepaper became more and more interesting.

A certain anxiety, however, continued to beset the Cardinal, as he confided to Madame de La Motte; he simply could not understand the Queen's continued disdain of him in public, which was in striking contrast to the cordiality and interest evinced in the little letters.

This latter complaint became His Eminence's daily refrain upon his return to Paris. Up to this point, Madame de La Motte, with her ingenuity for expedients, had always found a way to soothe away his uncertainties. Now she called upon all her fiendish genius to devise a strategy to cure the credulous Cardinal once and for all of this recurrent doubt.

This most recently conceived iniquity, however, required a series of careful preliminaries. In concert with her husband and Villette, Madame de La Motte proceeded with preparations for the staging of a strange farce the conception and perpetration of which revealed a diabolic imagination: She undertook to lead the Cardinal to believe that the Queen, though still unable to receive him in public audience as she desired to do, would meet with him privately. She would give him a midnight rendezvous in the palace park to tell him in person all the things she hesitated to trust to writing on the subject of his imminent public triumph.*

What the abbé is saying in "soaped pig" style is that the Countess de La Motte had further designs upon (and for) His Eminence, prestigiously illusory designs to beguile her eminently suggestible audience of one, for whose delectation (and delusion) the entire extravaganza was to be produced.

If the abbé is correct in crediting the Countess with being the illusionist, her conception was grandiose as well as "diabolic" and her hand masterful in manipulation of the magic lantern that wrought the celebrated phantasmagoria that would go down in history as the Grove of Venus impersonation.

Earlier, in Versailles's Hall of Mirrors, the Cardinal had been treated to the optical illusion of the Queen of France inclining her graceful swan (detractors said "goose") neck, nodding her high head to him in subtle sign of recognition. But that ardent, impetuous, petulant Monseigneur, not yet satisfied, demanded more, so more illusions must be forthcoming, more dazzling still to his bedazzled eyes.

The Cardinal was to be treated now to the sight he wanted most in this life to see: that of Her Most Christian Majesty walking, with "her caressing walk," along a secluded Versailles garden path—straight toward him! To keep, with him, a clandestine midnight rendezvous, or assignation, or whatever interpretation that mettlesome, libertine, overweening spirit of his attached to it.

The idea of an impersonation of the Queen might have been suggested in the first place to the perpetrator of the hoax by the fact that the Queen's double did exist, according to a story current at the time—a hush-hush story told to the Baroness d'Oberkirch in strictest confidence by the Duchess d'Orléans, to the effect that an illegitimate daughter of

---

* Here again, as with the Oeil-de-Boeuf incident in Chapter VIII, Georgel's memoirs do not agree with the eyewitness accounts as to the date. The abbé, erroneously, dates the above sequence and the subsequent Grove of Venus scene after the theft of the necklace, in 1785. The trial depositions of all those involved in the Grove of Venus scene attest to its having taken place in 1784, the year before the necklace hoax. As in Chapter VIII, I have shifted Georgel's passage to its proper chronological place.

Emperor Joseph's, "hidden away since birth somewhere on the Versailles grounds," was the living, breathing image of her royal aunt, Marie Antoinette.

Mythology, with its Olympians descending in a variety of guises for intercourse with mortals, offers ample precedent for the act of impersonation; but it is more likely that the idea for the Grove of Venus imposture was inspired by Beaumarchais's famous impersonation scene in Le Mariage de Figaro where the Countess Almaviva, disguising herself as her maid Suzanne, represents that soubrette at a midnight assignation in the castle gardens with her own husband, the Count—a scene with which the Countess de La Motte, a keen first-nighter, and Marie Antoinette, an enthusiastic amateur actress, were both familiar. (Her Majesty had performed the roles of both Suzanne and Countess Almaviva in her jewel-box Trianon theater.)

If the Queen herself was not a spectator to the midnight rendezvous in the Versailles gardens that moonless July night of 1784 (as French historians Michelet, Louis Blanc and Louis Hastier all think she was), and if Her Majesty was not privy to the plot for the impersonation of her majestic self, then the execution thereof—under her very nose, under her very windows—was as risky as an experiment in atomic fission and presupposed an agency of supreme intrepidity and outrageous audacity.

As every skillful illusionist knows, to create a successful illusion in antique or modern media of either the graphic or the lively arts, the artist cannot ask his audience to accept the preposterous, but must work his magic within a given framework of reality as it is known to and understood by, and so is acceptable to, his particular audience.

That framework of reality was not violated by the producer of the famous Grove of Venus performance staged on a midsummer night in the lower palace grounds. First of all, the mise en scène, a grove or arbor just below the Great Terrace, beyond the Orangerie and in the shadow of the Hundred Steps, was appropriate to the action that was to take place there and was entirely acceptable to the audience as the proper locale for an apparition of the Queen of France. It was one of Her Majesty's favorite garden spots and was known as such, known as the Queen's Grove—le bosquet de la Reine—as well as that of Venus, whose statue had given the spot its formal name. Access to the arbor was through a leafy labyrinth, a landscape vogue at the time, shut away behind a series of overlapping charmilles (walls of verdure, shrubs and

171

branches trained to wooden trellises) and planted recently to the Queen's specifications with rare, exotic trees and flowers "from the far ends of the earth," as a poet described the grove in 1776; a kind of summer salon, highly popular in that day.

"Now, it was common knowledge at Versailles," the Abbé Georgel intones, "that the Queen went, upon occasion, for an evening's stroll in the garden groves . . ." And Georgel's subtly censorious depiction of those summery Versailles nocturnes is confirmed by Madame Campan:

The Queen, on warm summery evenings, having spent the day in her apartments with the windows tightly sealed, simply could not sleep without a breath of fresh air, a stroll with the princes and princesses, her brothers and sisters-in-law, on the Grande Terrasse below her suite.

These outings at first caused no comment; that came later with the inauguration of open-air concerts and the erection of a dais on the Green Carpet Lawn to accommodate the royal-chapel musicians. The Queen delighted in these musicales under the stars, seated on a terrace bench, surrounded by the entire royal family with the exception of the King, who did not like to disarrange his scheduled hour for retiring.

It is true that the Versailles townspeople crowded the palace grounds until two or three o'clock in the morning; as to whether some indiscreet ladies of the court ventured to stray down into the dark gardens below, I cannot say; it may be so. But the Queen never left the upper terrace, walking arm in arm with the princesses, in their floating, diaphanous white lawn dresses, their wide-brimmed straw hats tied with gauze ribbons, the height of that summer's fashion.

No more innocent a diversion was imaginable, really—and yet all Paris, all France, all Europe was soon gossiping in serious detriment to the Queen's reputation, this criminal scandalmongering extending even to court circles, where the danger of disrespect to majesty should have been most clearly recognized.

In view of the widespread criticism, I presumed to discourage the Queen from this form of recreation. My admonitions, however, were disregarded. Carried away by enthusiasm, Her Majesty refused to believe that any real harm could come of it. This was a serious miscalculation on her part. It is highly probable that it was these moonlight promenades which inspired the plot for the impersonation which would result in Cardinal Rohan's fatal delusion.

I have held nothing back; my account is trustworthy. But it is not intended as a justification of the innocence of the diversions in which the Queen indulged. So disastrous were the consequences that the fault must have been grave indeed.

Results bear out this belief.

Cardinal Rohan, like the rest of the courtiers and townspeople of Versailles, was aware of the Queen's predilection for those summer night excursions into the park, and so he would not have been surprised at her choice of the park as the site for a rendezvous when, as Georgel tells it, there appeared "one of those little letters on gilt-edged notepaper announcing joyful news; this little letter actually set the night and the hour for a rendezvous with the Queen. Never was a meeting awaited with such impatience."

The Countess de La Motte, frequenting the palace and the gardens, familiar with the Queen's comings and goings, would unerringly have chosen the Grove of Venus for the secret audience for which she knew the Cardinal longed—and which she had long beseeched the Queen to grant that unhappy man, as she relates it in her memoirs.

One day when I was in converse with Her Majesty she announced to me, "On the subject of the audience you urge me constantly to grant Prince de Rohan, I have had an inspiration. Having reasons of my own to distrust him, and lacking confidence until after I have made a test, I will agree to meet him—without meeting him. Do you understand what I am trying to say? I would like the opportunity of knowing in advance what I may expect of the Cardinal's behavior at such time as I do actually grant him an audience. Would it not be possible—under cover of darkness, perhaps—to substitute, in my place, some woman whom the Cardinal would take for me? Meanwhile I would be close by to overhear the conversation and in that way could decide, according to his conduct, whether to grant or refuse him the interview. Could you not find someone who would agree to perform such a harmless little scene for me?"

Monsieur de La Motte and I slept not a wink that night, talking until all hours to decide whether or not to risk execution of the Queen's commission. My husband's final decree was that it should be undertaken only on the condition that the Cardinal be let in on the secret.

The Cardinal, informed, broke out into gales of laughter. "Good Lord!" he exclaimed. "Does the Queen really think that I could be

taken in by such a trick? No matter, I'll play along. If it's comedy Her
Majesty's heart desires, then, by all means, let her have comedy."

Everything thus disposed and agreed to by the Cardinal, it remained
only to discover a woman who would lend herself to our little game.*

*The Abbé Georgel considers that the Countess knew precisely where
to look to discover such a woman; indeed, he makes the Countess out
not only librettist but also impresario and even casting director for the
entire production, as in this passage from his memoirs:*

In her promenades at the Palais-Royal in Paris, the Countess happened to observe a girl with a beautiful form and a profile strikingly re-
sembling that of the Queen. Upon this girl fell the Countess's choice to
portray the role of leading lady in the Grove of Venus scene.

D'Oliva was the name of this young lady . . . a creature who trafficked in her charms.

*Any creature who trafficked in her charms was likely to be observed in
the Palais-Royal gardens, the haunt of ladies of the evening (in the
afternoon as well), that Orléans palace having recently become the
Rialto of the capital, with its wooden arcades, its shops, cafés, bars and
gambling houses.*

*"The Palais-Royal was by all odds the most popular promenade in
Paris that year of 1785," according to the Baroness d'Oberkirch, up from
Strasbourg on a visit to the capital. "One can already make the entire
circuit of the vast edifice under cover of the arcades, and it is at once the
resort of newshawks and idlers and the meeting place for court society
and the Parisian bon ton; crowds always gather at the foot of the grand
staircase leading up to the famous Orléans picture gallery to watch the
pretty and elegant ladies ascending and descending."*

*One such pretty lady who frequented the Palais-Royal that spring of
1784 was a Mademoiselle d'Oliva, although she had not entrée to the
Orléans collection and came in search of attractions more lively than
old masters.*

"The Palais-Royal was the scene of my daily promenade," she prattles

---

* The Cardinal, months later from his prison cell, would cry out in outraged denial
of the fact that he had been privy to the masquerade, in denial of the fact that it
had been a masquerade. "My eyes and ears could not thus have deceived me," he
moaned to the Abbé Georgel. "It was the Queen whom I saw and to whom I spoke
in the Versailles gardens."

naïvely through her mémoire—a legal memorial in her case, a trial brief published in the year 1786, signed by her and written at her dictation by her attorney, young Blondel. The latter, who had already made an outstanding reputation for himself before the Parliament of Paris, was perceptive (and susceptive?) enough to let his appealing little client tell her story in her own ingenuous words and style, with only now and again the trace of legal or literary editing:

I lived close by the Palais-Royal at the time of which I speak [the summer of '84], in a small apartment on the Rue du Jour, in the St. Eustache section, and often spent two or three hours of the afternoon in the gardens with various girls of my acquaintance, or, when I could find no one else to keep me company, a dear little lad of four of whom I was exceedingly fond and whose parents gladly entrusted him to my care.

One afternoon in July, I was seated at a small café under the arcades, unaccompanied except for the little child of whom I spoke, when I saw a tall young gentleman walking alone, passing back and forth before my table, time and time again. This gentleman was unknown to me. He looked at me, stared at me fixedly. I noticed that whenever he came close he slowed his step as if to gaze his full.

There was a vacant chair two or three feet away from mine; he seated himself in it. Until that moment, the young man strolling past, his approach, his repeated glances had made no great impression. But when he came to sit so close, I could not but take notice.

His eyes never left my person. His demeanor was serious, grave, though he seemed stirred by an ardent curiosity—seemed, indeed, to be making mental note of my dimensions, studying one by one every feature of my face and person.

But a more detailed account of this first encounter at the Palais-Royal would serve no purpose. Suffice it to say that, after we had seen each other at the same spot in the Palais-Royal three or four days in a row, the stranger ended up by addressing me; and I, I made the fatal error of replying to him. Indeed, I shall not claim to have conducted myself blamelessly in this affair. Soon enough I was to commit an error even graver than the first.

One evening shortly thereafter, I parted from the aforementioned gentleman to make my way back home. He must have followed without my noticing, for, all at once, there he was at my door. Presenting himself with protestations of respect and honorable intention, he begged only for permission to call on me, to pay me court. Those were his very words. I could not take it upon myself to deny him such permission, and once it was granted his attentions proved assiduous.

In all fairness, I must admit that he never gave me cause to regret the decision; never once did he transgress the bounds of honorable courtship. Only his inquisitiveness was extraordinary, his persistent questioning as to the state of my fortunes and my future—due to his great interest in my fate, as he explained, making reference to powerful patrons he would enlist in my behalf.

If, on occasion, he had a few words to say about my modest charms, if now and again some eulogy escaped his lips on the subject of what he termed my graces and my beauty, this was no more than common gallantry, empty compliments such as gentlemen traditionally pay to the ladies, who accept them as such.

And no one will find it difficult to believe my story when it becomes apparent, as it shortly does, that frivolously romantic objectives were the things furthest from this man's mind, that his objectives tended toward an entirely different goal. His designs on me were far more despicable, positively criminal.

But the reader is doubtless impatient to know who this gentleman was. It is time to name him. He was the Sieur de La Motte, the self-styled Count de La Motte, introducing himself as a high-ranking military officer with hopes for advancement higher still, thanks to the illustrious personages whom he could claim as patrons and whose favor he hoped to turn to my advantage. Thus he described himself in our first interview.

It was, I believe, as best I can recall, on the occasion of his ninth visit, one day in early August, that he entered my room with an expression of satisfaction such as I had never remarked before. He told me that he had the most interesting, most encouraging developments to report. "I have just come from the home of a personage of the highest rank in this kingdom—and you were the main topic of conversation. I will bring this lady to see you tonight."

"I have no idea who it can be," I answered, "for assuredly I have not the honor of knowing anyone connected with the royal court."

Sieur de La Motte took his leave without further explanation.

With what impatience I awaited the night, counting the hours, the minutes! I burned with curiosity to see this noblewoman of high station who had been mentioned to me with great reserve but, at the same time, great fanfare.

When at last evening came, the Sieur de La Motte returned. He told me that in just a few moments now I would meet the personage of whom he had spoken that morning. Then he went out, again without explanation.

Hardly had he left the room when I saw a lady enter; she was alone, without attendants. She approached me with the most straightforward, most gracious air.

"Since I am unknown to you, madame," she said, "you must be surprised at my visit."

To judge by appearances and by reports of her, I replied, it was a surprise which could not but delight me.

And who was this lady (whom I should have recognized, had I had even the slightest sophistication or worldly experience, as an archadventuress)? She was the wife of my so-called "protector"; she was the Lady de La Motte herself—although at this first meeting she was careful, as her husband had been, to conceal her name.

I offered a chair to the Lady de La Motte, who, drawing it up close to mine, seated herself. Then she leaned toward me, with a mysterious and confidential air and with glances betokening cordiality, yet with all the dignity to be expected in a woman of superior station condescending to confidences with her protégée. Thus she began the strange discourse now to be revealed to the reader. For I must reveal it, must write it down —so the law requires and my innocence demands! It is at this point that I must summon up my courage, for here my betrayers first profane an honored, a sacred name, a name at which I prostrate myself, so that it is on bended knee—yes, on bended knee—that I write down the facts which I must now relate.

"You may trust me, dear heart, in what I am about to tell you," the Lady de La Motte began. "I am a very highly placed person, attached to the Court of Versailles." As she spoke she took an envelope from her pocket. Opening it, she showed me several letters which she said were from the Queen.

"But madame," I answered, "I understand none of this. It is all an enigma to me!"

"Then listen carefully, my sweet. I am the Queen's confidante. She and I are just like this!" Smiling, she held up two fingers intertwined. "As most recent proof of her confidence, Her Majesty has commis-

sioned me to find for her a person to render her a service, and it is you
upon whom my choice has fallen. If you agree to perform this service—
the details of which are unimportant and will be told you at the proper
time—I will make you a gift of fifteen hundred francs, although the
present you will receive later from the Queen will be worth even more.
I cannot tell you my name as yet, but you will soon learn who I am. If
you do not care to take my word for this, we will go together to a
notary's office, where guarantees will be furnished you."

Now, I ask you, all you honest and simple souls, put yourselves in my
place! What was I to think? So young, in only my twenty-third year, a
simple girl of the people, knowing as little of intrigue as of finance!
What would you have said, have done?

The victim had been marked, carefully selected; my seducers could
not have made a choice more appropriate to their sinister designs. But
oh, what a fatal accident, one I shall deplore to the end of my days, that
out of all this great capital's teeming millions the La Mottes' search
should have led to me!

But to go on—for I must finish this painful story, and I promise not
further to interrupt myself, unless it be by my tears: From that moment
on, I was as clay in their hands; they had completely turned my head. I
would have given my life's blood for my sovereign. I could not refuse a
demand, no matter what, supposedly from the Queen herself.

I said then to the Lady de La Motte that I was only too flattered to be
able to render a service pleasing to the Queen, that no further pecuniary
inducements were necessary.

The Lady de La Motte, quick to seize upon my acquiescence, set the
date: "The Count de La Motte will come to fetch you in a carriage tomorrow night, to drive you to Versailles." She went out, leaving me intoxicated with joy and hope.

The next afternoon the Sieur de La Motte drove up to my door in a
hired carriage, in which we set out for Versailles.

Just before we reached the palace gates, we saw the Lady de La Motte
waiting for us, her maid at her side. Ordering our coachman to halt, she
told us to get out of the carriage and instructed the Count de La Motte,
"Show Madame to my apartments." Then she disappeared from view.

Her husband took me, along with the maid, to a hotel in the Place
Dauphine. Then he likewise disappeared, leaving us alone, the maid
and me.

Two hours went by without my seeing either the husband or the wife.

At last they returned, gay as birds, to advise me that the Queen, to whom the Lady de La Motte had announced my arrival, had expressed herself as highly pleased, that Her Majesty could hardly wait the morrow "to see how all this would come off."

At this point I could no longer repress my curiosity, and I asked the Lady de La Motte, "What, then, is this thing you would have me do?"

She replied, "Nothing, nothing at all, really. The merest trifle. You shall know very soon, dear heart."

Then it developed that I was also to have a title! The Sieur and Lady de La Motte instantly gratified me with that of Baroness d'Oliva* and forced me, against my will, to submit to the ridiculous metamorphosis which so ill accorded with my natural air, an infinitely simple and unpretentious one. But a mere plebeian "Mademoiselle" Oliva was scarcely fit to appear in the company of a "Countess de La Motte-Valois," and so it was as the Baroness d'Oliva, from that moment on, that the Countess introduced me to her friends, despite the fact that I myself would never have presumed to usurp such a title.

The rest of the evening was spent in inconsequential conversation. I stayed the night at their hotel, in a room to myself provided me by the La Mottes.

The next day the self-styled Countess de Valois personally took charge of my costume. She and Rosalie attired me in a dress of finest white linon moucheté [lawn] made, as best I can remember, en gaule, a popular style more frequently referred to now as a chemise; my coiffure was en demi-bonnet.

Next the Lady de La Motte handed me a little letter, folded in the ordinary way but without superscription. She told me neither what it contained nor to whom it was addressed, not even by whom written. Never once did the Sieur and Lady de La Motte tell me any of these things. All the Lady de La Motte said to me was, "Tonight I shall take you into the palace park, and you will hand this letter to a very great nobleman who will meet you there."

* Originally spelled Olisva, an anagram of Valois doubtlessly.

MEMOIRS
OF THE COUNTESS DE LA MOTTE-VALOIS

If here I simply cannot resist a brief digression, the reader will pardon me, since it is included expressly for his diversion.

That poor, silly girl was as elaborately decked out as a statue of the Virgin carried through the streets in a holyday procession. From the questions she asked me, it was clear that she was expecting some great romantic adventure—and had taken the necessary precautions!

"But tell me about this great nobleman," she insisted. "This seigneur, will he expect to embrace me? And if so, am I to allow him?"

"Undoubtedly," I answered.

"But what . . . what if he should expect still more?"

"I hardly think that probable."

Nothing could have been more amusing than that foolish creature's pretended embarrassment, whereas obviously she could have been disconcerted about such an eventuality only because she knew she would have the Queen as spectator.

TRIAL BRIEF
FOR THE DEMOISELLE LEGUAY D'OLIVA

Between eleven and twelve o'clock that night I left the hotel with the Sieur and Lady de La Motte, a white cape across my shoulders, a lace *thérèse* over my hair. I cannot remember whether I held a fan in my hand or not, so I cannot state positively yes or no. But the little letter was in my pocket.

The La Mottes led me into the palace grounds, down into the gardens . . .

MEMOIRS
OF THE COUNTESS DE LA MOTTE-VALOIS

The scene had been chosen by the Queen herself, but since I was not so familiar as she with the Versailles groves and paths, I went to reconnoiter, inducing the Cardinal to accompany me in order that our relative positions might be determined in advance.

To render the scene intelligible to the reader, the theater and the stage setting must be described. The comedy was to take place in the Grove of Venus—just below the Great Terrace of the château—which is surrounded by a maze of *charmilles*; these trellises of greenery fan out every three feet, so that to penetrate the labyrinth into the grove itself one must go all the way around to reach the one path that leads into it.

The Queen was to station herself between two trellises, at a spot to which there was no access from the grove. Her Majesty had taken her place there with Mademoiselle Dorvat, her maid of honor. The Cardinal was to enter by a path assigned him through two other trellises, and my husband was to guide Mademoiselle d'Oliva to her place.

TRIAL BRIEF
FOR THE DEMOISELLE LEGUAY D'OLIVA

As we were descending into the lower park, we met a man whom the Sieur de La Motte hailed with "Ah, there you are!" These were the only words spoken by the Count to the other man, who then disappeared into the darkness. (What should be noted here is that later on at the dinner parties I attended at the La Mottes' Paris house I recognized the Sieur de Villette as the individual the Count had addressed that night in the park of Versailles.)

Then the Lady de La Motte gave me a rose, with these instructions: "You are to hand this flower, along with the letter, to the great lord who will join you here, but you are to speak only these words, no more: 'You know what this means.' Now, remember that the Queen is close by, watching and listening. She is over there, just behind us, not ten steps away. You will even speak to her yourself, later on."

These words of the Countess de La Motte's so overwhelmed me that I felt myself shaking from head to foot. I could not but admit it to the Sieur and Lady de La Motte. Stammering, I asked what form of address was proper, whether I should say "Queen," "Madame," "Sovereign" or "Majesty."

The Sieur de La Motte answered, "You must always say 'Your Majesty.'"

Surely it is unnecessary for me to state that, far from having the honor of addressing the Queen, or of being addressed by her, I had not even that of beholding her. But, under the spell of the enchantment woven by my betrayers, my senses reeling, I remained firmly convinced at the time that I was being watched by the Queen.

The Lady de La Motte led me into an arbor and left me, with instructions to stay just where I was. Then she went off to find the great nobleman to whom I was to speak, but who had not yet come into view.

MEMOIRS
OF THE ABBÉ GEORGEL

The night of the rendezvous, the Cardinal, in a costume previously decided, went out on the palace terrace with the Baron da Planta. Madame de La Motte was to meet him there to advise him of the exact moment when the Queen would set out for the Grove of Venus.

The night was dark. The appointed hour had passed and Madame de La Motte had not yet put in an appearance. The Cardinal was growing anxious, when he caught sight of the black moiré domino by which he was to recognize her.

"I have just come from the Queen," she told the Cardinal. "She is highly disconcerted by word from Madame and the Countess d'Artois that they are joining her for a promenade. Nevertheless, you are to go immediately to the arbor. Her Majesty will find a way to escape the princesses. Although the meeting must be a brief one, there will be time enough for her to give you unequivocal proof of her interest and her favor."

The Cardinal betook himself promptly to the appointed place. Madame de La Motte and the Baron da Planta withdrew some distance away to await His Eminence's return.

TRIAL BRIEF
FOR THE DEMOISELLE LEGUAY D'OLIVA

Faithful to the Lady de La Motte's instructions, I did not stir from the spot where she had stationed me. Then the great unknown lord appeared and came toward me, bowing, while the Lady de La Motte stood off at the side, several feet away, as if to observe the scene.

I did not know who this great nobleman was—and no matter what His Eminence Cardinal Prince de Rohan says today when he claims that it was he, I know no more now than I did then. In short, in the man who came up to me I could recognize no one I knew, no one I had ever seen before. Besides, let the reader be assured that such skilled intrigants as the Sieur and Lady de La Motte had availed themselves of every favorable element, choosing the kind of night best suited for the playing out of that scene which needed to be hidden deep in shadows. The night was the darkest, without one beam of moonlight, so that I could distinguish nothing beyond the persons and objects familiar to me.

It is impossible for me to describe the state I was in. I was so nervous and excited, so confused by the strange scene itself as well as by the thought that the Queen was witness to it, as my seducers had convinced me—all in all, I was so tremulous, so shaky, that I still do not know how I managed to get through even half the orders given me.

Somehow I presented the rose to the great unknown lord and spoke the words I had been told to speak, "*You know what this means,*" or something similar to that. I cannot state positively whether he took the flower or let it drop. As for the letter, it remained in my pocket, completely forgotten.

At this moment the Lady de La Motte ran toward us, speaking in low but urgent tones: "Hurry, hurry! Leave quickly now!"

At least, that is all I remember hearing.

MEMOIRS
OF THE COUNTESS DE LA MOTTE-VALOIS

At that moment Mademoiselle d'Oliva gave the Cardinal the rose, which he pressed to his heart, pledging himself to guard the token all his life and naming it "the rose of happiness." (Later he had a box made to preserve it and renamed his favorite path at Saverne the Rose Promenade.)

On bended knee, His Eminence made the prettiest speeches imagina-

G*

ble to Mademoiselle d'Oliva, but took no liberty beyond that of gently raising the toe of her slipper to his lips for a respectful kiss.*

MEMOIRS
OF THE ABBÉ GEORGEL

Madame de La Motte could congratulate herself on a complete success. The scene had been played out exactly as she had composed it, the D'Oliva warned to keep the secret of the role she had portrayed and well paid for her compliance.

Monsieur de La Motte and Villette (whose off-stage assignment had been the simulation of the sound of approaching voices and of footsteps, precisely timed for the moment at which the interview was to terminate) joined with Madame de La Motte in applauding each other on having achieved exactly the effect desired.

The Abbé Georgel, having earlier ascribed to the Countess an imposing list of credits for the Grove of Venus melodrama, has here added to it those of sound and lighting effects as well.

How effective a production it was to the eyes of the distinguished, if lone, member of the audience his legal spokesman (legal light Target) would vouch at the trial the following year, telling it much as he had heard it from his client: "From now on there will be no more doubts, no more objections. His Eminence will believe everything this woman tells him, will execute her every command. For, in his eyes, the orders relayed him by Madame de La Motte come directly from the Queen and, as such, are sacred."

TRIAL BRIEF
FOR THE DEMOISELLE LEGUAY D'OLIVA

After I left the unknown lord in the Grove of Venus, I found myself a bit farther off with the Sieur de La Motte, while his wife and the un-

---

* Here, in her Mémoires, the second edition, the Countess de La Motte implies that Cardinal Rohan did believe it to be the Queen whom he met in the Grove of Venus and who gave him the rose he cherished and embalmed—in contradiction to her Mémoires, first edition, in which she claimed he was privy to the impersonation (see page 173 ff.).

known lord together departed in the opposite direction and disappeared into the dark. Only then did I remember the letter in my pocket. I drew it out and gave it to the Sieur de La Motte.

He escorted me back to the hotel. We sat talking, awaiting his lady's return. I feared she would reproach me for my remissness, but instead her compliments were generous. She told me she had just left the Queen, who had said, "I am highly pleased, my dear Countess, with the person you found for me. She acquitted herself of her role marvelously, and I authorize you to tell her that her future is assured."

I was in seventh heaven; I could not find words to express my gratitude to my two patrons. When it was time to retire, I went to my bed firmly convinced that my fortune was made and that what I had done was a completely innocent thing.

The next evening I was driven back to Paris in a court carriage. We all had supper together; the repast was gay. . . .

MEMOIRS
OF COUNT BEUGNOT

My presence at the La Motte supper table that night came about by sheer accident.

Invited earlier in the evening to a ball, with some exceedingly lovely ladies present, I had lingered there until after ten. When I came out I strolled along the Boulevard Beaumarchais toward the carriage stand on the Rue St. Louis, but at the corner of the Rue Neuve St. Gilles, the street where Madame de La Motte lived, I turned in automatically and, before I realized it, found myself at her door.

Giving my name at the porter's lodge, I inquired as to whether anyone was at home. The reply that Monsieur and Madame de La Motte were absent and only Mademoiselle Colson was in merely served to confirm my intention of paying a visit.

This Mademoiselle Colson was an orphan cousin of Monsieur de La Motte's whom Madame had taken in and promoted to the rank of *dame de compagnie* [lady's companion] and reader.* She was a young

---

* A reader on the Countess's staff implies a well-stocked library. This was indeed the case, as was established by a police inventory of the La Mottes' Bar-sur-Aube residence taken the following year. Beneath the marble glare of Voltaire and Rousseau, whose busts adorned the shelves, was an assortment of books beginning with Père Anselme's nine-volume Genealogical and Chronological History of the Royal House of France,

lady endowed with both intelligence and wit, and whenever we met she and I indulged in many a hearty laugh over the extravagances and affectations of the master and mistress of the establishment. They told her nothing, but she guessed it all.

"Their Highnesses seem to be involved in some grandiose scheme just now," she told me that evening. "All their time is taken up in secret conferences to which only First Secretary Villette is invited. His Reverence Father Loth, Madame's second secretary, is reduced to listening at keyholes. In further frustration, he makes three trips a day to the Palais-Cardinal without being able to make out a damned word of the confidential messages he has been sent to deliver. The poor little monk is beside himself; he is as curious as an old nun, you know."

Mademoiselle Colson and I thus spent two hours amusing ourselves at the expense of our mutual friends, guessing and prophesying.

Just as I was about to take my leave, Mademoiselle Colson, pointing to the clock, which indicated midnight, reminded me that I would never find a carriage on the streets at such an hour and said that since it was so late I had no choice but to await the return of Madame de La Motte, who would have her coachman drive me home.

Sometime after midnight we heard at last the sound of wheels on the courtyard cobblestones, and out of the carriage stepped Monsieur and Madame de La Motte, Villette and a young woman somewhere between the ages of twenty-five and thirty—a blonde, very beautiful and remarkably well built. Both women were dressed elegantly, but it was an elegant simplicity; and both men were in riding coats, which might indicate a party returning from a country excursion.

They began, of course, with the inevitable raillery on the subject of my midnight tête-à-tête with Mademoiselle Colson, and of the disappointment caused us both by so rude an interruption; and they continued talking foolishness, going off into sudden, inexplicable gales of laughter, humming snatches of tunes as they babbled, apparently carried away by each other's witticisms. The beauteous stranger shared the

---

a Royal Almanac for the year 1781 and Illustrious Men of France (required reading for a Valois, a Daughter of France, like the Countess de La Motte), ranging on through full sets of Rousseau, Voltaire, Crebillon, Racine, Boileau; including Plutarch's Lives, Cook's Voyages and an atlas, not to omit such pious texts as The Holy Week, Reflections on the Love of God and the Miserere; on to a pair of practical textbooks, a French-English and an English-French dictionary, such as might come in handy to a pair who contemplated the possibility of refuge in the British Isles.

prevailing mood of gaiety, but gave an impression of some reserve and timidity.

We all sat down to supper together. The high spirits continued undiminished; indeed, they soared higher still, becoming positively rowdy, boisterous. Mademoiselle Colson and I exchanged quizzical glances, uncomfortable as people always are at finding themselves surrounded by a hilarious band while excluded from the secret of the hilarity. Moreover, our presence seemed to disconcert this merry company, to prevent them from free discourse on the source of their merriment and from savoring its full delight.

I overheard Monsieur de La Motte question Villette as to whether it was risky to mention certain facts in our presence; Villette was just quoting, in answer, that "discretion is the better part of valor" when Madame de La Motte, seated beside him, placed her fingers across his lips and said in an imperative tone, "Hush! Monsieur Beugnot is too honest a man to share our confidences."

This remark I might have interpreted as a compliment had I not been aware that in Madame de La Motte's vocabulary the words "honest man" and "fool" were used synonymously.

Madame de La Motte managed promptly to change the subject and turned the talk—as was her wont with me—to Bar-sur-Abe, to my family, to the date of my next visit there. Everyone seemed eager to have supper over with.

I asked Madame de La Motte for her horses to drive me home, to which she raised only one slight objection: the beautiful stranger had also to be driven home. Madame de La Motte solved the difficulty by the decree that the one who lived at the greatest distance should drop the other off en route. To this I took exception, requesting permission of the beautiful stranger to escort her to her door, no matter how far distant—my only objection would be if it should prove to be too close by.

From the very first moment I laid eyes on her I had been puzzled, had felt the tantalizing little tug at memory that comes with sight of a face one is sure of having seen before without being able to remember where or when. I was hoping the mystery would be solved on our drive alone together in the carriage. I plied her with questions in the hope of leading her into giving me a clue, but I could get nothing out of her at all —whether because Madame de La Motte (who had taken her aside just before our departure) had recommended discretion to her or because, as was more likely, she was naturally inarticulate and was temperamentally inclined to depend for self-expression upon the pantomime of her graceful body rather than upon the spoken word.

I deposited the silent beauty upon her doorstep in the Rue de Cléry.

The thing that had been puzzling me about her all the evening was the striking resemblance she bore the Queen! For this lady was none other than Mademoiselle d'Oliva. And the joy that animated the guests at the supper table had been occasioned by the rousing success of the magnificent hoax just perpetrated in the gardens of Versailles, where Cardinal Rohan, deceived by the resemblance, had received from Mademoiselle d'Oliva's hand a rose and from her lips a few brief sentences which, in his delirium, he believed to have emanated from the Queen herself.

At the time, I had not yet the key to the enigma, but the moment the scandal broke it was supplied me. And from that moment on I could have no slightest doubt as to the identity of the guilty parties.

Historians, not invariably so cocksure as Beugnot in assigning the guilt, do not agree upon the degree of guilt to be assigned to the several parties involved in the guilty machinations.

France's great Michelet, for one, in his Histoire de France, *admits to doubts on the agency in the Grove of Venus impersonation:*

> I find it entirely within the realm of probability that the Queen, otherwise innocent, ordered the hoax . . . just such a farce as would have accorded with her known tastes. . . .
>
> It might well have been planned as a diversion for her, depressed as she was at the time (the summer of 1784) by the death of her brother, and discomfited in the first months of pregnancy. Figaro was all the rage and the Queen was a Beaumarchais enthusiast. The quid pro quos of the last act, were they reproduced in the shadows of Versailles Park? With Rohan a far more gullible subject than Figaro, standing in for the barber? It is not inconceivable. And with the Valois lending herself to the hoax unprotesting, since no harm beyond ridicule was to come to her benefactor and on the theory (not impossible in the light of the vagaries of human nature) that the Queen, having fooled His Eminence

and having, herself, been amused thereby, might come to feel less hostility for him—perhaps even sympathy.

Not only Michelet but also Louis Hastier, eminent modern-day French researcher whose historical works have twice been crowned by the Académie Française, is still doubtful as to what actually went on in the Versailles gardens that moonless July night of 1784, holding that "some member of the Queen's coterie, if not the Queen herself, engineered the intrigue." He adds, "In my opinion, Marie Antoinette and several members of her entourage were concealed behind a charmille in the Grove of Venus and participated in the scene, which had been mounted by Madame de La Motte with the consent—perhaps even at the instigation—of the Queen."

Thomas Carlyle, likewise dubious, rightly assumed that the doubts would never be resolved, neither by time nor by future research. Such dark implications loomed up in the adventure, Carlyle thought, "such adumbrations of yet higher and highest dalliances [hovered] stupendous in the background . . . whereof your Georgels, and Campans, and other official characters can take no notice." The truth, in Carlyle's estimation, was "known only to three persons: Dame self-styled Countess de Lamotte; the Devil; and Philippe Égalité—who furnished money and facts for the Lamotte memoirs . . ."

Of Carlyle's three who knew, only the Countess talked; talked freely of those "higher and highest dalliances" in this passage from her memoirs:

Thus was the farce played out. In accordance with the script, I had given the alarm, and the cast of characters had sped from the scene.

Cardinal Rohan, while congratulating himself on his performance, promptly availed himself of the opportunity to address further indiscreet messages to the Queen, who admitted to having been "royally entertained."

Up to now, using first one pretext and then another, Her Majesty had put off granting the Cardinal a real audience, but a few days after the Grove of Venus scene she finally did agree to receive His Eminence in one of her secret apartments in the palace. Although I accompanied him to the rendezvous, I remained in an adjoining room while they communed privately. Not until two hours had elapsed did he emerge.

As we descended by one of the concealed staircases that led down from Her Majesty's private suite, His Eminence told me, "I had to endure, of course, a variety of reproaches, but, all in all, the interview went off exceedingly well—surpassed my fondest expectations." And the following day I noticed that Her Majesty appeared in a considerably mellowed mood.

This, then, was how I came, by the most singular combination of circumstances, to find myself in a position so precarious, so ambiguous as inevitably to compromise my honor.

Although I had been flattered by appointment to the post of confidential messenger to two personages of the highest rank in all the kingdom, still the role of Cupid inevitably came to embarrass me, to offend my sense of delicacy. I could not dissemble even to myself the fact that the lavish gifts heaped upon me were no more than a stipend such as is paid to a domestic for his services. In the hands of these mighty patrons I was no more than a clay mold, to be shattered upon the ground after it has served its purpose.

If I am not mistaken as to the name, it was the Pavilion of Venus which became the trysting place for the Cardinal and the Queen. To satisfy the reader's curiosity as well as to identify the pavilion in case I have forgotten its proper designation, I will include a short description.

This elegant little pavilion, circular in shape and surmounted by a dome, is situated in the gardens of the Little Trianon, upon a hillock to which one ascends by a gentle slope. The building is surrounded by a sort of trench, which the Cardinal and I always crossed by means of planks laid across for that purpose.

In the center of the room, on a white marble pedestal, there stood the superb statue of Venus from which the edifice took its name; around the wall other smaller statues represented the Graces, Cupid and Psyche, as best I can remember. The doors were of glass, one of them leading, by way of four marble steps, into the gardens. The windows of the rotunda were draped in the finest silk, embroidered in a floral motif and designed to shut out prying sunbeams which, on certain occasions, might have been considered an indiscreet intrusion. The entire décor—the tapestries, the armchairs, the sofas—was in the most exquisite of taste.*

* There was no such pavilion, no such place, Madame Campan protested upon reading this passage in the Countess's memoirs; and the present-day curator's staff of the palaces of Versailles and Trianon echoes her sentiments, although the Belvedere is

This superb pavilion was open to visitors only on Saturdays, and even then only by a special permit bearing the signature of the Queen, a favor rarely accorded.

It was in the Pavilion of Venus that I generally awaited the Queen's arrival, although my anxiety and impatience prevented me from fully enjoying its beauties which I have just described. When the Queen had made her entrance, I would leave the room to fetch and to usher in the Cardinal, who usually appeared with a package tucked under his arm—the finishing touch to his disguise as a valet. Sometimes when the Queen was very late for the rendezvous, I had to search the gardens to find the Cardinal, who had restlessly wandered off. And often, despite the inclemency of the weather, despite the chill of night and early morning, I was obliged to spend long hours in the gardens waiting for the moment when the Queen and the Cardinal would be ready to separate.

Oh, why had I not the courage to free myself from such a servitude? Vain regret! It was I myself who thus furnished the weapons to be used against me. And those who should have protected me were the very ones who destroyed me—for my mistake in having served them too well.

The reader will doubtless be astonished by such an abrupt about-face on the part of the Queen who had hitherto proclaimed her violent animosity toward the Cardinal. I myself was astonished, and I was tempted to credit myself with the achievement. But, in that respect, I might well be likened to the fly in the famous fable, which buzzed about a coach, lighting now upon the wheels, now upon the horses, now upon the coachman's whip, and wound up considering itself responsible for making the carriage go.

What, then, was the real reason strong enough to have induced the Queen to admit the Cardinal into her good graces and probably far beyond? Was it love? Let the reader who suspects it promptly dismiss the illusion from his mind!

It was not love but politics which wrought that apparent reconciliation between the Queen and the Cardinal. And the seemingly romantic

---

just such a "pleasure dome" as the Countess describes—on its hillock to which one (still) ascends by a gentle slope, (still) surrounded by a sort of trench (which can still be) crossed by planks laid across for that purpose. It is octagonal, not circular as she describes it, but understandably her memory (for which, furthermore, she apologizes) may have been impaired by her harrowing experiences in the intervening years.

nocturnal rendezvous were devoted primarily to secret conferences on the secret correspondence which had long linked the Cardinal and the Emperor Joseph of Austria, the brother of the Queen.

It is, of course, a fact that the Cardinal, whose long-time obsession it had been to attain to the prime ministership of France, pressed me into service to intercede for him with the Queen, but never think that he relied solely upon my feeble efforts! It was the Austrian Emperor who, as a matter of political expediency, forwarded the Cardinal's cause; just how or why I cannot say, but doubtless Prince de Rohan argued convincingly that as head of the French government he could prove highly useful to Austria. And as for the Queen, who showed preference all her life for the interests of her native Austria over those of her adopted land of France, she felt constrained to sacrifice her personal prejudices upon the altar of patriotism, and she carried political expediency to the extreme by opening up her arms to a man for whose head she had been vindictively clamoring for many years—and would demand even more vehemently in the dreadful days of the dreadful trial to come.

Oddly enough, the Cardinal, despite his usual indiscretions, did not extend his confidences to me to include such international intrigues. But my suspicions were aroused by a number of things: an occasional inadvertent word by His Eminence, the frequent appearance at the Palais-Cardinal of German couriers, closeted in long and mysterious conference with the Cardinal, strange missions assigned my husband: the delivery of packets of papers to odd corners of Paris, to the St. Antoine Gate, to messengers with suspiciously foreign accents.

Although the Cardinal sought to make a mystery of it, my suspicions that the Austrian Emperor was behind it all were confirmed by an occasional boast of the Cardinal's that when his nomination to the prime ministership came, he would not owe it entirely to the Queen; rather it would be that he had forced her hand.

Whatever the basis for the reconciliation between the Cardinal and the Queen, it was inevitably of short duration. Fresh indiscretions, presumption and arrogance on his part rekindled in Her Majesty's heart the hatred which political expediency could only temporarily extinguish. Her desire for vengeance won out over all other considerations; from that time on, she was merely awaiting the opportune moment to bring about his ruin.

Gradually the Queen began to betray her impatience at his importunities; she could scarcely conceal her resentment of the diplomatic intrigue which forced upon her so unwelcome a co-conspirator. Only the Cardinal's influence with her Emperor-brother saved him—for a time. Held back only by this fragile thread, the sword of her vengeance dangled above his head.

But the Queen had nonetheless vowed his eventual destruction, and the fatal diamond necklace intrigue was shortly to present her precisely the opportunity she had so long awaited.

Thus the Countess's explicit statement of the Queen's motive in the diamond necklace intrigue, Her Majesty's vow to encompass the Cardinal's eventual destruction, becomes the leitmotif of all the Countess's self-justificatory threnodies.

Count Beugnot's voice rises in counterpoint: "Soon now the magnificent hoax of the necklace was to be essayed; every steppingstone leading up to it was so carefully aligned" (*by the Countess de La Motte, presumably*) "that success was assured . . ."

The Abbé Georgel's memoirs drum out his indictment of her:

If only the Countess de La Motte could have contented herself with those first embezzlements, she would have passed for a talented swindler who had skillfully hoodwinked an overcredulous Cardinal, and there the matter would have ended. For the Prince, suffering only superficial wounds to pride and pocketbook, would never have risked making himself a public laughingstock by prosecuting.

This woman, however, her soul deep-dyed in villainy, encouraged by the 120,000 francs which had cost her only a tissue of lies and a few sheets of gilt-edged notepaper, conceived of a new maneuver so daring, so fraught with danger as to have dismayed the most hardened and intrepid criminal.

Now, it so happened that there was a necklace, a superb diamond necklace, made by court jeweler Böhmer and valued at 1,800,000 francs. . . .

"A superb diamond necklace," Georgel calls it, "valued at 1,800,000 francs." If ancien régime francs d'or are translated into as yet unminted Yankee dollars at the late-eighteenth-century rate of exchange, $409,500 is the closest one can come to it. But that is scarcely a valid measure of the jewel's value in modern-day terms of reference, and so perhaps it is best to say that it was worth a king's ransom, in this case a king's mistress' ransom, since the diamond necklace had been originally designed for Louis XV's Du Barry.

At any rate of exchange, the price set upon it by court jewelers Böhmer and Bassenge was staggering, to judge by all references to it at the time. A formidable price tag dangled on the outsize jewel box (the size of a doormat, roughly), the gold-tooled red "Cardan leather case" wherein that "monument to the jeweler's art" reposed scintillating on its bed of tufted velvet, glittering with temptation to the eyes of various and sundry suspicious characters, according to various and sundry suspicious characters' accounts; flashing the eternal gemmy challenge to the hearts of the desperate, the daring, of whom more than one was known to be reconnoitering about that prodigious treasury; aglitter, aglow with challenge and temptation in every facet of its 647 brilliants, its 2,800 carats.

PART THREE

The Necklace

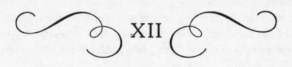

The Theft

(Winter 1784-1785)

THE DIMENSIONS OF THE JEWEL BOX into the confines of which Böhmer
and Bassenge could have fitted their opus magnum of a necklace must
have been, at the very minimum, fifteen by twenty inches; good showmanship would have extended the length of the case to a full two feet. For
the diamond necklace itself, extended, swinging at its full spectacular,
shimmering catenary, measured fifteen and thirteen inches from primary
multiple strand to nethermost tassel tip.

From a Drawing, as large as reality [Carlyle says], kindly
furnished . . . by the Abbé Georgel, in the Second Volume
of his Mémoires, curious readers can still fancy to themselves
what a princely ornament [the necklace] was. A row of seventeen glorious diamonds, as large almost as filberts, encircle,
not too tightly, the neck, a first time. Looser, gracefully
fastened thrice to these, a three-wreathed festoon, and pendants enough (simple pear-shaped, multiple star-shaped, or
clustering amorphous) encircle it, enwreath it, a second time.
Loosest of all, softly flowing round from behind in priceless catenary, rush down two broad threefold rows; seem to
knot themselves, round a very Queen of Diamonds, on the
bosom; then rush on, again separated, as if there were length

in plenty; the very tassels of them were a fortune for some men. And now lastly, two other inexpressible threefold rows, also with their tassels, will, when the necklace is on and clasped, unite themselves behind into a doubly inexpressible sixfold row; and so stream down, together or asunder, over the hind-neck—we may fancy, like lambent zodiacal or Aurora Borealis fire.

Carlyle's "row of seventeen glorious diamonds, as large almost as filberts," that "encircle . . . the neck a first time" are inventoried by Böhmer and Bassenge, in their official records, as "the seventeen stones comprising the choker—five to eight carats each." The "pendants enough" were precisely "six, pear-shaped," in jeweler's expertise; the two pendants dropping directly below the choker were "twelve and a half carats each"; the two pendants hanging between the festoons were "larger still than the first two." Of the two center pendants, "each set into a cluster of fourteen brilliants totaling ten carats in each case, the upper [was] a superb pear-shaped stone of nine carats, the lower a gem stone weighing eleven carats" (thus, seventy-five carats in the six pendants or pear-shaped stones alone), "with the trefoil to the lower pendant composed of three brilliants of great beauty, weighing five carats each."

In the center front of the necklace, the big round stone in the cluster center (which would have glittered at the cleft of the wearer's bosom), from which the two front tassels stream, is described by Böhmer and Bassenge as "an eleven-carat button stone valued at one thousand guineas" (better than five thousand dollars), and the cluster surrounding the button stones as "composed of eight brilliants of three carats each." *

"A glorious ornament," to put down the jewelers' inventory and pick up Carlyle's again, "fit only for the Sultana of the World. Indeed, only attainable by such; for it is valued . . . in round numbers, and sterling money, at between eighty and ninety thousand pounds." †

Intended originally for the sultana of Louis XV's world, the necklace was never to be clasped by his lavish hand about her "fairest throat," for the diamonds, unfortunately, were still on the worktables among

---

* The current valuation per carat weight is quoted roughly at $1,200, making a total of approximately $3,360,000 for the 2,800 carats in the necklace. (See Appendix)
† In the 1830s, when Carlyle wrote, this would have meant between $390,000 and $438,000 approximately.

their golden fittings in 1774 at the sudden setting of Louis XV's sun, at Du Barry's eclipse.

Böhmer and Bassenge, even as they beat their breasts at the loss of that magnifico of a customer, could not actually reproach themselves for missing the sale through any dilatoriness on their part. Confection of the diamond necklace had, necessarily, extended over many years; the financing alone had been tedious, time-consuming, an ambitious project in itself to which the partners had mortgaged not only their showplace showrooms on the Rue Vendôme but their private residences as well, even Madame Böhmer's cherished country place having been thrown in as collateral on one 200,000-franc loan negotiated with Baudard de Saint-James, official banker to the French Royal Navy.

Time and endless detail had been requisite, as well, to the execution of the design proper of the necklace. Countless hours and conferences had been devoted to the minutiae of craftsmanship, to such a detail, for example, as the clasp and the four bowknots from which the tassels depended—whether to execute them in gold or in the popular émail, and, if enamel was chosen, perhaps even a tactful change in 1774 from Du Barry rose to Nattier blue, Marie Antoinette's favorite color. Above all, however, limitless study and consideration had to be given to the basic proposition to which the necklace was dedicated: that it should be the greatest expression of majesty and magnificence ever made, the ne plus ultra of regal splendor and grandeur; what Louis XIV had proposed to state in marble and stone in his Palace of Versailles, Böhmer and Bassenge aspired to say in diamonds in their necklace. If it seems overstatement to more chaste modern tastes, one must remember that the jewel was calculated to appeal originally to the florid tastes of the Fancy Woman—and eventually, as it developed, to those of the Queen—of the Rococo.

But the financing and design, protracted as these processes had proved, had yet been mere preliminaries to the ultimate task of the assembly of that iridescent inventory proper. Consider the hours, days, weeks, months devoted to travel alone to all the world's diamond markets; to the scrutiny and appraisal of the thousands of stones out of which the final 647 flawless, first-water gem stones would be selected; to the cautious, painstaking balancing and rebalancing of the delicate diamond scales in test of each carat grain, each grain troy of that staggering 2,800-carat total.

Inevitably, years had gone into the making of what Carlyle termed "the famous and world famous" diamond necklace, although he caviled at the term "making" as applied to it.

Properly speaking, Carlyle insisted, the diamond necklace "was not made—only arranged and agglomerated." Of the diamonds composing it, the youngest was

> six thousand years of age and upwards . . . each with a history of its own . . . from the first making . . . first digging of them in the far Indian mines* . . . [where] they lay, for uncounted ages and aeons, silently embedded in the rock: [emerged] from it . . . when their hour came; served, next . . . as eyes of heathen idols, and received worship . . . ; had then, by fortune of war or theft, been knocked out; and exchanged among camp-sutlers for a little spirituous liquor, and bought by Jews, and worn as signets on the fingers of tawny or white Majesties; and again been lost . . . in old forgotten glorious victories; and so—through innumerable varieties of fortune—come at last to the cutting-wheel of Böhmer; to be united, in strange fellowship, with comrades also blown together from all ends of the earth . . . now being, so to speak, enlisted under Böhmer's flag —made to take rank and file, in new order . . . and parade there for a season. For a season only; and then—to disperse, and enlist anew ad infinitum. . . . This was what Böhmer called "making" his necklace.

And must have called it excruciatingly slow—must have vainly pressed his master craftsmen to speed the jewel to completion for the occasion of the coronation of the new King and Queen in 1775; this having failed, the necklace "was offered for the first time, in 1778, to His Majesty Louis XVI at the birth of the new monarchs' first child, their daughter Madame Royale," or so it was reported in a newsletter addressed to Catherine the Great of Russia by her well-informed Paris correspondent. "At first sight of the diamond necklace, the King was dazzled; he determined to present it to his Queen as a gift of relevailles" (maternity gift—literally, a getting-up-after-childbirth gift). "But Her

---

* The consensus among gemmologists is that the gem stones of the eighteenth century, including the necklace diamonds, came primarily from South American mines.

Majesty renounced the glorious jewel with the well-known phrase, 'At that price, we have less need of a necklace than a ship of the line.' "

A sentimental little "anecdote" to be discounted by the Countess de La Motte, in her memoirs, as completely out of character for the Queen; the noble words, expressive of preference for the national interest above the personal, were, she says, "expressed by His Majesty rather than Her Majesty."

Madame Campan, however, quotes them as gospel, and as the Queen's, although ascribing a more plausible, if less heroic, motivation for Her Majesty's renunciation of Böhmer's bauble. She writes:

The Queen, at that time, considered her jewel collection complete and told Böhmer that she had no intention of adding further to it.

She had at her disposal, first of all, the crown jewels of France, among which her favorite pieces were the twelve great "Mazarins," the diamonds so named in honor of the Cardinal who had bequeathed them to the national treasury; the exquisite pink diamonds, of which the most famous is the huge "Sanci"; and the string of matched pearls which had been the gift of Anne of Austria to the queens and dauphinesses of France, each pearl as large as a hazelnut and so rare as to be of inestimable value.

As to her personal jewels, the Queen had added to those brought with her as a bride from Vienna. Her first purchase from Böhmer, in 1774, had been a pair of girandole earrings at a price of 360,000 francs, which debt had been acquitted not too long previously with payment of the last installment of a series extending over several years. Later the King had given Her Majesty a ruby-and-diamond parure—matching necklace, bracelets, pin and earrings—and, still more recently, a pair of diamond bracelets, for which Böhmer had been paid in full a sum of 200,000 francs.

That jeweler, however, having worked for years to assemble an assortment of the very finest gems in world commerce to make a multiple-strand necklace, would not abandon his efforts to sell it to the Queen, and he took it to show to Monsieur Campan, with the request that my father-in-law speak of it to Her Majesty for the purpose of stimulating interest in the acquisition of the unique creation. This service Monsieur Campan properly declined, pointing out that he would be overstepping his place in recommending to the Queen an outlay of more than a million and a half francs. Nor could he suppose, he added, that either the Queen's maid of honor or her first lady in waiting would undertake the commission.

Böhmer did succeed, however, in inducing the King's first gentleman to display the necklace to His Majesty, who was so struck with its magnificence that he wanted the Queen to have it and sent the jewel case on to her apartments. But the Queen replied that she was unwilling to spend so huge a sum for personal adornment, especially in view of the fact that such elaborate ornaments were seldom worn at Versailles at this era—on only four or five state occasions in a year. The diamond necklace should be returned to Böhmer, the Queen concluded, noting that 1,800,000 francs would pay for another battleship for the French fleet.

Three years later, in 1781, undaunted by a first failure (*what was the birth of a mere Daughter of France compared to that of a Dauphin?*), Böhmer flew back to the King's antechamber on the wings of the stork. Wags amused themselves at his expense, calling him a very harbinger of royal lyings-in. Let the crown jeweler so much as appear in the Versailles corridors, the mammoth necklace case under arm, and the courtiers tittered, inquiring of one another whether Her Majesty could be pregnant again.

If the King of France would not buy, could not afford to adorn the mother of his son and heir, Böhmer had no choice but to take to the road with the paste copy of the necklace on a tour of all the courts of Europe, all the old "nine kingdoms"—only to discover with a shock that not a crowned head among them could afford it either. A nebulous interest evinced by the King and Queen of the Two Sicilies, a protracted chaffering with the ambassador from Portugal (where an Infanta was proposing to wed) might flatter Böhmer's hopes, but not his creditors'.

At which moment, once again, the best source of inside information is Madame Campan and her memoirs:

His hopes dashed after a year of fruitless endeavor, failing to find any court in Europe disposed to make so costly an acquisition, Böhmer returned to the King at Versailles with a proposal of new purchase terms on the necklace: only a part of the principal amount to be payable in cash (and that extended over a period of years), the rest in assignments of various royal revenues to the jewelers. This arrangement having been presented to the King as advantageous, he came to broach the subject once again to the Queen.

I happened to be present during this conversation. I remember the Queen's remarking to His Majesty that if he did not find the new terms onerous, he might consider making the acquisition to set aside for the future as a wedding gift for one of the royal children, but that as far as she herself was concerned, unwilling to lay herself open to public censure for such an extravagance, she would never wear the diamond necklace. The King replied that he would not consider so tremendous a current expenditure for an object which would benefit no one for years to come.

Böhmer bewailed his misfortune to everyone who would listen, although practical-minded people reminded him that he had only himself to blame for having gone to such expense in the creation of a jewel without having first received a definite order for it.

After several months of unsuccessful maneuvering and vain entreaty, he finally succeeded in obtaining an audience with the Queen; her daughter, the young Princess, was with her in the boudoir. Her Majesty did not know for what purpose Böhmer had sought this interview, but she never dreamed that it would be to bring up again the subject of the jewel which she had twice rejected, once personally and once through the King.

Böhmer fell to his knees, joined his hands in prayer, wept and exclaimed, "Madame, I am ruined, bankrupt, dishonored if you persist in refusing my necklace. I do not want to survive such terrible misfortune. I shall go direct from here to throw myself into the river!"

"Stand up, Böhmer," the Queen replied in a tone sharp enough to recall him to his senses. "There is no reason for honest men to get down on their knees to plead. If you were to commit suicide, I should pity you, as I would any deranged creature in whom I had taken an interest, but I would in no wise consider myself responsible. Not only have I never commissioned you to make a jewel such as presently causes your despair but, what is more, I have told you repeatedly that I would never add so much as another carat to my present collection of diamonds. I refused to buy your necklace for myself; the King offered to buy it for me, and I refused it as a gift. Never mention it again. Break up the necklace and try to sell the diamonds separately—then you will have no occasion to drown yourself!"

Marie Antoinette could not have guessed that she was wasting her royal breath and her pearls of wisdom on a man obsessed, a man with an idée fixe—a kind of temporary madness to which not even the soundest mind can claim permanent immunity. Böhmer may have marshaled for the Queen, for himself, for Bassenge and for their creditors an imposing array of entirely valid reasons for not breaking up that necklace: the ruinous loss to be sustained in a sale of separate stones as against the matched totality, and in a distress sale, to boot; the loss in labor, in the interest accumulating on the loans, etc. The most cogent argument of the lot, however, as it affected Böhmer, he would never have voiced, even to himself: that to have taken the Queen's advice would have been to make a mockery of his lifelong dreams and ambitions. The necklace was Böhmer's gaudy bid for immortality. Upon the necklace Böhmer would rest his claim to fame, as Cellini rested his upon a salt cellar—his claim to supremacy among the world's artist-artisans in precious stones and metals.

None of this was discernible to Marie Antoinette in the portly person of the crown jeweler sobbing at her feet. She dismissed him curtly, letting him feel the weight of her royal displeasure, according to Madame Campan's quote:

" 'I do not in the least appreciate your having indulged yourself in this exhibition of despair in my presence and in the presence of my daughter. Never let it happen again. Now go.'

"Böhmer withdrew, disconsolate," Madame Campan adds, "and we heard no more from him."

Madame Campan and the Queen may have heard no more from him, no more about his diamond necklace, but it was otherwise in the case of the Countess de La Motte, as the Abbé Georgel related in his memoirs:

Madame de La Motte had had occasion to see the famous diamond necklace, and she knew that the Queen, although she greatly admired it, had been reluctant to ask the King to buy it for her at a period when international complications imposed the strictest national economy.

The jeweler Böhmer had not concealed from Madame de La Motte the fact that, with the great jewel a drug on the market, he found himself in dire financial straits. He concluded with the remark that he was prepared to offer a generous commission to anyone who could help him dispose of it.

MEMOIRS
OF THE COUNTESS DE LA MOTTE-VALOIS

I had never even met the jeweler Böhmer, had never heard of his appointment as jeweler to the Crown, so how was I to know anything about his diamond necklace or his efforts to sell it to the Queen?

The first time I ever heard the necklace mentioned was by a man named Laporte. (Everything has its beginning which it is interesting to trace; here, then, is the beginning of my misfortunes.) This Laporte was a lawyer with whom I had been thrown in contact some time previously in connection with a financial matter. He was an aggressive, pushing, officious type; having once obtained an introduction to me, he was constantly underfoot. Every time I looked up, there was Laporte at my door.

Now it developed that he was an intimate friend of Böhmer's. Meeting him at Versailles one day, Laporte asked the jeweler whether he still had that necklace of his on his hands.

"Unfortunately, yes," Böhmer replied. "It is a millstone around my neck, and I would gladly give a commission of a thousand louis to anyone who could find me a buyer for it."

This, then, was probably the moment when my name came up and when Laporte promised Böhmer an introduction to me. For, shortly afterward, Laporte broached the subject to me, remarking that if I would "only agree to say a word or two to the Queen," tell her that the jewelers were ready to sell on any terms she might suggest, he was sure she would be interested in purchasing a piece of jewelry which she had so ardently desired that she had kept it once for an entire month. He added that I would be doing a tremendous service not only to Böhmer but also to him personally, because the jeweler had promised him a thousand-louis commission if he could put over the deal.

I replied that I knew nothing about the Queen's interest in the necklace, that, generally speaking, I avoided meddling in matters of this kind lest the Queen suspect me of having an ax to grind, that when I besought Her Majesty's influence and aid it was for my own far more important affairs and that I never wanted her to think me the type with my finger in every pie, trying to get in on everything, as she accused so many of her intimates of doing.

Nevertheless, within the week, there was Laporte back at my door, back on the subject of the necklace—only to receive a second rebuff. This time I forbade his mentioning it again. I wanted to hear no more about it.

But sharpers, speculators, commission men are not so easily discouraged. One day shortly afterward, while I was still at my dressing table, with Rosalie arranging my coiffure, a lackey announced Monsieur Laporte and also Monsieur Böhmer, upon whom I had up to this time never laid eyes.

Sending word that I was not at home, I tried to slip out of the house by a door on the landing, but precisely there on the stairway Böhmer and Laporte had stationed themselves. Forced, thus, to receive them, I civilly offered them chairs and inquired what brought them to me.

Laporte, who could be very ingratiating, was a glib talker. After having loudly praised my "generous heart," my "disposition to oblige friends and petitioners," he presented Böhmer to me, all the while protesting that he had come not to repeat his plea about the necklace but solely for the purpose of showing me this rare jewel as a curiosity, as a sight to see, before Böhmer shipped it off on approval to the court of Portugal.

After all, a look costs nothing, as these gentlemen laughingly declared, so, permitting Böhmer to unwrap the great leather case and open it on the table, I stood gazing at that superb, that unique necklace.

Laporte served as spokesman. "Is it not a shame," he asked, "that such a treasure should leave the kingdom, especially when we have a Queen whom it would so well grace—and who so covets it?"

"That's something I know nothing about," I replied. "Nor can I imagine why you come to me to relay your messages to Her Majesty, into whose presence, I repeat, I have not the honor of entrée!"

"Assuredly, madame, we have not come to pry into your secrets; still less to appear to doubt your word," said Laporte, with a meaningful wink and leer. "But, believe me, I know Versailles and what goes on there, and when I take the liberty of bringing my friend Böhmer to you it is because I am convinced that no one at court is in a better position than you to render us the service we presume to ask!"

Böhmer had his mouth half open, and I could see the words already forming on his lips, such words as "undying gratitude," "tokens of esteem," "gifts," "commissions." So, just to cut it short and be rid of them, I said that I would see whether I could help them indirectly, through friends of mine who were so fortunate as to have access to the Queen.

Drowning out the Countess's plaintive recitative "Not I, not I," the Abbé Georgel intones a direct indictment in his memoirs:

Madame de La Motte had already tested her talents on the credulous Cardinal; she would now undertake, by imposing still further upon his credulity, to appropriate not only the jewelers' commission on the neck-lace sale but the necklace as well.

The Countess, that is to say, would now cunningly contrive to corre-late one man's obsessive ambition with the other's. "The figurative hook and the figurative eye" (in Carlyle's metaphor) "which Böhmer and Rohan, far apart, were respectively fashioning for each other" were now to be hooked together by the deft fingers of that real-life, unmetaphori-cal seamstress, that needlewoman by trade, the Countess de La Motte. The "figurative hook" was Böhmer's "one mad object that he will attain or go to Bedlam," the preservation of his masterpiece intact and its ad-vantageous disposition to stave off bankruptcy—no secret ambition, this, but published by him abroad and at home to all who will listen, in-cluding the Countess de La Motte. The "figurative eye" was Prince de Rohan's own "mad object," the Queen's favor and the prime minister-ship—an ambition no more secret than Böhmer's, but worn upon the Cardinal's sleeve for all the world to see, including the Countess de La Motte, who, like any astute student of the human comedy, might arrive at the conclusion that here was a situation fraught with dramatic possi-bilities such as might be brought to a denouement personally profitable to a talented dramaturgist.

The "playwright of the comedy"—the Countess, in Georgel's meta-phor—taking advantage of the opportunity presented her by fate or by coincidence, promptly devised just such a clever plot, an outline of which is to be found in Georgel's memoirs:

In brief, what Madame de La Motte would now persuade the Cardinal to believe was that the Queen had her heart set on the diamond necklace; that, wanting to acquire it unbeknownst to the King and to pay for it in installments out of her own privy purse, she would do His Eminence the signal honor (in proof of her trust in him) of commissioning him to arrange the transaction for her; and that, in order to avoid any mention of her name in these negotiations, the contract was to bear his signature.

The first step, necessarily, was to summon His Eminence back to Paris. His removal to Alsace several months previously had been arranged for Madame de La Motte's convenience, to afford her the opportunity for a spending spree, for unrestrained luxuriation in her newcome prosperity; his recall from Strasbourg to Paris became, at this juncture, imperative to her new program of necklace negotiations.

Accordingly, she instructed the Baron da Planta to rush a courier to the Cardinal at Saverne, bearing one of those little letters on gilt-edged stationery, in which the Queen purportedly advised His Eminence, "The time is not yet ripe for your public triumph, but I urge you to hasten to Paris for a secret negotiation of great personal interest to me, one which I would entrust to none but you. The Countess de La Motte will speak for me to supply you the key to the enigma."

Cardinal Rohan, upon receipt of this little letter, envied the birds their very wings that they could fly more swiftly than he toward Paris.

He drove most unexpectedly into the courtyard of the Palais-Cardinal, in a flurry of sleigh bells, on one of those rare fine, frosty January days when the sun sets an icy world to glittering like diamonds. His sudden, unheralded arrival in the capital was as surprising to us as his sudden, unexplained departure for the provinces in April (in both instances upon instructions contained in those little letters).

No sooner had Monseigneur the Cardinal been furnished the so-called "key to the enigma" than he decided to proceed forthwith upon the mission, which could not but be regarded as highly flattering and honorable.

Madame de La Motte, having already dispelled his last lingering doubt, now embarked intrepidly upon her hazardous enterprise. She hastened to advise the jewelers Böhmer and Bassenge to expect the visit of a very great nobleman—and a very rich one—who would come shortly to inspect their diamond necklace and quite possibly to buy it.

"For my part," writes the Countess de La Motte, in direct contradiction to Georgel,

I gave so little thought to Böhmer and that necklace of his that it never occurred to me even to mention it to the Cardinal until some three weeks later, when he happened by my house and quite accidentally the subject of gems came up apropos of a new ring which he was flashing ostentatiously to elicit my compliments.

At the very mention of Böhmer's name and the story of the visit paid me, His Eminence sprang to attention. "Extraordinary! What a coincidence!" he exclaimed. Then he broke off as suddenly as he had begun, apparently plunged in reverie.

It is obvious now that he must have been thinking even then of taking me into his confidence on the subject of the necklace. Under the delusion that he would momentarily be appointed prime minister, the Cardinal considered no sacrifice too great to satisfy the fancy of her to whom he would owe that appointment. On the day in question, however, he abruptly dropped the subject of the necklace, apparently not yet ready to let me in on his great secret.

Two or three days later, at the early hour of seven in the morning, there came an urgent message from him, a request that I send him Böhmer's address as speedily as possible. The address being unknown to me, I was obliged to send my little *jocqui** running to Laporte, who jotted down the street and number on a slip of paper which my dusky African page boy sprinted on to deliver to the Palais-Cardinal.

"At the Sign of the Balcony," 11 Rue Vendôme, was the address, no more than a ten-minute walk from the Palais-Cardinal. Böhmer and Bassenge had set themselves up handsomely; their quarters were impressive, and the large courtyard was crowded with liveried grooms and coachmen and the fine carriages of their fine carriage trade.

January 24, 1785, was the date of Prince de Rohan's first visit, as Böhmer and Bassenge could distinctly remember some seven months later when the Queen demanded a written report on it from them. That wintry day's interview was indelibly imprinted on their minds; they could render it word for word in their "Memorandum Submitted to Her Majesty the Queen, August 12, 1785, signed by us, Charles-Auguste Böhmer and Paul Bassenge":

* A diminutive page or messenger boy (frequently a blackamoor, like Du Barry's and Madame de La Motte's). The word was borrowed from the English jockey.

On January 24 of this year Monseigneur Cardinal Rohan came to our place of business and asked to see our collection of jewels. We took advantage of the opportunity to show the Prince our great diamond necklace as the rarest assemblage of brilliants in the world.

The Prince, upon examining it, told us that he had heard of the diamond necklace and that he had been commissioned to come to us to inquire the very lowest price we would take for it.

We replied that our extreme eagerness to dispose of the necklace (as too heavy a burden over too long a time) had determined us to take a loss on it at the rock-bottom price of 1,600,000 francs, although it stood us, in time and labor as well as outlay of cash for the stones, far in excess of that figure. We added that this was the figure at which Messieurs Doigny and Maillard had estimated it some six years previously when the King considered the purchase, but that since then accumulated interest on our borrowing had caused us severe additional loss.

We explained that, even in its original conception, the creation of the necklace had never been undertaken as a profitable venture, but rather as a tribute to majesty, as an ornament to grace the greatest of queens; but that, doomed to disappointment in that hope, we had no choice but to send a sketch of the necklace to the Princess of the Asturias and were momentarily awaiting her order to send the jewel into Spain.

The Prince replied that he would report our conversation and would personally consider purchase of the necklace. He explained that although he was not speaking for himself he was certain that the terms suggested by the actual purchaser would prove acceptable to us. He went on to say he must further inform us that he did not know whether he would even be permitted to name the actual purchaser, but that in the event he was not permitted to do so he would give us his personal signature as guarantee on the contract. . . .

MEMOIRS
OF THE ABBÉ GEORGEL

A letter from Cardinal Rohan, delivered as usual into the hands of Madame de La Motte for transmittal to the Queen, reported his first visit to the jewelers and indicated that the deal might be consummated at the price of 1,600,000 francs (a reduction of 200,000 francs on the asking price) and upon the suggested installment plan.

A reply purportedly from the Queen, via the customary messenger, approved all the arrangements and authorized the Grand Almoner to proceed.

MEMORANDUM TO HER MAJESTY
FROM BÖHMER AND BASSENGE, AUGUST 12, 1785

Two days after Prince de Rohan's visit to our shop on the Rue Vendôme, he summoned us to the Palais-Cardinal, where he laid before us the proposal which he had been authorized to make for the acquisition of the diamond necklace, and of which we here render copy:

> That the price of 1,600,000 francs be subject to final appraisal by Messieurs Doigny and Maillard; to be reduced if their valuation should so indicate.
>
> The first installment, in the amount of 400,000 francs, not to be payable for six months; successive installments in similar amount to be payable every six months thereafter.
>
> If these conditions be accepted, the necklace to be ready for delivery as of Tuesday, February 1.

The Prince, having read us these proposals and having heard us signify our assent, requested us to affix our signatures to the contract.

This we did, as of date of January 29, 1785.

Herewith ended our second interview.

MEMOIRS
OF THE COUNTESS DE LA MOTTE-VALOIS

Purely by accident, a fatal accident indeed, was I drawn into a negotiation which the Cardinal was trying to keep secret from me.

His mysterious actions, his covert queries about the jewelers, his great hurry to get their address—all this, in addition to his well-known financial involvements, led me at first to suspect another of those "fast deals" he was so expert at "putting over," as the saying goes among speculators. A high-finance maneuver, in short, whereby he would buy the necklace to raise ready cash on it to pay off his most clamorous creditors! For to pay off his most pressing debts had been the Queen's advice to him as the surest means of regaining the King's esteem.

At first it had been the Cardinal's welfare which had given me concern, but suddenly I began to be concerned about my own, to ask myself whether the Cardinal's necklace dealings, if they were for the purposes I suspected, might not somehow compromise me. After all, it was to me the jeweler had come originally to seek help in disposing of the necklace. It was I who had given the jewelers' address to the Cardinal. It was possible that the Cardinal had mentioned my name in his dealings with Böhmer and Bassenge, and still more possible that they might lay the blame on me in the event the negotiations should turn out badly. For, after all, I was well aware of the Cardinal's financial involvements, and I simply could not see how he could handle an indebtedness of 1,600,000 francs.

After serious consideration, I went to the jewelers and told them that although the Cardinal had not taken me into his confidence, I had reason to suspect that he was contemplating the acquisition of the necklace; in which event, I implored them to remember that I had played no part in the transaction. And I urged them to insist on all their customary guarantees if the deal should be consummated.

Frankly, I did not foresee the difficulties I was laying up for the Cardinal, the obstacles with which I would beset his path. The fact is that the jewelers so literally followed my advice that they forced the Cardinal not only to admit that it was the Queen he represented but also to furnish proof thereof: a contract bearing Her Majesty's approval and her signature. It was the jewelers' insistence on this point that necessitated producing the so-termed contract forgery, which I shall take up presently.

But first I pause to ask whether the most prejudiced reader can consider it plausible that if I had had my eye on the necklace (as has been recklessly and illogically suggested), I would, by depriving the Cardinal of the means of acquiring it, have deprived myself of my surest means of appropriating it—which, clearly, was from him. If I had plotted the theft of the diamond necklace, was it not to my own best interests to have the Cardinal make the purchase in his own name instead of arousing the jewelers' distrust and thereby necessitating forgery of the Queen's signature?

Böhmer and Bassenge, desperate as they were to dispose of the necklace, would doubtless have come to terms with almost anyone who could show reasonably good credit and make reasonably good guarantee of payment. Now, the Cardinal, deeply involved as were his affairs, still enjoyed enormous Church revenues which he might have hypothecated in their favor and which the jewelers would hardly have rejected. If I had not gone to warn Böhmer and Bassenge, Cardinal Rohan would have been able to negotiate with them easily enough on his own. In which case, I could have stolen the necklace at my convenience and with a minimum of difficulty, without ever being obliged to resort to the dangerous expedient of forgery.

Now, is it not clear as day that had I schemed the theft I would never in this world have gone about it as I did—interfering with delivery of the jewel into the very hands from which I might hope to purloin it?

Several days went by without word from the Prince—rather unusual neglect, upon which I twitted him when next he came to call.

"Ah!" he exclaimed. "You're curious to know what I wanted with Böhmer and Bassenge! You know you can never keep a secret, so how could I trust you with one of this importance? But now the deal is nearly consummated, and I can reveal it to you: I have purchased that famous diamond necklace for the Queen. And don't start shrieking at my 'extravagance.' I would never have undertaken it without a private arrangement with the Queen. She is giving me her personal guarantee; she will sign and approve the contract I have made with Böhmer and Bassenge. I have it here, and I want you to rush it to Her Majesty. It must be signed tonight. Set out at once for Versailles, I beg of you."

I cannot express the relief I experienced upon learning that I had misjudged the Cardinal's motives: instead of his being involved in some shady, reckless manipulation, it was upon the Queen's business he was proceeding, honorably. Thus my mind was put at ease in regard to an affair which had originally caused me keen anxiety.

As messenger in the correspondence between the Queen and the Cardinal, I had in self-protection adopted the custom of making copies of their letters. In doing so on this occasion, I noted that the terms of the contract were in the Cardinal's own hand and that the instrument was complete except for the signature of the Queen.

Speeding by cabriolet to Versailles, then to the Queen's private apartments, I handed her the packet entrusted me by the Cardinal.

"But this is an unpardonable indiscretion!" the Queen exclaimed. "The Cardinal has named me to the jewelers! Had I been willing to let them know that it was I with whom they dealt, what need would I have had of Prince de Rohan to act as agent? I gave him positive orders to keep my name out of the negotiations."

I tried to explain the difficulties the Cardinal had encountered, and that the signed contract would only be shown to the jewelers—that it would remain in the Cardinal's keeping and in utter secrecy.

"Even so, it is impossible!" cried the Queen. "I have given the King my sacred word of honor never to sign my name to anything without advising him. But is there not some other way out of this impasse? It occurs to me that since this document is merely for form's sake, merely to be shown to the jewelers, and since they are not even familiar with my handwriting . . . Well, you and the Cardinal must think it over, see if you cannot devise some solution between you."

To interpret these words of the Queen's as an invitation to forgery may seem irreverent. It is possible that she had no clearer concept than I of the implications of forgery. It is possible that when she referred to the document as being "merely for form's sake," and to the jewelers as being unfamiliar with her handwriting, she may have meant something entirely different. But the fact is that it was thus I interpreted her remarks.

I have never sought to deny, from the first moment I picked up this pen, that I have been guilty of imprudent actions; this must be considered one of the most reprehensible. It may seem strange to claim ignorance as my justification, yet that is, in a sense, the truth.

Too little given to sober reflection, swept along, rather, by the whirlwind, formed and molded in the spirit of intrigue which prevailed as the mental climate of my day and world, product of a corrupt society, brought up on a somewhat lenient interpretation of the moral code, I could see in the act of forgery merely another example of the not uncommon subterfuge, the harmless expedient, to which a sophisticated society resorts and which it condones so long as the intent be not criminal—which mine was not, in that I knew the jewelers were not to be cheated, for the Cardinal stood guarantor to them, and the Queen to the Cardinal.

Reasoning thus (and never reasoning long enough—another of my bad habits), I decided that merely for "form's sake," then, we might show the jewelers something which they would take to be the approval of the Queen. If Her Majesty had not come out openly to suggest that someone sign for her, then she certainly seemed to be leaving up to me the choice of the means to the desired end.

While I was pondering the problem and wondering with whom to consult, a visitor was announced—my very special friend Monsieur de Villette. Being under obligation to me for a military appointment which I was about to procure for him, Villette could hardly refuse me a favor.

I related the turn affairs had taken, and Villette agreed with my interpretation of the Queen's remarks. "But," he added, "neither you nor the Queen seems to realize the risk of signing someone else's name. It is an act which the law categorizes as a crime, under the heading of forgery. Certainly you would not be asking me to commit a crime. Yet, without too much fear of compromising ourselves, here is what we might be able to do: First of all, I would make no attempt to simulate the handwriting of the Queen; I would not even attempt to disguise my own. And secondly, I would avoid use of her authentic titles; instead, choose a spurious one—one the Queen does not use in her official signature. Something like 'Marie Antoinette de France,' for example, which has absolutely no significance."

Driving immediately to the Cardinal's, I handed him the signed and approved contract. He examined it and then exclaimed, "So here it is at last!"

I burst out laughing and promptly related everything that had transpired.

"You're right," he said. " 'Marie Antoinette de France' means about as much as 'Queen of the Moon'—and yet I was taken in by it. And I'll wager that Böhmer and Bassenge will have no sharper eye than mine. I'll call them in immediately and bring the matter to a close. This document is only to be shown to them; it is my personal guarantee they are to hold."

MEMOIRS
OF RÉTAUX DE VILLETTE

Where to find a man bold enough, yet weak enough, to commit a forgery? That man was I, and well Madame de La Motte knew her hold over me. How could I resist her charms, her benefactions? How could I resist the command of a prince of the Church?

With that amiable, that seductive air of hers, Madame de La Motte said to me, "It is upon the altar of friendship, my dear Villette, that you must sacrifice your innate reluctance to such a task. Your whole future depends upon your compliance with our wishes, and you know how eager we are to see you make a place for yourself in the world. Now, here's the contract. Take the pen and write . . ."

I had opened my mouth in protest, but a look from the Cardinal, a look from Madame de La Motte sealed my lips.

It was she who dictated the words "Approved—Marie Antoinette."

And then, whether out of stratagem or out of ineptitude, the Cardinal said to me, "Add the words 'of France.'"

No sooner had I written than Monseigneur the Cardinal and Madame de La Motte promised me an annual pension of six thousand francs and a contract to support it. The very next day, the first installment was paid me by Madame de La Motte.

MEMOIRS
OF THE ABBÉ GEORGEL

Monseigneur Cardinal Rohan insistently demanded an authorization from the Queen as essential to the consummation of the necklace purchase. This document was shortly forthcoming; it was dated "Little Trianon" and signed "Marie Antoinette de France."

Had the darkest blindfold not bound the eyes of Prince Louis, the very form of the signature would have aroused his suspicions. The Queen never signed by any but her given name, Marie Antoinette. The addition of the words 'of France' betrayed gross ignorance of protocol.

How to account for the disparity between the accounts of Villette, the Countess de La Motte and the Abbé Georgel relative to the forgery incident? Once having admitted, as Villette did, that his had been the hand to wield the pen, why should he have lied about the technicalities incident to the act? Why, above all, should he have distorted the facts in 1791, the date of publication of his memoirs, at a time when he no longer stood in jeopardy of prosecution for the crime? Possibly Villette had his pride and used a set of pet euphemisms to protect it. This ne'er-do-well remittance man refers to himself as a "dilettante" whose family provided him "subsidies"; in this case he was "the pawn of criminals" rather than a criminal accomplice, and he uses the term "an exercise in penmanship" in preference to the harsher one of "forgery."

Conversely, there is also the possibility that Villette did not violate the truth in his version of the forgery. For, if Cardinal Rohan did actually participate in the commission of it, suggesting the form of the signature, as Villette claims he did, His Eminence would never have admitted that fact to Georgel, nor to Counselor Target; he would never have admitted to anyone that he had been an accessory to the crime of forgery, since his entire defense was to rest upon his claim to having been the innocent, unsuspecting victim of the criminals who perpetrated it.

Georgel, instead of clarifying the situation, further obscures it. Neither Cardinal Rohan nor the crown jewelers, he says, noticed the glaring discrepancy in the form of the Queen's signature.

If the crown jewelers did not notice the discrepancy (and even they, seemingly, should have been familiar with the Queen's signature from other contracts made with them by Her Majesty), how could it have escaped the eye of a great nobleman on familiar terms with royalty and royal protocol, a Grand Almoner to the court of France, a former ambassador to the court of Austria?

And yet Prince de Rohan failed to catch it, according to Georgel:

The Queen's signature—in the same handwriting as that which adorned the dainty sheets of gilt-edged notepaper—constituted for the Cardinal the ultimate proof of the Queen's good faith and confidence, to which he responded with the ultimate proof of his own.

Cagliostro, who had just reached Paris from Lyons, was impatiently awaited at the Palais-Cardinal; the High Priest must forthwith mount his tripod to consult the oracle.

Through all the hours of one long, candlelit night the Cardinal's own salon resounded to Egyptian incantations. Cagliostro, deep in trance and inspired by his demon familiar, pronounced his prophecies: Not only would the Cardinal's mission for the Queen be crowned with success, it would win him the highest honor in the power of royalty to bestow and would hasten the dawn of that glorious day which was to reveal to the world the Cardinal's rare talents, to the benefit of France and all humanity.

These are truths I here relate; yet it might well be thought I am inventing fiction. I might be inclined to think so myself had I not certain knowledge of every fact advanced.

MEMORANDUM TO HER MAJESTY
FROM BÖHMER AND BASSENGE, AUGUST 12, 1785

On the morning of February 1, we received a letter from the Prince, in his own hand but without signature, conceived in these terms: "I should like Monsieur Böhmer and his associate to come to me this morning as early as possible and to bring with them the object under discussion."

We went immediately to the Palais-Cardinal, carrying the great necklace with us in its case.

It was in the course of this interview that the Prince informed us that it was Her Majesty the Queen who was the purchaser of the necklace and showed us, in evidence, the contract with the marginal notation "Approved" alongside every clause and paragraph and, at the bottom, the signature 'Marie Antoinette de France.'"

We expressed our great joy and satisfaction at this advice, and the Prince told us that the necklace was to be delivered to Her Majesty that same day.

Thus ended the third interview.

Later that same day of February 1 we received a letter from the Prince, written in his own hand and signed by him, conceived in these terms:

> MONSIEUR BÖHMER:
> Her Majesty the Queen has advised me that it is her intention that, following payment of the first installment at the end of August, the interest due on the remainder of the agreed purchase price shall be paid concurrently with the scheduled payments on the capital amount, until the entire capital sum shall have been liquidated.
> *Signed*, CARDINAL PRINCE DE ROHAN
> AT PARIS, FEBRUARY 1, 1785

MEMOIRS
OF THE ABBÉ GEORGEL

The jewelers agreed to deliver the necklace to the Prince on February 1, the eve of Purification Day. The Countess de La Motte had specified this holyday, the day of the Cordon Bleu investiture, as the state occasion designated by the Queen for delivery of the jewel. The jewel case containing the necklace was to be taken to Versailles on February 1 and brought that evening to Madame de La Motte's apartment, whither the Queen supposedly would dispatch a messenger for it.

Madame de La Motte, intoxicated with joy at the fantastic success of her fantastic intrigue, had set the stage at her Versailles apartment for the grand finale, the transfer of the diamond necklace into the hands of the man who would present himself as the emissary of the Queen. Here were, in very truth, a stage and a performance.

The Cardinal, at the appointed hour of twilight on the appointed day, February 1, made his way to Madame de La Motte's, followed by his personal valet with the jewel case. This man the Cardinal dismissed at the door; then, taking the great leather case into his own hands, he went in alone. Here was the sacrificial victim, ready to be offered up on the altar of his own good faith.

The stage consisted of a room with a small alcove, a glass-paneled door serving as divider. The talented playwright of the comedy ushered the spectator to a seat in the alcove.

As the curtain rises, the stage is in semidarkness; one small lamp provides the only light. A door opens and a voice rings out:

"In the name of the Queen!"

Madame de La Motte advances respectfully, picks up the jewel case and hands it to the self-announced messenger of Her Majesty.

Thus was the transfer of the diamond necklace effected.

The Prince, the silent and concealed spectator, believed he had recognized the messenger; Madame de La Motte said it was the Queen's confidential valet from Trianon—the same one the Prince had observed escorting Madame de La Motte out of the palace gates one moonlit night. There was a similarity of stature, and both had worn the livery of the Queen.

The Cardinal felt complete assurance that the necklace had reached its proper destination.

MEMOIRS
OF THE COUNTESS DE LA MOTTE-VALOIS

He was, I can assure you, a man well known indeed to the Cardinal, this Lesclaux!* He was the confidential messenger who was so indispensable to the Queen's famous nocturnal dalliances and without whom it would have been impossible to have arranged the various gallant, if risky, assignations to which both the Cardinal and the Queen make reference in their letters (as printed in the appendix of the second volume of these memoirs). He is the same staff lackey who has been noted delivering Her Majesty's letters to me frequently in the past, the trusted emissary of Her Majesty, employed by her on countless missions requiring delicacy and tact.

It was nine-thirty, as I said, when Lesclaux reached my apartment; and it was the Cardinal himself who, picking up the necklace case, delivered it into the hands of the faithful Lesclaux.

If it was "in very truth, a stage and a performance," it was prestigious sleight of hand, the "presto chango" of magicians' patter, a dematerialization worthy of a Cagliostro (and inevitably credited to him).

If the Queen's hand was in it, juggling the diamond necklace as the instrument of her vengeance upon the Cardinal, she had, at the instant it was spirited away, moved inexorably to his destruction; and the Cardinal, voluntarily executing a "flattering commission" for and from the Queen, had, in the act of delivering the necklace into the hands of the Queen's messenger, delivered himself at one and the same time into hers.

If it was the Countess de La Motte (historians' favorite candidate for the honor) who had conspired to appropriate the prize for herself, she must have known that with that night's business she had taken the decisive, the irretraceable step, had set her foot upon a tightrope leading across an abyss. Thenceforward there could be no looking back, no looking down into the phalanxes of police with all their chains, dungeons, racks, stakes and gibbet wheels spread out for her should she trip and fall.

However it was—and theories by the dozen have been evolved from that day to this to account for the unaccountable in it—with the con-

* The Countess's spelling. The trial records give the valet's name as Desclaux.

veyance of the necklace case to the royal courier or criminal accomplice, the point of no return had been reached and passed.

Whoever it was—whether the Queen, to work her vengeance or gratify her passion for diamonds, or both; whether Cardinal Rohan, to win the Queen's favor by gratifying her whim or to maneuver to appease his clamorous creditors; whether Cagliostro, to enhance the size and value of the giant stones in alchemic crucibles (there was no theory too fantastic to be advanced); whether the Countess de La Motte, with the refreshingly simple motive of making off with a prize; whether a variety of agents with a variety of motives—whoever it was, up to the dusk of February 1, 1785, he, or she, or they, might yet have reconsidered, might yet have returned the necklace to the jewelers for them to dispose of as best they could in some one or other court of the old nine kingdoms of Europe, or beyond in some sultan's, to adorn his favorite houri. Up until that night of February 1, the purloining of the necklace had not yet been technically, finally, perpetrated.

But in the sound of the mysterious courier's receding footsteps, in the sound of the closing of the door upon him and the precious freight he carried off, there was a ring of finality audible—to the clairaudient a crackle, as of the crack of doom.

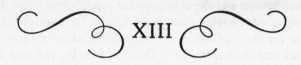

XIII

The Diamonds Disposed Of

(Early Spring 1785)

Fᴇʙʀᴜᴀʀʏ 1, 1785, was the date purportedly designated by Her Majesty for delivery of the diamond necklace, and the next day's Cordon Bleu investiture ceremony (traditionally performed in the Versailles chapel on Purification Day) the state occasion chosen by Marie Antoinette to adorn herself with the splendid new ornament.

Notice to this effect, purportedly from the Queen, was transmitted to Cardinal Rohan in messages delivered by the hand of the Countess de La Motte, according to Counselor Target, to whom His Eminence would shortly turn for sorely needed legal counsel.

Target's report upon this and other matters appears in his trial brief for Cardinal Rohan, which was published in 1786:

On February 2, the day after the delivery of the necklace, Monseigneur Cardinal Rohan instructed his personal valet, Schreiber [the same who has been noted carrying the necklace case, the previous evening, to the apartment of Madame de La Motte] to go to the palace at Her Majesty's dinner hour to take careful note of her attire.

Schreiber, upon his return from the palace, having observed Her Majesty at table,* reported that insofar as he could discern she was wearing nothing new in the way of jewels.

* Madame Campan on the subject of the "fishbowl of Versailles": "One of the traditions most disagreeable to Marie Antoinette was the royal family's daily dinner in public. The palace ushers admitted all visitors who were decently garbed. This spec-

The following day, February 3, at Versailles, the Cardinal encountered Sieur Böhmer and the lady his wife, and Sieur Bassenge. Instead of quaking, as a guilty man would have done, at the sight of the jewelers so near the Queen, Cardinal Rohan immediately asked them, "Have you offered your humble thanks to the Queen for her purchase of your necklace?"

When Böhmer and Bassenge replied that they had not yet had the opportunity, Cardinal Rohan urged them to pursue it promptly. And from that day forward, each and every time he saw them—from February 3, that is, through the following June—he continued to urge that they find occasion to thank the Queen. Continued procrastination on their part excited the Cardinal's impatience.

This fact was to be confirmed by Böhmer and Bassenge in their formal memorandum to the Queen.

MEMORANDUM TO HER MAJESTY
FROM BÖHMER AND BASSENGE, AUGUST 12, 1785

Shortly after February 1 we had occasion to see Cardinal Rohan, who told us that we should take advantage of our first opportunity to approach the Queen to offer our most humble thanks for the great kindness she had deigned to show us in the purchase of the diamond necklace. . . . Unfortunately, no such opportunity presented itself . . .

The jewelers were not thus dilatory in expressing their gratitude to the Countess de La Motte. According to the official depositions which they would later make, Monsieur and Madame Böhmer as early as February 3 were hosts at a dinner party honoring the Countess. And the very next day, February 4, the beaming partners Böhmer and Bassenge paid her a formal visit, bubbling over with gratitude and with substantial tokens of it—the latter, ostensibly, to the Countess's disdain, or so she professes in her memoirs:

---

tacle of the royal family at table constituted the main attraction for the provincial tourist. At the royal dinner hour, the Versailles staircases were always crowded with avid sight-seers, who, after watching the Queen drink her soup, ran up to see the princes eat their entrée and then sped, breathless, down again to reach Mesdames the aunts in time for the dessert. This custom of dining in public, under the gaze of a multitude of strangers' eyes, was, in the Queen's opinion, hardly conducive to a hearty appetite."

A few days after the sale of the diamond necklace, Böhmer and Bassenge paid me a visit to express their appreciation.

Go-between Laporte had been deputized to offer me 200,000 francs, half in specie and the rest in jewels, the 100,000 francs in cash to be divided between Laporte and me. This offer I had emphatically rejected on the grounds that, having played no part in the transaction, I could take no credit for it and would accept no gifts. A day or two later Laporte had come back again, this time to take the measure of my finger and that of my husband as well, and even that of Rosalie, my premier lady's maid, for the purpose of making rings for all of us. This proposition I had promptly vetoed; reiterated by Laporte, it was vetoed a second time. At this point I had really lost my temper and had forbidden Laporte my door, protesting for the hundredth time that since I had in no wise contributed to the sale of the diamond necklace I could not in good conscience accept either commission or reward.

"Noblesse oblige . . ." One can almost hear her say it, although her exact words were that she was "not the kind of woman to accept gratuities" for her favors; that for any indirect service she might have rendered in forwarding the negotiations, she found her reward in having "obliged" her "friends"; that it was her pleasure to exert her influence in exalted circles in their behalf, "in behalf of all worthy petitioners." The Countess would go so far as to grant permission to the maid, Rosalie, to accept a ring if the jewelers insisted; as for herself, she would accept no more than their protestations of gratitude—and, as on February 3, their lavish hospitality.

For the Countess and her friends, the early days of February passed pleasantly enough in socializing, but Cardinal Rohan grew restive when the first and then the second week of the month had elapsed and the Queen had still not appeared in public wearing the diamond necklace. Counselor-at-law Target in his trial brief describes his client's growing anxiety:

When time continued to elapse and the Queen had still not appeared in public wearing the diamond necklace, the Cardinal admitted to some astonishment at the delay. He was in a frame of mind, however, to accept any reasonable explanation rather than to open the door to anxiety and doubt; and for such explanations Madame de La Motte was never at a loss.

She was ready with the pretext, for example, that Her Majesty was still awaiting the final appraisal of the necklace by Messieurs Doigny and Maillard, as specified by the contract, to establish whether the price might not be excessive; or that the Queen's exquisitely delicate sensibilities precluded her adorning herself in public with an ornament which had not yet been fully paid for. Resourceful, drawing upon her fertile imagination for a rich fund of pretexts, explanations and excuses, Madame de La Motte had little difficulty in convincing the Cardinal.

As early as the month of February, only eight or ten days after the necklace had fallen into the hands of Madame de La Motte, her friend and confidant Sieur Rétaux de Villette was picked up for questioning by the Paris police and underwent interrogation on the subject of a considerable number of diamonds found upon his person.

MEMOIRS
OF THE ABBÉ GEORGEL

The diamond necklace once in her possession, Madame de La Motte busied herself with ways and means of enjoying the benefits of her prize with impunity.

The necklace was broken up. Madame de La Motte selected the least conspicuous gems to have mounted into bracelets, earrings and rings for her personal use, as has been since conclusively proven at the trial. Her friend and accomplice Villette likewise appropriated a number of stones for himself . . .

And was reported to the police by two suspicious Parisian diamond merchants, Adan and Vidal, whom he had approached with an offer to sell "three packets of diamonds worth twenty thousand francs."

Police Inspector de Brugnières duly filed a report on this incident at his Montmartre precinct station, dated February 16, 1785 (extant in the Necklace Trial dossier in the Archives de France), to the effect that "one Rétaux de Villette" had been "picked up for questioning on February 15." Questioned on this point, according to the Brugnières report, "Villette claimed that the stones in question belonged to a lady who had commissioned him to dispose of them for her, and to whom he had since restored them. He demurred at compromising said lady by naming her outright, unless at the express order of Police Lieutenant General

Lenoir." Such an order was forthcoming from Lenoir, before whom Villette was promptly taken, and "he was forced to the admission," Brugnières continues, "that the lady in question was the Countess de La Motte-Valois. But when a search of his person revealed no other brilliants, the man Villette was dismissed." The Countess's reputation as a "speculator in merchandise" being considered equivocal by the police, Lenoir checked further with the central station to ascertain whether any report of a recent jewelry theft had been filed, "but upon a reply in the negative, the matter was dropped."

MEMOIRS
OF THE ABBÉ GEORGEL

With the exception of the stones set aside for personal use by Madame de La Motte and Villette, the necklace diamonds were soon to be taken to London by Monsieur de La Motte, there to be converted into funds such as would provide revenues sufficient to place his wife at the highest level of opulence and maintain her in a style befitting a descendant of the Valois.

The Countess's disclaimer sounds the note that she was a woman much maligned, that it was not she but Marie Antoinette, that Queen of Diamonds personified, who had been tossing about diamonds by the fistful. The Countess writes:

Having acquired the necklace, the Queen had, indisputably, the right to do with it as she chose. But very shortly I was to have proof of what I had already suspected: that Her Majesty would remodel the necklace in such a fashion as to render it unrecognizable and thereby fool the King—an idea, for that matter, originally suggested by the Cardinal.

But at this point other developments were to alarm me. Meetings between the Cardinal and the Queen occurred ever more infrequently and, even then, ended in altercations. The Queen appeared glum and moody. I myself had occasion to suffer from her less amiable moods; it was as if she was punishing me for my role in her reconciliation with the Cardinal.

Her motivating impulse in an incident I shall next relate was doubtless to expiate her petty persecution of me, while biding her time to rid herself of me completely—for I am now convinced that the Queen planned that move at the same time she plotted the Cardinal's downfall. At any rate, one day Her Majesty, at her most charming, greeted me by handing me a small box and saying, "It has been a long time since I made you any gift. I want you to have these diamonds, but I forbid you, on pain of my displeasure, to mention it to the Cardinal."

After peeking into the box, I could not fly swiftly enough to the Cardinal—though swearing him to secrecy—to show him how rich I was. If I was guilty for the second time of betraying the Queen's confidence, as I had done in the Mademoiselle d'Oliva episode, it was because I always considered my first loyalty to be to His Eminence.

He spread the gems out upon a table, exclaiming, "This appears to be a highly valuable assortment." He told me that he would weigh the diamonds and give me an exact computation of their worth, but advised me meanwhile to speak to no one of the gift.

Even my husband knew nothing as yet of what I considered (oh, God, how ironical in retrospect!) my lucky windfall. Before confiding in Monsieur de La Motte, I set aside a number of stones to sell secretly so that I could indulge myself in several long-coveted luxuries.

The Cardinal, upon his return from Versailles, informed me that although he had succeeded in obtaining an interview with the Queen, she had failed to vouchsafe him so much as a word on the subject of the disposition she was making of the necklace, a silence he could not understand and found highly disturbing. It was not her decision to break up and reset the necklace which surprised him; it was the fact that she had not breathed a word of that plan to him.

Prince de Rohan likewise admitted to concern that Böhmer and Bassenge might discover what had been done to their creation. "That is exactly what would happen," he said to me, "should you try to dispose of such conspicuous gems in the Paris market, because in all likelihood they would find their way straight back into the hands of the crown jewelers. The Queen has probably little idea of the value of the gift she has made you; just because oval and flat stones are not requisite to the new design she has in mind, she passes them around as if they were mere trifles—whereas, I assure you, you have brilliants here worth three or four hundred thousand francs. I cannot overemphasize the need for precaution in disposing of them. You cannot proceed too swiftly or too secretly."

My husband, until now in the dark (he had only occasionally remarked, "What the devil! Where are all these diamonds coming from?"), upon being informed of the facts expressed himself as of the Cardinal's opinion, and that very day he contacted a diamond merchant named Frank, who accepted the commission to go to Amsterdam to arrange for the sale of the brilliants. A sudden outbreak of political disturbances in that city, however, precluded accomplishment of his mission.

It was then that my husband decided to take the stones himself to London, and he set out on April 12 upon that mission.

MEMOIRS
OF THE ABBÉ GEORGEL

At this time, then, Prince de Rohan, his little clique of confidants about him, basked in the illusion of royal favor, while from one side crime and from the other vengeance were gathering in the shadows to consummate his ruin.

It was with sharp regret that I watched His Eminence shut himself off from all his former company to confine himself to that of the Cagliostros and their band. The greatest part of his time was spent at their luxurious establishment, which was maintained at his expense.*

The group that gathered there was not numerous: the Baron da Planta, Ramon de Carbonnières, the latter's sister, whom the Cardinal had recently placed as dame de compagnie to the so-called Countess Cagliostro, and Madame de La Motte, who by now had reached terms of intimacy with the charlatan. Hers was the blithe spirit that enlivened all that company; to her these nightly gatherings owed their verve, their gaiety (while providing opportunity for her to make careful character studies of her fellow guests, to determine how each might best be enlisted into service in her sinister designs). The Grand Almoner daily congratulated himself on a friendship to which he considered himself so deeply bound in gratitude.

---

* Cagliostro would later deny under oath that his mansion on the Rue St. Claude was maintained by Cardinal Rohan. His Eminence, he said, might have come daily to sup, bringing members of his staff with him, but even so Cagliostro himself paid his chef daily "for daily provisioning of the kitchen; the Cardinal brought only an occasional sweetmeat or entrée, some special dish prepared by his own chef . . ." (His Eminence was a gourmet and his chef, according to Dumas, was second in fame only to Vatel, whereas chez Cagliostro the emphasis was on the crucible rather than the casserole.)

Cagliostro's secret doctrines were, at this time, making Masonic prose-lytes for him everywhere—although he was interested in attracting not so much a large following as a select one, with the result that eagerness was inspired in all the rest to join the company of the elect. Most highly prized as converts were peers of the realm of wealthy financiers. These were the very cornerstones of the Masonic lodges; the lofty titles gave prestige to the movement, while the millionaires gave the funds which ensured the grandmaster not only the necessities of life but also the far pleasanter luxuries.

In the last-named category came the international banker Saint-James, whose vast fortune constituted his sole recommendation. Madame de La Motte, one eye always focused on the future, on the next step in her complexity of purposes, had persuaded the Cardinal to admit Saint-James to membership in the Paris lodge on the theory that the million-aire, flattered at finding himself in such exalted company, might some-day prove useful in financing the Queen's exorbitant fancies and thus make a valuable ally to the Prince. The best method of gaining a hold over Saint-James, she pointed out, was by exposing him to the influ-ence of Cagliostro.

This suggestion of Madame de La Motte's was unanimously adopted.

However did one coterie accommodate both a Countess de La Motte and a Cagliostro? The thought of two such volcanic personalities smol-dering in the same salon brings up the intriguing question of how those two got on together.

According to Villette:

The Countess lived in dread of the sorcerer and his occult powers, but, her criticism of the charlatan and his wife having elicited a stern re-buke from the Cardinal, she sulkily resolved upon the course of dissimu-lating her antipathy by a show of friendship and cordiality. Cagliostro, on his side, quickly determining that the Countess de La Motte was too firmly entrenched in the Cardinal's affections to be dislodged by even his powerful influence, likewise made the best of a bad situation by as-siduously flattering the lady's vanity.

"It is generally known," the Countess de La Motte writes in her Story of My Life, "that the charlatan Cagliostro and I never really got along together. Certainly I never approved of that bag of sorcerer's tricks to which he resorted to maintain his hold over the Cardinal."

And Cagliostro in his memoirs: "I warned Cardinal Rohan over and over to beware of that deceitful woman and her nefarious stratagems, but he would take no heed."

Dislike at first sight, inevitably, and distrust the one of the other ("The raven loves not ravens"). But beyond that it was the sharp competition, the struggle between them for dominion over the Cardinal's heart and mind, with the Countess playing on his senses and Cagliostro on his sensibilities and superstitions.

The grandmaster's abstruse religious philosophies could have held little appeal for the giddy Countess, and his egalitarian Masonic ideology must have shocked her to the depths of her royalist soul. Why, the very "L.P.D." of Cagliostro's personal device and the insignia embroidered upon Masonic ritual aprons of the time—Lilia pedibus destrue, Trample the lilies underfoot—must have curdled her blue blood. Were not those royal lilies, the fleur-de-lis, emblazoned on her own Valois escutcheon as well as on the Bourbons'?

"The Grand Cophta's followers were so fanatic," she rants against him in her memoirs, "they would have erected a temple to him, breaking ground with their Masonic trowels, and raised an altar for him from which to preach his seditious doctrines. And—oh, tempora! oh, mores! —swinging their censers while they hailed him, they would have forced all the world to bend the knee and bow down before him!"

The Countess de La Motte, however, was never one to be overawed by a mere demigod, and if, as she suspected, his was only a new and glorified version of the age-old shell game, then she would try her luck against him, to see if her eye was not still quicker than his hand.

"She tried her utmost," Georgel writes, "to undermine Cagliostro in the Cardinal's esteem, but, unable to succeed at it, confined her rage and malice to the recesses of her heart, there secretly to hatch her plots of vengeance, awaiting only the propitious moment to come out openly against the man."

Count Beugnot saw the pair together, and he made his analysis of the situation in this passage from his memoirs:

As soon as I heard the news that Cagliostro had arrived in Paris and had ensconced himself in a suite at the Palais-Cardinal, I had no doubt at all but that an intimacy would shortly develop between him and Madame de La Motte. Thus I could hope that the latter would provide me the treat of inviting me to supper to meet so exotic a personality.

But such airs she gave herself about it—to the effect that Count Cagliostro had announced his intention of accepting no social engagements whatsoever; that otherwise he would be besieged with invitations from court and capital; that, having already turned down two highnesses, the Count d'Artois and the Duke d'Orléans, he could make no exceptions; that even at the Palais-Cardinal he declined to sit at table with His Eminence, but ordered his meals served in the privacy of his suite.

Thus Madame de La Motte put me off. I took up the matter with her again—again, unsuccessfully.

Shortly thereafter, her sister-in-law, Madame de Latour, outraged at last by her husband's wicked sense of humor, left Bar-sur-Aube and came to Paris to take up residence with the La Mottes, bringing her daughter, a young beauty of fifteen, an exquisite, fragile blonde who was soon to grace Cagliostro's cabinet of occultism in the role of the young innocent or clairvoyant indispensable to cabalistic formulae.

It was from the Latour ladies I learned that Cagliostro and Madame de La Motte having become close as peas in a pod, he was a frequent supper guest at her home—information which occasioned a loud complaint from me at her persistent refusal to invite me to meet the man. I availed myself of the opportunity at the same time to express my dissatisfaction with the lady's generally supercilious attitude toward me in recent months, announcing my resolve, as of there and then, never again to expose myself to her slights and her rebuffs.

This threat was to prove not entirely unavailing, for only a few days later came a letter from Madame de La Motte in which, although she protested that my criticisms were unjust, she issued a supper invitation for the following night, with the recommendation that I present myself at her house no later than ten o'clock.

I made my entrance upon the stroke of the hour specified. Madame de La Motte warned me that she might be obliged to mollify Count Cagliostro, who, temperamental creature that he was, would not stay on for supper if he came to suspect that an outsider had been invited there to stare at him. She requested me to avoid interrupting him and questioning him on any subject whatsoever, but to reply graciously to any question he might address in my direction. To these conditions I subscribed; to satisfy my burning curiosity I would at that moment have accepted terms even more stringent than these.

At ten-thirty Count Cagliostro was announced and accorded full honors—both sides of the salon's double doors swung wide. Madame de La Motte sprang up from her chair and rushed toward him, drawing him aside, presumably to ask his indulgence for my intrusion.

Cagliostro came forward and greeted the entire company without the slightest sign of embarrassment at the presence of a stranger.

The man seemed expressly modeled for the title role of Signor Tulipano in that popular Italian farce. He was of medium height, heavy-set and heavy-jowled, with olive complexion and an extremely short, thick neck; his moon face was ornamented with great, protruding eyes and a retroussé nose, the nostrils flaring.

Designedly, it might seem, Cagliostro affected the trappings of the charlatan. His coiffure was in a style known as the *catogan*, and new to France: the hair of his entire head parted and plaited into numerous small braids which were gathered and drawn back to the nape of the neck, where they erupted suddenly into a mass of curls. He wore that day a coat in the French style, steel gray with gold-braid trim—his sword thrust through the coattails—over an elaborately embroidered scarlet vest; his pantaloons too were red. A white plume nodded on his wide-brimmed hat, the mode of headgear traditional to the street-corner dental extractionist and all such practitioners who speechify and peddle their panaceas in the open air. Cagliostro's costume was, however, distinguished from that of the humbler mountebank by the froth of fine lace at his cuffs, by the numerous valuable diamond rings on his fingers and by the buckles on his shoes, flashing such fire as to create the illusion of Indian diamonds.

At the supper table were gathered only members of the family, a rather elastic heading under which I include a Father Loth, a monk from the monastery of the Order of Minims on the Place Royale,* who somehow reconciled (just how, I could never understand) his monastic robes with his position as assistant secretary and confidant to Madame de La Motte; he celebrated a private mass for her on Sundays and the rest of the week trotted back and forth from the Rue St. Gilles to the Palais-Cardinal on errands which Villette, the secretary in chief, considered beneath his dignity.

* Now the Place des Vosges.

There were, then, some nine or ten of us altogether at supper. Madame de La Motte had seated Cagliostro at her right; I was beside Madame de Latour, directly across the table from the great man. Reluctant to stare, I stole oblique glances. I did not yet know what to make of him, with that extraordinary face of his, that hair, that costume, and yet the man impressed me in spite of myself.

I listened to him as he held forth. He spoke in some indefinable jargon, half French, half Italian, liberally sprinkled with quotations presumably in Arabic, which, however, he did not trouble himself to translate for the benefit of a non-Arabic-speaking audience. He held the floor and had ample time to take up a dozen different topics, in view of the fact that he gave to each only such development as suited him. Every few moments he broke off to inquire whether he had made himself clear, whether we followed him. Whereupon, one by one, in turn around the table, every head bobbed and nodded dutifully in assent.

Each time he introduced a new subject, it was upon a fresh wave of enthusiasm; he tackled it with clarion voice and vigorous gesture, then just as suddenly dropped it to turn to the mistress of the house and pay her fondly comic compliments, banal gallantries, calling her his dove, his doe, his swan, his gazelle, borrowing his nomenclature from the most appealing denizens of the animal kingdom.

This same performance continuing throughout the meal, I was able to come to no conclusion beyond the self-evident one that our hero could discourse upon a multitude of subjects, including the heavens and the stars in their courses, the arcanum arcanorum, the temples of the Nile, transcendental chemistry, giants and behemoths, and a city in darkest Africa ten times the size of Paris with which he maintained constant contact through numerous correspondents. Upon all these and other fine esoteric matters, with every pertinent fact at his finger tips and with his audience in abysmal ignorance, he could speak freely and at length.

As we left the dining room, the great man deigned to direct a series of questions at me in rapid-fire succession. And although in reply to all I humbly protested a woeful want of knowledge, I later learned that he had expressed a highly flattering opinion of both my person and my intellect.

Declining several offers of a carriage, I insisted on making my way home alone on foot. It was one of those fine spring nights when the moonlight is at its mellowest to irradiate a world gently stirring out of winter's sleep. Paris was as silent and deserted as it always is after midnight in the Marais quarter. I stopped at the Place Royale, struck by a sudden urge to meditation on the strange spectacle I had just witnessed.

I found myself pitying the human race as I reflected on the lengths of folly and extravagance to which the "fortunate" of this earth are impelled in order to escape from the boredom induced by the very benefits which the social order heaps upon them in the cradle. I considered the case of poor Cardinal Rohan, caught up between Cagliostro and Madame de La Motte, who, as I could clearly see, had joined forces to push him to the brink.

But then I stopped to inquire of myself whether my own cynical curiosity could be considered wholly blameless. What had I been doing in that gilded den on the Rue Neuve St. Gilles among creatures at whom I merely scoffed whereas, more properly, I should have shrunk from them in horror? Recognizing my own shortcomings, I took the resolve to sever relations once and for all, unobtrusively but conclusively, with Madame de La Motte and her raffish crew.

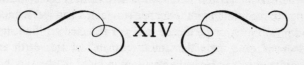

XIV

Suspicions

(Early Summer 1785)

MEMOIRS
OF THE ABBÉ GEORGEL

To MADAME DE LA MOTTE, involved in the execution of her plans for disposing of the necklace diamonds, the presence of the Grand Almoner in Paris and Versailles now proved embarrassing. To avoid his questions about Monsieur de La Motte's forthcoming voyage to London, it was necessary to bring about the Cardinal's return to Alsace. One of the little letters on gilt-edged notepaper wrought the desired effect; these little letters, in the hands of Madame de La Motte, were as a Circe's enchanted wand. "Your absence is indicated," this one said, "in order to afford me an opportunity to make my final preparations for your appointment to that high post to which you rightfully aspire."

It was at the time of the Cardinal's sojourn in Alsace that Monsieur de La Motte set out for England to undertake the sale of the diamonds which had composed the necklace. His reports from London fulfilled his wife's fondest expectations: the sale of the greater portion of the stones had been consummated and the funds invested in letters of credit.

A comprehensive report on the state of frenzied prosperity reigning in the La Motte establishment at this particular period was made later by Cardinal Rohan's legal counsel, Target (whose myrmidons ferreted out the titillating details), in his trial brief for the Cardinal:

The Countess de La Motte had originally made a secret of her husband's journey to London, but later spoke openly of it to her wide Paris acquaintance; and to prepare their eyes for the dazzling splendor that would manifest itself upon the Count's return, she spread the story of tremendous winnings made by him at English race tracks.

It was in early June that Sieur de La Motte returned to Paris, and there are witnesses aplenty to testify to the lavish display that followed his expedition across the Channel: horses, carriages, liveried postilions; magnificent furniture purchased from the shop of Gervais, Fournier and Héricourt in the Faubourg St. Antoine; statues and bronzes from Chevalier's on the Rue des Petits-Champs; marbles from Adam's, Rue de Popincourt, crystals from Sikes's. The clocks from Furet's were paid for outright in diamonds, and the pair of automatic singing birds in the gilt cage were bought with a single diamond valued at 1,500 francs. A shocking ostentation of diamonds was noticed during the couple's trip to the provinces, not only on the person of the wife but also on that of the husband, glittering on watch chains and on rings.

Treacherous as she was, the Countess nonetheless continued to accept from the Cardinal his customary generosities . . .

Not quite all caution had been thrown to the winds, however, since she made some effort—again according to Target—to shield the Cardinal's eyes from the more blatant symptoms of that opulence, "receiving His Eminence, on such visits as she could not prevent, in a third-story room under the eaves, most modestly furnished."

If she was the culprit, and overbold, it may have been that she felt secure—or, rather, felt she had the Cardinal securely in her toils; squirm as he might, it was unlikely that he would expose himself to scandal and royal wrath by publicly accusing her.

But, over and above such ratiocinations, what was one more risk among so many? What good were crisp letters of credit if not to indulge oneself, in her words, "in several long-coveted luxuries"?

MEMOIRS
OF THE ABBÉ GEORGEL

But July 30, the date specified for the first payment to the jewelers in the amount of 400,000 francs, was now only six or seven weeks away, and since the Cardinal's presence in Paris was imperative for that payment, His Eminence was summoned back from Alsace during the month of June. He arrived with all the eager impatience of a man who believes his goal to be at last in sight.

One of the little letters on gilt-edged stationery had assured him that all was now in readiness for realization of his fondest hopes—the Queen's promises to him were shortly to be fulfilled. Then ever so subtly, as if it were an afterthought, the little letter went on to mention that whereas funds were being assembled in preparation for the first stipulated payment on the necklace, unforeseen financial difficulties had cropped up to create some slight embarrassment, but it was hoped that there need be no delay in payment of that first installment on July 30.

This is how that female demon artfully graduated her plan of deception. The words "slight embarrassment" had been slipped into the text of that little letter to suggest to the Cardinal the idea for a new negotiation which, on the pretext of sparing the Queen that "slight embarrassment," would serve the purpose both of preserving him a little longer in his delusion and of putting off a little longer the inevitable moment when the hoax must come to light, thus affording Madame de La Motte precious time to put herself beyond the reach of the law.

Meanwhile, the exclusive soirées at Cagliostro's house were as charming as ever and even gayer than before, with the little band of the Cardinal's intimates in momentary expectation of the dawning of that glorious day whereon the Queen would gratify His Eminence's loftiest ambitions. Madame de La Motte was alone in knowing the secret that this was not to be.

Cagliostro's proselyte Saint-James had been admitted to that select coterie on Madame de La Motte's suggestion; she had plans for him. One day she said to the Cardinal, "I fear the Queen has encountered difficulties in raising the four hundred thousand francs for the payment due on the thirtieth of July, but I have thought of a wonderful way for you to solve her problem and at the same time insinuate yourself still further into her good graces. Speak to Saint-James; four hundred thousand francs will be nothing to him, especially when he learns that he would be doing a service to Her Majesty. You know how flattered he is by your attentions and Cagliostro's. Why not take advantage of the fact?"

The Cardinal thanked Madame de La Motte for her good counsel and confidently set out to win over Saint-James by revealing a full account of the necklace transaction, even showing him the contract with the signature "Marie Antoinette de France." He assured the banker that his financial assistance in this matter was the surest way into royal favor.

Saint-James, like all parvenus, was greedier for social standing than for money. He had long aspired to some government appointment and with it the royal decoration of the Cordon Rouge, but had not yet attained to the coveted honor. Speaking in the name of the Queen, the Cardinal promised it as a reward for this service to Her Majesty. The financier replied that he would deem it a privilege to offer his sovereign proof of his devotion, and that if Her Majesty would but honor him with her order to that effect he would relieve her of all anxiety on the score of the 400,000 francs.

The Grand Almoner forwarded to the Queen, via Madame de La Motte, a letter in which he rendered full account of Saint-James's favorable response. But the forger, the amanuensis for the little letters on gilt-edged notepaper, happened to be out of town; he was with Monsieur de La Motte in Bar-sur-Aube, where the two clever scoundrels were taking every possible precaution to consolidate the fortune derived from the scrapping of the diamond necklace.

The delay in this impatiently awaited reply from the Queen proved sheer torment to the Cardinal, who feared that Saint-James might think he was being tricked. Prince de Rohan communicated his anxiety to Madame de La Motte; he simply could not understand the reason for continued silence on the part of the Queen just when the date of payment was drawing near.

Once the forger Villette was back in Paris, the eagerly awaited reply from Marie Antoinette was forthcoming: Saint-James, the little letter said, must, in the near future, provide Her Majesty the opportunity of manifesting her appreciation of his service. Saint-James was away from the city at the moment, however, and the Cardinal could not get in touch with him for several days.

The banker's return to Paris would hasten—although Monseigneur Cardinal Rohan never dreamed it—the denouement of the necklace intrigue.

Encountering the financier at Cagliostro's, the Cardinal hastened to communicate to him the orders which had come—as he believed—from the Queen. Saint-James was ambitious, to be sure, but too cautious to risk a sum of 400,000 francs without proper guarantee; the Queen's letter, he insisted, must be given over into his keeping. The Cardinal replied that for this he would need authorization, which he would try to get without delay.

In the meanwhile, Saint-James, who had become suspicious (as he has admitted to me since), decided that he should confer with the Abbé Vermond, the Queen's chaplain, to request him to ask the Queen for her direct orders on the negotiation which had been proposed to him in her name through Cardinal Rohan.

Up to this point Madame Campan agrees:

Cardinal Rohan, who, with Madame de La Motte, was involved in the diamond necklace intrigue to an extent never entirely clarified to this day, approached Monsieur de Saint-James on the subject of making him a substantial loan, confiding to the financier the details of the necklace negotiation. The latter, famous for banking operations on the grand scale, collaborated with the government on naval and military financing, but his affairs must have been involved even at this period, for his total bankruptcy was soon to follow.

At any rate, Monsieur de Saint-James refused Cardinal Rohan the loan; he simply could not bring himself to believe that the Queen, who openly repudiated the Cardinal, would have chosen him to represent her in such a transaction; and he considered it his duty to inform Her Majesty of the confidence revealed to him by His Eminence.

I do not know whether sufficient emphasis was given this matter when it was mentioned to the Queen; I do not know how casual a reference may have been made; I do know it made too little impression on her. But, at the pinnacle of happiness and glory, how could she have imagined the sinister intrigue that was brewing?

All the Queen said to me that day was that talk of that confounded diamond necklace had cropped up again; that Monsieur de Saint-James had sent word to her that Böhmer still clung to the hope that she would purchase it; and that she would do well, for her own peace of mind, to discover what the jeweler had done with the necklace. Her Majesty therefore instructed me to speak to Böhmer about it the very first time I met him—to ask him, in an offhand way, what had become of the diamond necklace.

The following Sunday I happened to see Böhmer in one of the Versailles state apartments as I was on my way to Mass. I called to him, and he followed me to the chapel door. I asked him whether he had ever managed to dispose of his necklace, and he advised me that, happily, it had been sold. To my query as to which court had purchased it, he replied that it had been sent to Constantinople, where, at this very moment, it graced the Sultan's favorite. I congratulated him on the sale, although it was really for the Queen's sake that I rejoiced, in the knowledge that she would no longer be plagued by the jeweler's importunities.

That very evening I went to give Her Majesty an account of my conversation with Böhmer, eliciting an expression of her delight and relief (though she did express doubt that the jewel, designed to co-ordinate with French fashions and tastes, would be appropriate for the harem).

I had found Her Majesty in bed, where she was still confined after the birth of the Princess Sophie. She went on to chat with me at length on the subject of the startling change that occurs in women's tastes and inclinations between the ages of twenty and thirty, commenting that when she was ten years younger she had had a mad passion for dress and diamonds, but that now she cared only for the simple pleasures of country life, small informal parties among her intimates, reading and the supervision of her children's education.

It was true that the royal family life had changed from one of boisterous pleasures to a routine tranquillity. Indeed, as I think back now, this was the very happiest period in all the reign of Louis XVI and Marie Antoinette, these years between the end of the American war in 1783 and the birth of the Princess Sophie, the sovereigns' second daughter, in 1785—a time of clear, bright, untroubled skies. The storm clouds were gathering, but they were imperceptible on the day of which I speak. From the day of my meeting with Böhmer until the fatal one when the furious storm of scandal broke, not another word was heard about the diamond necklace.

These words were flatly contradicted by the Abbé Georgel, as we shall see later.

Meanwhile, the abbé says, the Cardinal again met Saint-James at the Cagliostros' and again pressed him to relieve the Queen of embarrassment by making the loan; he said that although he still was not authorized to turn over the Queen's letter, he would give the financier his own personal note. But something had happened to put Saint-James on his guard against the unsuspecting Prince, and he put the Cardinal off, saying that "unforeseen circumstances" made it impossible for him to lend the money at that time. He would not elaborate, but, Georgel says in his memoirs,

. . . he [Saint-James] could not refrain, finally, from asking, "Are you so very certain that you have correctly understood the Queen's orders in this affair? Is it not possible that you are mistaken, or that you have been deceived?"

But the Prince, still blinded by his delusions, merely interpreted these remarks as a defeat in the matter of the loan.

He repeated the conversation in one of his letters to the Queen. Nor was the response consoling: he was advised of his correspondent's disappointment at the financier's default, of her anxiety lest the 400,000 francs not be raised in time and of her hope that the Cardinal would somehow find the funds to meet the fast approaching July 30 payment date.

For the first time, suspicion was awakened in the Cardinal's mind . . .*

TRIAL BRIEF
FOR CARDINAL PRINCE DE ROHAN

One day toward the end of the month of June when Cardinal Rohan became particularly insistent in his questioning of Madame de La Motte as to why the Queen still postponed wearing the diamond necklace, that woman could actually meet his eyes with level gaze and reply, with utter composure, that although she had hoped to spare him the anxiety, she had no choice now but to reveal to him the Queen's real reason for not wearing the necklace: that Her Majesty wanted an appraisal made to establish whether the price of 1,600,000 francs was not excessive, such action being compatible with the terms of the contract. The Queen, herself considering the price too high, insisted that either it be reduced or a new appraisal be made; until such time, she would not wear the necklace.

The Cardinal complained that he had not been informed sooner. Hastening to advise Böhmer and Bassenge of this development, he took occasion to insist, as he had so often done before, that they present their humble thanks to the Queen. This time he made sure that they would

* It is a matter of curiosity that on July 27, 1785, Cardinal Rohan drew up an instrument giving the Abbé Georgel the equivalent of the power of attorney.

acquit themselves of that duty; this time he would no longer trust to the jewelers' promises, but insisted that they write then and there. Thus they wrote, their letter being prepared in Monseigneur the Cardinal's study, upon his desk. He himself corrected the composition, which was delivered to Her Majesty on July 12.

These are facts confirmed later by the jewelers themselves in their memorandum to the Queen on August 12:

In July, Prince de Rohan sent for us to come to him and informed us that the Queen considered the price of the diamond necklace excessive; that it was Her Majesty's intention to return the necklace to us unless we agreed to a reduction in price, which was set by the Prince in the amount of 200,000 francs—but on the condition that if Monsieur Doigny's appraisal of the jewel should set the value higher, we would be paid the higher price.

We heard this news with the greatest consternation. We represented to the Prince what irreparable damage such a reduction would cause us, into what disaster it would plunge us, reminding him that we had passed up the opportunity of sending the necklace to the court of Spain despite several requests from that quarter; reminding him also that, on the basis of our contract with him and on his guarantee, we had in turn made commitments to our own creditors to coincide with the dates upon which the Prince had assured us we could count on payments from the Queen.

The Prince promised to present our problems to Her Majesty. A few days later, when we were called back to the Palais-Cardinal Prince de Rohan told us that Her Majesty had approved our acceptance of the reduction in price and had sympathized with our position, and that therefore instead of the sum of 400,000 francs, as specified for the first payment on July 30, we were to receive the sum of 700,000 francs, the better to enable us to meet our obligations to our various creditors.

The Prince at the same time recommended that we render the Queen our thanks, and, fearful that we might not have the good fortune to be able to do so verbally, we wrote a letter which Böhmer delivered to Her Majesty.

A transcript of that letter, dictated by the Cardinal to the jewelers, is included in the Necklace Trial dossier in the Archives de France:

LETTER TO HER MAJESTY
FROM BÖHMER AND BASSENGE, JULY 12, 1785

MADAME,

We have attained to the pinnacle of happiness in presuming to think that we have expressed our respect and devotion to Your Majesty's orders by our submission to the latest terms which have been proposed to us, and we find vast satisfaction in the thought that the most beautiful jewel in the world is to grace the greatest and the best of Queens.

MEMOIRS
OF MADAME CAMPAN

The Queen had for a long time avoided Böhmer, fearing as she did his unpredictable follies, but the King had given the jeweler an order in 1785 for certain gifts for his nephew, the little Duke d'Angoulême—the traditional jeweled sword, buckles and epaulets for the child's baptism—and when these articles were ready for delivery, the Queen granted Böhmer an audience one day for the hour when she returned from Mass.

Along with the baptismal gifts, Böhmer handed Her Majesty a letter.

I was sitting in the library, reading a book, when the Queen entered with that letter in her hand, and with the remark that since I was so clever at solving the *Mercure de France* puzzles she hoped I would be able to solve the one that fool Böhmer had just handed her. Those were her very words.

She read me his letter, which contained some expression about his happiness at seeing her "in possession of the finest diamonds in Europe" and his hope that she "would not forget" him.* As she read, she commented that she could see in it only another proof of the man's madness, for she had not the remotest idea what he meant by complimenting her on the beauty of her diamonds or by his begging her not to forget him.

After reading the letter aloud to me, Her Majesty twisted the sheet of paper and burned it at the flame of the candle which was kept lighted on her library table for the sealing of letters.

---

* The fact that Madame Campan inaccurately quotes the Böhmer letter is not surprising, in view of the fact that she heard it read aloud, and only once, long years previous to the composition of these memoirs.

"That man's sole purpose in life must be to annoy me!" she exclaimed. "He is always off on some wild scheme or other. Do you suppose he has created some new piece of jewelry to sell me? If so, he will drive me to desperation. I am determined never to use him again; if I decide to reset any of my jewels, I will have the jeweler-craftsman on my household staff to do it—he, at least, will never try to sell me so much as a carat. Please remember," the Queen concluded, "to tell Böhmer, the very first time you see him, that I no longer like diamonds, that I will never buy another stone so long as I live, that if I have money to spend I prefer to add to my properties at St.-Cloud. Please go into full detail with him in order to get the idea through his head."

I asked the Queen if she wanted me to send for Böhmer to deliver her message, but she said that was unnecessary; it would suffice for me to avail myself of the opportunity when I first happened to meet him; with such a man, it was dangerous to give even such slight encouragement.

The Queen burned Böhmer's letter at her candle flame with the remark, "This is hardly worth keeping." But the time would come when she would regret having destroyed the enigmatic message.

Enigmatic, assuredly, the letter was, but if Marie Antoinette was innocent of knowledge as well as of guilt in the necklace negotiations, would not her normal reaction have been to attempt to solve the puzzle, to send a lackey trotting after the crown jeweler to summon him back into the royal presence, to ask him what "most beautiful jewel in the world," what "submission," what "latest terms"?

During the brief moment Marie Antoinette held the Böhmer letter in her hand, she had her finger on the clue to the necklace puzzle. Had she only troubled her elaborately coiffed, flighty head to pursue the matter further, she might have established the facts of the necklace negotiations long before the case erupted into a national and international scandal. But the irresponsible "featherhead," hastening to keep pace with her customarily frenzied schedule (having sandwiched Böhmer in between Mass and a supper party, a ball or a faro game), flibbertigibbeted off to her boudoir for a costume change and dismissed the troublesomely puzzling thoughts evoked by the jeweler's letter by the simple and convenient expedient of burning it in the candle flame. Not the crisic moment in the necklace drama's development, but a poignant one— one which, as Madame Campan says, "Her Majesty would live to regret."

This poignant moment was otherwise interpreted by the Abbé

Georgel, to such a degree that Madame Campan's editor, publishing her works posthumously, felt that it devolved upon him to rise to the defense of her version of the letter incident, and he added a footnote to that particular page to serve as a blast against Georgel (or, rather, against Georgel's devious, skulking shade, since his memoirs too had been published posthumously):

The reader will want to compare Madame Campan's frank and simple account of the letter incident with that involved, recondite passage in the memoirs of the Abbé Georgel [the footnote reads] wherein the Abbé supposes the Queen to have been already privy to the necklace negotiations. Surely it was not from the obscure wording of Böhmer's letter that Her Majesty could have derived her knowledge of that complex and shameful intrigue. To understand the diamond necklace drama, one must know the actors. A large cast of characters played out base and guilty roles. None was better informed than the Abbé Georgel, but none was more loyal to the Cardinal, none more ingenious in evolving defenses for the prelate; and none was more subtly clever than Georgel in misrepresenting the irreproachable conduct of the Queen, despite his profuse professions of reverence. In this passage of his memoirs Georgel allows the reader a glimpse of his respectful hatred of Marie Antoinette, if one can properly define the sentiment thus. Here he advances the theory that the Queen had knowledge of the Cardinal's machinations—at a time when, in the wildest flights of imagination, she could never have conceived of such a sinister plot. The reader who honestly seeks to penetrate the mystery that shrouds the truth before rendering judgment will do well to take a glance at Georgel's account, if only to convince himself that the Jesuit's theory in this regard is invalidated—nay, totally demolished—by Madame Campan's testimony.

The passage of Georgel's to which the Campan editor took such violent exception is the following:

How can I here withhold a fact which I would have preferred to omit? It is too integral a part of the terrible story for me to be able to pass over it in silence: The jewelers, who had frequent occasion to see the Queen, and who were, moreover, urged thereto by the Cardinal, certainly could not have left her for long in ignorance of the necklace transaction.

Despite the contract signed "Marie Antoinette de France," despite the

Cardinal's personal guarantee, it was clearly to the jewelers' interest to run no risks and to make sure that the necklace was for Her Majesty. Sieurs Böhmer and Bassenge did not admit this during the trial, but they made secret admission of it to a person who revealed it to me on the condition that he never be quoted or compromised. As for the Cardinal, he apparently never had the slightest doubt of the fact. Bassenge, when I happened to meet him in Switzerland in 1797, did not deny it; he made formal admission to me that during the trial his depositions and those of his associate, Böhmer, had been practically dictated by Baron de Breteuil, and that if he and Böhmer had not said all the things the Minister wanted them to say, neither could they say anything he did not want mentioned.

After a revelation such as this of Bassenge's, how is it possible to justify Her Majesty's connivance? How reconcile it with either her lofty principles or her lofty rank? A maneuver so indecent as that of Madame de La Motte's must have offended the Queen's delicacy and honor. Then how is it possible that, the moment the plot was revealed to her, the Queen did not manifest her righteous indignation? Had the Queen only followed the impulses of her own honest nature, surely she would have promptly warned the jewelers that they had been deceived and that they must take every precaution.

And even on the supposition that Her Majesty sought to wreak her vengeance on the Cardinal and to destroy him, even then the events which had already transpired and the evidence already in hand would have sufficed to force the Cardinal to leave the court and retire to his diocese. The Queen would have administered justice in a form beyond reproach. The Grand Almoner would have been justly punished for his credulity; the house of Rohan would have been hurt by the disgrace, but without being able to blame her. There would have been no world-shaking scandal, no Bastille, no sordid criminal trial.

Left to her own thinking, Marie Antoinette would surely have acted with such fairness. But she took counsel with two men who, from different motives, misled her.

Abbé Vermond was with the Queen when Böhmer and Bassenge took occasion to thank Her Majesty for the purchase of the necklace through the agency of Cardinal Rohan. The abbé, as astonished as the Queen, maintained his composure, questioned the jewelers on the transaction and instructed them to bring the contract to show the Queen and make a certified copy to leave with her.

When Böhmer and Bassenge later made admission of this interview, they could not agree as to the date when it took place, but they were in accord in the statement that nothing was said at the time to give them any suspicion that the Cardinal had not been acting at the Queen's command. Later, at the time of the trial, when the Cardinal reproached them for not having told him of what had transpired at this meeting with Abbé Vermond and the Queen, the jewelers replied that since the necklace transaction had already been consummated, they felt they should not bring up the matter until the date when the first payment fell due.

The Queen, with a copy of the necklace contract in hand, called Baron de Breteuil into secret council with the Abbé Vermond to confer on the action to be taken. Abbé Vermond wanted to denounce the Grand Almoner's actions to the King immediately as a clear-cut case of lèse-majesté which deserved swift punishment. Baron de Breteuil, motivated by the hatred he had vowed Prince de Rohan from their days of conflict over the Vienna embassy, pointed out that overt action would be premature; that, with the Cardinal's name alone appearing on the note held by the jewelers, he could not be accused of a crime for purchasing the necklace; that they must therefore bide their time and keep a close eye on the nest of intrigue until it hatched out, full-fledged; that the first payment date would probably bring matters to a head; that in the meanwhile he, Baron de Breteuil, would alert the Paris police to uncover the traces and the motives of such a machination.

If, in this conference, Abbé Vermond had exhibited less impetuosity and greater maturity, and Baron de Breteuil less animosity and greater prudence, the Queen might have received wiser counsel: to seek to penetrate the mystery of this strange negotiation, which to the Cardinal's enemies could only be either a desperate expedient of his to raise money or a hoax in which he might be victim rather than accomplice—in either case, they should have told her, such an indecency should be stopped immediately and kept from becoming public knowledge; consequently, Her Majesty should summon the Cardinal to her study, with his relatives the Prince de Soubise and the Countess de Marsan, and there, in privacy and with regal dignity, reveal that he had compromised his birth and rank in such a way as to make his resignation as Grand Almoner and his retirement to Strasbourg essential, but that out of respect for the house of Rohan this whole affair would remain forever shrouded in secrecy.

But Abbé Vermond wanted to vindicate his sovereign's honor spectacularly, and Baron de Breteuil wanted to give vent to his hatred; and so, swayed by their advice, the Queen brought about the total destruction of this man whom she regarded as her mother's detractor, a man she considered unworthy of the place to which he had attained against her wishes in the court of France. In such a way almost always do human passions, when bred on rancor and vanity, overrun the bounds of reason and moderation.

Baron de Breteuil, whose hatred never slumbered, soon discovered that Madame de La Motte had served as intermediary between the Cardinal and the jewelers, and he learned of the frequent conferences of the Prince, Madame de La Motte and Cagliostro. He summoned Böhmer and Bassenge and, as if it were a mere matter of personal curiosity, had them give him an account of all the events leading up to and following the sale of the necklace. Vindictive soul that he was, he persuaded himself that the Cardinal, whom he believed to be overwhelmed with debts, had conceived this transaction to free himself from his creditors. From this point of view, he considered the Grand Almoner's downfall as inevitable and imminent.

The Queen and Abbé Vermond, informed of all these circumstances, awaited with a kind of impatience the date of the first payment, when the web of intrigue should be exposed.

But before that day, Georgel says, the financier Saint-James, becoming suspicious of the Cardinal's attempt to borrow money in the Queen's name, approached Abbé Vermond to request that he ask the Queen for her direct orders in the matter. Georgel continues:

Upon learning of this second negotiation of the Cardinal's, Abbé Vermond ceased to doubt that the Prince was in financial difficulties and was resorting to this machination to extricate himself. Fanatically devoted to the Queen, he saw in such conduct an outrage to the name and the reputation of his august mistress. He confined himself, however, to the statement that he would take up the matter with the Queen and advise Saint-James of her intentions. Then he hastened to inform Her Majesty of the situation.

She, more indignant than ever, perceived a plot to compromise her in the most indecent manner. Reproaching herself for having already delayed too long, she wanted to move at once to stem the tide of evil. Honesty told her that her silence after first learning of the necklace negotiation had amounted to a kind of connivance, which had compounded the evil and which did not accord with her principles, her character and her rank.

Agitated by all these thoughts, she called in Baron de Breteuil, whom she had taken as counsel and guide in this affair. The Minister, who realized with secret joy that his old enemy was hurtling headlong toward his doom, urged moderation on the impetuous abbé and the indignant Queen. His hatred was hot, but he deliberated coolly, the more surely to prepare his blows.

"The crime is far too serious," he said, "to be dealt with hastily. Supreme authority would be censurable were it to act impulsively, without strict adherence to the forms prescribed by law. The culprit cannot now escape. The testimony of the jewelers alone might have been refuted by the Cardinal, who, by paying for the necklace, might have slipped out unscathed, but now we have a second witness in support of the first. I shall procure signed statements from Saint-James and from the jewelers. If when the first payment is due the jewelers' claims are not satisfied, that will be the moment to advise the King."

The decision was entrusted to Breteuil's zeal and experience. The Minister lost no time seeking out Saint-James for a conference and learned from him all the details of his conversations with Cardinal Rohan at Cagliostro's house. Breteuil demanded that Saint-James prepare and sign a statement for transmittal to the Queen; Saint-James gave him that statement. Saint-James's intention was to be accurate; neither threat nor promise could have induced him to a deliberate lie; but his undependable memory played him false on one or two points which later, at the time of the trial, constituted grave charges against the Cardinal.

In his statement, Saint-James quotes the Cardinal as saying, "I saw the Queen, who authorized me . . ." whereas His Eminence insists that what he actually said was: "You saw the letter from the Queen by which she authorized me . . ." Saint-James, at the time of his confrontation with Cardinal Rohan, did not retract his original statement, but he did add that he must surely have misunderstood the Cardinal's words. If Monsieur de Saint-James, whom I found to be a frank and honorable man, had been able to foresee (as he has since admitted to me) the use that would be made of his statement, he would never have given it to Breteuil without advising Cardinal Rohan of the fact, despite

Breteuil's insistence on secrecy. The Minister, however, merely offered
the financier the explanation that the Queen was curious to know how
the Cardinal had conducted and expressed himself in negotiating for
her.

*In the Countess's theory as well as Georgel's, it was "actually the
Baron de Breteuil who, behind the curtain, would play the leading role
in this horrible drama." And there are other striking similarities between the abbé's account of this episode and the one she gives in her
memoirs:*

I need not repeat that this thunder-bearer of despotism, armed with
the dread *lettres de cachet*, was the Cardinal's mortal enemy. Since he
was head of the police (as Governor of Paris), with fifty thousand
spies in his hire, it is hardly surprising that nothing in the kingdom
could long remain hidden from his Argus eyes. He had been informed
of the necklace negotiations almost from the beginning, and he had
early conceived the plan of using his information to bring about the
Cardinal's destruction.

He moved heaven and earth to arouse the jewelers' anxiety; and before ever establishing whether or not the Queen had actually authorized
the Cardinal to deal with them for her, he rashly took it upon himself to
make categorical denial, and to tell Böhmer and Bassenge that their
only recourse was to present the facts in a memorandum to Her Majesty. Thus intimidated, the jewelers rendered Baron de Breteuil a full
account of their dealings with Cardinal Rohan in the necklace transaction, the contract signature of "Marie Antoinette de France" constituting the most striking piece of evidence to hand. Breteuil seized upon it
eagerly and, affecting the outrage of a loyal subject, requested a private
audience of the Queen, in which he laid before her all the information
he had secured.

It is not difficult to imagine that the Queen, caught off guard, did not
judge it appropriate to make a confidant of the Minister; it was less
dangerous to pretend to echo his surprise and indignation; and the
necklace, having once been disclaimed, would have to be disclaimed
thenceforward for all eternity.

*The Queen's story, as Madame Campan expresses it—and Her Maj-
esty as well, in various letters of her own upon the subject—was to the*

effect that she had had no faintest inkling of the rascally intrigue brewing in the shadow of the throne, no slightest forewarning of the darkling conspiracy against her reputation until its culmination. It was Cardinal Rohan, that long-time antagonist, who had indecently victimized her by outrageous abuse of her sacred name in forwarding the desperate swindle whereby he hoped simultaneously to repair his hopelessly disordered finances; whether he had connived singlehanded or with the aid of co-conspirators was relatively insignificant from the royal point of view.

And the Countess's theory? That the capricious, treacherous, ruthless Queen had initiated the secret dealings with the Cardinal and the jewelers for the simple reason that she coveted the jewel. That, midway through the negotiations, she had suddenly recognized that the highly suspicious attendant circumstances, the series of self-incriminatory actions in which the Cardinal had become involved, afforded her precisely the opportunity, long awaited and more highly coveted even than diamonds, to consummate the Cardinal's disgrace (and incidentally to rid herself of an indiscreet, importunate and wearisome lover). That, finally, the Queen, caught off guard and panicky at Breteuil's untoward discovery of the necklace machinations, had lied—first, impulsively, to him and later, persistently, to the King and to the nation—as a measure of self-protection. As for the Countess de La Motte herself, stumbling innocently upon a queen and a cardinal partnered in a brief and deadly pas de deux, she had tripped and been trampled under by their flashing heels.

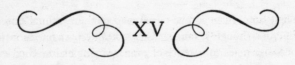

XV

Discovery

(Summer 1785)

TRIAL BRIEF
FOR CARDINAL PRINCE DE ROHAN

It so happened that Cardinal Rohan had opportunity, toward the end of the month of July, to examine a specimen of the Queen's official signature. The difference in the handwriting on this document and on that of the contract could not but strike his eyes, awakening, in truth, the first suspicions in his mind.

A host of horrid thoughts swarmed in upon him, but even these he was able to dispel by summoning to mind the facts upon which he founded his stubborn belief that the necklace was actually in the possession of the Queen. It was his natural, human instinct to cling to the conviction that he had not been duped in so delicate an affair.

He preferred to tell himself that it was his eyes that had deceived him, rather than ever to admit that it might have been Madame de La Motte.

MEMOIRS
OF THE ABBÉ GEORGEL

For the first time, suspicion was awakened in the Cardinal's mind; for the first time, his thoughts, ranging back over the past few months, discovered inconsistencies in a series of events which had seemed entirely natural and plausible to him at the time. The distrust manifested by Saint-James heightened the Cardinal's uneasiness; it was simply incredible that the millionaire, ambitious as he was for royal favor, should have point-blank refused a signal opportunity to oblige his sovereign.

In this distressful state of mind, Prince de Rohan called upon his oracle. Cagliostro, in his most inspirational tones, allayed the Cardinal's fears without entirely exorcising them. It was decided to summon Madame de La Motte.

"You have cruelly deceived me!" the Cardinal told her, his eyes fixing upon hers.

Even this strange and abrupt apostrophe from a man whose confidence in her had until then been limitless could not disconcert a woman so fortified by criminal instinct to dissimulation and effrontery.

"Monseigneur," she cried, "you insult me at the very moment I have succeeded in determining the Queen to rip aside the veil of secrecy which has hitherto shrouded her real sentiments for you. You will soon have reason to be ashamed of your suspicions!"

A ray of light had penetrated the labyrinth into which the Cardinal had been enticed, but Madame de La Motte's tone of self-assurance, the bright hopes she dangled again before his dazzled eyes, her promise of prompt delivery of the funds for the first payment for the jewelers—all these things plunged him back into the dark shadows of his former delusion.

Madame de La Motte, however, surveying the situation from her personal point of view, was not without burning anxieties of her own. What would be the denouement of her infernal intrigue? The necklace had been broken up, the stones pried loose and for the most part sold; part of the proceeds had been invested and part deposited in a London bank under an assumed name. A house at Bar-sur-Aube had been purchased and fully furnished, but there still remained certain steps to be taken to cover her traces. A mind dedicated to crime, no matter how brilliant, finds itself sooner or later, by the very workings of Providence, enmeshed in its own snares.

Dreading the imminent explosion, hoping to delay it yet a little while, Madame de La Motte determined to disgorge out of her ill-gotten gains the sum of thirty thousand francs.

Cardinal Prince de Rohan's attorneys, a sextet of the most celebrated legal minds of their day, would shortly direct their joint staff of secret investigators to tracing Madame de La Motte's every move through those crucial days of late July in 1785; and chief counsel Target, armed with these reports, would, figuratively, shake his accusing finger in her piquant face when she took her place in the dock.

TRIAL BRIEF
FOR CARDINAL PRINCE DE ROHAN

You yourself, madame, must have been trembling at the approach of that first payment date, July 30! What was the meaning of that distress so evident in your household, those feverish activities in which you were engaged on July 27—that day when you came rushing out of your door at dawn, not to come home again for dinner, nor for supper, not even to sleep? And that night of the twenty-seventh when you sought refuge at the home of friends and transacted your business during the hours of darkness? What was the significance of your visit to the office of Minguet the notary? Of the diamonds you left with him as collateral for a loan in specie?

Oh, yes! The tumult and the confusion at Madame de La Motte's that night of July 27 was noticeable—it attracted the notice of many people. She told one of her friends that it was imperative that she raise thirty thousand francs in gold that very day, and when said friend could not oblige, "Then I must get it from my notary!" she cried, and she rushed out of the house.

MEMOIRS
OF THE ABBÉ GEORGEL

Madame de La Motte dictated to Villette one of those famous little letters on gilt-edged notepaper in which the Queen was supposed to say that, although unable for the moment to raise more than thirty thousand francs, she could now promise to pay the entire purchase price of the necklace, the full 1,600,000 francs, by the end of August; that, in view of this development, she felt it should not be too difficult to obtain an extension from the jewelers, to persuade them to agree to a mere month's delay; and that the Cardinal must request it of them in the name of the Queen.

This little letter, delivered to the Cardinal along with thirty thousand francs in gold, constituted in the Prince's eyes irrefutable proof of the truth of all of Madame de La Motte's allegations. It never occurred to him that the proceeds from the necklace theft might have put her in a position to furnish such a sum herself.

With this on-account payment of thirty thousand francs in hand, he summoned the partners Böhmer and Bassenge . . .

MEMORANDUM TO HER MAJESTY
FROM BÖHMER AND BASSENGE, AUGUST 12, 1785

The end of July being the date specified for the first payment to us on the necklace contract, Prince de Rohan sent for us and announced that this payment must be deferred until the first of October, but that meanwhile he had received the sum of thirty thousand francs to be paid to us as interest. Such a sum not being as yet due us in interest, however, we made out a receipt showing it as partial payment on principal in Her Majesty's account.

MEMOIRS
OF THE ABBÉ GEORGEL

The jewelers obstinately refused to agree to the postponement requested, insisting that the total amount of 400,000 francs was necessary to them on the specified date of July 30 in order to enable them to fulfill their own obligations, in which they could not be remiss without suffering the loss of their credit, their clientele and their reputation.

For the next three or four days in succession, they appeared at the Cardinal's bedside as early as six in the morning; and every day, after heated discussions, they went direct from the Palais-Cardinal to report to Baron de Breteuil.

TRIAL BRIEF
FOR CARDINAL PRINCE DE ROHAN

The turmoil at Madame de La Motte's house on the Rue Neuve St. Gilles reached its peak during the first days of August. Those apartments were being methodically stripped of furniture.

Madame de La Motte, after closeting herself for hours with Villette in an attic room, came down to announce that she had sent that confidential secretary of hers to Bar-sur-Aube to fetch her husband. Monsieur de La Motte returned to Paris with Villette on August 3.

Shortly thereafter Monsieur de La Motte, accompanied by a person who has since testified to that effect,* made a visit to the office of the notary Minguet on the Rue du Mouton, where he counted out six banknotes of five thousand francs each, still in the presence of the aforementioned witness; in return for which, the notary restored to Monsieur de La Motte a jewel case, that of Madame de La Motte—and valued by the jeweler Régnier at 100,000 francs.

On that same morning of August 3, after what Georgel termed a "heated discussion" at the Cardinal's bedside, jeweler Böhmer decided to go to see Madame Campan at her country estate of Crespy just outside Paris, a visit described by her in her memoirs:

On the first of August, I left Versailles to go to my country place at Crespy. It was my father-in-law's custom to invite guests out from Paris for dinner on Sundays; Böhmer was invited out once or twice each summer. On August 3 he appeared and, obviously very upset at having received no answer from the Queen, inquired whether she had given me any message for him. Replying that she had given me none because she had no further orders for him, I went on faithfully to repeat all she had instructed me to say.

Evidently petrified with fear, he asked me how the Queen could have failed to understand the purport of his letter to her.

"I read it myself," I replied, "and I could not understand it either."

"You are not expected to," Böhmer said, "since you are not in on the secret." Then he requested a private interview with me to explain what had transpired between the Queen and him. This I could not promise

---

* Target's witness was the black-frocked Father Loth.

him until evening, after the hour at which our guests from Paris usually took their departure. Not until all these persons had gone was I free to leave the salon and walk with Böhmer down into the garden.

I think I can remember our conversation word for word. I was so horrified by his disclosure that every word of it was graven deep in my memory. I could foresee such perils stretching out before the Queen no matter which path she chose to extricate herself from involvement in this vicious intrigue, and I was so shocked, so distraught, that a storm came up and broke without my even noticing it at the time. Thunder crashed, lightning flashed about our heads, while Böhmer and I stood there talking in the driving rain.

"Now tell me," said Böhmer, "to whom shall I address myself for a reply to the letter I handed the Queen on Sunday after chapel?"

"No one," I told him. "Her Majesty burned your letter without ever being able to determine what it meant."

"Oh, madame," Böhmer cried, "that isn't possible! The Queen knows very well that she owes me money!"

"Money, Monsieur Böhmer? We settled the Queen's account with you in full a long time ago."

"Madame, you are obviously not in her confidence. A man can hardly be said to have been paid in full to whom one million six hundred thousand francs are owing—a man who is being ruined because he cannot collect!"

"Have you lost your mind?" I asked. "For what jewel could Her Majesty owe you such an exorbitant sum?"

"For my diamond necklace, madame," Böhmer replied coldly.

"What?" I exclaimed. "That necklace about which you have vainly tormented her for so many years? But you told me that you had sold it in Constantinople for the Sultan's favorite."

"It was the Queen who sent orders to make that reply to any question on the subject," the dangerous imbecile explained. And then he went on to tell me that the Queen had decided she wanted the necklace after all and had sent Monseigneur Cardinal Rohan to handle the transaction for her.

"You must be mistaken!" I cried. "The Queen has not addressed a single word to Cardinal Rohan since his return from Vienna ten years ago. No man at court is in such disfavor."

"It is you who are mistaken, madame," Böhmer insisted. "He is so much in her good graces that she receives him in private. It was to His

Eminence that she entrusted the thirty thousand francs which were delivered to me as first payment for the necklace. It was in the Cardinal's very presence that she took the money from a purse which is kept in the little Sèvres porcelain desk by the fireplace in her boudoir."

"And was it Cardinal Rohan who told you this?"

"Yes, madame, the Cardinal himself."

"Oh!" I groaned. "I do not know what dreadful intrigue is afoot, but I do know you have been robbed!"

"In truth, madame, I begin to be frightened myself, for His Eminence assured me that the Queen would wear the necklace on Pentecost, but I have not yet seen her with it on. That is what decided me to write the letter to Her Majesty."

Then Böhmer asked me what course of action I could suggest to him, whereupon I advised him to go at once to Versailles to request an audience with Baron de Breteuil, who as Minister of the King's Household was keeper of the crown jewels, and from then on to be governed by Breteuil's advice. I warned Böhmer that, in my opinion, his having acted in so important a matter without direct orders from the King or the Queen constituted a betrayal of his oath of fidelity to the monarchs taken at the time of his appointment as crown jeweler.

He answered me that he had not acted without orders; he had read them in the letters signed by the Queen; he had even been forced recently to show them to several bankers in order to prevail on them to extend his credit.

I urged him to set out at once for Versailles, and he assured me that he would. But instead of following my suggestion, he went to Paris, to the Cardinal's. It is a report of this visit which His Eminence made in a memorandum which was later found by the police in the drawer of a desk which Monsieur the Abbé Georgel must have overlooked when he ransacked the Palais-Cardinal for papers. The memorandum bore the words: "Today, August 3, Böhmer went to the country house of Madame Campan, who told him that the Queen had never received his necklace, and that he had been tricked."

After Böhmer left, I wanted to follow him and go to the Queen at Trianon. My father-in-law prevented me, contending that there must be some sinister intrigue afoot which was best left to the Minister to handle, that I had given Böhmer the very best possible advice and should take no further action.

TRIAL BRIEF
FOR CARDINAL PRINCE DE ROHAN

Böhmer came to tell Cardinal Rohan that one of the Queen's ladies in waiting had made the statement that Her Majesty had no idea of the meaning of the letter the jewelers had delivered to her on July 12. But the Cardinal, firm in his delusive convictions, contended that either the Queen's lady in waiting had not said what she was quoted as having said or she was not in the Queen's confidence; in either instance, all that could be deduced from her remarks (if, indeed, she had actually made them) was that the Queen still wanted secrecy maintained on the subject of the necklace's purchase.

On this same eventful day of August 3, Böhmer's associate, Paul Bassenge, received a message from the Countess de La Motte, as he describes in the jewelers' memorandum to the Queen on August 12:

On the third of August, 1785, Madame de La Motte-Valois sent a priest to Sieur Bassenge with a message requesting that he and Madame Böhmer come at once to her house, 13 Rue Neuve St. Gilles. Madame Böhmer being away from the city on a visit to the country, Sieur Bassenge went alone to Madame de La Motte's.

Madame de La Motte asked Bassenge if he had seen Cardinal Rohan recently; to which Bassenge replied that he had just come, that morning, from a visit to the Palais-Cardinal. Madame de La Motte inquired whether the Cardinal had given him any news, and Bassenge said No. Thereupon she advised him that the Cardinal presently found himself in a dreadful dilemma: The signature on the contract he held, supposedly that of the Queen, had proven to be a forgery.

Madame de La Motte told Bassenge that she had no idea how the Cardinal would extricate himself from his predicament, but that her advice to us, if we sought to avoid further risk, was immediately to exercise our rights, fall back on the guarantees given us by Prince de Rohan and call upon him to fulfill his pledges; in view of the Prince's vast personal fortune, he was assuredly in a position to pay us in full.

Madame de La Motte had reckoned accurately, as Cardinal Rohan would himself confirm in his own words before his judges in Parlia-

ment: "*It was part of Madame de La Motte's far-range planning to come out openly and tell the jewelers that the Queen's signature on the necklace contract was a forgery. She could pride herself on having jockeyed me into a position where I had no choice but to pay for the necklace and do so without a murmur. And that is precisely what I would have done, had it cost me my entire fortune, had it necessitated enlisting the aid of my kinsmen.*"

If only the jewelers had not panicked, upsetting Madame de La Motte's most brilliant calculations! But, as they state in their memorandum to the Queen, "*After so alarming a piece of news as that confided to Bassenge by Madame de La Motte, we decided to go straight to the Queen and throw ourselves at her feet and upon her mercy by revealing our position. Unfortunately we were unable to obtain an audience with Her Majesty at that time and were obliged to wait . . .*"

The sun was about to set on that eventful August 3, but before it sank at the end of the Champs Élysées several items still remained on Madame de La Motte's agenda. There was Villette to be paid and packed off on "*a voyage to Italy, which,*" he told her, "*I have always yearned to visit.*"

MEMOIRS
OF RÉTAUX DE VILLETTE

Madame de La Motte herself insisted on my leaving Paris. Yielding to her instances, I agreed to flee before the coming catastrophe and head for the Swiss border at Geneva. Madame de La Motte, in accordance with our agreement, made me a six months' advance payment on my yearly pension of six thousand francs. She urged me to maintain strictest secrecy on all these matters and to write to her by every post, promising to answer my letters promptly, to keep me advised of everything that happened day by day and to send for me to join her in Bar-sur-Aube just as soon as possible.

I joined the La Mottes and their guests at supper that night. Sometime after midnight the company disbanded, and, the house having already been stripped of beds and furniture, I went down to my cabriolet in the courtyard to sleep till dawn, prepared to be off to an early start in the morning. Madame de La Motte had already packed up nearly all her furnishings into wagons to be dispatched to Bar-sur-Aube . . .

According to Rohan's chief counsel, Target, however, by midnight of August 3 Villette was sprawled sleeping in his cabriolet across the luggage, and Madame de La Motte and Rosalie had slipped out the door and crossed the quiet courtyard. As Target reconstructed it in his trial brief for the Cardinal:

Toward midnight, you steal out of the house with your maid. Fear and trembling apparent in your every step, you hardly dare trust the shadows to shield you from spying eyes; you shrink from even the candle beam in the porter's lodge and will not pass the gate until he and his wife have gone off to bed, snuffing out the candle. You and Rosalie pull down the hoods of your capes and, faces hidden, make your way swiftly, mysteriously, keeping always to the shadows of the buildings, along the silent and deserted boulevard that leads to the Palais-Cardinal, where you will go seeking refuge . . .

MEMOIRS
OF THE COUNTESS DE LA MOTTE-VALOIS

Unfortunately, I had long since formed the habit of confiding everything to the Cardinal. He now hastened to Cagliostro, and that quack gave him advice which would prove fatal to himself as well as to me.

Here is a résumé of that advice: First of all, on the premise that the Queen would never dare open her mouth about this affair, but would do all in her power to shut it up, Cagliostro discouraged the Cardinal from entering into private arrangements with the jewelers such as would have reassured and effectively silenced them. In the second place, he suggested to the Cardinal the idea of frightening me into flight, so that in case the Queen denied receiving the necklace the theft could be imputed to me and my flight across the borders put forward as convincing proof of my guilt.

This, then, was the dastardly advice proffered by the scoundrel; this was the decision adopted by the dupe.

When Rosalie and I reached the Palais-Cardinal that night, we were shown into a top-floor suite at the end of a long, dark corridor, an apartment usually occupied by the Abbé Georgel.

That Jezebel in his celibate bed! The servants must promptly have re-
ported this to the abbé upon his return from Strasbourg, where he had
gone on diocese business.

MEMOIRS
OF THE ABBÉ GEORGEL

Madame de La Motte arrived at the Cardinal's in the middle of the night. Face distorted, eyes bathed in tears, she cried out to him, "I have just come from the Queen, who, forgetting all her former tenderness, tells me that she will flatly deny ever having received the necklace, that she will likewise deny ever having given you authorization to act for her, that she will issue orders for my arrest—and that she will encompass your destruction. You see me still atremble, reeling under that thunderclap. I dare not go back to my house; I believe the police already surround it. Give me asylum here until I can make secret arrangements with my husband for our escape."

MEMOIRS
OF THE COUNTESS DE LA MOTTE-VALOIS

Monsieur de Carbonnières, with two of the Cardinal's bodyguards armed to the teeth, went out on the boulevards to search for Monsieur de La Motte and bring him—almost drag him forcibly—to the Palais-Cardinal.

Monsieur de La Motte had no idea that the situation was about to explode in our faces. Indeed, he had the air of a man walking in a nightmare. He asked me to explain the mystery; I did, and endured his well-deserved reproach for having allowed myself to become involved in so reckless a business with the Cardinal. Oh, that unfortunate weakness of character of mine! That fatal tendency to action without forethought! But actually these failings of mine should serve to remind the reader how ill-fitted I was by nature for the intrigue into which I had been insidiously inveigled, how my own credulity and naiveté provided my enemies the very opportunity they needed to consummate my ruin.

The Cardinal's locking the doors of our apartment, his air of satisfaction in leaving us—all this gave rise to Monsieur de La Motte's suspicion that His Eminence was conspiring against us.

We went to bed, but not to sleep—instead, to talk in whispers of the dangers all about us, to make plans and consider means of executing them. This is how we spent the hours of that dreadful night.

MEMOIRS
OF THE ABBÉ GEORGEL

On the Cardinal's own admission, Madame de La Motte's tragic scene was played with such artistry that he took all her horrible lies for fact.

"If that woman," he asked himself, "was not acting in good faith, would she ever have come here and delivered herself into my hands?" But her move in coming to the Palais-Cardinal was yet one more stepping-stone carefully set in place by that villainous, conniving woman in her long-range plan of defense should she happen to be arrested.

The Cardinal, touched by her plight, suggested that he might be able to send her to his estates across the Rhine, where she would be safe from persecution. As for himself, he feared nothing. Had he not in his possession proof to justify his actions and his conduct? In addition, he was convinced that the Queen, if she was well advised, would never dare expose herself to a scandal which might so strangely compromise her in public opinion.

STORY OF MY LIFE
BY THE COUNTESS DE LA MOTTE-VALOIS

The Cardinal, having decided to accuse me openly, planned it so that appearances should be against me. It was with this purpose in mind that he offered me asylum in his residence and then made every effort to persuade me to try to escape from the kingdom, which would serve as convincing proof of my complicity.

But my husband could not be talked out of his projected trip to Bar-sur-Aube. He declared that he did not yet know to what extent my imprudence had involved me in this terrible affair, nor could he yet foresee the consequences in view of the mighty enemies I might have raised up against myself; that he was resolved not only not to abandon me, but even to accompany me into exile should this prove necessary, but that he was determined first to go to Bar-sur-Aube, as he had planned, and to give notice there of his departure so as to avert gossip, scandal, etc.

Our belongings had nearly all been packed. The wagons stood waiting in our courtyard for the journey to Bar-sur-Aube—another circumstance which proves our innocent tranquillity.

The Cardinal contradicted my husband's statements; the argument grew heated. In the face of my husband's firm stand and unalterable decision, the Cardinal at length fell silent. Monsieur de La Motte having threatened to jump out the window if the Cardinal did not unlock the door, His Eminence was finally obliged to let him go.

MEMOIRS
OF THE ABBÉ GEORGEL

Thus it was that Madame de La Motte spent twenty-four hours at the home of Monseigneur the Cardinal. She emerged after nightfall, accompanied by the Baron da Planta and young Ramon de Carbonnières, who escorted her back to her residence. From there she and her husband set out for Bar-sur-Aube, having first made sure that nothing which might incriminate them had been left behind in their Paris house.

August 6, then, was the date the La Mottes, Rosalie and the last of the heavy-laden wagons pulled out of the courtyard, past the porter's lodge, through the gates and away from the empty house on the Rue Neuve St. Gilles.

And three days after that, on August 9, "it pleased Her Majesty, the Queen, to send for Sieur Böhmer to come to her at Trianon," according to the jewelers' official memorandum. "Until that date, we had been unable to secure an audience with Her Majesty or to render her our account of the necklace transaction . . ."

On August 8, Madame Campan had been summoned to the Queen at Trianon "to assist Her Majesty by hearing her lines in rehearsal of her role of Rosine for the new Beaumarchais comedy, The Barber of Seville, which was to be performed in the Queen's Trianon theater the following day, August 9." Madame Campan writes:

I found the Queen alone in her boudoir, and we sat together on her couch while going over the lines of her role. For an entire hour, Her Majesty concentrated on the play; then she turned to question me about Böhmer.

"Did you know that imbecile came here a week ago to ask to speak with me, claiming to have been sent by you? The man is crazy! Having nothing to say to him, I refused him an audience."

In this way I discovered that Böhmer had disregarded my advice to go direct to Baron de Breteuil.

"What in the world can he want of me?" the Queen inquired. "Do you know?"

Then I related to her all that Böhmer had told me, withholding nothing, distasteful as it was to me to broach such an infamous subject to my sovereign. She made me repeat the sordid story to her several times without omission of so much as a word of my interview with the jeweler, although several times she could not refrain from interrupting with expressions of her distress at the thought that forged letters in her name were being circulated. What she could not understand was how Cardinal Rohan had become involved in such a nefarious business. It was all an enigma to her, beyond her powers of conception.

I implored her to see Böhmer at once for her own security, in view of the fact that there was such an intrigue afoot.

Ordering me to stay with her, the Queen dispatched a message to Böhmer in Paris, summoning him to Trianon on some pretext I can no longer remember.

He came the next morning, August 9, the day for which the performance of the comedy was scheduled. (It was the last of those popular theatricals ever to take place at the Petit Trianon theater, although none of us surmised it at the time.)

The Queen had Böhmer ushered into her study and asked him how it happened that she must again hear talk of that diamond necklace on the subject of which she had forbidden him ever again to approach her. He answered that he had been forced to come to her because he could no longer put off his creditors.

"And what have your creditors to do with me?" Her Majesty exclaimed.

Then it was that Böhmer made admission of the entire necklace negotiation. As the plot unfolded, the Queen's astonishment mounted —as did her fury.

Her words to Böhmer were in vain; that importunate and dangerous man simply kept on saying over and over, "Madame, the time for pretense has passed. Deign to admit that you have my diamond necklace and give me assistance! If not, my bankruptcy will bring the whole affair to light."

The Queen's distress may well be imagined; I found her, after Böhmer's departure, in an alarming state. The thought that anyone could believe that she would have entrusted to a man like the Cardinal the mission of dealing for her with a tradesman, unbeknownst to the King, for the acquisition of a jewel which she had refused as a gift from the King himself—this was the thought that drove her to despair.

Böhmer had not once mentioned the Countess de La Motte; her name would be pronounced for the first time by Cardinal Rohan during his interrogation by the King.

The Queen called the Abbé Vermond and Baron de Breteuil into council. Unfortunately, the deep-rooted, implacable hatred for Cardinal Rohan which motivated both these men made of them the very counselors most likely to mislead the Queen in the course of action to be followed in this affair; their personal antagonism toward the Prince made them forget the fact that a man of such high rank, no matter how guilty, must be shielded by all those who have the honor to share that rank, made them forget, as well, that a personage of such prominence is bound to rally a powerful party to his standard, even to attract a large following from among the perennial malcontents of court and capital. The Minister and the abbé too readily persuaded themselves that the Cardinal Prince could be stripped of his high positions and his orders and delivered over to public contumely for his ignoble conduct. In this they were mistaken.

I saw the Queen after the Baron and the abbé had left her, and I trembled for her.

"Such hideous vice must be unmasked," she cried. "When the Roman purple and the title of prince are used to cloak a common thief so desperate for money that he dares compromise the wife of his sovereign, then all France, all Europe must hear of it!"

It is clear that, as of this moment, the fatal plan of action had been decided. The Queen could read my fright in my face; I made no attempt to hide it. Knowing her to be surrounded by so many enemies, I could not but fear that, should she publish the intrigue to the world, attempts would be made to embroil her still further in the sordid business.

I begged her to seek less prejudiced, more dispassionate advisers. But she commanded me to silence.

If only Count de Vergennes, the Minister of Foreign Affairs, had been called in to advise the Queen, his great experience of the world and of human nature would have brought him immediately to the conclusion that the very first consideration in handling such a rascally intrigue as this—compromising, as it must, the august name of the sovereign—was to keep it quiet. Instead, Her Majesty continued her deliberations with the Baron and the abbé over a period of several days. All they could see was the opportunity to encompass the Cardinal's downfall at court and his disgrace in the eyes of Europe; they were oblivious to the fact that delicacy and tact were prime essentials in the handling of such a delicate matter.

MEMOIRS
OF THE ABBÉ GEORGEL

Meanwhile, Böhmer and Bassenge notified the Cardinal that they would exercise all their rights under the terms of his personal guarantee in order to collect the total amount due them on the necklace.

The Cardinal, who had acted in good faith throughout, was outraged by the threat. "You are entitled to exercise your rights," he told the jewelers, "but I shall exercise my own. My honor being impugned, I must protect it by proving that I have acted only as agent of the Queen."

"Ah, Monseigneur!" cried Böhmer. "I have had the honor of seeing and talking to the Queen, and she tells me that she never commissioned you to act for her in this transaction, that she never received the necklace. To whom, my Prince, could you have delivered it?"

The Cardinal, thunderstruck, replied that he had delivered it to the Countess de La Motte and that he had himself witnessed the transfer of the jewel case to the Queen's messenger on February 1. "Moreover," he continued, "I have in hand the authorization signed by the Queen. That shall serve as my safeguard."

"In that case," Böhmer said, "it is clear that you have been cruelly deceived."

This was the Cardinal's last interview with the jewelers; they did not come again to the Palais-Cardinal. They reported everything to Baron de Breteuil, who ordered them to write out a memorandum of all the facts relative to the necklace purchase, and to sign it with both their names. This memorandum, fully detailed—and drawn up under the Minister's direction—was delivered to him promptly.

He then conferred with the Queen and the Abbé Vermond on the preparation of the report to be handed to the King, one calculated to affect the monarch's heart with the same indignation that burned in Marie Antoinette's: a presentation of the Cardinal's conduct as an affront to the probity and honor of the sovereign's wife, and an exposé of a negotiation offensive to the very majesty of the throne—in sum, the crime of lèse-majesté, which could be expiated only in public punishment. It was a delineation every brush stroke of which betrayed the Baron's hand.

But the crowning blow—the finishing touch of refined cruelty which could have emanated only from Breteuil's malevolent soul—was the idea of deferring the date for making the report to the King until August 14, so as to make his enemy drain the bitter cup of humiliation to the dregs. For thus it would be on the fifteenth, Assumption Day, before the entire court and the throng of visitors from Paris assembled at Versailles for that solemn holyday, that the blow would fall upon the Cardinal's head.

In the meantime, Monseigneur Cardinal Rohan, although reassured by the pledge in his possession which he thought to be that of the Queen, was nonetheless prey to the anxiety inevitable to a position so critical as that in which he found himself. The abrupt departure of Madame de La Motte from Paris, the silence of Böhmer and Bassenge and the sudden cessation of their visits, their frequent interviews with Baron de Breteuil, the persistent rumor to the effect that Saint-James had made a statement damaging to the Cardinal—all these things together were enough to rattle the clearest and coolest head.

The Cardinal's conviction that he held his commission from the Queen discouraged constantly recurring doubts about Madame de La Motte. On the other hand, his loyal and forthright soul could not conceive of the possibility of a plan on the part of the Queen to destroy him by denying facts which seemed to him as clear as day. But he did suspect that his implacable enemy, Baron de Breteuil, was capable of conspiring with the highest authorities in the land to bring about an open scandal.

In his perplexity, he was tempted to throw himself at the feet of his King to make open confession of his activities. But fear of arousing the monarch's suspicions of the Queen—and the possibility of danger-ous complications for both himself and her—deterred him.

Why did he not tell everything to those members of his powerful family who could have given him helpful counsel and forestalled—by going direct to His Majesty—the terrible explosion being prepared in the Queen's little committee?

He preferred to go and pour out his heart to his oracle, Cagliostro. That prophet of the universal religion succeeded, through a series of prognostications, in finding some basis for consolation and for comfort.

"Not so! Not so!" Cagliostro would later claim in his own defense plea:

I had always prided myself as a student of human nature and connois-seur of physiognomy. When Prince de Rohan introduced me to the Countess de La Motte and asked me what I thought of her, I told him repeatedly that in my opinion she was a cheat and an adventuress. With this the Prince invariably took issue, protesting that she was a strug-gling but honest woman. He clung fast to his opinion; I, to mine. In the last few months he had been coming to my home even oftener than was his wont, and I noticed that he seemed troubled, distracted, grim. Respecting his privacy, I made no attempt to pry. But every time Mad-ame de La Motte's name came up, I told him, with my customary forth-rightness, "That woman is deceiving you."

About the first week of August His Eminence said to me, "My dear Count, I am beginning to think that you are right and that Madame de Valois is indeed an intrigante."

Wherewith he related to me for the first time the story of the diamond necklace and admitted his suspicions. When the Prince asked my ad-vice, I told him that he now had no choice but to turn the woman over to the police, and to go himself to relate the facts to the King and the Cabinet ministers. When Prince de Rohan protested that his devotion and his affection for the Countess precluded resort to so violent a meas-ure, I suggested that he send one of his friends or family to do it, but this he could not bring himself to do.

"In that event," I replied, "you must put your trust in God. He will have to do the rest, and I can only wish you luck."

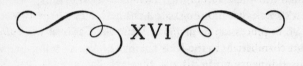

The Cardinal Arrested

(August 1785)

Aᴜɢᴜsᴛ 15 ᴡᴀs ᴀɴ ɪᴍᴘᴏʀᴛᴀɴᴛ ᴏᴄᴄᴀsɪᴏɴ at Versailles: it was both Assumption Day—a major holyday—and the Queen's official birthday, her jour de fête. High Mass was to be celebrated by the Grand Almoner of France, Cardinal Prince de Rohan. The palace was thronged with visitors from Paris and sight-seers from the provinces, for no occasion in the year offered a better view of the pageant of royalty. The procession would include the entire royal family: the King and Queen, with the four "Children of France," the Counts of Artois and Provence with their wives and children, Mesdames (the three old-maid aunts) and all the princes of the blood. The populace crowded into the public rooms and corridors, lining the Hall of Mirrors, through which the majestic parade would pass on its way to chapel. The high and the mighty of the kingdom—the highest-ranking members of the nobility and the King's ministers—took their places in the Oeil-de-Boeuf, as was their right and privilege.

This was the day "selected by Baron de Breteuil, the Cardinal's implacable enemy, as that on which the thunderclap of royal wrath should strike the Cardinal down," the Abbé Georgel tells us in his memoirs. For, he says of the Baron,

It was his idea that the blow should strike the Prince at a moment when he was clad in the Roman purple, in pontifical vestments—on Assumption Day, when the Grand Almoner with all the emblems of his ecclesiastical dignities would accompany the monarchs to the chapel.

At ten o'clock that morning, one hour before His Majesty was scheduled to go in procession to divine services, the Cardinal was summoned by a court chamberlain to the King's study.

As His Eminence made his way there, he had an idea that the King had been informed of the diamond necklace affair, but never for a moment did he foresee the coup de théâtre his enemy had prepared for him.

Baron de Breteuil, in whose judgment the Cardinal stood already convicted by Böhmer and Bassenge's memorandum and by Saint-James's statement, had proposed that Prince de Rohan be arrested the moment he entered the King's door to accompany the monarch to Mass; but Louis XVI (whose heart was as kindly as his judgment was sound), although profoundly affected by the evidence submitted, refused to pronounce condemnation before the accused had had an opportunity to be heard.

His Majesty, moreover, desired, in so serious and delicate a matter, to avail himself of the counsel of two of his ministers whom he knew to be not inimical to the Cardinal. Consequently Monsieur de Miromesnil, the Keeper of the Seals, and the Foreign Affairs Minister, the Count de Vergennes, were summoned into the presence of the King and Queen in His Majesty's study, where Baron de Breteuil informed them of the jewelers' memorandum and Saint-James's statement and read a report of his own findings.

The Queen spoke with a moving and eloquent emotion which was product of her innocence and of the gravity of the offense. Carried away by a resentment uncriticizable except as it was uncontrolled, she expressed the sentiment that such an outrage merited immediate and public condemnation. The two ministers who had been called into conference, impressed by the evidence shown them, could not resist sharing the Queen's indignation; they did, however, advance the opinion that the evidence pointing to his guilt should be laid before the Cardinal and thus all decision as to subsequent action delayed until His Eminence had been heard.

This reasonable suggestion Baron de Breteuil opposed but the King, with his inherent sense of justice, adopted, and the Grand Almoner was shown into the royal study.

Imagine his astonishment at seeing such a tribunal in assembly, presided over by the King and Queen! Calling upon all his inner resources, he braced himself to take a stand indicative of both respect and confidence.

A secret meeting behind locked doors, in the private study of the King, a meeting of six persons in all, constituting the highest council in the land: three top-ranking Cabinet ministers, the King, the Queen and, called up before them, Cardinal Rohan; six persons in all, and yet two detailed reports exist of the words spoken in that inner chamber, one by the Abbé Georgel, to whom Cardinal Rohan described the scene, the other by Madame Campan, to whom it was described by the Queen— reports in some instances supplementing the one the other, in other instances contradictory:

MEMOIRS

OF THE ABBÉ GEORGEL

The King, handing the jewelers' memorandum and Saint-James's declaration to the Cardinal, said to him, "Read these."

After His Eminence had finished reading the document the King asked, "What have you to say in your defense against such grave charges?"

"Sire," answered the Cardinal, "the facts contained in the jewelers' memorandum are correct, but Saint-James's statement is inaccurate. I purchased the necklace for the Queen."

MEMOIRS

OF MADAME CAMPAN

The King asked the Cardinal, "Is it true that you purchased the diamond necklace from Böhmer?"

"Yes, Sire."

"What have you done with it?"

"It was my belief that it had been delivered to the Queen."

"Who instructed you to make this purchase?"

"A lady named the Countess de La Motte-Valois. I thought I was paying my court to the Queen in undertaking the commission for her."

At that point the Queen interrupted, saying, "How could you have believed that I would choose you to conduct this negotiation for me—and with such a woman as intermediary?"

"I now realize that I have been deceived. It was my great desire to please Your Majesty that blinded me. I only re-

"And who commissioned you to do so?" the Queen interrupted.

"You, madame."

"I? I, who have not spoken so much as a word to you since your return from Vienna? I, who openly manifest the most glacial coldness, the most obvious disfavor toward you? I, who have refused to grant you an audience despite your almost stubborn insistence?"

"Your Majesty authorized me to make the purchase," the Cardinal replied, "by means of a document signed in your own hand."

"Where is this document?" the King demanded.

"Sire, I have it in a portfolio in my Paris residence."

"That document," the Queen cried out in tones revealing a noble though impetuous wrath, "that document is a forgery!"

At that word, the Cardinal, who still felt sure of his facts, darted a glance at the Queen which was, perhaps, not duly respectful. Marie

gret that I did not perceive the ruse."

Then he took out a pocketbook containing the letter supposedly from the Queen to Madame de La Motte in which Her Majesty had supposedly commissioned him to act for her.

The King, taking the letter, exclaimed, "But this is not in the Queen's handwriting—and the signature is not even in proper form! How is it possible that a prince of the house of Rohan, a Grand Almoner of France, could have believed that the Queen would sign herself "Marie Antoinette de France"? Everyone knows that queens sign only their baptismal name. Not only is this not a good imitation of the Queen's handwriting, it betrays ignorance of protocol. But now, monsieur," the King continued, "explain to us this whole enigma. My hope is that I need not find you guilty, that you can offer justification of your conduct. Tell me, what is the meaning of your actions with regard to Böhmer—your letters and pledges to him?"

At these words the Cardinal blanched visibly and clutched at the table edge for support.

"Sire, I am too overwhelmed to be able to answer Your Majesty coherently."

"Try to pull yourself together, Monsieur Cardinal, and go into my library, where you will find paper, pens and ink. Write out what you have to tell me."

The Cardinal went into the King's library to put his statement into writing.

The Count de Vergennes and the Keeper of the Seals concurred in the opinion that this affair should be hushed

Antoinette, who noticed this, felt herself imbued with a mighty ire. The King, who had also perceived that glance of the Cardinal's, said to His Eminence, "Now go."

up immediately in order to prevent scandal; but Baron de Breteuil's opinion prevailed, the Queen, in her great bitterness, supporting him.

Her Majesty was at such a loss to explain the motive behind this strange intrigue apparently directed against her that, even as the King was questioning the Cardinal, a terrifying thought flashed through her mind: What if the hidden purpose of the conspiracy were to discredit her in the eyes of the King and the French nation? What if the Cardinal were to announce that the necklace was at this very moment in her possession and point out a certain spot in her apartments where it would actually be found, having been secreted there by some person in her suite who had betrayed her? (But no, the motivation was less complex: it was a case of financial desperation and common thievery!)

The Cardinal came back into the King's study a quarter of an hour later with a written report as confused as his oral response had been.

Thereupon the King said to him, "Now leave our presence."

MEMOIRS
OF THE ABBÉ GEORGEL

The Queen, tears mingling with her anger, resolutely demanded justice. Her expression imposed silence on the Keeper of the Seals and the Count de Vergennes; they sat by, mute.

Baron de Breteuil proposed that the Cardinal be arrested immediately. The King, moved by the Queen's tears, gave the order to Baron de Breteuil and to the Duke de Villeroi, his captain of the guards.

The Grand Almoner, who had just come out of Louis XVI's apartments, was walking down the Hall of Mirrors waiting for His Majesty to leave for the chapel. His face betrayed no change of expression when, suddenly, he heard Breteuil cry out in a loud tone of voice, "Arrest Cardinal Rohan!"

This cry and the approach of the Duke de Villeroi, who notified Prince de Rohan of the arrest order issued by the King, attracted the attention of the great throngs in the Hall of Mirrors and fixed every eye on perhaps the strangest scene ever to take place in that historic gallery.

The Cardinal was immediately surrounded by the captain of the guards, the lieutenant of the Royal Bodyguards and Baron de Breteuil. It was remarked by all present that the Duke de Villeroi's face showed distress, that Baron de Breteuil's was beaming with satisfaction and that the Prince's mien was calm.

The Prince, in that terrible moment which might well have overwhelmed his senses, gave astonishing proof of his presence of mind. Taking advantage of the confusion and the crowd surging round, he halted, leaned down facing toward the wall, as if to straighten his buckle or his garter, and seized a pencil and a scrap of paper; shielding them within his square red cardinal's hat, he scribbled off a few hasty lines, then straightened up again and continued on his way.

When the Cardinal reached his house his servants were drawn up in double file before the door, and as he passed between he managed, totally unobserved, to slip the scrap of paper into the hand of his confidential valet, Schreiber.

Schreiber rode at breakneck speed for Paris and galloped into the courtyard of the Palais-Cardinal sometime between eleven and noon; his horse dropped dead at the stable.

I was upstairs in my apartments. Schreiber, horror written on his face, rushed in to me with the words, "All is lost! The Prince has been arrested!" Then he fell to the floor in a faint, letting drop from his limp fingers the slip of paper he had ridden so furiously to deliver.

When he regained consciousness, he rendered me an account of what had transpired that morning at Versailles. I realized the urgency of executing instantly the order contained in the Cardinal's penciled note, which had been so hastily scrawled that one could scarcely recognize his hand. The valet Schreiber, initiated into his master's secrets, furnished me the key to the enigma.

Shortly that small red leather portfolio was put out of reach of searching hands and prying eyes; it had been the repository for all those little letters on gilt-edged notepaper addressed to the Cardinal. It was then that the valet, amidst groans, narrated the details of the necklace affair (of which at the time I knew nothing) and of the all too intimate liaisons linking the Prince, Madame de La Motte and Cagliostro.

At about three o'clock that afternoon the Cardinal drove back from Versailles to Paris in his carriage, accompanied by the lieutenant of the Royal Bodyguards, Count d'Agout, whose orders specified that he was not to allow his princely prisoner out of sight or to permit him speech with anyone until the arrival of Baron de Breteuil and the lieutenant of police, who were to come to the Palais-Cardinal to put the Cardinal's papers under seal. The Count d'Agout, who disliked having to carry out so strict a surveillance, purposely lingered in the courtyard on some pretext or other when he stepped out of the carriage, in order to afford Prince de Rohan the liberty of entering his house alone.

I hastened to meet the Prince, using a secret door which opened into his dressing room. As I came in, the valet, Schreiber, was just reassuring the Cardinal on the score of the small red leather portfolio. It had cost him his sharpest anxiety.

His Eminence's first words to me were these: "You must be greatly astonished, but you may rest assured that I am no fool and that I was authorized to do all that I have done. Of this I have proof in hand, so do not be uneasy. Perhaps we can manage to meet and talk again to-night."

Our conversation could not be prolonged; the Count d'Agout had come up the stairway, and the Cardinal, to demonstrate his appreciation of his guard's courtesies, was unwilling to be further separated from him.

Baron de Breteuil and Monsieur de Crosne, the lieutenant general of police, arrived at 4 P.M. and the entrance gates of the Palais-Cardinal were ordered opened in the name of the King. The Baron, upon his arrival at the Vienna embassy in 1775, ten years previously, had predicted to me that he would one day be in a position to issue orders to Prince Louis de Rohan and make him feel the full weight of the ministerial powers. He had prophesied accurately, and he reveled that day in his cruel advantage, presenting himself at the Cardinal's with the air and tone of a conqueror who has overwhelmed his enemy. That enemy, although in chains, never bore himself with greater dignity or grandeur.

The Minister first demanded, by order of the King, the document which the Cardinal had described as the Queen's authorization for purchase of the necklace. The Cardinal handed the paper to him, but requested a receipt for a piece of evidence which he considered vital to his justification. Actually, it was a piece of evidence which might have consummated his ruin instead, had not Providence brought to light the forger and with him the clue by which the infernal intrigue was eventually to be solved.

Next, the royal seals were affixed to the Cardinal's papers. After that, Baron de Breteuil and Lieutenant General de Crosne appeared in my apartment to put my papers under seal as well. As they were about to withdraw, the Minister fixed me with a gloating eye and said in an ironical tone of voice, "Monsieur Abbé, you can see that we are no longer in Vienna."

"Monsieur," I replied, "of that I am well aware. In those days you could only threaten; today you have the power to execute your threats."

Just before leaving, Baron de Breteuil advised Count d'Agout that the King had granted the Cardinal permission to receive visits from his family and household staff. Shortly thereafter, his numerous and shocked relations arrived. His Eminence, alone among them all, maintained his air of serenity and composure.

Prince de Soubise, the Cardinal's cousin, succeeded in obtaining a private audience with the King at seven o'clock that night, to beseech His Majesty, in the name of all the house of Rohan, to deign to enlighten them on the crime which could have brought about so shocking a scandal. Louis XVI appeared troubled and said, "I do not wish to see Prince de Rohan's downfall. It was for his own sake that I felt I must arrest him." Later His Majesty revealed to Prince de Soubise the Queen's grievances against the Cardinal, and the story of the necklace transaction.

I joined His Eminence and the Count d'Agout as third member at the supper table. At eleven o'clock I retired for the night.

It was not until eleven-thirty that Count d'Agout showed to His Eminence the *lettre de cachet* delivered to him that afternoon by Baron de Breteuil and bearing the order under the King's seal that the Cardinal be conducted that very night to the Bastille. At midnight Count de Launay, governor of that state prison, arrived to escort the Cardinal thither in his carriage.

The Cardinal was stunned by so extreme a measure. When I left him an hour or so before, he had expected, at worst, to be put under house arrest or exiled to his diocese of Strasbourg. Nevertheless, he would now exert the self-control necessary to show himself ready, with no loss of dignity, for the sacrifice of his liberty as exacted by his King. Indeed, His Eminence, summoning up all his reserves of strength, had perhaps never exhibited greater dignity and courage than at this moment when he found himself at grips with the full force of royal and ministerial power unleashed against him.

Of course, before setting out for the Bastille Cardinal Rohan had the comfort of knowing that the little letters in the red leather portfolio had all been consigned to the flames—all, that is, save one or two which had been confided to my care in case of an emergency.

MEMOIRS
OF MADAME CAMPAN

The Abbé Georgel's destruction of the Cardinal's entire correspondence, especially that with Madame de La Motte, had the effect of plunging the whole intrigue into impenetrable obscurity. The resultant mystery left the field open for wildest conjecture, opened the way for imagination to run riot in countless irresponsible memoirs written on the subject. From the very beginning of this fatal affair, ineptitude and lack of foresight seemed to have dictated the court's every move.

As for the La Motte woman, she was undoubtedly descended from a bastard branch of the royal house of Valois, but one which had not appeared at court for many years. Hereditary vices in generation after generation had plunged them into utter destitution.

I have heard it said that the last known member of this Valois branch had occupied the estate of Grosbois and that, appearing only rarely at court, he was asked by Louis XIII how he occupied himself spending all his time in the provinces; to which this Baron de Valois had replied, "Sire, I keep busy trying to make enough money to live on." Shortly thereafter, to the general merriment, it was learned that he was a counterfeiter!

Madame de La Motte had married some insignificant bodyguard of a husband and lived at Versailles in modest furnished rooms. It is really inconceivable that so obscure a person could have succeeded in creating the impression that she was on terms of intimacy with the Queen, who, despite her graciousness and kindness, rarely granted private audiences, and then only to persons of the highest rank.

The only member of the royal family who had accorded protection to this La Motte woman was Madame the King's sister, and that consisted merely in helping her to obtain a slim pension of some 1,200 to 1,500 francs. Neither the Queen nor any of the Queen's entourage had ever had anything at all to do with this adventuress.

The Queen, indeed, racked her brain to try to recall the face of this woman whom she had heard spoken of as an intrigante who was often seen in the Versailles gallery on Sundays. (As is well known, the general public, with the exception of those whose dress betrays them as the lowest class, is admitted to the Hall of Mirrors and to certain state apartments, as to the park.)

Later on during the trial and its attendant publicity, when pictures of the Countess de La Motte-Valois were on sale at every Paris street corner, Her Majesty requested me, one day when I was going to the capital, to purchase for her a certain etching of the Countess which was said to be a fairly good likeness, so that she could see whether the portrait would recall to her mind anyone she might ever have seen before in the Hall of Mirrors.

K*

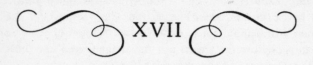

XVII

The Countess Arrested

(August 1785)

MEMOIRS
OF COUNT BEUGNOT

ALTHOUGH it was as yet only early July, I decided to return to Bar-sur-Aube. I went to bid goodbye to Madame de La Motte, who, vivacious as ever, twitted me coquettishly on my precipitate departure for Bar-sur-Aube without consulting her calendar, which precluded departure from Paris until October.

So I was greatly surprised to see her arrive in Bar-sur-Aube at the beginning of August along with her entire household staff, including even her husband. (Only Villette was missing, left behind in Paris like an abandoned sentinel.) And, what seemed stranger still, every day more wagons rolled into town, heavily laden with household furnishings—magnificent pieces all, and in greater supply than any one house could hold. Two complete silver services and the most exquisite porcelains added the finishing touches to the lavish ménage. As a final symbol of imprudence, a jewel collection was displayed, containing more than 200,000 francs' worth of diamonds. Even the husband was gem-bedecked beyond the point befitting an honest man. And there was not a carriage in their stables which had not been custom-made in England to specifications so elaborate and exacting as to advertise the fact that expense was the very last consideration. Noteworthy in the midst of all this splendor were certain costly fantasies such as the decorative arts devise to tempt the most lavish and most jaded tastes: a pair of mechanical canaries, for example, their gilded throats harmonizing in a popular operatic air; golden music boxes, common enough today but still a curiosity at that time; and clocks with highly complicated mechanisms, such as one on whose dial a different scene appeared with every hour that chimed.

Before such an array, the observer must conclude that these *objets d'art* could have been purchased only by people whose money was burning holes in their pockets—people who could not toss it out the window fast enough. In any case, it was the consensus that Monseigneur Cardinal Rohan was paying the bills for this dazzling prodigality, and everyone admired the worthy cause to which the Grand Almoner was applying the philanthropic funds of the Grand Almonership.

The first exhibition of splendor by the La Mottes had astonished Bar-sur-Aube; this one produced a consternation verging on indignation. Neither husband nor wife, however, betrayed the faintest symptom of concern. Their table was superb; they entertained at a series of parties, one after the other in rapid succession. They were making every effort to attract the best society of the town, and to extend the circle of their acquaintance to the châteaux of the region. They enjoyed only moderate success in either direction; to this I can attest out of a sad personal experience.

Of all the châteaux in France at that period, Brienne was the most frequently occupied. Prominent Parisians, including distinguished men of letters, often visited there, and the local nobility paid assiduous court to the Count and Countess. Amateur theatricals were a featured entertainment at the château, as everywhere in France. Monsieur de La Motte told me one day that he had been invited by the Count to attend a comedy, and he offered me a seat in his carriage if the play appealed to me. I accepted, but no sooner had his flashy English-made carriage—with four horses in harness and three lackeys riding behind—drawn up before the door than I was tempted to back out. I had a premonition that I would share the ridicule of such an ostentatious equipage.

The reaction of those who witnessed our arrival at Brienne confirmed my fears. Luckily the curtain was about to rise, which temporarily attracted the attention of the party, including the host and hostess. But when I took my seat beside Monsieur de La Motte in the theater, I noticed that within seconds every lorgnette in the hall was trained upon him maliciously and passed from hand to hand to the accompaniment of mocking laughter and supercilious shrugs.

I could not deny that my companion merited attention. He was dressed in singularly recherché style and had even managed to work a number of diamonds into his attire—the acme of poor taste at a period when simplicity was the ruling fashion. What he was actually wearing that day was a sky-blue cloth coat over a white vest trimmed in gold braid, and a pair of canary-yellow taffeta pantaloons. The picture thus far might merely indicate an exaggerated foppishness, but now comes the feature of the costume which marked it as an outright absurdity: Inspiration had come over Madame de La Motte in the form of a decorative motif embroidered on her husband's left lapel, a bouquet of roses and lilies intertwined, an ornamentation such as has never been seen (much less worn) before or since and which offered a challenge to all those present to interpret the floral symbolism; the obvious conclusion was that it represented the union of the La Motte and Valois coats of arms, roses being emblazoned on the one and the royal fleur-de-lis on the other. The quintessence, surely, of vanity and fatuousness.

The performance over, the guests—a brilliant gathering composed of neighboring nobility and Parisian literary lights—returned to the salon. I bowed to the Countess de Brienne, who barely nodded in return before she turned her back upon me; my greeting from the master of the house was confined to a bare "Good evening, monsieur." One is ill at ease in a large company after so chill a reception by the hosts. I remained standing, uncertain where to turn in this enemy camp, when my lucky star led the Count de Dampierre into the salon and to my rescue. If it was fortunate for him to come upon so good an audience for his endless accounts of his countless inventions, it was no less fortunate for me to come upon so distinguished a bore to attend and fasten on during supper.

Only later did I learn, from various guests, the tricks played on Monsieur de La Motte during supper: how, despite all the splendid repast spread before his eyes, hardly a morsel of food had been allowed to reach his plate; how he had left that groaning board as hungry as Sancho Panza getting up from his first banquet as governor of Barataria. This trick could never have been brought off except through the concerted efforts of a band of practical jokers, all exultant at their success and claiming tribute for the achievement.

"Very funny, very funny indeed!" Monsieur de Dampierre fumed at their interruption of his monologue. "But leave us in peace; we are wearing neither canary-yellow pantaloons nor embroidered boutonnieres. There's your man over there, trying to crawl up the chimney. Go laugh at his expense, if he's in the mood to tolerate it, but allow us to continue our more rational conversation."

At this point Monsieur de La Motte screwed up his courage to approach and propose our departure. I acquiesced wholeheartedly, but was fated to drain the chalice to the bitter dregs.

I went out with him, and we stepped into his magnificent equipage, with two lackeys behind, brandishing lighted torches, and on the step a small blackamoor draped in silver cloth from head to toe. The windows of the grand salon at Brienne open onto the north terrace, which forms the court of honor of the château. Madame de Brienne and all her guests had gathered at the windows to contemplate the splendor of our departure and to hail it with clapping of hands and gales of laughter which floated out into the night and, distinctly, to our ears.

For my part, the horses could not start up swiftly enough!

Back home again, both Monsieur de La Motte and I maintained strict silence on the subject of the reception accorded him at Brienne—if out of modesty on his part, out of generosity of heart on mine. But the story of the adventure made the rounds soon enough, embellished in the telling by those who prided themselves on having taken part, until it became so absorbing a topic of conversation in all the châteaux of the region as to supersede in interest and curiosity, for a week or two at least, even the Mercure de France puzzle.*

Several days after the embarrassing expedition to Brienne with Monsieur de La Motte, Madame de La Motte suggested my accompanying her on a visit to the Duke de Penthièvre, in residence at the time at his nearby estate of Châteauvilain.

The wound to my pride suffered at Brienne was not yet healed, and

* For an account of this adventure and of the La Mottes' reception in the provinces at this particular period, see the passage from the memoirs of the Vicomtesse de Loménie, a member of the Brienne family, in the Appendix.

I had sworn by all the gods not to be caught making the same mistake a second time. So I refused.

And Madame de La Motte insisted.

I pointed out to her that, having no title in prefix to my name to recommend me to the Prince, nor any favor to seek of him, I did not relish the prospect of sitting through a dozen preliminary courses with his gentleman of honor, all to attain to the postprandial privilege of coffee with His Highness!

To clarify these comments, I should explain that in none of the households of the princes of the blood was etiquette so rigorously observed as in that of the Duke de Penthièvre; nowhere was the royal tradition so zealously preserved as in this lateral branch of the family of Louis XIV. The Duke de Penthièvre was all the more exacting of the honors due him as prince of the blood in that he was a legitimized—in contradistinction to a legitimate—grandson of the Sun King.* Genial and casual as he might generally appear in his contacts with the world, on certain points he carried his pretentiousness to extremes no longer even fashionable.

When one presented oneself at Châteauvilain of a morning to pay one's court, one requested the honor of presentation to the Prince through one of his gentlemen of honor, and audience was granted the selfsame day at the hour His Highness came from Mass (leaving not only his prayer book behind him in the pew but also any trace of Christian humility the divine services might have instilled in him). The Prince received with a uniform benevolence all who presented themselves, but whereas the nobility was invited to dine with him at his own table, the non-nobility was ushered to that of his first gentleman, Monsieur Florian, a model of gracious urbanity.

Dinner over, Monsieur Florian offered his guests the alternative of staying on for coffee with him or going to take it with His Highness. There could be little hesitation, and one came at last to the grand salon to join the haughty crew who had had the honor of stretching their legs beneath the same board as the Duke. Their greeting to the newcomers was full of condescension. There were, to be sure, quite a few among them who were not particularly well dressed (some, indeed, who did not appear particularly well bred), but all of them, to a man, for fear of being confused with the untitled had buckled on an old family sword

---

* His father, the Duke de Maine, was the son of Louis XIV by his mistress the Marquise de Montespan.

or hunting knife, either of which two ornaments constituted an acceptable symbol of nobility at the court of Châteauvilain.

The Duke overdid his attentions to the late arrivals. The touching serenity of his face, the sound of his voice, his noble bearing—all harmonized in expression of the loftiest virtues. One recognized in him the last living link with the glory that was Louis XIV (any slight irregularity in transmission having been long since sanctified by the Church).

No price should have been too great, perhaps, to pay for the privilege of basking even momentarily in that radiant presence. Yet untitled folk avoided Châteauvilain unless they were dependents of the Prince or sought a favor. I had gone there once on the latter mission, though the favor sought was not for myself. I suppose I should not have been dissatisfied with my reception at his hands, but I had no intention of subjecting myself thereto a second time.

Thus, I resisted Madame de La Motte's entreaties to escort her on her visit to the Duke and proposed instead that she drop me off at the Abbey of Clairvaux, which was on the road between Bar-sur-Aube and Châteauvilain, and stop back to pick me up once her visit was over.

Things thus arranged, we set out at eight o'clock in the morning on August 17, 1785—a day I shall never forget.

Madame de La Motte left me at Clairvaux as agreed and went on to Châteauvilain, where she dined with the Prince and received a welcome that was to astonish all the courtiers there: His Highness personally escorted her as far as the door of the second salon, to the top of the grand staircase—an honor he accorded not even to duchesses, but reserved solely for princesses of the blood—so thoroughly imbued had he been from youth with the principle that illegitimacy was no excuse for relaxation of royal standards.

While Madame de La Motte visited at Châteauvilain, I remained at Clairvaux, where I had often been a guest. The abbot invited me to stay on for the St. Bernard's Day festival, holding out the added inducement of hearing that celebrated speaker the Abbé Maury, who was to drive in from Paris that very evening to deliver the saint's official eulogy.

I accepted with pleasure. St. Bernard's Day, the birthday of the abbey's patron saint and founder, was quite a celebration at Clairvaux. Alms were distributed to the poor at the abbey gates, and the bourgeoisie from Bar-sur-Aube was admitted to a dinner in the refectory over which the abbot, a handsome figure of a man, a gallant with the ladies and a prodigious bore, personally presided—a once-yearly honor due the community, as it were.

Madame de La Motte drove into Clairvaux at about eight o'clock that evening, and when I told her of the abbot's dinner invitation she indicated a disposition to join our company. The abbot urged her to remain —indeed, fell all over himself bowing and scraping, paying her his respects, his worship. He was well aware of the intimate liaison existing between Monseigneur Cardinal Rohan and Madame de La Motte, and he accorded her the full honors of a princess of the Church.

A numerous party gathered then for a stroll in the gardens while awaiting the arrival of the guest speaker and the announcement of supper. Nine o'clock chimed and still Abbé Maury had not appeared. At nine-thirty, it was decided to wait no longer.

But no sooner had everyone taken his place at table than the sound of carriage wheels was heard; it was the guest of honor from Paris. The abbot darted out to greet him and insisted on his coming straight to the dining hall without even changing from travel garb.

There had scarce been time to unfold the napkins before the abbot asked the traveler for the latest news from Paris—what was going on, what people were talking about in the capital.

"What people are talking about? What news?" the Abbé Maury echoed the words. "Where are you living, then, in darkest Africa, that you have not heard the news which shocks and rocks all Paris? The most amazing, the most bewildering news—Monseigneur Cardinal Rohan, Grand Almoner of France, arrested last Tuesday, Assumption Day, in his pontifical vestments, as he emerged from the King's own study!"

"Does anyone know the reason for such a shocking arrest, so violent an action?"

"Not exactly. There's talk of a diamond necklace which the Cardinal was supposed to have purchased for the Queen but didn't. What no one can understand is why they should have arrested the Grand Almoner of France for such a trifle—in his pontifical vestments, mind you, and coming out of the King's own study."

The moment the words reached my ear, I turned to look at Madame de La Motte. The napkin had dropped from her hands; her face blanched, transfixed, she stared into her plate. After that first paralyzing moment of shock, she rose from her chair with visible effort and rushed out of the refectory, one of the dignitaries of the establishment following her. A few seconds later I left the table and went to find her. She had already called for her horses, and we took our departure.

Here is the gist of our conversation:

"I suppose it was a mistake to have left so suddenly, especially with the Abbé Maury there?"

"Not so. The mistake would have been to linger over your supper at Clairvaux. After all, your liaison with Cardinal Rohan is no secret, it's a matter of public knowledge, and this may be a question of his very life. Certainly the safest course for you to follow is to take to flight before couriers or letters or further word can reach Bar-sur-Aube from Paris. But tell me, can you explain the Cardinal's arrest?"

"I can't—unless it's some deviltry of Cagliostro's. The Cardinal is hopelessly under his spell. It's not my fault. Heaven knows I've warned him over and over—"

"Let's not go into that just now. Tell me, what is this tale about a necklace the Cardinal supposedly bought for the Queen? How does a cardinal come to be involved in a jewelry transaction? And how is it that the Queen would appoint as her agent a man whom she openly scorns?"

"I repeat, it must be Cagliostro's doing."

"But haven't you entertained the man yourself? Are you sure you're in no way involved in this?"

"Absolutely not! What's more, I'm completely unconcerned about the whole affair. My mistake was to go bolting out of the dining hall as I did."

"I consider that no mistake. If you have no concern on your own account, then you should have on the account of your good friend who is in serious difficulties."

"Oh, fiddle-de-dee! You don't know the Cardinal. If he's got himself into a jam, he has a dozen tricks up his sleeve for getting himself out again."

"Madame, you are making me confidences I would prefer not to share. But there is one last service I am prepared to render you. It is now ten o'clock, and we are coming into the village of Bayet; I propose leaving you here at the home of a friend for whom you know I can vouch, while I go on in your carriage to Bar-sur-Aube to give the alarm to Monsieur de La Motte. Within an hour, he should be able to gather up your valuables and come to get you in your fastest carriage, to which your best horses have been harnessed, so that the two of you can take, this very night, the road to Châlons, and on to the Picardy or Normandy coast. You would do well to avoid Boulogne, Calais and Dieppe, where they are possibly already on the lookout for you. Instead choose one of the dozens of small ports, where for ten louis you can get a small boat to England."

"Monsieur, you have finally succeeded in annoying me! If I have allowed you to proceed this far, it is because I was thinking about something else. How many times must I repeat that I am in no way implicated in this affair? For the tenth time, then, I tell you: My only regret is for the unceremonious way I dashed out of the refectory, as if I had been an accomplice in the follies of your Cardinal Rohan."

"Madame, let us speak no more about it. I will only say that you have often in the past, and on your own admission, regretted spurning my advice. I only hope and pray that this may not prove an instance in which you will rue it more bitterly than ever before."

We rode along in silence for an hour.

At the gates of Bar-sur-Aube, I begged her at least to burn any papers in her possession which might be compromising to herself or to the Cardinal. "This is a measure," I declared, "dictated by honor on the one hand and by your own personal safety on the other."

To this she agreed, and when I offered to assist her she did not refuse. Upon leaving the carriage in the courtyard, we went directly upstairs to her suite. Her husband, who had gone out early that morning on a hunting party, had not yet returned.

We opened a large sandalwood chest, which was stacked high with papers of every size and color. I was in a hurry to get it over with and asked whether the chest contained any legal instruments, deeds, mortgages, notes or the like, and upon her response in the negative I suggested throwing the entire batch at once into the fire. But Madame de La Motte insisted on at least a cursory examination. So we proceeded to it, very deliberately on her part, summarily on mine.

It was then, as I cast hurried glances over some of the hundreds of letters from Cardinal Rohan, that I noted, pityingly, the ravages to his soul wrought by the fatal combination of two such passions as love and ambition. While it is fortunate for the memory of the Prince that these letters were consigned to the flames, it must be considered a distinct loss to the study of the human passions. What a century, in which a prince of the Church did not hesitate to write and sign his name to love letters which, in our day and time, any self-respecting man would blush to so much as read!

Amidst this conglomeration of papers and documents there were heaps of bills, some marked paid, others demanding payment; offers of property for sale; advertisements of costly merchandise of every variety; prospectuses of novelties just devised—all the world reaching greedy fingers to dip into the Pactolian stream swirling about Madame de La Motte.

And then I came across letters from Böhmer and Bassenge, letters about the necklace, receipts for money paid and urgent claims for payments past due. I asked Madame de La Motte what she wanted done with these. When she hesitated in her reply, I seized my opportunity and tossed that whole lot into the flames.

It was a slow process.

When I left Madame de La Motte, in the early hours of morning, I urged her more strongly than ever to make ready for her getaway; but the only rejoinder, which came through laughter, was to the effect that she would indeed make ready—but for her bed instead.

And so I left her in her apartments that reeked of burning paper, of sealing waxes impregnated with a dozen different perfumes.

That was at three o'clock in the morning. By four o'clock she had been arrested and by four-thirty was on the way to the Bastille!

The superficial examination I had made of her papers had resolved none of my doubts, but from what I had seen of the Cardinal's letters I considered the two of them hopelessly lost, the one through the other.

MEMOIRS
OF THE COUNTESS DE LA MOTTE-VALOIS

Since that portion of the story next to be developed is known to me only through the report of my husband, I now request him to take up my pen and recount those events to the reader with the simplicity, the veracity with which he recounted them to me. While he takes up my task, I shall catch my breath and summon up the strength to finish it.

So now it is the Count de La Motte who speaks:

The next morning, the morning of August 18, the first thing I saw when I awakened was a great mound of ashes and blackened, scorched scraps of paper, which I swept back into the fireplace. I had hardly finished when my bedroom valet announced that two men were at the door, asking to see me. I told him to show them in.

One of them, warning me to make no outcry, told me that they had been sent on orders from the King to seize all our papers. Offering no resistance, I turned over to them the keys to the wardrobes, chests, desks, etc. By the time they had collected all my papers and put them in a box, to which I was required to affix my seal, the Countess had awakened.

One of the two policemen took me aside and told me that their orders were to take the Countess with them to Paris to be present at the breaking of the seals; that there was no reason for alarm, however; that they were to take her to Baron de Breteuil's, where the business would be concluded in short order.

The Countess, informed of these developments, took the news quite calmly and requested time to dress, to breakfast and to gather up a few personal effects necessary to the voyage.

While she was thus occupied, I inquired of the police whether I would be permitted to accompany my wife. When they replied that they saw no reason to prevent it, I went to my apartments to dress and to order up my horses and carriage. But when I returned to the room where they waited, they observed to me that if I went off with them it would serve to create the impression that they had orders to take me as well as the Countess, and that for appearance's sake it might be better for me to show myself about town after they left, then follow later.

"Besides," they said, "your horses are faster than ours. We can get no farther than Nogent tonight; you can easily overtake us there."

So, acting on this advice, which struck me as sensible, I decided to follow them in about two hours. Would to heaven I had done so!

I escorted the Countess to the carriage, but no sooner had it pulled out of sight than I went up to my apartments, located in the wing of the house across from my wife's suite. There was a desk there which I had had specially made in Paris with a secret compartment for valuables, so ingeniously concealed that the policemen's search had failed to discover it. Now, when the police had ransacked this desk they had come across a purse containing 31,000 francs' worth of Farm Bank notes and had seized them. To my protest that they were authorized to confiscate only papers, not money, they replied that their orders were to seize any and all papers with writing of any kind—but without reading what was written! Baron de Breteuil, who was well acquainted with every aspect of the intrigue, well knew that the search would yield up letters from the Queen and had taken this step to ensure that no profane eye should desecrate them. He alone would thus remain master of the Queen's secret, with all the power and influence such an advantage must provide. But fate decreed otherwise.

It so happened that when we were packing up to leave Paris the Countess had used the secret compartment of the desk for papers which she meant to conceal even from me. Fortunately, in her search for papers for the bonfire the night before she had forgotten those in the secret drawer. Now as I inspected that desk of mine, so recently and scandalously despoiled, the thought occurred to me to look in the secret compartment—where, to my surprise, I found a packet of letters, wrapped and tied in an old money bag!

I locked the doors while I examined them. Fearful that they might prove compromising, my first impulse was to burn them like the rest. Providence restrained my hand.

MEMOIRS
OF COUNT BEUGNOT

I heard the news of Madame de La Motte's arrest from her husband, who came at six o'clock in the morning to tell me of it in a calm, matter-of-fact tone of voice.

He had not taken part during the night in the review of his wife's documents, since just as he came home she had announced her intention to retire, closing the door of her suite on one and all alike, her husband no exception. He did not learn until morning—and then from her, after her arrest—what was going on in Paris and why she was being taken there.

With me he affected nonchalance. "Madame de La Motte will be away for only three or four days at most; she has gone to give the Minister some information which he needs. I figure she should be back by Wednesday or Thursday. You and I must get together to arrange to meet her along the road and make it a triumphal homecoming."

"Monsieur," I replied, "I must tell you, since obviously your wife did not, that only last night I strongly recommended to her that she set out with you for England and by the shortest route. Had she taken that recommendation, she would not now find herself on the high road to the Bastille. So I offer the suggestion that you put into execution yourself, alone, the plan I counseled for the two of you together. It will be far safer, I assure you, than to waste your precious time hereabouts in cultivating your own exotic illusions or attempting to inspire the like in the minds of others. I am sufficiently well acquainted with your situation to tell you that you are playing the role of either a lunatic or an ass."

"My, what a high and mighty tone you are taking with me today. What in the world could Madame de La Motte have told you to justify such an overbearing attitude?"

"She told me nothing. All the more reason for me to urge your prompt retreat."

Monsieur de La Motte shrugged his shoulders and went off, whistling jauntily. But either he had come to pull the wool over my eyes for the purpose of inducing me to perform that service for him with the rest of the citizenry or my advice finally struck home; at any rate, later that night he hopped into a carriage and headed for the Channel coast and England.

That was August 18. Not until the twenty-second did the police show up in Bar-sur-Aube with orders for his arrest.

With every event of that eventful August 18 impressed so vividly in Beugnot's mind, it is surprising that he fails to mention in his memoirs the La Motte family conclave to which he was summoned by the Count just before the latter went galloping off to Boulogne.

Whether Beugnot forgot or preferred not to recall that council called at the La Motte mansion on the Rue St. Michel, the minutes of the meeting are preserved in a report made out and signed by Paris Police Inspector Surbois, dated August 22, 1785, and now in the Necklace Trial dossier in the Archives de France.

If Count Beugnot, in his memoirs, chose not to talk, the family had no choice but to do so, under oath—and under protest—to Inspector Surbois, their depositions revealing that the circle at the council table had included Beugnot, the fugitive Count de La Motte, Uncle Surmont, First Citizen and head of the police of Bar-sur-Aube, his lady, Madame de Surmont, Monsieur and Madame de Latour, the Count's sister and her husband, and Monsieur Filleux, cousin and business manager to the Countess.

In the first business on the agenda of that committee, one thinks to discern Beugnot's fine legal hand: formulation of an ingenious instrument, a bill of sale impeccably executed, signed and sealed, and predated as of July 4, 1785, conveying the La Motte residence in Bar-sur-Aube to Monsieur de Latour for the sum of twelve thousand francs, marked paid, the Count and Countess de La Motte, however, reserving "the right to occupancy of said premises and to any alteration thereto deemed appropriate during their lifetime."

Cousin Filleux would admit to having "arranged for safekeeping" of the La Motte silverware—"two large wooden crates and six or seven chestfuls" (the police would never find the seventh, so perhaps there were only six)—six feet underground, under a shed on Filleux's farm, with a manure pile of masterly design for further camouflage. As for the La Motte collection of diamonds, these were divided into two lots, the Count carrying off one with him to London and Madame de Surmont undertaking to secrete and safeguard the other.

The only diamond remaining from that collection to sparkle openly in Bar-sur-Aube at the date of Inspector Surbois's arrival, according to his report, sparkled on the finger of memoir writer Beugnot's hand—"a stone worth three thousand francs, set in a handsome ring." The inspector's inquiries among the citizenry elicited a variety of conjectures as to the nature of the services rendered Madame de La Motte by the gallant young attorney to warrant so costly a gift, the consensus being to the effect that it was a reward for his professional services in the moment of emergency subsequent to her arrest.*

For her adventures subsequent to that arrest, the Countess takes back the pen she relinquished briefly to her husband and herself resumes the account in her Story of My Life:

And now I come to the moment when the plot against me thickens. A wicked *lettre de cachet* surprised out of an unwitting King will serve as instrument of vengeance, and I will be dragged off to that dread prison the very name of which brings a shudder to this day. It is the Bastille of which I speak.

There countless victims of arbitrary power languished amidst groans,

* Beugnot's memoirs fail to shed any light upon the subject, making no reference whatsoever to a diamond ring.

tears, and curses for the day that gave them birth. There, in the Bastille, death, which affrights every other breathing creature, was welcomed as a blessing and a consolation. There the innocent victim, denounced at the whim of any government minister or any powerful enemy, expiated the crime with which he was charged without ever learning what it was.

Into this fortress I was led at four o'clock in the morning, never guessing it to be my destination. Indeed, so little did I suspect—the police having told me I was being taken to Baron de Breteuil—that I slumbered peacefully throughout most of the trip.

When we reached Paris's St. Antoine Gate, my captors placed themselves in such a position as to shut off my view, but their precaution was in vain; just then I stuck my head out the carriage window—and there was the Bastille!

"What!" I cried. "Is it there you are taking me? How you have deceived me, then!"

My captors tried their best to calm me, telling me they did not think my imprisonment would be of long duration—two or three days at most.

At the first inner gate, leading to the governor's residence, the postilion knocked and guards came to open. The carriage stopped at the governor's door and the Count de Launay himself appeared, clad in a dressing gown, and with apologies for such attire extended his hand to help me from the carriage. He led me to a great hall, where the King's lieutenant inscribed the date and hour of my entry in the Bastille registry and requested my signature for my papers, which were deposited in the archives.

Next Count de Launay most courteously inquired whether he might offer me some refreshment and gave me assurance that I would be treated well. When I told him that Baron de Breteuil was to visit me in the morning, he said that was likewise his understanding. He then instructed the King's lieutenant to show me to my quarters, suggesting the Comtée Tower as the most suitable since it provided the maximum of light and air. The King's lieutenant offered me his arm, and we set out.

The first thing to attract my attention was the sight of the Army veterans who served as guards. Their uniform, a blue cape with a hood concealing almost the entire face, and their behavior, whirling away from us the moment we came near, struck me as so strange that I burst out laughing, asking my escort whether courtesy was against the rules of the Bastille, that the guards should all turn their backs upon a lady!

Saint-Jean, the turnkey, told me later that these veterans had managed nonetheless to steal a glance at me, and he commented that never had they seen a prisoner so undismayed at incarceration. To tell the truth, once I was past the moat, the drawbridge and the main gate [enough to dismay the stoutest heart!] nothing much disturbed me; and perhaps not even the moat, the drawbridge and the gates, formidable as they were, had ever been contemplated with such composure as mine.

Gaily I traversed the courtyards; with a light step I climbed the stairway leading to my tower. It was my innocence which warded off the terror that strikes the guilty soul. Not even the horrid spectacle of the Bastille could trouble the serenity of mine.

The King's lieutenant, climbing the steps beside me, suddenly lowered his voice to a whisper, leading me to believe that the Cardinal must be in a cell close by. If my escort hoped to induce me to follow his example so that the Cardinal should not hear my voice, he had never been more mistaken. I raised mine higher still. Thereupon he informed me that it was a rule of the Bastille to talk in whispers loud enough only to make oneself heard. But what cared I for his rules and regulations? Was I ever one to be regimented?

Finally he showed me into the apartment assigned me. One look was enough!

"Monsieur," I inquired, "is it this Gothic cavern the governor expects me to occupy? And am I supposed to be grateful for his consideration? If so, kindly convey my thanks." Whereupon I proceeded to inspect the bed and, noting that it corresponded exactly with the rest of the elegant décor, advised the King's lieutenant that if they expected me to sleep they had better remove that miserable pallet and substitute a proper bed, one at least as good as that furnished the Cardinal.

To this remark the King's lieutenant replied that he had no idea what I meant, for it was likewise a rule of the Bastille not to answer a prisoner's questions about any fellow prisoner in that living tomb. And if it was traditional to make a mystery of the names and crimes of the other inmates with whom the questioner had no connection, then how much more rigorously was secrecy preserved in regard to prisoners whom the same crime—or the same accusation—had united in that temple of despair.

It was a good thing I had registered a complaint about the bed, for shortly after I saw my jailer come in the door, carrying excellent linen sheets, neat bed curtains and a fine, deep feather bed. As soon as Saint-Jean had arranged these things in the best order possible he went out, and I to bed, trusting to sleep to repair the fatigues of travel and to bring sweet forgetfulness of my woes.

But no sooner had I laid my head upon the pillow than I saw Saint-Jean come back, followed by the King's lieutenant. The turnkey went through all my dresses, emptying the pockets. He and the officer confiscated one gold case and another made of tortoise shell, an ivory rouge box, gold-banded, with an exquisite miniature painted on the lid and a mirror inside, an English portfolio, a gold knife with tortoise-shell handle and, last but not least, my purse containing eighteen gold louis. As final insult, they unpinned from my gown my superb diamond-studded watch and jeweled chain.

The reader may be sure that I did not sit quietly by while this outrage was perpetrated! But my visitors proceeded to their task as calmly as you please, displaying a maddening indifference to my threats.

Unable to sleep after they had gone, I prowled my cell. It was evident all too soon that it offered little of interest for examination: two chairs and a table, nothing else; no tapestries, no rugs, no pictures. The only thing left to do was try to raise myself up to the high, barred window slit, to see what was to be seen from there or to try to make myself seen by others. I pulled myself up by the bars and managed to peer out, but there was nothing. All I could make out were high, stone prison walls —no more.

At eight o'clock I heard the turnkey at my door, but he would not reply when I called out. As only answer to my cries there came the grating of the key in the great lock, the rasp of the heavy bolt pushed in—horrifying, terrifying sounds, clutching at my heart.

And that was the moment at which my gaiety deserted me, though it had accompanied me thus far into the very depths of the Bastille, mine being a blithe spirit such as that grim fortress had never known before.

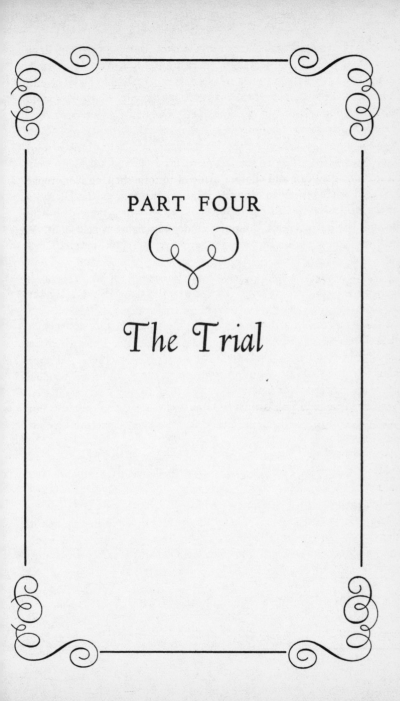

PART FOUR

The Trial

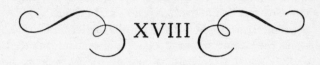

XVIII

Accusations and Counteraccusations

(Fall 1785)

In the Austrian imperial archives there is a letter dated August 22, 1785, addressed to the Emperor Joseph and signed "Marie Antoinette":

You will have had news already, my dear brother, of the catastrophe involving Cardinal Rohan. I take advantage of the courier being dispatched to Vienna today by Count de Vergennes to give you a résumé of the affair.

The Cardinal admits to having purchased, in my name and through the use of a signature which he believed to be mine, a diamond necklace valued at 1,600,000 francs. He claims that he has been tricked by a Lady Valois de La Motte. This common adventuress has no standing at court and has never had access to my company. She has been in the Bastille for two days now, and although in her first interrogation she admits to intimate relations with the Cardinal, she formally denies having played any part in the necklace transaction.

It should be noted that the terms of the sale contract are written entirely in the Cardinal's hand. In the margin alongside each paragraph the word "Approved" appears in the same handwriting as that of the signature below, "Marie Antoinette de France." Presumably, this signature and the "Approved" notations were written by the aforesaid Valois de La Motte. Comparison is being made with specimens of her handwriting. It is also noteworthy that no attempt was made to imitate my script, and of course I never sign myself "of France."

To all the court here it is indeed a mystifying tale, in which I am supposed to have confided to the Cardinal a secret mission.

All decisions relative to the handling of the matter were made by the King and me; the Cabinet ministers knew nothing about it until the moment the King sent for the Cardinal and questioned him in the presence of the Minister of the King's Household and the Keeper of the Seals. I was present at that meeting and was really touched by the reason and firmness the King displayed in so trying a session. When the Cardinal made a plea that he not be arrested, the King replied that he could not spare him without failing in his duty as both sovereign and husband.

I hope that this affair can be wound up shortly, but I am determined that the whole horrid business be clarified before the eyes of the world. . . .

There is extant, in a private collection, another letter signed "Marie Antoinette," dated a month or so later and addressed to the Queen's sister, Maria Christina, Regent of the Austrian Netherlands:

I have never so much as laid eyes on the La Motte woman, who is apparently an intrigante of the basest order, although not without a measure of attraction and ton, a dashing sort of creature.

People say that they have encountered her more than once on the secret back stairway leading from the Princes' Courtyard to my private apartments—obviously a stratagem of hers (and not new among intrigants) to trick her dupes into believing she is on terms of intimacy with me.

STORY OF MY LIFE
BY THE COUNTESS DE LA MOTTE-VALOIS

On August 20, just as the bells chimed noon, the King's lieutenant appeared at my door to request me to put on my cape and follow him to the council chamber at the far end of the Court of the Six Towers.

Instead of Baron de Breteuil, whom I had been led to expect to see, I found Monsieur de Crosne, the lieutenant general of police, and Monsieur Chesnon, commissaire of the Châtelet Court, in his robes of office.

After due observance of the social amenities, these gentlemen asked my permission to get down to business, handing me a crucifix upon which to swear to speak the truth in reply to their questions. This first interrogation lasted three whole hours; a second examination, later that evening, went on until 1 A.M.

Then it was that Monsieur de Crosne said to me, "You are accused, madame, of having taken flight from the kingdom with a diamond necklace which you appropriated illegally."

The lieutenant general could hardly keep a straight face as he spoke, and I, with my naturally zany sense of humor—I promptly burst out laughing.

(It was obvious that the Cardinal had not been told I was in the Bastille. Obvious, as well, that Monsieur de Crosne was a novice at his profession. His predecessor, Monsieur Lenoir, would never have come thus directly to the point, but would instead have sought to trap me with an infinitude of insidious questions.)

"How utterly ridiculous!" I exclaimed. "How patently absurd! Monsieur must be amusing himself at my expense! Now, really, I ask you, gentlemen, had I been guilty of such a crime, is it reasonable to suppose that I would have remained quietly at home in Bar-sur-Aube, all my jewels with me? And why, pray tell, if I was suspected of such larceny, was a search not instituted to establish whether the necklace was or was not in my possession? I beseech Monsieur de Crosne to send police immediately to Bar-sur-Aube to investigate."

From the transcript of a statement by Cardinal Rohan dated August 20, 1785, at the Bastille, written and signed by the Prince for an investigative commission of Cabinet ministers:

Madame de La Motte's behavior in going to Bar-sur-Aube was not so daring, so inconsistent as might appear at first glance; she relied on the fact that she had implicated me so deeply that I would never dare speak out. And she was right. I would not have. I would have preferred to pay for the necklace and keep silence . . . while she enjoyed her ill-gotten gains . . .

"In her very first interrogation at the hands of Lieutenant General de Crosne," says the Abbé Georgel, "Madame de La Motte named and implicated Count Cagliostro. . . ."

The Countess's choice of Cagliostro as scapegoat was entirely predictable: an irresistible impulse, surely, stemming from the old feud between them. But over and above the motivation of impulse and resentment, he was eminently eligible for the role of "fall guy," this mountebank with his broken French and bizarre make-up, with the mystery of his origins and of his fortune, doubly suspect as necromancer and Freemason, as foreigner and spy. Small wonder that at her very first quizzing on August 21, the Countess de La Motte charged the "alchemist," the "Rosicrucian" with the crime of the theft of the diamond necklace.

TRIAL BRIEF

FOR COUNT CAGLIOSTRO,

PUBLISHED BY ATTORNEYS BRAZON AND THILORIER

On the fifteenth of August I learned, along with the rest of Paris, that Monseigneur Cardinal Rohan had been arrested. Several persons came to warn me that as a close friend of His Eminence I might well be arrested too. But, firm in the conviction of my innocence, I replied that I was resigned to stay patiently at home, there to await the will of God and of government.

On August 23 a court commissaire, an officer and eight policemen appeared at my door.

The pillage began before my very eyes. They forced me to open wardrobes, chests and desks. Papers of great importance out of my green portfolio were lost, as well as rolls of Venetian, Roman and Spanish gold coins and forty-seven bank notes of France in the amount of a thousand francs each. Priceless elixirs, precious potions and balms fell prey to their depredations.

I implored Monsieur de Chesnon, the commissaire, to permit me to be driven to my destination in my carriage; but he had the inhumanity to refuse, and I was dragged along on foot, to the scandal of the entire neighborhood, halfway to the Bastille. At that point a fiacre happened along, and I obtained the grace of being allowed to hire it.

The terrible drawbridge was lowered across the moat, and I saw myself swallowed up inside . . .

Chesnon, the Châtelet Court commissaire, point-blank denied any irregularity in his procedure; it had been strictly according to the letter of the law, he insisted.

OFFICIAL REPORT
OF THE ARREST OF THE SIEUR AND LADY CAGLIOSTRO,
THE SEARCH MADE OF THEIR PREMISES, PAPERS, JEWELS, ETC.

On August 23, 1785, at 7 A.M., we, Marie Joseph Chesnon fils, attorney at law and King's counselor, did proceed to the residence of the Cagliostros. Accompanied by Paris Police Inspector de Brugnières, we found the couple in their bedroom on the second story. . . .

[And subsequent to the departure of Cagliostro under guard of Brugnières] . . . all the jewels, money and papers having been gathered up by the Lady Cagliostro and put by her into a box, we bound it up several times securely with a green silk ribbon to which at one end we affixed our red Spanish wax seals, requiring Madame Cagliostro to affix her own personal seal at the other end of said ribbon.

As we were about to depart, we inquired of the Lady Cagliostro whether she did not intend to take any precautions as to the safety of her household and personal effects. To this she replied in the negative, stating that she had the greatest confidence in her first lady's maid, with whom she would leave the keys; whereupon we observed to the Lady Cagliostro that there seemed to us no necessity to leave the servants access to the entire house, and that it would be more prudent to take the keys to her personal apartments with her. Madame Cagliostro having adopted this proposal, we ordered all the windows to be fastened throughout the house, and the Lady Cagliostro, to ensure the safety of her furnishings, locked the door of her apartments and put the keys in her pocket. . . .

> CHESNON fils,
> Commissaire of the Châtelet Court
> BRUGNIÈRES,
> Inspector of City Police
> The Lady Cagliostro, being unable to write, has affixed her mark: X

L

TRIAL BRIEF
FOR COUNT CAGLIOSTRO

Now my wife has suffered a fate similar to mine. At these words, I falter. I shall spare the sensitive reader the horrors I have suffered and confine myself to the statement that, as heaven is my witness, given a choice between death and six months in the Bastille, I would unhesitatingly cry, "Lead me to the scaffold in the public square!"

A resident of this country for six years now, dwelling among a generous, hospitable and witty people, I had come to believe that in France at last I had found my adopted land, and I congratulated myself in advance on all the good I could perform for my new fellow citizens. A thunderbolt has destroyed that sweet illusion, and I find myself hurled into the Bastille.

My wife, that most gentle, most amiable, most virtuous of women, has been dragged into the same black pit. Thick walls, iron bars, mighty locks separate me from her. She moans, and I cannot hear. I question my guards about her; their lips are sealed. Perhaps, alas, she may be no more. A frail and delicate creature, could she survive six months in a keep where even a man needs all his courage, all his inner resources to fight off despair?

What crime have I committed? Who has denounced me? Of what am I accused? Are there witnesses who testify against me? I am refused even the bare knowledge of the nature of the complaint lodged against me. I am told nothing. How can a man ward off the blows of invisible attackers?

The only answer I can obtain is that the criminal ordinance so decrees. I fall silent and bow my head, moaning, before a law so alarming, so rigorous to the innocent.

According to the August 23 entry in the zestful, detailed journal (unpublished) of Simeon Hardy, whose bookshop on the Rue St. Jacques was the resort of authors and journalists and buzzed with the gossip of the rialto, the greenroom, the salon and the boudoir:

Count Cagliostro, a newcomer to the capital, where he flaunts his so-called occult sciences and a new species of charlatanism—passing also,

The Count de La Motte

The Countess de La Motte

The Count Cagliostro

The Countess Cagliostro

Marie Antoinette

Cardinal Prince Louis de Rohan

Louis XVI

The little scene below this portrait shows
Mademoiselle d'Oliva with Count de La
Motte at the Palais Royal

Mademoiselle Leguay d'Oliva: note her marked
resemblance to Marie Antoinette

The Queen's Necklace, composed of 647
diamonds weighing a total of 2,800 carats

Above: Countess de La Motte escapes from the Salpêtrière prison: crossing the Seine near the Bastille

Left: The Countess and her maid, disguised as peasants, continue their journey on foot

The Queen in favour: A contemporary engraving showing Marie Antoinette, surrounded by an admiring entourage, shortly after the birth of her son on October 22, 1781. A song, specially written in honour of the event, is inscribed below

Je ne refpire plus que pour toi...
un baifer, mon bel Ange! *Acte 1.er Scene 1.re*

The Queen maligned: '*I live only for you . . . a kiss, my
beautiful angel!*' A scandalous little vignette, showing Marie
Antoinette and the Duchess de Polignac in deep embrace.
This first appeared as an illustration to the contemporary
prose drama, *La Destruction de l'aristocratisme*

A cartoon: Marie Antoinette is represented as a harpy, tearing up *The Rights of Man* with her claws

A cartoon: 'The holy family steps across from the Tuileries to Montmidy.' Beneath the royal personages stand Countess de La Motte (*'Here's a very well-known object!'*), the Cardinal (*'I'll stick to La Motte!'*), and the Duke de Coigny (*'If I mounted her* [the Queen], *she'd jump the tracks!'*)

The Palace of Versailles by Jacques Rigaud; members of the Court strolling through the formal gardens between the Grand Terrace and the Chapel

The Bastille by Jacques Rigaud: the Porte St. Antoine is in the foreground

incidentally, for a spy—has just been arrested along with his wife, who is reputedly the Cardinal's mistress.

And the Paris correspondent of the Imperial Court of St. Petersburg reported:

When Police Lieutenant General de Crosne began questioning Cagliostro, the latter insolently remarked that he could think of no misdeed to account for his arrest, unless it might be the assassination of Pompey —although even as concerned that antique crime, he had acted under the Pharaoh's orders!

Whereupon Monsieur de Crosne, displaying admirable *sang-froid*, observed that he would refrain from going into criminal matters that had transpired under his predecessors in office.

MEMOIRS
OF THE ABBÉ GEORGEL

One thing that surprised the Cardinal himself was that Madame de La Motte in her early interrogations had not implicated the Cardinal's secretary, young Ramon de Carbonnières (with whom she had had close contact), as she had implicated Cagliostro and the Baron da Planta. This was what saved young Carbonnières from the Bastille.

Another young man with whom Madame de La Motte had had "close contact" admits to trembling in his boots. Count Beugnot writes:

I fully expected to be arrested any minute. At that point I could not guess how strangely Baron de Breteuil would mismanage the whole case; I could only base my conjectures as to what he would do on what I thought he properly ought to do, and that included a *lettre de cachet* made out in my name. Remembering the secret horror I had experienced all my life every time I passed the Bastille, I interpreted it as a premonition.

I dared not leave Bar-sur-Aube, and yet I was afraid to stay, thinking of the anguish it would cost my loved ones if the police should appear to drag me out from beneath the paternal roof.

A happy circumstance rescued me from the horns of my dilemma.

The town of Bar-sur-Aube was at the moment engaged in a serious lawsuit, which was about to be judged before the Council of State. The attorney insisted that someone be sent to the capital to keep up with the case at court. The choice of the municipality fell on me, and thus I could afford to return to Paris without arousing suspicions as to the reason for my departure.

My position in Paris, however, was not without its embarrassments. The necklace affair, which was a complete mystery at that point, was the consuming interest of the day, and I could not make my appearance anywhere without being put on the witness stand. I decided to shut myself away from all society. I did not even attend the sessions at the Palais de Justice, but occupied myself solely with the Bar-sur-Aube case before the Council.

This matter had split the citizenry of the town wide open, as such internal litigation is apt to do in a small community. The opposition party, the side against which I was directing the complaints and petitions, seemed to find my presence in Paris highly importunate and made a determined effort to run me out. I received a flood of anonymous letters warning me to make my getaway before I was consigned to the Bastille, advice I was all the more disposed to follow for the reason that, as I have said, I regarded my arrest as inevitable. And I think I might actually have taken to flight had only my personal interests been at stake. But I had been deputized by my native town and entrusted with its defense in a case where judgment was momentarily to be rendered. To fail such a trust, to flee in the face of a sacred duty, would have constituted open admission of guilt.

In the final analysis, I had not committed a single action with which to reproach myself, had given no word of counsel for which an honorable man need blush, and thus had nothing to fear even if, as first seemed unlikely, the case should be tried before a regular tribunal. If, on the other hand, it were to be treated as an affair of state, the worst that could happen to me would be to spend six months or a year in the Bastille. You came across people every day who had had such an experience, and who had not lost standing thereby.

My decision to stay on in Paris once taken, I set out to reconcile myself to the thought of the incarceration threatening me. As a matter of fact, I began to pack a Bastille overnight case, starting off with those small paperbound volumes of the classics referred to as "Cazins" from the name of the publisher. To this stack I added a mathematics text, an atlas, paper and pens and ink, and a supply of body linen. All this I arranged in a small valise, which I set at the foot of my bed, like a friendly sentinel ready to accompany me at a moment's notice.

I went further: I walked up several times to the Faubourg St. Antoine, to the Arsenal Gardens, to accustom myself to the sight of the Bastille by studying it from a distance. Counting the narrow slits which served that fortress as windows, I tried to guess the one through which a seldom ray of sunlight would filter in to me.

This, then, was how I gradually inured myself to an idea which had originally panicked me.

Monsieur de Launay, the governor of the Bastille, was from my part of the country. I have heard men rise to his defense more than once in answer to the calumnies published against him by Linguet in his *Memoirs of the Bastille*. At the time, I had heard from authoritative sources that the governor carried out his unpleasant functions with all the courtesy and consideration compatible with those duties. As it developed, I had not been misled, for among those persons arrested during the Necklace Trial the innocent vied with one another to render justice to Count de Launay for their treatment at his hands. Thus I arrived at the conclusion that I had nothing to dread on his account.

It was at this time that I came to a realization of the importance of making a decision and abiding by it. Having completely shaken off the incubus of fear, I could get back to work on the Bar-sur-Aube case, and I settled down to write what turned out to be the very best brief of my whole career.

The case was tried at Fontainebleau, and I won it. My brief, forwarded to Bar-sur-Aube along with the news of the favorable decision, won me a little local triumph which went a long way toward changing the opinion of those townspeople who had been prejudiced against me because of my liaison with Madame de La Motte.

I had refused any fee for professional services, but my fellow citizens, in expression of their appreciation, elected me—although I was not yet twenty-five—town notable, a position corresponding to that of municipal councilman today. This was the first elective office with which I was honored by my fellow citizens, and none has ever brought me so keen a sense of satisfaction, although since then I have won their votes for the highest public offices in the land.

If Councilman Beugnot lived in the dread that he might be heading for the dungeons of the Bastille, the Abbé Georgel knew for certain that he was eligible:

The Count de Launay himself has told me since that Baron de Breteuil ordered him to make ready a cell for me. At the royal meeting where it had been decided to incarcerate the Cardinal and the others in the Bastille, the Minister had requested of the King that I be arrested also. It was impossible, he had argued, that a man who had been the Cardinal's confidant for more than twenty years should not be implicated in this affair.

From the lips of the Keeper of the Seals and the Minister of Foreign Affairs I learned that they had seen fit to defend me on the grounds that I no longer enjoyed the confidence of the Cardinal, who, without depriving me of his esteem, had become noticeably estranged since the beginning of his liaison with Cagliostro and the Countess de La Motte, and that, the Grand Almoner's recent conduct being irreconcilable with my desire to serve him usefully, I had advised them of my imminent resignation. (Indeed, my friends had been critical of me in recent months for continuing my association with Cardinal Rohan, warning me that the Prince's frivolousness, selfishness and financial involvements did not augur well for my future. My friends and associates knew how disillusioned I was, how hard I had tried, though vainly, to persuade His Eminence to a conduct better befitting his birth, rank and personal talents.) The arguments in my defense presented by the Keeper of the Seals and the Minister of Foreign Affairs won out over the recommendations of Baron de Breteuil. Thanks to them I escaped the Bastille.

Actually, I had never known or even seen Madame de La Motte, but I had been well aware of her relations with Monseigneur the Cardinal, and all I could learn about that immoral and conniving woman had given me concern as to the outcome of such a liaison. Ever since he had become deeply involved with her and with Cagliostro I had had only such contact with the Grand Almoner as was indispensable to the business of the Grand Almonership and the Quinze-Vingts,* of which I was the administrator.

I could not close my eyes to the change that had come over the Prince's

* A hospital for blind gentilshommes, in Paris, with three hundred (fifteen times twenty) patients.

personality. That courtesy which had been so natural to him, that noble affability which had won all hearts, had disappeared from his face and from his lips alike; a harsh and imperious tone had come to tinge his daily intercourse with his subordinates. I do not know at what school he had learned the philosophy he so often quoted, that men must be driven like slaves—shocking words from a man endowed with all the qualities of heart and soul to inspire response to his need to love and to be loved. Unable to reconcile this metamorphosis in the Prince's character with my way of thinking, I had been preparing, after twenty-two years of the most loyal and unselfish service, to leave the Prince—who at that time would probably have seen me go without a regret, even though from the day I joined his staff I had never drawn a breath, so to speak, except in dedication to his glory and welfare.

This was the state of affairs at the moment of his catastrophe. It was the moment, surely, to forget that my zeal and devotion had gone unappreciated. Up to that point I had found myself rather coolly detached, in that the warmth of my affections had been chilled by the above-mentioned considerations; but in the actual crisis I felt my old affection and my energies surge back, and, without a moment's hesitation, I devoted myself wholeheartedly to the cause of the illustrious prisoner.

News of that extraordinary stroke of royal power by which the Cardinal, Madame de La Motte, Cagliostro and the Baron da Planta had all been imprisoned in the Bastille traveled quickly from Versailles and the capital to the provinces, across all Europe. To most people, it was a complete enigma, everyone reacting according to his personal prejudices and opinions.

Those who judged the event by the rules of prudence and political policy might have wished that the King and Queen, even in supposing the Cardinal guilty, had adopted a method less characterized by personal animosity, precipitation and vengeance. It was the consensus that it behooved the throne to proceed to the administration of justice as objectively and rationally as does the law. The birth, the name, the episcopal character of a bishop and cardinal, the dignity of a prince of the house of Rohan seemed to deserve consideration, which would in no wise have detracted from the severity of the punishment had such been judged necessary after an investigation conducted in accordance with the due processes of law.

The blame fell upon the Baron de Breteuil, who had taken advantage of the Queen's emotional instability and of the King's youthful immaturity to destroy his personal enemy, Cardinal Rohan.

The Abbé Georgel and Madame Campan are in agreement on this point. Madame Campan writes:

The moment the Cardinal's arrest became known, a universal clamor went up. All the trial briefs published by the defendants during the trial served only to augment the furor and confuse the issue; no word was written or spoken to clarify the secret motivations.

Immediately upon the Cardinal's arrest, the Prince de Condé [who was married to a Rohan princess], Marshal de Soubise and the Countess de Marsan set up loud cries of indignation. The clergy, from the youngest seminarian to the most venerable cardinal, promptly expressed distress at the scandalous arrest of a prince of the Church—a stand which should have been foreseen. In fine, the clergy and the majority of the nobility were, at the moment, openly defiant of authority and particularly bitter against the Queen. You heard censure of the throne in the halls of Versailles as well as in the cafés of Paris. Even Mesdames were critical of the King their nephew. The mood of people everywhere was such as to welcome the discomfiture and humiliation of the monarchy and the court.

From the Amsterdam Gazette, September 27, 1785: "Everyone is outraged at such a blatant act of absolute despotism as the seizure of His Eminence Prince Louis de Rohan, an act attributed by many people to the personal animosity of a vengeful Cabinet minister."

The general sense of outrage was well analyzed by the Cardinal's fellow Academician Gaston de Lévis in his Souvenirs et Portraits, *published some twenty years later:*

At the arrest of Cardinal Rohan, all France, all Europe, watching breathlessly, concluded that it must have been a question of a conspiracy on a scale threatening the national interests, an emergency permitting of not so much as an hour's delay in counteraction. But when it turned out to be only a sordid intrigue concocted by a charlatan and an adventuress to fleece a vain and gullible prince, thoughtful minds found the Minister as much to blame as the Cardinal.

The Queen's name had been compromised; the publicity given the case by the handling of it compromised her reputation, and the trial staged later did more to harm her prestige than all the libels published against her.

Even Count von Fersen, that most gallant, most devoted of all the Queen's admirers—lovers? one true love?—in a letter (now in the Swedish Royal Archives) to his King, Gustavus III of Sweden, dated September 9, 1785, was critical:

The tales about the Cardinal, especially in the provinces, are fantastic. Most people seem to think that the necklace transaction and the forgery of the Queen's name are not the real reasons for his imprisonment; instead they attribute it to secret political motives, which is certainly not the case.

In Paris the most popular theory is that it was all an intrigue between the Queen and the Cardinal; that she pretended to dislike him, the better to conceal their little game; that actually he was very much in her good graces and that she did commission him to arrange the necklace purchase for her; that the King finally heard about it and made a scene, whereupon she feigned to faint away, claiming the excuse of pregnancy. . . .

There were, then as now, three possible constructions to be placed upon the Cardinal's actions in the case: one, that he negotiated for the necklace in the Queen's name in order to appropriate the jewel to his own purposes; two, that the Queen ordered the necklace purchased for herself, using the Cardinal as intermediary; and three, that the Cardinal was the gull of a fiendishly clever adventuress.

To the first of these three possible interpretations the Queen herself, of course, subscribed. On September 19 she wrote to the Emperor Joseph:

The Cardinal has used my name like a vile and clumsy counterfeiter . . . The probability is that, temporarily pressed for cash, he thought he would be able to pay the jewelers the first installment without anyone's ever discovering the fraud . . . For my part, I am delighted to have heard the last of this horrid affair . . .

It seems impossible that even the "featherhead" could have been so flighty as to believe she had heard "the last of this horrid affair." At any rate, the Austrian Emperor did not share his sister's opinion on the score of the Cardinal's guilt in the Necklace Case, subscribing rather to theory number three, according to his letter of September 2 to Count Mercy at Versailles:

News having just reached me of the affair involving Prince Louis de Rohan, I am exceedingly annoyed, all the more so in view of the fact that the Queen is so disagreeably compromised in the matter.

I have always known the Grand Almoner to be the most frivolous and improvident of men, the worst spendthrift imaginable, but I must admit that I would never have believed him capable of a swindle or of misconduct as grave as that of which he stands accused. . . .

"Of course, as concerns Cardinal Rohan's associates, I could believe anything I heard. His is a character to which adventurers and adventuresses might precisely be expected to appeal," Emperor Joseph later remarked to the French ambassador to Vienna, Count de Noailles, —and was quoted by the latter in a prompt (September 5) dispatch to his superior, Count de Vergennes.

As for that astute Minister of Foreign Affairs himself, he could not agree with Emperor Joseph in subscribing to theory number three, although he does not make clear which of the other two he leaned toward. "It is a rare occasion when a man of such intelligence as the Cardinal is so easily duped," Vergennes wrote to Count de Noailles on August 22; and again on August 31: "It is simply inconceivable that the Cardinal could have been as easily taken in as he claims to have been."

Count Beugnot, who said that those who tried to make the Cardinal out an imbecile were wrong, for "that he assuredly was not," was critical of the technique of the criminal procedure in the case (a criticism that is significant in view of the fact that Beugnot would himself one day serve as director general of the national police under Louis XVIII):

From the very beginning, I could never understand Baron de Breteuil's conduct of the case. With Cardinal Rohan's arrest on August 15 and his charge that a woman named the Countess de La Motte-Valois had tricked him, there was no excuse for delay. Twenty-four hours should have sufficed to arrest her in Bar-sur-Aube, whereas, with the advance notice given her at Clairvaux, she—if only she had taken advantage of it—could easily have made her escape, leaving the Cardinal in truly desperate straits.

But to go on with the story: Madame de La Motte was arrested—no one else. Not until five days later did the police show up to seize her husband—as if he, warned by her fate, would have sat quietly at home, packing his kit for the Bastille! And not until eight days after his flight to England did the authorities get around to the diamonds, coming to Bar-sur-Aube to look for them—apparently in the hope of finding none, for how could anyone imagine that Monsieur de La Motte, with ample time to execute his plans, would not have carried them off with him or deposited them in a secure hiding place?

So much for Bar-sur-Aube. In Paris, Villette, the Countess's confidential secretary in chief, the most imprudent, lethargic, slow-moving of men, was allowed time and enough to get across the border to Switzerland; and even Father Loth, that shameless monk, the Countess's confidential assistant secretary, was given opportunity to bury himself under an assumed name in some remote monastery of his order.

How explain such conduct of the case on the part of Baron de Breteuil? Is some portion of the blame attributable to the extraordinary incompetence of Lieutenant General de Crosne, a kind but gullible fellow? One fact is incontestable: The notorious necklace affair in its very earliest stages was handled by the Minister with such ineptitude as to justify the Cardinal's supporters in their supposition that Baron de Breteuil had managed it expressly as a triumph over his hated enemy. I myself have reason to believe it to have been one of the two motivating factors. . . .

Suppose, on the other hand, that the case had been handled with intelligence and decisiveness. As early as the fifteenth of August, arrest orders would have been issued, in Paris, for the Countess's two secretaries and all persons intimately associated with the household. By the sixteenth, at Bar-sur-Aube, Monsieur and Madame de La Motte would have been seized along with all their jewels, papers, relatives and boon companions. Once the whole lot of them had been rounded up in the Bastille, the investigation might have proceeded smoothly and expeditiously enough.

They would have found, for instance, in Madame de La Motte's jewel case a certain *bonbonnière* which I had admired a dozen times: a round tortoise-shell box encircled by a band of enormous diamonds, evenly matched and perfect in color; the lid, on which a rising sun was painted, would fly up at the touch of a certain secret spring to reveal a portrait of the Queen in the very costume and pose assumed by Mademoiselle d'Oliva in the Grove of Venus scene.*

MEMOIRS
OF THE ABBÉ GEORGEL

The investigative commission appointed by the King, which consisted of Police Lieutenant General de Crosne and three Cabinet ministers, proceeding to an examination of the Cardinal's papers, discovered absolutely nothing pertinent to the necklace—a factor contributing to Baron de Breteuil's ill humor.

Meanwhile, at the Bastille, Lieutenant General de Crosne began taking depositions from Madame de La Motte, Count Cagliostro and the Baron da Planta. The last two both showed great reserve in their statements to avoid being implicated in a case with such connotations as to render the end results unforeseeable.

One of the three Cabinet ministers appointed by the King to his investigative commission in the Rohan case was the Marine Minister, Marshal de Castries,† whose journal (a day-by-day account dictated to his secretary, and thus in the third person) carries this report under the dateline of Friday, August 19:

On August 19 Cardinal Rohan sent word from the Bastille that he wanted to talk to the Count de Vergennes and the Marshal de Cas-

---

* Something Beugnot did not know was that the bonbonnière was found in the search of the La Motte house at Bar-sur-Aube, according to a report by Police Inspector Surbois—"a candy box with a miniature of the Queen on the lid . . . we had been ordered to seize it and to remove the portrait." The bonbonnière was not listed among the other personal effects put up later at public auction. If an order to search for it had been issued, the existence of the object must have been known to the authorities.

† This same Marshal de Castries had preceded the blackhearted Marquis d'Autichamps as commander of the Count de La Motte's cavalry corps at Lunéville four years previously when the Countess came there as a bride. His promotion to the Cabinet post had deprived La Motte of his best friend in the corps; Castries' removal was, in the Countess's words, "one of the first in our long series of misfortunes."

tries . . . He excluded Baron de Breteuil, his ancient enemy, who was proving himself such in this affair . . .

The Cardinal, upon seeing the two Cabinet ministers, inquired of them, "But in the event my revelations might compromise another, what, then, would be my duty?"

"To tell the truth," replied Monsieur de Castries. "We will take down your statement in writing; it shall serve as basis for the entire investigation and procedure. It shall serve either to clear you or to inculpate you . . ."

"Very well, then," said the Cardinal, "I will tell you the whole story."

MEMOIRS
OF THE ABBÉ GEORGEL

Monseigneur the Cardinal wrote out his statement covering the events which he had interpreted as authorization for the necklace purchase. His simple recital of facts was truthful in every detail; his reticence on the subject of the little letters on gilt-edged notepaper was a precautionary measure dictated by discretion, rather than a guilty omission. If he decided to make no reference to the correspondence which had motivated his actions, it was because this appeared to him too delicate a point to mention and he wished to avoid compromising the name of the Queen unnecessarily.

JOURNAL
OF MARSHAL DE CASTRIES

"So there, gentlemen," said the Cardinal, "is the whole story and all the facts—the exact truth."

"But," said Monsieur de Castries, "have you no receipt [for the necklace], no letters to support your story?"

"No," the Cardinal replied. "I burned them all."

"But," inquired the Marshal, "what if Madame de La Motte-Valois denies your account?"

"She will not dare deny it," said the Cardinal. "Not when we meet face to face. However," he continued, "we will soon know what she has to say, since I hear that she has been arrested and brought here within the last few hours." Whereupon he inquired whether this was so.

To this the ministers (although they knew very well that she had actually been brought to the Bastille that very night) replied that they could tell him nothing about it.

At her very first interrogation Madame de La Motte gave the case an unexpected development by blaming the whole business on Cagliostro. Her depositions were in direct contradiction to those of the Cardinal. . . .

On Thursday, August 25, the King summoned Marshal de Castries, Count de Vergennes, Baron de Breteuil and the Keeper of the Seals [Miromesnil]. The Queen, who was present, told the conference, "I am compromised in this case. It seems to be the consensus that I received a necklace for which I have not paid. I want to discover the truth of this matter in which someone has dared to use my name. The Cardinal's family seems to want the case tried by a regularly constituted court of justice. It is likewise my wish that the matter be referred to the Parliament of Paris for judgment."

This remark was received in total silence. Finally, Monsieur de Castries, although not called upon to speak, took the floor and said, "Since the preliminary investigation of the case has been initiated through extrajudiciary channels, it seems to me it would be well so to continue, and I am of the opinion that a confrontation of the prisoners would serve to clarify the situation promptly."

"But it would be very embarrassing," the Keeper of the Seals interposed, "to deal with a cardinal in this way. It is simply going too far to confront a cardinal with other witnesses."

"I don't see why," Monsieur de Castries replied. "It is against my own best interests to persist, for the moment this case is transferred to the regular courts it would be out of the jurisdiction of the Cabinet ministers—and, from a selfish point of view, that is the best thing that could happen to us. But, thinking of the national interests, I feel strongly that temperate action should be our course . . ."

Monsieur de Vergennes had little to say during this meeting, but it was clear that he agreed with me . . .

Marshal de Castries was right. Vergennes had already expressed himself to the King to the effect that Louis should in this instance act as

supreme *judge, as was his right*—rather than turn the *case over to
Parliament and to national publicity*—as is *evidenced by an autographed
letter from the King to Vergennes:*

I have weighed your reasons. Come tomorrow before Mass, and I will
hear you once more upon this subject. It is necessary that a decision be
arrived at so as to conclude this intrigue initiated by a man in financial
straits, who has so scandalously compromised the name of the Queen,
and who, in order to clear himself, has no other recourse than to allege
his connection with an adventuress of the worst sort. He dishonors his
ecclesiastical character. He may be a cardinal, but he is none the less a
subject of the Crown.

JOURNAL
OF MARSHAL DE CASTRIES

Baron de Breteuil spoke not a word at the Cabinet meeting.
"Very well," the Queen resumed, "it is my opinion that the choice
should be left to the Cardinal. Let him confer with all his family and
come to a decision as to whether the case should be judged by the King
or by the courts; let him present his request to the King in writing
so that, whichever method of justice he chooses, we may get on with the
matter promptly, for it is one in which my name is compromised."
Whereupon the King said to Monsieur de Castries, "You will go,
then, tomorrow, with Monsieur de Vergennes—and Baron de Breteuil
too—to submit this choice to the Cardinal. I shall expect his reply
within three days."
The King's ministers then went to the Bastille. The Cardinal's face
remained expressionless as he heard them state that Madame de La
Motte flatly denied ever receiving the necklace, ever so much as mentioning having known or been associated with the Queen. The Cardinal maintained his composure as he listened to the ministers report that
Madame de La Motte had contradicted his entire account of the sequence of events.
But "Oh, my God," he cried at last, "if only I were granted permission to be confronted with that woman face to face, I am positive that
I could make her admit the truth!"

STORY OF MY LIFE
BY THE COUNTESS DE LA MOTTE-VALOIS

The Cardinal's perfidy (if it was true that he had actually imputed the necklace theft to me) disgusted me, but, even so, I had an idea that Baron de Breteuil was resolved upon the Cardinal's ruin; and knowing full well that the Queen had sworn him her undying hatred, I could clearly see that I was to be used as the tool to serve the hatred of the one and the vengeance of the other.

Lieutenant General de Crosne insisted that I sign the deposition he dictated to me. Seeing my reluctance to betray the Cardinal, he said, "Very well, then, madame, I suppose I shall have to tell you that it is the Baron de Breteuil himself who invites you to follow this plan in order that the Queen not be compromised in the affair."

"But what will happen, then, to me? Will it not be said that I have wickedly tricked the Cardinal?"

"Absolutely not, madame. At any rate, I assure you that we will see to it that you are cleared of blame, that it will be the Cardinal upon whom it falls. I undertake personally to safeguard your interests. . . ."

MEMOIRS
OF THE ABBÉ GEORGEL

The ministerial commission returned shortly to the Bastille to announce to the Cardinal that, with Madame de La Motte's deposition directly contradicting his, the King was unable to reach a conclusion as to the facts, and therefore offered the Cardinal a choice: either to throw himself upon the mercy of the King as supreme judge of the nation or to take his case before the judges of the Parliament of Paris, there to defend himself against the indictment to be drawn up against him and Madame de La Motte. The King accorded him three days in which to arrive at a decision.

Madame de La Motte's unexpected and disastrous betrayal revealed her as either a witch who had viciously deceived him or a tool in the hands of some powerful enemy determined on his ruin. In either case, the Cardinal could see only dishonor, or perchance even the scaffold, confronting him unless he could succeed in establishing proof of the facts as he knew them.

His Eminence's most dread concern was for the letters he had turned over to Madame de La Motte for delivery to the Queen. When he wrote them, his conviction that the Queen had authorized open expression of his sentiments had given rise to a freedom of thought and emotion which, while not transgressing the bounds of respect, might well be misinterpreted.

If Madame de La Motte, he reasoned, is a monster of ingratitude who took advantage of my trust to appropriate the necklace, she surely plans to escape retribution by forcing me to silence through the threat of exposing these letters of mine, which (in response to the encouragement in the messages she had previously transmitted to me) naturally include certain expressions on my part which are bound to bring down upon my head the wrath of the King and Queen. If, however, Madame de La Motte is only a tool in the hands of my enemies, then these letters, already in their possession, will ensure their triumph over me; in the opinion of the public I will stand convicted of criminal temerity, whereas, led on by the graciousness and cordiality of the Queen, I was only respectfully familiar. In this dreadful dilemma, if I throw myself upon the mercy of the King I can hope at best for exile and loss of my court positions; and since it would be a secret trial, I must inevitably suffer in public opinion, because I would not be permitted to publish the facts of the case.

Monseigneur the Cardinal chose to make a detailed account of all the circumstances preceding and contributing to his disaster in my presence and in that of his staff of attorneys, chief counsel Target,* Maître de Bonnières and Maître Tronchet, the greatest legal lights of their day, and Maîtres Collet, Laget-Bardelin and de Préameneu. His legal advisers did not minimize the dangers inherent in entrusting himself to the clemency of a youthful king who was necessarily influenced by an outraged and beloved wife as well as by a vindictive minister. On the

---

* Chief counsel Target, an ugly giant of a man, renowned both as an athlete and as a savant, was the first lawyer in 150 years to be elected to membership in the French Academy and was so distinguished an orator that Dr. Franklin made a point of attending court on the days he pleaded before the bar. Target later was one of the chief authors of the new French Republic's constitution, and in 1792 he refused (on grounds of age) to serve in the defense of Louis XVI before the National Assembly —a defense undertaken, hopeless though it was, by Maître Tronchet, who was ten years Target's senior.

other hand, they could not but sketch a fearsome picture of the severe, protracted and humiliating procedure of criminal court cases.

Vacillating thus themselves, his legal counsel dared not influence the Cardinal's decision. They told him, "If we can find and produce evidence of your innocence, then trial by Parliament is preferable; but if your powerful enemies in government block our efforts to establish such proof, then it would be better to throw yourself upon the King's mercy. You must consult your own courage and your own conscience in reaching this decision."

Monseigneur Cardinal Rohan himself drew up his reply to the King; it was brief and noble:

> SIRE,
>
> I had hoped, through the method of direct confrontation with the other accused and with witnesses, to have secured proof whereby to demonstrate conclusively to Your Majesty that I was merely the dupe of the fraudulent machinations of others; in which case, I would have asked no other judge than Your Majesty in all your well-known justice and mercy. But since denial of the privilege of confrontation has deprived me of such a hope, I accept with respectful gratitude Your Majesty's permission to prove my innocence by the regular judicial processes. Consequently, I beseech your Majesty to issue the orders necessary to refer my case to the judgment of the Parliament of Paris, before a joint session of the Grand' Chambre and the Tournelle.*
>
> If, however, even now I could hope that further clarification of the issue might convince Your Majesty of my innocence of any implication in the case beyond that of having been cruelly deceived, then I would of course implore Your Majesty to pronounce such judgment personally out of your ineffable kindness and sense of justice.
>
> My cousins, in accord with me in this decision, have added their signatures to this letter along with mine.

---

* Two Parliament courts which adjudicated criminal cases. The Grand' Chambre derived its name from the Great Hall of the Palais de Justice, where it sat; the Tournelle was so called because its sessions were originally held in a small tower (tournelle) of the Palais. In cases involving important personages the two courts deliberated together.

THE TRIAL

CARDINAL DE ROHAN

ROHAN, PRINCE DE MONTBAZON
PRINCE DE ROHAN, ARCHBISHOP OF CAMBRAI
MARSHAL PRINCE DE SOUBISE

One of the ministers of the investigative commission has since admitted to me that the court had not expected such bold resolution from the Cardinal; that the King, and above all the Queen, appeared disturbed because of the sensational publicity that the juridical process would entail. Louis XVI must additionally have been reluctant to play the role of accuser, for by doing so he would make a spectacle of himself in the eyes of his people and of all Europe; and by invoking the vengeance of the law against the presumed authors of outrages to the name and dignity of the Queen he would make a spectacle of himself before a tribunal of which he himself was the lawgiver and the sovereign. It was tantamount to relinquishing his sovereign power to struggle in the judicial arena against one of his own subjects.

Thus it was that the King referred the case to his Parliament of Paris, to the Grand' Chambre and the Tournelle in joint session.

Letters patent signed by Louis XVI and countersigned by Minister de Breteuil at St.-Cloud on September 5, 1785, and registered with the Parliament of Paris on September 6:

We have been informed that two men named Böhmer and Bassenge are supposed to have sold a diamond necklace to Cardinal Rohan; that the aforementioned Cardinal, unbeknownst to the Queen, our very dear wife and companion, is supposed to have declared himself authorized by her to make the purchase at a price of 1,600,000 francs, payable in installments at regularly scheduled intervals; and that, to that intent and purpose, he is supposed to have shown Böhmer and Bassenge certain so-called terms of purchase as having been approved and signed by the Queen; that the aforementioned necklace having been delivered by the aforementioned Böhmer and Bassenge to the aforementioned Cardinal, and the first payment date agreed between them not having been met, they thought to have recourse to the Queen . . . Not without a righteous indignation have we been able to contemplate such an unheard-of temerity, such an audacious effort to trade on an august name (a name dear to us on so many counts), such a daring violation of the respect due the royal majesty.

We deemed it only just on our part to summon before us the afore-mentioned Cardinal; and upon his statement that he had been deceived by a woman named La Motte de Valois, we judged it indispensable to seize his person and that of the aforementioned Madame de La Motte de Valois, and to take such other measures as our wisdom dictated, for the purpose of discovering all those who might have been authors and accomplices in such a plot; and we have deemed it appropriate to refer the case to you, for investigation and for trial by you, the Grand' Cham-bre and the Tournelle in joint session.

MEMOIRS
OF THE ABBÉ GEORGEL

The King charged his prosecutor general, Joly de Fleury, to enter complaint in his name against Cardinal Rohan and Madame de La Motte, accusing them as authors and agents of criminal maneuvers tend-ing to compromise the honor and dignity of his wife, the Queen; to secure evidence on all the facts as advanced in his complaint; and, in compliance with all necessary legal formalities, to proceed to trial and judgment.

This is a summary of the voluminous charges presented to the Parlia-ment of Paris by the prosecutor general.

MEMOIRS
OF MADAME CAMPAN

Oh, fatal moment, when the Queen would find herself in open con-test with one of her own subjects, upon whom justice should have been pronounced by the King alone, the King himself, as sovereign and su-preme judge and lawgiver! But in the confusion around the royal coun-cil table, false standards of equity, poor judgment and blind hatred com-bined upon a course of action undermining both royal authority and national morale.

Napoleon, in 1818, with plenty of time for musing on St. Helena, would analyze other rulers' mistakes (more caustically than his own), among them those of Louis XVI in the diamond necklace affair: "The Queen was innocent and, to ensure the greatest possible publicizing of the fact, wanted the Parliament of Paris to proclaim her innocence in its judgment. But instead, as it developed, she was deemed guilty and the monarchy discredited."

"It was Napoleon's opinion," adds General Gourgaud, from whose Sainte-Hélène the above quotation is taken, "that Louis XVI should have acted as supreme arbiter in that case, as was his right and privilege."

Napoleon's was an accurate diagnosis of Louis's greatest blunder, submitting the Diamond Necklace Case to his Parliament of Paris, his courts, for trial—literally his Parliament of Paris, his courts, his judges (appointed by him for life), for these regular juridical channels administered justice only by virtue of the powers delegated to them by the King. Traditionally and legally, the King was the first, last and supreme judge over his subjects. If ever a case called for the monarch's personal judication, it was this one where the honor and reputation of the monarch's own wife were at stake; if ever he should have performed—with expedition and delicacy—his traditional role of judge, it was in the Diamond Necklace Case, where the Queen of France's dignity and virtue had been compromised.

Baron de Breteuil, if not the King, should have sensed that the centuries-old hostility of the Parliament of Paris toward the throne had been intensified by recent clashes in Louis XVI's reign.

The parlements of France were, in actual fact, courts of justice only, appointive, not elective, bodies; in no sense, therefore, representative of the people, and with no trace of legislative power. One of the functions of the parlements was to keep a record of royal edicts and ordinances, to record or register any new law promulgated by the King, any new levy imposed by the King's Minister of Finance. This function of registering or recording or ratifying new legislation was construed by the Parliament of Paris as the right to interpret the fundamental legal code of the monarchy (in the sense that the Supreme Court of the United States interprets the Constitution—with the difference, of course, that no constitution had ever been promulgated in France); and the right to remonstrate, the refusal to record or ratify, came to constitute Parliament's sole means of defying the monarchy, a defiance that took the form of a national judiciary strike which paralyzed the law courts of the land.

The weaker the monarch, the more fractious the parlements became

—as with Louis XVI when they flatly refused to record or ratify the tax legislation proposed by a succession of his finance ministers; in this circumstance, Louis had recourse to the ancient royal prerogative of exiling such a refractory assembly.

A proud, hereditary caste system unto itself, this assembly of learned, wealthy judges seized, in 1786, upon the Diamond Necklace Trial as the opportunity to humiliate the King and to impair the arbitrary power of the King's Cabinet ministers.

As a contemporary, Count Beugnot displayed keen perspicacity in his analysis of the subtleties of the conflict between the Parliament of Paris and the Court of Versailles on the eve of the diamond necklace scandal:

It so happened that Count de Calonne, the King's Minister of Finance, had offended the Marquis d'Aligre, the president of the Parliament of Paris. The latter, while lacking the qualifications of a great jurist, was yet endowed with extraordinary talents of persuasiveness and leadership, with a singular dexterity in manipulating his company of fellow judges, and had thus since 1774 been able to assure a majority on the bench favorable to the Court of Versailles. On that basis, the ancient form of government might have endured for some time. But if in 1786 Aligre did not actually encourage an opposition party in the Parliament, he allowed it to form—an opposition party which found support, strangest of all, in Versailles itself, upon the very steps of the throne.*

At the time of the Rohan trial this opposition had not yet organized or coalesced, but it was certainly already in existence, awaiting only the opportunity to come out into the open. It might be said that the unfortunate Diamond Necklace Case constituted that party's first trial of strength, a strength so great as to have surprised the party itself and to have dealt a severe blow to the monarchy. History has proved how catastrophic was the aftermath of these first parliamentary maneuvers against the central government. Without an examination of these complex undercurrents of conflict, it is impossible to understand all the strange, devious and scandalous intrigues connected with the diamond necklace affair.

* Beugnot's reference here is to the King's brothers, the treacherous Count de Provence and Count d'Artois—the future kings Louis XVIII and Charles X—and to the King's still more dangerous cousin, the Duke d'Orléans (Philippe Égalité), father of France's last king, Louis Philippe.

While I was in Fontainebleau to attend the hearings on the Bar-sur-Aube litigation, Madame de La Motte's case was turned over to the Parliament of Paris. People were surprised that more summary judgment had not been pronounced, but there was reason to expect another example of severity, since the preamble of the letters patent by which the King formally conveyed the case to the Parliament flatly stated as fact that the Cardinal had purchased the diamond necklace in the name of the Queen and that he had been hoodwinked at the hands of Madame de La Motte. Thus on those points there appeared no further need for investigation by the Parliament; they must stand as irrefutable truths in that they had been so advanced by the King in his letters patent, and in that the letters patent had been accepted without any protest by the Parliament.

It is easy to see how absurd it was, under the principles of absolute monarchy, to expect the Parliament of Paris to debate or even to question the facts advanced by the King in the letters patent. To do so would constitute an affront to the principles of absolute monarchy; would verge, indeed, on the crime of lèse-majesté. The Parliament, in accepting the case under the letters patent and on the basis of the truth of the charges contained therein, was legally bound to proceed on the premise of the Cardinal's guilty involvement. The only question before the court was to ascertain the degree to which majesty had been offended.

The negotiations and purchase of the diamond necklace constituted more or less guilty machinations, but, in the last analysis, were merely common criminal expedients. The important fact that dominated the whole sordid business was this: that Monsieur and Madame de La Motte had had the audacity to pretend that the Queen of France, the wife of their sovereign, had granted a clandestine midnight rendezvous in the gardens of Versailles to Cardinal Rohan, had spoken to him, handed him a rose and allowed him to throw himself at her feet; and that, for his part, a cardinal, a ranking officer of the Crown, had dared to think that such a clandestine midnight rendezvous had been granted him by the Queen of France, the wife of his liege lord; that he had gone to keep that appointment, had accepted a rose and had thrown himself at her feet.

Therein lay the real crime, the outrage to Church, to royal majesty, to morality; as such, it called for swift, stern retribution. There might, indeed, still have been time to check, by a striking example of severity, the as yet almost imperceptible trend toward mockery of principles hitherto sacred. I was convinced that Madame de La Motte would draw the death penalty.

At ten o'clock one night, shortly after my return to Paris from Fontainebleau, a letter was delivered to me from Police Lieutenant General de Crosne, an invitation to present myself without delay at his offices.

I had no idea to what to attribute such a summons, but it gave me concern. I glanced at my Bastille overnight case, still packed, still in readiness at the foot of my bed, and I had an idea that this time I would be needing it. In view of the fact, however, that the case had been transferred into the hands of the Parliament, I could console myself with the thought that my imprisonment would not be of long duration.

I went directly to the police lieutenant general's office.

"Monsieur," he greeted me, "it is on the subject of Madame de La Motte that I wish to speak to you. I regret having disturbed you at this hour of the night, but I was in a hurry to see you." An opening gambit I could hardly consider reassuring! Then Monsieur de Crosne went on to say, "Madame de La Motte, whom I have just left, has chosen you as her defense counsel. Here is your pass for entry to the Bastille. I urge you to be there as soon as the gates are open, between nine and ten in the morning. That poor lady has not seen a friendly face in over two months now, and I have promised her that tomorrow morning without fail you will be there at her orders."

I thanked Monsieur de Crosne for his Bastille pass, but replied that I could not accept Madame de La Motte's choice of me as her barrister; that hers was a case of the gravest import, for which I had neither the necessary experience nor the talent. I remarked that it would be presumptuous on my part to undertake it, and that therefore I must decline.

Monsieur de Crosne insisted, arguing that if I felt I needed assistance (a theory to which he did not subscribe), I could call in as many of my colleagues as I chose; above all, he made a point of the fact that this was an affair which was bound to be so highly publicized as to ensure making the reputation of a young attorney. Waxing eloquent for perhaps the first time in his life, he yet failed in his effort to seduce me, and we parted.

The next day, another message from Monsieur de Crosne; another visit to his office.

This time he handed me a letter from Madame de La Motte, in which she stated that she could not understand why I was making such difficulties about taking her case and urgently requested me to come at least to discuss it with her. Monsieur de Crosne, in adding his own urging, observed that he could not but reach the conclusion that my refusal must be due to fear of the danger inherent in the proposed role of lawyer for the defense, and he sought to reassure me on that score, winding up with the request that I discuss it with Minister de Breteuil.

Again I demurred, this time on the grounds that I had nothing to say to Baron de Breteuil which I had not already said to him, Monsieur de Crosne, and that neither could the Minister persuade me to do what I had refused to do for the police lieutenant general.

Monsieur de Crosne, ever more insistent (for what reason, I cannot imagine), implied that a readier compliance on my part with the wishes of the authorities could not but be helpful in forwarding my political and legal career, his constant refrain consisting of the words "Go and have a little talk with the Minister," to which I protested that I could see no point in availing myself of that honor.

I left him after having requested his permission to send a letter in reply to that of Madame de La Motte's to me.

He must have later learned from one of his confidential agents with whom I went into greater detail on the matter that whereas I viewed the necklace chicanery as merely a sordid incident, I considered the impersonation of the Queen in the Grove of Venus scene to be a capital offense. It was in this same light, apparently, that he considered it, so it would have suited his book exactly to have had Madame de La Motte's legal counsel share his views on the subject.

I wrote my letter of reply to Madame de La Motte, basing my refusal solely on my lack of experience and talent for so serious an affair; but I added that any further insistence on her part would be vain, because my refusal came as the dictate of my conscience and was thus unalterable.

And that was the last I heard from her or from Monsieur de Crosne.

In my stead, Police Lieutenant General de Crosne recommended Maître Doillot, his own family lawyer, to serve as defense attorney to Madame de La Motte.

Did Beugnot suspect that Monsieur de Crosne had succumbed—yet another victim—to the vaunted charms of Madame de La Motte?

Her remarks, taken in conjunction with Beugnot's, sound suspiciously like it:

Justice demands that I make clear that Police Lieutenant General de Crosne conducted himself toward me with all the delicacy and consideration which any unfortunate soul in custody of the law has a right to expect. And, incidentally, let this statement stand as rebuttal to my enemies' criticism that I never have a kind word to say about anyone!

"The Cardinal has already chosen a large staff of lawyers," Monsieur de Crosne advised me. "It is high time you selected your legal counsel. Baron de Breteuil suggests this list of renowned attorneys for your consideration." Whereupon he handed me a letter apparently written by Baron de Breteuil himself. In fact, the Minister seemed to take a particular interest in my case, and I rather imagine it was he who had recommended me to Monsieur de Crosne's good graces.

All in all, this visit from the head of the police seemed to augur well for my future, and it left me in an optimistic mood. Reassured as to my fate by my innocence and by the talents of my prospective defender, from that moment on I reconciled myself more and more to my situation. Peace of mind had succeeded to anxiety. I laughed, I sang away the days, as if I were anywhere at all rather than the Bastille.

As gay as all that? It must have been in the course of this same interview that Crosne told Madame de La Motte that Beugnot had refused to undertake her defense, breaking a promise made in the heyday of their romantic interlude, when, in his own words, he promised to "reserve my good will and zeal to serve her until such time as she would have an important case to take before a court of law—words of mine which Madame de La Motte apparently never forgot, for two years later, from the depths of the Bastille, she would write to remind me of that promise and hold me to it, asking me to defend her . . ." Unblushingly Beugnot quotes himself and his broken promise in his memoirs—but then, young Beugnot had his political career to think of, and early experience in the great world had proved that this is not most expeditiously accomplished by the espousal of unpopular causes. Quick as Madame de La Motte was, generally, to vivid denunciation of the fair-weather friends who turned their faces away from her in her peril and agony, she makes not so much as a mention anywhere of

Beugnot's repudiation of her and of his own promise. For that matter, there is not so much as a mention of his name to be found throughout all her numerous volumes.

MEMOIRS
OF COUNT BEUGNOT

Doillot had been in practice before the Paris bar for many, many years, and not without renown. Deep in his sixties or beyond, he had retired to his study, where he was still consulted as an eminent jurist.

Even a sage old gentleman such as this could not with impunity survive close contact with the Countess de La Motte. She completely turned his head. He believed implicitly all the tales she spun him, became emotionally involved with his client and put up an impassioned defense of her innocence, making his debut in the case with the publication of a trial brief, the most extravagant defense plea ever to flow from the pen of an attorney in all the years since attorneys first began composing defense pleas. Fantastic as a tale out of *The Arabian Nights*, it enjoyed, nonetheless, a sensational success. And to think that it was the composition of a venerable white-wig of seventy summers!

MEMOIRS
OF THE COUNTESS DE LA MOTTE-VALOIS

My defense plea created quite a stir in Paris.

Doillot, my barrister, had finally convinced me that I must reveal the truth and lay the blame where it belonged, upon the Cardinal. Doillot's insistence, above all, that I deny my intimacy with the Queen and never so much as breathe her name led me to surmise that this line of defense had been suggested to him by Her Majesty through Baron de Breteuil.

"You will be lost," Monsieur Doillot warned me, "if you do not follow my advice. Where would you be without Her Majesty's protection? You will be a mere insect to be crushed beneath her foot if you allow your loyalty to the Cardinal to blind you to the necessity of protecting yourself." ·

Monsieur Doillot more than once barely escaped assassination. He had been warned to be on his guard lest the Cardinal's family make him rue the day he had agreed to undertake my defense.

On December 4, 1785, he published my first trial brief, which aroused so keen an interest throughout Paris that he had to call in the police to keep order among the crowds around his house during the distribution. The reader can guess at the furor when I say that in one week my attorney passed out ten thousand copies gratis, and that he issued three thousand more in response to written requests—not to mention five thousand copies sold by the printers.

A furor indeed, as confirmed by that week's issue of Observations de Père Tranquille ("Father Tranquil's Comments"), one of the most popular broadsheets peddled by the newshawkers on the Paris streets:

Never having been the kind of man who is in such a hurry for the news as to be willing to fight my way through a crowd or get myself smothered or trampled to death just for the privilege of buying the latest edition, there I was, yesterday, going along quietly minding my own business, when where should I find myself but on the very block where Lawyer Doillot lives.

All of a sudden, up rushes a law clerk, panting, sweating, to inquire breathlessly, "Monsieur, did you get one? Are there any left?" Upon my reply that I neither knew nor cared, my man went dashing off . . .

As I turned the corner of that cursed street, I narrowly missed being run down by a doctor's carriage, Aesculapius shrieking loudly enough to burst his lungs, "Stop, coachman, stop! Right there in front of Doillot's door—over there!"

And no sooner had I recovered from that fright than a cabriolet brushed by me so closely as to fray the cloth of my jacket sleeve. Cursing that damned Doillot and that damned trial brief of his, I congratulated myself on having got clear of the mob, when still another fellow accosted me.

"Sir," he cried, "no need to ask what mission brings you here. Just tell me, did you succeed in getting one?"

On my word of honor, at that point you would have thought, like me, that what they were handing out in front of Doillot's door was not a legal document but a fifty-franc gold piece to every Frenchman who could prove he had use for one.

According to the Abbé Georgel, Doillot's defense plea for Madame de La Motte was "a tissue of lies, of striking improbabilities, contradictions and anachronisms." (An opinion in which Doillot's own brother, a notary at the Châtelet Court, concurred: "The man has either gone stark raving mad or Madame de La Motte has bewitched him as she did the Cardinal!") Fuming, the abbé writes in his memoirs:

Nevertheless, her formal denial of all the facts which constituted the Cardinal's sole defense, the tone of confidence and effrontery characterizing this publication, the self-assurance and boisterous gaiety displayed by the woman even behind bars—all this heightened the anxiety of the Cardinal's counselors and defenders.

This *mémoire* of Madame de La Motte's was widely distributed among the populace and won many partisans.

It was a curious custom, this one of printing and publishing a legal mémoire (memorial)—a trial brief, or defense plea, technically addressed by the defense counsel to "Our Lords of the Parliament," formally registered with the court and forming an integral part of the dossier of the trial—and of selling copies or distributing them gratis to the public months before the judges ever took their seats upon the bench to begin deliberations on the case.

But then, the whole tradition of jurisprudence of the ancien régime seems strange to twentieth-century eyes. The procedure in a criminal case was essentially secret—and remained thus, in France, as late as 1897. The defendant had to face the examining magistrates alone, unsupported by legal talent; the witness, likewise, was called upon to appear alone to make his deposition. According to an ordinance of 1670, "The accused, regardless of rank, will be expected to make his response to questioning by the magistrates without benefit of legal counsel, which is not necessarily permitted him even after confrontation with other accused and with witnesses," and legal commentary on this ordinance indicates that no exceptions were made, not even for personages of the loftiest station, not even for dukes or princes.

Scarcely any parallel may be said to exist between the ancien régime's curious concept of the role of defense counsel and our own present-day interpretation of the lawyer's function. No defense counsel was permitted to attend his client's interrogations in a criminal case;

the examining magistrate conducted the investigation, as it was intended, in utmost secrecy. The defense counsel, generally speaking, did not obtain access to the facts and the evidence of the case until the inquiry was concluded, and not always then. Ignorant of the developments of the preliminary judicial proceedings, the attorney. had nevertheless to draw up a trial brief for his client, basing it on what meager information he could garner through the indiscretions of magistrates or the venality of court clerks and reporters. Quotations from as yet unreleased depositions or confessions might appear in the form of such circumlocutions as "the witness is supposed to have said . . . ," "the defendant is reported to have claimed . . ."

It was the custom, in important cases, for a succession of trial briefs to be published for each client—at no specified phase, no regular interval in the procedure, but haphazardly, sporadically, when and if surreptitious information leaked out from the closed courtroom to the ears of the counselor at law. The purpose of these publications was, of course, to ensure maximum publicity for the case and for the client and to stir up public sympathy for the defendant, since public opinion exercised an inevitable influence on the parliaments.

Considerable public sympathy was stirred up by the Countess's first trial brief, which presented her as (in Georgel's words) "the innocent victim of intrigue and cupidity."

TRIAL BRIEF
FOR THE COUNTESS DE LA MOTTE-VALOIS

It is upon the unsupported statement of Cardinal Rohan that the Countess de La Motte-Valois has been implicated. As the sole complainant, it will be up to him to prove his accusations that she stole the diamond necklace.

The depositions of the jewelers show clearly that throughout the negotiations they dealt solely with the Cardinal, never with the Countess. He it was who showed them the contract with the notations "Approved" and the signature "Marie Antoinette de France." As if a cardinal, a prince of the house of Rohan, an expert courtier, could be ignorant of the fact that the Queen never signed thus!

And what could be more patently absurd than Cardinal Rohan's claim that he looked to the Countess for intercession with the Queen—

to a woman so obscure as never to have attained to the honor of a court presentation? (Not that the qualifications of name and rank were lacking; rather, the fortune was insufficient to finance so costly a formality.)

An allegation still more preposterous: that the Countess de La Motte arranged for the Cardinal—guess what? An audience with the Queen! Where? In the park of Versailles. When? In the month of July, 1785, at the hour of midnight, mind you—a grossly indecent suggestion. Now, really, a man of the Cardinal's rank and position, a prince of the Church and of the realm, the King's own Grand Almoner, the first officer of the Crown, to look to an obscure woman such as this for presentation to his sovereign!

MEMOIRS
OF THE ABBÉ GEORGEL

Personally, I am convinced that Madame de La Motte spoke a highly significant truth when she hinted that Cagliostro, beyond any other man alive, held the key to the enigma: knowledge of the secret motives behind it all. . . .

TRIAL BRIEF
FOR THE COUNTESS DE LA MOTTE-VALOIS

Last April the Countess de La Motte was introduced by the Cardinal into a veritable witches' Sabbath in the Cardinal's own boudoir in the Palais-Cardinal, a somber spectacle in eerie light, having as its object the final disposition of the necklace diamonds.

Kneeling before a table laden with cabalistic symbols, with crucifixes of every shape and kind, with crossed swords and daggers, was the innocent young medium, the Countess's own niece, Mademoiselle de Latour. . . . The Cardinal was in ecstasy at the feet of the magician, kissing his hands. . . .

"You shall see," he said to Madame de La Motte, "what miracles this man can perform; he has strange powers, but if you dare speak of these mysteries you will discover to your sorrow that he has the power not only of good but of evil."

"Swear, madame!" said the prophet in his most oracular tone of voice, laying his naked sword upon the head of the kneeling medium. "Swear upon this cross that you will never speak of the scene you are about to witness." And then to the Cardinal, "Go now, Prince, go now to fetch the diamonds."

Upon these words, Prince de Rohan ran to pick up a large white box and laid it open on the desecrated altar. "Your husband is to take these stones," he said to the Countess de La Motte, "and dispose of them in England. . . ."

MEMOIRS
OF THE ABBÉ GEORGEL

Lacking all evidence beyond the Cardinal's own unsupported story, we had to stand silently by while the tide of public sympathy flowed strongly in Madame de La Motte's direction.

We had pitifully few facts upon which to base the Cardinal's case: the Count's trip to England shortly after the necklace transfer, the La Mottes' sudden transition from poverty to affluence, the Baron da Planta's knowledge of the Grove of Venus scene . . .

Saint-James's and the jewelers' depositions, copies of which I managed to obtain despite the government's efforts to keep them from us, served only to further embarrass the Cardinal's attorneys, for the reason that they charged the Prince without in any way inculpating Madame de La Motte.

The legal staff, which met daily, agreed that it was impossible to plan a strategy of defense until we had settled with the jewelers, to prevent their bringing civil suit against the Cardinal for payment of the necklace or testifying against him at the trial. It was only proper that the Cardinal should pay for the necklace; nor did he ever hesitate upon that point. The difficulty consisted in getting Böhmer and Bassenge to agree to terms proportionate to His Eminence's present financial situation, in persuading them to accept an assignment of 300,000 francs yearly on his revenues from the Abbey of St. Waast until the capital debt and the interest had been paid in full.

Finally I concluded such a settlement with the jewelers. This done, there were the cries of still other creditors to be stilled, for the Prince's indebtedness at that period amounted to over two million francs.

Wielding extensive powers and acting in concert with the princes of the house of Rohan, I effected great reforms in the Cardinal's various establishments, reduced the household expenses in both Paris and Alsace to the barest minimum and made arrangements with the creditors for the gradual liquidation of the debts. As a result of these arrangements, a revenue of eighty thousand francs remained to the Cardinal. The liquidation plan called for payments to begin in January 1786 and to continue until 1794, at which time the Prince, totally disencumbered of debt, would see his vast revenues restored to him.

I have learned since that the Cardinal, upon his return to Alsace from exile, reproached me my arrangements; but, at the time, the schedule was adopted out of dire necessity. Ah! Was it nothing that I had managed to wipe out such a crushing indebtedness? It meant, of course, a reduction in his personal income over an eight-year period, but with a heart so noble, with sensibilities so keen as his could he ever actually have enjoyed his full income amidst a din and clamor such as his creditors would have put up?

As if there were not complexities enough confronting us, this was the moment chosen by the Pope to write to signify his extreme displeasure with Prince de Rohan for having compromised the dignities and rights of the Sacred College, for having besmirched the Roman purple by submitting to a secular tribunal rather than to the mercy of the King. The Supreme Pontiff added that this blow to the august prerogatives of the cardinalate might force him to strike the Prince's name from that roster.

Consternation spread through the house of Rohan at the threat of such a blemish to a name long revered in the Sacred College. Still more important, such action on the part of the Pope would be highly prejudicial to the Cardinal's cause at a trial in which not only his honor but his life might be at stake.

The Cardinal could well justify his action to the Pope. He had not failed to lay claim to the privileges of the Sacred College and to his rights as a bishop; he had petitioned the King for trial before an ecclesiastical court, albeit in vain. At first there was talk of sending me to Rome to present the case for him, but the Cardinal's family and legal staff decreed that my presence was too urgently needed in Paris. Instead, I managed to persuade Count de Vergennes, the Minister of Foreign Affairs, to use his good offices in Rome to plead with the Pope to suspend judgment until satisfactory explanation and apology could be made by Cardinal Prince de Rohan. His Holiness finally agreed to postpone a report on the matter to the Sacred College.*

The prospect of adverse action in Rome might well have dismayed Cardinal Rohan, but no one was in a better position than I to judge how heroically he met the peril.

His Eminence had by now restored me to his full confidence. I saw him twice daily and reported to him all my actions and the results of all my investigations. Often we dined together tête-à-tête, discussing affairs while we ate, a precious time-saving device during those arduous days. It was from him alone, from his explanations and recollections, that I could hope to discover the thread that would lead us out of the dark maze in which we were blindly groping.

I had never been a man of robust constitution, yet, during those seven months preceding my exile, I found myself charged with both the spiritual and the temporal administration of the Grand Almoner-ship and the Quinze-Vingts, the bishopric of Strasbourg and the abbeys of St. Waast and Chaise-Dieu, as well as the management of the Prince's personal affairs and the daily correspondence with the govern-ment ministers, the judges, the lawyers and the Prince's family, who honored me with their confidence. In pursuance of my errands in a single day, I usually required six or seven horses. With the assistance of two secretaries, and by limiting myself to three or four hours of sleep, I was able to encompass it all. A man's zeal and devotion redouble his physical and spiritual stamina when the life and the honor of a person to whom he is attached are, so to speak, entrusted to his vigilance.

* Pope Pius VI's opinion on Cardinal Rohan's involvement in the diamond necklace scandal comes to us through a report from Cardinal Bernis, France's ambassador to the Vatican. According to Bernis, the Pope made no effort to defend Cardinal Rohan, but he did tell Bernis that his correspondents indicated that whereas Car-dinal Rohan was a man who might well have been guilty of frivolity and blindly misplaced confidence, it seemed inconceivable to them that he could have com-mitted an actual crime. The powerful Rohans managed to circumvent drastic action against their cousin in the Sacred College; twenty-six cardinals in solemn conclave on February 13, 1786, voted merely to suspend their fellow member from the exer-cise of his cardinalic rights and privileges.

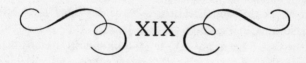

XIX

Witnesses, Defense Pleas

and New Evidence

(Late Fall 1785)

LETTER FROM THE PARIS CORRESPONDENT
OF THE IMPERIAL COURT OF ST. PETERSBURG

> Prince Rohan, clad in his cloak of red,
> Was called to the Vatican for a chat.
> Asked the Pope, "If you've lost your head,
> Where will you wear your cardinal's hat?"

So goes the popular jingle that has been put to music and is sung, whistled, hummed all around the town, this verse and a dozen more. The incorrigibly frivolous Parisians follow the Necklace Case and Trial in typically Gallic style, making of it a vaudeville, a satirical song.

The affair of the Cardinal is the sole object of public interest; no one here any longer cares what goes on in the rest of the world. The Cardinal's friends are worried; the case seems to be going against him. One rumor is that he conceived a criminal and audacious passion for his charming sovereign, and that thus it was easy to persuade him that his homage, in the form of the gift of the diamond necklace, would be acceptable to her. The poor Cardinal seems to have been the dupe of the scoundrels that surrounded him.

The secret history of the Roman emperors offers few examples of excesses such as those in which Cardinal Rohan has indulged. In Paris alone he maintained twelve love nests, which were the scene of orgies to shock the most licentious. He has dissipated his substance— physical, spiritual and material—in vain pursuit of the evanescent pleasures of the flesh. One of his favorite (and most costly) erotic divertissements was the private staging of Aretino's lascivious comedies with prima donnas of the Comédie Italienne so prominent that their performance and their silence could be commanded only at ruinous fees.

Prince de Rohan's partisans claim he is the victim of a court intrigue; others term him the victim of his own frivolity and gullibility. Paris lays the guilt upon the Cardinal and Madame de La Motte; the Court of Versailles, upon the Queen—although it is now considered unwise to discuss the case in public, several arrests having taken place for indiscreet comment, oral as well as written.

It was a newsletter with a style and subject matter well calculated to titillate the ear of the recipient, Catherine the Great. Small wonder that this "Paris correspondent" continued his reports to the imperial Russian court for over fifteen years.

It seemed there was no news except news of the diamond necklace scandal. Simeon Hardy wrote in his journal entry of September 6, 1785:

. . . This trial at the moment holds the attention of not only all of France but all of Europe.

People seem now to consider the whole case an injudicious action on the Minister's part—another such rash move as his arrest and incarceration of Caron de Beaumarchais in St. Lazare prison last March, with only this distinction: that in the case of a prince-cardinal he is dealing with a personage of far greater importance than a mere playwright, no matter how popular a one.

The great ladies of the court are the Cardinal's most ardent supporters. They rise to his defense, grateful for the tact and consideration he displayed at the very moment of his arrest by his order to the Abbé Georgel to destroy the billets-doux which might have compromised a number of the grandest of grandes dames.

The ardor of these ladies accounts for the latest fashion furor: the high-style bonnet of this spring season, known as "the Cardinal in the Straw," in the shape of a cardinal's hat, with cardinal-red-ribbons on a straw brim—symbolic of the heap of straw on the floor of the Bastille cells.

Gross exaggeration, this last, or else inaccurate information, for "Monseigneur Cardinal Rohan was never confined in a tower cell at the Bastille," according to the Abbé Georgel, who adds:

Nor was the door to his apartment ever fastened with the triple locks customarily used at that royal prison.

Baron de Breteuil had assigned His Eminence one of those hellish dungeons, those tombs for the living, but the King countermanded the order, designating an incarceration less humiliating to a man of the Prince's rank. The King's lieutenant at the Bastille yielded up his own apartments to the illustrious prisoner, and a single guard was posted at the exterior door of the suite.

Permission was accorded the prisoner to choose any two of his personal valets to serve him; to receive daily visits from his family and legal staff; to take his promenades in the governor's garden. His table was served in a manner befitting his rank and station; Count de Launay lavished upon the Cardinal every attention which might mitigate the unpleasantness of his situation.

The official Bastille register on one day alone, August 29, 1785, lists more than thirty visitors to Cardinal Rohan—princes and princesses, dukes and duchesses. Hardy noted in his journal:

To accommodate such a stream of noble guests, the Bastille drawbridge was left down over the moat throughout the day, a thing never known to happen before. Cardinal Rohan, in his Bastille apartments, gave one dinner party, at which oysters were opened and champagne swizzled, for twenty guests. . . .

STORY OF MY LIFE
BY THE COUNTESS DE LA MOTTE-VALOIS

While Cardinal Rohan enjoyed every comfort and consolation imaginable, I was confined to a narrow, gloomy tower cell and served on pewter dishes.

The turnkey, coming to remove my supper tray and finding it untouched, remarked, "Ah, Madame is not hungry tonight. She does not care to eat?"

"It's not that, my friend," I replied, "but I'll wager the Cardinal is treated more respectfully and served on silver instead of common pewter. Just tell Governor de Launay, please, that a descendant of the Valois kings is entitled to the same consideration as a Rohan."

Astonished, the turnkey looked at me with a new respect, protesting that he had had no idea who I was, or he would have served me differently.

No sooner said than done. The pewter service was removed and was replaced by dishes of the finest porcelain, with silver covers, and I was given a menu appropriate to the table appointments. From that time on, I had no cause for complaint on food or service; Monsieur de Launay was quick to provide me anything I required.

Actually, during the first six months of my detention, I had no complaint with Count de Launay's conduct; it was only later that he revealed himself as my enemy. He was a handsome man—too bad his heart and soul did not match his appearance!

At first he paid me daily visits, often sending for his tapestry loom and stitching at it for an hour or two in my room while we chatted. Of course, never once did he discuss the charges against me, and once only did he mention the Cardinal's name, and then reluctantly. It so happened that at times, when things seemed to be going well, I nourished my natural optimism by bursting into gay and exuberant song. The astonished guards having reported to Governor de Launay that I gave voice to a minimum of sixty arias a day, he came into my room and, struggling to repress his smiles, requested me to oblige him by discontinuing my concert at noon, the hour of the Cardinal's daily promenade in the governor's garden.

Once, when Governor de Launay and I were strolling together there, I questioned him about some of the popular notions concerning the horrors and mysteries of the Bastille, the most prevalent being that its subterranean cells were filled with prisoners who would never again see the light of day—their family and friends never knowing what had become of them. I let him talk, but his denials could not convince me; too many instances are known in which a man or a woman is suddenly seized by the police and dragged away, never to be heard of again—disappearing, as it were, off the face of the earth. Such examples of barbarity are bound to astonish my readers, the foreigner especially finding difficulty in believing that a people so tender, so spiritual as the French could have endured these outrages of authority as long as they did.

To one such example of barbarity I can attest out of personal experience. A week after my arrest, Madame de Latour, my husband's sister, requested permission of Governor de Launay to visit me. Shown into a room, she heard the bolts pushed to behind her and found herself a prisoner. Her pleas to the governor to tell her the reason for her detention brought the reply that he merely carried out the orders issued to him, never inquired into them. Madame de Latour spent six months in the Bastille without ever ascertaining why. Particular anguish for a tender mother and fond wife, whose three children and husband were inconsolable.

The sweet comfort of friends and family enjoyed by the Cardinal was denied to me. Attorney Doillot, to provide my sister and me a glimpse of each other, arranged for her to station herself at a certain spot upon the boulevard at the hour I took my promenade atop the tower. I climbed up to the platform, accompanied by a single guard, and saw my sister and two gentlemen appear below (one of them the Count de Barras,* who was to have wed Marianne had not fate, in striking me down, inflicted misfortune on all those near and dear to me). The three of them fluttered their handkerchiefs; I fluttered mine in return and blew them a kiss. The guard did not see, or pretended not to.

I had caught sight of my sister's beloved face, and I made myself satisfied. I asked no more. My sojourn in the Bastille was teaching me to discipline my wayward heart.

MEMOIRS
OF THE ABBÉ GEORGEL

The president of the Parliament of Paris at that time was Monsieur d'Aligre, famous for his opulence, his avarice and a special knack for getting his money's worth out of every transaction. He was reputed to be slavishly loyal to the Crown, a fact that did not go unnoticed by his

---

* The future chief member of the Directory, which governed France from 1795 to 1799.

fellows in the Parliament, where he was tolerated rather than respected. He was a man of ambiguous principles and easy morals.

Georgel's estimate of Aligre's loyalties was accurate, although he certainly never saw the following letter from Count Mercy to Emperor Joseph in Vienna:

The Cardinal's trial gives rise to great intrigues aimed at rescuing him; Count de Vergennes and the Keeper of the Seals are both suspected of favoring him, but fortunately the president of the Parliament does not share their prejudice. My friendship of long standing with that magistrate places me in a position to maintain him in this highly satisfactory frame of mind.

Since it is important to the Queen's interests that there be nothing to arouse public suspicion in the conduct of this case, I took occasion to point out to the president that there seemed to be developing a tendency to becloud the main issue with irrelevancies. At his request, I have now drawn up a brief outline of suggestions as to the proper approach to the matter—after first showing this list of directives to the Queen to make sure she subscribed to my point of view and would co-operate.

MEMOIRS
OF THE ABBÉ GEORGEL

President of Parliament d'Aligre appointed Titon de Villotran and Dupuy de Marcé as the examining magistrates in the Diamond Necklace Case inquiry, to conduct and preside over the preliminary hearings, the taking of depositions from the witnesses and the interrogations and confrontations of the accused.

Titon de Villotran was the Grand' Chambre magistrate most frequently appointed, in cases of national importance, to conduct the investigations and draw up the reports thereon for the Parliament of Paris. What Titon lacked in integrity, he made up for in personality and persuasiveness; he enjoyed a reputation for presenting his view of a case so superbly as invariably to win over the majority of his fellow judges.

Marcé, the second member of the investigatory team nominated to conduct the Diamond Necklace Case inquiry, was considered a mediocrity; he subordinated himself in all matters to his illustrious colleague, who was his guide and compass.*

A recess of the Parliament, occasioning a long delay, afforded us precious time for preparation of the Cardinal's defense. My every waking hour was devoted to investigation and to the gathering of sorely needed evidence. But Providence was watching over the Cardinal's honor, and when the first ray of light broke through to illuminate the case, it came less through my efforts and vigilance than through a stroke of unforeseen good fortune.

An Abbé Juncker, a man of intellect and some renown, approached me to volunteer his good offices. It was he who gave me the first hints for a course of investigation by which Madame de La Motte's infernal intrigue would be laid bare.

What the Abbé Juncker told me was that a monk named Father Loth had come to him and told him that, at the dictate of his conscience and of his gratitude to Cardinal Rohan, he had important revelations to make to me; that he had been on terms of intimacy with Madame de La Motte and could no longer hold back highly significant information pertinent to the diamond necklace investigation.

As business administrator of the monastery of the Order of Minims on the Place Royale, he had been a neighbor of Madame de La Motte, who in her lean years had known how to play upon his sympathies. He had made frequent contributions to the lady in her distress, and she had responded later by taking him into her confidence concerning her sudden affluence, which she attributed to the liberality of the Cardinal and the Queen. Admitted soon to the most intimate familiarity, Father Loth had seen and heard things in her home to arouse his suspicions: words inadvertently let slip, mention of a handsome gift expected from the court jewelers because she hoped to find a buyer for their expensive necklace, compliments paid by Madame de La Motte to a tall beauty named Mademoiselle d'Oliva on the success of a role played in the gardens of Versailles; the appearance of little letters which she said were from the Queen to the Cardinal and from the Cardinal to the Queen, the similarity of the handwriting on these little letters to that of Madame de La Motte's friend Villette, who was often closeted for hours with Madame and her husband, busily plying his pen. Father Loth

---

* Marcé followed Titon's lead even up the scaffold steps, climbing "Sanson's ladder" only a few months behind Titon in the second year of the French Republic.

had been witness to the alarm and confusion in the adventuress's house in the early days of August just prior to her flight. He was able to give me helpful information about Villette's personal life and to turn over to me some specimens of his penmanship, and he recalled the time Mademoiselle d'Oliva was taken to Versailles by Monsieur de La Motte in a rented carriage.

This was the gist of the story Father Loth came to confide in me one midnight, after having donned a disguise at the house of the Abbé Juncker so as to avoid any suspicion of collaboration in the event he should later be called to testify in the trial proper. He added, but in a way that made me suspect he was not telling all he knew, that he had reason to believe that Madame de La Motte had taken advantage of the Cardinal's good faith to bilk him of great sums of money and even to appropriate the diamond necklace. These were important revelations, to be sure, although there was as yet little or no evidence to substantiate them.

The Cardinal still refused to believe that Madame de La Motte had conceived and carried out a plot so wicked and so daring.

"I am positive," he insisted to me, "that I saw and spoke with the Queen in the gardens of Versailles. My eyes and ears could not have thus deceived me. This fact alone contradicts the idea that the correspondence with Her Majesty was an invention of Madame de La Motte's imagination."

A comparison of the samples of Villette's handwriting with that of the two little letters which I had preserved from the flames for just such an emergency convinced all six lawyers of Madame de La Motte's guilt and of the fact that the Queen's letters and the contract signature were forgeries.

The Cardinal, shaken at last, awaited with a burning impatience the results of my inquiries concerning Mademoiselle d'Oliva and my efforts to discover Villette's hiding place.

Meanwhile, the prosecutor general continued taking depositions from the witnesses called—all notably hostile to the Cardinal. The assistant prosecutor openly told the Rohan family to resign themselves to the fact that their kinsman's was a lost cause. We learned that the prosecutor general and the president of the Parliament, Monsieur d'Aligre, had met in secret with the Queen, who, probably unaware at the time of the Countess de La Motte's criminal intrigue and considering the Cardinal alone as guilty, directed all her resentment against him. Persuaded as she was of his offense against her name and dignity, it is not astonishing that she personally intervened with a number of the most influential of the judges. As for the malicious insinuation that the sovereign promised immunity to Madame de La Motte for her co-operation in bringing about the Cardinal's ruin, that blasphemy would never have soiled my pen if the horrible charge had not gained credence and if the infernal La Motte woman had not voiced it at the time her verdict was announced. Still, such mighty opposition could not but alarm the Cardinal's partisans, particularly since our only arms as yet consisted of conjectural and presumptive evidence.

At long last, however, factual evidence was forthcoming. Father Loth had made new admissions to Target; there was the proof I had obtained of Mademoiselle d'Oliva's excursion to Versailles with Monsieur de La Motte the very day of the Grove of Venus scene, the testimony of the coachman hired to drive them there, and witnesses to the visits paid and the presents given to Oliva by the La Mottes.

Father Loth's reticence, it developed, had been due to his fear of being brought to justice as an accomplice of Madame de La Motte's; but upon Target's assurance that only complete honesty on his part could save him from indictment, he finally ripped aside the veil shrouding the truth. He confessed that he had had knowledge of the whole fraudulent scheme from its inception; that, beguiled by the most potent of feminine wiles, he had felt constrained to keep the secrets of a woman who had acquired too strong a hold over him; that he had been ready, at her urging, to flee Paris with her and her husband, but that the inner voice of conscience had held him back and determined him, instead, to break away from that vicious band and withdraw from the world into a solitude where he could meditate upon the proper course of action; that, torn by remorse, he had at last reached the decision that he must not add to his other sins the sin of a criminal silence; and that he had come to dedicate himself to the Cardinal's defense by revealing the series of crimes to which he had been a guilty witness, in the hope that he would be afforded means of escaping legal retribution.

That there had indeed been a conspiracy Father Loth confirmed, a conspiracy only too real, only too expertly complotted by Madame de La Motte, her husband and Villette.

STORY OF MY LIFE
BY THE COUNTESS DE LA MOTTE-VALOIS

Oh, that serpent I had warmed against my breast! To have turned upon me, sunk its fangs into my flesh, my heart! He against whom I harbor the deepest resentment is a monk named Father Loth, from the monastery just across from my house on the Rue Neuve St. Gilles.

This monk wormed his way into our family circle by the expedient of making himself indispensable to us. Officious creature that he was, he acted as agent for a number of people who used him in sales, purchases, trades, deals of all kinds, for which he had a special talent. He often said that young people like my husband and me needed someone they could trust at the head of their establishment to watch out for their interests and supervise the domestic staff. He cited a Count and Countess So-and-So, just our age, who had confided management of their affairs to him.

"I expect nothing at all out of this, mind you!" he exclaimed. "It is my pleasure to do favors for my young friends. Their satisfaction is the only reward I seek or would accept."

Unfortunately, we allowed ourselves to be persuaded, and the monk took over our household, personally interviewing and engaging our cook, attending to the payment of wages, keeping our keys when we left the city . . .

When we set out for Bar-sur-Aube in August of 1785, we left Father Loth in charge of our Paris residence with a sum of money more than sufficient to discharge our outstanding debts; he appropriated half that sum, leaving half our bills unpaid. And as if that were not knavery enough, he auctioned off to his personal benefit two wagonloads of our furniture which were packed and ready for dispatch to us in the provinces.

All these operations of his were performed, of course, at the direction of Cardinal Rohan's lawyers, with the intent and purpose of impairing my reputation.

MEMOIRS
OF THE ABBÉ GEORGEL

Father Loth's strange revelation came to serve as an outline for the Cardinal's defense. The only problem was how to present these facts so that, without altering the truth all mention of the correspondence between the Queen and the Cardinal could be avoided. With Father Loth's assurance that the Prince's letters to the Queen had been burned in his presence by Madame de La Motte on the eve of her flight from Paris, a terrible weight was lifted from the Cardinal's troubled mind. The little letters in his red leather portfolio, those written purportedly by the Queen to the Cardinal, having likewise been fed to the flames, we felt justified in suppressing a point which could only have served as fuel for calumny and would assuredly have become more detrimental than beneficial to the Cardinal's cause. Father Loth himself felt he should keep this in mind when making his deposition.

My first attempts to have him called as a witness by the prosecutor general and the examining magistrates were fruitless. Finally I went to Keeper of the Seals Miromesnil, who saw the justice of my request, and Father Loth was called and heard. As we learned soon, his deposition, which we had envisioned as a double-edged sword for the Cardinal's defense, did not make that impression on Prosecutor General de Fleury and Examining Magistrate Titon. They held that since its allegations were not supported by proof, it could not invalidate the depositions of Böhmer, Bassenge and Saint-James, who had testified unanimously that Cardinal Rohan had received the necklace, which he had acquired by using the Queen's name and her supposed signature.

The Cardinal's attorneys, while admitting that this was so, decided nevertheless not to hold up publication of his defense plea until the necessary proofs were obtained, but to issue it based on what we had. Meanwhile I was to bend every effort toward securing the persons of Sieur de Villette and Mademoiselle d'Oliva.

Counselor-at-law Target lost no time in publishing the justification, which was read avidly. Prolix and interminably long, it did not live up to the author's reputation, but, even so, the combination of this defense plea and the undeniable evidences of the Cardinal's good faith (so infamously abused)—evidences such as his having urged the jewelers to speak to the Queen about the necklace—produced a sensation.

Madame de La Motte's second brief was not long in following. The facts alleged by that brazen, that ingeniously wicked woman plunged the impartial reader back into uncertainty, distressed the Cardinal's well-wishers and encouraged his enemies.

"I had absolutely nothing to do with the necklace purchase, never acted as intermediary," she claimed in this publication. "All I know is that the Cardinal purchased it himself to get his hands on a valuable piece of jewelry; that he and Cagliostro later broke it up and sent my husband to London to sell the stones and bring back the money."

She added that, having been so fortunate as to attract the Prince's fond interest, she had received from him considerable sums of money and a great many diamonds, which had enabled her to make her various acquisitions in Bar-sur-Aube. As for the Grove of Venus scene, that was a wild tale concocted by Cagliostro, to whom the Cardinal had given part of the money from the sale of the necklace.

It was obvious that Madame de La Motte had not yet learned of Father Loth's defection—much less, the extent of his revelations—and that with her husband and Villette safely out of France, she felt it would be impossible to verify the charges against them.

Father Loth having discovered Mademoiselle d'Oliva's address for me, I assigned secret operatives to keep her under constant surveillance until I could secure an order for her arrest. But a clandestine visit from Madame de La Motte's lawyer persuaded the girl to decamp. My spies advised me of her sudden midnight flight to Brussels.

The girl's presence in Paris was essential to our strategy of defense, to furnish proof of Madame de La Motte's criminal fraud. With no hope of assistance from the Minister of Paris, I again had recourse to the good offices of the Count de Vergennes, who secured a request, directed to the Austrian governmental authorities in the Low Countries, for the extradition of Mademoiselle d'Oliva.

And of her gentleman friend, a gay blade by the name of Toussaint de Beausire, a young scion of petty nobility who was running through his modest patrimony at a rapid clip. The pair were incarcerated in Brussels' Treurenberg prison on the night of October 20, but there the difficulties began, for the Brabant authorities proved finicky on the subject of international law and the right of asylum.

"To overcome these difficulties," Foreign Affairs Minister de Vergennes wrote to the Abbé Georgel on October 24, "an expedient has

been suggested to which the French Foreign Office has resorted several times previously: that is, to persuade the prisoners themselves to petition the authorities to be returned to Paris for the purpose of undertaking their own defense there."

Obviously a very clever operative was required to perform the trick of inducing Oliva and Beausire to request their own extradition, and Paris Police Inspector Quidor was the man Count de Vergennes chose for the delicate mission. Quidor, supervisor of the police force that patrolled the Paris streets and the girls who walked them, reported later to Vergennes, "At first glance I recognized the Demoiselle d'Oliva as being registered in my files for a long while under the name of de Signy. A rather retiring creature, she never made much of a reputation even as a demimondaine. I would characterize her as silly rather than criminal or vicious."

Quidor must have been eloquent indeed, for on October 31 Oliva and Beausire signed their names to a petition addressed to the Sovereign Council of Brabant setting forth that their presence in Paris had become "absolutely imperative"—"as a result of which," Quidor reported to Vergennes, "all that was needed on my part was a bit of tact and finesse, and I had the two prisoners over the border and on their way to the Bastille."

To casuist Georgel, it was the end that was significant, not the means. He sums it up in his memoirs:

There were difficulties, but the negotiations were conducted zealously and Mademoiselle d'Oliva was finally brought to the Bastille . . .

As for Villette, all our investigations failed to yield the slightest clue as to his whereabouts. I gave a description of our man to the Count de Vergennes, who recognized the importance to our case of producing at the trial a man who had served as tool to Madame de La Motte in the forgery of the famous contract signature "Marie Antoinette de France."

It was of equal importance to us to secure information from the London jewelers to whom the necklace had been sold. For such research, an active, skillful and intelligent man was needed, one who spoke English and whose devotion to the Cardinal was unquestionable, a man with the talent to procure valid, legal proof of the sale of the necklace stones by Monsieur de La Motte. All these qualifications I found united in the person of young Ramon de Carbonnières, the Prince's secretary. His dangerous intimacy with Cagliostro had totally alienated me from him, to be sure, but, deeming him useful at this juncture, I had no hesitation whatsoever in choosing him for the London negotiations. I had every reason to congratulate myself on my choice; no one could have accomplished the mission more skillfully or successfully.

Another example of Madame de La Motte's diabolical genius was her naming Cagliostro as the Cardinal's confidant and accomplice in the acquisition of the diamond necklace, as the one in all the world who could reveal the motives behind the strange intrigue. . . .

Cagliostro, seriously incriminated by the charges in the trial brief, demanded legal counsel to present his justification. The publication made intensely interesting reading. The author displayed all the graces of a flowery and imaginative style; it was a dramatization of a Cagliostro séance. As far as the Cardinal's cause was concerned, the important point was Cagliostro's testimony to the effect that Madame de La Motte had made confidences to him about her intimacy with the Queen and her mission as intermediary between the Queen and the Cardinal in the necklace purchase for Her Majesty.

The Cagliostro defense plea enjoyed a tremendous success.*

TRIAL BRIEF
FOR COUNT CAGLIOSTRO

Arraigned before the Parliament, I can still only guess at the crime of which I am accused. If I am mistaken in my surmise, then I am tilting at shadows, but at least I will have voiced the truth and given the saner element of the general public some idea of the libels being published against me. Oppressed, accused, calumniated, I look into my own heart and conscience to find the peace which men deny me.

I have traveled widely; I am known throughout all Europe and in most of Africa and Asia, and I have everywhere proven myself the friend of mankind. My knowledge, time and fortune have all been spent in succoring suffering humanity.

I have studied and practiced medicine without ever degrading that noblest of all arts by monetary considerations. An innate, irresistible impulse drew me toward the suffering; thus I became a doctor.

* So great a success that eight soldiers had to be posted at Attorney Thilorier's door in the Notre Dame cloister.

The rich have enjoyed my remedies gratuitously. The poor have enjoyed both my remedies and my largesse. Rich enough to be able to afford to bestow my benefactions on all alike, I have indulged myself in the supreme luxury of the independent spirit, that of giving generously and accepting never, carrying such delicacy to the point of rejecting even the proffered rewards of grateful sovereigns.

I have never anywhere in the world contracted debts; my morals are pure to the point of austerity. I have given offense to no one, neither by word nor deed. Such injury as has been done me I have pardoned. My philanthropies have been performed in anonymity. A stranger in every country of the world, I have everywhere fulfilled the duties of a citizen, have everywhere respected the established religion, the law and the government.

And there you have the story of my life.

My infancy was spent in the town of Medina in Arabia; there I was brought up under the name of Acharat in the palace of the Mufti Salahym. From earliest days, I can remember three servants in attendance and a preceptor named Althotas.

The latter told me that I had been orphaned at three months and that my parents were Christians and nobles, but always he maintained strict secrecy as to their names and the name of my birthplace. A word now and then escaping his lips gave me reason to suspect that I had first seen the light of day at Malta or Trebizond.

Althotas, with the loving care of a father, taught me almost all the languages of the Orient and cultivated my early disposition toward the sciences, he himself possessing knowledge of them all, even the most abstract. He it was who taught me to worship my God and to love and serve my fellow man. He and I wore Mohammedan garb, but the true religion was in our hearts.

When I reached my twelfth year, Althotas and I began our travels. We spent three years at Mecca as guests in the palace of the Sultan, who manifested the most tender symptoms of affection toward me. From Mecca our caravan headed for Egypt and the Pyramids, with their great subterranean vaults, whither no ordinary traveler ever penetrates, excavated by the ancients to conceal and preserve for all time the most precious cache of occult knowledge revealed to man in the course of the centuries. The priests of the temples of the Nile initiated me into those mysteries.

In the course of the next three years, Althotas and I journeyed through all the principal kingdoms of Africa and Asia. In 1766, we set sail for the island of Rhodes. Grandmaster Pinto of the Order of the Knights of Malta received me in his palace, treating me with great distinction and offering me rapid advancement in the order should I determine to remain. There, for the first time, I donned European dress; nor was I surprised to see Althotas appear in the ecclesiastical robes of the order, decorated with the Maltese cross.

In Malta it was that I suffered the loss of my tutor, Althotas, wisest and most enlightened of mortal men. After his death I bade Grandmaster Pinto farewell and set out on my wanderings through Europe, preserving everywhere my incognito of "Count Cagliostro."

In 1770, in my twenty-second year, while I was visiting Rome, chance brought me the acquaintance of a young lady of quality named Serafina Feliciani. She was hardly more than a child, but her budding charms lighted in my heart the fires of a passion which sixteen years of marriage have only kindled higher. This is the unfortunate creature whom neither her virtues nor her innocence could save from an arrest as cruel as it was unjustified.

Having neither the time nor the inclination to write a tome, I shall not go into detail concerning my travels throughout the kingdoms of Europe. I invoke the testimony of the persons I have met in all these lands to say whether I have ever committed an action unworthy of a man of honor, whether I have ever asked a favor of any man, of even the sovereigns who expressed their curiosity and eagerness to meet me.

REFUTATION OF THAT SECTION OF THE COUNTESS DE LA MOTTE'S
BRIEF WHICH DEALS WITH COUNT CAGLIOSTRO

Whatever one's opinion of the predominating style of the brief published for the Countess de La Motte, one must admit that it is at least remarkable for the incredible number of insults compressed into a few paragraphs. It is not my intention here to act as literary critic of this popular opus; I would never have mentioned it had the Countess only contented herself with a massacre of the French tongue and not gone on to affront truth and decency.

Let us take up her insults one by one.

"Quack,," she calls me. Quack? I have often heard the word without ever ascertaining its exact meaning. Does it designate a man who, without holding a doctor's certificate, yet has extensive medical knowledge; who heals the sick, rich and poor alike, accepting money from neither? If this be the definition of a quack, then I agree I have the honor of being one.

"Experimenter after the philosopher's stone." Whatever my views on the philosopher's stone, I have kept them to myself. I have never importuned the public with a description of my experiments.

"Lowly alchemist." Alchemist or no, the adjective "lowly" befits only those who crawl on their bellies, seeking favors, whereas it is a matter of public knowledge that the Count di Cagliostro has never sought, never accepted a favor or pension from any man.

"False prophet." Not always. Had Cardinal Rohan only heeded my prophecy to beware of the Countess de La Motte, he and I would not be where we are today.

"Self-designated Count Cagliostro." I have borne the name Cagliostro through all Europe. As to the designation "Count," one may judge by the education given me and by the reception accorded me by the Mufti Salahym, the Sultan of Mecca, Grandmaster Pinto, the Pope and most of the crowned heads of Europe whether the title of Count is not rather an incognito for a far loftier one.

"Guardian of the diamond necklace." I could hardly be in possession of the diamond necklace, since I have never so much as laid eyes on it. The contract was signed January 29, 1785; I did not reach Paris until January 30 at nine o'clock in the evening, a fact easily verifiable. Thus all negotiations were consummated before my arrival except the delivery of the necklace, which was made thirty-six hours thereafter. I was in Lyons at the time the negotiations were going on; I was in Bordeaux at the date of the apparition of the pseudo Queen in the Trianon gardens. I would have arrived in Paris, then, expressly to pluck the fruits of an intrigue cultivated by another. How preposterous!

"Cagliostro used the necklace to swell the treasures of his incredibly vast secret fortune." If my secret fortune is incredibly vast, what need had I to swell it?

In her own inimitable style, the Countess de La Motte goes on to describe a horrendous séance at which I practiced animal magnetism on her niece, and ties it into the story of the diamond necklace affair with flagrant inverisimilitude and awkwardness. In a bizarre spectacle bathed in an eerie light I am supposed to have sworn the Countess to secrecy on the subject of her husband's mission to England to dispose of the diamonds.

Either the Countess has completely lost her head or she trusts to the credulity of the judges if she hopes to extricate herself from the affair by reeling off such nonsense.

She has the effrontery to quote my valet as boasting that he has been in my service for over 150 years, to quote me as laying claim to an age of three hundred years and more—a guest at the wedding feast at Cana, who seeks to multiply the stones of the necklace the way the loaves and the fishes were multiplied and transmuted!

On one page the Countess calls me a Greek; on another, a Mohammedan; on still another, a Portuguese Jew. I have already stated that I was brought up as the son of Christian parents; I have never been either a Jew or a Mohammedan. Those two religions leave an ineffaceable mark upon their male followers, so the truth of my statement may be verified; I am ready, if necessary, to submit to an examination, for it will be more humiliating to those who exact it than to him who suffers it.

Elsewhere in her brief, Madame de La Motte refers to me as "one of those extravagant knights of the rose cross who possess the secret of summoning up the dead"; again, she terms me "an Egyptian from Alexandria," whence I brought into Europe my witchcraft and sorcery; and she only regrets the fact that we do not live in a century when I would have expiated a sorcery charge in flames at the stake.

Then, having justified arraigning me as both a "swindler" and an "astral entity," the Countess de La Motte goes on to speak of the "so-called Countess Cagliostro, the woman who shares his couch and fortune." Was it not enough, then, for the Countess de La Motte's defender [Doillot] to slander and to insult me? Must he attack me at my most vulnerable point, my wife? The attack upon myself I could have forgiven, but never that upon my wife! What harm has she done him? What harm has she done the Countess de La Motte? How to account for a man in public life who would wound an innocent and virtuous creature who is not even an adversary in the case, against whom he has no complaint, no charge, against whom his only reproach can be that she has had the misfortune to have linked her life with mine? As for the Countess de La Motte's demand for proof of our marriage,

I hereby guarantee to produce and publish those papers the moment they are restored to me by the police.

And yet, on the subject of Madame de La Motte, I am convinced that the grave harm she has done me she has done less out of hatred for me than out of desperation to shift the blame from her shoulders onto those of another. Whatever her motive, insofar as I can find forgiveness in my heart I forgive her. Indeed, once I am assured that my own innocence has been recognized, I shall petition His Majesty the King to grant clemency to the unfortunate La Motte. Nor would clemency constitute an offense to justice. For, no matter what the Countess's guilt, she has already been punished. Ah, you may take my word for it, there is no crime in this world which is not expiated by six months in the Bastille.

And, now, Frenchmen, I would ask you: Are you motivated solely by morbid curiosity that you would go on reading such recklessly malicious publications as hers, designed to heap shame and ridicule upon the Friend of Mankind? Or would you, instead, prove yourselves men of good will and justice? Then inquire no further, but listen, and love him who has always respected monarchy and government because they are in the hands of God, who has always respected religion because it is the law and the law because it supplements religion, who has always respected other men because, like him, they are the children of God.

So once again I say to you, Inquire no further, but listen, and love a man who has come among you doing good, who suffers attack with patience and defends himself with moderation.

MEMOIRS
OF COUNT BEUGNOT

One of Paris' most eminent attorneys, Maître Thilorier, appeared in the legal arena to defend the Man of Miracles; he set the sedate halls of the Palais de Justice ringing with exotic names from the banks of the Nile and the Euphrates, the place of origin of that fabled hero who was enshrouded in an aura of religious mysteries presaging marvels likely, one day, to astound the universe.

Thilorier, with his ready sense of humor, was the first to chuckle at his own composition. Fantasy was apparently the order of the day, however, and it evoked no protest of outraged credibilities but, rather, an enthusiastic acclaim.

Next Cagliostro's wife was flung into the Bastille, and in rushed Lawyer Polverit to champion the cause of the lovely Serafina Feliciani with a well-composed if high-flown and sentimental defense plea:

> Her origins are as mysterious as her husband's . . . She is an angel in human form sent upon this earth to brighten the days of the Man of Miracles. Her face is endowed with a beauty such as has never before been granted mortal woman. Tender, gentle, patient, she is a very model of virtue—nay, more than a model, since that implies the existence of the virtues' converse defects or vices, the existence of which she does not even suspect. Her character offers the ideal of perfection which we other poor sinners can only regard with awe, never hope to emulate. Yet it is this angel to whom Sin is unknown who finds herself today behind bars. What an incongruity! What possible connection can there be between this rare soul and a criminal trial? . . .

This latest fantasy, like all the others, enjoyed a tremendous vogue. Indeed, each of the trial briefs in turn attracted sensational publicity for the attorney-author as well as for the client.

In this fashion, one of the most serious cases ever to be brought for judgment before the Parliament was turned into a circus. How could the Parliament of Paris have ever permitted the carnival spirit thus to invade one of the gravest forms of juridical defense? Could it have been a predetermined policy for dealing with a crime into which it was considered indiscreet to probe too deep, a crime, rather, to be buried deep under ridicule and scandal? There is reason to think that such was the case.

At any rate, next to appear in the lists was Lawyer Blondel, representing little Mademoiselle d'Oliva.

Compact, clever, skillfully written, his proved a very model of a defense plea, touching but lightly upon the demoiselle's character (no innocent like Serafina, to be sure), presenting her as a young woman only too easily taken in who played out her role in the gardens of Versailles without the faintest conception of its sinister implications. Such was the artistry of the author that the general public was promptly stirred to sympathy for this demoiselle in distress, a sympathy that spread from the populace to Parliament itself. . . .

If it has been seen that a legal veteran like Doillot could not with impunity come into too close contact with his pretty Countess client, no more could young Blondel (a debutant at the bar, fresh out of law school) with his pretty "Baroness." But with this distinction, that Doillot lost his reputation in the Diamond Necklace Case, while future Judge Blondel's was made thereby. In his defense plea for "Baroness" d'Oliva he soared to literary heights on the wings of infatuation for his winsome client, who managed somehow—lady of the evening though she was, habituée of the Palais-Royal cabarets—to maintain her amateur standing. All Paris saw her now through Blondel's dazzled eyes:

TRIAL BRIEF
FOR THE DEMOISELLE LEGUAY D'OLIVA

My story is as simple, as naïve, as artless as I am myself, as has been my deportment through all the strange role set me to play by my seducers.

Born in Paris in 1761, of honest if humble family, my first misfortune was to be orphaned at too tender an age, deprived of parents' care and vigilance which would have warded off the dangers inevitable to an unprotected girlhood, abandoned to faithless guardians who robbed me not only of youth's sweet illusions but even of my modest patrimony.

A woman young, weak, untutored, timid—poor me, I stand today indicted in a criminal case where I must defend myself against the mightiest of accusers; must contend with shrewd and powerful codefendants; must struggle against hostile or treacherous witnesses. And worst of all, without knowing who brings the charges against me, how can I prepare my defense? What, I ask, oh, what is the accusation brought against me? Have I been merely imprudent or have I committed some grievous error, even, perhaps, a crime? To judge by the cruel plight in which I find myself, I must somehow, unknowingly, have offended both the throne and society.

Snatched from my bed in the middle of the night of October 16, 1785, by the head of the Brussels police, three policemen and five town guards, I asked by what order they seized me, demanding my rights as a French citizen in the name of my sovereign—only to be told that it was my sovereign himself who had ordered my arrest. Dragged off brutally and ignominiously, I learned only in the Brussels prison, from the jailer's newspaper, that my arrest was in connection with the Diamond Necklace Case. Even then, it was with astonishment rather than fright that I found myself implicated in an affair of which I had not the slightest knowledge; my innocence reassured me.

Finally I was brought to Paris and imprisoned in the Bastille.

I have told my story to the police lieutenant general and the examiners, have stated the facts with the candor, the unswerving veracity appropriate to innocence; thus I shall repeat them in my confrontations with the witnesses and the other defendants throughout the entire investigation and the trial.

Innately incapable of crime as I am (an act cannot be said to be criminal unless there is criminal intent behind the deed), my very innocence has served to bring the guilty to light. If fate ordained me to be the unwitting instrument of their criminal intrigues, it ordained me likewise to be the one to unmask the criminals themselves and deliver them over to legal retribution. It was into my frail hands that an inscrutable fate chose to place the thread by which the judges would find their way to the truth through the tortuous paths of the criminal maze.

No matter what Monseigneur Cardinal Rohan says, he has nothing to reproach me with and must answer for the consequences of his denunciation of me. I never had the honor of knowing him. I do not know, never knew, never even saw Sieur Cagliostro or the Lady Cagliostro, his wife, or Sieur Böhmer or Sieur Bassenge. I never saw the diamond necklace. I never even knew such a necklace existed.

Of all the defendants, I knew only Sieur and Lady de La Motte, who were intrigants far too clever, you may be sure, to share their confidences with a girl so obviously unsophisticated, so unworldly. To see, to talk with me for a moment is to know that I am incapable of telling a lie, much less of sustaining or enacting one. Had my seducers even breathed the Cardinal's name or the august name of the character I was to portray, I would have recoiled in horror at such sacrilege. To resist would have required no sophistication, no intellect, on my part; inherent respect and fear would have sent me flying off in panic.

What I want to say is that if the Cardinal Prince de Rohan, the highest officer of the Crown, a man of the loftiest rank, of mature age and great intellect, argues that he was taken in by the impostures of the Lady de La Motte, then he only proves how much more easily I could have been deceived—I, a simple plebeian, in my early youth, with no knowledge of the great world, timid, credulous, trusting. Despite the vast gulf separating us in the social order, Cardinal Rohan and I have one thing in common: we have both given the world a memorable example of the dangers of indiscreet liaisons.

They tell me that the Lady de La Motte denies having coached me for the nocturnal scene in the palace gardens, that she arrogantly denies having associated with a woman of my class. Oh, vile and haughty woman! Come down from the branches of your lofty family tree, whence you defy the law and insult your codefendants. I am a mere nobody, as I well know, but you are only my equal when you stand beside me at the bar of justice, before which name and rank and honors must all be laid aside.

But what matter if she denies me? There are three important witnesses to the truth of my deposition: the Sieur de La Motte, the Sieur de Villette and Rosalie, the Countess's lady's maid. . . . If the police could come almost two hundred leagues to Brussels to capture me, why have these witnesses not been searched out and apprehended? Good heavens, what kind of world do we live in that I am deprived of the very testimony that could clear me? I demand that these arrests be made today! I demand it in the name of the law, the law of the land, the safeguard of every citizen, great and small alike. Shall I arouse no answer in the courts of justice?

At the thought of such injustice, my blood seethes, my heart cries out in indignation. Is not this the century that boasts of its advances to new frontiers of science, of philosophy? Are not men become aware today of the rights as well as the duties of citizenship? Have they not come to expect justice for all, regardless of station, of fortune?

I refuse, then, to believe that our legal system can be corrupt; this would constitute an insult not only to the majesty of the law but to public intelligence as well.

Walled off as I am from all humanity, shut up in these high towers away from the world, still I await with trust and confidence the decision on my fate. Even here in this dark prison of the Bastille, this dread fortress cut off from sight and sound of mankind, like a desert wasteland of silence and solitude enclaved within the very heart of the teeming capital—even here I cling to my faith that I will hear those words of cheer and solace ring out: "She is a citizen of France and, as such, entitled to the protection of the law. She is innocent and shall so be declared by the due processes of law."

"Twenty thousand copies of Maître Blondel's defense plea for the Demoiselle d'Oliva were sold out in a few days' time," the Amsterdam Gazette reported; and "Manuel" was inspired to verse in his popular news bulletin, Le Garde du Corps ("The Royal Bodyguard"), putting these stanzas on the ruby lips of the Palais-Royal belle:

> It's been proved by them both that I saw nothing well:
> "Dark as night," said Target. "Black as ink," quoth Blondel.
> Of one thing I'm sure, for my very own part,
> In this little story laid bare is my heart.
> For, naïve as I am, and so simple too,
> Oliva knows best how to vanish from view.

MEMOIRS
OF THE ABBÉ GEORGEL

Mademoiselle d'Oliva's defense plea won her universal sympathy; sensitive souls responded to the naïve and ingenuous admissions of the beauteous courtesan. The style of the trial brief was imbued with all the dewy freshness, the delicacy of coloring attributed by the poets to the Paphian goddess herself. . . . Mademoiselle d'Oliva's forthright and honest account gave the general public its first inkling of the plot which had victimized the Cardinal. The Countess de La Motte lost completely the sympathy that her two defense pleas had won her. It was possible at last to discern her as the fiendish schemer of a series of incredibly daring maneuvers.

A great stride had been made toward the truth, but the presence of Monsieur de La Motte and, above all, of Villette was of still greater importance to the Cardinal's defense strategy. We had ascertained that Monsieur de La Motte had left London after consummating another sale of highly valuable diamonds brought from Bar-sur-Aube. His wife claimed in her second trial brief that her husband would shortly arrive in Paris with proof that he had acted as agent for the Cardinal, but we were not deluded into expecting his voluntary return. We already had evidence that he had sent letters of credit to a Paris bank, where they had been cashed by Madame de La Motte. We had also established the fact that Monsieur de La Motte had large sums on deposit in London banks under an assumed name.

Despite the zeal of our investigations, however, Monsieur de La Motte's hiding place remained a mystery.

MEMOIRS
OF THE COUNTESS DE LA MOTTE-VALOIS

The Rohans, resolved on avenging their honor at any price, had sworn to pursue my husband to the far corners of the earth, insistent that only his life could appease their wrath. If cold steel and poison failed them in their evil designs on him, it was not for lack of trying.

Sword blades thrust in at the Count de La Motte through the window of his carriage as it rolled along the main thoroughfares of London, hired assassins jumping him outside his Jermyn Street hotel, "countless assassination attempts stemming from the hand of either the Queen or the Cardinal": such are the charges made by the Count for fifty-odd pages of his memoirs. All this derring-do was scoffed at for years as typical La Motte mendacity and exaggeration, but it was later substantiated by a correspondence file that turned up in the Foreign Affairs Archives on the Quai d'Orsay: a stack of rejected extradition petitions to the Court of St. James's from the Court of Versailles for the return of the elusive Marc Antoine de La Motte, letters to and from the French embassy in London on the subject of spies set on his trail, on the subject of kidnap and murder plots attempted, frustrated and reinstigated —exactly as the Count de La Motte had described them in his memoirs:

Emerging from a theater on London's Haymarket Square one rainy night, I hailed a cab, but hardly had the horses turned into Piccadilly when I saw a naked sword blade shatter the glass of the rear window just at eye level. Had I been sitting upright or toward the center of the seat, the murder weapon would have pierced my throat.

Having only a swagger stick with which to defend myself, I pulled the cord to summon the coachman, but when I pointed out the broken windowpane and the bravo, who, having leaped from the back of the carriage, was running off as fast as his legs would carry him, the coachman understood not even my efforts at sign language—understood nothing, that is, beyond the damage to his vehicle, for which he demanded indemnity of me. Not until I reached my hotel could I find someone who spoke French, and then the fellow had nothing constructive to offer beyond the recommendation that I be more cautious in the future!

My lawyer, Linguet, only confirmed what I already knew: that since my existence constituted a threat to both Cardinal and Queen, my life was in danger in London. He advised me to take to flight to the wildest, remotest region possible—to Ireland, as it was finally decided—traveling under an assumed name. . . .

Dublin was gay and I had entrée to the best society, but, fearful that I had been recognized by the Viceroy, who also had entertained me, I determined to leave for Scotland. . . . Little did I suspect that my melancholia and my loss of appetite betokened a cause more direct than mental anguish and gloomy premonitions. Being visibly altered in appearance, however, and eighteen days having gone by without my body's performing its normal and indispensable functions, I consulted the eminent medical faculty of Edinburgh, who assured me that had I presented myself twenty-four hours later they would have been unable to save my life from the poison in my system. The same hand that had directed the murderous sword in London had administered the deadly dose in Dublin, a fact to which Count d'Adhémar, the French ambassador to England, later admitted. . . .

Loneliness and ennui dragged along in my wake wherever I went. . . . At that point, I would have walked into a veritable den of thieves for just one word of news from Paris about my wife or on the subject of the Necklace Trial. Unable to speak or read the English language, I yielded to my valet's suggestion that I take lessons from a man named Costa.

Whereupon the plot begins to thicken. Ambassador d'Adhémar could show to Marie Antoinette a letter that had reached him from Edinburgh, signed by a man named Costa, "instructor of modern languages to the dukes of Buccleuch and Gordon," as he described himself. "My economic situation," Costa had written, "obliges me to an action re-

pugnant to my tender heart. But if I sacrifice the Count de La Motte to the welfare of my family which is in want, I do it in the knowledge that he is guilty and should be delivered over to justice. I do not feel that my act is criticizable, when the world is full of people who have built their fortunes upon the bodies of innocent victims."

In brief, for the sum of 260,000 francs Costa offered to deliver the person of Count de La Motte, together with any diamonds he might be carrying on his person, at a specified British seaport.

The Queen handed the letter to Foreign Minister de Vergennes, who advised Adhémar to proceed—although cautiously, so as not to offend the English authorities, who were far more finicky than the Brabantine on the subject of the rights of refugees

"The crafty Vergennes wrote to Adhémar in London," Count de La Motte's memoirs state, "to say that they wanted me dead or alive, preferably the former. The plot was to get me to Newcastle, where I was to be drugged, abducted and taken aboard a French ship at anchor in the harbor."

Police Inspector Quidor, who had acquitted himself so well on the Brussels expedition, was Count de Vergennes's choice for this delicate kidnap mission. He was placed in command of a ship which sailed from Dunkirk for Newcastle, purportedly to pick up a cargo of coal, manned by a crew of twenty—ostensibly mariners, actually the flower of the Paris police force. In this assignment, however, Quidor betrayed nervousness, "mentioning several times that he did not mind risking his life on the streets of Paris whenever called upon to do so," according to a letter from Ambassador d'Adhémar to his Foreign Office superior, "but that he did not relish the idea of operating in England, where discovery by the English authorities could land him on the gallows tree."

Costa, too, apparently lost his nerve at the last minute. In Count de La Motte's version, "After meeting with Ambassador d'Adhémar at a Newcastle tavern, Costa came and admitted to me that there was a plan afoot to abduct me. I advised him to pretend to continue to cooperate and thus get hold of the promised 26,000 francs' advance, which would come in very handy." Thus, it would appear, the Count joined with his would-be abductor in reaping the reward for a kidnap plot of which he himself was the victim-designate.

As Adhémar explained it later, Costa protested that he had not been given sufficient time or funds to complete the necessary arrangements and that the wary Count de La Motte had somehow got wind of the plot.

"The thing was simply impossible," Quidor wrote in his final report to the Foreign Office. "The kidnaping could never have been brought off under the very noses of the Newcastle port authorities. The Tyne river front swarms with sailors, watchmen are posted all night every fifty steps along the docks, and foreign craft particularly are kept under twenty-four-hour surveillance by the customs inspectors to prevent smuggling; lastly, the coastline is so treacherous that a pilot is assigned to all outbound vessels. Even so, it was with great reluctance that I abandoned both the plan and Costa at Newcastle and returned to London, thence to Dunkirk, whence I am now taking the road back to Paris, distressed at the realization that all my zeal and devotion to this mission have been in vain." Distressed as well, no doubt, to have forfeited therewith the fifty thousand francs cash and the life pension that had been held out to him by Count de Vergennes as reward for a mission successfully accomplished.

In Paris, meanwhile, the Queen appraised the situation as she saw it on December 27, 1785, in a letter addressed to Emperor Joseph of Austria:

From the moment of the Cardinal's arrest, I was sure that at least he would never again appear at our court, but the trial, which will last several months, may have consequences even more serious.

The judicial procedure of the Parliament began with the issuance of writs of arrest suspending all his civil rights and functions until the pronouncement of judgment in the case. Writs were issued at the same time for the charlatan Cagliostro and his wife, for the La Motte woman and for a streetwalker named Oliva. What company for a Grand Almoner of France, a cardinal of the house of Rohan!

On December 15, 1785, the "writs setting a day for a hearing" (décrets d'ajournement pour être ouï) issued by the Parliament of Paris in September for the prisoners in the Bastille were converted into writs of capias, or arrest (prise de corps, "taking the body," in this case taking the body of the prisoner from the King's jurisdiction), made out in the names of Cardinal Rohan, Madame de La Motte and Cagliostro, the latter having barely missed winning a Grand' Chambre majority for acquittal. As to the writ for Countess Cagliostro to which the

Queen refers, she was on this point mistaken, none ever having been indited against the Roman beauty.

It is apparent that it was a matter of policy to ensure that the trial should proceed in strict accordance with the law. By a special decree, the King transformed the Bastille from a state to a judiciary prison in order to give the Parliament of Paris full jurisdiction over the Necklace Case prisoners. The conduct of the investigation was meticulously correct in every detail, at least as concerned outward form; all reports, records, interrogations and depositions were complete, were signed by all parties thereto and were duly filed with the court registrar.

As of December 15, the Cardinal discovered that a prisoner of the Parliament endured a more rigorous captivity than a prisoner of the King. His chief counsel, Target, registered a loud protest upon being advised by the governor of the Bastille that he and his client could no longer consult in privacy; there is extant a letter from Launay to Breteuil requesting further instructions on this touchy point. The Countess de La Motte must have smirked to learn that Prince de Rohan now suffered the loss of the special privileges of which she had been so envious, that he could no longer hold court as if the Bastille were another Palais-Cardinal, receiving and entertaining a stream of prominent visitors and conducting the business of his Strasbourg diocese, the Grand Almonership and the Quinze-Vingts hospital. Whereas it had hitherto been the Cardinal's custom to take his midday stroll on the platform atop one of the six towers, his promenade grounds were now changed to the triangular inner garden in Governor de Launay's private quarters in the bastion of the fortress; this was done in order to put a stop to the public demonstrations among the crowds which collected on the streets below to catch a glimpse of the illustrious prisoner on his eyrie. According to a contemporary reporter, Nougaret, the Prince was so affected by this action of the Parliament that he suffered "repeated attacks of the nephritic colic to which he was subject."

MEMOIRS
OF THE ABBÉ GEORGEL

Meanwhile the Cardinal's defenders learned with dismay that the two examining magistrates had voiced it as their opinion that the affront to the Queen's honor could be requited only through punishment of the

Cardinal—if not as author and accomplice of the outrage, then at least as having been involved in an association that could not but be considered indecent for a man of his rank and station. Such a point of view alarmed us.

Still further to heighten our anxiety, Baron de Breteuil went about openly soliciting the judges, in the name of the Queen, against the Cardinal. The Queen herself, doubtless embittered by a publicity that focused the eyes of all Europe upon her, no longer took the pains even to conceal her hostile activity. I did not question the integrity of the judges of Parliament, but it was difficult to believe that they were not shaken by the hints of a sovereign to whose influence no Frenchman could consider himself impervious.

At this point, fortunately, young Ramon de Carbonnières returned from England bringing important new evidence that supported the Cardinal's claim to innocence and left no further doubt as to Madame de La Motte's larceny.

For his visit to the London jewelers young Ramon had been provided by Böhmer with a drawing of the necklace and a list of all the stones, described by carat weight, cut and color. His inquiries proved conclusively that most of the necklace diamonds had been sold by Monsieur de La Motte on his own account to two jewelers, Grey and Jefferyes, payment being made partly in cash, partly in merchandise. These facts appeared in legally valid affidavits, sworn to and signed before a London judge and a notary.

AFFIDAVIT OF WILLIAM GREY,
JEWELER, NEW BOND STREET, LONDON

The diamonds sold to me by Monsieur de Valois so perfectly resemble, both in carat weight and cut, the stones of the diamond necklace made recently in Paris by Böhmer and Bassenge, insofar as that necklace is known to me through a sketch and description, that no slightest doubt exists in my mind but that these were taken out of the Böhmer and Bassenge necklace. All the brilliants were loose when Monsieur de Valois brought them to my shop, and several were so severely damaged as to lead me to conclude that they had been pried loose from their setting with a knife or similar crude instrument. . . .

Judging from the Böhmer design and description provided me, I now conclude that the stones shown me by Monsieur de Valois were those which had formed the festoons of the necklace.

In addition to £6,090 cash, the Count de Valois received another £4,000 in merchandise, according to this true extract from my ledger:

Delivered to Monsieur the Count de Valois, London, May 20, 1785:

	£	s.	d.
A Medallion set with diamonds	230	0	0
A Diamond Ring	94	10	0
A Pearl Knot for a Lady	52	10	0
A Fire-Screen	1	4	0
A Purse	4	14	6
A handsome Steel Sword	100	0	0
Ditto Ditto	45	0	0
A Diamond Hoop Ring	13	13	0
Setting a Diamond Ring	1	8	0
A Ring Case	0	8	0
A Handsome Star-shaped Diamond Brooch	400	0	0
A Pair of Asparagus Tongs	2	12	6
A Gold Watch	38	0	0
A Pair of Scales for Diamonds	1	1	0
A Watch Chain	6	16	0
A Handsome Pair Diamond Girandole Ear-rings	600	0	0
A Diamond Ring	100	0	0
A Diamond Snuff Box	120	0	0
Diamond Shirt Buttons	28	0	0
A Parcel of pearl-seed and other Pearls for embroidery	1,890	0	0
A Pearl Necklace	170	0	0
1,800 Pearls	270	0	0
A Diamond Aigrette in the Form of a Rose	60	0	0
Steel Buckles, Purses, Needles, Toothpick Cases, &c	—	—	—
	4,281	6	0
Paid in Cash	6,090	0	0
TOTAL	10,371	6	0
Credit by value received in various diamonds	10,371	6	0

AFFIDAVIT OF NATHANIEL JEFFERYES,
JEWELER, LONDON, NOTARIZED DECEMBER 16, 1785

On a visit to my shop on April 23, 1785, Monsieur de Valois told me that he had recently inherited these diamonds from his mother, who had worn them as a stomacher, but I was suspicious that so great a treasure in brilliants could not have come by honest means into the possession of a private individual, and so betook myself to the Bond Street police station to inquire whether reports of any robbery or swindle had come in from France. The tremendous value of these diamonds, and the considerable loss suffered by Monsieur de Valois in exchanging them for other merchandise and then converting that merchandise into cash in another transaction—all this fully convinced me that he could have only acquired the stones through criminal action.

MEMOIRS
OF THE ABBÉ GEORGEL

It took all the influence the Keeper of the Seals could bring to bear to overcome the prosecutor general's reluctance to admit these notarized depositions from London into evidence in Paris. I do not know why such resistance was encountered in the sanctuary of justice whenever there was a question of admitting proof of the Cardinal's innocence.

The taking of depositions being completed, all witnesses having been heard by the prosecutor general for the Crown, Fleury, and by the Parliament-appointed examining magistrates, Titon and Marcé, the latter were to go to the Bastille to begin the interrogation of the defendants imprisoned there, and the confrontation of these accused with each other and with the various witnesses.

The Cardinal, being duly advised of the procedure, was notified that from this point on until the day of judgment all communication with his counsel and family would be severed. This legally imposed isolation period could not but alarm the Cardinal's defenders. It was feared that the Prince, a captive, distraught and preoccupied with the perils of his position, and a stranger to the rigorous forms of criminal procedure, might become confused during the interrogations and confrontations, to the point of contradicting himself or making admissions damaging to his cause. His relatives and legal staff expressed their acute anxiety on this score.

To counteract, insofar as possible, the embarrassing situation confronting us, I conceived of an expedient that proved the solution of our difficulties. In my position as administrator of all the Cardinal's property and revenues, I petitioned for authorization to report to him by letter on these matters and to receive his written recommendations in return. Baron de Breteuil at first rejected the request but finally came around to granting it—albeit reluctantly, and with the proviso that all such correspondence be subject to censorship by Governor de Launay and the two court examiners.

Having surmounted these obstacles, I rushed to perfect my plan, with only twenty-four hours remaining before the moment when all other communication would be cut off. Using place names and personal names connected with the diocese and the various estates, I worked out a secret code that defied detection and aroused no suspicion; it was a code similar to one which the Cardinal and I had used successfully during the Vienna embassy days. That last night, I stayed at the Bastille until midnight, rehearsing it with His Eminence.

The Cardinal's lawyers, appreciative of the inestimable advantages of this innocent subterfuge, never ceased to express their admiration of the ingenious and useful system I had devised. And thus it was that despite the curtain that was lowered to separate Cardinal Rohan from his legal advisers, we succeeded in keeping in close touch with daily developments inside the Bastille and in guiding the illustrious prisoner in his course of action. . . .

Suddenly those days of anxiety and concern were brightened by the sweetest, most unexpected of consolations. Foreign Affairs Minister de Vergennes had spared no effort in his search to discover the hiding place of Villette and had forwarded descriptions of the fellow to every French embassy and consulate on the Continent. Baron de Castelnau, our resident at Geneva, located the wanted man in that city, disguised and living under an assumed name.

Castelnau so efficiently spied upon the fugitive in his little excursions to a suburb where he went regularly to play the mandolin, and he seized so opportune an hour to effect the arrest, that the Geneva magistrates could find no cause for complaint on the score of violation of international law.*

MEMOIRS
OF RÉTAUX DE VILLETTE

Despite all my precautions, I was arrested in Geneva and dragged off to the prisons of Paris.

It was the era of despotism, when the people were weighted down under the chains of slavery. Government ministers more tyrannical than the sultans of Tunis or Algiers wielded power of life and death over the French populace. In vain might a citizen cry out against injustice; let him so much as displease a man of rank or position—even his wife, his relatives greedy to get their hands on his fortune—and he would be snatched off, abused and flung into a dungeon whither neither the sun nor the human voice could penetrate.

The reader can imagine my distress at my arrest, aggravated as it was by the coarse jeers and taunts of the constabulary, which seemed to take a positive pleasure in its cruel assignment. Trembling, I endured it all in silence, speaking not a word, despite the dastardly methods to which the police resort to make a prisoner more talkative.

More talkative than he would lead us to believe, Villette, judging by the police report received from Geneva and now in the Foreign Affairs Archives. The report, signed by Paris Police Inspector Quidor (just back from the abortive Newcastle kidnap expedition), makes interesting reading. Villette's revelations about his relations with Madame de La Motte were so lurid as to impress even case-hardened Quidor, whose beat was the Paris red-light district:

* The Queen's faction was not unaware of the Foreign Office's services in behalf of Cardinal Rohan which might be interpreted as disservices to the Queen, as is shown in a letter from Austrian Ambassador Count Mercy to Emperor Joseph: "Count de Vergennes has just given another signal example of his sympathy for Cardinal Rohan, a sympathy which tends to save the prelate at the expense of the Queen . . ." One explanation for Vergennes's pronounced sympathy for the Cardinal may be that they were, in all probability, fellow Masons in Cagliostro's Paris lodge; another may lie in the fact that the Foreign Affairs Minister was miffed at Marie Antoinette's persistent refusal to permit his handsome Greek wife to be presented to her at the Court of Versailles.

The prisoner describes himself as "stud bull to Madame de La Motte," it being obviously on the basis of his physical endowments that the lady made choice of him as her lover. Of insatiably amorous temperament, he cannot apparently afford to be invariably discriminating, resorting occasionally to prostitutes of the lowest ranks.

Quidor's report concludes with the following dialogue excerpt from the interview with Villette in the Geneva jail:

"Any news of the Oliva girl? Has she been found or apprehended?"

"She's in the Bastille!"

"Do you know whether she has said anything about me? Or made any public statements? She's the only one who could involve me in this business. Madame de La Motte will never mention my name, I know, but if this girl talks I'm a lost man."

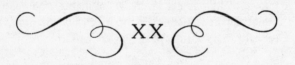

Interrogations and Confrontations

(Winter 1785-1786)

THE PARADE OF WITNESSES in the Diamond Necklace Case, in and out of the Bastille, in and out of the halls of the Parliament of Paris, went on through all the fall months of 1785, from September well into late December. It was a parade that began immediately after Madame de La Motte's first questioning in the Bastille (August 19 or 20) at the hands of Police Lieutenant General de Crosne, who could not have hoped to find her more voluble; the Countess talked freely, loosely, naming names, scores of names (always with the notable exceptions of Oliva and Villette, of handsome young Ramon de Carbonnières and handsome young Jacques Claude Beugnot).

Cardinal Rohan, in his examination at the hands of the commission of Cabinet ministers, had mentioned the names of still other parties whom he indicated as having knowledge of the series of events leading up to the necklace transaction. As an aftermath of these disclosures, a dozen or so witnesses were subpoenaed and others were less ceremoniously seized and clapped into the Bastille in a highhanded measure to ensure obtaining their testimony: witnesses such as Countess Cagliostro, Baron da Planta, Grenier (the Countess de La Motte's premier jeweler) and Rosalie Briffault (her pert premier lady's maid); as Marie Jeanne de Latour (the niece of Count de La Motte, the child medium of Cagliostro's candlelit séances), thrown into a cell alongside her mother,

Madame de Latour, whose incarceration the Countess has earlier described.

This parade of witnesses, proceeding willy-nilly, with good grace or with ill, cheerfully or sullenly, in and out of the Palais de Justice (which shares the Île de la Cité with Notre Dame and continues into the twentieth century as the seat of France's highest court), in and out of its inner chambers, where Examining Magistrates Titon de Villotran and Dupuy de Marcé were waiting to take their depositions—this parade was led off, quite properly, by Böhmer and Bassenge. After the jewelers came the banker Saint-James, commission-man Laporte and Desclaux, the Queen's Trianon lackey; and after them, to no one's surprise, the Abbé Georgel, who, in mid-September, produced his surprise witness, Father Loth. In Loth's wake came the Countess de La Motte's entire domestic staff and all her purveyors, notaries, bankers, jewelers—even her admirers, including the current favorite, the Count d'Olomieu, fiercely twirling his mustaches at the process server. While among the government witnesses summoned by Prosecutor General de Fleury there suddenly appeared, one wintry night, to the enormous gratification of the curiosity seekers thronging the Palais de Justice courtyard, no less a celebrity than Madame du Barry, immediately recognizable even in the flickering torchlight as she alighted gracefully from her elegant carriage at the foot of the great staircase, the forget-me-not blue of her eyes unfaded, her golden head untarnished. The Du Barry's was an appearance to start the rumors flying, to stimulate speculation as to her possible connection with the Diamond Necklace Case (beyond the known fact that the prodigious jewel had been originally designed by Böhmer and Bassenge, in the late years of the last reign, with her and her indulgent royal lover in mind).

Even Madame Campan had offered to go into Paris to give her testimony, as she writes in her memoirs:

Speaking to the King, I offered to go to testify to what Böhmer had told me of the Cardinal's complicity in the necklace negotiations, but the King was so considerate as to say that he preferred to spare me that disagreeable experience, especially since he could not see that it would serve the Queen's interests.

"For it appears," His Majesty explained, "that all the Cardinal's papers have been destroyed save one scrap of memorandum in his handwriting found in a desk drawer of the Palais-Cardinal, dated the end of

July and showing the notation that Böhmer had mentioned seeing Madame Campan, who had warned him to be on his guard against an intrigue designed to victimize him; that Madame Campan had told him that she would lay her head upon the executioner's block in maintaining that the Queen had never even coveted the diamond necklace, much less commissioned its purchase. Did you have such a conversation as this with Böhmer?"

Confirming this, I went on to quote Böhmer's statements to me concerning the Cardinal: to wit, that His Eminence had explicitly stated to Böhmer that he held his commission directly from the Queen and that it was from the Queen's own hands that he had received the thirty thousand francs destined as payment on account for the jewelers.

"Were you alone with Böhmer when he made that statement?" the King inquired. On my response in the affirmative, he continued, "Well, then, the man could simply deny ever having said it, for here he is now, assured of being paid his one million six hundred thousand francs on the guarantee of the house of Rohan. Thus we can no longer count on his sincerity; and besides, how could he ever explain his own strange conduct—why he wrote that enigmatic letter to Her Majesty and then, receiving no response, waited three full weeks before making another effort to contact either Her Majesty or me? No, I shall advise my Parliament that I prefer no one so close to the Queen as yourself to be subpoenaed. They have sent word to inquire whether I should object, and I do, on the ground that your going into Paris might give the impression that you had been sent to testify by the Queen; that would be unseemly."

As for the Queen herself, any information relative to the necklace transaction in her power to furnish had to be forwarded to the magistrates in a roundabout fashion. The Parliament of Paris had originally conceived some idea of sending a delegation to Versailles to take Her Majesty's deposition, but this the King promptly vetoed, and not without reason: it would have constituted a clear case of lèse-majesté for Her Majesty to have been subjected to an interrogation by representatives of His Majesty's own instrument of justice, his own judicial appointees.

Instead, the King decided, Her Majesty should graciously deign to forward to Parliament, by the hand of the Keeper of the Seals, a résumé of the information in her possession which might be considered pertinent to the Necklace Trial.

This manuscript was accordingly delivered to the Parliament by the Keeper of the Seals and became a part of the official dossier of the trial, numbered, listed and filed by the court registrar along with all the other documents and exhibits, under the title "Information Considered of Sufficient Importance to be Communicated to the Keeper of the Seals for the Purpose of the Enlightenment of the King and of his Parliament of Paris in the Cause of Justice in the Diamond Necklace Affair."

The document is described by the court registrar, in filing, as "being comprised of fifteen separate articles, and consisting of seven pages, bound and laced with a narrow blue silk riband."

Unfortunately, only the description survives; the document itself is missing (misplaced, misappropriated?) along with two other items, categorized in the dossier as "exhibits for the prosecution."

Meanwhile, the Parliament's duly appointed examining magistrates, having completed the hearing of witnesses in the Palais de Justice, removed to the Bastille for the questioning of prisoner witnesses and prisoner defendants. Memoirist Nougaret describes the first questionings:

Examining Magistrates Titon and de Marcé, accompanied by Court Clerk de Frémyn, launched into the interrogation of the accused with a determined effort and great zeal, coming to the Bastille to conduct these sessions. The day of Cardinal Rohan's initial interrogation, the magistrates continued the hearings from nine o'clock in the morning until 1 P.M. and, in a second session that same day, from four in the afternoon until midnight.

There were elaborate formalities to be observed in the interrogations vis-à-vis a cardinal; a rigorous etiquette had to be preserved by the functionaries of both the Bastille and the Parliament as well as by Prince Louis himself. Upon the appointed examination days, the Prince donned ceremonial garb, his scarlet cardinalic robes, scarlet calotte, scarlet hose, all the attributes of his office. The governor of the Bastille in person came to escort His Eminence to the council chamber of the fortress, where he left the noble prisoner with the magistrates and other court personnel, Monsieur de Launay remaining in the adjoining room

N*

so as to be immediately available should Prince de Rohan have need . of anything. At the end of each séance, the governor awaited his prisoner at the door, thence to escort His Eminence back to his apartments.

The Cardinal's initial interrogation began on Wednesday, January 11, at 9 A.M., according to the official record of the hearings, penned in the court clerk's cramped script across a sheaf of folio sheets:

On this day, Wednesday, January 11, 1786, there was brought before me, Jean Baptiste Maximilien Pierre Titon, magistrate of the Parliament of Paris, in the government council chamber of the fortress of the Bastille, Cardinal Rohan, decreed a prisoner by writ of capias issued by the Parliament of Paris on December 15 of last year. . . .

Interrogated as to his surname and given names, age, rank, station and residence, the respondent replied that he was Louis René Édouard, Cardinal Rohan, Prince-Bishop of Strasbourg, Grand Almoner of France, aged fifty-two, residing in Paris at his Hôtel Rohan in the Rue Vieille du Temple. . . .

The necklace contract, bearing the signatures "Böhmer and Co." and "Marie Antoinette de France," having been shown to the Cardinal, we called upon him to state whether the five terms of purchase of the contract were not entirely written by his own hand and whether it was not the contract submitted to Böhmer and Bassenge, accepted and signed by them as Böhmer and Co.; and if so, we required of him that he identify the contract by initialing it.

Cardinal Rohan recognized the propriety of our request, admitting readily that the first five paragraphs of the terms of payment were in his hand, and that he was ready to initial it as such. This done, he added, however, that he was constrained to call to our attention that he was astonished to see this document included as a state exhibit in view of the fact that it had not been discovered or seized among his papers, but had been voluntarily submitted by him to the Minister de Breteuil for transmittal to the hands of the King personally and thus should be construed as a proof of the good faith in which he had acted throughout—an exhibit for the defense, therefore, rather than for the prosecution. . . .

When called upon to declare whether the six "*Approuvés*" noted in the margin of the contract at the side of the articles, and the signature "Marie Antoinette de France," were actually the handwriting of the

Queen, the respondent stated that whereas he had originally been firmly convinced that they were in the hand of the Queen, he was now convinced that they were not. Asked whether he knew by whose hand these words and the signature had been written, he declared that he could not positively state whose handwriting it was.

Cardinal Rohan was next shown the depositions made by Bassenge and the financier Saint-James, which constituted the most serious indictments against him: first, Saint-James's testimony to the effect that the Cardinal had told him that he himself had seen in the hands of the Queen the sum of 700,000 francs, destined for the first payment on the necklace; second, Bassenge's testimony to the effect that the Cardinal had told him that he had dealt directly with the Queen in the necklace transaction.

As regarded the first deposition, that of Saint-James, the Cardinal replied to his inquisitors:

Even Saint-James admits that our conversation was not a serious one, but rather a casual chat at a social gathering, on an open terrace surrounded by a press of people and a deal of noise—a chat, moreover, in which both Saint-James and I spoke in whispers so as not to be overheard by the other guests. Now, under such circumstances, and with several months having since elapsed, it is easy, as Saint-James must recognize, to confuse what he thought he heard me say with what I actually said, a great similarity existing between the two. What he thought he heard me say was, "I saw the sum of seven hundred thousand francs in the hands of the Queen," whereas what I actually said was, "I saw a letter in the handwriting of the Queen in which she said that she had put aside the seven hundred thousand francs for the first installment due to Böhmer and Bassenge . . ."

In regard to Bassenge's deposition, Maître Target had coached Cardinal Rohan to say in the rebuttal that "the witness Bassenge must simply have made an honest mistake" about what he thought he had heard the Cardinal say. This defense stratagem was hooted by the Countess de La Motte: "When Saint-James and Bassenge produced testimony highly incriminating to the Cardinal, his defenders tried to make both witnesses out defectives—the first, Saint-James, as hard of hearing, the second, Bassenge, as a half-wit."

The Abbé Georgel, while admitting these two particular depositions to be the most telling indictments brought against the Cardinal, yet manages to explain away, to some extent, these "most highly embarrassing points in all the evidence" against his master. This exercise in dialectics appears in his memoirs as: "The Cardinal's confrontations with Böhmer, Bassenge and Saint-James diminished to a great extent the damaging effect of their earlier testimony. Without actually retracting their original statements, they did modify several expressions which, taken literally, had produced an impression unfavorable to the Cardinal."

And so the Cardinal's first official interrogation came to an end.

MEMOIRS
OF THE COUNTESS DE LA MOTTE-VALOIS

Our first interrogations and confrontations began the first day of January, 1786.* And from that moment on, we were deprived of all legal counsel.

At eleven o'clock that morning, the lieutenant of the guard came to escort me down to the council chamber, where Titon de Villotran, along with Court Clerk de Frémyn, waited. I knew Monsieur Titon and was charmed to find that he was the magistrate appointed to conduct the inquiry and render the report thereon to the Parliament.

Knowing how high-spirited I was, how sensitive and touchy, he begged me—banteringly, of course—to hear him out with calm. "I will, in truth," he said, "be putting some rather disagreeable questions to you, but try to control yourself, I implore you, and reply with moderation."

The first hour having been devoted to the social amenities and various preliminaries, he embarked upon the interrogation proper. The questions being the same, however, as those put to me earlier by Police Lieutenant General de Crosne, my responses were identical.

The official record reads:

---

* The actual date of the Countess's first appearance in the legal arena, according to the official trial record, understandably more accurate than the Countess's memory, was January 20; her first series of interrogations continued through nine sessions, well into February.

On this day, Thursday, January 20, 1786, there was brought before me, Jean Baptiste Pierre Maximilien Titon, magistrate of the Parliament of Paris, in the council chamber of the fortress of the Bastille, the Lady de La Motte de Valois, accused, decreed a prisoner by writ of capias issued by the Parliament of Paris on December 15 last. . . .

Upon taking oath to speak the truth, the respondent was questioned as to her surname, given names, age, rank, station and residence, to which she replied that she was called Jeanne de Valois de Saint-Rémy de Luz, wife of Marc Antoine Nicolas, Count de La Motte, that her age was twenty-nine and her residence in the Rue Neuve St. Gilles, Paris. . . .

Questioned as to whether it was not because she had foreseen that the necklace swindle would all shortly come to light that she had removed from Paris to Bar-sur-Aube, taking all her personal and household effects with her, the respondent stated that when she had bought the Bar-sur-Aube house in 1784 it had been with the intention of spending part of every year there, and that it was to that purpose that she had sent various furnishings there; and that she had done so openly, with no attempt at concealment, all the world, including Monseigneur the Cardinal, having seen the wagons packed and pulling out of her courtyard. The respondent further stated that had she been visited with any premonition of impending doom such as being arrested in connection with the diamond necklace transaction, she would never have made so public an entry into the provinces, but would have removed instead with her husband to a foreign country like England, where he was well acquainted. . . .

Questioned as to whether she and her husband had not carried off with them from Paris the remnants of the diamond necklace, and whether they did not display these brilliants at Bar-sur-Aube, the respondent stated that the only brilliants she took with her to Bar were the ones she had been wearing in Paris openly and in full view of all who cared to look, including Monseigneur the Cardinal, who had given them to her. But, she said, what she could not understand was why, if the police had been sent to arrest her on the Cardinal's accusation of having stolen the diamond necklace, they had limited themselves to searching and confiscating her papers, without ever having so much as broached the subject of diamonds, without having seized those in her possession and unconcealed. The respondent further stated that, having dined the previous day at the Duke de Penthièvre's and supped at the

Abbey of Clairvaux, she had been bedecked in all the jewelry she owned; and, not having returned from those entertainments until three o'clock in the morning, she had not made the slightest effort to put away, much less hide, her jewels, but had simply tossed the pieces into a dressing-table drawer which she did not lock and which was later opened by the police. She observed to us additionally that these diamonds which she had had with her at Bar-sur-Aube were those which had been given her by the Cardinal and with which she had frequently adorned herself in Paris and at Versailles, at the theater and at balls and other gala occasions; and that the trial had thus far produced only suspicions and unsubstantiated accusations as to the provenance of her jewels' being the diamond necklace, whereas, on the contrary, when the Cardinal had given them to her—some as outright gifts, some to sell for him—he had told her that they had come from Rohan heirloom pieces which he no longer wore now that he was growing older. . . .

Questioned as to whether she had told the Cardinal that she would try to arrange a rendezvous for him with the Queen, the respondent stated that our imaginations must be running riot, and that whoever had conjured up such a fantastic tale must either be dreaming or raving mad; that she was astonished that the Cardinal would even claim to have needed an obscure woman like herself to obtain an audience for him with his sovereign, when his own high rank and his position as Grand Almoner brought him almost daily to court and into contact with Their Majesties, so that he had opportunity to know better than any other what was going on at Versailles, including the fact that she had not the honor of entrée to the Queen; that if the Cardinal had actually uttered such nonsense, then the French Academy should henceforward close its doors to him. . . .

Shown the necklace contract and questioned as to whether the "Approuvés" and the signature were in her hand, the respondent stated that she had never seen the instrument before, much less had anything to do with writing it; that, after all she had heard on the subject, she was glad to get a look at the famous document at last; and that she recognized the Cardinal's handwriting in the text, the five articles entitled "terms of sale," but did not know the handwriting in the six marginal notations or in the signature "Marie Antoinette de France." On this basis, the respondent agreed to initial it.

MEMOIRS
OF THE ABBÉ GEORGEL

Thus it came about that a prince of the royal blood of Brittany, a sovereign prince of the Holy Roman Empire, a prince-bishop, a Grand Almoner of France, cloaked in the Roman purple, fell subject to the cruelest of humiliations and was forced to appear in the attitude of a presumed prisoner, to be confronted with whom? with a fury, the wickedest of wicked women, whom, out of misplaced charity and excessive compassion, he had rescued from the depths of destitution; a woman whom he had indiscreetly trusted, whom, in a burst of confidence which cold reason finds it difficult to condone, he had made the repository of his innermost hopes, dreams, ambitions and affections; a woman, who, after dragging herself through the slime of intrigue and of crime, after bilking her benefactor of 120,000 francs and a diamond necklace, had climaxed her treachery by labeling him the author of her own criminally dishonest machinations.

The confrontation, the procedure whereby accused persons are brought face to face with each other to answer each other's charges, or are confronted with the witnesses who have testified against them, was an important feature of ancien-régime jurisprudence and, necessarily, a provocative one, for inevitably the sparks would fly.

"For her confrontations with Monseigneur the Cardinal," says Georgel, "this inherently immoral woman made her appearance armored in insolence; her expression, defiant, shameless, dared to assume all the confidence of innocence; her tongue, tipped with venom and contumely, was unchecked by honesty."

MEMOIRS
OF THE COUNTESS DE LA MOTTE-VALOIS

The morning of my first scheduled confrontation with the Cardinal, I awaited his arrival with an impatience which the reader can imagine more easily than I can describe.

Upon entering the council chamber, I had found Monsieur de Marcé presiding, assisted by Monsieur de Frémyn, the court clerk. To the latter I expressed my pleasure in seeing him again, but there was a somber air about him that day, a distant manner that could scarcely be construed as a favorable omen; he went so far as to affect not to notice me. As for Monsieur de Marcé, the examining magistrate, there was an indefinable something in his expression that alarmed me, a hint of the severity to be expected in his judgment of me.

At last, through the door at the far end of the room, I saw the Cardinal enter. He, after cordial greetings to the gentlemen and chilly ones to me, seemed inclined to linger in chitchat with the court functionaries; if so, I cut it short with the remark, "Come, gentlemen, I am waiting. Let us get on with our business."

Monsieur de Marcé and his colleague came forward and, with the Cardinal, seated themselves around the table, where I had already taken my place. The examining magistrate instructed me to raise my right hand and swear to tell the truth, at which word the Cardinal and I startled and, for the first time, looked directly at each other.

As I raised my hand, I resolved to try to clear myself without involving the name of the Queen, which I was determined at all costs to avoid. Attorney Doillot had warned me that the Cardinal would be trying to trap me, to lead me into naming the Queen so that she would turn against me. And it will be noted that, despite my pointed questions to the Cardinal, I framed them in such a way as never to compromise the Queen. In speaking of events even indirectly connected with the necklace matter, I referred to it only as a tale told me by the Cardinal, a fanciful one which I had never really believed.

Nor should anyone be shocked that I availed myself of this, the sole means of defense left me. No, the reader must try to put himself in my place, try to realize the delicacy of the situation in which I found myself, a woman, alone, frail, without defenders as without influence, faced with the problem of clearing my name without implicating that of the Queen. Let the reader consider my plight before he renders judgment.

While the court clerk was inscribing our oaths into the record, my eyes sought those of the Cardinal, but he averted his and, in a distracted manner, pretended to be absorbed, endlessly rolling and unrolling a twist of paper between his fingers as if he would never have done.

Then it was that they handed me the transcript of the Cardinal's previous interrogations in order that I might read them over before being questioned upon the various articles contained therein. Imagine my indignation and distress when I saw a formal accusation drawn up against me, complete with the signature of the Cardinal himself! As I came to the end of each paragraph of the charges, I stopped reading and raised my eyes to stare at him. But he dared not meet my gaze; it would have abashed him. . . .

Indeed, anyone listening to us during those first days of our confrontations would have thought that each had resolved upon the destruction of the other.

The questions on the list presented to me by the Cardinal added up to a total of no less than 183! Mine to him I had limited to eighty-nine.

From the official record of the interrogations and confrontations, January and February 1786:

Questioned as to whether she had not, in November of 1784, asked Cardinal Rohan for sums totaling 120,000 francs, purportedly for charitable donations, in the name of the Queen, and whether the Cardinal had not sent her these monies in two remittances by the hand of the Baron da Planta, the respondent declared that if the Cardinal said he had, or if the Baron da Planta said so, they were all getting crazier and crazier; that she did not understand such foolishness; that the supposition that a man with so much as a grain of common sense would have handed out such sums as that without requiring a receipt, without retaining the written request for the loan, was utterly preposterous and she resented the insult to her intelligence. . . .

Questioned as to whether she had not shown the Cardinal a letter purportedly from the Queen in which Her Majesty expressed a desire to acquire the diamond necklace, the respondent declared that if the Cardinal claimed she had shown him such a letter, then let it be produced in evidence.

A good point, and she hammered away at it throughout her interrogations and confrontations, insisting that any such letters "purportedly written by her or transmitted by her to the Cardinal as bearing instructions from the Queen be forthwith produced in this courtroom—above all, the one described by the Cardinal as instructing him to deliver over the necklace box to the messenger supposedly sent by the Queen," for surely "any man with a brain in his head would have demanded and held fast to a receipt for well-nigh two million francs' worth of gems."

Later, in the course of the Countess's second series of confrontations with the Cardinal, came a question calculated to cut her to the quick: "whether she had not solicited and received from Cardinal Rohan, during the years 1783 and 1784, such modest sums as four and five louis at a time," as the official trial record puts it.

As might have been expected, the reaction flashed swift and sharp. "Upon my word, Madame de La Motte, you are a hothead!" Madame de La Motte herself quotes Magistrate de Marcé's ejaculation, describing the scene in her Story of My Life:

How dare Cardinal Rohan state that I solicited and accepted such piddling sums from him! What would I have wanted, pray tell, with those four and five louis—I who succored the widow and the orphan, befriended the needy, allotted monthly pensions to family retainers? I who maintained a residence in Paris, an apartment at Versailles, a country house at Charonne, all three establishments well staffed and having stables stocked with blooded horses and fine equipages! I kept a staff of twelve to serve me at my town house on the Rue Neuve St. Gilles, as all Paris knew and as the Cardinal could not have failed to observe, my house being no more than a hundred paces from his own; each time His Eminence came to call, he could not but have noted that I had a liveried porter to open the carriage gates to him, liveried footmen to announce him at the salon door. His Eminence was bound to have seen the courtyard filled with my splendid carriages, and to have known that they were mine by the fleur-de-lis of my Valois coat of arms emblazoned upon the doors.

Having seen all this, Cardinal Rohan yet dares to claim that he was doling out four and five louis at a time to me. Now, is it not incredible that at the period of my greatest prosperity, I would have deigned to accept alms—the only proper words for such paltry sums? No, I was not the type of woman to accept charity, nor was Cardinal Rohan the type of man to offer it to the woman to whom he was paying court. No one knows better than he his own largesse to his own mistress.

From the official record of the confrontation of Madame de La Motte and Cardinal Rohan on April 24, 1786:

. . . To this Cardinal Rohan made answer: "I have hesitated up to now, out of a natural and understandable repugnance, to reply to Madame de La Motte's *double-entendres* about the nature of the relations between herself and me. If she has so little respect for herself and her own reputation as to imply indecencies which are not factual, then I must reject the suspicions she seeks to raise; it would be beneath my dignity to elaborate on so unsavory a theme.

"Here, thus, we have to deal with a new atrocity from the lips of Madame de La Motte, like all the rest devoid of likelihood, beyond the realm of possibility and probability, accomplishing no purpose save that of inspiring the same disgust as have her other attempts to arouse odious suspicions. At such a charge I can only sigh, turn away my eyes and thoughts and, in closing, call to your attention the fact that Madame has waited an unconscionably long while to launch this particular libelous attack. Perhaps she has been preparing it as a last resort to bolster the falsehoods she has hitherto advanced, which she now sees crumbling away beneath the weight of the testimony of the witnesses and the other accused."

STORY OF MY LIFE
BY THE COUNTESS DE LA MOTTE-VALOIS

It was when we had come to the fifth article of my deposition that a sharp contest arose between the Cardinal and me. He had prepared a set of stock answers, all evasive, which he parroted incessantly, with only some minor variations, until I insisted that he make a direct answer to a direct question. Thereupon he lost his temper—and I mine—setting off a dispute that raged for some three hours. It was I who came off winner in that first trial of strength between us. My replies were short and simple, but so direct, so to the point that those present could not keep the smiles from off their lips—as clear a form of applause as a clapping of hands.

The Cardinal, for his part, must have been equally convinced that he had emerged the victor in that verbal fray, or at least so he must have retailed the incident to the Abbé Georgel, whose memoirs relate that "Monseigneur the Cardinal, stirred to the keenest indignation, yet managed to preserve his calm superiority, forcing Madame de La Motte to admissions and contradictions which shook to its foundations the towering edifice of lies she had built up in her two defense pleas."

STORY OF MY LIFE
BY THE COUNTESS DE LA MOTTE-VALOIS

Those constant, interminable interrogations and confrontations, with their eternal, insidious questions, were enough to bewilder a clearer head than mine. That is the only explanation I can offer for the frequent contradictions and inconsistencies into which I was trapped and upon which my enemies seized gleefully.

But from my first day in the Bastille, I had been harassed by agents and emissaries of both parties, the Queen's and the Cardinal's. Commissaire Chesnon, as early as August 18, 1785, gave me to understand that the Queen would protect me on the condition that I tell my story without involving her, and when I cried that I simply did not see how that could be done when she herself had been the very heart and soul of the affair, Chesnon replied, "If you name her, you are lost."

And if my own counselor, Doillot, urged the same tactics on me, it must be remembered that he had come to me at the recommendation of Baron de Breteuil and, like the Baron, had only two concerns at that point: first, to bring the Cardinal's head upon the executioner's block; second, to keep the Queen's name out of the affair.

This brings me to the question I have asked myself a thousand times: If the Queen never knew me and if I had deceived the Cardinal, why were such infinite and elaborate precautions taken to keep the Queen's name from being so much as breathed aloud in the Diamond Necklace Trial? This is the question that I shall never cease to ask myself, and that I would now ask of those readers who dare to think for themselves, those to whom these memoirs are dedicated.

On one side, then, the Queen's faction and on the other that of the Cardinal sought to win me over, to shape my testimony to their advantage. Count de Launay, governor of the Bastille, had assigned the chaplain of that horrible prison as intermediary between the Cardinal and me, informing us of the subjects to be covered in the next day's interrogation or confrontation, so that the Cardinal and I might harmonize our stories. (The Cardinal could claim as his creatures almost the entire personnel of the Bastille, from the governor down.) The chaplain explained that the Cardinal, in charging me, had yielded most reluctantly to the insistence of his family and his legal counsel, and only upon being convinced by them that he did not thereby imperil me, for the reason that the Queen wanted only one victim in this case —the Cardinal himself. This explanation I accepted the more readily, perhaps, because I was loath to believe him guilty of such perfidy.

"I am sure," the pernicious abbé continued, "that after all His Eminence's good offices in your behalf, you would not want to be the one responsible for the stroke of the executioner's ax upon his neck—for that is precisely what will happen if you co-operate with his enemies in proving that he carried on a clandestine correspondence with the Queen."

"Then what in the world am I to do?" I asked. "If I can accuse neither the Cardinal nor the Queen, that leaves only me to shoulder the burden of guilt." My shoulders being precisely those upon which Maître Target proposed to shift the blame.

"If I were in your place, madame," the chaplain insinuated, "I would speak the truth. I cannot see what harm could come of your admitting the gift of some diamonds from the Queen."

"No, that's no good either," I replied. "It would be dangerous for me to make that claim, because it implies that the Queen actually received the necklace, and that is precisely the point to which Her Majesty does not choose to admit . . . Alas!" I cried. "My God, to whom can I listen?" I could not trust even my own defense counsel, who, being Breteuil's man, quoted me on every page of the trial briefs he prepared and published in my name as saying that I had never laid eyes on the Queen—and further persuaded me to repeat that lie myself to the judges on the floor of the Parliament, whereas my natural, my best defense would have consisted in speaking the truth as to our relations. No consequences, surely, could have been so cruel as those incurred by the lie.

By a fatal and almost inconceivably fantastic set of circumstances, the Queen and I actually made common cause in the Necklace Trial, for I was, in a strange sense, actually only representing the Queen in a case in which she could not appear openly; while the Cardinal, trying desperately to conciliate Her Majesty and at the same time save his skin, blamed everything on me—a dodge conceived, as usual, by his precious Maître Target. Thus it was I found myself in mortal struggle not only against the openly exerted influence of the powerful house of Rohan but also against the secret influence of the all-powerful Queen, who was to turn upon me when she saw she could not bring me to do her dirty work in her deep-laid plot for the destruction of the Cardinal. Is it any wonder that I succumbed to such overwhelming odds?

There were pitfalls everywhere I turned; to be discreet was not enough; I could not open my mouth, could not make a move without being told, "If you say thus or do so you are lost."

"Say it's black," the first person would tell me, "or you're done for." So I said, "Yes, it's black." "Call it white," a second insisted, "or it's all up with you." So I said, "No, it's white." Then, "Don't even mention such and such," a third party warned, "or the game is up." So, when they questioned me on that particular point, I beat about the bush. Although I never guessed it at the time, all these contradictions, discrepancies, tergiversations served to tip the scales of justice and public opinion against me. I was like the patient in the fable to whom one doctor says, "Eat, or you'll perish of starvation," whereas the next practitioner to come along insists, "Don't eat a morsel, or you'll die of indigestion."

Thus it can be seen that I was misled by friend and foe alike; from my very first day in the Bastille, not a step, not a word was suggested to me that did not eventually contribute to my downfall.

Actually, I had powerful arguments in my favor; truth and innocence were on my side, and my arguments should have pulverized those of the Cardinal. But he, on his side, could claim such overpowering advantages as family fortune and influence, plus a mind more highly trained than mine, and his position was further bolstered by the depositions of witnesses bribed and coached by his lawyers.

At my second confrontation with the Cardinal the social amenities were dispensed with, and when the magistrate inquired of us whether we desired our respective depositions of the preceding day to be read back to us, it was agreed likewise to dispense with that formality.

The Cardinal, who had lacked the hardihood to look at me, much less address me, proved that he had audacity enough to continue to incriminate me. At that point I lost my patience.

"Monsieur," I cried, "you have gone too far!" And, my exclamation having effectively silenced him, I launched forthwith into a dissertation on the subject of his correspondence with the Queen, devoting at least half an hour to it and all without the Cardinal's daring to interrupt. The very mention of that exchange of billets-doux had reawakened all his terrors; he sat frozen into immobility, like a man struck by an unexpected blow.

As for Titon and Frémyn, passive spectators to the scene, they sat, content merely to smile, arms folded—consequently, writing down not a word of my testimony. Such conduct on their part was proof positive that they had no intention of putting down in black and white any evidence which might serve to involve the Queen; in this doubtlessly they were acting on instructions from Baron de Breteuil (unless, won over by the Rohan family, they had a double motive in recording nothing of what I said).*

At length, the Cardinal's confusion having become visible to all, Magistrate Titon spoke up, saying, "We will skip over this article, and go on to another."

At these words I did not spare Monsieur Titon my reproaches, but told him point-blank that it was not up to the presiding magistrate to offer any comment; that his duty was purely and simply to make a record of the depositions of the various parties. There could no longer be any doubt in my mind but that the Cardinal had won him over, along with Marcé and Frémyn. I saw them all tremble when he hesitated over a response, for fear he blunder into some contradiction. I watched them straining toward him, every nerve and muscle tense, hands and feet twitching, their eyes fixed upon him, as if willing him with every ounce of their strength into saying what they wanted him to say. Thus one sees sharpers pressing close about the gaming table, concentrating on signaling their accomplices, to compel them toward that certain card upon which all their hopes are riding.

As I was to learn in the days that followed, whenever the Cardinal found himself in an awkward situation and the magistrates failed, despite glares and glances, to silence him or to prompt the proper response, then they had a way of cutting him off in midsentence and suddenly breaking up the meeting by rising abruptly from the conference table.

Every iota of evidence favorable to the Cardinal was inscribed into the record with alacrity and exactitude, whereas whenever it was a ques-

---

* It was widely said in Paris at the time that Examining Magistrate Titon had been royally remunerated for his zeal in "acting on instructions." The Paris correspondent of the Imperial Court of St. Petersburg said it in one of his newsletters: "Louis XVI has appointed Titon de Villotran to the post of King's magistrate in the civil courts, accompanying this recompense for his services with a transfer of 500,000 francs, to be applied to the purchase price of that coveted post."

tion of testimony tending to compromise His Eminence I had to go into a tantrum to make the court clerk take it down. Even then that underhanded Frémyn needed only to resort to any of a dozen stratagems in his repertoire to alter the official minutes: by adding here and suppressing there; by omitting one word and substituting another; by excising whole sentences; by inserting long speeches that were never spoken into the text of a sheet after it had already been signed by all present and stamped with the Parliament's official seals. Once I overheard that "worthy" Marcé, scandalous prevaricator that he was, whisper to that "honest" Frémyn, "Remember to space your lines farther apart today." That was one of their favorite dodges; several times, in rereading the minutes of the preceding day's session, I noticed that additions had been made between the lines.

After having repeatedly made vain objection to this performance, I took my turn at jumping up incontinently from the table, vowing never to return and declaring that, since these gentlemen were determined in advance to find me guilty, my presence was not required and they could just as well condemn me without further hearing. Once I stood my ground for a solid week, and it took all Governor de Launay's pleas and promises to persuade me to take my seat again at that conference table —which I had dubbed the "sacrificial altar," it being obvious that I had been selected as the sacrificial victim to be offered up in the Necklace Case.

But although a sense of humor was lost on Court Clerk de Frémyn, he was quick enough at twisting my droll expressions to my disadvantage and at construing my refusal to appear as resistance to orders and contempt of court and making note of it as such for the judges of the Grand' Chambre.

It was an occasional flare-up such as this, a fit of temper, a brief lapse into ill humor that led these venal men to label me temperamental and intractable. But such transitory flashes of temperament cannot surprise the reader; the long months and hours of almost daily questioning, the constant strain, had considerably altered my basically pleasant disposition.

I began to fluctuate between heights of exaltation and valleys of depression, between my inherent optimism and a dark foreboding. In the beginning, all those about me, even the magistrates, seemed convinced that the Queen would surely intervene in my behalf. That general impression, together with my firm resolve to shoulder the burden of a crime which I had not committed rather than to compromise my sovereign, gave me the right to hope that Her Majesty would spread the wings of her protection above me, would never allow me to fall victim to my loyalty to her. This consoling thought restored me to my natural exuberance. I sang all day, enjoyed my promenade and slept the tranquil sleep that is the product of a tranquil conscience.

But when I discovered that word had gone out that the honor of the Queen was to be safeguarded at any price, and that a formidable league was organizing to avert the royal thunder from the Cardinal, when I discerned the storm clouds all gathering above my innocent head—at that moment I lost my courage, my taste for food, my disposition for sleep. Despair succeeded calm in my soul.

Additionally, there had come a tragedy to distress my already distressed heart, all the more difficult to bear in that it was totally unforeseen. In November Maître Doillot had, none too gently, broken to me the news of my brother's sudden death.

"He died and lies buried in India. The frigate of which he was a commander put back to sea immediately after the funeral." This was the frigate on which he had served so brilliantly and so heroically as to win, before his thirtieth birthday, the King's own decoration of the Royal Cross of St. Louis.*

I tried to console myself with the thought that my dear brother had thus been spared the humiliation of learning the calumny, the persecution and the shame to which his sister was being subjected, that he had died thinking her safe and happy. "Oh, God," I prayed, "perhaps this is one of Thy blessings?" For so overwhelming were my misfortunes that I was reduced to thanking Him for having taken away the dearest of brothers!

But this was a philosophical attitude I could not long sustain. A kind of frenzy gripped me: I could not sit still, I paced my cell. A vision of the lifeless body of my brother flashed before my eyes, and when I covered them with my hands there came the image of him as I had seen him last in life, and I heard his voice bidding me sternly to defend my honor and his.

Between the hours of three and four that morning, I was shaken by

---

* Count Beugnot must be considered flippant in this passage from his memoirs dealing with the Countess's brother: "The Baron de Valois, a punctilious and dedicated officer in the Navy, had attained the rank of lieutenant when he suddenly died in 1785, in the very midst of his sister's trial—not, surely, without some resentment at being unable to postpone his demise at least long enough to learn the outcome."

convulsions so violent that I fell from my bed and would have expired, had not my cries attracted the attention of the officer of the guard, who found me on the floor, naked and unconscious, beneath a table that had been overturned in my fall. By the time I regained consciousness, Governor de Launay had summoned a physician. A terrible tremor, a chattering of teeth had followed in the wake of the convulsions, to the accompaniment of a torrent of tears. The tears the physician made no attempt to stay, in the hope that they would relieve the oppression upon my heart, but he prescribed a bloodletting and a calming potion. While he administered all the remedies known to the physician's art for the relief of the body, that scoundrelly Bastille chaplain appeared to offer his ministrations to the soul, even he apparently being moved at finding me in extremis.

Upon awakening next morning, with only the vaguest recollection of the horrors of the previous night, I was surprised to find my turnkey, Saint-Jean, and a guardsman at my bedside, a vigil to which they had been posted by Launay. The latter returned shortly afterward with the physician, who prescribed two more bleedings, which brought some relief to my agonies; to this day, however, none of the resources of the materia medica have ever alleviated the periodic headaches to which I have since been subject.*

Several days later when I saw His Eminence again, he came toward me with concern evident in his expression, telling me that he had daily inquired after me of the chaplain. His eyes seemed now to be imploring my forgiveness; gone was that air of chilling pride and hauteur which he had affected at our previous encounters in the council chamber. As he gently took my hand to escort me toward the fireplace, I could not hold back the tears, at which he blanched, exclaiming, "Ah, Countess, to what a sad pass we are come! How unfortunate a pair we are!"

Indeed, throughout the entire course of that day's confrontation the Cardinal and I were so emotionally overwrought that we could scarcely attend the questions of the magistrates when they addressed us. Those

* Several eminent modern-day practitioners of the "physician's art" have essayed a diagnosis based upon the Countess's own account of her symptoms; the seizures constantly recurrent from childhood on, the headaches, the "heights of exaltation and valleys of depression" suggest the possibility of a brain tumor—if epilepsy is to be ruled out, as the Countess says specifically that it was, and on no less an authority than "the eminent medical faculty of Her Royal Highness, Madame Elisabeth, the sister of the King, after extensive examinations."

two, Argus-eyed as they were, pretended not to notice the goings-on between the Cardinal and me, although the manner in which we were mutually affected at this meeting could not have been more clearly discernible. At this meeting, as at others to follow, the Cardinal's air of interest toward me, the warmly affectionate tone of voice with which he addressed me, could have escaped no observer; anyone looking on must have wondered to what cause to attribute the harmony which manifested itself so openly between accuser and accused.

This harmony between them was subject to observation and to frequent comment, as Nougaret remarks in his Anecdotes du règne de Louis XVI, citing in this passage what he terms "extracts from Madame de La Motte's main volume of memoirs":

"One day when the Cardinal and I were being questioned upon a delicate point which neither he nor I had the slightest intention of clarifying, I made some answer which was not in strict conformity with fact. 'Ah, Madame Countess,' exclaimed the Prince, 'how can you advance a statement you know to be false?' 'As with all the rest, monsieur,' I replied. 'You know as well as I that from the first question put to us by these gentlemen, neither you nor I have uttered a word of truth. Indeed, it was never intended that we should, else why would they have supplied both our responses and our questions to us? And all our statements have had to be made in just such or such a fashion, according to instructions; if not, as you and I well know, we could have expected to wake up with our throats slit the first dark night in the Bastille.'"

If it is impossible to locate, among the Countess's numerous publications, the particular passage quoted by Nougaret, still she expresses much the same sentiment on page 118 of the first edition of her Mémoires justicatifs: "It is now common knowledge that during the course of our interrogations at the Bastille, neither the Cardinal nor I uttered a word of truth—and for the very best of reasons: we dared not . . . lest we be murdered." A dose of that deadly brew, perhaps, to which, on page 136 of the same volume, she refers as a "Versailles bouillon"? She continues:

Both of us having been warned that we were not so much as to breathe the name of the Queen, what could we possibly have said that bore even the faintest resemblance to fact?

As for the depositions of the witnesses at the trial, the signs of perjury leap from the page to strike the eye. To substantiate my charges of subornation, it is appropriate that I enter into some detail concerning the character of those who brought false witness against me, and concerning their relations with me and with the other defendants. They were, as a group, highly amenable to reason; originally ferreted out and approached by Laporte and Father Loth, they were coached by Target and bribed, coaxed, pampered, rewarded and guaranteed protection by the house of Rohan.

Laporte, a lawyer licensed to practice before the Parliament as well as a financial promoter and speculator, had frequently benefited by my good offices and my influence exerted in his behalf in court and government circles; his first-born I had held in my arms, as godmother, above the baptismal font. Yet when they read me his deposition, it proved a curious composition, at once conciliatory and treacherous, in betrayal of several confidences I had been so indiscreet as to make him on the subject of the Queen's favors.

Brought face to face with me, Laporte could not conceal his agitation and the fact that my presence intimidated him.

"Monsieur," I addressed him, "I have always considered you an honorable man. Forget for a moment what is written in that deposition, and reply honestly to my questions." Then, leading him along gradually, question by question, I secured his admission that I had consistently rejected his offers to share in the 200,000-francs sales commission proferred by Böhmer and Bassenge, and that, annoyed by his repetitions of the offer, I had ordered him out of my house.

His final admission was gratifying to my cause: "Not only did Madame de La Motte play no part in the necklace negotiations, but she refused to take any credit for it. On the contrary, she went so far as to try to dissuade the jewelers from delivering the necklace to the Cardinal."

Indeed, out of all that throng of witnesses, not a single one could actually connect me with the necklace transaction. Moreover, throughout the whole course of the investigations, Böhmer and Bassenge, in their depositions, never once brought any charge against me, and in the detailed formal report they drew up at the behest of Baron de Breteuil to present to the Queen on August 12, 1785, there did not appear so much as a mention of my name.

. . . Another "honest" man for you was that Régnier, a jeweler, who had been seduced into rigging the total of my purchases to a staggering sum. When I demanded that his account books be entered in evidence, that satisfaction was never granted me.*

. . . And then there was Grenier, goldsmith, clockmaker and speculator, who had come to my house originally with Laporte to seek my aid in one of their financial schemes and whose deposition was dictated to him in its entirety by Maître Target. This was obvious from the fact that Grenier, with his limited intelligence, could never have authored such a masterpiece, the main object of which was to prove not only that I had told him I had the honor of entrée to the Queen, but that I had showed him, one day while seated in my bath, letters purportedly from Her Majesty.

There is on record a deposition by Mainguet, one of the Countess's notaries, to the effect that on July 28 of the preceding year he had lent her the sum of thirty-five thousand francs, the implication being that this was the source of the thirty thousand francs which the Countess delivered to the Cardinal a day or two later, purportedly from the Queen, as an interest payment on the necklace account. On the subject of this loan the Countess, who was rarely nonplused, commended the court on having the facts, for once, correct, taking exception only to the purpose of the loan, which, according to her, was not the one indicated. What it was, she said, was "a favor to a friend, the distinguished wife of the Portuguese ambassador," who, finding herself in a tight squeeze financially, had applied to the Countess, who had obliged by borrowing the sum from Mainguet "to tide her over."

Admitted into evidence were affidavits sent up to the capital from Bar-sur-Aube by Police Inspector Surbois and containing statements by the Countess's local "business agent," Filleux, along with inventories of the La Mottes' provincial properties taken September 9-12 of the preceding year, showing household effects appraised at fifteen thousand francs (approximately four thousand dollars) and silverware (six cases

* Target, on the other hand, says that Régnier did produce his ledgers, "whereupon Mme de La Motte admitted to the purchases, exclaiming loudly upon the frailty of the human memory and posing herself the rhetorical question, How could she have forgotten, in less than a year, the details of her dealings with Régnier?"

out of the original seven, grudgingly excavated by Filleux from under his farm's loftiest dunghill) appraised at thirty thousand francs. All this wealth in the hands of Madame de La Motte, Target would say, could be accounted for only as coming from the proceeds of the sale of the necklace diamonds, a charge that would be countered by the Countess's counterproposition that the fortune at her disposal represented, rather, the "generous gifts of an indulgent lover," along with other sums contributed by "princes and princesses of the blood and by a succession of Cabinet ministers toward the endowment of a daughter of the Valois in distress."

The court record of the third interrogation of Madame de La Motte, that of January 23, 1786, shows that the examining magistrate opened the session by informing her that "the court found her testimony of the previous day's session to be extraordinary." Maître Target echoed that sentiment in his first published trial brief for Cardinal Rohan, with the words:

Fable follows fable upon her lips, as the need develops; and if you dare to ask her to prove her statements, she will present you with a proposition still more outlandish than the one it was designed originally to support, and in a tone more positive even than that in which she voiced the original. Thus a first misrepresentation is buttressed by a second, the second by a third, and, what with that imaginative genius of hers and that air of utter self-assurance, she will wind up persuading you that it is you who are confused by the conflict in her testimony.

The Baron da Planta, still a prisoner in the Bastille, got off on the wrong foot in his very first confrontation with the Countess. "That poor benighted equerry of the Cardinal's," she comments scathingly in her memoirs, "made statements ill calculated to support his master's—for instance, mentioning that he had several times met me at Versailles with the Cardinal, at the foot of the little staircase leading down from the Queen's private apartments."

When the Baron, in his testimony, inadvertently mentioned having "read a trial brief published in the Countess's defense," she demanded of him, the magistrates, the court clerk and all others present, as she tells it, "How came the Baron da Planta to procure a publication of that or any kind when he was supposed to be shut off, like the rest of the prisoners in the Bastille, from all contact with the outside world?" To *this, she says, "Planta gave a reply typical of the courtesy one may expect from boorish Germans: 'And what is it to you how I came by it, madame, so long as come by it I did?' "*

Although German-speaking, the Baron da Planta was, more accurately, "a surly Swiss from the eastern Alps," as the Abbé Georgel describes him. The abbé gives this version of the scene in his memoirs:

The Baron da Planta, disdaining to look at the woman or take notice of her taunts, addressed her with *sang-froid* and precision:

"I swear in the name of justice that I have often heard you say that you enjoyed the honor of meetings with Her Majesty, and that Her Majesty desired the Cardinal to purchase the diamond necklace for her. I swear that I walked with you on the Versailles terrace the night of the Grove of Venus impersonation, and that you came, in my presence, to tell the Cardinal that the Queen was on her way to meet him in that arbor. And I take oath upon my head and honor that I brought you, in two installments, sums totaling one hundred twenty thousand francs which you had requested of the Cardinal in the name of the Queen."

The Countess's retort stands inscribed in the official record of that day's stormy session:

To this Madame de La Motte made reply that the Baron da Planta was a madman; that, having forced his attentions on her, he had at last, in October of 1784 in her Paris residence, cornered her in a small room without a bell pull, where he insisted wildly that she yield to his passions, promising to make her fortune if she would . . . ; that, suddenly substituting actions for words, he had threatened her with his cane and, making all manner of lewd and menacing gestures, had flung himself upon her; that, taking to flight, she had sought refuge in her salon, where she found the Count d'Olomieu, her sister and several other persons whose names she could no longer remember; that she had rushed in, pale, trembling, almost fainting; and that not until she had recovered from her fright had she been able to recount the incident to those present, whereupon Count d'Olomieu had said, "You had only to call out, and we would have rushed to your assistance."

To what fiercer defender could a woman have looked than to a Captain Count d'Olomieu, that formidable martial figure, that mus-

tachioed, high-ranking military person? Villette, usually only sulky or spiteful about his rivals for Madame de La Motte's affections, waxes positively vicious about this, the final and undisputed victor in the amorous contest:

Count d'Olomieu climaxed her succession of lovers. Known as a man without shame as without integrity, he was likewise without esteem among his troops and fellow officers. He was a man without a virtue, unless reckless courage—or, rather, disdain of danger—be counted one; his could not properly be termed courage, for courage implies overcoming fear, whereas Olomieu was fearless. Having chased his last challenger around his mistress's table and out of her house with a pair of fire tongs, Count d'Olomieu reigned supreme at that time, holding undisputed dominion over Madame de La Motte's heart and senses.

The service of the subpoena to appear as a witness in the Diamond Necklace Trial spelled finis to Olomieu's brilliant and promising military career; the ensuing scandal compelled him to resign his captain's commission in the Royal Guard.

"The witnesses annihilate her." This quotation is from Maître Target's indictment of Madame de La Motte in his defense plea for Cardinal Rohan. "They march against her in long and steady procession—Sieurs Böhmer and Bassenge, Laporte, Régnier, Grenier, Furet [her clockmaker], her own servants . . ."

STORY OF MY LIFE
BY THE COUNTESS DE LA MOTTE-VALOIS

When it came to the subornation of my own servants I was so outraged that I could not control myself even in the presence of my judges. Monsieur de La Motte, desperately hungry for news, had sent his valet, Lessus, from London to Paris, where he was seized for questioning. His was a deposition too adroitly drawn up, you may be sure, to be the product of a humble and inexperienced body servant. Target's hand, it was plain to see, had guided the pen.

Target's hand was discernible again, the Countess vowed, in the deposition of Rosalie Briffault, that pert soubrette of a lady's maid who is pictured in the popular contemporary series of Necklace Case portrait prints—twenty-two copperplate engravings which became collectors' items overnight—as wasp-waisted in her fluted, ruffled uniform, her towering cap settled coquettishly upon her curls, earrings dangling to her shoulders. Her retroussé nose up in the air but her wits about her, Rosalie might have stepped over the footlights of the latest Beaumarchais comedy; she was another Suzanne or Rosine, up to as many tricks and just as tart in her observations about her betters.

Rosalie could tell the court—and did—about the bare cupboards chez La Motte in 1782 and 1783 ("Let us retire early, madame—sleep takes the edge off hunger pangs"); about the Cardinal's visits to Madame ("The door to the boudoir was always left ajar"); about the Grove of Venus episode ("I assisted Madame at the toilette of Mademoiselle d'Oliva, slipping the chemise-dress over her shoulders, draping the shawl, arranging the coiffure").

Even Deschamps, that faithful La Motte footman, was dragged into the Bastille to describe his errands to the stationers' for the purchase of that special pattern of notepaper, those dainty gilt-edged sheets upon which Villette—as Target sought to reconstruct the crime—had penned the billets-doux which were delivered by Madame de La Motte to the Cardinal in the name of the Queen.

The Queen's footman, Desclaux (in Her Majesty's own special Trianon livery of silver and scarlet), was called as a witness too. Though the King had refused to allow his Parliament of Paris to summon the Queen's lady in waiting, Madame Campan, he could not hold back the Queen's lackey when request was made by the judges for Desclaux's appearance in court.

In the Cardinal's version of the necklace story it was Desclaux who had been named to him by Madame de La Motte as the messenger sent by the Queen to pick up the necklace. Villette, commenting on this in his memoirs, says, "The Cardinal should have recognized him, having seen him several times, on errands from the Queen, at Madame de La Motte's." But according to Desclaux's deposition, made December 2, 1785, "The truth is that I had not so much as spoken with Madame de La Motte in over three years." He had last seen her, he said, "at the home of a mutual friend in Versailles, a male midwife."

To Madame de La Motte this was "much what might have been expected" from the Queen's "own creature" (further identified by the Countess, it will be remembered, as the confidential messenger whom she claimed the Queen had used in arranging her "trysts and assignations" with Cardinal Rohan in the Trianon grottoes and mazes). To Madame Campan, on the other hand, he was an "honest and upright man."

One of the most amusing episodes of the whole bizarre necklace affair, in the opinion of Nougaret, was the state visit paid by Madame du Barry to the Parliament of Paris. As he describes it in his Anecdotes:

She arrived at the Palais de Justice on the evening of December 7, 1785, and was received with all the pomp and ceremony usually reserved for the most exalted personages of the realm. The records officer came into the courtyard to open her carriage door, and ushers brought their torches to light her way up the staircase, the entire ceremony being repeated at her exit.

This is the gist of the evidence she gave: The Countess de La Motte had had herself announced to Madame du Barry, with the proposition that Madame du Barry take her on as dame de compagnie. But after the Countess de La Motte had concluded her dissertation on her own genealogy and illustrious ancestry, Madame du Barry concluded that the applicant was far too exalted a personage for the post in question. She thanked her, but declined the offer of her services on the ground that she was not in need of a companion and, besides, was not of such noble lineage herself as to aspire to a Valois in her retinue.

The Valois scion did not surrender after so polite a defeat, but returned a few days later to enlist Madame du Barry's good offices in bringing a petition of hers to the attention of the King. It was a petition soliciting an increase in her pension from the Crown, and she had added the words "de France" at the end of her signature. When this elicited an exclamation of surprise from the Du Barry, the Countess de La Motte explained that, having been officially recognized by the Crown as a descendant of the royal house of Valois, she always signed herself thus, "de France." Madame du Barry could not repress a smile at such pretentiousness, but agreed to exert such influence as she had at court to further the Countess's cause.

Nougaret's anecdote bears only the faintest resemblance to the way the story is told by the Countess de La Motte in her memoirs:

Even at the risk of boring the reader with the details of so long and complicated a juridical procedure, I cannot resist a word on the role assigned to the "Dowager Queen," the Immaculate Du Barry, the Du Barry of hallowed memory. That woman testified that I had gone to her house to solicit her favor and patronage, leaving with her a petition signed "Marie Antoinette de France"! The fact is that I did go to Louveciennes, but purely out of a natural curiosity to see that notorious former favorite; I went not as a suppliant but in high style, in a fine coach-and-four.

In the course of our interview, the Du Barry remarked that she had thought the Valois line extinct, whereupon I handed her a copy of my genealogical table, certified and signed by *Marie Antoine* [sic] *de Sérigny*, judge-at-arms of the nobility *of France*; this last was the name she twisted into "Marie Antoinette de France," adding that *I* had signed myself that way.

When she and I came face to face at the confrontation, she gave herself all sorts of impudent and haughty airs, but I quickly put her in her place by reminding her of the great gulf between her origins and mine, at which she exclaimed, "I do not appreciate being brought here to be subjected to insults by Madame!"

All in all, according to this version it was a thoroughly unpleasant experience for the Du Barry, enough to make her regret her original impulse to oblige the royal family by volunteering her testimony.

A third version of the Du Barry day in court comes from the Paris correspondent of the Court of St. Petersburg (who describes the whole episode as "fort gai"):

When the examining magistrate asked Madame du Barry her name she retorted, "It is one you can scarcely have forgotten, having been so long renowned in France." And to the magistrate's question "What is your age?" the Countess du Barry snapped, "Now, really, messieurs, your questions are not very courteous. Since when do gallant gentlemen ask a pretty woman her age?"

"Very well, then, if Madame refuses to state her age, we have no choice but to record it as fifty."

"Why not sixty? That would make this interrogation even more absurd!" came Madame's last word in that exchange.

Catherine the Great's correspondent obviously did not have access to the official record of that interrogation, which reads: "Brought before us . . . this seventh day of December, 1785, Jeanne Gomard de Vaubernier, Countess du Barry . . . residing at Louveciennes, aged thirty-five" (proving that chivalry was not dead, after all, in France, for the Countess had been born in 1743).

The name of an old enemy of the Countess de La Motte's pops up in the necklace investigations. From out of the mists of her girlhood there reappears the villainous figure of the Marquis de Boulainvilliers— still pursuing her, across the moat and into the Bastille ("From the fatal day he first beheld me, the man had never ceased his persecutions").

Now, to refute the Countess's story—a true one, verified by all others concerned—that the Marquise de Boulainvilliers had presented her to His Eminence at Saverne in 1781, the Marquis wrote a letter to the Cardinal in which he said, "Grateful for this opportunity to be of service to Your Eminence, I hereby testify that my late lamented wife and I were denied the pleasure of accepting Your Highness's invitation and never visited Saverne."

"Since, however, it was public knowledge," the Countess de La Motte's memoirs comment, "since even the newspapers had carried accounts of the Boulainvilliers' visit to the Cardinal's château, since His Eminence himself had admitted that our meeting took place there and then, the examining magistrate, Monsieur de Marcé, very wisely decided to omit the Marquis's malicious missive from the official dossier of the Necklace Trial."

TRIAL BRIEF
FOR CARDINAL PRINCE DE ROHAN

On occasions when Madame de La Motte could no longer brazen it out with the witnesses and the other accused, she burst into tears; at other times she resorted to fainting spells or went off into convulsions. Tremulousness succeeded a show of bravado, sobs following upon shrieks. She ran the gamut of emotions, varying her performance from day to day depending on whether she felt up to a big dramatic scene or merely a passive, pathetic tableau of injured innocence.

MEMOIRS
OF THE ABBÉ GEORGEL

She seemed to revive at the sight of Father Loth.

"You too?" she demanded of him. "You too have sold yourself to the highest bidder to ruin me?"

The monk, lowering his eyes to escape the flashing fire of hers, and refusing to be distracted by her vituperative apostrophes, weighed his words and measured his phrases so carefully that he managed, without compromising himself, to limn a clear and damning picture of the series of intricate, infernal maneuvers practiced by Madame de La Motte upon the Cardinal, from the theft of the 120,000 francs up to and including that of the diamond necklace.

Father Loth's major contribution to the Rohan defense strategy was his identification of Villette as the forger of the little letters purportedly from the Queen which had contained the orders purportedly from Her Majesty to Cardinal Rohan in the matter of the 120,000-francs loan and the necklace negotiations.

Loth's official deposition, at a confrontation with the accused in the Bastille on March 16, 1786, indicates that even Villette's secretarial duties were performed at bedside:

I remember that once, when paying Madame de La Motte a visit, I was kept waiting outside the boudoir, on the explanation that she was momentarily occupied with Sieur Villette. A little later, when the door was opened briefly, I saw Villette hovering about her pillow, writing at a small table which had been drawn up to her bed and upon which were spread pens and ink and those dainty sheets of blue-bordered notepaper.*

Up from off the official trial records in the Archives de France comes the full blast of Madame de La Motte's reply to Father Loth:

* There was no unanimity among the witnesses upon even so minor a point as the color of the notepaper. Loth described it as "blue-bordered" and Georgel as "gilt-edged," while lackey Deschamps, who should have known, having been the one sent to fetch it from the stationers', insisted that it was "embossed with a fleur-de-lis emblem."

. . . You stole from me, you rifled my money boxes. You made trouble between my husband and me; as major-domo of our household, you hand-picked cooks for my kitchen—and harlots for my husband's bed.

Three years later, when the Countess wrote her memoirs, she could still clearly recall that particular March 16 confrontation with Father Loth:

I buried him under a stream of invective, even as I had earlier heaped him with my favors.

Of all the perjurers of the Necklace Trial, him of whom I have cause for most grievous complaint is that monk of the Order of Minims known as Father Loth, who was so unpopular with his brothers that he had to seek friends beyond the walls of his monastery—just across the street, as ill fate would have it, from my house on the Rue Neuve St. Gilles. Oh, had I only listened, before it was too late, to those who tried to warn me against that little black-frocked monster!

He it was who most zealously served the Rohan interests, running around Paris searching out witnesses for Target, including Laporte, Régnier and Mademoiselle Colson, that ingrate orphan protégée and pensioner of mine,* who later admitted to me that it was the perfidious monk who had instructed her in her testimony.

TRIAL BRIEF
FOR CARDINAL PRINCE DE ROHAN

A great chorus of voices rises and swells against her: all the witnesses of France; all those of England, where her husband is spreading the same fables she originated here . . .

---

* "When Mlle Colson signified her decision to quit her post of reader and dame de compagnie in my establishment to take the veil," the Countess also says in her memoirs, "I continued my patronage by securing her a pension and a place in a desirable convent from Monsieur de La Luzerne, the worthy bishop of Langres, upon whose affections I had never lost my hold."

STORY OF MY LIFE
BY THE COUNTESS DE LA MOTTE-VALOIS

When the great Target ran out of false witnesses in France, he sent off to England for a fresh lot, assigning Monsieur de Carbonnières to that honorable mission . . .

A mission accomplished, in that it procured the London jewelers' affidavits regarding their purchases of diamonds from the Count de La Motte in April and May of 1785; but it must have been considered a failure in another sense, for the British authorities were not to be budged from their adamantine opposition both to confiscation of the aforesaid diamonds and to extradition of the aforementioned Count. To back up the affidavits, however, Carbonnières brought back a Sieur O'Neal, a captain in the French Army, who had accompanied the Count de La Motte to England and could personally testify to the diamond sales in Bond Street: a hostile witness who yet escaped the Countess's excoriations—nay, won her commendations as "a sensible, dependable kind of man whom I thought I could trust to hold down my husband's extravagances on the excursion to London," according to the official record of that confrontation.

"And now just a word or two on the subject of poor Oliva," the Countess says in her memoirs. And she goes on:

I want, first of all, to make the observation that she was such a naïve and simple creature that not all the connivings of all the Launays, Marcés, Titons and Frémyns combined could bring her to say "yes" for "no" or "black" for "white"; not all of them together could get her to change a word of her ingenuous recital. So when the time came for her to be brought face to face with me, the reader may easily imagine the intensive coaching that went on.

Uncertain of what the girl might come out with in front of the other witnesses and defendants, the magistrate was careful to frame his questions to Oliva in such a form as to elicit only "yes" or "no" answers— a strategy that did not escape my attention, prompting my observation to Monsieur de Marcé that it would better serve the interests of justice were he to desist from putting words in her mouth and allow her to speak for herself. At this he blushed fiery red, broke off speaking, abruptly rose and suspended the hearing in open fury.

That was the hearing the record of which begins:

There was summoned before us, . . . this nineteenth day of January, 1786, . . . Marie Nicole Leguay d'Oliva (or de Signy), . . . aged twenty-four, a bourgeoise, residing in Paris formerly on the Rue Thiroux . . . replying that she did not understand how the Lady de La Motte could stand there and arrogantly claim that she scarcely knew her or that their meeting had been accidental, when the way it was was that the Count de La Motte had come nine times in a row to visit her at her apartment in the Rue du Jour and then had brought the respondent, his wife . . .

The Countess's reply to this, as paraphrased by the court clerk, was that:

She had run across the Oliva purely by accident at a Palais-Royal café and, the girl having made a nice enough first impression, appearing polite and well behaved, the respondent had offered to drive her home when the Count de La Motte should arrive in their carriage; and although the latter pretended not to know Mademoiselle d'Oliva, pretended even to resent going out of the way to drop her off on the Rue du Jour, the Countess had not been taken in thereby, noticing his winks and leers in the stranger's direction and his boot toe edging up against her slipper. . . .

Questioned as to whether she had not shown Mademoiselle d'Oliva letters purportedly from the Queen, the Countess inquired whether it would not have been an extraordinary procedure on her part to have shown letters from her sovereign to a person she had met for the first time; and she replied further that had she ever been so honored as to receive letters from Her Majesty, she would have shown them only to trusted friends, whereas no such confidants had testified that she had ever done so.

Questioned further as to the Grove of Venus episode, the respondent scornfully dismissed that whole business as "great barefaced lies," saying that if she and the Count had taken the Oliva to Versailles, it was only because the girl had begged them to show her the château; that she had lent Mademoiselle d'Oliva a white net veil "only because the poor thing's bonnet was so horribly soiled" and certainly not as part of any elaborate costuming for an impersonation; that, as a matter of fact, while Oliva went into the palace grounds to walk with the Count de La Motte and Villette that night (July 24 or 25, she could not be sure which), she herself had taken a stroll with the Cardinal, their stroll taking them as far as Trianon, where they had rested a while on chairs under the colonnade of the gallery before starting back at midnight; and that, not finding the others yet at home, she had gone out again with Rosalie, her maid, and with her "*jocqui*," going as far as the palace gates to look for the missing trio, though to no avail.

To the judges' questions concerning the rose and the letter that Oliva said the Countess had given her to transmit to the Cardinal, the Countess replied, the clerk tells us,

that they must be drawing on their imaginations to concoct such fantastic, incredible, ridiculous tales as these; that it must be the work of the cabal formed to victimize her; that such nonsense as this, however, she took as an insult to her intelligence.

Let the haughty woman deny it as often as she chose, said Mademoiselle d'Oliva in her trial brief. For:

To back up my word on the nocturnal scene in the Grove of Venus, there is Cardinal Rohan's, given in all his depositions and confrontations, whereas the Lady de La Motte's voice alone speaks out in denial of it. As to what went on between Cardinal Rohan and the Lady de La Motte prior to and subsequent to that night, I do not know and do not want to know; I confine my testimony to those events in which I actually participated.

The time of illusions is past; the law takes over and must find that the Lady de La Motte's testimony is entirely unsupported, while I can prove that I drove to Versailles and back with Monsieur de La Motte. I can prove it by the testimony of Sieur Lenau, who rented him the carriage for the trips and submits his stable register book in evidence. I had two other witnesses, but I have lost them: first, Sieur de Villette, whom I later recognized at the La Mottes' as the man I had seen and heard in the Versailles gardens—the boon companion of my seducers, who heard and saw it all; and second, the Count de La Motte himself, who paid me assiduous court in order to render me receptive to the dastardly deception about to be perpetrated upon me by his wife and him. These two witnesses have disappeared, gone into hiding, whereas what light might they not have shed upon the purity and innocence of my intentions and my conduct! . . .

How does the Lady de La Motte propose to deny her visits to me, when she was seen by the porter at my house and even by the neighbors, all of whom stand ready to identify her as well as the coachman and the lackeys of her equipage? And how about her many friends to whom she presented me in public places and in private—and by the name of *Baroness d'Oliva*, despite my constant protests? To her friends such as Sieur de Villette, Father Loth, Sieur Davesne [an artist commissioned to paint the portraits of the Count and Countess] and a high-ranking Army officer [Captain Count d'Olomieu] who came daily for his game of tricktrack with the Lady de La Motte, bringing his own liveried lackey to serve him at table; and, in addition to these most frequent visitors at the Countess's, many others of her friends whose names I have since forgotten.

It must be clear, however, that the Lady de La Motte sought me out, that she went about everywhere with me and insisted that I accompany her constantly, that she wined and dined me at her Paris residence and at her Charonne country house, that she feted me and invited me to balls and to the theater—to the Comédie Française once, I remember, when *Le Mariage de Figaro* was playing. . . . Thus it was unmistakably she who sought my company and who paid me, as I have already proved, 4,268 francs (a mere fraction of the fifteen thousand francs promised me, but enough to prove that she recognized an obligation), a sure sign that an arrangement existed between us. Thus, if she would now deny me, it devolves upon her to explain to the court the nature of our former relationship and the basis of the financial obligation.

The law gives me the right to interrogate you, Lady de La Motte, and commands you to reply to my questions!

Beginning in August of 1784, shortly after the nocturnal scene in the Grove of Venus, the Countess paid me varying amounts at various times until September of that same year, when a fifth and last remittance of three thousand francs brought the total to 4,268, which she declared to be all she could do for me at the time. That moment marked the beginning of a great change in her attitude toward me; where she had been all cordiality before, she became suddenly cold and distant. She issued me no more invitations to her table; she paid no more visits to my house; at length I began to find her door closed against me. Our liaison had been of short duration. She had no further need of my complaisance. What could she find in common then with an obscure and fortuneless girl whose very presence became an embarrassing reminder of sinister intrigues and unfulfilled obligations?

For thus suddenly dropping Mademoiselle d'Oliva from her society, the Countess de La Motte could reel off a string of reasons. From the official record of her interrogation:

The Lady de La Motte replied that it was because, for one, she had discovered that Mademoiselle d'Oliva had a police record, being known to them by the name of de Signy, as a courtesan living a life of sin.

The respondent further stated that her friends had reported instances of the girl's improper conduct in company, but that when she had finally run Oliva off the premises it had been primarily because of the flagrant goings on between her and the respondent's husband; that Cardinal Rohan had even summoned the Count de La Motte to reprimand him for such disrespect to his wife; that he and Oliva had been sleeping together for quite some time before the respondent learned of it in September of 1784, when she forbade the girl her door thenceforward.

Then it was Cagliostro's turn to raise his right hand and swear to tell the truth, the whole truth—although the official record of the confrontation of Monday, January 30, 1786, shows the Man of Mystery as reticent as always about vital statistics:

. . . name, Alexander [Count]* Cagliostro, residing in the Rue St. Claude, in the Marais quarter, . . . [occupation] healing the sick without having made medicine his profession . . .

Called upon to state whether he had seen the necklace contract with

---

* In every instance (and they are innumerable in the hundreds of pages of the trial dossier) where Cagliostro's full name appears, someone—presumably the prosecutor general—struck out the title "Count" with the heavy, black, incisive pen strokes of an indignant hand.

the marginal notations, "Approved," and with the signature "Marie Antoinette de France," the respondent declared that he had not been shown that instrument until the end of July 1785, at which time he had told the Cardinal that he would wager it was a forgery, that as Grand Almoner His Eminence should have known better and that the Queen did not use such a signature; but that when the respondent made further remarks along these lines, His Eminence had cut him short with the words, "It is too late to look back now," to which the respondent had replied, "Then it is too late to seek my advice upon the matter. I warned you over and over against that woman. Now it is clear that she has taken you in and fatally deceived you."

At Cagliostro's confrontation with the Countess de La Motte, violence flared—according to the version she gives in her memoirs:

We came to grips one day, Cagliostro and I, when that charlatan, who was as common as he was impudent, took it upon himself to give me a mouthful of impertinence, to the obvious amusement of Messieurs Titon and de Marcé. I put a speedy end to that comedy by hurling a candlestick at the empiric's head. Then, turning to the snickering magistrates, I remarked that if they wanted to make a real farce of it they need only provide me with a broomstick so that I could all the more convincingly play the witch that they were trying to make me out to be. That was a day upon which I really lived up to the reputation which those gentlemen always attributed to me.

But according to the Abbé Georgel:

Count Cagliostro, resorting to his most sonorous and pontifical tone of voice in inveighing against Madame de La Motte, drowned her out with a tidal wave of awesome invocations wherein the name of God was indiscriminately mingled with that of the infernal legions, of which he termed her the messenger.

He was unshakable in his story of the confidences she had made him about her liaisons with the Queen, about the Queen's wish to acquire the necklace and about the thirty thousand francs which the Countess had delivered to the Cardinal in the Queen's name as a payment on account. To this the Countess could find no reply beyond a volley of invectives such as "mountebank," "charlatan," "impostor" and "fraud."

MEMOIRS
OF THE COUNTESS DE LA MOTTE-VALOIS

"Tell me, Grand Cophta," I said to him, "among all your amulets, charms and incantations is there not an abracadabra to whisk us both up over the Bastille walls? And, if so, pray tell why you have not used it to get yourself out of here!"

At this point Cagliostro took fire and screamed a prophecy at me, foaming with rage:

"Someone else will be here soon—your Villette! He's on his way from Switzerland now. And when he gets here he'll talk, that fellow. He's one who will talk!"

Villette signed the Bastille registry on March 16, 1786, fulfilling the first half of the prophecy; the second was fulfilled shortly thereafter, when he began to spill all he knew. (The Countess, however, refused to give Cagliostro the satisfaction of attributing the accuracy of his prediction to supernatural powers or clairvoyance. "How, you may well ask," she apostrophizes the reader in her memoirs, "did Cagliostro, supposedly held incommunicado like the rest of us, come by that piece of news unless, as I have claimed, it was via the Bastille whispering gallery and thanks to the Cardinal's clique of co-conspirators and hirelings?")

From the official record of Villette's first interrogation:

This day of Friday, April 7, 1786, . . . summoned to a hearing . . . the prisoner Louis Marc Antoine Rétaux de Villette, aged thirty-two, former cavalryman . . . stated that he had come to the capital in 1784 to solicit an officer's post in the mounted police. Interrogated as to whether he had not lived upon the bounty of the La Mottes, the respondent replied that this was not the case, that he had come up from the provinces with the sanction of his family, who had provided the money necessary for his needs. Interrogated as to whether the Lady de La Motte had not, since the necklace transaction, bestowed upon him various sums upon various occasions, the respondent replied that if she had done so it had been merely a matter of small loans of which he had kept scrupulous account, reminding her of the amounts to be re-

paid although she had been so gracious as to forbid the very mention
of it.

MEMOIRS
OF THE ABBÉ GEORGEL

In the belief that no direct evidence linking him with the crime had
yet been produced by the investigation, Villette persisted, throughout
his first interrogations, in a flat denial of everything that might tend to
incriminate him, admitting only to his former intimacy with Madame de La Motte. Questioned on the basis of testimony given by
Father Loth, he conceded that he had occasionally served that lady in
the capacity of secretary,* copying out letters from her notes or writing
them at her dictation; then he went a bit further and admitted to
having been advised by her of the fact that Cardinal Rohan had purchased the diamond necklace from Böhmer and Bassenge.

His confrontation with Father Loth, however, disconcerted him.

MEMOIRS
OF RÉTAUX DE VILLETTE

Loth, that perfidious and ingrate monk, who, like me, owed everything to Madame de La Motte, yet joined with all the rest in bringing
about her downfall. He, along with the Abbé Georgel, Ramon de Carbonnières and others of the Cardinal's agents, engaged in endless,
shameless intriguing.

No sooner had I landed in my Bastille dungeon than Messieurs de
Marcé and de Frémyn hinted strongly that my only hope of avoiding
the gibbet lay in confessing all I knew—but confessing in such a manner as not to compromise Cardinal Rohan, but, rather, to show him as
the innocent victim and Madame de La Motte as the authoress of
the intrigue. From Governor de Launay down to the lowliest jailer,
everyone with whom I came in contact had, in fact, the same advice

---

* While admitting to having been secretary and lover to Mme de La Motte, Villette
made the distinction between that and having been her friend. "She had no friends,
in the true sense of the word," he said in his petition to the Parliament. "No one,
actually, was ever admitted into her full confidence. She kept her business to herself."

to offer. At last, lured on by promises and intimidated by constant threats of torture, I agreed to testify against Madame de La Motte.

MEMOIRS
OF THE COUNTESS DE LA MOTTE-VALOIS

No sooner had Villette landed in the Bastille than the Rohan faction began to suggest to him the nature of the testimony he should give. Indeed, to save him the trouble of preparing his depositions, they supplied him with ready-made drafts. Just as Baron de Breteuil, Commissaire Chesnon, Count d'Adhémar and all the Queen's party were constantly impressing it upon my husband and me to blame it all on the Cardinal, the Rohan partisans were indoctrinating their witnesses with the suggestion to lay it all to the account of Madame de La Motte.

MEMOIRS
OF THE ABBÉ GEORGEL

When the necklace contract was handed to Villette by the magistrates for his examination, and he was required to state whether or not he recognized the handwriting of the signature "Marie Antoinette de France" and the "Approuvés" in the margin, he noticeably paled, trembled and stammered; but, regaining his self-control, he stubbornly repeated his denials of having any knowledge thereof.

Back behind the bars of his cell, however, with time to reflect upon the questions put to him and upon the handwriting comparisons that had been made at the interrogation, Villette came to the conclusion that proofs strong enough to convict him had therewith been offered in evidence.

At the petition of Prosecutor General de Fleury, the foremost handwriting experts in France, Messieurs Harger and Blin, were called into consultation in the case. Studying the contract, they gave it as their considered opinion that the "cramped motion and unnatural deliberation manifest in the pen stroke reveal a definite attempt at dissimulation of the author's hand"; and comparing the contract signature to a specimen of Villette's script, they opined that, despite the attempt at dissimulation, there were "clear similarities." Harger's report, with which Blin concurred in a separate affidavit, ends:

Thus, in good conscience, the aforesaid expert, Harger, arrives at and expresses it as his conclusion that the author of the handwriting specimen submitted to him for examination is undoubtedly the same one who wrote the words "Approved" and "Marie Antoinette de France."

Although one might wish that a specimen of the Queen's handwriting, along with that of Villette, had been submitted to Harger and Blin for comparison with the contract signature and the "Approuvés," still one realizes quickly enough that that would have been far too delicate a measure to have expected either the judiciary or the handwriting experts to tread.

It was at this juncture that Villette capitulated and confessed to having committed the forgery; so the Abbé Georgel relates it in his memoirs:

Prodded by remorse and, even more, by the assurance that he would not render himself liable to the death penalty if he limited himself to saying that he had only copied some writing given him by Madame de La Motte for the purpose of having a duplicate made, Villette admitted that the signature "Marie Antoinette de France" upon the document shown to him in court was the product of his pen. He was careful to emphasize that he had made no attempt to reproduce the handwriting of the Queen, that Madame de La Motte often gave him the originals of papers and letters to copy out, and that in this instance he had seen nothing criminal in making such a copy, having no inkling of the use to which the instrument was destined.

He was careful to explain also at this second appearance before the magistrates, on May 5, 1786,

that he had not willfully given any false testimony in his previous interrogation, but, rather, had not previously entered into full detail in the hope that these facts need never come to light and that thus he need not compromise other persons; but that now, having reason to fear that juridical proof against him had been acquired by the court, he felt it his duty to render homage to truth.

Thus reads the official record of his statement; but to hear him tell it unofficially in his memoirs, his "duty to render homage to truth" cost him mortal anguish:

Spineless as I was in allowing myself to be brought to name Madame de La Motte as the sole instigator of the directions to affix the false signature of the Queen upon the necklace contract, for the express purpose of deceiving Cardinal Rohan, still, at sight of her at our first confrontation, I fell prey to bitter remorse and blurted out that I had been forced to that accusation to save my neck. Before I could get all the words out of my mouth, however, the magistrates adjourned the session; and back in my cell my jailers were quick to offer me condolences on the fate in store for me as a result of my recantation. In despair at what I had done, I swore to follow instructions faithfully in the future and implored pardon of Court Clerk de Frémyn, whose very face so terrified me as to bring on the ague, chills and fever.

Even Cagliostro, in his confrontation with Villette, took a turn at softening that far from obdurate heart, claiming in his memoirs that he had

delivered a sermon an hour and a half long to impress Villette with the duty of a man of honor, with the long reach of the arm of Providence, and with the love owed by man to his fellow man. I led Villette to hope for the mercy of God and of the court, my discourse becoming so protracted and impassioned that when it was over I could not have uttered another word. The magistrate presiding at our confrontation was so touched that he termed it a "celestial discourse" and told Villette that I had talked to him as a brother, as a man of God and of morality, and that only a monster could fail to be moved thereby.

Following Villette's confessions the Countess de La Motte was recalled to the council chamber for reinterrogation. According to the record for May 8, 1786:

The magistrates pointed out to her that she could no longer deny these facts, because it had been proved before the court that the handwriting of the "Approuvés" and of the signature on the contract was that of Villette, he himself having now testified not only to the authorship thereof but also to the fact that he had acted at her, the respondent's, behest; to which the respondent replied that assuredly it had not been she who had directed him to it and that, furthermore, she did not consider that conclusive proof had been established insofar as concerned the court's claim that the handwriting on the contract and Villette's were one and the same . . .

Cornered but indomitable, the Countess made light of the testimony of the prosecution's team of handwriting experts. As for Villette's motives in confessing, she had her own ideas on that score, and she voices them in her memoirs:

Villette had made a deal whereby he could save his skin by slavishly following the instructions of the cabal formed to destroy me; and when he seemed to be having difficulty in opening up, he was subjected to torture, or the threat of torture, to set his tongue to wagging freely about everything he knew—everything, that is, save mention of the Queen.

Villette went so far, then, as to admit to "having copied off a signature onto a document at the behest of Madame de La Motte sometime in January of 1785, and on her assurance that said document would never leave the hands of Cardinal Rohan." So far Villette would go, no farther—at least not in the May 5 interrogation record, where he is officially quoted as saying that,

having in no wise profited by the deception, he could not be considered technically to have acted with criminal intent nor, therefore, technically to have committed a crime of forgery; that, as everyone knew, he was the most impractical of men, the last in the world to be influenced by the profit motive, his involvement in this miserable business being attributable, rather, like all his other follies and peccadilloes, to his eternal weakness where women were concerned.

Questioned as to whether the Cardinal knew the contract signature to be a forgery, and whether that was the reason for the Cardinal's refusal to deliver it into the jewelers' keeping, the respondent asserted that as to that he had no idea, although, as Grand Almoner, Cardinal Rohan might have been expected to know the form of the Queen's signature; and that as for himself, although lacking His Eminence's well-known intellectual endowments, the respondent did not think he could have been so easily taken in.

What had happened between April 7 and May 5, the dates of Villette's first and second interrogations? As he himself puts it in his memoirs:

Those who compare my first deposition with the succeeding ones cannot fail to note the difference. The first was honest and forthright; the rest were dictated to me by the Minister of Foreign Affairs, Count de Vergennes, who threatened me with the rack if I failed to frame my testimony so as to exonerate the Cardinal.

His Eminence's legal staff had concluded that his only defense consisted in, first, denying everything, and, second, suborning both the witnesses who could bring charges against him and the magistrates who would deliberate thereupon. Once set in motion, the machine began to roll along, and by its very momentum it soon swept along in its wake both the examining magistrates and the court clerk, with the result that these functionaries tampered with the depositions throughout the hearings; and at such times as they were fearful that the Cardinal might blunder or contradict himself in his testimony, they called suddenly for a recess without even giving His Eminence time to finish his sentence.

Suborned or no, Villette showed himself evasive when the judges came to question him on the subject of the little letters on gilt-edged notepaper purportedly from the Queen to the Cardinal. Here at first he would not admit authorship; then he hedged by saying that, even if someone had seduced him into committing such an act, "no effort had been made to copy the handwriting of the Queen—thus, no forgery proper had been committed and there could be no lèse-majesté."

But once having admitted writing these musk-scented billets-doux, Villette admitted to having written "a hundred-odd"—which must have struck the judges as exceedingly strange in view of the fact that the Cardinal, throughout the whole course of the trial, would never admit to having received one. (If the Countess de La Motte was correct in her theory that it was the Rohan faction which had induced Villette to "open up," then his avowals on this particular topic must have struck them as carrying a good thing too far.)

Questioned as to the tenor of the Cardinal's letters to the Queen which Madame de La Motte had shown him in dictating the replies, Villette first described it as "intimate and tender," later changed the adjectives to "cordial and friendly" and then, according to the record, added that,

judging by what he had seen of those letters handed by the Cardinal to Madame de La Motte for transmittal purportedly to the Queen, it was his, the respondent's, opinion that if Cardinal Rohan had fallen prey to a hoax in the necklace transaction, it could be attributed to His Eminence's consuming desire to regain royal favor and his overweening ambition to become prime minister; that these obsessions Madame de La Motte had recognized and known how to turn to her own advantage . . .

At this third interrogation, on May 11, 1786, Villette emphatically denied that he had played the role of the Queen's messenger at Madame de La Motte's Versailles apartment on the night of February 1, 1785, and that he had received the necklace in Her Majesty's name. That role he would deny consistently to the end—as well he might, considering its inescapable implications of larceny. (He would deny it even when Rosalie Briffault, the Countess's maid, identified him as the man to whom she had opened the door and whom she had clearly recognized.) On the subject of that particular incident in the necklace transaction, the record says, Villette insisted to the magistrates that he

had no knowledge whatsoever, not the faintest inkling, had never even heard it spoken of; and he pointed to the fact that the Cardinal's own description of that messenger as a man with heavy black brows and thin, pale face bore no slightest resemblance to his, the respondent's, person, as the judges could clearly see; this constituted further proof that he had not performed that role.

In that third interrogation, Villette was likewise still denying having played any role at all in the famous Grove of Venus scene. "No. . . . No. . . . No," reads the official record of May 11. No, his had not been

the running footsteps; not his the voice warning, "Hurry, hurry! Mad-
ame and the Countess d'Artois are coming!"—the words spoken to
break up the midnight rendezvous. No, Villette had "not the vaguest
idea, at the time, of what was going on." As the record puts it, he said

that he had been limping that night, due to a sore heel, and so had sat
down upon a marble bench on the great terrace of the château to wait
for the others, who had gone down by the Hundred Steps to the park
below; that he had only learned later about Oliva's impersonation of
the Queen, which, he admits, struck him at the time as hilariously
funny, so that, unconscious of the enormity of the offense, he had
laughed and laughed—a giddy reaction he had since come to rue.

But what Villette stoutly denied in the interrogation of May 11 he
admitted to at a confrontation on May 12.
The Abbé Georgel's version of that May 12 recantation is contained
in his memoirs:

The confrontation of Villette, Mademoiselle d'Oliva and Madame
de La Motte developed into a scene of tragicomedy, what with the torrent of outrageous expressions pouring forth from the lips of Madame
de La Motte at the height of her fury and the ingenuous responses
issuing from those of Mademoiselle d'Oliva, not to mention the tears
into which the latter constantly dissolved.

Mademoiselle d'Oliva called upon Villette to corroborate her statement that he had been with her in the Versailles gardens that July
night. This Villette did; he confirmed her statement concerning all that
had transpired in that farce which, he said, Madame de La Motte had
assured him was being enacted to gratify a whim of Her Majesty's.
Bracing himself, he endured without a murmur the stream of abuse
Madame de La Motte vomited against him. His set face, his persistence
in maintaining the verity of his testimony finally overwhelmed her.

After all, there had been not only Villette and Oliva to testify that
the Grove of Venus incident had actually transpired, there had been
Cardinal Rohan as well, and the Baron da Planta, even the Countess's
Rosalie.
But if Madame de La Motte was forced to an admission on that
point, it was as a "practical joke" that she admitted it. She was not
yet at a loss for ingenious explanations, as is shown by the official rec-

ord, which tells us that she described the impersonation as "a trick she had played upon her lover to pay him off for an infidelity," and that she said

it had been easy enough to persuade that girl, such a silly little' fool, to undertake the role; it was the Cardinal himself who had given her [the Countess] the idea for the prank by telling her, toward the end of June 1784, that he and the Queen were at odds over one of his indiscretions, and that he yearned for a rendezvous to effect a reconciliation.

But that the "jest" had been intended as a ruse to extort money from the Cardinal she denied; rather, she said, she had "only a few days thereafter shattered any illusion he might still entertain as to having actually enjoyed an interview with the Queen, by telling him that it had all been in fun."

Hard pressed at that crucial May 12 confrontation, the Countess de La Motte gave ground in permitting herself some oddments of confession. In response to Villette's recorded statement that Cagliostro should be "considered innocent of any involvement whatsoever in this whole affair," she conceded that her "only reproach of the sorcerer" was for his advice to the Cardinal to prosecute her for the necklace theft." Then, as concerned Villette's skittering off to Italy on her money and her urging (as he had testified), she granted the court that she had lent him four thousand francs on condition that he not mention the Oliva incident, but, she insisted, the trip to Italy had been Villette's own idea in order to escape from his family, who were trying to have him locked away somewhere "to prevent further drain on their resources by his shiftlessness and escapades."

This confrontation with both Villette and Oliva at one and the same time "proved too much for even Madame de La Motte," says the Abbé Georgel. "Physically and emotionally spent, she fell silent and finally fainted dead away."

The Leyden Gazette, which evidently had news sources within the Bastille, printed a sensational account of the scene in which it informed its public:

Madame de La Motte's confession was forthcoming only after a thousand shrieks of rage and hideous convulsions, which eventuated in a fainting spell. Someone was sent running to fetch smelling salts. Saint-Jean [the turnkey in her tower], having been summoned, picked her up from the floor to carry her to her cell, at which moment she came to and sank her teeth into his shoulder, deep enough to bring blood. Saint-Jean emitted a howl and dropped her.

Maître Target's comments on the final sensational developments in the Bastille investigations appeared, that spring, in another published trial brief for Cardinal Rohan, partly in the form of a high-flown apostrophe to the Countess's defender, Maître Doillot:

How do you explain a client who would have us forget in the courtroom what she declared to be the truth in her first trial brief, and who later asks that we forget her testimony in the courtroom in favor of what she is now saying in her second trial brief? How do you explain a client whose defense plea on the eve of judgment retains scarcely a trace of those arguments which constituted her defense plea at the time the hearings began?

The eve of judgment (to borrow Target's phrase) was actually at hand, for the hearings in the Bastille were drawing to a close.
At the last confrontation between Villette and Madame de La Motte, he pleaded with her to join him in a confession of complicity.

It is useless for you to go on with your denials [the record quotes him]. You refuse to recognize the fact that everybody accuses you, and that your lone voice fails to carry conviction. When you try to shake me in the confession I make of my own guilty acts, you are only harming your own cause. It is clear that you do not realize where your best interests lie . . .

The Countess's riposte is officially recorded as:

Monsieur Villette's observations are made only to frighten me, but I fear nothing. To all his remarks, I persist in the reply that I never urged him to affix the "*Approuvés*" and the signature upon the necklace contract or to any other writing purportedly coming from the Queen. If Monsieur Villette chooses to claim that he did write these various items, it is obviously because he has been intimidated by being told that the handwriting experts of the court have found that his ordinary handwriting bears a striking resemblance to that on the necklace contract, and that he could be condemned to death by reason of this identification alone.

It is obvious, as well, that Villette has come to terms with someone, that he has been promised that if he confesses to this, his punishment will be materially lightened. If I were guilty, I suppose I might also make a confession for the same reasons, but I repeat that I am in no wise guilty, and I therefore await with calm the judgment of the Parliament of Paris, asking no grace of any man.

Despite his courtroom expressions of impatience with Madame de La Motte's stubborn refusal to admit her complicity, Villette in his memoirs pays tribute to her for that stand:

Madame de La Motte, alone of all the defendants, stood fast in the face of the storm that raged about us. Caught up between the Parliament's conspiracy and the secret agents of the Queen, she persisted in denying all guilt and in charging the Cardinal with the crime. It was the Queen's will that the Cardinal be ruined for his complicity and that Madame de La Motte be spared for hers; the Parliament, in a spirit of vengeance and defiance of royal authority, willfully assumed a stand of opposition to the throne.

A rumor seeped out of the Bastille, however, to the effect that Madame de La Motte was withstanding the storm less staunchly than Villette's description would give to believe. The Abbé Georgel reports it in his memoirs:

Bowed down beneath the crushing weight of testimony against her, for which she could no longer find any reply save that of invective, Madame de La Motte cried out in a fury, "I can see that a complot has been joined to encompass my destruction. But before I succumb, I vow to reveal evil mysteries and to pronounce the names of lofty personages who are still lurking behind the scenes."

This threat, for some unknown reason, was not inscribed in the official record of the Bastille hearings, although, as shall be seen and as is well known, Madame de La Motte was on the verge of putting it into effect at the very moment judgment was pronounced upon her.

Another rumor from the fastnesses of the Bastille appears in Hardy's journal entry of March 9, 1786: "Rumor has it that His Eminence persists in the claim that the famous diamond necklace had indeed and verily been delivered over to the Queen; and that he continues insistently to demand to be brought face to face with Her Majesty."

Nevertheless, that spring of 1786 was a time for rejoicing in the Cardinal's camp, as the Abbé Georgel writes:

That great and providential confession of Villette's saved the Cardinal. Just as it fully supported the evidence submitted by His Eminence in proof of the good faith in which he had acted throughout, so also did it serve to shed light upon those dark and devious criminal ruses of Madame de La Motte's, whereby she had purloined the necklace.

The Cardinal's counsel decided to inform the public of this fortuitous development in the case—one, indeed, which those legal minds regarded as decisive; and so they rushed into print a brochure entitled *Rapid Reflections*, wherein Target summarized the facts with such precision as to eliminate all remaining doubt from the public mind as to both Madame de La Motte's guilt and the Cardinal's innocence.

Georgel here reflects Target's professional appraisal of the situation. Among that counselor at law's manuscript notes and papers in the Bibliothèque de la Ville de Paris are memoranda in which Target contrasts the Cardinal's position before Villette's providential arrival on the scene with his situation after Villette's confessions. Target's notes show that he reasoned that:

In the beginning—and as long as only Madame de La Motte, Mademoiselle d'Oliva and Cagliostro were numbered among the accused—the sole, and the logical, conclusion was that Cardinal Rohan had to be considered guilty.

There could be no certainty as to whose hand had committed the forgery, but the text of the contract was entirely (and admittedly) in the Cardinal's handwriting; and it had been upon the Cardinal's assurance that the signature was genuine that the diamond necklace had been delivered to him.

Bassenge's deposition had established the fact that Monseigneur Cardinal Rohan had spoken and acted throughout as if he had been directly commissioned to the purchase by the Queen.

Under such conditions as these which prevailed at the opening of the court hearings, the Cardinal's defense counsel could not have hoped to exonerate him. In vain might they have claimed deception (practiced upon him) and gullibility (on his own part) as the excuses for his actions. The counterargument inevitably must have been that such gullibility on the Cardinal's part was highly improbable and totally incredible, and that there was no proof to substantiate the claim of deception, since Madame de La Motte denied the fabulous Grove of Venus episode—despite the affirmation of Mademoiselle d'Oliva, whose testimony, in view of her unsavory reputation, was necessarily suspect.

But from the moment of Villette's arrest, it became evident that he had been the forger of the contract signature; that the Grove of Venus scene, fantastic as it might seem, had actually taken place; that Villette had written, at Madame de La Motte's dictation, the series of letters which had been transmitted to the Cardinal and represented as coming from the Queen.

From that point on, the elaborate deception alleged by Cardinal Rohan as having been practiced upon him could be envisioned as a distinct possibility; and if he had been deceived by such stratagems, he could no longer be considered an accomplice to the forgery and theft. His offense, representation of a false signature as genuine, monstrous abuse though it was of the name of the Queen, was yet limited to *lèse-majesté*. For such an offense, the amende honorable might be expected to consist of an open apology to Their Majesties—becloud though it must the honor of the Rohan name, precluding the possibility of all future national dignities for the Cardinal.

On this last point, Georgel takes issue with the opinion of the eminent jurist:

Villette's confession should have completely absolved His Eminence and restored him his liberty, and it was in this light that the public viewed it. Instead, at the very moment of his triumphant justification, he was to find himself subjected to the cruelest humiliations.

Those last spring months of 1786 were the most trying times of all for Cardinal Rohan. Deprived of communication with the outside world, painfully dragging out his miserable existence, His Eminence was draining the bitter cup to the dregs.

His agonizing situation affected his health, though never his courage;

severe colic and other disquieting symptoms aroused suspicion of poisoning. Governor de Launay took alarm and instituted inquiries which indicated that the attack had been caused by verdigris on a saucepan in which His Eminence's whey had been prepared. Weakened by this attack, the Cardinal became subject to severe headaches that persisted throughout the rest of his incarceration, with the result that his left eye filled up constantly with an acrid pus, which gave Dr. Portal cause for concern lest the eyesight be impaired.

Dr. Portal, the Cardinal's personal physician, who had been issued a rare laissez-passer into the Bastille by an alarmed Launay, combined the role of Aesculapius with that of Mercury, slipping scraps of messages from Maître Target to the Cardinal and notes in invisible ink from the prisoner to his counselor, who preserved them in his files (where they can be read today, for the invisible words penned over 150 years ago become visible again when held close to heat). The Cardinal wrote in one of them:

There are usually nine hours of interrogation every day, and, just between you and me, I grow very weary. I send you the rest of the text of my last confrontation, but I warn you again that if so much as a hint of this communication were to reach their ears there is no telling to what lengths they might not go to punish those responsible. I hope I will not be called back for confrontations until Monday, but the sooner you can send me your directives the better. I was able to make out your last message, but hope the paper need not be folded quite so small next time.

I have adjusted myself here to horrors such as I never dreamed I would be called upon to become accustomed to. I am more and more depleted by fatigue, but that only spurs me on to redouble my efforts, lest my enemies suspect it. I am determined to appear fresh and composed, to staunch the blood of my wounds whenever I descend into the arena. I would not give anyone the satisfaction of seeing me otherwise.

Vale, vale. May heaven soon diminish my agonies.

And in another invisible-ink letter to his counselor:

That wicked woman created quite a scene today with Count Cagliostro, hurling a candelabra at his midriff when he called her a "damned cheat." But retribution was swift, for in doing so she struck herself in the eye with a candle. I am to be confronted with her tomorrow, but I will answer for it that she will dare throw nothing at me. Nor does she any longer have the power to disconcert me. I see her now for the horrible creature that she is.

We have not yet seen the end of this extraordinary affair, but I can now face the future with equanimity. I thank God for having rendered my position in the case so different from what it was at the outset. My mind is tranquil now, because my honor is redeemed; all the rest are personal indignities which I can endure.

Adieu. If I cannot express fully here my gratitude to you, your own sensitive heart and soul will plumb its depths.

In still another letter Cardinal Rohan asked the legal mastermind to bestow the benefits of his counsel on Maître Thilorier, Cagliostro's attorney, and to exert his influence to ensure that the title "Count" was not omitted from the legal documents, which might constitute a slight to his dear and touchy friend.

And in one of these letters penned in sympathetic ink there appears the question, a strange one for a prisoner of the Crown to ask his counselor, "Have you had any recent news of the Q[ueen]? Please tell me if it is true that she still appears so sad.

They were all languishing and repining now, the Bastille prisoners, some of whom had been immured for more than eight months in that fortress; they were unnerved, on edge. Villette had his "ague, chills and fever"; the Countess was greensick and prey to a succession of "black moods, tantrums, convulsions and migraine"; and Cagliostro's morosity become so pronounced as to give Launay another alarm, prompting him to write for advice in the emergency to Police Lieutenant General de Crosne, who obliged with the following letter:

If you deem it advisable to place a guard in the cell with the prisoner Cagliostro to relieve the monotony and to alleviate the effects of despair to which he has succumbed, then I suggest that you choose from among your officers one whose rectitude and benevolence are known to you and assign him, from this date forward, the duty of passing the nights in the cell with the prisoner.

Cagliostro's despair in great part stemmed from the incarceration of his Countess. On February 14, 1786, Maître Thilorier presented a petition to the Parliament of Paris in the name of his client, printing and releasing it for public distribution ten days later:

MY LORDS OF THE PARLIAMENT:

The humble suppliant, Alexander, Count Cagliostro, addresses you on behalf of and in the name of his wife, Serafina, declaring that he has every hope that the premier senate of France will not reject the petition of a foreigner imploring the liberation of his spouse, who is presently on the verge of death in the dungeons of the Bastille.

The petitioner seeks no favor for himself; he patiently awaits, in his shackles, the moment when justice shall proclaim his innocence to the world. But his spouse has been neither arraigned nor accused, nor even (so he hears) summoned as a witness, and yet she has been incarcerated for more than six months.

The suppliant asks that the Parliament of Paris exercise its noblest rights, those of enlightening supreme authority and relieving oppression. The suppliant has sought in vain to bring this appalling injustice to the attention of those in whose hands national authority lies.

The eyes of all Europe are fastened on this famous trial. Public curiosity battens upon the most trivial detail concerning it. Both the innocence and the imprisonment of Countess Cagliostro are known to the Parliament; the suppliant now publicly advises the Parliament of the malady which presently threatens her life.

Will she be allowed to perish without even the benefit of the healing arts of her husband? And if it is true that his arts have succeeded in snatching a thousand Frenchmen from the jaws of death, is he to be condemned to the torture of knowing that she lies expiring within a hundred feet of him, in the same prison, without being permitted to render her either medical attention or human solace?

Advised of these circumstances, may it please you, My Lords of the Parliament, to take Countess Cagliostro under your jurisdiction and to use your good offices with His Majesty to obtain the revocation of the *lettre de cachet* by virtue of which she is held in the Bastille.

ALEXANDER, COUNT CAGLIOSTRO

From Hardy's journal for that week:

THE QUEEN'S NECKLACE

Count Cagliostro's petition to Parliament was a touching exposé of Countess Cagliostro's critical condition; and by it, all Paris learned that the life of an angel was endangered through the misapplication of arbitrary power—a paragon of virtue and of beauty fallen victim to royal despotism.

From the anonymous Compte Rendu de ce qui s'est passé au Parlement . . . *("The Account of What Happened in the Parliament concerning the Cardinal Rohan Case"), published in 1786, the author of which was either a judge of the Parliament or a spectator in the gallery:*

The Parliament of Paris took alarm at this eighth petition from Count Cagliostro, and the assembled Chambers were promptly called into joint session.

Monsieur d'Éprémesnil, councilor in the Grand' Chambre, expressed astonishment that the Lady de Latour, sister of the fugitive Count de La Motte, had already been released from the Bastille, while the wife of Count Cagliostro (who himself scarcely figured in the case) should still be held prisoner.

By a vote of thirty-two to twenty-six, the motion carried that the president of the Parliament should be deputed to seek audience with the King to supplicate His Majesty to take the petition of Count Cagliostro under consideration, and to be so gracious as to accede to his request.

The government itself, at length disturbed, bestirred itself to require a report from Governor de Launay on his delectable prisoner. Launay's reply, dated February 23, 1786, is addressed to Police Lieutenant General de Crosne:

I have been advised of the concern of our lords of the Parliament with regard to the illness of Madame Cagliostro. You should know, monsieur, that had she suffered the slightest indisposition you would have been advised, as it is my custom to advise you daily of all developments in this fortress.

The lady in question is not ill at all. She takes her promenades daily —is out walking at this moment on the platform of the tower. She did suffer a slight sprain to her left wrist some two weeks ago, but even that was so minor an accident as not to have kept her from her embroidery.

428

Nevertheless, the doctor has been summoned to examine her, and as soon as he issues a report I shall forward it to you.

A month later, on March 18, the main gates of the Bastille swung open and the drawbridge was lowered to allow Madame Cagliostro to pass over, to return to the Rue St. Claude mansion upon which she had so precipitately bolted the doors in mid-August of the previous year.

According to an anonymous pamphlet entitled La Dernière Pièce du fameux collier *("The Last Word on the Famous Necklace Affair"):*

It is all the rage in Paris this week to flock to the Rue St. Claude to pay one's respects to Madame Cagliostro. It is not unusual on any one night to see the names of three-hundred-odd visitors inscribed on the register at her porter's lodge.

Those who are so fortunate as to be received by the lady herself assert that her eyes have been well-nigh washed away by the flood of tears shed during her confinement at the Bastille; but fortunately, what remains of those velvety orbs is still beautiful. Others say she talks too freely for a "victim of despotism" and insists that the Count de Launay's treatment of her was eminently correct, even her own lady's maid, Francine, having been permitted to stay on there to attend her.

Her path is strewn with flowers when she makes a public appearance on the streets. Her first visit, a few days after her release, was to the Palais-Royal arcades, where she laughed hilariously at the engraving purporting to be a likeness of herself, on sale with those of the other Necklace Case personalities.

The most prominent hostesses in the capital dispute with one another for the privilege of claiming Countess Cagliostro as their guest of honor, and the gentlemen callers at her door vie with one another for that of consoling the lady for the grief she suffers at the continued confinement of her husband. Indeed, some Paris wags go so far as to claim that Count Cagliostro is presently engaged in drawing up another petition even more piteous than the last, beseeching the Parliament to take his beloved back into custody and restore her to her cell in the Bastille.

That grim keep seemed to be ridding itself of superfluous Necklace Case prisoners. The great drawbridge was lowered on February 7 for Madame de Latour and on March 18 for Madame Cagliostro; Rosalie

Briffault and Régnier the jeweler, the Baron da Planta and Toussaint de Beausire, Mademoiselle d'Oliva's cavalier, had crossed to liberty earlier. But there was one new arrival, who was signed in on May 12 as "Jean Baptiste Toussaint"—the son born to Mademoiselle d'Oliva and legitimized by his father, Toussaint de Beausire. He was the only prisoner in all the Bastille who had entered it without benefit of the lowering of the drawbridge, and the only Necklace Case prisoner of whom it could ever be positively stated that he had been guilty of no complicity whatsoever in the diamond necklace affair.

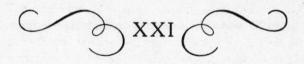

On the Eve of the Trial

(Early Spring 1786)

AT THE MOST CRUCIAL MOMENT of the hearings in the Bastille," the Abbé Georgel recounts in his memoirs, "I was suddenly exiled to the town of Mortagne, thirty-six leagues from the capital."

The lettre de cachet came on March 10, 1786, signed by Baron de Breteuil over the King's seal.

The immediate reason for the action by the abbé's ancient enemy was, very probably, although Georgel professes to doubt it, the Lenten message for 1786 that he authored in his capacity of vicar general to the Grand Almoner—a message printed and posted, as was the custom, on the doors and in the sacristies of the churches under the jurisdiction of the Grand Almonership, including the chapels of the Quinze-Vingt and the Convent of the Assumption in Paris and the King's chapel at Versailles. It began:

I, François Georgel, Doctor of Theology, vicar general of the Grand Almonership, . . . am sent unto you, dear brethren, as the disciple Timothy was sent unto the people when Paul, in chains, could not come before them to teach them. And I say unto you that it is permitted to you to eat butter and eggs throughout this Lenten season of 1786 until the advent of Palm Sunday . . .

The "butter and eggs" part was innocent enough, but the rest of that Lenten message was temerarious in the extreme, and Baron de Breteuil made sure that the King should not miss the point of the odious comparisons.

This interpretation of the message is denied by Georgel in his memoirs:

That Lenten message of 1786, which enjoyed some success, was no more than a fortuitous collection of texts from Holy Scripture adapted to the current situation. The opening paragraph, which constituted the crime in the eyes of the sovereign, was a direct quotation of the words of St. Paul himself, taken from his Second Epistle to Timothy, in which he exhorted his disciple not to blush for his master's chains and captivity. This forceful opening, simple and natural as it was, was interpreted in sinister fashion by Baron de Breteuil, who told the King that I had compared Cardinal Rohan to St. Paul and myself to Timothy and had likened His Majesty unto Nero, who had put the apostle into irons.

Actually, had I been guilty of such a reprehensible thought, is it likely that I would have had the effrontery to post this Lenten message under the King's very eyes, on the doors of his own chapel? Furthermore, had this been the true reason for the action taken against me, is it reasonable to assume that they would have waited a full month after the publication of the message, long after all the talk relative thereto had subsided? And is it not too much of a coincidence that my exile order was dated, rather, two days after a threat made by me to use information which had reached me concerning a flagrant irregularity of conduct on the part of the Baron de Breteuil?

My contacts with Böhmer and Bassenge since the day when I had arranged with them for payment of the necklace debt had put me in a position to learn from the jewelers themselves of the hints that Baron de Breteuil had made both to them and to Saint-James to word their depositions in a way that would be detrimental to the Cardinal. Certainly I do not presume to sit in judgment on the soul of that minister; let him, rather, be judged by a recital of the facts.

In a burst of confidence, Bassenge revealed that Baron de Breteuil had even sent his secretary to them to promise full payment on the necklace if, during the confrontations, they would go beyond what they had said in their depositions. "What he wanted us to add," Bassenge told me, "was that the Cardinal had given us positive assurance that he had seen the Queen, talked with her, and received her direct orders for the purchase of the necklace. Such a lie," he continued, "seemed altogether too odious for us to lend ourselves to and thereby contribute to the destruction of a prince against whom we had no cause for complaint—who, himself cruelly deceived, had acted in good faith toward us." By their refusal, he said, the jewelers had incurred the Minister's displeasure.

Baron de Breteuil's action in this matter had constituted an out-and-out case of subornation, and I did not conceal from Böhmer and Bassenge that the information they had just given me seemed too advantageous to the Cardinal's cause to omit using it. Taking fright at the thought that their disclosure to me would thus be publicized, the jewelers implored me to abandon such a project, adding that if I persisted in it they would be obliged to deny that they had ever said such a thing.

I demonstrated to them, however, that I had taken care not to be the sole witness to their disclosures: having divined, from earlier conversations with them, that more confidences might be forthcoming on the score of Baron de Breteuil's machinations, I had taken the precaution of stationing two witnesses of unimpeachable veracity behind my office door, where they could hear but not be seen.

When the *lettre de cachet* was delivered to me forty-eight hours later, there remained little doubt as to what hand had hurled the bolt. It was clearly to the interest of the vindictive Minister that I be removed from the scene of action before I could put to use the evidence so recently acquired about the illicit expedients to which he had resorted to encompass the Cardinal's downfall. By means of my exile he deprived Prince de Rohan, at the most critical moment, of the man who had become the very mainspring of his entire defense strategy, the one who could best serve His Eminence's cause in the perilous days of the trial proper immediately ahead.

Delivered at eight o'clock in the evening, the exile order allowed me barely twenty-four hours to prepare for my departure; foregoing sleep, I devoted them to making arrangements with the Prince's relatives and attorneys to compensate for the loss of my hand at the helm. I chose the Abbé Juncker to be put in charge of affairs in Paris; by bringing Father Loth to us he had given proof of his zeal for the Cardinal's cause. Plans were devised to keep me in constant touch with the developments in the case through channels that were safe from detection, so that from my place of exile in Mortagne I could continue to direct the Cardinal's defense through the man I had chosen to substitute for me during my absence. That much of the plan the Abbé Juncker meticulously executed. His disloyalty to me personally I did not at the time suspect.

Arriving on March 12 at my destination, I met with a most cordial reception. The society of Mortagne, which was composed of retired military and well-to-do nobility, was justly renowned for its hospitality. Indeed, I found this so delightful a spot that, had not my birthplace always represented, for me, the terrestrial Paradise, I might have adopted Mortagne as my home.

My sojourn there during the remaining ten weeks of the Cardinal's imprisonment was not spent idly, however, nor without assiduous service in His Eminence's cause. I remained in constant correspondence with both Maître Target and the Abbé Juncker.

The hearings having been concluded, the examining magistrates set a day [May 22, 1786] upon which to make their report to the Grand' Chambre and the Tournelle of the Parliament of Paris in joint session. The text of this report, along with the records of the proceedings, was submitted to Prosecutor General de Fleury so that he could prepare his conclusions and his recommendations to the Parliament.

The abbé thus summarizes the next step of the procedure in criminal cases. When the preliminary hearings were over, the examining magistrates who had conducted those hearings—in this case, Titon de Villotran and Dupuy de Marcé—fulfilled their role as rapporteurs by drawing up a detailed report which would be delivered to the Parliament. Before the report was formally presented to the assembled Chambers, however, it was submitted to the prosecutor general together with the full dossier of the case—the official records of all inquiries, depositions, interrogations and confrontations, all the evidence acquired in the months of investigation—on the basis of which he in turn would prepare his recommendations. Traditionally the latter were handwritten and kept in a sealed envelope, to be opened only after the reading of the magistrates' report and after the final interrogation of the accused upon the floor of the tribunal by the assembled judges.

Concerning what might be expected of Prosecutor General de Fleury's recommendations Georgel says:

These conclusions and recommendations would, presumably, be not unfavorable to the Cardinal, in view of the fact that it had been proved in the course of the inquiry:

1. That the Cardinal had been convinced that he was purchasing the necklace for the Queen.
2. That the signature "Marie Antoinette de France" had been forged by the hand of Villette, at the instigation of Madame de La Motte.
3. That the necklace had been delivered to Madame de La Motte.
4. That Madame de La Motte's husband had transported the loose stones taken from the necklace to London for sale, the proceeds going to his personal gain.
5. That Madame de La Motte had wickedly taken advantage of the Cardinal's good faith by a series of criminal machinations.

With proofs so favorable to the Cardinal as these established in the inquiry, legal retribution might have been expected to fall upon the head of Madame de La Motte alone; yet, to our dismay, we learned that the examining magistrates and the prosecutor general were in favor of convicting the Cardinal as well as Madame de La Motte.

It developed that, a few days prior to the date set for presenting the report, Titon, Marcé, Fleury and the president of the Parliament, Marquis d'Aligre, had had a conference with the Queen at the Tuileries, the purpose of which, beyond a doubt, had been to convince them that the affont to the sacred honor of Her Majesty demanded the imposition of a penalty upon Cardinal Rohan—a severe penalty involving public dishonor and the loss of all his offices. As a result of this meeting the Queen was assured of the support of the two examining magistrates and the president, which, she was certain, would win over a majority of the judges.

"I find it extraordinary," the Emperor Joseph wrote that month to Count Mercy, "that the verdict of a court should become known days before the court even begins deliberations. It is proof that in France even justice is brought into the sphere of politics."

The occasion for the surprise expressed by the Emperor was a communication sent him by Count Mercy on May 23, the day after the convocation of the Parliament of Paris to begin examination of the evidence. "Thanks to a rather extraordinary confidence made me," Mercy had written, "I was able to obtain the enclosed memoranda. One is a list of the various judges of the Parliament, showing the opinion of each with regard to the Necklace Case; the other is a rough outline of the verdict that may be expected—subject, of course, to last-minute changes."

Count Mercy could likewise send his imperial master an exact copy of the prosecutor general's draft (amended by the Queen) of his conclusions and recommendations to the court—which, incidentally, confirmed Georgel's surmises as to the prosecution's severity toward the Cardinal.

The main change made by the Queen in Fleury's text had been the elimination of his recommendation that the Cardinal be required to declare openly before the Parliament that it was temerity on his part to have put credence in even the possibility of a nocturnal rendezvous with Her Majesty on the Versailles terrace.

The Queen herself, in a holograph letter to the Austrian ambassador on May 19, had told Count Mercy of her decision to eliminate that particular paragraph from the prosecutor general's recommendations. The letter, which came to light in the mid-nineteenth century in the Vienna State Archives, reads: "I will not here enter into any discussion of the all-important affair. The Baron [Breteuil] will give you my thoughts on the matter—above all, my determination to allow no mention whatsoever, at the trial, of the midnight rendezvous, the terrace incident. The Baron will explain my reasons."

What Her Majesty's reasons were for suppressing all reference to the Grove of Venus incident, or even whether Baron de Breteuil ever explained them, Count Mercy in all his voluminous correspondence with Vienna never mentions. Equally strange is the fact that despite the Queen's express orders to Prosecutor General de Fleury to delete this article and any and all reference to the midnight rendezvous, he nevertheless retained it in his conclusions just as it appeared in the original draft.

Count Mercy wrote in another report to Vienna that spring:

Her Majesty deigned yesterday to discuss the notorious Rohan affair with me, and she remarked that the cabaling and intriguing designed to exonerate that distinguished defendant had become more vigorous than ever. The Rohan partisans are determined, at any cost, to ensure that the Cardinal be spared the accusation of swindling—to have it, rather, that he acted out of incredible folly and indiscretion.

One of the first maneuvers on the part of the house of Rohan was to win over a number of honorary councilors of the Parliament who, although they have not put in an appearance there in many years, nevertheless retain the right to sit and cast their vote.

Madame Campan had reason to believe that the Rohan maneuvers had gone far beyond the honorary councilors, as she relates it in her memoirs:

Monsieur de Laurencel, the assistant prosecutor general, sent the Queen a list of the names of all the judges of the Parliament; alongside each was a notation of the means by which his vote had been solicited by the Rohan faction. I held that list in my possession along with other secret papers later entrusted to my safekeeping by Their Majesties, but it was burned eventually, like all the rest, in the holocaust of Revolution; I still remember, however, that women played a shocking role in the subornation of justice—a sad commentary on the morals of the times. It would appear that the judges of that august tribunal, even the most venerable and respected among them, had succumbed to the fatal combination of feminine wiles and bribery.

Count Mercy addressed another report from Paris to the Austrian Foreign Office on May 23, 1786:

The trial of Cardinal Rohan, still the focal point of interest here, builds inevitably to its climax. The reading of the official report to the Parliament by the examining magistrates who conducted the Bastille hearings was begun yesterday on the floor of the tribunal and is expected to continue for several days longer, in view of the extensive proceedings it covers. Despite the mystery and involvements that complicate the case, the verdict is expected before Pentecost. Thus, as is easily comprehensible, the curiosity of the Parisian public is at fever pitch in anticipation of the terms of the judgment to be handed down in this trial which is unprecedented in the annals of French history. As I have indicated, that feverish curiosity should now be shortly satisfied.

Meanwhile still another trial brief for Cardinal Rohan has been published by Maître Target, claiming more or less to exonerate His Eminence, and so preparing the general public to accept him as chief victim, to be pitied, rather than chief culprit, to be penalized. Target's trial brief is entrusted to this same courier, and whenever new ones appear I shall consider it my duty to procure copies for forwarding to you.

No mean achievement, that, for Necklace Case publications were bringing premium prices and people were rudely jostling one another on the street corners for the privilege of paying such prices to the newsvendors, whose cries of "Du nouveau, du nouveau! The latest news! Read the latest on the Necklace Case!" were the most familiar in Paris in the spring of 1786.

The government had evidently made some effort to suppress the flood of Necklace Case publications—although unsuccessfully, to judge by a letter on the subject from Marie Antoinette to her sister Maria Christina: "There seems a possibility that the Lawyers' Association itself will prevent the printing [of Target's trial brief]. We feel that its publication should not be permitted until it has been passed by the national censors, but the Lawyers' Association claims to have the right to print and publish without submission to censorship."

Count Beugnot, himself a member of the Lawyers' Association, expressed outrage at the "carnival spirit pervading the Necklace Case publications," likening the endless series of trial briefs to a "legal tourney" in which the counselors at law were breaking pens instead of lances in defense of their clients: Maître Doillot, never suspecting, perhaps, that he had been the Countess de La Motte's second choice as attorney (after Count Beugnot), gallantly entered the lists with the publication of three defense pleas in her name; the defenders of Mademoiselle d'Oliva and of Cagliostro came out with two apiece for their clients; Villette's malicious Maître Jaillant-Deschainets made do with merely one; while Maître Target outstripped all the rest with a grand total of five trial briefs for Cardinal Rohan.

Target, who considered himself a literary as well as a legal light, had given several private prepublication readings of his fifth and last Necklace Case composition to his fellow members of the French Academy, who, in the tradition of the Forty Immortals, pronounced it a masterpiece; and before the printed version appeared, manuscript copies were grabbed up at the sky-high price of thirty-six francs each. With such advance publicity, it is small wonder that three separate printings could not satisfy the public demand. All three editions were distributed gratis: one in the vast colonnaded court of honor of the Hôtel de Soubise, the handsome palace of Cardinal Rohan's cousin the Marshal (causing such a riot as to necessitate the summoning of the patrol and the mounted guard), another at a publisher's in the Palais-Royal and the third at the Claude Simon bookshop, and all three editions were exhausted by sundown of publication day. The brochure brought up to five francs on the first resale, and there was simply no limit to what a really ardent bibliophile might pay to complete his collection of Necklace Case memorabilia.

The competition was not limited to literati. It was considered that no more treasured gift could be presented to one's fiancée or mistress, to one's prosperous bachelor uncle or valued business associate in the provinces, than a Necklace Trial memento: a trial brief by the renowned Target, a copy of the Amsterdam Gazette or the Courrier de l'Europe, an engraving of Mademoiselle d'Oliva, the highly popular etching of the Count de La Motte paying his first formal call upon her (with a bed in the background, its coverlet turned down), a gutter-press ode or jingle, cartoons of the Countess de La Motte in pornographic poses plastiques with an assortment of partners chosen from the list of her former lovers—with Cardinal Rohan, with Villette, with the Count d'Olomieu, with the Marquis d'Aligre, president of the Parliament of Paris.*

An outraged government and its police did not sit idly by while the clandestine press operated. Two part-time barbers, Dupré and Chambon by name, who had published the twenty-two engravings of the Necklace Case star performers (a best-selling series despite the fact that half the likenesses were not those of the persons represented), were arrested and "embastilled" on March 21, 1786; and in February of that same year the police had managed to detect and seize the author-editor of the popular pamphlet Le Garde du Corps. But for every one ar-

---

* Not only does Aligre's name figure prominently on Villette's list of the Countess's lovers; she herself implicates him in her memoirs, with lengthy tributes such as "President d'Aligre's great services to me in my days of financial difficulty . . . the benefit of his sage counsel in addition to his generosity, amounting to some ten thousand francs—which he refused to let me repay in times of prosperity and Queen's favor, despite my lively urgings . . ."

rested a dozen fly-by-night journalists and publishers evaded the police net. At the very first hint of surveillance a small hand press could be jerked out of a cellar on the Left Bank at midnight, to be clattering away by dawn in an attic on the Right Bank, turning out newssheets, broadsheets, handbills: *Réflexions de Motus* or *Observations de Père Tranquille* or any one of a score of equally scandalous issues. The police were not to be censured for lack of trying, but they could not cope with hawkers who, having done a brisk business in contraband on the Champs Élysées, scuttled off before the constabulary could catch up with them and, by the next day, had attracted a new clientele under the Palais-Royal arcades with a fresh stock of *Le Conte Oriental, La Dernière Pièce du fameux collier* or *La Lettre de l'abbé G—— à la comtesse ——,* one more libelous, more titillating than the other. (An example, from Bachaumont's *Mémoires secrets:* "Her head beside his on the pillow, Mademoiselle d'Oliva, in granting the Cardinal her favors [at the Grove of Venus rendezvous], convinced him that he enjoyed those of the Queen. No wonder His Eminence's ambitions soared accordingly.")

Every wag strove to outdo the others with his bons mots. On March 26 Hardy entered this one in his journal: "The Count de La Motte has been run out of London by the Lord Mayor and has taken refuge in Constantinople, in the bosom of Allah, doffing his foreskin and donning the fez—or so it is widely said."

"It is widely said . . . On dit . . ." The rumors were flying thick and fast. Catherine the Great's faithful Paris correspondent reported to her on May 8:

In Paris they are saying that the government is undertaking research to disprove the Countess de La Motte-Valois's claims to Valois heritage, which the King's own official genealogist had previously authenticated. If they are now sufficiently determined to invalidate it, it is thought that they will not suffer frustration in their effort.

People say that an example must be made of someone in this nasty business, and that Madame de La Motte will be called upon to pay the piper for two. His Highness the Count d'Artois is quoted as saying recently, "I suppose I resemble our Lord Savior to the extent that I am always sympathetic to the magdalens of this world, but in this instance I very much fear that my dear Valois cousin may be hanged by her pretty neck."

And in another dispatch to St. Petersburg, the correspondent quotes an epigram which he attributes to the lips of no less a personage than the King of Prussia: "Cardinal Rohan will be obliged to call upon all the resources of his not inconsiderable intellect to convince his judges that he was a fool."

Catherine also received the lyrics of more new songs, including this one, which had a hundred choruses:

> Oliva says, "He's such a goose!"
> La Motte insists, "He's morally loose."
> His Eminence claims he's just obtuse.
> Hallelujah!
>
> Red are his robes from the Holy See.
> "Black is his heart," said Queen Marie.
> "We'll whitewash his name," the judges agree.
> Hallelujah!

Another popular quatrain called for a duet between Oliva and the Queen:

> "Vile damsel, it becomes a harlot ill
> To play at my role of queen."
> "Now do not be wroth, my sovereign,
> Have you not often tried mine to fill?"

"This unprecedented scandal of a case, with its web of intrigue and counterintrigue," said the Leyden Gazette, "holds all Europe spellbound, breathless, waiting for the denouement"—a denouement about which the Abbé Georgel had this observation to make in his memoirs:

The notoriety attendant on a trial in which the honor of the Queen of France was involved, and in which the King himself brought accusation against his own Grand Almoner, a prince, a bishop and cardinal of the Holy Roman Church, for the crime of lèse-majesté, had considerably augmented the normal complement of judges in the Grand' Chambre and the Tournelle of the Parliament of Paris. All the honorary councilors and other officials who had the right to participate in the sessions of that tribunal availed themselves of it in the Diamond Necklace Case, betaking themselves to the Palais de Justice to hear the report by the examining magistrate and to cast their votes, as was their privilege. More than fifty judges were seated.

The sessions were lengthy and numerous; the official report of the entire preliminary investigation had to be read aloud on the floor of the Parliament. A certain member of the Grand' Chambre, a friend of the Cardinal's [Éprémesnil], took notes of all that was said and done throughout these proceedings and transmitted that priceless information to His Eminence's legal staff, who, accordingly, designed a plan of conduct for him to follow in his appearance before the court.

The Palais de Justice, on its island in the Seine at the very heart of Paris, has been a center of government and of justice since the very earliest days of the French monarchy, when the Capetian kings lived and held court there; and earlier, as ancient remains imply, the site it occupies was used for the same purpose by the prefects of Roman Lutetia. There in the thirteenth century Louis IX, Saint Louis, built a new palace, of which the jewel-box Sainte Chapelle was a part. The fourteenth century saw the addition of the four towers of the Quai de l'Horloge and the superb Gothic chambers of the Conciergerie, the prison which was to play such a grisly role during the Reign of Terror. Abandoned as a royal residence in the 1300s, the Palais was turned over to the Parliament of Paris as the seat of the nation's highest court.

It was here, in the Great Hall—"still in all its medieval splendor," as Berryer was to describe it, "with its great stone columns, its arched roof springing from gilded brackets, . . . with two upper galleries for distinguished spectators"—that the extraordinary joint session of the Parliament's Grand' Chambre and Tournelle to try the Diamond Necklace Case opened on May 22, 1786.

The official transcript of the minutes of that extraordinary session lists the number of participating jurists as, variously, sixty-two and sixty-four. Not all the honorary judges of the Parliament had availed themselves of the privilege of taking part, as Georgel thought. The princes of the blood and the peers of the realm, whose right to a vote in the Parliament of Paris was hereditary, had voluntarily abstained from appearing.

Titon de Villotran began the reading of the examining magistrates' report to the assembled judges on the opening day. The reading took until May 29. Its conclusion was the signal for the prisoners to be transferred from the Bastille to the Conciergerie in preparation for their final hearing before the tribunal.

MEMOIRS
OF THE COUNTESS DE LA MOTTE-VALOIS

Throughout all the long months of the interrogations and the confrontations, not one visitor had been allowed inside the Bastille. That part of the proceedings over, I rejoiced at the sweet privilege of seeing my legal counsel, Monsieur Doillot, once again.

As he entered my cell, however, he knit those heavy brows of his and, trying to suppress the twinkle in his eye, growled, "People in Paris are saying that you've been exceedingly naughty, Madame la Comtesse—that in one of your little tantrums you sank your teeth into poor Saint-Jean's hand, taking off half the thumb. And another rumor has you desperately ill, dying—although, judging by appearances, the latter report is grossly exaggerated."

It was obvious that my enemies had tried to make something out of my occasional moments of hysteria, which should not too greatly surprise the reader. Was it not natural that the monotony of prison routine, the strain and harassment of those grueling months of questioning, should have affected my mood and disposition?

Saint-Jean, the turnkey, being present at this interview, broke in to say, "In my opinion, Madame has been only too patient with her hecklers."

One evening in May, a few weeks later, Maître Doillot came to see me and informed me that the case would come to trial within the next day or two. "It is possible that the prisoners will be transferred tonight from the Bastille to the Conciergerie, so hold yourself in readiness—I hear you'll be taken there before midnight."

This news, far from dismaying me, struck me as encouraging. I interpreted it to mean that my long captivity was coming to an end. No gloomy premonitions came to mind. Alas, I was far from dreaming what fate awaited me!

Monsieur Doillot's face betrayed no forebodings, though he did question me as to whether I had any comprehension of the juridical procedure. My reply was in the negative.

"Well, then, to begin with," he explained, "the accused in a criminal trial is obliged, when he comes before his judges, to sit upon a kind of stool, called a *sellette*."

"Oh, I may have heard the name somewhere," I said airily. "What of it?"

"The custom may seem strange," Doillot continued. "It is a relic of medieval court procedure preserved into modern times for the reason that, the defendant's position being necessarily so disagreeable and unpleasant, he might be overcome and faint if he had not a seat of some kind. And don't be miffed if they make you use the small back stairs to go up to the courtroom."

"Heavens above, Monsieur Doillot!" I exclaimed. "You're wasting your breath with this talk of *sellettes* and back and front stairs. It's all Greek to me."

Alas, these mysterious terms were a prediction of the humiliations in store for me, but at this point I could not guess the dreadful connotation and shrugged it all off nonchalantly.

At eight o'clock that evening Saint-Jean, bringing me my supper, said to me in that brusque, rude style typical of men of his profession, "My, what a gay mood we're in tonight! Upon my word, madame, you're a queer one. Hasn't Doillot told you what's going on? Good Lord, things don't look too good for you. It wouldn't surprise me at all to see this business end up at the scaffold in the public square."

Although the humor of his remarks struck me as rather crude, I read no dire portents into them.

"Hurry along, Saint-Jean," I replied coolly, "and ask Governor de Launay whether I'm to be taken to the Conciergerie tonight. If not, I should like to make ready for bed."

At 10 P.M. Saint-Jean returned. "It's set for eleven o'clock," he said, "so make ready. All the prisoners are to be removed to the Conciergerie tonight, and you're scheduled as the first to leave."

At eleven sharp he came to fetch me.

"Farewell, my friend!" I cried. "All I hope is that I never lay eyes on you or your horrid Bastille again."

In the council chamber, whither Saint-Jean conducted me, I found Governor de Launay and two officers, who demanded my permission to search my pockets—with the explanation that this was an ancient custom to which all must submit before passing on to the Conciergerie.

444

Finding nothing in my pockets to confiscate save a packet of papers, they escorted me out to the carriage.

The drive to the Palais de Justice, down the boulevard and across the Seine, seemed all too short. Before ever we pulled into the Cour de Mai, the great courtyard of the Palais de Justice, I could see that the huge building was ablaze with light from every window of every floor and that there were thousands of people milling around the area.

An officer of the guard came to the carriage to offer his arm to help me down the steps and into the large room known as the Hall of Records, into which, as we entered, four or five hundred people crowded after us. Every room, every corridor of the Palais was jammed; people were sitting in the window embrasures, standing on the tables.

The concierge of the Conciergerie and his wife hurried forward to greet me with every courtesy, offering me refreshments of which I felt it was only gracious on my part to partake. And, listening with pleasure to the compliments paid me by most of the spectators assembled to see me, I went out of my way to express my appreciation of their sympathy and encouragement.

At two o'clock, succumbing finally to fatigue, I asked to be allowed to retire, and after bidding goodbye to that large company I was shown by the concierge's wife to my quarters. As she left me, she graciously assured me that she would be on hand early in the morning to help me with anything I might need before I was called into court.

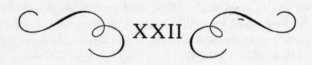

XXII

The Verdict

(May 1786)

MEMOIRS
OF THE ABBÉ GEORGEL

The examining magistrate having made his summation before the court, the time had come for the defendants to appear before the bar . . .

From the Leyden Gazette:

Villette, dressed in black silk, his eyes swimming in tears, was the first of the accused to face his judges on the morning of May 30. This is a quick-witted man, ready with his answers almost before the judges have the questions out of their mouths, replying with a tone and air of utmost exactitude.

MEMOIRS
OF THE ABBÉ GEORGEL

Villette admitted that the signature "Marie Antoinette de France" was in his hand, but insisted that he had written only at the dictation of another. Villette was not being honest: he had been well aware of his fair friend's guilty intrigue; he it was who, costumed as a Trianon valet, had received from the hands of Madame de La Motte the jewel case containing the necklace.

When she, to avoid implicating herself, persisted in denial of all these facts, Villette seized gratefully upon the opportunity provided him by her silence to escape incrimination as her accomplice in the theft. It was in this fashion that he managed to escape the punishment which is generally meted out for forgery and larceny on such a scale. On the other hand, it was Villette's confession that saved the Cardinal; without it, His Eminence must have been presumed guilty of forgery.

Madame de La Motte appeared with a boldness and effrontery that disgusted the judges, who were familiar with her infamous machinations through the report of the court investigations. She brazened it out, however, admitting nothing. Involving herself in a maze of contradictions, she denied the facts attested by other witnesses and defendants in the various depositions and confrontations.

STORY OF MY LIFE
BY THE COUNTESS DE LA MOTTE-VALOIS

The judges began to gather in the courtroom at six o'clock that morning. I was up and dressed by half after six.

Madame Hubert, the concierge's wife, having advised me that Oliva was in the cell next to mine, I asked to see her. I found her nursing her baby and tried to cheer her up a bit, although I could not refrain from chiding her for the injustices she had done me in testimony given at her lawyer's advice.

Sometime between ten and eleven the concierge and his son came to fetch me and led me down the narrow, dark back stairs to which Monsieur Doillot had referred. At the foot of the steps waited Monsieur de Frémyn, who escorted me into the Great Hall, where the full Parliament was assembled.

Oh, dreadful moment! What a spectacle awaited me! Here, then, was come the hour when some sixty judges, white-wigged and robed, gathered to decide upon my fate, would for all time sully my honor and besmirch my name. Have I the courage to continue this painful story? Yes, righteous indignation and innocence lend me the strength to finish the doleful task I have set myself.

All too quickly, then, I came to understand Monsieur Doillot's veiled allusions to the famous *sellette*. He had tried to prepare me for the humiliation awaiting me, and I had not understood what he meant; but when the moment came to submit to that shameful custom, I recoiled in horror. Whispered words of encouragement from persons close beside me, however, revived my courage.

"Must I be seated," I cried out, "in a chair designed for the guilty?" How could I have foreseen such indignities? Confronted, alas, with the inevitable, I obeyed.

Monsieur de Frémyn took advantage of the situation to humiliate me further, approaching me to tell me curtly that I must throw back the hood of my cape. Managing to control my temper, I merely glared at him, remarking that any man with an ounce of chivalry in his soul would have shown more consideration for a lady in distress. There was a scattering of applause at my reply, a murmur of censure for Frémyn's boorishness.

I shall not attempt to describe in full the anguish of my hours before the bar. My knees, my whole body trembled violently. So great was my state of confusion that, though I sat in full view of the multitude, I saw little of what went on around me. Then the words "Courage, madame —take courage," reaching my ears from all corners of the hall, from the lips of some of the judges themselves, restored my confidence and soothed my troubled spirits. My thoughts became clearer and I was able at last to reply to the questions put me with the precision and vigor appropriate to innocence.

The president of the Parliament, the Marquis d'Aligre, ordered the reading of my interrogations and confrontations, on the completion of which I arose and, bowing respectfully, remarked that I was dismayed to discover to what extent these official documents had been abridged and censored. I protested that such glaring omissions deprived my judges of evidence vital to any decision as to my guilt or innocence.

"I therefore beseech the judges themselves to question me on the facts relative to the necklace transaction," I declared, "so that I may have the opportunity of stating the facts as I did originally, as I have stated them a hundred times since and as I shall continue to state them for all the future."

Pointing out the number of contradictions apparent in the Cardinal's testimony, I reminded the court that His Eminence had identified Villette, at their first confrontation, as the man to whom I had turned over the necklace. "Whereas if my judges will only compare the Cardinal's original description of the Queen's messenger with the person of Monsieur Villette," I urged, "they will know what value to ascribe to the Cardinal's testimony in general. The Sieur Villette's appearance before this court is a contradiction incarnate of the Cardinal's delineation of that mysterious figure."

I can no longer today remember all the questions asked me on that occasion nor all the revelations forced from me under duress. One thing is certain, however: my replies seemed to create a great sensation among the judges as well as among the spectators.

At least one of the judges, Mercier de Saint-Léger, was not so impressed as Madame de La Motte would lead us to believe they all had been:

The La Motte woman made her appearance with an air of bravado, with all the self-assurance in the world—her eyes, her expression indicative of a woman whom naught could dismay. She did, however, command attention by her straightforward and confident manner of speech.

Reluctant at first to take her seat in the *sellette* indicated to her by the sergeant at arms, she visibly blushed and drew back involuntarily; but she finally settled herself so gracefully upon it, arranging the folds of her satin skirt about her, as to give the impression that she was comfortably ensconced in her favorite armchair in her own salon.

The Leyden Gazette reporter wrote for the delectation of his feminine audience:

Madame de La Motte . . . was meticulously groomed, exquisitely and elegantly attired: her dress, a blue-gray satin banded in black velvet; at her waist, a black velvet belt sparkling with steel beads; a black hat trimmed with black lace and ribbon; and, about her shoulders, an embroidered muslin cape edged with net.

In a hearing that lasted over three hours, Madame de La Motte launched forth with the startling declaration that she was "about to expose a great scallawag"—which all present took to mean the Cardinal. . . . She spoke in terms of theory rather than fact, but she undoubtedly scored a point when she insisted that none of the letters, none of the written material which should properly have been submitted in evidence at the trial had been produced.

Despite her fetching appearance, her grace and her beautiful figure, despite her air of breeding and distinction, she failed to win sympathy because, I think, the evidence pointed too clearly against her.

Her presence of mind was astonishing. Questioned by an ecclesiastical judge the Parliament, the Abbé Sabbatier, whom she knew to be hostile to her, Madame de La Motte replied, "That is a highly insidious question. But I know you, Monsieur Abbé, and it is just what might have been expected from you."

This sally the Countess reports somewhat differently in her Story of My Life:

"I know you abbés are in league against me, but it's not that to which I take exception; the thing I criticize is that your question betrays a total lack of common sense."

"Enter it in the record!" a voice called out. "Enter it in the official record of the Parliament that Madame de La Motte says the Abbé Sabbatier has no common sense!" At which, smiles and chuckles momentarily erased the frowns from the judges' brows and there were bursts of laughter from the spectators.

Monsieur de Bretignières, one of the judges, then asked me a question which was as misplaced as that of the abbé, but to which I was forced to give a direct reply. "Madame," said he, "you saw a great number of letters in the hands of the Cardinal, so you should be able to tell us what was in them, and whether the Cardinal wrote letters in reply to those he received."

"Monsieur," I answered, "I consider that a highly indiscreet and dangerous question. Besides, is not Cardinal Rohan himself the person who could most properly answer it? Why not ask him to produce the letters of that correspondence so that you may read them and satisfy your curiosity?"

My readers can see how careful I was to try to avoid compromising my sovereign. But the judges, whether they wanted merely to gratify their curiosity or whether they were sincere in seeking to elicit all the information I could give them, insisted that I make specific answer to the questions asked me on the subject of the little letters. Thus I had no choice but to tell the court the subject matter of the correspondence.

They asked me whether I was personally convinced that these letters had come from the Queen or whether I considered the tenor of the little letters too familiar to have been written by a sovereign to one of her own subjects. My reply was that this had been the very observation I had made to the Cardinal when he first showed them to me.

"And what answer did he make to that?"

My judges continuing insistent that I give specific answers to their queries concerning these letters, I was obliged to go into some detail on the matter, although I cannot now remember all the many questions that were asked or the answers given.

From the anonymous Compte Rendu de ce qui s'est passé au Parlement:

To persistent questioning about one certain letter shown her by the Cardinal as coming from the Queen, the Countess manifested a sudden reluctance, remarking with an air of mystery that she did not wish to reply, because by so doing she might offend the Queen.

"The truth cannot offend Their Majesties," Parliament President d'Aligre objected, "and the truth is what you owe to justice."

Thereupon the Countess replied that the letter in question had begun with the words, "I send to *thee* . . . ," and she added that the Cardinal had shown her more than two hundred letters sent him by the Queen in which future rendezvous were appointed or past rendezvous commented on, and in which she addressed him as "thou" and "thee."

At these words a very clamor went up among the magistrates.

STORY OF MY LIFE
BY THE COUNTESS DE LA MOTTE-VALOIS

I concluded my testimony with a few general observations on the charges against me as a whole. . . .

All the questions put to me, along with my replies, having been duly inscribed in the official trial record, I insisted on having them all read back aloud to ensure that the recording clerk had been more faithful to his duty than the two court examiners in the interrogations made at the Bastille.

When President d'Aligre asked if I had anything further to tell the court, I replied that it only remained for me to entreat my judges to consider carefully all the circumstances of the case involving me, that I resigned my fate into their hands in full confidence that, with their reputed wisdom, enlightenment and impartiality, they could not but find in my favor.

Having rendered the reader a full and truthful account of the happenings in the Parliament, I have only one last comment to make—on the injustice done me in the news reports of the trial at the hands of journalists in the hire of influential and powerful enemies. Even these hostile newspaper accounts had to admit that I defended myself vigorously and capably, with a feminine logic and forcefulness astonishing to the judges. It was the truth which made me eloquent; it was innocence which inspired me with the courage to meet the occasion.

"Madame de La Motte," said the Leyden Gazette, "on the day she appeared before her judges was meticulously groomed, exquisitely and elegantly attired . . ." Now, my readers will know how much of that to believe when they remember that my appearance in court took place between ten and eleven o'clock in the forenoon! I call upon Madame Hubert, the concierge's wife, and upon my judges themselves to support me in my point-blank denial of the statement.

A white batiste waist, a short cape, an untrimmed net bonnet, a white net veil over my face, my hair simply coiffed, not even powdered—there you have a description of the costume it pleased the Leyden Gazette reporter to refer to as "elegant."

That same irresponsible newssheet went on to censure my "intrepidity" and my "unseemly urge to self-justification" and did not hesitate to apply to me the epithet of "audacious woman." Would they make a crime, then, of my pride? That I am proud I do not deny; that same pride—that nobility of soul, rather, which prevents me from flinching before my equals when they seek to outrage me—manifests itself as benevolence or generosity when any man comes to ask my aid. So exquisite are my sensibilities in doing favors for others that I seek even to make them forget the fact that they are not my equals, seek even to spare them the embarrassment of putting their request into words. If these be deemed expressions of vanity and pride, then let my enemies make the most of it. I call upon those persons whom I have had the opportunity to oblige; let them say whether they have ever found me a proud or haughty woman!

That same Leyden *Gazette* reporter mendaciously ascribes the following remark to me: "I am about to expose a great scallawag." I challenge him to name a single person of integrity in the Great Hall of the Parliament that day who will admit to having heard me make such a statement!

But I fear I have too long preoccupied my reader with proof of the fact that my enemies misrepresented my conduct before the Parliament of Paris.

To resume, then: When my judges had signified that I was to withdraw from their presence, I bowed to them respectfully and withdrew. Monsieur Hubert, the concierge, escorted me back upstairs, a great throng of spectators following at my heels all the way to the Huberts' apartment.

Everyone paid me compliment, observing that I had defended myself very well, that even an experienced lawyer could not better have pleaded my cause. And everyone wished me well.

From the Leyden Gazette, June 2, 1786:

As soon as Madame de La Motte had left the courtroom, the *sellette* was removed and Cardinal Prince de Rohan was ushered in. He was dressed in long violet robes [the official mourning color for cardinals], with a red calotte on his gray hair, red stockings, red heels on his shoes, a mantelletta of violet cloth lined in red satin, across his chest the blue riband of the royal Order of the Holy Ghost and on a golden chain about his neck the bishop's cross.

MEMOIRS
OF THE ABBÉ GEORGEL

The Cardinal, calling upon all his inner reserves of strength and courage to meet so decisive a test, presented himself before the court as a man deeply moved but nobly calm. The expression on his face, one of modesty, respect and great dignity, could not but favorably impress the magistrates.

He remained standing before the bar, his extreme pallor showing the inroads of a recent malady so serious as to have aroused concern for his life. President d'Aligre invited him to take a seat before the long interrogation should begin. The Prince expressed his deep appreciation of that signal honor by a deep bow, but did not accept the president's invitation until it had been extended him for the third time.

Questioned on several points still requiring elucidation, the Cardinal astonished the judges by the clarity, the precision and the vigor of his responses. Remarking the keen sympathy inspired by his humiliating position, he took advantage of it to explain, with the utmost frankness, the grievous mistakes into which his credulity had led him.

"I was utterly blinded," he exclaimed, "by my overwhelming desire to regain the Queen's good graces."

This touching scene caused a veritable sensation among the judges who were about to decide the fate of one of the kingdom's mightiest figures.

From the Leyden Gazette:

The interrogation of Cardinal Prince de Rohan lasted for more than two hours. . . .

An expression of indefinable sorrow and weariness on his face, the Cardinal bowed to the court and withdrew. His judges bowed in return; the High Bench itself stood up to salute him, an extraordinary distinction to be paid a prisoner.

The court had not yet shaken off its reaction to that moving scene when Mademoiselle d'Oliva was summoned. But the sergeant at arms returned to the courtroom without her; the prisoner was nursing her newborn babe and humbly begged the indulgence of our lords of Parliament for a few moments more for her little son to finish his feeding. The Grand' Chambre and the Tournelle of the Parliament of Paris in joint and formal session thereupon hastened to send word to the young mother that she should take all the time she needed.*

At last she appeared, her simple dress in sweet disarray.

The reporters in their newspapers, the judges and spectators in their respective diaries, journals, memoirs, all float off on a tide of unabashed sentimentality at the sight of Mademoiselle d'Oliva: "her appealing face," "her wayward chestnut curls escaping from under her little round bonnet," "poor Mademoiselle d'Oliva, all tears and trouble," "almost impossible to reconcile such disarming candor and ingenuousness with a

* "The Law bows to Nature," the official court record reads.

reputation for dubious morality." As for Monsieur de Bretignières, an art collector as well as a judge, Mademoiselle d'Oliva reminded him of the lovely model in Greuze's latest painting, "The Broken Pitcher," and the Abbé Sabbatier, beside him on the bench, "agreed that the likeness was startling." In the words of fellow judge Mercier de Saint-Léger, "When the pretty creature appeared about to faint, half the members of that austere tribunal were on their feet to rush to her assistance. Of course, she could never get out so much as a word in response to any of the queries put to her; her sobs choked them off in her throat. But the judges could well dispense with words—there was more than enough to convince them of her innocence. When, dismissed, she rose to withdraw, it was to the accompaniment of universal, overt sympathy, manifest in face and voice throughout the courtroom." As one of the numerous reporters might have put it, not a dry eye in the house.

Next came Cagliostro, "swaggering, dashing, in a gold-embroidered green taffeta coat, his hair in the catogan style," and, with him, a change of pace and mood, according to Nougaret:

"Who are you and whence do you come?" inquired President d'Aligre.

"I am a noble voyager, Nature's unfortunate child," Cagliostro intoned, to the judges' intense amusement, bringing smiles to their set faces.

It was anything but an occasion for merriment to the defendant, however. With imperturbable gravity he began the story of his life in that blaring metallic voice likened by the Baroness d'Oberkirch to "a trumpet veiled in crepe," in that indefinable jargon described by Count Beugnot as a burlesque jumble of French and Italian with flourishes of Arabic.

DEFENSE PLEA
OF COUNT CAGLIOSTRO

As I have told you, the names of my parents and of my birthplace are unknown to me. I cannot state as a certainty whether I saw the light of day at Malta or at Medina. I had with me always a preceptor who told me that I was of noble birth. . . .

But what matters it whether I am the son of a monarch or of a peasant, whether I travel the world without making known my identity? Choosing to preserve my incognito, I have on various occasions made use of the titles of Count Harat, Count Fenix and Marquis d'Anna, although generally throughout Europe I have been known as Count Cagliostro. . . . I have always considered it my privilege to refuse to gratify public curiosity with regard to my name or my origins, no matter what is said of me, no matter whether people call me the Wandering Jew or the Antichrist or any other libel which malice can invent.

But if since my arrival in the kingdom of France I have given offense to any man, let him now stand and say so. Inquire of the governors, the judges, the populace of every city, every town, every village in France in which I have sojourned, as to whether I have ever given rise to so much as a breath of scandal, whether any action of mine has ever been in violation of the law or of morality or of religion. Question the curates of the parishes; they will tell you of the charity I have done among their poor. Question the jailers; they will tell you of the relief work I have done among their prisoners. Question the commandants of the artillery regiments at Strasbourg; they will tell you of the wounded soldiers I have healed.

Inquire of the King's own Cabinet ministers; here are letters of recommendation in my behalf from two of them which I submit to the attention of this court and the general public, letters of recommendation all the more honorific in that I solicited them neither directly nor indirectly. Quoting from that of Count de Vergennes, Minister of Foreign Affairs: "Such uniformly laudatory reports as reach me of Count Cagliostro's humanitarian services in France recommend him, surely, to the most respectful and courteous reception among us." . . . And Minister of Justice de Miromesnil: "Count Cagliostro has devoted his life to comforting the poor and the afflicted. I have personal knowledge of good deeds so numerous performed by this stranger in our midst as to have earned him a very special consideration among Frenchmen." . . .

And now you have heard me, judges and citizens; you have the story of my life. Such is the man who has made himself known at Strasbourg, at Bordeaux, at Lyons, at Paris, under the name of the Count Cagliostro.

Will you say that it is not enough? Will you insist upon still further information as to my native land, my name, my motives, my resources? As to the source of my fortune, it can have no bearing on this case, yet

I shall here reveal to you more than I have ever before revealed to anyone, anywhere. Hear, then, the secret of my resources: know that in whatever country I travel, a banker comes forward to provide me all I may require. In Basle I need only call on Sarrasin; in Lyons it is Sancostar; in Rome, Bellone. . . .

Is not this enough to satisfy the law—to satisfy all questions, indeed, save those of idle curiosity? When, to heal the sick and to feed the starving, I apply for membership in your medical and philanthropical societies, then you will have the right to question me further. Surely, however, the right to do all the good within one's power for one's fellow man requires neither citizenship nor title nor proofs nor guarantees. Not that I seek credit or self-glorification. I do good because such is my mission in life. I must do good.

And yet what harvest have I reaped for the services I have rendered the French nation? Out of the bitterness of my heart I tell you: My rewards have been slander—and the Bastille.

Cagliostro, willy-nilly, had supplied the comic relief to the May 30 session. The next one opened on a somber note, according to a Dutch newspaper account:

At half past four the next morning, Wednesday, May 31, nineteen members of Cardinal Rohan's family—princes, princesses, an archbishop and a grand marshal of the armies of France—all dressed in mourning attire, took their places in a row on either side of the entrance to the Great Hall of Parliament.

Speaking no word, but merely bowing to the magistrates filing past into the hall, they employed no means of solicitation save their mournful silence, in which might be discerned their grief, their fortitude and their respect for the majesty of the law and the throne. This mode of solicitation so noble, so worthy of the illustrious houses of Rohan, Soubise, Guéménée and Lorraine, made a deeper impression upon the judges than all the eloquence exercised in the Cardinal's behalf.

From five o'clock on, not only the Palais de Justice but all the streets and bridges for blocks around were thronged with people. The Paris foot guard and mounted guard patrolled the area.

That same day, May 31, Count Mercy wrote to Emperor Joseph:

The closer we come to the judgment day in this world-famous Rohan case, the higher public curiosity and excitement mount.

Parliament is expected to reach a verdict this very day. It will probably not come, however, until late tonight and will not become known until early morning. Thus I will be obliged to wait until the next courier to send you word of the outcome.

From the official trial records and the notes of Prosecutor General Joly de Fleury:

Shortly after 6 A.M., the assembled Grand' Chambre and Tournelle of the Parliament of Paris having been declared in session, Prosecutor General Joly de Fleury opened proceedings by unsealing and reading his recommendations to the court:

RECOMMENDATION 1:

That the word "*Approved,*" repeated six times in the margin of the contract with the jewelers Böhmer and Bassenge, and the signature "*Marie Antoinette de France*" be herewith declared to be forgeries and falsely attributed to the Queen; that these words shall be struck out and expunged from said document (hereinafter referred to as PROPOSITIONS AND CONDITIONS OF PRICE AND PAYMENT FOR THE DIAMOND NECKLACE); that notation of the present decree shall be made upon the aforesaid instrument, after which it shall be deposited in the criminal-records file of this court, affirmation of which shall be made by the court registrar.

(First recommendation of the prosecutor general unanimously adopted by voice vote of sixty-two judges in session.)

Certainly a finding consistent with the evidence submitted; for, in addition to the testimony by Harger and Blin to the effect that the contract signature and the marginal notations were forgeries of the Queen's hand, these notations and the signature offered two striking anomalies to the Queen's: first, Her Majesty signed her name with no paraph, no squiggle at the end, whereas the contract signature displayed such a final flourish; second, the Queen (in all documents extant) consist-

*ently signified her assent to terms by the marginal notation "Bon"
(Good), rather than "Approuvé."*

RECOMMENDATION 2:

That Marc Antoine Rétaux de Villette be condemned to
banishment for life from the kingdom of France, his goods to
be forfeit to the King.

*(Second recommendation of the prosecutor general unanimously adopted
by voice vote of sixty-two judges in session.)*

RECOMMENDATION 3:

That Nicole Leguay d'Oliva be acquitted on the grounds
of insufficient evidence to convict, acquittal to be accompanied by a reprimand from the court for criminal presumption in impersonation of the sovereign.

*(Third recommendation of the prosecutor general unanimously adopted
by voice vote of sixty-two judges in session.)*

RECOMMENDATION 4:

That Alexander Cagliostro be acquitted without reprimand from the court, totally exonerated.

*(Fourth recommendation of the prosecutor general unanimously
adopted by voice vote of sixty-two judges in session.)*

RECOMMENDATION 5:

That Marc Antoine Nicolas de La Motte be condemned
in absentia to be flogged and beaten, naked, with rods; to be
branded with a hot iron on the right shoulder with the letters G.A.L. by the public executioner; to be conducted to the
galleys, there to be detained to serve our King for life; that
all goods of the said La Motte be forfeit to the King; this
sentence, by reason of the contumacy of the said La Motte,
to be written upon a tablet to be affixed to a post in the
Place de Grève [the place of public executions].

(Fifth recommendation of the prosecutor general adopted unanimously by voice vote of sixty-two judges in session.)

RECOMMENDATION 6:

That Jeanne de Valois de Saint-Rémy, Countess de La Motte, be condemned to be flogged and beaten, naked, with rods by the public executioner; to be branded upon both shoulders with a hot iron with the letter V [for *voleuse*, thief]; to be imprisoned in the female house of correction of the Salpêtrière for life; all of the goods of the said Jeanne de Valois de Saint-Rémy, Countess de La Motte, to be forfeit to the King.

(Sixth recommendation of the prosecutor general adopted unanimously by voice vote of forty-nine judges.)

The number of judges had been reduced from sixty-two to forty-nine by the enforced withdrawal of the thirteen clerical councilors upon the proposition by the pro-Rohan judges Saint-Vincent and Du Séjour that the Countess de La Motte-Valois be sentenced to pain of death. The death penalty being legally inapplicable in this instance, the recommendation thereto was merely a technical maneuver to effect the retirement of the clerical party (the majority of whom were known to be unfavorable to the Cardinal), who were under ecclesiastical charges prohibiting their participation in cases involving capital punishment. The forty-nine remaining judges voted unanimously for condemnation of the Countess *ad omnia citra mortem*, the severest penalties short of death.

RECOMMENDATION 7:

That the Cardinal Prince de Rohan be sentenced to appear eight days hence in the Great Hall of the Palais de Justice to make public statement to the effect that he has been guilty of criminal temerity, of disrespect to the sacred persons of the sovereigns, in betaking himself to the Grove of Venus in the belief that he was there to meet Her Majesty the Queen of France; and to the effect that he has contributed to the deception of the jewel merchants by allowing them to believe that the Queen had knowledge of the necklace transaction; that the Cardinal Prince de Rohan be sentenced to express his repentance publicly, and publicly to seek the pardon of the King and Queen; that he be condemned to divest himself of all his offices, to make a special contribution of alms to the poor, to be exiled for life from all the royal residences and to be held in prison until execution of said sentence.

If there had thus far been a semblance of unanimity in the judges' voting, it was disrupted immediately upon Prosecutor General de Fleury's reading of this recommendation to the court concerning Cardinal Rohan, when an uproar broke out upon the floor, according to the accounts that appear in the notes of Joly de Fleury himself, of Parliament President d'Aligre and of Maître Target. As the last-named tells it:

Prosecutor General de Fleury had drawn up his summation and his recommendations to the court against the express advice of Advocate General de Séguier, to whom, by court procedure, he was committed to submit them for approval. This conflict between the King's prosecutor general and the advocate general of Parliament brought on a scene of violence which revealed to what white heat passions had been fanned.

The advocate general, advocating the Cardinal's outright acquittal without court reprimand for criminal presumption, declaimed to Fleury, "Close as you are to the tomb, how can you have agreed to dishonor your ashes? How can you have agreed to try to involve this court in your venality?"

"Such an attitude on your part does not surprise me," Fleury replied. "It is only to be expected that a libertine like you would rise to the defense of another such, a Cardinal de Rohan."

"I do not deny," Séguier said, "that I occasionally visit public women. I do not even care if people see my carriage waiting before their door. But people will never see me so base as to sell my vote for power and fortune."

President d'Aligre expressed himself as favoring the prosecutor general's recommendation in principle, but with the proviso that the penalties on the Cardinal be lightened in view of extenuating circumstances. Had the president taken the floor to explain his opinion, as did most of the judges in voicing their vote, he would very probably have succeeded in winning over many members of the Parliament to his views; but the monarchy and the Cabinet had recently slighted President d'Aligre, so that while not actually hostile to the Court of Versailles, he did not consider himself duty-bound to exert his influence in its behalf.

Aligre's summation was legally sound and strictly impartial: "By any analysis of the evidence relative to the crimes of forgery and larceny, it is impossible to establish any complicity on the part of Cardinal Rohan, or even any knowledge by him of criminal machinations. Inevitably, one must conclude that there can be no doubt of his innocence of these two crimes. Having admitted this fact, there remains solely the crime of lèse-majesté, offense to the sacred persons of the King and Queen. Reparation for this crime consists properly of a public apology to be made by the Cardinal to Their Majesties. It will then devolve upon the King, as supreme judge of the nation, to decide whether or not to accept said apology, or to impose such conditions thereto as may please His Majesty."

At two o'clock in the afternoon the magistrates interrupted their work to go into the Hall of St. Louis, where President d'Aligre had ordered a great table set up for dining. Most of the judges ate standing up, and by three-thirty the session had been resumed.

MEMOIRS
OF THE ABBÉ GEORGEL

Despite the favorable impression made by the Cardinal upon the court, despite the preponderance of evidence in his favor, the prosecutor general refused to relax the severity of his recommendations to the court.

The two examining magistrates, Titon and Marcé, first in the order of voting, opted in favor of the recommendations in their entirety; fourteen other judges followed suit.

Vice-President d'Ormesson proposed an amendment whereby the public apology by the Cardinal would be retained but all the other punitive clauses omitted; eight judges supported this amendment.

Councilor Fréteau [de Saint-Just], whose integrity, erudition and persuasive oratory had won him great influence in Parliament, took the floor and, explaining his opinion with a brilliant analysis of the case, offered a resolution that the Cardinal be fully acquitted without reprimand or penalty of any kind. Fréteau spoke with an electrifying effect.

Robert de Saint-Vincent, who was known as a magistrate of the highest principles and of unimpeachable character, immune to any dictate save that of law and justice, not only supported Fréteau's resolution with his vote but seized the occasion to speak out in open criticism of the scandalous publicity given the case by the government's method of handling it, beginning with the ill-considered public arrest of the Cardinal on August 15 in the Hall of Mirrors at Versailles. Saint-Vincent went so far as to deplore the fact that the youthful sovereign lacked Cabinet ministers wise and courageous enough to have steered him away from actions so sensational as to undermine the prestige of the Church, compromise the dignity of the throne and outrage the laws guaranteeing personal liberty.

The discourses by Fréteau and Saint-Vincent, imbued as they were with all the prestige emanating from men of such great renown, won over the majority of the votes.

The decision narrowed itself down to two propositions, as five of the eight judges who had supported Ormesson's amendment went over to the side favoring complete exoneration of the Cardinal, while the three others voted for the prosecutor general's recommendations [not guilty of forgery and larceny, but guilty of *lèse-majesté*, with public reprimand and loss of office]. At long last, on May 31, 1786, at nine o'clock in the evening, after an eighteen-hour session, came the solemn verdict acquitting the Cardinal of all the charges against him. The famous judgment, for which France and all Europe had waited in suspense, was decided by a vote of thirty to twenty.*

What a memorable day for Cardinal Rohan—the longest day in his life, interminable hours of anguish and dread uncertainty; a day that had seen him appear, head bare and bowed, in the position of a criminal before a court holding power of life and death over him; a cruel day which was, however, to end in triumph for him with the proclamation of his innocence in terms forceful enough to be heard round the world. To have lived through such a day was to have passed through the fires of dread and doubt, to emerge at last into the glory of total vindication. What a supreme moment it was for the Prince when he was called before the magistrates who had sat in judgment on his fate and heard from their lips the words assuring him liberty and victory!

* Georgel notwithstanding, the official count on the vote was twenty-six to twenty-three.

The thousands of people thronging the Palais de Justice and all its environs sent up reverberating applause and joyous cries of "Bravo! Bravo!"

STORY OF MY LIFE
BY THE COUNTESS DE LA MOTTE-VALOIS

Suddenly, at nine o'clock that night, I heard shouts and cheers ring out from the main courtyard of the Palais de Justice. Running to the window of the concierge's apartment, whither I had been invited to take supper, I could see huge crowds of people gathering on the great staircase. . . .

The uproar continued unabated, but the only word I could make out was the oft-repeated "Bravo! Bravo!" Just then Madame Hubert and her son came in, and I inquired of them what the excitement was all about.

"Oh, there's a to-do about a pickpocket caught red-handed," they replied. "Some fool was so bold as to try to snatch a watch out of the vest of an onlooker—in the very shadow of the statue of Justice, mind you."

The explanation sounded plausible; I was unsuspicious.

The tumult, however, far from subsiding, swelled louder and louder. An anxiety which I could not suppress drew me back to the window. I listened, and finally out of the confusion of voices one rang forth distinctly: "It's good news for the Cardinal, all right. But what is to become of that poor Madame de La Motte?"

No sooner had these words reached my ear than my knees gave way beneath me and I fell into a chair which was luckily close by. The concierge and his son came rushing to my assistance, and when I had regained consciousness they helped me, one on each side, back to my room.

A few moments later they left me to go down into the courtyard to try to discover the meaning of the words that had so alarmed me. Returning shortly, they betrayed by the expression on their faces the fact that they had only bad news for me; their silence constituted proof more striking still.

Feign indifference, I told myself; if they believe you to be resigned to your fate, they may reveal the truths which their fear of hurting you has thus far kept them from speaking.

And so at last they told me the news of the terrible verdict of guilty—which was yet a thousandfold less terrible than that part of the sentence which they kept from me, or which possibly they themselves had not yet heard at the time.

"The Cardinal, Cagliostro and Oliva are all acquitted," they told me. "Villette—and you, madame—are condemned to banishment."

"For how long? How many days, months, years?"

"For three years, according to the first reports—although, with everyone criticizing the judges, there is perhaps still hope of modification."

My valiant efforts at self-control only proved to the concierge and his wife the extent of my inner agitation. They advised me to take to my bed. What a cruel night I spent! Searing my eyeballs was the vision of that humiliating scene before the court, of scenes of future humiliation at which I could still only guess.

Like a drowning man clutching at any straw, I clung to the only hope remaining me: that the Queen would not allow degradation to be the lot of a woman whom she had honored with her intimacy and confidence. Was there not good reason to hope for her mercy? Had I not spared her name throughout the whole long investigation? Had she not, herself, a fond and tender heart?

But what if she should turn a deaf ear to my cries for help? Then, I swore I would publish the truth to the whole universe: that I had been the victim of my respect for her, that my only crime had been to serve her too loyally, that she had inhumanly abandoned me.

MEMOIRS
OF COUNT CAGLIOSTRO

The judges rise from the bench. The verdict has been rendered, and report of it flies from mouth to mouth. . . . The members of Parliament, as they leave the hall, are surrounded by jubilant crowds who applaud them, press their hands, strew their path with flowers. A universal rejoicing resounds through the corridors of the Palais de Justice, out and into the streets of Paris.

The Cardinal, clad in the Roman purple, is released in response to the vociferous demands of the populace and is escorted by them to the gates of his Palais-Cardinal. They share his triumph as they shared his tribulations.

I left my prison cell just before midnight. A dark night it was, and the district where I lived was normally silent and deserted at that hour. Imagine, then, my surprise at being greeted by a throng of some eight to ten thousand men and women! They had pushed through the entrance gates, surged into the courtyard, up the stairways, into every room of every floor.

Arriving in my carriage, I was lifted out, carried inside the house, upstairs, into the very arms of my wife. My heart could not withstand the press of so many tumultuous emotions welling up simultaneously to claim dominion. My knees gave way beneath me and I fell to the floor unconscious. My wife, uttering one piercing cry, fainted dead away.

Trembling friends pressed about us, fearful that this finest moment of our lives might well also be the last. Anxious word spread from room to room, into the streets. The rataplan of the drums was hushed. A mournful silence replaced the gleeful uproar.

I recovered consciousness. A torrent of tears escaped from my eyes, and then at last I could reach out my arms and clutch to my heart her whom—but no, I will say no more. Only you privileged beings whom heaven has endowed with the rare and fatal gift of ardent soul and sensitive heart, who have known the delights of an early and single love in life—only you can fully appreciate the meaning of that first moment of joyous reunion with the beloved after ten months of torturous separation.

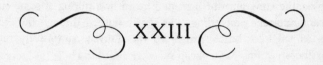

XXIII

Sentences Executed

(Spring and Summer 1786)

MEMOIRS
OF MADAME CAMPAN

THE MOMENT word of the verdict reached me, I went to the Queen. I found her alone, weeping, emotionally distraught.

In a voice choked with tears she said to me, "Come and sympathize with your sovereign who has been insulted, a victim of cabals and injustice.* The schemer whose purpose was to destroy me, or perhaps to get his hands on some ready cash by trading on my name and by forging my signature, has just been acquitted without so much as a reprimand. Condolences are in order. You may offer me yours, and in return I offer mine to you, a native Frenchwoman, for if *I* have failed to find justice in a case in which my reputation was at stake, then what chance would you have in one involving your honor and your fortune? A nation has come upon bad times indeed when its supreme tribunal is composed of men swayed by personal prejudices and passions, half the lot susceptible to corruption, the other half tinged with that spirit of audacity that expresses itself in open defiance of authority."

At that moment the King came in. He went to the Queen and took her hand in his.

* For an aprocryphal letter in which, purportedly, Marie Antoinette *implored "dear heart"* Polignac to come and weep with her too, see the Appendix.

I wanted to withdraw, but His Majesty told me, "Stay! You are one of the few around your mistress who sincerely shares her grief. You find her in deep distress, and she has good reason for it. This whole trial has been an outrageous proceeding. The Parliament refused to see Cardinal Rohan as anything but a prince of the Church and of the realm, whereas he is nothing but a cheap swindler and this whole business nothing but a shady, disreputable scheme of his to hoodwink the jewelers out of the necklace—only to be hoodwinked out of it himself in the end, as it turned out. To give him the benefit of the doubt, he may have hoped eventually to pay off the jewelers, but certainly, familiar as he was with our court, he could not have been such an idiot as to believe that Madame de La Motte was an intimate of the Queen's or her intermediary in the transaction. No, this was a case easily enough resolved; it was no Gordian knot requiring an Alexander to cut it."

I do not pretend, in repeating the King's considered judgment, to offer any final solution of the mystery. The opinion of a subsequent generation tends to view the Cardinal as the innocent dupe of Madame de La Motte and Cagliostro; the King could have been mistaken in considering him a guilty accomplice.

And so at last the famous Diamond Necklace Trial came to an end. The happy years of the Queen's life ended with it; the carefree, joyous days were gone, never to return. It was farewell forever to those tranquil and informal holidays at her beloved Little Trianon; farewell forever to those brilliant fetes and galas which served as showcase for all the glittering splendor, the sparkling wit, the exquisite good taste of French court life.

More than that, it was farewell forever to respect and reverence for the institution of monarchy. The traditional forms and ceremonies continued to surround the throne, to be sure; but it was an empty ritual, since it no longer emanated from the heart and soul of the nation.

MEMOIRS
OF THE ABBÉ GEORGEL

As soon as the Parliament had pronounced its verdict, a friend of mine on the Cardinal's staff set out for Mortagne on the first mail-coach, with His Eminence's authorization, to bring me the happy tidings. The news thus reached me within twenty hours, inspiring a joy beyond expression. A holiday was declared in the town of Mortagne; the society and nobility of the entire region hastened to join me in rejoicing.

Who would have believed it possible that the Cardinal's day of triumph would be followed by a day of exile and disgrace? Might one not rather have expected that the King, gladdened to find innocence where guilt had been presumed, would have manifested his love of justice by showering marks of the highest favor upon his Grand Almoner? Such action would have done credit to Louis XVI.

But then, a king is to be pitied whose council lacks a tutelary genius who can ward off the thunder of royal wrath from innocent heads, who can convince the sovereign that a show of arbitrary power in the face of the solemn judgment of a tribunal convoked by the sovereign himself constitutes a blemish difficult to cover over when the annals of that reign come to be written. Even a sovereign is accountable for his actions to the tribunal of posterity.

And will the reader not find it incredible when I reveal that the news of the Cardinal's vindication had to be broken gently to the Queen? No one, indeed, cared to undertake the mission; it was delegated finally to the Duchess de Polignac, Her Majesty's closest friend, who sought to soften the blow by all the tactful means that fondness could improvise.

On behalf of Madame Campan, her editor answered Georgel in this footnote in one of the posthumous reissues of her memoirs after the abbé's had appeared:

"And will the reader not find it incredible"—to paraphrase Georgel's question—that the venerable abbé should have been surprised at the Queen's distress at the outcome of the trial? Must it not have been a proper, a profound source of sorrow to Her Majesty to witness the triumph of a prelate who had compromised her name before all France, all Europe by the scandal of his liaisons, by his imbecilic gullibility, by a presumptuousness, a hopefulness, in regard to his relations with her, too indecent to be repeated?

Actually there is a more maliciously subversive implication in this one subtly phrased question-exclamation of Georgel's than in all the frontal attacks upon the Queen in the Abbé Soulavie's openly inimical *History*. What, then, does the Abbé Georgel think a woman, a wife, a queen holds dear, if not her honor and the dignity of the throne?

MEMOIRS
OF THE ABBÉ GEORGEL

The day after the verdict had been pronounced, Baron de Breteuil, ministerial instrument of the Queen's vengeance, appeared at the Palais-Cardinal to demand of His Eminence in the name of the King his resignation as Grand Almoner and his Cordon Bleu, and to deliver a *lettre de cachet* by which His Majesty ordered the Cardinal to depart from Paris within three days and go into exile at his Abbey of Chaise-Dieu.

The King's orders were respectfully received and obeyed. Cardinal Rohan, whose public triumph enabled him to rise above petty persecution, made dignified surrender of the offices and decorations which had come to him from the hand of his sovereign.

Before leaving Paris for his exile in the mountains of Auvergne, His Eminence wrote me a letter which I preserve to this day. It proves that, at that period, the memory of my zeal and my services to him had not yet faded from his mind; he wrote me in tones of lively, if modest, rejoicing at the flattering public acclaim that had greeted his triumph, saying that his only regrets were that I had not been on hand to share it with him and that the King's disfavor should have struck him at the very moment of his vindication.

Even Marine Minister de Castries expressed censure of fellow Cabinet Minister de Breteuil, in his journal entry of June 1, 1786:

Baron de Breteuil, so crippled with gout that he had to be carried into the Palais-Cardinal in a sedan chair, insisted on delivering the King's *lettre de cachet* in person, an action that brought down universal criticism upon his head.

Indignation at the monarchy's punitive measures against the Cardinal was widespread and outspoken. Cries of "Tyranny!" went up from every rank of society, directed primarily against the Queen.

The King had had no choice but to punish the Cardinal, Count Mercy wrote to Emperor Joseph on June 11:

Clearest proof of the Parliament's despicable attitude toward the throne is to be found in the Rohan faction's entire satisfaction with the verdict. The judgment rendered in the Cardinal's favor was clearly intended as a slap at the Queen. The King being understandably indignant and the Queen wounded by the Parliament's conduct, the monarchy had no choice but to express its disfavor of the Cardinal, who had most certainly merited it. But despite the fact that the throne was entirely justified in its action, the Cardinal's partisans have stirred up vigorous public resentment.

And Marshal de Castries added in his journal for June 1:

The Parliament of Paris, carried away by its resentment against the Court of Versailles and the government, refrained from voicing so much as a word of reprimand to the Cardinal for his follies, for his guilty credulity, for (worst of all) the indecency of what he suspected, even admitted, as possibilities with regard to the Queen.

MEMOIRS
OF COUNT BEUGNOT

When the Diamond Necklace Case was first turned over to the Parliament, no one would have believed such a verdict possible. I, personally, was convinced that Madame de La Motte would be treated far more rigorously; that is to say, I fully expected her to draw the death penalty.

But the mighty house of Rohan was determined to save the Cardinal at any price. The family exerted its terrific influence not only in the upper ranks of society but also among the middle classes. It was their hope that the weight of public opinion would make itself felt in the Parliament; and actually, that great judicial body seemed to lose its poise under pressure. The elements of opposition to the throne and to the government were growing stronger day by day.

In the case of the Necklace Trial, the actual larceny was of secondary importance; the real crime was that of *lèse-majesté*, disrespect to the hitherto sacred persons of the King and Queen, and, as such, cried out for prompt and stern disciplinary measures. An example of severity, at that critical point, might well have nipped the spirit of anarchy in the bud, might have stemmed the fast-running but still subterranean tide of disrespect for all the political and ecclesiastical institutions hitherto held sacred.

Even today, when the Revolution has only too thoroughly eradicated every trace of reverence for the royal person—even today it is difficult to conceive of the fact that the Parliament of Paris in 1786, under an absolute monarchy, would have dared to dismiss so lightly an offense against the sacred person of the Queen, would have dared to treat the impersonation of the Queen in the Grove of Venus as a simple case of fraud and the parties responsible for the fraud as merely so many rascals. The Revolution must have already begun in the minds of men who could have so insolently shrugged off a grave offense to their sovereign in the person of his wife.

The very point that the antiroyalist, liberal—indeed, revolutionary—factions in the Parliament has intended to make, startling though it was to the eighteenth-century mind: that the person of the Queen was not, in their opinion, necessarily sacrosanct.

The heresy of lèse-majesté, the full impact of the gravity of an offense to the sacred person of royalty, is lost on the mind of the twentieth century, when the institution of monarchy has shrunk to that of a vestigial organ on the body politic. It is difficult for the modern mind even to recall that monarchy was originally a religious concept: the crown was a materialization of the nimbus, kings were kings by divine right, divinely appointed—and divinely anointed, as the ritual of coronation offers rare and faint reminder.

The French philosophers of the eighteenth century—Voltaire, Rousseau—had dared to theorize that the monarchical system was not the sole, divinely willed form of government, nor even the best. The American Revolution had been the New World's practical statement of that radical theory; ten years later, in 1786, the Parliament of Paris made the first such statement for the Old.

Attack on the monarchical principle must come, necessarily, through attack on the person of the monarch; in the case of the French Revolution it was on the person of the Queen, who offered a far more likely target than the King, as those who fomented, plotted, and directed the Revolution early diagnosed. A negative personality such as that of Louis XVI might be irritating, but it was not infuriating; he was, at worst, a dullard, blinking, bumbling, irresolute, but, withal, modest in his tastes, gentle, decent-living, sober, pious. Marie Antoinette, on the other hand—upon whom the glaring spotlight of publicity in the Diamond Necklace Trial now focused, picking her out as the primary, the vulnerable, the dazzlingly splendid object of attack—had personality traits aplenty to serve as material for battle cries: "the Austrian Woman," "Madame Deficit," "the spendthrift," "the pleasure-mad," "the gambler," the "bejeweled," "the bedizened," "the haughty," "the proud," "the coquette," "the harlot."

A "sacred person"—this?

What the verdict of the Parliament of Paris on May 31, 1786, really said was this: "We cannot find Cardinal Rohan guilty of 'criminal presumption' in accepting the idea that the Queen of France appointed a midnight rendezvous with him in the dark thickets of the Versailles gardens. With Her Most Christian Majesty's reputation for frivolity and indiscretion, with her succession of male and female 'favorites' of dubious repute, we find it entirely plausible that Cardinal Rohan did so presume."

Marie Antoinette seemed to have grasped the significance of the verdict intuitively. "The Queen's distress at the outcome of the trial was greater than seemed reasonably justified by the cause," Count Mercy reported to Vienna.

Shortly after the Diamond Necklace Trial—and for the first time in her reign—hisses greeted Marie Antoinette when she entered her box at the Comédie Française in Paris. In the autumn of 1786, Madame Vigée Le Brun's latest portrait of the Queen was withdrawn from exhibition at the Salon "lest it provide occasion for outbursts of public antagonism." And finally, that same fall, came a letter from Paris Police Lieutenant General de Crosne so hazy with circumlocution, so cryptic with tactful illusion, that it must needs be deciphered before the meaning becomes clear: that Her Most Christian Majesty the Queen of France, to avoid any possible unpleasantness in the form of public demonstrations, might best postpone any contemplated visit to Her Majesty's capital city.

MEMOIRS
OF RÉTAUX DE VILLETTE

What a terrible moment for the Queen, when she learned simultaneously of the acquittal of the man she had sworn to destroy and the sentence pronounced upon the woman she had sworn to protect, the woman who had pandered to her lusts. . . . The poor King, duped to the very end, demanded to see the trial records, but, on the pretext that the original documents were illegible, false copies were substituted.

As for me, I could reach the ear of no one influential enough to help me; I was condemned to banishment for life and run out of Paris. The public executioner and the guard at the city gates recommended that I keep my mouth shut and keep going, putting as many miles as possible between me and the city limits before nightfall.

After the gates had closed behind me, a tall man came up and called me aside, giving me the impression that he was a member of Cardinal Rohan's retinue. He handed me a purse containing fifty-five gold louis and a sheet of paper with the name and address of an Abbé d'Aimar, to whom I could apply for further assistance, should the occasion arise. Occasion did arise and I did apply, but without ever eliciting a response from the aforementioned cleric. . . .

Eventually, my wanderings led me to Venice.

MEMOIRS
OF THE ABBÉ GEORGEL

Villette was escorted by the authorities across the French frontiers, and Mademoiselle d'Oliva returned to Paris society, where, rumor has it, she followed a more respectable way of life than heretofore. Upon her release from prison, there developed among the young bloods of Paris an assiduous rivalry for her hand, sullied though it was—a shocking commentary on the morality of our times. The victor in that shameful competition did not, however, long enjoy his supposed good fortune, for we are to see him perish on the Revolutionary scaffold.*

Of all the rivals for her favor the one who had the inside track was clearly Maître Blondel, the attorney who had conducted her inspired defense throughout the trial. Upon her release from the Conciergerie the night of May 31, 1786, Blondel bundled her up and took her home with him to his house on the Rue Beaubourg.

As for Cagliostro, he very shortly departed the kingdom.

---

* Georgel is far ahead of the story. Monsieur de Beausire, Mademoiselle d'Oliva's escort on her flight to Brussels and father of the baby boy born to her in the Bastille, deserted wife and child long before the guillotine was set up in the Place de la Révolution; and Mademoiselle d'Oliva perished, destitute, forlorn, in a convent at Fontenay-sous-Bois in 1789, at the age of twenty-eight.

Departed it by invitation of the King, by lettre de cachet of June 1, 1786, to the Baron de Breteuil: "You will order Cagliostro to be out of my city of Paris in eight days' time, and out of my kingdom of France within three weeks. You may show him this letter bearing my seal."

Police Inspector de Brugnières presented the exile order to the Cagliostros on June 2; they closed the doors of the mansion on the Rue St. Claude and departed, the Countess Cagliostro going promptly to St.-Denis, the Count to the Paris suburb of Passy, where the Boulainvilliers château crowned the hill above the Seine, where founding Mason Helvetius had lived and where his widow lived still, where Benjamin Franklin had resided for most of his seven years in France—a very hotbed of French Masonic activity. A band of Cagliostro's most faithful lodge members mounted guard over the house in Passy where their leader had taken refuge, and "all Paris came to say goodbye: authors, journalists, judges of the Parliament, fellow Masons," according to a contemporary report.

On June 13, Count Cagliostro went through St.-Denis to pick up his wife, and together they set out for Boulogne, from which port they took ship for England on the sixteenth. In his memoirs Cagliostro writes:

The shores I left were lined with crowds of citizens from every walk of life, who blessed and thanked me for the good works I had performed for them and their fellow countrymen. They bade me a touching farewell. The winds were already wafting me far from shore, but even when I could no longer hear their voices I could see them still, their hands raised toward heaven.

I blessed them in my turn and cried out to them again and again as though my words could reach their ears, "Farewell, Frenchmen! Farewell, my children, my country, farewell! Sought after by many nations, I chose France as my adopted land, used my fortune and my talents to their full extent in benefit of your countrymen. Yet an order of exile is my reward. Oh, you who dwell in that fair land, people of graciousness and tender hearts, receive now the adieus of an unfortunate man who has, perhaps, earned your esteem and your regrets. He has gone, but his heart remains with you. No matter what region he shall inhabit, he will show himself eternally the friend of France, hoping only that such injustices as he experienced in your land fall upon himself alone."

In London, on June 26, Cagliostro published his celebrated open letter to the French, Lettre au peuple français:

I have been hunted, like a criminal, from France. A *lettre de cachet* of the King has banished me from the kingdom, although the King has never heard my case; an unworthy minister of the King wielded that dread instrument of royal power.

The question has been asked of me whether I would return to France if the King's exile order were to be rescinded. "Assuredly yes," I replied, "on one condition—that the Bastille, where I languished for six interminable months, be razed to the ground and a public promenade erected on its ruins."

Ah, Frenchmen, you have all the ingredients for national felicity: a fertile soil, a gentle climate, a verve, a national genius—all that you could ask, dear friends, all the ingredients save personal security, respect for the dignity of the individual, the rights of man, so that a Frenchman may close the door of his house at night and lay his head upon his pillow, secure from tyranny, from injustice, unafraid. To work toward this happy revolution in the order of things is a task worthy of your *parlements*. Only timid souls would be dismayed at the task ahead.

And so I prophesy to you: One day a prince will govern in France who will abolish arbitrary powers and *lettres de cachet*, who will consult all three estates, who will convoke your States-General. Such a ruler will act upon the principle that abuse of power destroys power itself.

The newsvendors of Paris could have sold ten times the number of copies available of Count Cagliostro's Lettre au peuple français. Even the author admitted, "It was with difficulty that a printer could be found in England to print this tract, which was written with a liberalism bordering on republicanism."

It was regarded as the confession of faith of an Illuminati or a Freemason. The court of the Inquisition was later to state that Cagliostro's open letter to the French was "conceived in a spirit calculated to excite revolt." And Paris Police Commissaire Chesnon noted, "We still remember the terrible effect of Cagliostro's letter, not only on the French public but throughout all Europe. Its sale hastened the Revolution."

If Cagliostro ever claimed for himself the gift of prophecy, his open letter to the French was signal proof of it. Three years later, almost to the month, the Bastille was to fall, "razed to the ground" by the bare hands of the first mob of the Revolution, and still later a "public promenade" would be erected on its ruins—the present-day Place de la Bastille, with its 170-foot-high statue of Liberty atop the great bronze Colonne de Juillet, the most popular public gathering place in Paris even in these days of the Fifth Republic. And further in fulfillment of Cagliostro's predictions, on May 5, 1789, the States-General was to be convoked in Versailles by order of Louis XVI.

But this is getting ahead of the story.

In the early weeks of June 1786 the Countess de La Motte was still in the Conciergerie, as she relates it in her Story of My Life:

The days passed rapidly enough in the pleasant company of Monsieur and Madame Hubert. A steady stream of visitors relieved the monotony of prison life, rendering me almost oblivious to the disagreeable aspects of my situation.

The Huberts being in the habit of retiring early and I never before midnight, their eldest son kept me company in the evenings at a game of piquet or a chat in our favorite station in the window seat, the best place in the Conciergerie to catch a breeze on warm June nights. Later this gallant young man would escort me back to my quarters, stopping in the courtyard on the way, at the foot of the central staircase, to feed the rabbits he kept there in a little hutch.

Another agreeable companion was the priest from the Sainte Chapelle just beyond the Palais courtyard, a friend of the Huberts', a witty, highly educated and widely traveled gentleman, who, expressing his appreciation of my talents as a conversationalist and raconteuse, showered me with courtesies and attentions, such as a dozen bottles of his finest cider—a brew he knew to be a favorite of mine.

Occupied thus with a variety of people and diversions, I permitted my imagination to make excursion along only pleasant paths and promptly banished from my mind any thought threatening to trouble my fool's paradise. The only disturbing factor was that Attorney Doillot had not once come near me since my removal to the Conciergerie. Though I had written him several letters, his replies continued evasive; he managed somehow always to elude my invitations to come to visit me. But if I occasionally exclaimed aloud in expression of my surprise and astonishment at his neglect, it was only to forget all about it a moment later, for were not his messages always couched in terms of hope and solace? And, with a nature like mine, what more was needed to restore me to equanimity?

I would go dashing down to Madame Hubert's apartment to dispel in her company and that of her friends any trace of melancholy Monsieur Doillot's curious behavior might temporarily have inspired. The Huberts and their guests made it plain that they considered my vivacity, my high good humor, my repertoire of jokes and stories ample recompense for their assiduous attentions.

As for the future, I gave thought only to plans of what I would do after I had regained my liberty. I decided that I would go first to Bar-sur-Aube to sell my house and properties; then, on to England to take up residence. Monsieur Doillot had often spoken to me, during those long months at the Bastille, of that sweet land of liberty where just laws, impartially administered, protect the weak from oppression by the strong, protect the peasant from the overlord; where no man is condemned without a hearing, where every man dares speak the truth. It was from England that I planned to write to the Queen of France, with the further resolve that if my letter should go unanswered I would submit my case to public opinion.

These were the lines, then, along which I was thinking and planning, with never the slightest premonition of the doom awaiting me.

After some two weeks at the Conciergerie, at the supper table one evening the conversation turned to the subject of my trial and prospects.

"You have every reason to be hopeful," Monsieur Hubert remarked. "Rumor has it that Monsieur Doillot will soon publish another brief for you so as to clear you completely in the eyes of the King. The only thing to fear is—that is, some people are predicting—that His Majesty will issue a *lettre de cachet* in your name, relegating you to a convent."

At those dread words, "*lettre de cachet*," I let out a shriek and, in the throes of hysteria, began throwing cups, plates, forks, knives off the table onto the floor. I broke, overturned everything within my reach, heedless of the pleas and entreaties of my hosts and fellow guests. Finally I seized upon a large porcelain vase close at hand and struck myself in the head with it, using all the strength of which I was possessed.

The others crowded round, trying to pry loose my fingers from the jagged fragment of the shattered vase, which I held clutched in my hand.

"No!" I cried. "Rather death than the prolonged torture of life in a convent cell, deprived forever of the right to denounce the outrages committed against me!" Blood streamed from my self-inflicted wounds. I fell into convulsions from which I could not be rallied for more than three hours.

Several days later, when I had regained my strength, Madame Hubert besought me to give her my word of honor to exert greater self-control in the future. A letter from Monsieur Doillot likewise exhorted me to patience and announced his intention of visiting me the following day. Thus reassured, I agreed to accept Madame Hubert's invitation to join her guests at dinner.

The next day Monsieur Doillot did, indeed, come to the Conciergerie, but only as far as the door, where he handed the concierge a letter to be delivered to me with the excuse that he was in travel garb, on his way to his country estates, and that his carriage was waiting. To calm my fears, his letter reported a highly satisfactory interview with Baron de Breteuil the previous day and announced an appointment a few days hence with Keeper of the Seals de Miromesnil. In the meanwhile, Monsieur Doillot wrote, he urged me to hold fast to my courage.

The concierge's wife asked whether my attorney's letter offered any hope that the Queen might soon come out openly as my protectress. "That's the rumor one hears everywhere," she said. "People are wagering that Her Majesty will never allow the sentence to be carried out."

Oddly enough, I attached no particular significance to those ominous words, although I did begin to feel a sharp anxiety in regard to Monsieur Doillot's strange reluctance to meet me face to face.

A sudden malaise overcame me. The Huberts, their visitors and all their kind attentions had come to pall on me. I simply could not sit through another supper or card party. I had to tell the concierge's wife, for whom I had developed a genuine affection, that I had lost my taste for society and that I preferred to retire from contact with the world.

"And why do they keep me on here at the Conciergerie?" I asked her. "Is it a *lettre de cachet* they are waiting for, to determine the place where I am to be sent?"

I decided to write to the advocate general of the Parliament to ask him that question directly, calling to his attention the fact that my

house in Bar-sur-Aube had been left in the hands of servants and that
I hoped soon to be permitted to go there to straighten out my affairs
before leaving for England—provided, of course, there was truth to the
report that I was to be exiled.

I also drew up a petition to the King imploring him to reconsider. my
case and reminding him of my many claims to his mercy, not the least
of which was the blood royal of the Valois coursing through my veins.
And then I wrote to Baron de Breteuil to remind him of his pledge to
plead my cause before the King, to reveal the injustices to which I had
fallen victim.

As late as June 11, Austrian Ambassador Count Mercy, with all his
inside sources of information, could not discover what fate might be in
store for the Countess de La Motte, according to his report to Vienna
of that date:

There is as yet no definite news on the fate of the Countess. The
Parliament has been forbidden to publish any in extenso text of the
sentences pronounced. No one knows for certain whether the rigorous
sentence against the Countess will be applied, or whether she will be
spared the flogging and the branding. I have been unable to establish
the situation in further detail as concerns this case, which must be considered to be as unfortunate as it is famous. And I might add that I am
far from convinced that we have heard the end of the miserable business. Still further complications, intrigues and machinations are sure to
come to light.

Marine Minister de Castriès heard the rumors and jotted them down
in his journal: "It is said that Baron de Breteuil has seen Madame de
La Motte, that he has promised her his protection and that the sentence
against her will not be carried out with any degree of severity."

And in the Archives de France is this letter, unearthed from the
Ministry of Justice files for 1786, unsigned and with no superscription
save a simple "Monseigneur" (probably meant for Keeper of the Seals
de Miromesnil):

MONSEIGNEUR

Attorney Doillot asks me to assist him in reaching you with a message.

He states that he has seen Baron de Breteuil to request a stay of execution for his client, only to be told by the Minister that the matter is out of his hands. Doillot therefore beseeches me to bring it to your attention.

I asked him whether he had drawn up a petition for me to forward to you with a statement of the grounds upon which he bases such a request, but his answer was that he has no way of making proper preparation, in view of the fact that he is denied access to his client; that this is simply a last service which he feels it his duty to render her.

STORY OF MY LIFE
BY THE COUNTESS DE LA MOTTE-VALOIS

I inquired of the concierge, one day in conversation, who would be the person to notify me of the judgment pronounced upon me. It would be one of the secretaries of the Parliament, he told me, either Monsieur de Frémyn or Monsieur Breton; the sentence, as he explained, was customarily read aloud to the prisoner in the Hall of Records.

"Just let them try to come and read that infernal exile order to me!" I cried. "I'll snatch the damned paper out of their hands and tear it into a thousand pieces before their very eyes." Alas, what would I have said had I dreamed that a sentence a thousand times worse than exile was to be my lot? Had I only known, only guessed, suicide would have saved me from dishonor. But I was innocent of guilt and simply did not believe they could condemn me.

The three days preceding my public opprobrium were spent in a state of extreme nervous agitation. Not that I had any idea of the fate about to befall me. No, it was, instead, some strange premonition of impending disaster that evoked a state of alarm such as I had not experienced until then.

At last that doomsday dawned, that day of June 21, that day of infamy, the crowning blow to my life of grim misfortunes. At five o'clock a jailer appeared at my door to give me the message that Monsieur Doillot was asking for me in the Hall of Records below, excusing himself for disturbing me at such an hour of the morning on the grounds that he was about to depart the city on a voyage.

I told the jailer to tell my attorney that I deeply regretted my inability to come down to see him, but that I had spent a wretched night and felt too weak to stir; that I would look forward to seeing him another time in the near future.

The jailer replied that Monsieur Doillot had brought me a letter from Versailles and had been instructed to deliver it to me in person that very day.

"A letter from Versailles!" I whispered the words to myself. "Can it be a message from the Queen?" The moment that thought came to mind I hesitated no longer, but told the jailer that I would get up, get dressed and come down immediately to join Monsieur Doillot.

"It's really foolish to go to the trouble of getting all dressed up," the jailer said. "Besides, there isn't time, Monsieur Doillot is in such a hurry to be off. Just come along as you are."

MEMOIRS
OF RÉTAUX DE VILLETTE

If ever it behooved a monarch to preserve one of his subjects from barbaric punishment, it was in the case of that good old Louis XVI with regard to the Countess de La Motte.

Execution of the sentence was scheduled to take place at daybreak without public announcement of any kind, specific orders having come to advance the hour of the torture to the earliest morning before crowds could collect.

Orders from Police Lieutenant General de Crosne, who was fearful of popular demonstrations and mob violence. With the erection of the scaffold on June 19 in the courtyard of the Palais de Justice, where such public executions traditionally took place, a brisk traffic in reserved seats for the spectacle had begun, seats in the windows and standing room on the rooftops of the houses across the street from the Palais going at premium prices. Judges of Parliament and the lawyers connected with the case were besieged with inquiries as to the precise date and hour—inquiries such as that of the Duke de Crillon, who wrote to Attorney Target, "I am consumed with curiosity to see this woman scourged with the rods which you, in a manner of speaking, have prepared for her."

STORY OF MY LIFE
BY THE COUNTESS DE LA MOTTE-VALOIS

So I took off my nightcap, hurriedly slipped on a simple morning dress and cape and followed the jailer down the back stairs by which I descended daily to visit the Huberts.

The jailer, walking ahead of me, went through a small door across from the concierge's apartment, closing it behind him. Intending to follow, I opened the door, but no sooner had I passed through than it was slammed and locked behind me, as if I were some ferocious jungle beast which the hunters feared would turn and maul them.

At that moment my arms were seized and I was dragged into the Hall of Records. There they bound me fast with cords. Alas, what did I not say while my captors subjected me to this indignity!

After the first moments of shock, anguish and despair, the figure of Court Clerk Breton caught my eye. Seeing him, I remembered what the concierge had told me in regard to the official reading of the sentence.

"No! No!" I cried to him. "I will not listen to that wicked verdict! I refuse to bend my knee to hear you read a judgment rendered against me by a band of corrupt judges bribed by my enemies to find against me!"

But no sooner had I uttered these words than I felt myself seized by cruelly strong arms, which tried to force me to my knees. I put up violent resistance, whereupon two of the ruffians held me up between them by the elbows—suspended in mid-air, so to speak—while the court clerk read out the terms of my sentence. But his words were never heard; my screams drowned out his voice.

My frantic struggles against overwhelming force were soon exhausted. Triumphing all too easily over the weakened resistance I could offer, the dastardly crew dragged me outside into the courtyard. There my shrieks rent the air anew. Again and again I cried out to the crowd of onlookers, imploring them to save an innocent woman, a descendant of France's former kings.

With my last reserves of strength, I tried to pull loose from the executioners. My cries, my sobs, my fury, my despair robbed me of my senses. I saw nothing, heard nothing after that, until those savages began to . . .

Despite the fact that noon was the traditional hour for public executions, despite the precautions taken by the authorities to preserve the utmost secrecy in the hours of dawn, still some two or three hundred people from the neighborhood had gathered in the Palais courtyard by 5 A.M. and hundreds more arrived later, pressing against the twelve-foot-high, gilt-tipped black iron railings and entrance gates.

Every foreign correspondent in Paris, apparently, arose early that morning of June 21; the London Courier and the gazettes of Amsterdam, Leyden and Utrecht all carried eyewitness accounts during the week of June 23 to 30. Every Parisian reporter was on hand as well, to describe the gruesome spectacle for the local newssheets.

A distinguished English spectator, William Eden, the British special envoy to the Court of Versailles (and ancestor to Sir Anthony), reported to Prime Minister Pitt:

Madame de La Motte had no suspicion of the judgment, which, in France, is not communicated to the accused except in case of capital punishment. . . . She went in an undress, without stays, which proved convenient. . . .

The bourreau [executioner] and his assistants . . . carried her into an outer court, where she was fastened to a cart with a halter round her neck. The bourreau talked to her like a tooth-drawer, assuring her most politely that it would soon all be over.

And according to a Parisian reporter:

Immediately she perceived the instruments of torture, she sank to the ground in convulsions even more violent than those she had suffered previously. Her screams were so loud as to be audible through the entire Palais.

"It is the blood of the Valois that you are desecrating!" she shrilled, addressing the spectators. "Snatch me from my executioners! It is my own fault that I suffer this ignominy—I had only to speak one name and I could have made sure of being hanged instead."

Did she speak it? Some say she did—Hardy, for one: "She vomited out insults against all the judges of Parliament, against the Cardinal and against still another person, a person still more sacred."

That was the version the Abbé Georgel heard and recorded: "A delirium overcame her, accounting doubtlessly for her ravings. She inveighed with unbridled tongue against the Queen and Baron de Breteuil with imputations and imprecations so obscene that the presiding officer was obliged to order a gag put into her mouth."

And Villette, in his memoirs: "People had been hired to station themselves in the Palais courtyard to put up a din for the express purpose of drowning out any reckless accusations that might issue from the lips of their victim as she writhed in agony."

STORY OF MY LIFE
BY THE COUNTESS DE LA MOTTE-VALOIS

"It is the Queen," I cried, "the Queen who should be here in my place! My only crime is that of having served her too well!"

"The flogging was slight and pro forma," the report of Mr. Eden continues, "but the branding was done with some severity. It is a good idea that the V branded on her shoulder stands also for Valois."

"When they tried to disrobe her she defended herself like a lion," another eyewitness reports, "so ferociously, with tooth and claw, that the executioners were forced to cut her clothes off her, down to her chemise—a spectacle highly indecent in the eyes of those thousands of onlookers."

Not in the eyes of Nicolas Ruault, describing the scene in his journal:

Her whole body was revealed—her superb body, so exquisitely proportioned. At the flash of those white thighs and breasts, the rabble broke the stunned silence with whistles, catcalls, shouted obscenities.

The prisoner slipping from his grasp, the executioner—branding iron in hand—had to follow her as she writhed and rolled across the paving stones of the courtyard to the very foot of the grand staircase. . . .

The delicate flesh sizzled under the red-hot iron. A light bluish vapor floated about her loosened hair. At that moment her entire body was seized with a convulsion so violent that the second letter V was applied not on her shoulder but on her breast, her beautiful breast.

Madame de La Motte's tortured body writhed in one last convulsive movement. Somehow she found strength enough to turn and sink her teeth into the executioner's shoulder, through the leather vest to the flesh, bringing blood. Then she fainted.

STORY OF MY LIFE
BY THE COUNTESS DE LA MOTTE-VALOIS

Later I learned that I had been transported by carriage, in a state close to death, from the Palais courtyard to the prison of the Salpêtrière, across the Seine.

Since I remember absolutely nothing of my arrival in that vale of tears and dishonor, I shall supplement my narrative with this account given by Mother Superior Victoire, the head of that house of correction for females, a woman notable for her virtues—above all, for her compassion:

ACCOUNT BY MOTHER SUPERIOR VICTOIRE OF THE SALPÊTRIÈRE

Monsieur Breton and the guards hired a carriage to take Madame de La Motte to her destination, a most considerate gesture on their part—the dictate of kind hearts if not of custom.

We were fearful she would expire in our arms before we could get her inside the institution. She was carried from the carriage directly into the registry office where the women prisoners are signed in upon entry to the Salpêtrière. For some three quarters of an hour she remained in a state of total unconsciousness, her face so covered with cuts and bruises that human features were almost indistinguishable.

Monsieur Breton recommended her to my care, though I hardly had need of recommendation from him to interest myself in the poor creature's fate. As soon as possible she was moved to a single bed in the dormitory, most kindly yielded to her by one of the other prisoners—else Madame de La Motte would have been obliged to share one of the large communal beds for six, which would assuredly have contributed to her discomfort.

Shortly after Madame de La Motte had been put to bed in the dormitory I went to inquire whether she had need of anything, but she lay speechless, her eyes fastened on the crucifix at the foot of the bed. She raised her hands and folded them in prayer, but so swollen were her lips and tongue that she could not articulate a word.

When she began to recover, I showed her the institutional uniform she would be expected to don. I requested her to empty her pockets and to take off the gold hoop earrings fastened in her ears. She could only roll her head from one side to the other in a mute plea to me to remove the ornaments." *

* "Dr. Louis of the Academy of Surgeons happened to be in the Salpêtrière on an errand of mercy and stopped by to minister to the cruelly wounded inmate. He offered twelve gold louis for her gold hoop earrings. At the doctor's words, Madame de La Motte revived sufficiently to say, 'Twelve louis! Why, the weight of the gold alone is worth more than that.' The transaction was concluded for eighteen louis, which Sieur Louis took from his pocket and counted out then and there."

PART FIVE

The Aftermath

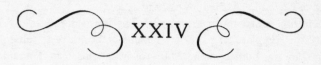

XXIV

The Countess Escapes

(1786-1789)

MEMOIRS
OF THE ABBÉ GEORGEL

BARON DE BRETEUIL, who had exiled me to Mortagne to prevent my producing evidence of his maneuvers and machinations to convict the Cardinal, deemed it inadvisable to restore me too promptly to liberty upon termination of the trial lest his motive in exiling me appear too obvious.

His cousin, the Duke de Châtelet, an old and good friend of mine, did, however, succeed in persuading the Minister to soften the blow. A *lettre de cachet* was issued on June 9, eight days after the verdict, substituting as my place of exile my native Bruyères, in Lorraine, where my family was and where I had a charming home. On June 29, I departed Mortagne, after proper expressions of gratitude for the courtesies and attentions lavished on me there.

Since the *lettre de cachet* expressly forbade an overnight stay in Paris, I spent only twelve hours there before continuing on to Coupvrai, a country estate of the Cardinal's nine leagues beyond the capital, where I remained for several days. I summoned the Cardinal's business agents to meet with me there and worked out with them a statement of his financial situation, of the arrangements I had made with His Eminence's creditors and of the schedule of administration adopted in consequence. At the same time, I made a detailed report on these matters to the Cardinal himself in a letter which I sent by personal messenger to the Abbey of Chaise-Dieu, then his place of exile.

Therewith ended my relations with His Eminence Cardinal Prince de Rohan. His place of exile, for reasons of health, was subsequently changed by royal order to the Abbey of Marmontier, in Touraine, and eventually to his own residence at Saverne. Home again myself, in Bruyères, and receiving no reply to my letter to the Prince, which I knew had been delivered to him, I felt that it behooved me to follow his lead and remain silent. I was no longer useful to him.

I had devoted twenty-four years of my life, in unflagging zeal and boundless enthusiasm, to the glorification of his name. It was an established fact that I had never sought personal benefit from our association. To the Cardinal's generosity I owed but a single benefice of one hundred louis from the Priory of Ségur in Auvergne. During his captivity in the Bastille, His Eminence had offered me another living with six thousand francs' revenue, as provost of the chapter of Lauterback in Alsace. This I had refused despite his urging; he expressed most graciously his appreciation of my services, but I took pride in emphasizing the fact that no selfish motive prompted my labors and my vigils. At that particular period I had been granted by the Foreign Affairs Ministry a pension of five thousand francs and a revenue of ten thousand francs on the Abbey of Lucelles in Alsace as reward for my diplomatic services to the nation [as secretary to the French embassy in Vienna during Prince de Rohan's term as ambassador, and as chargé d'affaires for the year following the Prince's recall]. I considered myself rich enough to be happy.

This, then, was my status as my exile in Bruyères began. The exile order remained in effect only while Baron de Breteuil remained in office; his successor restored me to full liberty.

Then it was that I learned that the Cardinal's silence was a manifestation of his displeasure. Certain persons, bent on dissolving the bonds which my services during the trial should have rendered indissoluble, had depicted me to His Eminence in the most odious colors; these persons had told him, as His Eminence himself has since told me, that I had entered into a secret understanding with Baron de Breteuil, a compact prejudicial to the Cardinal's interests, and that my exile had been merely a maneuver arranged between the Minister and me, my purpose being to put the Cardinal under guardianship and to appropriate unto myself, as his vicar general, the administration of his Strasbourg diocese.*

That such a charge might have been leveled against me out of malice and perversity is at least conceivable; but that the Prince should have credited it without hearing my side of the story, without verifying a charge which metamorphosed me so suddenly and so infamously—this is the fact which is inconceivable to all those who had opportunity to observe the zeal, the fervor, the self-sacrifice with which I had served him throughout the twenty-four years in which he honored me with his confidence.

When this extraordinary piece of news finally reached me, I permitted myself no murmur of complaint, however shocked I was at such injustice. I could have deemed it a point of honor to search out the calumniator and deny the calumny, but, feeling that my lifelong demonstration of loyalty should have placed me beyond suspicion, I reached the decision that to attempt to justify myself would be to demean myself; and so I chose the part of silence, trusting to time and to my conduct to unmask this wicked fraud sooner or later.

It would never have occurred to me that the guilty party could have been the Abbé Juncker. The Cardinal himself later revealed to me the treachery of that cleric whom I had favored with my friendship and esteem. I have since engraved my pardon upon the abbé's tombstone, and I like to think that the tears of his own repentance washed away the traces of his black ingratitude. Today Monseigneur Cardinal Prince de Rohan, no longer under any illusion concerning the Abbé Juncker's character, displays greater justice in evaluation of my loyalty, which there was never reason for him to doubt. His letters, his attitude, his restoration of good will and confidence to me in recent years persuade me that the clouds of misunderstanding have blown away.

In my case, as it developed, the rupture proved a distinct advantage. Once again my own master, propelled by both my natural inclinations and a general world-weariness toward the peaceful pleasures of rustic retreat, I reached a better understanding of the vanity of worldly affairs and the ephemerality of the favor of the mighty of this earth. The happiest days of my life have been those spent since my retirement in

* *Michelet's dictum on Georgel (colored by that historian's violent antipathy to the Jesuit, to which the grave had put no term) is that he was "clever, dangerous, without fear as without scruple," and that he "played on the fears of Rohan and Rohan's family so as to acquire full control over the administration of the Cardinal's estate."*

the society of my friends, in the bosom of my family, beside my paternal hearth, which it has pleased me to beautify still further. The original ardor of my ambition to win a high place for myself in the world has been so completely extinguished that I would not today exchange my independence and leisure for the loftiest of posts or the most glittering of fortunes.

If my rupture with the Cardinal was effected quietly, all too much publicity attended the breach between him and his secretary, young Ramon de Carbonnières, who, great as had been his former devotion, resigned immediately after the trial. Whatever the cause of Carbonnières's dissatisfaction, it would have been more becoming in him to have sealed his lips rather than to indulge in open recrimination and in disrespect to his former patron. A man whose services to his patron are rewarded with ingratitude has but one recourse if he would avenge himself nobly: that is, to maintain silence, waiting for the passage of years and the natural course of events to vindicate him; any expression of prideful disdain for his former patron is as improper as any expression of hope for reconciliation.

Subsequent to his severance of relations with Cardinal Rohan, young Carbonnières, withdrawing to his father's household in Paris, won nomination as deputy from the capital to the second Assembly, where he distinguished himself both upon the rostrum and in the committees to which he was appointed. Impetuous by nature, he obviously set his sights too high and thought to make his reputation by fervid opposition to the royal prerogative; his political principles were neither sufficiently mature nor sound, with the result that he has been seen to go astray in his chosen career of national politics. Let it be said in his favor, however, that he was never guilty of disrespect to the person of the monarch and that he never indicated, in even his most fiery oratory, any intent to dethrone the King and establish a republic, still less to shed the blood of the unfortunate Louis XVI.

On June 21, the sentence upon Madame de La Motte having been duly executed, she was transferred to the prison of the Salpêtrière, where, with her head shaven and wearing penitential garb, she was committed to solitary confinement—shut off from all communication with mankind save for those attendants assigned to bring her nourishment and to restrain, by means of repeated castigation, the disordered flux of her envenomed tongue.

Not even the Countess herself lays claim to such maltreatment in her Story of My Life:

The day after I had been transported, dying, to the Salpêtrière, a crowd of female prisoners came flocking round, in a great clatter of wooden shoes and with cries of "Oh, there's that poor lady! How sweet she is, poor soul—not a hardened criminal like us, and never meant to survive in such a hellhole!"

Alas, I did not yet realize where I was, but wondered vaguely who they were, this troupe of scarecrows in the same costume that had been presented me upon arising—dresses of coarse gray drugget, hose of the same shade, brown wool petticoats and rough linen chemises, round caps, sabots. Several approached to offer me consolations of a nature unlikely to reconcile me to my lot; but when they seized my arm I allowed myself to be pulled along into a prodigiously vast and cavernous room.

"This," my new-found friends informed me, "is the dormitory by night and the workhouse by day."

It offered a horrid sight of some one hundred unfortunate creatures in direst misery, a sight so revolting that I turned away my eyes, could scarcely catch my breath and would have keeled over backward had not strange arms reached out to hold me up. The shock was too great for one in my weakened state, and I could barely summon the strength to exclaim, "Unhappy Valois, is this, then, to be your fate?"

I shudder still at the recollection, but must somehow summon up the courage to continue my humiliating narrative.

It seems appropriate to give the reader here a brief description of that tomb for the living and the pitiful females buried alive there. If those who owed their sentences to crime and debauch found a sojourn at the Salpêtrière insupportable, then imagine how frightful an experience it must have been for those who owed theirs to frailties of human nature or to a miscarriage of justice, as in my case!

Actually, the Salpêtrière consisted of three separate and distinct divisions. The first was a place of detention for women of ill fame; this was the Salpêtrière proper. The second was a correctional institution for girls and women whose parents or husbands or guardians found their presence at home inconvenient or embarrassing, and who were thus "denounced" to Cabinet ministers or police officials by inhuman relatives with influence in those spheres; some such septuagenarian victims of family cruelty had spent forty years in that reform school. The third, the division of the prison to which I had been assigned, was that for female criminals under life sentence; it occupied the innermost keep, nine courtyards removed from the exit gates.

To accommodate the hundred-odd prisoners, our dormitory held six beds, each five feet wide, covered with straw and some old coverlets. Pine boards spaced out along the walls held the inmates' daily portion of bread and other pitiful possessions. High up in that gloomy hall were windows with neither glass panes nor shutters, but only iron bars to shut out the sun while allowing free passage to wind and snow and rain.

The rations for each inmate consisted, supposedly, of three ounces of meat thrice weekly, on alternate days two sous' worth of cheese and watery soup, and a weekly allowance of one and a quarter pounds of bread; but even these rations were subject to arbitrary diminution, thus adding the peril of starvation to that of death by freezing and conditions of general hardship and privation.

To see those women of the Salpêtrière, you would have taken them not for human beings but for wild beasts. Armed with stones, with broken bottles, with chairs, they were always ready to spring into battle against one another. It is impossible to imagine anything so horrible as the blasphemies and the filth pouring from their lips. Those who had come there before losing the normal gentleness and timidity of their sex were in peril of their lives amid that pack of savages, who would have cut to ribbons any creature that dared defiance. Either the newcomer had to join in the state of general depravity, renouncing all decency and delicacy of sentiment, or suffer fiendish persecution. An unarmed man in a tiger-ridden jungle had as much chance of survival as a decent woman in that vicious mob.

Sexual perversion was rampant. If any creatures came there virtuous, their virtue could not long survive, whereas the original vices they brought with them were developed further and multiplied. Although I had at first scarce comprehended what was going on before my very eyes, the prison chaplain, at my second trip to the confessional, commiserated with me, explaining that all these poor females were abandoned to the same abomination—which was designated, indeed, "the sin of the Salpêtrière." The modesty of my sex and my reluctance to offend that of my reader forbids me from entering into further detail here.

"Oh, why do they not burn down this infamous prison?" I cried out, revolted at the revelations and struck with astonishment that France would suffer such penal conditions to endure in the very heart of the nation—whole generations of women depraving one another, entering a prison to expiate one sin and emerging capable of every crime—instead of following England's lead in sending prisoners to colonize the New World, there to recover the self-respect and virtues forever lost in the homeland. The penal system in France and in all the world should have as its primary goal not castigation of the individual but benefit to society as a whole.

Even so, in justice to those lost souls of the Salpêtrière I must add that they showed me all the respect and consideration of which they were capable. And therewith I conclude my description of the notorious prison to which a descendant of Henri II was consigned and wherein she languished for eleven months and seventeen days—for crimes, moreover, of which she was innocent!

I succumbed to many maladies during the time I served in that vale of tears; my constitution, naturally delicate, and my soul, naturally proud, could not resist such a succession of staggering blows. My existence became intolerable, and, cheated of weapons for ending it by violence, I resolved to perish by starvation and by exposure. I refused nourishment for days and slept on the cold floor at night. "Oh, let me die!" I replied to the remonstrances of the mother superior. Only the chaplain succeeded in dissuading me from my efforts at self-destruction.

I had become frightfully weak and thin. It seemed as if scarcely a breath of life remained in my emaciated frame. I was a walking skeleton, a ghost of my former radiant self, with the pallor of death upon my face, cheeks hollow; my eyes, sunken deep into their sockets, had lost their natural gleam and sparkle.

The prison chaplain, throughout these long and cruel months, sought ceaselessly to relieve my piteous plight. He instructed the mother superior to allow me a decent bed and a cell to myself, and he himself sent a superb engraving of the repentant Magdalen to hang at the foot of my bed and an ivory crucifix to adorn the headboard. Thanks to that worthy Monsieur Tillet, whose name I can never speak without the fondest gratitude, my cell was transformed into an oratory.

The Leyden Gazette made capital of the repentant Magdalen in a story which described Madame de La Motte as showing "the true spirit of Christian humility and resignation to her dire fate" by "employing the better part of all her waking hours in reading and in meditation upon that manual of asceticism, The Imitation of Christ." A mystic, a saint, a martyr, the Gazette implied; this was the woman whom the Queen had dared call a criminal!

Public opinion had veered sharply round, by now; the tide of sympathy was running strongly in Madame de La Motte's favor once again. The brutality of the spectacle in the Palais courtyard, the giant, black-clad public executioners manhandling a lone, frail and appealingly pretty woman, the wanton mutilation of fair female flesh—all this had stirred up indignation, which was further heightened by the report of the imprecations against mysterious, exalted personages which had flowed from the victim's bleeding lips in a stream that only a gag could stifle. Hardy commented in his journal:

Hardly had the sentence upon Madame de La Motte been put into execution when a certain element of the populace, touched to compassion for a victim of court intrigue, ventured to lay the blame at the door of the Parliament for the undue severity of its sentence. Popular sentiment ran strong against our lords of the Parliament and the unnecessary violence done a weak and hapless woman. Theirs had become a highly unpopular verdict.

Not only the Parliament but the Queen became unpopular. Even the Queen's dear friends admitted it. Even the Princess de Lamballe, Her Majesty's very dearest friend (save only the Duchess de Polignac, who had usurped Lamballe's place as favorite) admitted it in her memoirs:

It is not surprising that fickle Paris—which till this moment had idolized the Queen as its benevolent deity, the sight of whose lovely face brightened the faces of even the wretched—now turned against Marie Antoinette for what was construed as heartless abandonment of Madame de La Motte to the horrors of her fate. And as it is the Gallic nature to be extremist, so now the Parisians' idolatry of Her Majesty was transformed into indignation against her. Public opinion began to vacillate, and the private enemies of the Queen, who were legion, treacherously stimulated the growing discontent. The Queen no longer saw her people pressing about her carriage to catch a glimpse of her royal person, no longer heard the flattering cries of "*Vive la Reine!*" which had formerly accompanied her progress through the streets of the capital.

No one warned the Queen that the populace's new hostility might have fatal results, and so, far from seeking to allay it, she withdrew, offended, into chill silence. Her expression, hitherto so sweet and gracious, manifested henceforward only a haughty disdain for the opinion of that populace which she never dreamed would one day acquire the power to dispose of her destiny and that of her family.

The Princess de Lamballe never dreamed it either—never until it was too late and she had returned loyally though recklessly from the safety of emigration, risking her head (which would decorate a pike) to share the last, desperate, agonizing days of her sovereign friend's peril and imprisonment—unlike that other friend, the Duchess de Polignac, who discreetly sat out the Revolution across the border.

But even the Princess de Lamballe, loyal to the death though she proved herself to the Queen, evidently could not resist the impulse of sympathy toward the Queen's "victim," Madame de La Motte, for she sought admittance to the Salpêtrière to commiserate and to make a contribution for relief of the prisoner's hardships, an attempt that inspired a spate of epigrams. The mother superior was widely quoted as denying the Princess admission with the words, "Madame de La Motte is serving out her sentence, true enough, but she is not condemned to receiving visitors—not even a princess of the blood—whom she is unwilling to admit."

The Princess' abortive visit to the prison gave rise to a spate of rumors too (upon which her memoirs do not elaborate) as to the mysterious purpose behind it: whether she had gone on a secret mission from the Queen with offers of recompense or escape; whether she had gone on a secret Masonic charge of the Lodge of Isis, into which she and the prisoner had been initiated by Countess Cagliostro; whether she had gone on a simple mission of personal charity to a woman whom her haughty father-in-law, the Duke de Penthièvre, had chosen to welcome into his salon with all the honors due a princess of the blood; or whether, finally, she had gone because it was the thing to do, because it was bon ton to make a pilgrimage to see the famous prisoner of the Salpêtrière—as the prisoner herself pridefully relates in her *Story of My Life:*

The crowd of prominent personages who flocked to see me at the Salpêtrière was prodigious. Here is what the Leyden Gazette had to say about it:

Never has there been seen in the environs of the Salpêtrière such a glittering array of elegant carriages as streams there since the detention of Madame de La Motte. Among those who seek permission to enter the institution, however, there are precious few who satisfy their curiosity by so much as a glimpse of the unfortunate victim of despotism, who sometimes shuts herself away behind the closed door of her cell and sometimes obliterates herself among the throng of her companions, hiding her face to avoid recognition—no difficult trick in view of the fact that she wears the same uniform as the other inmates.

A lady of the highest rank in the realm only recently met with frustration in her attempt to satisfy her curiosity, winding up in an altercation with the sister who had conducted her on a tour of the buildings. . . .

I will not here quote the rest of that article, although it presents a most interesting picture of my incarceration. Those of my readers who choose to read it in its entirety will find it, however, in the September 20, 1786, edition of the Leyden Gazette, in the column headed "Letter from Paris" and dated as of September 14; and there is a similar account in the Journal de France.

It is an established fact that no less than fifteen hundred persons of the greatest distinction in the kingdom came to see me at the Salpêtrière, a list thereof having been sent by the mother superior to the police.* Although these visitors were advised as they alighted from their carriages that I would see no one at all, neither friend nor relative, not even a sister, they all contributed at least a louis to a fund to be employed by the sisters toward the alleviation of my misery.

The Gazette of Utrecht would emphasize, however:

It is quite a mistake to believe that the unfortunate Madame de La Motte enjoys any preferential treatment in the Salpêtrière. While it is

---

* A list reading like the Almanach de Gotha: princesses, duchesses, marquises, baronesses de Duras, de Mouchy, du Bourg, de Joigné (niece of the Archbishop of Paris), as well as Her Highness the Duchess d'Orléans, who personally took up a collection for the relief of the famous prisoner.

true that beneficent hands have flown to her succor, still the prevailing custom of the institution decrees that any contribution to one of the inmates be distributed among them all.

(A kinder interpretation than that of Madame de La Motte herself, who states, "It is the prevailing custom for the good sisters to appropriate all such gold pieces for themselves.")

Not only the hearts of the great ladies of the court and the capital had been touched by compassion for the "unhappy Valois," but even those of the hardened criminals who shared her lot . . . as the Utrecht Gazette sentimentalized in another special edition:

Even such scum of the earth as these are touched by so much virtue and resignation, by such gentleness and grace, and have clubbed together (one forgoing her snuff, another withholding from her pimp her three-sou weekly contribution) in order to provide the Countess, as they respectfully address her, with a variation from the institutional rations—such as, last week, a special treat of peas and bacon.

Whereas the Gazette de Hollande joined in the maudlin chorus with the lines, "Poor, simple, primitive creatures! Christ well knew the human soul when, at Golgotha, scorning the rich, He bent His head toward the repentant thief."

But since the Gallic tongue, even with the salt tang of tears upon it, cannot resist wagging a bon mot, so the Paris correspondent of Catherine the Great retailed the very latest version for the diversion of his imperial employer:

Here everyone's heart melts with pity at the thought of the horrible fate suffered by Madame de La Motte-Valois. Even the King, it is said, is disposed now to show her some indulgence.

Apropos of which a bon mot making the rounds is said to have amused His Majesty highly; it is to the effect that in his company one day, the talk turning as usual to the dreadful plight in which a scion of the royal house of Valois finds herself, a blithe and witty prince in the King's entourage spoke up, saying, "But think, Sire, of what difficulties you may encounter in arranging a marriage contract for the Dauphin when it becomes known that his own cousin is a jailbird in the Salpêtrière!"

Rumor was rife in Paris concerning plots to effect the deliverance of the Dauphin's cousin from her prison bars. The Utrecht Gazette reported as early as August 1, 1786:

The Countess de La Motte-Valois has attempted to escape. She dug a hole through which her head would go, but she became stuck in it, unable to move forward or back, whereupon panic seized her. Struggling in vain, she cried out and thus brought up the warders, who discovered her in that impasse. Her attempt at flight has served only to increase the severity of the conditions of her detention.

This bulletin was premature, although escape plots were certainly being formulated in November, when contact was made with the notorious prisoner through the agency of a fellow inmate, Angélique— "a poor soul imprisoned on a false charge of murder of her illegitimate babe, a crime of which that tenderhearted girl was utterly incapable," the Countess writes, adding, "Angélique was at that time the talk of Paris as my devoted maid and servitor. In her affection I found my only solace."

It was toward the end of November 1786 that one of the sentinels on night watch in the courtyard slipped the barrel of his gun through the bars of Angélique's cell to nudge her awake. She started up, but he quickly quieted her with these words, according to Madame de La Motte's Story of My Life:

"Do not fear me. Are you not she who serves Madame de La Motte? Well, then, here are writing materials, pen and ink and paper, and a letter for Madame. Tell her she can trust me!"

At five the next morning, as soon as the inner doors of the prison were opened, Angélique came running to me to pour out the story of her bizarre nocturnal adventure. Upon reading the letter, my astonishment was acute; I could not believe my eyes.

"Unfortunate lady," the message read, "hold this letter up to the light. C'est entendu [It's agreed]."

As soon as I was alone, I held the paper up to the sun and made out these words in sympathetic ink:

MADAME: Your friends are working zealously to find means to ameliorate your unhappy fate. We exhort you not to abandon hope, but to try to build back your strength to undertake a long and arduous journey.

Advise us what disguise will be needed, and indicate the day you wish to set out. . . . You will find a boat and two oarsmen waiting beyond the King's Gardens, at the riverbank. Seek to procure a pattern of the key used to unlock your corridor. . . .

Put all your trust in the messenger who brought this letter.

At first I was tempted to believe the letter an optical illusion. More than twenty times I read and reread the magic lines to convince myself I was not dreaming. No, I told myself then, it is no dream, it is a sweet and happy reality.

Yet who, I asked myself over and over, was the benevolent mysterious being who was taking such interest in my fate? The writing seemed to be that of a person who sought to disguise his hand. The expression "*C'est entendu*" made me think it must be the Cardinal or the Queen, for this had been a catchword known only to them and me, a password in the private code developed in their letters (as the reader may establish for himself by a perusal of that correspondence in the Appendix to this story of my life). I could scarce contain myself for joy. Perhaps, I told myself, they have both come to repent the wrongs they have done me and seek to expiate their injustices to me!

At nightfall, alone, I wrote my reply, beginning it: "O secret correspondent, whoever you are, I put my faith in your sincerity. Give me further details, and I will set the date . . ."

Angélique having found an opportunity to slip this note to our sentinel, I sought ways of obtaining an outline of the key, as I had been requested. After weeks and months of scheming, I managed to make a reasonably accurate facsimile, with every jagged indentation reproduced, of that object as it dangled from the chatelaine at the waist of the warder. Finally it was ready to be delivered by Angélique in a letter to the sentinel.

And at last, on February 15, 1787, that sentinel handed Angélique a key made in strict accordance with my sketch, an exact representation of which herewith follows. Imagine my transports of delight when, alone with Angélique in the corridor, I reached out a trembling hand to insert that key into the lock and, merciful heavens, it fitted, it turned, the door swung open!

Then I began to devote myself to working out the costume best suited to that perilous flight. After long meditation I reached the decision to adopt masculine attire and passed that word, through Angélique, to our sentinel. Angélique, meanwhile, throwing herself at my feet, had persuaded me to allow her to accompany me.

Ten days later the sentinel brought the first items of the chosen disguise, which was to consist of blue redingote, black vest and breeches, pigskin gloves, a high round hat and a cane. Two days thereafter he completed the delivery, along with final instructions for escape.

At first I floated on clouds of joy; even the faint hope of shedding my shackles dissipated the deep melancholy which had brought me wellnigh to the grave. At last I could see my bondage coming to an end. I considered myself directly under the protection of the Queen, never doubting that it was her hand which was to deliver me from the abyss into which my excessive loyalty to her had plunged me, and that it was Baron de Breteuil (who had always appeared favorably disposed to me) who was acting as her agent. Courage revived within me to assure success to the bold enterprise ahead.

But illusions of happiness were fleeting; grave doubts beset me upon the heels of the sweetest reveries. When news reached me that the Cardinal had been exiled, I knew it could not be he who was my secret correspondent; and how could I imagine that the Queen, after suffering the severest punishment to be inflicted upon me, would now attest my innocence? What if the unknown correspondent was a mortal enemy, luring me into ambush?

A visit from Lieutenant General de Crosne further alarmed me. Interested and sympathetic though he had shown himself at our first meetings in the Bastille, yet I reasoned that he must be acting on instructions from higher up to ascertain whether the reports of the Salpêtrière wardens that I was talking too much were true, and whether it would be wiser (as the whispers went) to exile me to some remote convent for life, where no one could hear my revelations, where even my name would remain unknown.

Such were the agonizing doubts that cooled my hot impatience to set out in flight. They have sent me a key and a disguise, I told myself, but it may well be a decoy; and if I make the break for freedom, even if

I find the promised boat and oarsmen waiting on the riverbank, how do I know they are not cutthroats hired to assassinate me before I cross the Seine? What if someone is offering me escape only as a means of ensuring my eternal silence, a silence such as only my death can guarantee, regarding a secret which the Queen is determined at all costs to keep?

Thus I vacillated between hope and fear, unable to overcome gnawing doubt and uncertainty, until June 2, 1787, when I finally brought myself to set the date and hour for escape. . . .

MEMOIRS
OF THE ABBÉ GEORGEL

When Madame de La Motte's husband, who was in London enjoying the fruits of his crime, learned about the severity of the punishment inflicted upon his wife and about her imprisonment in the Salpêtrière, he made so bold as to bring threat of publishing an exposé in which the Queen and Baron de Breteuil would be strangely compromised, unless his wife was promptly restored to liberty and to him.

On December 7, 1786, the British Foreign Office notified Mr. Eden, its special envoy to France, of a threat by the Count de La Motte to publish an exposé of the diamond necklace affair and instructed him to suggest that the Court of Versailles make a public refutation to counteract the inevitable repercussions of the forthcoming charges.

On December 29 the London Morning Chronicle carried a letter from the Count de La Motte claiming that repeated pledges to him by French Ambassador Count d'Adhémar for a proper hearing before the Parliament of Paris had been violated, and that, unless the promised opportunity for belated testimony before the French courts was now provided him, he would have no choice but to publish the justification of his conduct to the world in his promised exposé—an exposé substantiated, he claimed, "by a highly significant packet of letters which, having been preserved by a very Act of Providence, are today in my possession."* The statement continues:

* This was the packet of letters so providentially retrieved by the Count from the secret compartment of his desk the night of the Countess's arrest in Bar-sur-Aube.

And so the world shall be informed; I shall make clear and concise account of the whole diamond necklace transaction and tell what actually happened to the necklace itself by making special mention of the Party in whose hands it presently reposes—the Party who, while making my wife a gift of some of the lesser stones, which I later disposed of in England, retains by far the most considerable portion of the gems, which might easily be worn by that very Party today in revised design and settings without ever being identified by anyone, not even the jewelers. I shall relate in full how my wife and I were inhumanly sacrificed by this Party!

Nor am I to be discouraged by the threat that my memoirs, if published, will raise up a powerful host of enemies against me. Whatever my fate, I shall have had the satisfaction of having published the justification of my honor, of having unveiled the whole sordid intrigue. . . .

And who knows but that one day, for the benefit of my own native land, my memoirs will unseal the eyes of him who has been so long kept blindfolded! Oh, they warn me, to be sure, that my memoirs will never be allowed to reach his hands, that every avenue of approach to His Majesty will be blocked. Of this I am well aware. But on the other hand, I herewith make the observation that there exists a powerful party in France whose goal is to forward justice, who have, for long years, been preparing a mine which awaits only the propitious moment to be exploded.

If the forthcoming publication of my memoirs hastens this moment, serves as the match to light the mine and set it off, then I shall look upon all the misfortunes I have encountered upon my path as leading directly to the explosion, and shall consider myself sufficiently rewarded for the injuries and persecutions I have suffered.

With this statement, sir, I trust I shall no longer be reproached for a timidity alien to my character.

The following spring (under date of May 11, 1787) the British Foreign Office advised its Paris envoy that the Duchess de Polignac had arrived in London, "being seen on Tuesday at the opera," and implied that music could scarcely have been the purpose of the Duchess's Channel crossing, but, rather, that it was to the intent of negotiating with the Count de La Motte for purchase of that now famous packet of letters.

That packet of letters was evidently the cause of considerable consternation at the time in the Court of Versailles, judging by a series of dispatches from the Paris correspondent of the Imperial Court of St. Petersburg, the first of which is dated June 27, 1787:

Madame de Polignac and the Count de Vaudreuil, her *amant en titre*, have set out for England to negotiate with the Count de La Motte for the purchase of the famous letters, supposedly written by Her Majesty to Madame de La Motte, the full text of which her husband is prepared to publish in justification of her conduct and his in the necklace business. . . .

It is said in Paris that Madame de Polignac returned from English shores triumphantly bearing the packet in question, although at a price steeper still than the four thousand louis [more than twenty thousand dollars] originally quoted, necessitating the dispatch of a courier for another purse of French court gold.

Channel traffic continued brisk throughout July, according to further reports from Catherine the Great's correspondent that summer. The Princess de Lamballe was off next on a sudden and mysterious voyage to London, "a mission thought to be similar to that of La Polignac in the preceding month: to treat, that is, with further demands of the Count de La Motte and of former Finance Minister Count de Calonne." And on July 26 "the Abbé Vermond, Marie Antoinette's father confessor and secretary, crossed from Calais to Dover."

While the Count de La Motte, in London, treated arrogantly with the Queen's emissaries (one of his conditions for negotiating on the letter packet was, reportedly, that such emissaries come to him), the Countess, in Paris, plotted to escape from the King's prison of the Salpêtrière, as she writes in her Story of My Life:

June 8 at 11 A.M. were the date and hour set with my anonymous correspondent for the great enterprise of my escape from the Salpêtrière.

Before setting out that morning, Angélique and I hurriedly gulped cup after cup of coffee by way of stimulation.

At the Red Gate [the gate leading from the women's courtyard to that of the superintendent] the gatekeeper was known to be in the habit of going twice daily to fetch her bowl of soup. On this day at eleven o'clock, when she left the gate to go to the kitchens, a prisoner named Dubois, whom I had enlisted in my service, delayed her by some excuse, thus affording us time to slip through that gate and the two beyond it. As we opened the gate to the fourth courtyard, a throng of workmen and servants confronted us, but they merely nodded to us in passing and went on about their business.

Angélique, familiar with the layout of the institution, and thinking me close behind her, took a short cut—losing me in doing it. Suddenly she was out of sight! Panic-struck at being separated from my guide, still I called to mind the saying, "All roads lead to Rome," and forged steadily ahead, although the courtyards seemed to succeed one another endlessly; only nine in all, they seemed like ninety! At each, handing the gatekeeper a tip, I passed through unquestioned.

At length I came to one astonishingly large courtyard where I encountered throngs of visitors on a sight-seeing tour of the Salpêtrière. To avoid calling attention to myself, I deemed it wise to melt into the group which was entering the church. It was hardly the moment I would have chosen for sight-seeing, but I seized the opportunity to send up a fervent prayer to heaven for guidance in so ticklish a situation, and, still following the crowd, I came at last upon the answer to that prayer—the main gate, the gateway to freedom! But scarcely had I passed that formidable barrier and come into the King's Gardens, crowded and busy at that hour, than I found myself confronted by another dilemma: whether to turn to the right or to the left to reach the Seine.

No sooner had I taken my first step to the right than I spied the river—and Angélique awaiting me! I trembled with joy at sight of that good creature, who promptly stepped into a boat drawn up at the bank, with two men at the oars. I followed her aboard and, my finger to my lips, signaled Angélique to silence. Fearful that my voice, if not my distinctly feminine form, might belie my masculine attire, I stood silently, my back to the oarsmen, throughout the crossing.

The sight of Paris was wondrous to behold, although greatly changed since my last glimpse of it en route to the Conciergerie from the Bastille, eleven months previously. I shall not attempt to describe the tumultuous emotions that shook me—transports of delight, primarily, at sweet liberty regained after long and shameful captivity. But as I stepped out of the boat on the Right Bank of the city, near the Arsenal, the six towers of the Bastille rose to confront my eyes, chilling me with fear. Uncontrollable trembling seized my body; I thought those dreadful gates were swinging open to swallow me up again.

Angélique, reassuring me, led me through tortuous back streets and alleys to the city gates, where I hired a carriage to take us as far as Charenton. There, at a shoemaker's shop, I exchanged my painfully heavy boots for a pair of slippers. We rented another carriage to take us seven leagues beyond and then continued on foot, putting another six leagues between us and Paris before midnight.

Oh, how wondrous is God's mercy! He loosened the iron bars behind which my enemies had confined me; leading me by the hand, He directed my faltering footsteps through the direst perils.

That night we slept in a village called Maison Rouge; the next morning at six we took to the road again. Despite my swollen feet, I plodded on till ten that night, when we took shelter at a roadside inn. Next morning, since there were no carriages for hire and Angélique was no horsewoman, we had no choice but to continue walking on to Provins. It was there I decided to exchange my masculine attire (in which, sooner or later, my saliently feminine characteristics were bound to betray me) for a peasant costume. Angélique went out to purchase all the items for the new disguise: a skirt of pink, blue and white striped linen with blouse and apron to match, a stout pair of shoes with dainty buckles, and a wicker market basket to match her own, containing eggs and butter neatly covered over with a linen napkin.

I had hoped to rent a carriage at Provins, but these were available only at relay stations, and I feared the questions that might have been asked us there. To avoid the stares of the curious, we took our way through the town by the least frequented thoroughfares; but even that precaution could not save me from attracting the attention of a group of Army officers we encountered at the edge of town.

Whispering among themselves that I was a woman in man's disguise, they quickened their pace to catch up with us. One of them approached and spoke to me, ogling and winking broadly, "Handsome little cavalier, were you to do me the honor of accepting my escort, I would follow you anywhere—to the very gates of hell."

Embarrassment overwhelmed me. What could I say?

"I have guessed who you are," he continued, "You are—" at these words a violent trembling seized me—"you are a romantic young lady who has run away from her convent to keep a rendezvous with the lucky fellow who has won her heart."

At this conclusion, I could breathe again; courage and voice returning to me, I replied, "Monsieur, since you have guessed my secret, then
I beg you, spare me the embarrassment of forcing your attentions upon
me."

The officer, satisfied with my implied confession of a disguise which
he could congratulate himself upon having divined, insisted no further
and withdrew.

A league beyond the town, Angélique and I came upon the perfect
secluded spot for my costume change: a long alley of willows at the foot
of a mountain, beside a stream winding its way through lush green
meadows. Withdrawing beneath the willows' leafy tent, I managed in
the briefest moments' time to transform myself from a Paris dandy to a
provincial peasant lass. Filling the pockets of the pantaloons and the
coat with rocks, we tossed the clothes into the stream, watching them
sink beneath the ripples. Then, slipping the handles of the little wicker
baskets over our arms, Angélique and I set off, looking for all the world
like a pair of farmers' daughters returning from the village market.

By nightfall, although we were in sight of Nogent, my feet were pain-
ing me so acutely that I could not drag myself another step. Angélique
carried me into a stable, where we curled up gratefully upon a haystack
for the night.

The next day a young farmer, a youth in his twenties, stopped his
cart and invited us to ride as far as his village, beyond Troyes. But
when I offered to pay him, he made me an offer instead; in utter serious-
ness, he offered me his heart, his hand and his fortune, giving me an
exact accounting of the latter, along with his name and address.

Although the gravity, naiveté and presumption of this young peasant could not but strike me as infinitely amusing, still under any
other circumstances I would never have thus cruelly toyed with his affections; but in that perilous flight across France I dared take no slightest
risk, and so I promised the good peasant lad to become his bride! Not
until we had plighted our troth in wine at a roadside inn, not until we
had embraced and embraced again, would my rustic swain agree to part
with me or allow me to continue on my journey.

The conquest of this country bumpkin did, however, win me a recommendation to another farmer of the region, who took Angélique and
me in his cart as far as Vendhurst, within a short distance of Bar-sur-
Aube.

From there I sent Angélique to deliver letters to my husband's family.

Several proved to be away from home; his uncle and aunt, Monsieur and Madame de Surmont, were at home but gave Angélique a chilly reception. Only upon her urging did Monsieur de Surmont agree to meet me at midnight in a secluded spot beyond the town.

He seemed to greet me cordially enough, and we sat down at the edge of a ditch to talk. Before we parted he pulled four gold louis from his pocket, expressing his regret that he could not be more generous, but explaining that recent disastrous speculations had so impoverished him that he had been obliged to borrow even that modest sum.

As we said goodbye, he inquired as to my plans.

"I am going to England," I replied, "where I hope to find my husband—if the latest newspaper reports are correct." I very carefully omitted telling him that I was heading for Switzerland via Luxembourg. I knew too well the character of his wife to trust her with information as to my plan of flight. I was convinced that only in Switzerland would I be safe while trying to establish contact with Monsieur de La Motte and make arrangements to travel to London to join him.

Another cautious figure slipped out the gates of Bar-sur-Aube and past the city walls that night to meet the fugitive: Madame Beugnot, mother of the Countess's good friend and erstwhile suitor. Count Beugnot writes in his memoirs:

My mother never ceased to champion Madame de La Motte, even after the verdict of guilty brought against her by the Parliament of Paris. And when the unfortunate prisoner, in flight from the Salpêtrière, came to hide in the rock quarries near Bar-sur-Aube, my mother had the courage to go to seek her out in the darkest hours of the night. It so happened that Madame de La Motte, in her brief days of prosperity, had made liberal contributions to my mother's favorite charities, and my mother now took to her an equal or even greater amount. But she brought Madame de La Motte a gift more precious than gold; such a gesture of confidence and loyalty on the part of a lady of the highest integrity and unassailable virtue must have restored a measure of self-respect to the publicly dishonored, mutilated and humiliated creature hiding in the shadows of the quarries.

In return, the Countess de La Motte may be said to have made a very decent gesture of her own. In all the hundreds of pages of her memoirs devoted to her flight, she sedulously avoided mention of Madame Beugnot's name; nor did she mention the name of Madame Beugnot's son in any one of the four autobiographical volumes that were to flow from her pen. The Beugnots she knew to be retiring, eminently respectable gentlefolk; she would not involve them in even the shadow of her notoriety.

"Beyond Metz, beyond Thionville—" after countless brushes with the Gendarmerie, after countless hair-raising, hairbreadth escapes from storms, from bandit-ridden forests, from villainous coachmen and overinquisitive, leering local Lotharios—"beyond Thionville," the Countess's narrative continues in her Story of My Life,

the young man driving our carriage pulled up one day at a roadside inn, to rest the horses, he explained, but above all to greet the proprietor, whom he had learned to respect and admire in his days there as a stable-boy.

Madame Schills (the name of this worthy innkeeper to whom a kindly Providence had guided me!) informed me that the name of the town was Olerisse, and that I now found myself within the borders of the Grand Duchy of Luxembourg, in the Austrian Empire. My emotional reaction to this news must have been clearly visible upon my face, for Madame Schills inquired gently, "Have you reason to rejoice at leaving the French frontier behind?" Then she pressed my hand in hers and whispered, "I have guessed who you are—but do not be afraid! In my house you will find safety; in me, a sincere and devoted friend. From here you can write to your relatives and await word from them."

An offer so unexpected and so kind could not be refused. As events were to prove, I could congratulate myself for having given my confidence to this noble woman. Madame Schills, at thirty-six, is a paragon of female virtues; her face is better than beautiful—it is interesting.

To my letter to Monsieur de La Motte came a reply within ten days: For him to set foot on the Continent was too great a risk; he was searching for a proper and trustworthy person to send to fetch me and escort me across the Channel. But when three weeks had gone by without another word from him, I grew fearful that our letters had been intercepted; I trembled at every carriage that pulled up before the inn, lest it be bringing police to carry me off, back to the hideous prison I had escaped.

The Luxembourg newspapers carried stories from Paris about my escape; one report was to the effect that I had been arrested at Calais and shipped off to the Île Ste.-Marguerite. Then rumors began to fly in the neighborhood: talk of the two strange women at the inn of Madame Schills, one of whom might well be the famous Countess de La Motte! What if the stories circulating in Luxembourg reached Paris? My position had become perilous; and still no word forthcoming from London!

At last, on July 28, late in the afternoon, a strange lady drove up to the inn, giving her name as Mrs. MacMahon and asking for me. Madame Schills, having satisfied herself as to the newcomer's credentials, ushered her in.

I could not prevent a flush of fright at sight of this unknown, but I was quickly reassured when, embracing me and producing a letter from my husband, she told me she had come to lead me to the land of liberty!

Our departure was set for the very next day. My generous and emotional hostess burst into tears, thus starting mine to flow. Still, these were happy tears; if I was leaving her, it was to join my husband in the sanctuary of the oppressed, to put myself forever out of reach of the snares and plots of my deadly enemies. Showered with her blessings, I departed. My tears then were not to be the last I shed over parting from my friend; how could I ever forget my benefactress?

After a forty-eight-hour crossing by packet from Ostend to Dover, we set out for London on August 4 at seven in the evening, arriving early the next morning at the home of Mrs. MacMahon, No. 80 Haymarket. At nine o'clock, I saw Monsieur de La Motte appear!

I will not attempt to describe the poignancy of that reunion, the inexpressible blending of joy and sadness—delight, tenderness, anguish all at once. There was primarily, of course, the thrill of seeing my husband after years of separation, of joining him in a land where the rights of the individual are sacred, where a man is safe from the disfavor of the powerful. Even so, there were undercurrents of fear. How could we shake off the haunting fears of the dreadful past? How adjust to the uncertain future, to the anomaly of our present position? All these anxieties were inherent in the circumstances of our reunion in a foreign land. My heart could not but be stirred by a thousand conflicting emotions, one following pell-mell upon the other.

During the two weeks I stayed at Mrs. MacMahon's I dared not go out for even a breath of air unless accompanied by my hostess, and then not until ten o'clock at night, so as to avoid the stares of the curious, foreigners as well as Englishmen, who crowded the coffeehouses of the Haymarket.

Was freedom for the Countess de La Motte stipulated by her husband as part of the purchase price for the packet of letters? There was widespread belief that this was so; the Abbé Georgel voiced it in his memoirs:

One would have thought that threats by the Count de La Motte to publish an exposé unless his wife were restored to him merited mere scorn and disdain from the authorities. Instead, to the astonishment of the entire world, news came shortly thereafter that Madame de La Motte had found means to escape her narrow cell, to cross all France unapprehended and to make her way to London.

Such an escape—for which, significantly, no one was ever punished—could have been accomplished only through the connivance of the authorities.

With which opinion the Leyden Gazette concurred in its June 19 issue: "There can be no doubt that the female prisoner was aided and abetted by a powerful hand in her escape and throughout her flight."

The superficiality of the subsequent police inquiry further confirmed the general opinion. The only remaining question was whose hand it had been—whether the Baron de Breteuil's, acting for the Queen, or the sinister hand of the Duke d'Orléans, raised always against his cousin's interests. The finger of suspicion pointed, as well, to the prison chaplain, worthy Father Tillet, for men of the cloth apparently were particularly susceptible to the Countess's charms.

The Countess herself, as has been previously seen, speculated on the possibility of its being either the Queen or the Cardinal, but she drew no definite conclusion, calling it "an unknown but benevolent hand" that had snatched her "mysteriously from the pit." She continues in her Story of My Life:

No sooner had I recovered from the fatigues of that perilous flight than I began to devote all my energies to a consideration of ways of justifying my conduct in the eyes of the world—of presenting the facts certain to vindicate me and my grievously offended honor. I proposed next to submit my case to world opinion, never doubting for an instant that I would be totally exonerated by that supreme tribunal.

But the same relentless fate was to hound me in England and involve me in a series of fresh disasters I had never expected to be called upon to face. Heaven marked me in the cradle as a victim, a prize example of the vicissitudes to which the human race is subject, and I am doomed to drag out the cruel burden of existence upon this earth until death delivers me.

Upon my arrival in London, I found my husband in dire financial straits, awaiting the moment when it should please his family to restore the remnants of our fortune which they had promised to safeguard for us. His uncle, Monsieur de Surmont, had promised to forward our valuables from Bar-sur-Aube to London immediately upon request, but not until the following October was the promise fulfilled. Furthermore, Madame de Surmont (a dishonor to her sex) spread ugly rumors about us in Bar-sur-Aube and went so far as to pretend that we owed her gratitude for not having turned over to the police those pitiful remnants of our fortune—diamonds, silver, laces—which had escaped seizure and the public auction of our effects.

But scarcely had Monsieur de La Motte laid hands upon these few valuables remaining to us in all the world (amounting to some sixty thousand francs) than a crowd of so-called "creditors" gathered on our doorstep, brandishing court warrants for collection of their claims. Five times I saw him arrested; five times he extricated himself from the arms of the law through the efforts of Mr. Grey, the jeweler, with whom Monsieur de La Motte was obliged to deposit our jewels to induce him to act as guarantor. His trusted lawyer, leading him on with false hopes, had advised him to avoid the courts at any cost and to quiet first one and then another of these so-called creditors with sums of 100, 150, 200 guineas at a time. The lawyer himself demanded and collected twenty, thirty, forty pounds sterling at a time for his disservices.

As net result of all this fine advice, I never saw the proceeds from so much as a carat of my own diamonds. I saw myself stripped of my jewels without realizing a sou. In short order, my overcredulous husband had frittered away a sum equivalent to the total value of our jewelry.

It was not poverty which frightened me; life had inured me to privation as well as to suffering. No, it was rather despair at the dissipation of those last resources upon which I had counted as the means of publishing my justificatory memoirs!

Gullible, headstrong, indiscreet, Monsieur de La Motte withdrew his confidence from me and followed no counsel but his own. Those who know him know well that it requires no student of human nature to read into his soul; his physiognomy is a mirror for his every thought and emotion. It is a sad reflection indeed upon the human race that candor and generosity expose a man to betrayal by the first false "friend" or schemer who comes along. After this brief character sketch of Monsieur de La Motte, all his follies and blunders become self-explanatory.

Plunged in deepest melancholy, I came to curse the day upon which I was born, and Monsieur de La Motte to curse the one upon which he first laid eyes on me. It was his misfortune that his fate was linked with that of a woman prideful of her Valois heritage. Alas, my sorrows are multiplied by those of the people near and dear to me. The curse of the Valois fell not only upon me but upon all connected with me. The tears caused me by my husband's misfortunes have been a thousand times more bitter than any I have shed for my own.

And yet here I must make the sad admission that since my disgrace I no longer find in Monsieur de La Motte the tenderness to which I was accustomed. Indeed, he has become so unjust and cruel as to blame me for our common misfortunes.

Unmistakably, a rift within the lute. And the memoirs of the Count de La Motte give evidence that, just as his Countess found a change in him, he found a change in his Countess:

When my wife rejoined me in London, I quickly perceived that the great misfortunes she had suffered had much altered her disposition; constant tact and caution were needed to keep her in good humor. But, though I avoided every occasion of causing her displeasure, even so, several times during the period I spent with her she tried to destroy herself, and for the merest trifles.

Twice I held her back by her skirts when she attempted to throw herself out a window. But in spite of all my patience and consideration, I could not refrain from saying one day that her woes were for the most part the product of her own waywardness and extravagance. No sooner had I uttered these words than she flung herself upon a dagger which she happened to be holding in her hand, and despite my promptness and that of other members of the household in rushing toward her, we could not prevent her from stabbing herself below the breast and were horrified to see her fall unconscious to the floor.

And, in plaintive duet, the Countess's Story of My Life:

Cease, oh, cease your unjust reproaches, you who won my heart from the moment my eyes first beheld you! Her head bowed down today under shame and injustice, your unhappy wife has not forfeited her rights to your compassion!

But the Count de La Motte, whether the proverbial last to learn of his wife's infidelities or whether grown suddenly squeamish, had a reproach more grievous still to register against his Countess: "For a long time before this, the Countess's way of life and her liaisons with other men had alienated me from her."

Among such liaisons to be noted, first came that with a British milord, of whom all that is known is that he "rushed forward to proffer his protection to the charming victim of foreign despotism"; thanks to that inherent respect for his betters bred in the bone of the British journalist, he remains forever nameless.

As for the Countess's liaison with her fellow expatriate, the once "beau" Calonne, that affair was so flagrantly conducted as to inspire one columnist, "Julie Philosophe" (Philosophizing Julie) to report, "It was soon obvious that the liaison between Monsieur de Calonne and the by-blow of the Valois had reached a stage of deepest intimacy."

It was not surprising that the two most notorious members of London's French colony should have revived a friendship dating from the days when the Countess had solicited Calonne's aid as Minister of Finance, dismissal from which post he properly attributed to the Queen's cabals. Mutual hostility to Marie Antoinette furnished not only an added bond between Calonne and his vivacious mistress but the incentive for his collaboration on her forthcoming memoirs (first edition), although for such a pair of stormy petrels, any collaboration, literary or otherwise, was destined to a violent end.

As such "Julie" describes it in her tattle column—with one eye to the keyhole, to judge from her gory details:

Finis to the affair between the two notorious refugees was written in bloody violence. To tell it briefly:

The fond pair were seated one day at the card table for their regular game of piquet, when the Countess made a play which elicited from Calonne the exclamation, "That card gives your entire hand away! You are a marked woman!"

Calonne's tone of voice and choice of words revealed beyond the shadow of a doubt that this was a deliberately malicious allusion to the mark [the red and puffy scar] left by the branding iron of the public executioner upon her white flesh.

The Countess, sensitive to the extreme on the subject of that blemish [just below the swell of her lovely breast], reacted violently to the taunt. A stream of invective poured from her lips, to which the ex-Minister replied with a tirade equally vicious.

Beside herself with rage, the Countess overturned the card table separating her from Calonne and hurled herself upon him, her hands, hitherto so caressing, clawing at his mocking mouth, ripping the skin and bringing the blood to her aging lover's cheek.

MEMOIRS
OF THE ABBÉ GEORGEL

Restored thus to the arms of her husband, Madame de La Motte, that enduringly wicked woman, joined with him in concocting new libels by means of which to extort large sums of money from the Queen and Baron de Breteuil.

Marie Antoinette, presumably above suspicion, should have been in a position loftily and scornfully to wither the impotent threats directed at her by a woman held in public contempt. And Baron de Breteuil, if he had nothing with which to reproach himself, was hardly the type of man to allow himself to be intimidated by a refugee from the Salpêtrière. It is therefore difficult to understand why someone should have undertaken to buy the La Mottes' silence by dispatching gold to them in London.

But the Duchess de Polignac, on the pretext of making a visit to the fashionable resort of Bath, set out suddenly for England and personally delivered the specified sum to Monsieur and Madame de La Motte, who in turn delivered to the Duchess what purported to be the sole manuscript extant of the threatened diatribe against the Queen.

The fact that the deal was consummated by the Duchess de Polignac is confirmed by Madame Campan in her memoirs:

I can attest to having seen in the hands of the Queen herself the manuscript of the infamous memoirs that issued from the pen of Madame de La Motte.

The manuscript had been brought to the Queen from London. The corrections appearing upon it in those passages where glaring errors in court etiquette betrayed the ignorance of the authoress were in the handwriting of Monsieur de Calonne. The Queen feared Calonne, and with reason. She had proof that this former Minister of Finance had become her bitterest enemy, and that there was no expedient to which he would not stoop to blacken her name.

"How could the Queen's party have put faith in the word of that disreputable La Motte pair?" Georgel asks rhetorically. "The mission [of the Duchess de Polignac] served only to postpone the catastrophe. The famous memoirs, of which the La Mottes claimed to have turned over the sole existing copy, nonetheless shortly appeared in print."

No connotation of blackmail is to be found in the Countess's Life Story; if she set a price on withholding her memoirs and the packet of letters from the press, it was for "reluctant renunciation of the publication of her vindication"; if French gold was paid over, it was "indemnification for confiscated properties, damages for miscarriage of justice and for lost honor and reputation." Or so she rationalized it for her reading public (and for herself?) in her Story of My Life:

From the moment of my arrival in London, my first and only thought had been publication of my justification for the eyes of all the world. To this my husband made objections.

There was a great deal of talk, at the time, of a possible plan of reconciliation whereby I would renounce publication of my memoirs in return for certain pecuniary considerations to be accorded me by the French court. Actually, was there gold enough in the world—much less in the treasury of the French monarchy—to compensate me financially for my ravished honor, my tortured soul and body?

Still my husband urged me: "Our only recourse is to force the French government to indemnify us for their injustices. For the suppression of the memoirs, the only terms to which we will agree will be a total restitution of our fortune and properties. Such action on the part of the French authorities would constitute our moral vindication in the eyes of the world."

I too would have preferred to spare the honor of the Queen, and I tried to warn Her Majesty that I was in possession of certain letters miraculously preserved from the ruins, letters incriminating her and exculpating me (the originals of which, I might add, have been deposited for safekeeping in the Tower of London, where my readers may consult them at no extra charge). All I asked in return was restitution of property rightfully mine which had been seized, after an iniquitous verdict, to enrich the coffers of the King.

But I really never considered it likely that the French court would capitulate on those terms, and besides, my main goal was public vindication. To this purpose, then, I eagerly took up my pen, denying my feeble, tortured body even the minimum physical requirements of nourishment and sleep until my memoirs should be ready for publication.

Although we were obliged to borrow money to defray the costs of printing, five thousand copies in French have now come off the press, and three thousand more in English; the latter went on sale at a guinea each in New Bond Street shops.

These Memoires justificatifs de la Comtesse de Valois de La Motte, *to give them their full French title* ("a cesspool of calumny" *is what Georgel called them*), *began:*

I invoke God as my witness as I write!

Before Him, I take a solemn oath that were I upon my deathbed I would reaffirm every word of this, the first true statement I have been able to make, speaking at last freely and openly here in England, safe from my mortal enemies. All previous defense pleas made in my name, all depositions and court testimony made by me under duress are herewith repudiated as part of that travesty of justice known as the Diamond Necklace Trial. . . .

And then:

With my dying breath I will maintain that illicit relations existed between the Cardinal and the Queen. . . . I have already mentioned the efforts I made to reconcile that pair of illustrious lovers, but the Cardinal had been unpardonably indiscreet on the subject of his liaison with the Queen. Unfortunately he had extended the circle of his confidants far beyond me, to include his uncle the Prince de Soubise; his aunt the Countess de Marsan, the Baron da Planta, Cagliostro, even the jewelers Böhmer and Bassenge, not to mention a dozen others, making a conversation piece of the favors granted him by the Queen, making sport of the prowess demanded of her lovers.

A physical as well as a moral wreck at the age of fifty-one after a life of excess and debauch, His Eminence found it strenuous to live up to the amatory standards of his royal paramour and made arch admission that he resorted to a variety of stimulants: first fortifying himself with a dose of Cagliostro's famous aphrodisiac, then stimulating himself further by a visit to the love nest he maintained in Passy, where the fledgling occupant obliged by parading before him costumed as Mother Eve—all this elaborate ritual to perk him up, to put him "in the proper mood," as he put it, "to keep a rendezvous with the royal redhead in the Salon de Venus."

But the prize in the memoir package was tucked away in the Appendix: the collection of billets-doux purportedly exchanged by the Queen and the Cardinal, which the Countess introduces by apostrophizing the Queen:

And so now at last you know! Today, herewith, I confirm the dread certainty—full, grim proof confronts you from the pages of my memoirs. Yes, that licentious correspondence exists, has been preserved—if not in full, then in part, examples enough to set your perfidious heart to quaking! Will you dare to deny that the letters are yours? I doubt that you will try it; there are too many people who know, who will recognize your style, your mannerisms, your special secret catchwords and phrases.

And she tells her readers:

It is, of course, regrettable that out of the two-hundred-odd letters comprising the correspondence between the Queen and the Cardinal, only some thirty-one fell into my hands. None have been suppressed; I promised my public to publish these billets-doux, and I herewith fulfill the pledge. The correspondence—all that I could salvage of it—is printed in the Appendix of this volume, immediately after my genealogical table.

If the reader will cast an eye upon Number 1 of that collection, an exact copy of the very first letter written by the Cardinal to the Queen, he will discover the impetuous fellow this early in the game referring already to "the hope glimmering" in his heart, to Her Majesty's "luscious lips," to his "enslavement" to her charms. In Number 6 he has become "the Slave begging kisses from the adorable mouth" of his "dear Master." And to think that the Queen of France permitted this!

According to the Countess's annotations, a whole secret lovers' code had been developed: The Cardinal was referred to as the Slave, the Queen as the Master, the King as the Prime Minister and Baron da Planta as the Savage; and "C'est entendu" was used as an upper-stratum Gallic "O.K." One example should suffice to gratify "the reader's curiosity" as to the subject matter and epistolary style of this member of the French Academy. At random, Number 15: "A little gem of a letter," the Countess writes, "already full of 'thees' and 'thous.' Baron da Planta's code name might more appropriately have been the 'Shadow,' since he accompanied the Cardinal everywhere; at any rate, upon the night in question, the shadow had evidently followed the substance to Trianon. Let the reader draw his own conclusions as to the rest."

LETTER 15

I could not resist, last night, stealing back to the scene of our blissfully happy rendezvous to kiss the very blades of grass upon which your adorable feet had trod an hour earlier. I could not tear myself away from reminiscing, when suddenly, from behind a hedge, there issued sounds to make me think someone was about to spring upon me. Affrighted, I made one mighty leap to escape the ambush and, leaping before I looked, plopped into a deep and muddy ditch!

The Savage, awaiting me on the other side and seeing only the ridiculous predicament in which my clumsiness had landed me, burst into gales of laughter, with mirthful grimaces such as have never been seen on that glum face before, subsiding only long enough to assist me out of my muddy hole before he went off into fresh bursts of laughter, holding his sides, rolling on the grass, shaking so hard he could not utter a word.

Hearing no further sound, seeing no sign of ambush, I waited for the paroxysm of mirth to subside; whereupon I told him rather sternly that I would in the future dispense with the services of an equerry who proved himself so indiscreet in an emergency.

"Do not condemn me without a hearing," he implored. "It must have been a rabbit or a partridge that alarmed you into thinking you had the whole Polignac clique on your traces. Try to see it from my point of view: I had heard nothing, seen nothing to account for your wild plunge into the ditch. Suddenly there you were, sprawled out, your legs in the air, mud in your hair, your breeches split from waist to knee!"

My sense of humor once restored, we joined in a chorus of laughter. After all, no damage had been done beyond a mudbath and a rip in my breeches. It was only later that the discovery of a gash in my hand sobered us in our hilarity. The Savage having capably served as surgeon, the wound is less painful today. Indeed, I was scarcely conscious of its throbbing through the night—my heart throbbing more violently still at thought of your adorable person, causing me even in my sleep the most delicious dreams.

The Countess, on a visit here this morning, spied my bandaged hand and heard the narrative of my nocturnal adventure, although I could foresee the inevitable banter with which she would greet it. What I had not foreseen was that her mirth would become so immoderate as to oblige her to go rushing from the salon. I dared not follow her lest I set off a fresh deluge. And I can only hope that when our charming mutual friend comes to give you her version of what she terms my "misadventure" her rippling laughter will leave no such traces in your boudoir as it did in my salon.

MEMOIRS
OF THE COUNTESS DE LA MOTTE-VALOIS

Another promise I make the reader is that in these memoirs he will find the clue to the mystery, the key to the enigma, the only logical explanation of the case ever offered—because it is the only true one. Woe betide those who have forced me to it!

How, otherwise, make sense of the romantic adventure in the Grove of Venus, the disappearance of the bulk of the necklace diamonds, the strange coincidence of the Queen's involvement in all?

The question that must inevitably arise is why the Queen, having once decided that the time was ripe for the Cardinal's destruction, did not first restore the necklace before striking him down with her wrath, as any private individual, any normal person, would have done? Well may you ask. The only answer is that her intellect is on the same plane as her sensibilities, her tastes, her affections—impulsive, inconsistent, illogical.

But, the reader is sure to ask, is it possible that the Queen of France is capable of such pettiness? The answer to that question is a simple one: If the Queen of France were what she ought to be, these memoirs would never have been written. If the Queen of France were not what she is, would I ever have known her on such a footing? Would I ever have been, in her hands, like a poor quivering bird in those of a vicious child who, after an hour's sport, plucks it alive, feather by feather, and throws it to the cats?

If the Queen of France were not what she is, would France today find itself in a state of combustion?

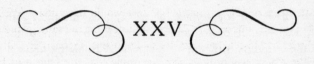

XXV

The Countess Triumphs

(1789-1791)

July 14, 1789:

The mob seethed through the city, collecting muskets, axes, pikes and constant reinforcements, snowballing, swelling, surging toward the most dread, most hated symbol of oppression in all France . . .

It was nightfall when the world-shaking news reached Versailles, where the Assembly—the original, nonviolent example of defiance of royal authority—still met.

"The Bastille has fallen!"

The Assembly, terrified of royal reprisal but bitter at royal obstructionism, acclaimed the bloody exploit with cries of "Victory!"

It was midnight when the Duke de La Rochefoucauld-Liancourt, Grand Master of the King's Wardrobe and one of the titled liberals, left the Assembly for the palace to awaken the King.

"Sire, the Bastille has been taken! The garrison has been overwhelmed, massacred. Governor de Launay's head is being brandished on a pike through the streets of Paris."

"But . . . but then it is a revolt?"

"No, Sire, it is a revolution."

It did not take long for the news of the fall of the Bastille to cross the Channel and reach the ears of its most celebrated former prisoner *save only the Man in the Iron Mask. The Countess de La Motte exults in her* Story of My Life:

Where, my fellow countrymen, oh, where today are those forbidding towers, those symbols of despotism? Liberty has put them to the torch and to the sword, and they have disappeared from the horizon. That hellhole of a Bastille has vomited forth the last of its victims; naught remains but dread memories and rubble! Immured, myself, behind its grim walls, I had firsthand experience of those cavernous vaults, which left on my mind an impression so horrifying that it could be erased only by the joyous news of its total destruction.

But then, before the celebrated Revolution, France was literally covered with state prisons, correctional institutions and convents. No wonder horror of the Old Regime fills all men's hearts. Abolished, too, is that other abuse of arbitrary power, the *lettre de cachet*, the very mention of which still sets me trembling like a leaf. Thanks be to God, those days are gone forever. Despotism never again, I pray, will rear its head in France.

Of the death of the Bastille's governor, who had had the distinction of being the first victim of all the Revolution's thousands, the Countess's Story of My Life, *curiously enough, contains not a single gloating word. There were malicious tongues, of course, to wag the suggestion that Launay's name had lengthened the Countess's already lengthy list of lovers. This momentous month of July, however, was no time for reminiscing; rather, it was a time for action, and the Count de La Motte was off for Paris—the more readily, perhaps, in view of his Countess's steadily "deteriorating" disposition. The Countess writes:*

My husband arrived in Paris on August 20, four years to the day from that one on which he had quitted France in 1785.

And now I am hoping with all my heart that the nation from which he seeks justice will act upon his case and swiftly vindicate his honor. It is hardly the action of a guilty man to turn himself over to the authorities when a life sentence still hangs over his head.

Our detractors, to be sure, accuse us of being "publicity seekers" and spread reports that "a certain party" has turned up in Paris "to stir up trouble," to rehash a "certain case" which was originally the scandal of the century.

The Countess, impetuous, importunate, impatient, found it difficult to wait; she simply could not sit quietly by while the Assembly—now calling itself the Constituent Assembly—proceeded to its interminable business of drafting France's first constitution. The Countess could count numerous friends on those benches: Count d'Estaing, Ramon de Carbonnières, Jacques Claude Beugnot (delegate from Bar-sur-Aube) and, on the tribune itself, as first president of that august body, a close personal friend from girlhood days, "that worthy prelate" the bishop of Langres.

The Countess proceeded to the business of drafting a document of her own and sending it off—a petition to the Assembly for revision of her sentence:

Oh, generous and compassionate nation, deign to suspend for a moment your sublime labors, the great affairs of state which have first claim on your attention, to listen to the account of my distress.

Hear me, wise legislators who astonish the universe with your wisdom in framing laws to guarantee the rights of man and the liberty of the individual, in abolishing forever the old France of slave and tyrant! You whose name shall be blessed by future generations will surely not refuse me this act of justice. France no longer has two scales of justice, one for the poor and humble, another for the high and mighty.

I appeal to you, worthy representatives of the people, who, having overthrown the despots, will surely extend a helping hand to one of despotism's most famous victims. Noble patriots that you are, not even you have suffered such tortures at the hands of the tyrants as have I—after having first felt their perfidious caress; mine is the unique experience of having been flung from the arms of a queen into the hands of her executioner!

But now the day of reckoning has come. I shall appear in the arena; and as for her who victimized me, I shall make her descend and appear there with me. Pridefully, now, I shall bare my breast and display those horrible scars, the once ineffaceable marks of shame, which today have become the glorious stigmata of a patriot.

Tremble, villainess! Tremble!

The Queen trembled. She thought they should start for Metz, near the border, or at least remove from Versailles to the palace at Rambouillet, four leagues farther from Paris.

The King thought today that he should abdicate; the next day, that he shouldn't. "He asked advice of everybody," Malouet remembered, "and seemed to be saying to every soul who approached him, 'What should be done? What can I do?'"

He asked the question of Rivarol, who sent the reply, "Play the King" —precisely the role of which Louis XVI was incapable. With no talent for governing and none for meeting a crisis, he could only clutch clumsily at the crown, a well-intentioned, kindly, decent, but an ir-resolute and vacillating man—whose ancestors had bequeathed him a revolution.

The exodus of the unpopular was on. The Count d'Artois, the Baron de Breteuil, the Abbé Vermond and all that select, once envied coterie of the Queen's intimates, the detested, profligate Polignacs, above all—were taking the hint of the people's displeasure. The Versailles court-yard was crowded, those July nights, with carriages, with mountains of luggage, with passengers in a last mirthless, dead-serious fancy dress (masked to escape the angry mobs along the roads) passing one after another through the great gilded gates, never to return.

The Queen, alone, lonely, in her suite, "unnerved, restless," as Mad-ame Campan saw her, "sent messenger after messenger to summon to her presence this or that lady or gentleman of the court, only to find their apartments empty, echoing, with locks fastened upon the doors. Terror had sent them scurrying to the border and across. The silence of death reigned throughout the palace."

In October of 1789, published in Oxford in both French and English for distribution on both sides of the Channel and sure to enjoy a brisk sale in that hour of hot political crisis, there appeared An Open Letter from the Countess de Valois de La Motte to the Queen of France:

Listen, you evil, deceiving woman! Read this without shuddering, if you can. Today perhaps you are to be pitied even more than me—you, a princess, powerless Queen of the finest empire in the universe.

You have resorted to every expedient within your power to prevent the publication and distribution of my memoirs, which shall imprint upon your brow a mark of shame as red and ugly as that which your in-famous executioner branded upon my breast.

Queen of the once most loving and loyal people in the world, every tongue in France today is cursing you! The nation demands that you desist forever from your political conniving, your wicked meddling, your mysterious intrigues. If ever, now is the time to show yourself worthy of wearing a crown, else it will be snatched from your head any moment, now that you have driven your people to recover by force their inherent rights. But why should I try to teach you? The French nation, on July 14, gave you a lesson you will not soon forget.

Today liberty has restored me to strength and courage, and you may expect attack. Dread, above all, the forthcoming publication of my second memoirs. I have been criticized for being thus far too discreet in my revelations, but now the whole story, down to the last syllable, goes to press.

The Countess signed herself "your mortal enemy, the innocent Valois, Countess de La Motte," and it was precisely as mortal enemy to the Queen that Mirabeau saw her, from his vantage point at the head of the Revolutionary council table. "Madame de La Motte's voice alone," he wrote, "brought on the horrors of July 14 and of October 5" (the storming of the Palace of Versailles by the Women's Army).

"The insurrection of October 5 was directed primarily against the Queen," wrote Madame Campan, who had stood shuddering in the Place d'Armes of the château as the vanguard of that ferocious "female" army marched upon it from Paris, "eight to ten thousand strong, bursting through the gates, past the guards, overflowing into all the courtyards—" brandishing muskets, pikes and axes in suspiciously muscled forearms, and with a suspicious shadow of beard beneath the wigs and bonnets—"screaming obscene threats to tear out Marie Antoinette's heart to make a stew and her liver and gizzards for cockades to trim their bonnets."

"It so happened that I was not on duty at the palace that night of horrors," Madame Campan's memoirs relate. And so it was to Madame Campan's sister and another lady in waiting that Marie Antoinette owed her life when, at about four-thirty in the morning, there was an outbreak of horrifying shrieks and shots:

The multitude had swarmed in and slaughtered the Queen's guards! My sister and her companion bolted the outer doors behind them, ran to Her Majesty's bedroom and rushed her from her bed, barefoot and in nightdress, through secret doors and along back corridors to the King's suite, where she was reunited with him and the children [the Dauphin and Madame Royale, the Princess Marie Thérèse Charlotte] even as the attackers were battering down the paneled doors of the adjoining Oeil-de-Boeuf. There were many people later to testify [at his trial in the Châtelet Court] that they had recognized the Duke d'Orléans pointing the way for the mob to the entrance of the Queen's apartments.

(There were likewise many to insist that they had recognized the Countess de La Motte marching at the head of the Women's Army from Paris to Versailles; it was a headlined story in the Paris newssheets that October of 1789. The Countess's denials were more convincing than the Duke's, however: no evidence was ever produced that she had left English shores.)

"A staccato of gunfire" from the courtyard below the King's balcony where the "army" was bivouacked, Madame Campan tells us, "signaled mob approval and mob victory at the moment His Majesty pronounced his words of surrender—his promise to remove with his court from Versailles to Paris."

"We have the baker and the baker's wife and the baker's son! Now Paris will never want for bread again!" chanted the "female monsters swarming around the royal coach" as it rolled out through the great gilded gates for the last time into the Avenue de Paris. As they chanted, says Madame Campan, "that exultant troupe of cannibals pranced in a danse macabre about the carriage wheels, flaunting their grisly trophies, the heads of the slaughtered guards impaled on pikes."

Madame Campan rode with the palace staff in one of the hundred carriages bringing up the rear of that torturously slow procession—"Oh, God, what a procession—the funeral cortege of monarchy!" she writes in her memoirs:

The Queen had sent for my father-in-law and me a moment or two before her departure for Paris, early that morning of the sixth, to turn over her valuables to us for safekeeping; she herself was taking only one jewel case. Her courage in the face of the mob had been magnificent, but alone with us in the privacy of her apartments Her Majesty could scarcely speak and tears coursed down her cheeks. She did me the honor of embracing me and extended her hand to Monsieur Campan to kiss, saying to us, "Come to me at once to Paris, to the Tuileries, and never leave me! Faithful servitors, in moments like these, become the most precious of friends. We are lost, dragged off—it may be, to death. Prisoner kings are always very close to it."

In Paris, all the approaches to the Tuileries were thronged with vicious ruffians from the streets, jeering and insulting us and all who came in or out of the palace. From the streets beyond could be heard that exultant tumult of wildly excited crowds that is almost as frightening as the roar of fury. Occasionally a dreadful racket came up from the terrace of the palace itself; twice the Queen and the children were forced to come in from the gardens; they could no longer even go out for a breath of air.

News and book vendors cried out their licentious wares under the Queen's very windows, shouting out such titles as "The Scandalous Life of Marie Antoinette" and holding up and waving infamous cartoons and pictures to capture the attention of the passers-by.

One title the Queen heard hawked by the book vendors in the autumn-sere gardens below her windows was that much ballyhooed Second Mémoire justicatif de la Comtesse de Valois de La Motte, which had been rushed to press before the end of October 1789.

> The terrible truth with vengeful eyes
> Flies upon the wings of time, reads in the depths of hearts,
> Its fearsome torch inevitably lighting up the abyss
> In which crime has taken refuge from retribution.*

Thus, with a quotation from Voltaire's Ériphile, the Countess began her second memoirs. And the terrible "truth" with vengeful eyes—and sixteen appropriately pornographic copperplate engravings—followed swiftly:

In my first memoirs I lifted only a corner of the veil, merely hinting at the horrid truth, and I suffered reproach from my reading public for having wielded too timid, too gently probing a pen, my meaning having been thereby obscured.

If my first account was discreetly ambiguous, it was because I sought

---

* La vérité terrible, avec les yeux vengeurs,
Vient sur l'aile du temps, et lit au fond des cœurs.
Son flambeau redoutable éclaire enfin l'abîme
Où, dans l'impunité, s'était caché le crime.

to shield a woman—a woman who might have become the idol of twenty-five million Frenchmen but whose name has become instead anathema on their lips: another Medici, a Messalina, a Fredegund. Very well, then, O insatiably curious reader! I will speak out, tell all. I owe it to my fellow citizens, to myself, to posterity. Indeed, I must warn the reader that some may be shocked by my courageous candor in respect to various illustrious personages, especially the cruel Antoinette and the imbecilic Cardinal.

Everyone knows with what audacity Antoinette has always claimed that she has never so much as seen me. I will here prove that not only has she seen me but she has known me, caressed me, called me by the fondest nicknames, overwhelmed me with the favors of her sweetest intimacy.

The reader will remember my description of the flattering reception with which the Queen first distinguished me, the interest so cordial as to elicit from the Cardinal the exclamation, "Why, she has taken a fancy to you!" I was prompt, the reader may be sure, at the first rendezvous appointed me by Her Majesty, but even so, she was awaiting me with the liveliest impatience, giving rise to conjectures in my mind along the lines of the Cardinal's. She received me with that graciousness, that friendliness of hers which makes her so utterly irresistible to those she smiles upon. So seductive was she that I may say I literally idolized her. Even today I must forcibly expel the vision of her lovely face from my mind's eye if I am to continue.

Our first interview was taken up, however, by Her Majesty's questions on the score of my genealogy and financial status—and, above all, her repeated warning that any breach of confidence on my part would be under pain of swift disgrace. I pledged inviolate silence on the subject of our liaison.

At parting I was honored by a tender kiss, a gift of ten thousand livres in notes on the Bank of France and the words, "Farewell, we will meet soon again."

The Cardinal's first question to me was just what might have been expected of an old libertine, a debauchee, a man with no faith in virtue, and I suppose I must have been naïve in insisting that Her Majesty's tender emotion had been merely a reflection of her desire to relieve the plight of a daughter of the Valois. At any rate, the Cardinal, refusing to believe that that first meeting with the Queen had passed chastely, urged me to secrecy and, above all, to compliance with the Queen's any and every wish—repeating over and over again that not only my fortune but his as well depended on it.

The next day a note in the Queen's handwriting summoned me to Trianon: "Come this evening by the avenue of chestnut trees, where one of my ladies will be waiting to lead you to me . . ."

Following instructions, I was shown through the Trianon gates and into the boudoir of Her Majesty, where I was shortly to receive clear and precise explanation of all I had been led to suspect—the full meaning of the Cardinal's "She has taken a fancy to you!"

My God, to what depths the high and mighty of this earth will stoop! No humble shepherdess could have displayed a more ingratiating manner, a greater eagerness to please than the Queen of France in that delicious moment. I trembled at the proximity of majesty, but my inherent awe and respect were the very last sentiments my sovereign hoped to inspire at that instant. Seeking to put me at my ease, she rallied me with compliments, with pet names and with no-longer-ambiguous caresses.

Ingenious at corruption, past mistress at the arts of perversion, she directed first her eyes to dwell devouringly on what she smilingly called my "outstanding attractions," then her lips, her kisses following her greedy glances over my quivering body. And I . . . I blush as I confess that here were undreamed-of delights—and satisfactions * * * * * * *

Her embraces were mingled with protestations of eternal friendship. How could I dream, that night of intoxicating pleasure, that she would one day allow those "outstanding attractions" of mine, which she praised and gazed at with such voluptuous enthusiasm, to be profaned and mutilated by the branding iron of her public executioner?

After two hours of such communion, the Queen dismissed me with another sheaf of bank notes and the same phrase: "Farewell, we will meet soon again."

Three days later, another note, another rendezvous at Trianon. I here confess, and for the first time, that that night was the most glorious of my life! I was assisted with my disrobing, and then began that unforgettable night which raised me to the rank of the gods of this earth, as the voluptuous Princess, awaiting me between the royal sheets, invited me to share the royal couch! And I can assure the reader that she lost no time, but took full advantage of the five hours of freedom afforded her by the King's absence on a hunting trip to Rambouillet. What a welcome substitute I made, she laughed, for the lumpish, repulsive body of the

* The asterisks are the Countess's.

"Prime Minister"—her mocking name for that poor King to whom the Parisians serve today as guardians and jailers.

Forced at last to take leave of me to return to Versailles, the Queen "adjourned the meeting" until the following Sunday at the same time and place.

Oh, my august sovereign, now it is to you alone I whisper: Can you recall both the glamorous setting for those enchanted hours we spent together and the grim, bare stage upon which I was sent to expiate them alone? No matter with what cruelty you later struck me down, you cannot have completely banished those memories from your heart, those nights when you raised me up to share your dizzying heights—or was it you who condescended to my level? No matter which. In my eyes, you sought in vain to shed the traces of imposing majesty—I recognized it even in your moments of most passionate abandon and told myself, "This is the Goddess Flora disporting herself, whiling away an idle hour with a humble floweret!"

MEMOIRS
OF MADAME CAMPAN

"Calumny is a deadlier dose than any poison," the Queen remarked to me one day in the Tuileries, shortly after an attempt to poison her food had been frustrated. "In this century poison has become unfashionable. My enemies will bring about my destruction by calumny instead."

The La Motte memoirs, the first edition and the second, swelled the chorus of hatred and obscenity aimed at the Queen and accelerated its tempo. The Countess's "insatiably curious readers" gobbled up the love letters from the Queen to the Cardinal and the Cardinal to the Queen published in "unexpurgated form, as promised, in the Appendix." Public appetite, whetted by scandalous titbits, called for more.

There were pamphlets, leaflets, brochures, booklets, caricatures. Hawkers cried titles one more licentiously titillating than the others: "The Scandalous Life of Marie Antoinette," "Rustic Scenes at Trianon," "Fureurs Utérines," "The Nymphomania of Marie Antoinette," "A List of All the Persons with Whom the Queen Has Had Debauched Relations" (thirty-four names, including those of princes, actors, musicians, lackeys, the King's brother along with his groom, plus the Duchess de

Polignac, the Princess de Lamballe and the Countess de La Motte, as coryphees of the feminine troupe)—an eructation of such vicious filth that the researcher leafing through the stack of pages written by men long dead about a long-dead woman draws back, sickened, at the rank blast that comes up off the yellowing sheets. (Paris' Bibliothèque Nationale, in recognition of the fact, sets the collection apart, inaccessible even to the scholarly rank and file, in a section referred to formally as la Réserve, less formally as "l'Enfer"—the Inferno.)

Out of all the deluge of calumny, the Countess's offerings proved the most devastating to the reputation of the Queen. In the opinion of Marie Antoinette's biographer Pierre de Nolhac, "The Countess de La Motte's pamphlets caused definitive acceptance of the legend of the Queen's vices." There were other attacks perhaps more obscene, but they were published under noms de plume and therefore were never as pungent and convincing as those signed by a real-life name, a name famous, moreover, throughout Europe ever since the Necklace Trial, the name of an accredited member of the nobility, a scion of the blood royal, a pensioner of the Crown, the intimate of cardinals, princes and Cabinet ministers. Her name on a pamphlet, signed with a flourish, carried conviction.

The leaders of the radical revolutionary parties—Robespierre, Marat, Hébert—were quick to spot the publicity value of the Countess's name and exploits, and they issued her a cordial invitation to come to Paris to appear in the "arena" she had herself suggested, the arena of the courtroom, for a retrial of the Diamond Necklace Case, this time with the Countess on the witness stand and the Queen in the dock. It was tempting.

Royal intelligence agents, scenting danger, investigated rumors that there was an intrigue afoot involving the La Mottes. They reported their suspicions to Mirabeau, the dominant figure of the Assembly, who, though he had discarded his title of Count, was a strong supporter of the cause of constitutional monarchy (his support being attributed by some of the radical members to the King's gold or the Queen's charms).

Mirabeau considered Madame de La Motte's activities as clear and present danger to that cause. In a note to the court, dated November 12, 1789, he wrote:

Change your tactics with the La Motte woman; her arrest would only create fresh scandal. Confine yourselves to keeping an eye on her; find out her plans, connections, resources, ambitions. Crafty as she may be, it should be possible, using some ingenuity, to deceive her by offering her protection and defenders whom she does not suspect. This intrigue, whether the Duke d'Orléans is author of the plot or whether he is merely the agent for Lafayette, is dangerous only if we show ourselves afraid to probe into it. The current agitation to bring Madame de La Motte's case into court for revision of her sentence has an aim more sinister than that of merely stirring up public curiosity and sentiment: a direct attack on the Queen is intended. Her Majesty's firmness and clarity of mind being well known to these conspirators, they consider her the first and strongest defense of the throne; ergo, she must be eliminated first. If these politically artful men succeed in bringing the La Motte case to public trial, in transforming the La Motte woman's libelous charges into "legal proof," they can then claim justification for raising the question of royal divorce proceedings on the Assembly floor, leaving the King only the alternatives of regency or abdication. In this light, the La Motte case becomes a definite threat, forms the very basis of the conspiracy.

The King's expiring government executed Mirabeau's plan of action with surprising ability and success. With almost its last gasp, it talked the Count de La Motte into taking as his lawyer their own man, Marivaux, head of the royal secret police. There is evidence to suggest, however, that the revolutionary agents likewise contacted the Count and that he showed himself equally amenable to their suggestions. It is entirely possible that he sold his services to the highest bidder, or to both. At a moment of touch and go as concerned the political future of France, the Count was providently protecting himself against any and all eventualities: restoration of the Old Regime, constitutional monarchy, republic. His sister-in-law, Marianne, reported from her convent near Paris to the Countess de La Motte in London that her husband was "leading a gay life in Paris, ensconced in a very expensive suite on the second floor of the Palais-Royal."

When the Count himself wrote the Countess to urge her to join him in Paris, it is not clear whether it was at the behest of the revolutionary agents who wanted her there for the retrial of the Necklace Case or at the promptings of lawyer Marivaux in behalf of the counterrevolutionary party, eager to keep her under surveillance and to come to terms with her for her silence. It must have been tempting to her, the thought of returning in open triumph to the city she had departed in shame and by stealth. There were promises of a decree to be enacted by the Assembly, a public "proclamation of valuable services rendered the nation by Madame de La Motte"; there were hints of an official welcome to be rendered her by the city of Paris. All very, very tempting.

And yet the Countess proved very, very wary. In reply to her husband's letter she wrote him:

What I want to know is: If it is true that certain people in high places are so eager to come to terms with me for my silence for the sake of dear 'Toinette, then why do they not come here to London to take up the matter? Why do they insist that I come to Paris instead? The Bastille may be in ruins, but the Salpêtrière still stands—and I'll take no chances on being thrown back into that hellhole of a prison!

In another letter to her husband, dated January 11, 1790, the explanation of why the Countess would not go to Paris to join him takes on a more personal note: "My sister Marianne writes me that people in Paris are saying that you have deserted me, and she elaborates upon the fact with a hundred spicy details."

The Countess confides plaintively to the reader of her Story of My Life:

Alone, destitute, I have been thrown entirely upon my own resources. And despite the sensation my memoirs have created throughout Europe, not a penny of revenue from them comes into my hands. Instead I am dunned by publishers and booksellers to repay them for advances made to the Count—advances, needless to say, in regard to which he kept me entirely in the dark. After the short character sketch I have earlier drawn of my husband for the reader all his blunders, follies and extravagances are self-explanatory.

On May 14 of last year, a month after the Count's departure, a New Bond Street bookseller named Coup descended suddenly upon my house in Chester Place with half a dozen bailiffs in his wake, brandishing a warrant for the seizure of all my household and personal effects to satisfy a claim of three hundred pounds sterling against Monsieur de La Motte—despite the fact that the sale of nine hundred copies of my memoirs, at a guinea apiece, must have netted the man twice the amount of the claim.

Oh, I think I could better bear the curse that blights my life did it not also fall upon every life attached to mine, down to my lowliest dependent. Even faithful Angélique, my fellow prisoner of the Salpêtrière, companion of my flight, was constrained at this juncture to seek other service. As I look back, however, I refuse to believe that her heart prompted her to the action she has taken against me. No, I shall always believe that it was my enemies who took advantage of that simple soul and put her up to suing me for twenty guineas in back wages.

Yet why should I have expected more from that poor creature than from the relatives and friends upon whom I had showered benefits and favors in the days of my prosperity? Alas, when a man loses his fortune, his position, his prestige, he soon discovers that his friends have been swept away along with all the rest. . . . My former friends, to be sure, rationalizing their rejection of me, are ready with a dozen different excuses: the taint of my dishonor would rub off on them; my powerful enemies might become their own; their careers and their children's would be jeopardized. Who could expect such stoicism of a man that he should offer up such weighty considerations as these upon the altar of friendship?

But if there is one person in all the world who owes me gratitude and devotion, it is my sister Marianne. After all I have done for her, to think that she now refuses to share with me in my hour of need that which is actually my own! For the rich revenue she selfishly enjoys today comes to her not through any generous royal gesture but from the proceeds of the sale of my confiscated properties, out of the 35,000 francs cash taken from me at the time of my arrest.*

Here, then, it would seem, the story of my misfortunes should terminate. Have not the executioners consummated the sacrifice of the victim? Has not the victim succumbed to their blows? What more remains to be said?

That the persecution of my enemies continues!

To make me the butt of public ridicule and scorn, I have been spared

---

* "That pious, self-righteous hypocrite of a sister!" is the Countess's less elegant term of reference in a letter for her husband's eye alone. "Only two letters from her in reply to all my pleas for help. In the first, she suggests that she and I finish out our lives together, incognito, in some small Swiss or Italian town where we could live not only cheaply but 'respectably,' 'out of the public eye.' All her offers are based on the one condition: that I write no more memoirs. How ill it becomes her to attach strings to her offers, when everything she has is rightfully mine! She may insist that it is the King who awards her the pension from his privy purse, but only to the extent of what he has snatched from mine."

nothing malice can devise: vulgar cartoons, anonymous letters and, scurviest trick of all, the circulation of scurrilous books and pamphlets over my name such that I blush even to read them. Indeed, I must warn the public to be on guard and to spurn such hoaxes from the pens of my enemies. Falsely attributed to me are such examples as a spurious supplement to my memoirs and a recent leaflet entitled *Address to the National Assembly of France by the Countess de La Motte.*

The leaflet which so outraged the Countess purported to be a "petition for vindication of her honor and restoration to active citizenship," and was printed in London in 1790. By "honor," it was careful to explain for the benefit of the gentlemen of the Assembly, the petitioner did not mean the "sterner virtue which prompts some women to fierce resistance of the advances of the Creator's premier creation, man." Further "clarification" followed:

And as for the qualification "active citizen," who can lay better claim to it than I? You must admit, gentlemen, that it was an activity nothing short of amazing which I displayed, popping in and out of so many beds in such record time in Paris, Trianon and Versailles. Not to mention similar extraordinary amorous activities here in the British Isles. Indeed, from both sides of the Channel you can call in gentlemen to witness that the Countess de La Motte is not only active but has little movements all her own! And a constitution, gentlemen, almost as remarkable as yours.

By its bylaws, then, I beseech you to issue a decree restoring me to the rights and privileges of active citizenship; and I pledge you that I will faithfully live up to the honor every night—I mean every day—of my life, just so long as my youthful charms endure.

STORY OF MY LIFE
BY THE COUNTESS DE LA MOTTE-VALOIS

To protect myself and my public from hoaxes such as these, I shall in the future personally sign every copy of every work I publish.

A fresh rash of libelous pamphlets has erupted here in England in recent months, and there have been newspaper attacks against me more virulent than before, such as the recent story that "the Countess de La

Motte's fondness for memoir-writing for mercenary motives has cost her the affections and patronage of a certain English lord who had hitherto showered her with benefactions." And will my reader find it possible to believe that my relentless enemies, spying upon my every move, have tracked me down to this last poor retreat into which I have crawled to hide from a scornful world?

One day, several weeks ago, hired agitators gathered at the door of this house in which I lodge and put up a hideous racket to intimidate my landlady. "Did you know you are harboring a dangerous character?" they demanded of her. "Did you know that your mysterious female tenant is none other than the notorious Countess de La Motte, who is engaged in libel of the French monarchy? Better get her out if you don't want your name and house involved in an international incident!"

The next day, the same uproar, with warnings to my landlady to chase me out and threats that a French regiment was on its way to carry me off by force. Such threats might well have terrified anyone not conversant with England's policy toward refugees, and this despicable farce might have ended with my being turned out upon the streets had not a gentleman of my acquaintance, an Englishman of some renown, intervened to reassure my trembling hostess.

In my husband's case, physical violence has been succeeded by libel, attempts upon his reputation instead of upon his life: newspaper stories to the effect that "petitions to the Assembly by Monsieur de La Motte are rejected without so much as a reply," a charge constituting more of an insult to that illustrious legislative body than to my husband and me. Those valiant and enlightened representatives of the nation cannot be indifferent to the moans of the oppressed. A Frenchwoman, I love my native land and revere those patriots who work to ensure the nation's welfare and glory. No matter how urgent our claims for justice, I would not want a personal issue to interrupt their deliberations on the constitution, upon which the eyes of all Europe are focused.

And while I wait eagerly, though with my usual resignation, to discover what fate has in store for us, I address myself to the most difficult task I have yet undertaken: the full, unexpurgated story of my life, beginning with my earliest years as beggar girl in rags and tatters, shrinking from a cruel mother's blows, on through the subsequent misfortunes of my life, which, in comparison, would make mere thirst and hunger appear an enviable estate.

In early 1791 the Countess wrote to her husband in Paris:

You may tell your Lawyer Marivaux that the story of my life will ere long be ready for the press. If Marivaux could read it, he would see for himself that it is a new thunderbolt ready to be hurled at the heads of those monsters, those authors of my disgrace. As for your requests to me, my dear, not to go on with this life story "for fear of offending the authorities," I simply cannot understand what you are afraid of. Follow your lawyer's advice yourself, if you like, but don't try to impose it on me. I am still fond of you, to be sure, but in this instance I shall follow my own inclinations. I consider the matter of my life story none of your business.

As for your talk of despair, blowing out your brains and such, I can only say that you are a disgrace to your sex. Act a man! Look at me: I am a walking skeleton, with sorrow gnawing at my vitals (my liver is especially distressful), and yet I would not give my enemies the satisfaction of dying! Courage keeps me alive; above all, it is the hope of seeing my enemies overwhelmed which sustains me.

Not for long. Even with that indomitably vindictive spirit to animate it, her small wiry frame could not survive mortal injuries. But the Countess de La Motte would live to hear and to rejoice at news of "enemies overwhelmed"—in the debacle of Varennes.

MEMOIRS
OF MADAME CAMPAN

In the spring of 1791, four or five months before the flight to Varennes, the Queen began a series of mysterious preparations, giving me a long list of secret commissions which included the packaging of her jewels for forwarding to Belgium. Her personal jewels, that is to say. The crown jewels had already been surrendered to the Assembly in accordance with the decree to that effect, the Queen having delivered them over by her own hand to the commissioner sent to the palace for that purpose—even the Anne of Austria pearls, which, despite the commissioner's protests, Marie Antoinette insisted be considered as national property. "The decision is mine to make, and I have made it" were Her Majesty's noble words.

Her Majesty and I spent one whole evening together in the month of March, packing her jewels. Locked in a study off the stair landing, a small room everlooking the Tuileries Gardens, we spread the jewels out between us on the couch—all her diamonds, rubies, pearls—wrapped them separately in cotton and managed to fit everything into one small-ish box. This was the box that would be entrusted to Léonard, the Queen's hairdresser, whose departure from Paris would be timed to co-incide with hers. Léonard's carriage, it will be remembered, sped through the village of Varennes a bare hour or two before the road block was set up to halt the royal coach; fate would reserve its obstacles for the un-fortunate monarchs.*

From among her personal jewels the Queen kept out only one pearl necklace and a pair of hoop earrings with pear-shaped diamonds. These earrings, along with several other pieces of trifling value, were all the jewels that remained in Her Majesty's dressing table and must have been seized by the committee which took over the Tuileries after the second, fatal attack on August 10.

The Queen did me the honor of confiding the date tentatively set for their momentous project of escape, a day sometime between the fif-teenth and the twentieth of August. She even deigned to express regret that my regularly scheduled term of service with her in the palace did not happen to fall within that period, thus precluding my accompanying her on the expedition. Instead, she explained, she was arranging for me to join her as soon as she reached the border, and she insisted that Mon-sieur Campan and I leave Paris before news of their flight could break. She was fearful that there would be rioting and that all connected with the monarchy would be in danger.

But on the eve of my departure with my father-in-law for our Au-vergne mountain retreat all my fears were for my sovereign and her pre-carious undertaking. I was somehow not overly sanguine as to the suc-cess of it; I feared that by treachery or bad luck it might come to disaster.

Disaster came by bad luck rather than by treachery, but primarily it came by botching, by bungling, by overemphasis on just such frivolous

* "The Queen's jewel box," Madame Campan added, "remained for long years in Brussels, where Léonard had delivered it, and came at last into the hands in which it belonged, those of the Queen's only surviving child, her daughter; the Austrian Emperor turned over the mother's jewels to the girl years later, when she finally reached Vienna."

trivia as Madame Campan has described. If only the rubies, the diamonds and the pearls and Léonard's curling irons had been jettisoned—if only the royal caravan had traveled light, swiftly and on schedule—the escape might have been carried out successfully. But then, the whole piteous fiasco must be written off in one long agonizing subjunctive of had-onlys and might-have-beens.

The tolling of tocsins, the rataplan of drums sounded the news of the royal family's frustrated flight and capture at Varennes on June 21, 1791 —a signal that the monarchy was now clearly and openly the prisoner of the people and was doomed, and that the Republic was looming up. France had not realized these facts, had not understood where the Revolution was going, until Varennes.

Madame Campan's heart broke with the news, as her memoirs tell it. She was in the Auvergne mountains on the afternoon of June 25, making ready for her journey to Brussels to join the Queen, when she heard the news "proclaimed, to a tattoo of drums, by a messenger shouting, 'I come to bring you the joyful word that the royal family has been caught and arrested, and a hundred thousand armed men are standing guard!' "

If she hoped against hope that the report of their capture might be untrue, the grim truth was confirmed in a letter that came to her

. . . on June 28, from Paris, bearing no signature, but in a handwriting which I recognized, and dated June 25, the day of the Queen's return from Varennes. Her Majesty's message read:

> We have just arrived. I write you from my bath, where I try to find some repose and comfort for my weary body. As to our state of mind, I will refrain from comment. We are still alive—and that is about the most that can be said for us . . .

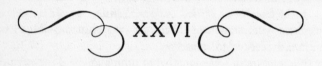

XXVI

The Fate of the Principals

(1791-1803)

I WAS BASKING in the delights of retirement in my natal village of Bruyères when the French Revolution broke out, shaking the carefully constructed edifice of my tranquil way of life to its foundations and expelling me from the earthly paradise I had created there for myself. But how could I hesitate to sacrifice it all and emigrate, when the alternative was to take an impious oath [the required oath to observe the 1790 Assembly-decreed Civil Constitution of the Clergy] by which I would abjure the holy bonds of allegiance to Church and King?

The historian who seeks to describe these events finds himself wandering, disorientated, among the ruins of the finest monarchy in Europe. The ruffian cries of "Liberty" and "Equality" have so deranged men's minds that the gentlest, most polished, most highly civilized people of the universe has become overnight a people of ravening tigers and anthropophagi: citizen slakes his thirst on the blood of fellow citizen, daggers smoke from the murder of a thousand victims, the guillotine's corpses are stacked high in gory piles; the most precious and most illustrious blood of France gushes forth to drench its soil.

O France, my native land, what a spectacle you present to a stunned universe! Here in Germany, land of my exile, I find that I have neither the strength nor the talent to undertake a history of this horrendous Revolution, which can be writ only by a pen dipped in tears and blood.

Despite this protestation of inadequacy the abbé promptly took up his pen and proceeded to the redaction of copious notes for that very history, six volumes of "memoirs by an unprejudiced observer to serve as a history of the late eighteenth century." Taking refuge in Freiburg in 1793, Georgel dedicated himself to this work and to "a life of pious devotions" until the year 1799, when, at the age of seventy, affairs of State and Church reclaimed his peculiar talents for a mission to the Court of St. Petersburg on business of the Knights Hospitalers with Czar Paul I, who accorded Georgel a cordial and flattering reception and also that order's Maltese Cross and a suitable pension to accompany the decoration.

The abbé, later given an equally cordial and flattering reception at the court of Louis XVIII in exile at Mitau, was discouraged from paying further homage to that émigré monarch by reason of a contretemps involving Marie Antoinette's daughter, Marie Thérèse Charlotte, by then the Duchess d'Angoulême, who visibly blanched, quivered and turned away her head when he was presented, her memory stabbed by the very mention of his name, by his connection with Cardinal Rohan and the diamond necklace affair, with all its fatal repercussions for her martyred mother.

Georgel returned to France after Waterloo and the second Bourbon Restoration and rejected a proffered bishopric to accept the humbler duties of provicar general of the bishopric of Nancy, "to which post he devoted his unflagging zeal and sterling executive talents until his death in 1813 at the age of eighty-three," according to his nephew-executor, who, entrusted with the manuscript of the Georgel memoirs, published them in 1817; the author himself had been unwilling to do so during his lifetime, "lest slumbering passions be thereby aroused."

Georgel's reluctance to rehash the old necklace scandal was not out of consideration for the "mighty personage" of the Cardinal Prince de Rohan, whom he had survived by ten years. The abbé had kind words to say of that former friend and patron's latter days:

The Revolution had caused Cardinal Rohan to abandon France [in 1790] for his estates on the right bank of the Rhine, where he led a frugal and modest life, generously sharing the benefits that remained to him with French priests who had emigrated in distress and poverty to the German territories of which he was sovereign prince. Far from the tumult and intrigues of the court, Cardinal Rohan consecrated himself heart and soul to the welfare of his diocese and his subjects.

Cardinal-Bishop Prince de Rohan, as it developed, could no more pronounce the words of the oath to the Civil Constitution of the Clergy than could his fellow cleric Georgel. The Cardinal had been nominated by the clergy of Hagenau as its deputy to the States-General convoked by the King in Versailles in 1789, and he had taken his seat in the National Assembly two months after the fall of the Bastille. The Assembly had shown a disposition to enshrine him among its early Revolutionary heroes as a signal victim of despotism and court intrigue, but he had declined to capitalize on his involvement in the diamond necklace incident. After passage of the bill decreeing the Civil Constitution of the Clergy, he had signaled his dissent by withdrawal, not only from his seat on the benches of the legislature but from French soil altogether, to his estates at Ettenheim, in Baden, across the Rhine from Strasbourg —where Georgel has described him in the midst of his pastoral life and duties, "a man no longer stirred by any ambition save the noble one of service to his fellow man."

Pope Pius VI himself, in a letter written in April 1791, would "commend his dear son Cardinal Rohan for his episcopal valor in denunciation of perfidious anticlerical legislation—for the heroism of his conduct in voluntarily renouncing his native land and his great birthrights in defense of the Mother Church." Pontifical encomiums more glowing still were to appear in the Pope's pastoral letters published toward the end of the century (perhaps in compensation for his public castigation of the Cardinal during the days of the Necklace Trial scandal):

The Rohan establishment at Ettenheim was turned into one vast seminary, where the bishop himself mingled with the hundreds of French ecclesiastics flocking across the border. His Eminence sat beside them at table, shared their meager fare and consecrated all his revenues to the maintenance of that multitude of refugees. Thus Cardinal Rohan renounced all the splendor that once heralded the foremost prince of the realm and the century, to take his place on the world stage as the

simple servant of Jesus, indistinguishable from the other priests about
him save for his greater ardor and humility.

There in Ettenheim, full of good works and in a veritable odor of
sanctity, Cardinal Prince Louis de Rohan died in 1803. The young Duke
d'Enghien, his niece's husband and the last of the Condés, was at his
deathbed and later wrote home, "Cardinal Rohan, fully conscious as he
took the last sacraments, died a death so noble as to be truly edifying to
all present—a fact that may astonish you as much as it did me."

Even more astonishing—in view of Cardinal Rohan's volte-face from
the fleshpots to the viaticum, from the liberal republicanism of Cagliostro's Masonic ideology to the ultraconservative, promonarchical, pro-
clerical side, in view of his estrangement from former intimates such as
Baron da Planta, Ramon de Carbonnières and the Abbé Georgel—was
the fact that his loyalty to Count Cagliostro personally continued unim-
paired, long after the trial, long after the time of illusions was past.
Cardinal Rohan in late 1789 could still write with all his original ardor
in behalf of his friend in need, in a letter addressed to the Archbishop
of Lyons:

MONSEIGNEUR:
You have often heard me speak of the Count Cagliostro, and you
know that I have consistently extolled his humanitarian endeavors, those
superior qualities, those virtues of his which won him the esteem of the
most distinguished personages of Alsace and in my case a deep personal
attachment.

I cannot highly enough recommend this benevolent soul to your favor.
It has been with actual veneration that I have, through the years, observed his unswerving adherence to the principles he holds to be righteous and just.

I have told you enough to ensure him a cordial reception at your
hands, but I have not actually even begun to tell you all the good I
know and think of him. . . .

But his letter of recommendation, dated December 7, came too late;
by December 29, 1789, Cagliostro was locked hard and fast in the papal
Castel Sant' Angelo.

The wonder of it is how Cagliostro, foremost prophet of Masonry in Europe, founder of lodges across the Continent, "grandmaster of the godless craft" and, as such, "revolutionary agent" and "Antichrist"—how Cagliostro ever came to the decision to beard the papal lion in his den of Rome. Was it some secret revolutionary or Masonic oath or "charge" that exacted some secret mission of him there? Or the man's desperate choice of death by martyrdom in preference to immortality as a buffoon?

Cagliostro, quitting France in 1786 after the necklace trial, by exile order of the King, had taken refuge first in England. But even that "sanctuary of the out-of-date" had failed him: the Scottish Rite lodges repudiated the Grand Cophta of the Egyptian Lodge and publicly derided him with a wickedly malicious cartoon and a jingle. So, "his glamour torn, his mysteries in rags, and, worst of all, hopelessly unfashionable," as William Bolitho writes, "Cagliostro totters out of history. He and his Serafina set off from London, rolling like dismasted caravels in strange seas."

They came first to Basel, to the banker Sarrasin, whose debt of gratitude to Cagliostro ("for having bestowed on him the blessings of a belated paternity," Cagliostro had told the Parliament of Paris) was so great "that he would give me the whole of his fortune were I to ask him for it." Under Sarrasin's auspices Cagliostro founded "the Mother Lodge of the Helvetic States," but this Swiss refuge would not be his for long. For reasons unknown (unless it was police persecution), the Cagliostros moved on to Turin, where "the Count had no sooner set foot than he was ordered to leave it instantly."

The next report is from Vicenza, where his Countess was "obliged to pawn a diamond of value." (In hardship and poverty, Serafina's beauty vanished with her jewels; "nothing was left of her but her eyes.") There was rumor of a lodge founded in the obscure village of Roveredo, in the Austrian Tyrol, but soon abandoned by the Grand Cophta at the urging of the local constabulary, after the publication of a stinging little satire entitled "The Gospel According to St. Cagliostro."

In Trent he found another prince bishop who was, like Rohan, a seeker after the philosopher's stone. But from Emperor Joseph came swift orders expelling Count Cagliostro from Austrian soil.

No fanfare of trumpets now; all the clouds of incense and Oriental splendor had been dissipated in the mean, dreary and sordid peregrination from frontier to frontier that was traceable only by a paper trail of pretentious Masonic prospectuses, of police warrants and expulsion orders, back to its point of origin, the city of Rome. Was it Serafina's homing instinct, with Rome as the only place she could think of to pick up her bearings? That theory does not seem good enough to account for such a desperation measure; more convincing is the theory that the one-time star performer, reluctant to abandon the boards and join the ranks of the supernumeraries, settled for the role of corpse, his only proviso being that it lie at center stage.

The incontrovertible fact is that the Cagliostros re-entered the Papal States toward the end of the year 1789, and that there, engaged on some obscure Masonic mission, they were apprehended by the agents of the Inquisition and locked away pending trial.

"Cagliostro on trial in Rome," says the Paris Moniteur in December of that year, "evoked as much interest in the Eternal City as he had formerly done in the French capital. Interception of a cryptic message from him to an Italian priest led to the detection of a conspiracy to overthrow the Papacy."

At any rate, the papal government thus justified its series of mysterious arrests, its doubling of the guard at the Vatican and its dispatch of troops to surround the Castel Sant' Angelo. Of course, it may well have been the papal government itself which spread the rumor linking Cagliostro with the French revolutionaries, the rumor that his followers in Rome were pledged to rescue him by setting fire to the Castel Sant' Angelo. At the time, the Moniteur reported, there was even talk of exiling all French citizens from Rome.

Although the verdict of the Inquisition court could never have been in doubt at a moment when two papal bulls were issued decreeing Freemasonry a crime punishable by death, still the Cagliostro trial dragged on for almost two years. Though the forms of justice were observed, Cagliostro's privilege of choosing two legal defenders was a mockery; his choice was confined to a pair of officials appointed by the apostolic court, whose defense of him consisted solely of the advice that he acknowledge his guilt and throw himself upon the mercy of the court. (The Inquisition, a byword in every language of the world for torture and religious tyranny, justified the stigma more than ever in the eighteenth century, when the Church found itself in mortal contest with world revolution, anticlericalism and Freemasonry.)

At his first hearing before the apostolic court, Cagliostro's spirit was not yet broken, as we know from an account by one of the Inquisition judges who later turned biographer, writing of the man upon whom he had sat in judgment:

He [Cagliostro] burst into invectives against the court of France, to which he attributed all the misfortunes he had experienced in the Bastille. And when told that his wife had confessed and testified against him, he denounced her as a traitress . . . [but later] burst into tears, expressed the liveliest tenderness for her and implored the favor of having her as his companion in his cell. One may well imagine that this request was not granted.*

When, after months of imprisonment, questioning and possibly torture, Cagliostro "confessed that Freemasonry was a veritable crime, and contrary to the Catholic religion, no one believed him," the biographer-judge relates, "and if he flattered himself on recovering his liberty by this means, he was mistaken." Later the prisoner declared that "everything he had done in his life had been done with the consent of the Almighty." He demanded to be brought before the Pope: " 'If His Holiness would but hear me, I prophesy I would be set at liberty this very night,' " the court biographer further quotes the prisoner. Cagliostro confessed, retracted and "confessed again, drowning the truth in a flood of words." As to his religious convictions, the Inquisition judge continues: "Cagliostro replied that his beliefs were those of the enlightened men of his century." Questioned further, the prisoner declared that he believed "all religions to be good, and that providing one believed in the existence of a Creator and the immortality of the soul, it mattered not whether one was Catholic, Lutheran, Calvinist or Jew." And as to his political opinions, "he confessed to a hatred of tyranny, especially all forms of religious intolerance."

On March 21, 1791, the Holy Office rendered its verdict. The judges of the apostolic court, unlike those of the Parliament of Paris, had been unamused by their prisoner's antics; his oratory had evoked no glimmer of a smile on their grim faces, and their verdict was grim, deadly serious:

Giuseppe Balsamo, otherwise known as Count di Cagliostro, attainted and convicted of many crimes, and of having incurred the censures and penalties pronounced against heretics, dogmatics, heresiarchs and propagators of magic and superstition, has been found guilty and condemned to the said censures and penalties as decreed by the apostolic laws of

* Translated from Vie de Joseph Balsamo (Paris, 1791), which in turn was translated from the original Italian.

Clement XII and Benedict XIV against all persons who in any manner whatever favor or form societies and conventicles of Freemasonry, in Rome or in any of the dominions of the Pope.

Nothwithstanding, by special grace, the sentence of death is hereby commuted to perpetual imprisonment in a fortress, where the culprit is to be strictly guarded, without any hope whatsoever of pardon.

The manuscript book "Egyptian Masonry" is solemnly condemned as containing rites and principles . . . which open a road to sedition and destruction of the Christian religion. This book, therefore, shall be burned by the executioner.

By a new apostolic law, we shall confirm and renew not only the laws of previous pontiffs which prohibit the societies of Freemasonry, but we shall also decree that the most grievous corporal punishments shall be inflicted on all who associate with these societies.

The papacy intended the sentence against Cagliostro as a sentence against Freemasonry, as a declaration of a war in which no quarter would be given.

The Countess Cagliostro's sentence was, likewise, imprisonment for life—in Rome's penitentiary for women, the Convent of St. Appolonia, where, rumor had it, she died in 1794.

The publication in 1791 of the Inquisition judge's "biography" of Cagliostro (or Giuseppe Balsamo, as the anonymous author called him) stirred up a hornet's nest in Europe; a Masonic pamphlet published in riposte "produced such a sensation throughout Italy, and particularly in Rome," according to the Paris Moniteur, that "the Conclave, terrified at the revolutionary fury it had aroused, instructed its agents to buy up every copy they could find."

Rumors as to the fate of Cagliostro ran riot. One day he was reported to have committed suicide in his cell; the next, to be chained to the wall, a raving maniac. A story made the rounds that he had predicted the fall of the papacy and that he expected the Roman populace to march on the Castel Sant' Angelo to deliver him. The Moniteur relates that during a night of terrible storm "all Rome was stricken with fear as if the end of the world had come, and Cagliostro, mistaking the thunder for the cannon of insurgents, was heard shouting, 'Here I am—here! Come deliver me!'"

In any event, the papal government decided to remove its troublesome prisoner to safety; he was secretly transferred "in the middle of the night" from the banks of the Tiber to the dread fortress reserved for heretics and radicals, Castel San Leo, almost inaccessible on its rocky eyrie near Montefeltro in the Apennines.

A Napoleonic agent was later to describe San Leo:

Its galleries were cut out of solid rock and divided into cells, and old dried-up cisterns had been converted into dungeons for the more dangerous criminals. It was in one of these cisterns that the celebrated Count Cagliostro was interred alive in 1791. The Holy Office had taken care that commutation of the death sentence should be tantamount to the death penalty. Cagliostro's only communication with mankind came when his jailers raised the trap door to his dungeon to lower food to him. Here he languished for three years without air, movement, or intercourse with fellow human beings. During the last months of his life his condition excited the pity of the prison governor, who removed him to a ground-level cell, in which the curious visitor may read inscriptions and sentences traced upon the walls by the unhappy alchemist; the last bears the date March 6, 1795.

On October 6, 1795, the Moniteur carried a report that Cagliostro was dead, adding that Roman gossip hinted at the probability that "his jailers had put him out of his misery."

In 1797, during the French Army's invasion of the Papal States, Cagliostro's prison of San Leo was taken by the Polish Legion. The first act of the officers was to search for Cagliostro, who was regarded as a martyr in the cause of liberty.

"They thought to rescue him," writes Figuier, "and perhaps even to give him an ovation similar to that he received in Paris after his acquittal by the Parliament in the Diamond Necklace Trial. But they had arrived too late; Cagliostro, the jailers declared, had recently died."

According to another, and more macabre, version of the French capture of San Leo, the officers demanded to be shown Cagliostro's grave and, having exhumed his skeleton, filled the skull with wine and toasted his memory as a martyr of the French Revolution.

The mystery that had enshrouded Cagliostro's life veiled his death as well.

Among those whose imagination has run riot on this theme, Madame Anna Blavatsky, founder of the Theosophical Society in London in the 1800s, offers the most colorful version: that Cagliostro had escaped from

San Leo into Russia, where he resided for some time at her father's home and where she saw him "produce in the midst of winter a plate of fresh strawberries to satisfy the whim of an invalid who had expressed a craving for that fruit."

The Abbé Georgel's imagination was less undisciplined than Madame Blavatsky's, yet he too betrayed an obsession on the subject of Cagliostro, on the recondite implications of the man's philosophy and its influence on the times; Cagliostro's Masonic mission loomed up on Georgel's Jesuit horizon in the form of that perennial bugaboo, the world-wide conspiracy. So Georgel states it in his memoirs:

The great conspiracy against throne and altar had its beginnings in the reign of Louis XV. It brewed its poisons and sharpened its poniards in the shadowy meeting halls of the Encyclopedists and economists, in the lodges of the Illuminati and the Freemasons. . . .

Personally, I am convinced that Madame de La Motte spoke a highly significant truth when she hinted that Cagliostro, beyond any other man alive, held the key to the enigma: knowledge of the secret motives behind it all [the Necklace Case]. And perhaps I myself should respect that secrecy, out of consideration for the men who risked their lives to preserve the veils of mystery. Never a word relative to it was spoken by Cagliostro or by Cardinal Rohan or by the Baron da Planta or by the Cardinal's secretary, young Ramon de Carbonnières, or by any other of their confidants or initiates. This secrecy is all the more astonishing in view of the fact that these same men came later to be alienated—to the point of open hostility after the Revolution.

Cagliostro's Egyptian Lodge had doubtlessly, like Freemasonry, its impenetrable sanctuary and formidable oaths beneath which its secrets lay forever buried.

That Goethe was likewise obsessed with Cagliostro and his mysteries, with the significance of Cagliostro's connection with the Necklace Case —and the connection of the Necklace Case, in turn, with the Revolution—we know from Carlyle, who said that Goethe was "in a state of mind alarming to his friends." The German scientific and literary genius, his curiosity not yet satisfied despite an assiduous correspondence with Baron de Breteuil on the subject, pursued the investigation in Palermo, personally tracking down the story of Cagliostro's identification with Balsamo, as he himself describes in his Travels in Italy.

Goethe, a Mason (very possibly a Rosicrucian, one of the Illuminati), could not have been unaware that the Masonic mission in the eighteenth century was revolution, the overthrow of the despotism of both King and Church. He saw dark portents in the diamond necklace affair, because he read into it far more than the surface significance, far more than a clever jewel theft and a sordid intrigue: "The affair is as horrifying to me as a sight of the Medusa's head. The intrigue was utterly destructive to royal dignity. The Necklace Case is the prelude to revolution."

Dumas, romanticizing Cagliostro as the "liberator," the grandmaster of Masonry and the architect of the French Revolution, represented the occult Masonic ideal as the great motivating influence of the revolutionary age. And for the latter theory there exists some foundation in fact: although Freemasonry maintained an official silence on its role in both the American and the French Revolutionary movements, the Masonic hand is clearly discernible in both; in both France and in America, the list of self-acknowledged Masons reads like a roll call of the great Revolutionary leaders. The lodges in both nations were closely allied: General Lafayette had been initiated in America by General (and Grandmaster) George Washington himself; Benjamin Franklin, "champion of Masonry and its living symbol," used his long years of residence in France unofficially to forward the Masonic cause as zealously as any of his official diplomatic missions. Freemasonry in America tacitly acknowledged its responsibility in the French Revolution; the excesses thereof, deplored by Masonic leaders on both sides of the Atlantic, dealt a serious blow to Freemasonry in the United States.

The mind of a man with a deep strain of mysticism, a mind like Goethe's, might easily have become involved in esoteric ramifications. The Freemasons, as Goethe knew, considered themselves the spiritual heirs of the Knights Templar, who considered themselves the spiritual heirs of the priests of the Temple of Solomon and, through them, the priests of Luxor and Karnak. If Freemasonry was the repository of the arcanum for that particular eighteenth-century world, then was it in a divine design and destiny that the agents of the brotherhood were employed?

While Carlyle's approach was certainly not that of a mystic, still he sensed something contrived in the diamond necklace affair in its relation to the French Revolution; he caught the trace of a supernatural agency: "Perhaps the upper powers, minded that a new chapter in universal history shall begin here and not farther on, may have ordered it all." He may have been thinking in terms of the deus ex machina, the stage machinery of Greek drama by which the figure of a god was lowered onto the stage for the purpose of resolving the dramatic action when that action had bogged down and the human protagonists appeared incapable of bringing it to its inevitable denouement.

The long-overdue denouement that was the Revolution in France, for example. All the necessary elements and causations of revolution were present in 1785: absolute monarchy, incompetent, despotic, despised; a galling and outmoded feudal system with its castes, privileges, burdensome tributes; anticlericalism and antimonarchism, ideological preparation by reform-philosophers Rousseau, Voltaire, the Encyclopedists; injustice, inequality, poverty and even, presently, famine; and yet action had bogged down, had hopelessly stalled. Here was the classic situation calling for the introduction upon the scene of the deus ex machina, the definition of which further reads: "any contrivance for dramatic presentation, especially, a supernatural agency."

Might the Greek stage prop have been symbolic, suggestive of a divine agency, messengers of the gods or of God? Agents, acting consciously or unconsciously in effecting divine missions? The Oriental religions, Buddhism and Confucianism, state the proposition, as do theosophy and Freemasonry.

A proposition which might have brought Goethe to the ultimate question in his enduring mental debate on the historical and occult significance of the diamond necklace affair and of Cagliostro: Was Cagliostro to be considered such an agent of destiny in the Diamond Necklace Case, in the Revolution? And if so, acting consciously or unconsciously? An imperfect prophet, with psychic powers imperfectly understood even by himself, and so indiscreetly practiced?

The Rosicrucians and the Illuminati at the time, and the theosophists in the early twentieth century, resorted to such extravagant terms as "prophet," "adept" and "apostle" in description of Cagliostro and offered an esoteric explanation for his guarding the secret of his origins from the judges of both the Parliament of Paris and the Inquisition— even at the cost of his life.

An agent conscious of his role of destiny? The Countess de La Motte in her Story of My Life supplied an answer with the ring of truth to it when, commenting on Cagliostro's imprisonment in Castel Sant' Angelo (news of which had reached her in London in early 1791), she wrote gloatingly that he was "unlikely ever to emerge from that grim fortress unless to be led out to the scaffold upon the public square, there to fulfill that high destiny upon which he always claimed he had been sent into the world."

These glad tidings of another of her "enemies overwhelmed" reached the Countess de La Motte in London just a month or two before "the vengeance of heaven" struck upon her wicked head—which was the Abbé Georgel's interpretation of her untidy end and was taken by him as his text in this passage in his memoirs:

As for Madame de La Motte, that viper who hissed out her venom in a series of malicious memoirs, she did not live long to enjoy the fruits of evil. She perished in London in a fatal accident: during a night of orgy and debauch she was thrown out of a third-story window to the street below. The vengeance of heaven strikes upon the heads of the wicked when human justice proves too lenient or too slow.

The abbé's fire-and-brimstone version of the Countess's final catastrophe is contradicted by that of the lady's husband, as it appeared in the posthumously published memoirs of the Count de La Motte:

It was not, as first reported in the British newspapers, a London bailiff come to arrest the Countess on a court order for debt but the secret agents of the Duke d'Orléans who terrified my wife and drove her to such desperate measures of self-defense when she found herself a hapless pawn in his sinister game—to get her to Paris as a witness against Marie Antoinette, which was considered essential to the Orléans conspiracy to seize the throne from the Bourbons.

Their schemes thus far frustrated by the Countess's refusal to set foot off English shores, the Duke's henchmen conceived the plan of contriving her arrest on trumped-up charges of debt, on the premise that once they had her in their clutches they could coerce her to play their game by promises to arrange her release and by assurances of a public triumph over her enemies in Paris.

To this evil purpose, one of these ruthless men went before a justice of the peace and swore upon the Holy Bible that Madame de La Motte owed him one hundred guineas. Armed with a warrant for her arrest, they presented themselves at her door and notified her that she must follow them. She knew not so much as the name of the devil who had brought false witness against her; and besides, had she actually incurred such a debt, she would not have been liable to arrest, since it is legally the husband who stands responsible for his wife. Madame de La Motte was sufficiently well informed upon the laws of the land to have recognized that fact, but she would have had to furnish proof that she was a married woman, and unfortunately she had not her marriage papers with her—all her family documents had been confiscated in 1785 in the Bastille.

When these villains insisted on leading her off with them, she warned them that if they resorted to force she would throw herself upon the mercy of the English populace, who were certain to rise to her defense. Meanwhile she found opportunity to send her maid running off to fetch her lawyer instantly to defend her and to serve as guarantor, whispering to the girl that if she could not find said lawyer she was to make a certain signal as she returned to the house so that Madame de La Motte would be forewarned and could determine what step to take in that eventuality.

While the maid rushed off upon this errand, the Countess, playing desperately for time, enacted the role of solicitous hostess: she set out a collation and a choice bottle of Oporto wine and walked around and around the table, carrying on a sprightly conversation, all the while keeping an eye upon the window and the street in an anxious lookout for the maid's return.

At long last that girl reappeared, but she was unaccompanied by the legal counselor and gave the preappointed signal to inform her mistress that hope for help from that quarter was to be abandoned. So the Countess, watching her chances, finally made her move: she rushed suddenly out the door, slamming and bolting it behind her.

If only the Countess had not panicked, she might have leaped into one of the public conveyances on the street and driven to safety in another canton of London where the arrest order would not have been applicable. But instead of availing herself of this tactic, she made a mad dash for the adjoining house, never suspecting that her tormentors were spying on her every move through an open window.

In no time, these bravos were battering at the neighbor's door, demanding that he yield up their prey. The proprietor, a friend of my poor wife's, insisted that he was harboring no fugitive and that he knew no one by the name of Madame de La Motte, to which the intruders replied that if he spoke the truth and they failed to find her on his premises, they would suffer the legal consequences and pay the penalty for illegal entry. This was how they bullied their way in to ransack the house. A search of the ground floor and the first floor having availed them naught, they climbed up to the second story, with the proprietor following behind, still protesting loudly. Coming finally to a locked door, the housebreakers demanded it be opened to them. Vainly did the homeowner explain that that particular room was rented out and that the tenant had the only key; the Orléans agents, convinced that Madame de La Motte was concealed behind that door, threatened to break it down.

Madame de La Motte, who was actually hiding in that room, heard the threats and was convinced that it was all a plot to drag her forcibly back to France to a second cruel incarceration. That was the point at which she completely lost her head. Opening the window, she slipped through the aperture and out, to dangle by her hands from an iron bar on the window grating—desperate, determined to let go her hold and hurl herself to the street below should her pursuers succeed in forcing the door.

Unfortunately, the door was made of light-weight wood, and the attackers encountered little difficulty in kicking out the panels. The moment Madame de La Motte saw the heads of her enemy appear through the door, she relaxed her grasp on the window railing and fell to the pavement three stories below.

It was her misfortune not to have been killed outright, for she had suffered mortal injuries: her hip fractured in two places, her left arm splintered, one eye half out of its socket, her whole body shattered. In this piteous state she lingered on for several weeks. Indomitable as was her spirit, she actually expected to recover from the fatal accident, according to a fairly lengthy letter I received from her at the time, describing the details of the tragedy and announcing her plans for a removal to the country, where she hoped to convalesce.

Thus came death, at the age of thirty-five, to a woman whose entire history was one of misery and calamity. She might have lived out a normal life span and ended her days in tranquillity and content had not the peculiar distinction of her ancestry gone to her head, causing her delusions of grandeur that were responsible for the overweening pride and ambition which brought her to disaster.

Despite the Count de La Motte's claim to having received a letter from his wife during her last illness, his account may carry little more weight than Georgel's, for, never having bestirred himself to travel to

London to the bedside of his Countess, he may have known no more than what he read in the newspapers or heard the newsvendors shrilling out beneath the windows of his Palais-Royal suite.

The only firsthand bedside bulletins turned up years later among the papers of a gentleman named Longchamps, officially a Paris Postal Department administrator, unofficially a secret agent of the royalist party, assigned to contact the Countess to dissuade her from publication of her latest, most ambitious literary project, the two-volume Story of My Life, for which prepublication announcements had appeared in the London newspapers during the early summer months of 1791.

There was no time to lose, and on the eve of Varennes the royalist cause could ill afford another blast of scandal against the Queen from the pen of that best-seller authoress. Monsieur de Longchamps, presuming on a somewhat better than nodding acquaintance with the Countess, opened correspondence with her by a letter introducing his emissary, a certain Monsieur Bertrand, who was en route to London.

One week before Varennes, on June 13, Bertrand mailed his first report of the Countess de La Motte's accident, which had occurred the night before his arrival in London. In his search for her, he had been directed to a street near Westminster Bridge, to the home of a Mr. Warren, a perfumer by trade, the Good Samaritan who had picked up the Countess's mangled body from the road.

According to Bertrand's first report to Longchamps:

From the moment I entered the room where she lay, Madame de La Motte began to play upon my sympathies, lifting the bedclothes to show me her frightful injuries. I have never seen anything so horrible. Her thigh is broken, both legs in splints, her entire body black and blue. The surgeon was obliged to make incisions to allow suppuration.

On June 21, Longchamps received a letter from Warren the perfumer (and reluctant host):

I simply have not the means to continue caring for this desperately ill woman, with the constant expenses of doctors and nurses—not to mention bed linen. My duties as a husband and father must supersede those of friendship and charity.

By June 23 the news of Varennes had reached Paris, whence it flashed on and across the Channel to England. It was news momentous enough to rouse the Countess de La Motte to struggle up on her pillows, to hear and to savor every last gruesome detail of the indignities suffered by the royal family in their capture and their long, slow, prisoner's progress back to the capital, tongue-lashed, openly insulted, heaped under with contumely, soiled with their own sweat and others' spittle. News of such cruel retribution to the Queen of France gave the Countess strength to hang on to life.

But the news also meant that, the royalist cause being lost and the royalist party in confusion, no funds were forthcoming for Longchamps to forward to London; nor was he likely to go into his own, despite Bertrand's urgent entreaties:

The Countess is destitute; she says she must have immediate assistance if we want her to hold off any longer on distribution of her life story. She claims to have no other source of revenue. I keep trying to persuade her to postpone action on issuing the edition, with the promise that you will take care of her, but I am as astonished as she at receiving no word from you in all this time.

The Story of My Life had come off the press, six thousand copies: four thousand in French for the Paris bookshops, a thousand for Holland, and a thousand copies of the English translation for sale in London.

The Countess was committed by a recent pledge to her readers to sign her name to every copy. That herculean task Bertrand managed to persuade her to postpone from day to day, but by July 29 he was reporting to Paris that Warren was becoming more and more nervous:

It is easy to see that the only thing that keeps him even civil to Madame de La Motte is the fear that she will not reimburse him for what she has cost him to date. She made me such a scene yesterday as required all my courage to endure. I tone it down considerably in this report.

She said we were trying to cheat her of her hard-earned bread, that proceeds from the sale of her life story were her sole means of subsistence, that we were trying to rob her of even that, and that she held us responsible for her terrible plight and would have her revenge for this latest perfidy on the part of her old enemies.

"What faith can I have in your lies?" she demanded. "Tell your friends in Paris that as of tomorrow morning I start signing the copies of my life story!"

I let her cries and tears pass in silence. At that moment the fever came on her and her body was racked with trembling from head to foot.

I have given you only a hint, the barest outline of this overpowering scene.

Then, by letter of August 5: "The patient is nearing an end . . ." On August 26 both the Courier and the Chronicle of London carried the death notices: "Jeanne de Saint-Rémy de Valois, Countess de La Motte, on Tuesday, August 23, 1791, at eleven o'clock in the evening . . ."

And: "Burial in the churchyard of St. Mary's, Lambeth, on August 26 . . ." (The parish register records that tongue-twister of a Gallic name as "Jean St. Rymer de Valois."

Not that finis is thereby written to the life of the Countess de La Motte-Valois. Like Cagliostro, she constituted newspaper copy too good to be so easily relinquished by the yellow press. Furthermore, many of her contemporaries not only found the circumstances incident to her fatal fall mysterious (murder? suicide? accident?) but seemed suspicious even as to whether she had actually expired in London in 1791, pointing out that the line in St. Mary's parish register was not proof conclusive that she lay beneath its sod; and so sensational stories on her account continued to circulate throughout Europe. It was entirely credible to the general public that, with so many powerful, fanatic enemies on her trail, the Countess might have expressly obscured it by false death reports to escape to safety and anonymity in some remote region of the earth. If the general public had been uncertain as to what to make of the Countess de La Motte from what it had read of her prior to her reported demise, it was likewise uncertain as to what to believe thereafter. Irrepressible, never a one to subside beneath a mere spadeful of sod in a Lambeth churchyard, the Countess would be joining Cagliostro as a revenant well into the next century.

Mr. Warren, the Countess's last and reluctant earthly host, promptly addressed himself to the widower in Paris: "I had your wife buried in Lambeth Churchyard, but reserved the right for her family and friends, if they are so disposed, to erect a monument over the remains of the most affectionate Wife, Sister and Friend that ever lived."

Failing to elicit a response, Warren sent off an itemized statement of expenses incurred in the Countess's last illness. But he had still not struck the responsive chord in the heart of the Count, who preferred to pay to his wife's memory another kind of graceful tribute, one far less costly than a monument, the annexation of her patronymic at the cost of a mere hyphen, neat and stylish, small: Count de La Motte-Valois henceforward. (The gloom of his mourning period was considerably brightened, according to that omniscient, omnipresent Paris correspondent of the Court of St. Petersburg, by the charms of "la Seymour," a renowned Parisian courtesan better known to the profession as "la Belle Impure.")

By the late fall or early winter of that year of the Countess's death, the four thousand autographed French-language copies of her Story of My Life were shipped by the London publisher, J. Bew of Paternoster Row, to the Continent, consigned to Paris bookseller Gueffier. They were not, however, sent directly to his Quai des Augustins libraire, on the Left Bank; the precious contraband was stored temporarily in a secret warehouse.

"I can face death with equanimity . . ." The Countess de La Motte's words leap out at you from Volume II of her Story of My Life:

. . . if I can but die in the certainty that this vindication of my life and innocence will be published.

For I honestly believe that those who will take the trouble to read the full story of my life, and thus come to know my characteristics and my personality, will be convinced that I was simply not the type, was temperamentally incapable of the diabolically clever machination of which I was accused.

Intrigue on such a scale is an art for which I have not the talent and presupposes a methodical, coolly calculating brain, a carefully conceived scheme, a deep-laid plot and a sure, steady, untrembling hand to carry it through—all qualifications foreign to my make-up, incompatible with my disposition. I am a creature, rather, of impulse, flighty, erratic, unstable emotionally, as my reader has come to know me. And, young as I was at the time of the necklace affair, in my twenties, still a debutante on the great stage of Versailles, unversed in the ways of that complex, lofty court world, how could I have dared even attempt so audacious a flight on fledgling wings?

My enemies will not be satisfied with having harried me to the tomb, they will harass my memory beyond it. To safeguard their illustrious names for history, they must make of mine a byword of shame and scorn, must make out the Countess de La Motte as the archadventuress, archvillainess of all times. And they may yet succeed in this, their plan for deceiving posterity. But no, no! They shall not triumph—not if I can reach with this story of my life the open minds of this generation and generations to come.

May God see and hear me as I write. If this were to be my last testament, I would not change a word, a syllable of it.

Strong words—and, propped up against the pillows of her deathbed, she signed her name to them, on hundreds of copies. Strong words for a devout, or at the very least a practicing, Catholic; this she was, as even hostile witness Father Loth had brought out before the judges of the Parliament of Paris when he related under oath that the Countess de La Motte had missed not a single morning at her devotions—he himself had unlocked the back door of the chapel of the Order of Minims regularly at 10 A.M. and had celebrated a private mass for her there in aristocratic seclusion.

The evil men do lives after them, and the malign influence of the Countess's recently published Story of My Life was to make itself felt in Paris shortly after her death, directly affecting that particular phase of the Revolution, making dread impact upon the prisoner monarchs in the Tuileries, as Madame Campan relates dramatically in her memoirs:

Having barely escaped an arrest order issued against me in the Auvergne mountain village of Mont-Dore, I managed to make my way back to Paris and returned to the Queen's service in the Tuileries on September 1, 1791, a week after the catastrophe of Varennes.

I was shocked by the terrible change in Her Majesty: her hair had turned white in a single night on the road back to Paris. Even the basic comfort of sleep had been lost to her in those turbulent, tocsin-filled hours of darkness throughout the autumn of 1791. The sovereigns were guarded like real prisoners now; a strict watch had been set up not only at the palace gates but in the family's innermost apartments.

A false flicker of hope came briefly in September, when the final draft of the constitution was nearing completion and the King's acceptance was assured.

Early the next year, however—in 1792 it was—a prominent and highly respected priest sent word to me requesting a private interview. He explained that he was acting upon information which had reached him concerning a posthumous libel from the pen of Madame de La Motte and stated it to be his impression that the London agents who were preparing to publish it in France were interested solely in pecuniary gain; these agents had indicated that they would deliver the manuscript to him for a thousand louis in gold, if he could find some friend of the Queen's ready to make such a sacrifice for her protection. The cleric added that he had thought of me, and that if Her Majesty wanted him to act for her he believed that he could make a deal with these parties on the basis of 24,000 francs.

I relayed his proposition to Her Majesty, who rejected it, authorizing me to tell the priest that in the days when it had been within her power to punish purveyors of such libel she had disdained the use of force to stifle them, and that if she were now to show herself so imprudent or so weak as to buy off even one blackmailer the zealous Jacobin espionage system would ferret it out, with the result that the libel not only would be published but would become all the more damaging when the public was informed of her desperate measures to keep it from their knowledge.

One evening a few weeks later the Baron d'Aubier, a close personal friend of mine, told me a very curious story about an incident which had created great excitement that day in the National Assembly: "The Assembly was in an uproar today over a denunciation turned in by the workmen of the Sèvres porcelain manufactory," he said. "They brought up to the tribune, to the president's desk, a stack of copies of a purported *Life of Marie Antoinette*. The Sèvres factory manager, called before the bar, stated that he had received orders to burn these books in the porcelain kilns."

I reported this to Their Majesties at the supper table. Blushes suffused the King's face; he hung his head so low his chin very nearly touched the plate.

The Queen asked him, "Monsieur, do you know anything about this matter?"

The King made no reply.

Then Madame Elisabeth inquired of her brother whether he could offer any explanation of the mystery. Still no reply.

I withdrew from Their Majesties' presence.

A little while later the Queen came to me to tell me that it had been the King who, in anxiety on her account, had bought up the entire edition printed from the La Motte manuscript which had been originally offered to her through me, and that the King's intendant, Monsieur Laporte, had found no better method for disposing of those thousands of copies than to make a five-hour bonfire of them in the Sèvres porcelain kilns—to the mystification of two hundred Sèvres workmen, of whom eighty per cent were indubitably radical revolutionaries.

Her Majesty told me that she had concealed her dismay from the King; he had been distressed enough, and she had no reproach to make when it was his fondness and concern for her which had brought about the misadventure.

The King had made the purchase privately at the bargain price of fourteen thousand francs from the authoress's widower.

The Count de La Motte, in early May, had written the King that he could lead the authorities to the warehouse where the thousands of volumes were stored: "I can lay claim to the whole edition and wrest it from the hands of a group of malicious subjects who plan to use it as an instrument of their subversive purposes."

One single copy, escaping the Sèvres kilns, was found in the house of the King's intendant, Laporte. Had it remained through negligence on his part in tying up the thirty bundles, or treachery, or simple curiosity? Whatever the reason, the Committee of Public Safety of the National Convention claimed it from him, read it, no doubt smirked through its spicy passages, and came to the patriotic decision to turn it over to the Libraire Garnéry on the Rue Serpente for reprinting.

This second French edition, which appeared shortly thereafter, carried a foreword:

This book has been reprinted from the copy found among the papers of Sieur Laporte, intendant of the King's civil list, and later turned over to the Committee of Public Safety of the National Convention. The lengths to which the court has gone to prevent publication of this work clearly prove how greatly the monarchy feared its publication, how many facts it contains which the royalist party would have preferred to keep from public knowledge. *Nota*: This, the sole copy remaining from the London edition which was burned at Sèvres, is signed, by hand, "Jeanne de Saint-Rémy de Valois, also known as de La Motte."

(". . . if I can but die in the certainty that this vindication of my life and my innocence will be published.")

The publication date of the second French edition of the Countess's Story of My Life is noted as "the Year One of the French Republic"— the end of 1792. Had the Countess lived but one more year, she would have achieved both of her burning ambitions, the publication of her life story and the retrial of her case and her husband's. For on July 20, 1792, the Paris court had quashed the six-year-old sentence.

The Count in his petition to the court had not failed to play up the significance of the case to liberated France: "The sentence by which Madame de La Motte and I were condemned served as a signal for revolution. There is a Providence which delights to direct the destiny of mortals and, working in mysterious ways, transmutes the blood of the innocent into a poison to the tyrants who shed it!"

How could a revolutionary Paris deny him? The court's decision was: "Whereas the prosecutor general's indictment, as presented to the quondam Parliament of Paris on September 7, 1785, is signed in only one place, at the end, and not upon each separate sheet as is required, a violation of the law exists . . ."

Sentence reversed—on a technicality, true, but it was still gratifying assurance to the Count de La Motte that he need no longer tremble at the horrid thought of bending his shoulder to the oar of the King's galleys.

"The King's situation was by then so desperate, through all those last months leading up to the August 10 attack," writes Madame Campan, "that the Queen actually wished for the end to come, no matter how dread a form it took."

The monarchy could still count a few, a pitiful few, defenders in the Assembly; one of them strode to the tribune to deplore the cries of the rabble-rousers:

When crime comes out into the open, when there is loud and open incitement to regicide at the very doors of this Assembly, on the terrace of the Tuileries, then how, I ask you, can we hope to restore order and confidence in the nation? . . . I indict the bloody propaganda sheets of Marat and Carra, demagogues deliberately provoking public disorders. . . .

This speech, printed in the May 4, 1792, issue of the Moniteur, was attributed to an up-and-coming newcomer, young Delegate Jacques

Claude Beugnot, representative from Bar-sur-Aube. Beugnot, self-described in his memoirs as having been a member of the "young liberal" political movement some ten years earlier, was finding in 1792 that his liberal principles were now considered conservative, nay, reactionary, and that his place was with the Right.

Most of the original Left, the constitutional-monarchy party (to which Beugnot belonged) had by now been pushed far over to the Right by the new radical, republican, regicidal Left—the fanatic Terrorists, against whom Beugnot dared publicly to inveigh in 1792:

These Terrorists are not representative of the nation. The nation is represented by peace-loving workers and farmers, by citizens of all the provinces of France, who look toward us in the Assembly with respect and with hope for peace and order under the constitution. If we hope to assure government by that constitution, it is high time for us to unite to combat these Terrorists, and therefore I propose a decree, to be brought to a vote in this very session, for the prosecution of the authors and disseminators of incitements to violence, to defiance of law and order.

Beugnot won, that day of May 3, 1792, not only the vote he called for against the Terrorists but a personal victory as well: nomination to the post of secretary of the Assembly.

But that was only May.

By August his open denunciation of Marat, Carra and the other radicals had marked him for the Terrorists' vengeance: an anonymous warning convinced him that it would be the part of discretion to resign his secretariat and henceforward vacate his seat on the well-nigh deserted right bench of the Assembly.

MEMOIRS
OF MADAME CAMPAN

At last came the terrible night of August 10.

At midnight the tocsins sounded . . . The Swiss Guard drew up into a veritable wall about the Tuileries . . . By four o'clock great mobs had filled the Place du Carrousel and all the streets leading to the palace, the bloodthirsty Marseilles men heading the columns . . .

All hope for defense abandoned, the King was warned that unless he and his family sought refuge with the Assembly they would inevitably be slaughtered. We watched the royal family walk away through the gardens between a double row of Swiss Guards . . .

That night saw almost all the eight hundred Swiss massacred . . . The handful of noble men who had made a valiant last stand in defense of their monarch fled under the Louvres colonnades, to be stabbed or shot. Water from the palace's shattered fountains mingled with the blood on the parquetry floors, staining the hems of our white court gowns crimson.

With a group of the Queen's attendants, I was caught on a palace stairway by a band of Marseillais and had already felt a terrible hand upon my throat when a cry came up from the floor below: "What's going on up there? We're killing no women today, remember!"

It is rare to see death so close and live to tell it. . . .

Upon my arrival at my sister's, our family was reunited, which was more than any of us could have hoped. But I could not stay on and endanger them; there were already crowds at the door shouting for "the head of Marie Antoinette's confidante." In disguise, I managed to reach the house of my friends the Morels and hid there overnight. The first panic past, I gave no more thought to my personal misfortunes. I could think only of the terrible plight of the Queen.

Next morning my sister and I went to the Feuillants' convent and secured entry cards to the four small cells to which the Assembly had assigned the royal family. I see it still—I think I shall see it until the day I die—that narrow convent cell, the peeling green paper on the wall, the miserable cot on which my dethroned sovereign lay stretching out her arms to me.

In all that I have recounted here on the subject of that most tragic of women and of queens, those who did not live close to her, those who knew her only slightly, and especially those who knew her not at all except through infamous libels, may think that I have felt it my duty to sacrifice truth to loyalty. Fortunately, there are those still living who can stand unimpeachable witness to the truth of what I speak; they can say whether what I have seen and heard and believed seems to them true or false.

Most of that day I spent at the Feuillants' convent. Her Majesty told me that she would request permission for me to accompany her to whatever place the National Assembly should decree as their prison, and I went back to the Morels' to gather up some of my things in preparation for following her.

That same night of August 11, at nine o'clock, I returned to the convent, only to be turned away from every door. I was told that the Queen had "enough people with her." My sister, I knew, was there, and a second lady in waiting. On the twelfth I returned to the Feuillants' to renew my solicitations for entry to the royal family's quarters; by neither entreaties nor tears could I move the guards at the doors.

Shortly afterward I learned that Louis XVI and his family had been transferred to the Temple.

A visit to the mayor of Paris was unavailing, eliciting only the threat to imprison me in La Force if I did not cease my importunings. . . . From that time on I sorrowed, receiving no further word from my noble and unhappy mistress beyond what I read in the newspapers and what details I could coax from the National Guardsmen on patrol around the Temple. . . .

Forgive me, majestic spirit, tragic Queen, forgive me! I look upon your portrait as I write. My eyes, responding to the tenderest thoughts, constantly seek out your well-remembered face. In your eyes I try to read the answer as I ask, Has this work of mine served your memory well? That proud and noble head, fallen to the cruel steel of the executioner —my eyes cannot dwell upon it without blinding tears that make me drop my pen. Yes, I can speak the truth without offending your spirit. Truth shall serve her best whom falsehood has so cruelly outraged.

"What can I add to these eloquent words of Madame Campan's?" her editor, Barras, wrote in 1824. "Madame Campan is dead. Let those who libeled her while she lived assail her memory if they must. Her own words will defend her better than could any of mine."

What Barras called the libels that blighted the last years of Madame Campan's life issued from the lips of the Old Regime nobility, returned from long exile with the restoration of the Bourbon monarchy in 1814. It was said that Madame Campan had fraternized and collaborated with the enemy, the upstart Directoire and Empire hierarchy. But, then, what would they have had Madame Campan do toward the end of the Revolution, "after the fall of Robespierre, when I found myself faced with the problem of providing, singlehanded, for an aged mother, an invalid

husband,* a nine-year-old son and all the rest of the family in hardship?
I chose the town of St.-Germain to establish my school for young
ladies. . . . In 1795 Madame Joséphine de Beauharnais placed her
daughter Hortense with me, and six months later she entrusted to me
the delicate commission of breaking the news to the girl that her mother
had married a Corsican gentleman, a graduate of the Military School, a
general."

Did the hard-core, die-hard dowager duchesses reproach Madame
Campan for having traded on her Old Regime prestige to make an overnight success with the New? Fortunes had changed hands, titles been
lost in the upheaval of the Revolution; Directoire society in the early
1800s was like a library, "its volumes, old and new alike unmarked,
tossed back on the shelves at random." Nouveau riche, arriviste—what
else but elegance of speech and manner could give a man distinction?

Madame Campan could hardly have been expected to reject Emperor
Napoleon's honor: appointment to the post of directress for his imperial
school at Écouen for the children of Legion of Honor veterans. But her
enemies could make her rue it after Waterloo.

"In that moment of rejoicing for all faithful servitors of the royal
family, in that moment which saw their devotion rewarded by a grateful
Louis XVIII—in that moment, Madame Campan suffered her cruelest
humiliation," Barras writes. "Absurd but vicious calumnies and libels
pursued and plagued her even in her final woodland retreat at Mantes.
The accusation leveled against Madame Campan was far more serious
than ingratitude; she was accused of treason."

Ugly rumors sounded in the Tuileries whispering galleries: whispers
about Madame Campan's brother, Edmond Charles Genêt, a leading
Girondist.† But: "I myself had told the Queen about him," Madame
Campan's memoirs protest, "and I offered to resign my post because of
the embarrassment of my position, but Her Majesty would not hear of
it."

There were other, uglier whispers: the coincidence by which Madame

---

* Madame Campan's second and last (and succinct) mention of her husband in all
three volumes of her memoirs.
† Better known as Citizen Genêt, the first French minister to the United States
(appointed in 1792), whose outfitting of privateers in American ports and whose
intrigues to involve America in France's war with Britain and Spain led to his being
replaced at the request of President Washington—who then refused to extradite him
when the Jacobins, who had meanwhile come to power in France, ordered his arrest.
Genêt remained here, married a daughter of New York Governor George Clinton
and became a naturalized U.S. citizen.

Campan was always off duty at all the most critical moments: off duty the night of the march of the Women's Army on Versailles; off duty the date of the Varennes flight. And as to August 10, 11 and 12, at the Feuillants' convent, Madame Campan's sister, it was pointed out, had found a way to get past the guards to the side of her royal mistress, had never left the Queen those three days, was still there and was arrested there on the thirteenth, after the monarchs' transfer to the Temple. And two other ladies in waiting had found a way to follow their Queen even into the Temple—had been willing to pay for their devotion with a prison sentence in La Force. But the ugliest rumor of all started later, upon the discovery of a Prefecture of Police record dated August 11, tending to prove that Madame Campan had not left the Morels' house on the Rue St. Pierre that entire day—the day her memoirs claim she spent with her sovereigns in the convent; a record stating that only at nightfall had Madame Campan emerged, and then to take a hired carriage, not to the Feuillants' but "out of the city, to a destination unknown." Madame Campan had written:

When I saw the King and Queen at the convent on August 11 they failed to give me any word of instruction with regard to the portfolio of secret papers which they had entrusted to my care; doubtlessly they expected to see me again later. Minister Roland and his Girondist government instituted assiduous search for those papers; the Tuileries were ransacked from attics to cellars, and fifty armed men forced their way into my sister's house and searched it after my departure. For days and nights I struggled to decide what to do with the papers given into my hands for safekeeping by Their Majesties.

Like those of the American Revolution, these were "times to try men's souls." According to Madame Campan's editor's account, "Madame Campan, with several denunciations out against her, with Robespierre on her traces, with that portfolio of papers highly incriminating to the King and Queen, went to hide her dangerous secret and her sorrow at the Château de Coubertin in the Valley of Chevreuse."

MEMOIRS
OF COUNT BEUGNOT

I had warning during the early days of October 1793 that an arrest order had been issued against me. I was faced with the choice between flight and the guillotine.

By then the torrent of blood which was to drench France had begun to flow. A hive of savages swarmed over the nation, let loose how and whence no one will ever know, infesting the Republic with spies, informers, judges and executioners. Courage was shaken, souls shattered, faces distorted; men were afraid to stop along the street to look, to speak, so much as to listen.

When two weeks had passed without further word of the arrest order, I was weak enough, I admit, to dare to hope. But on the eighteenth Vendemiaire, at nine o'clock in the morning, came the knock at my door. . . . We rode off in style, in a hired carriage which my police escort was thoughtful enough to summon, arriving at our destination [the Palais de Justice] shortly before noon.

From top to bottom, the whole great flight of stairs, the grand stairway of the Palais, was covered with women—taking their seats on the steps as at a Roman amphitheater, impatiently waiting for their favorite gory spectacle to begin. Indeed, the chariot of death, the tumbril, was already at the door, awaiting the two poor wretches condemned that day to be thrown to the lions.

As I stepped out of the carriage the whole circus audience rose to its feet, emitting one long howl of joy. Clapping of hands, stamping of feet, convulsive laughter signaled the audience's ferocious glee at the sight of new prey. The short way I had to go on foot from the carriage to the prison door was time enough for me to be stained with spittle and pelted with filth from every direction; judging by the reception given me upon my entry, I could easily surmise the kind I might expect upon my exit.

The door swung open, and I was swallowed up in that vast anteroom to death more commonly known as the Conciergerie.

On the left as you come in is the registry office, partitioned into two sections by a wooden lattice. The registrar's chair, desk and register are in the part nearest the courtyard; here the new prisoner enters, is committed, signs in; the space on the other side of the partition is dedicated to the use of the condemned for those few, endless hours between the pronouncement of the death sentence and the execution of it.

The newcomer sees the condemned, even speaks to them if he has the courage; the frail barrier of separation serves as a reminder that there is no more than one short step between him and the scaffold. The day of my entry there were two men on the other side of the partition, awaiting the arrival of the executioners. They had shed their coats; their heads were already shaven, their neckbands loosened. . . .

What a spectacle was that anteroom to the guillotine! There, as the pallets on the floor indicated, the condemned had endured the long torment of the night. You could see the remnants of the last meal they had taken, the clothing they had scattered here and there and the two guttered candles which they had not troubled to extinguish—as if that pale flame was more suitable than the sun for funeral lighting.

I was taking in every detail of that horrible sepulcher for the living when, with a great burst of sound from the courtyard, the door flew open and I saw the policemen, guards and executioners come in. That was all I saw; a sudden faintness overwhelmed me, and I threw myself, face down, on a bench, to shut out sight of the elaborate apparatus of public execution. . . .

I was supposed to consider myself a privileged character to have been assigned to share one of the forty or fifty pallets on the floor of the prison infirmary, a space a hundred feet long by twenty-five wide with barred iron gates at either end and seemingly carved out of solid rock, blackened with centuries of smoke, dank. Two narrow windows high up in the high vaulted ceiling let in the only light; night was distinguishable from day only by the rasp of bolts, the clank of keys, the howling of dogs. All around me in the dark I could hear half-stifled moans and choked sobs; from farther down the line, some dream-haunted creature cried out with cries that chilled my soul. I could make out the words well enough: "blood . . . executioner . . . guillotine . . ." These were to become familiar words of nightmare soliloquy from up and down the long row of funeral couches. Hour by hour the metallic voice of the Palais clock marked interludes in an eternity of anguish. Dogs bayed back at it. If you have never spent a night in the Paris Conciergerie, you can never know what hell exists aboveground.

The day after my arrival, a quick tour of the prison turned out to be a reunion with old comrades from the benches of the National Assembly.

The trial of the Girondist deputies was just drawing to a close. Their mass execution [some twenty-two of them] on November 2 spread terrible dismay among the prisoners in the Conciergerie. And posterity would sternly demand an accounting of the strange chain of circumstances by which these founders of the Republic had been brought to the scaffold.

By that autumn of 1793 the Revolutionary Tribunal had begun working at sickening speed; an arrest order and a death sentence were, by then, one and the same.

Madame Roland's trial had been announced to follow her Girondist associates, and her arrival at the Conciergerie constituted an event. I, for one, was curious to know the woman who in fifteen brief months had emerged from obscurity to high rank in the national councils, to fame, chains and death, all in little more than a year. Personal egotism had sparked her meteoric rise; she openly attributed to herself the greater portion of her husband's literary and political glories. But, in all fairness to her, I must admit that she knew how to extend her empire even unto the depths of the Conciergerie, where she held benevolent sway.

The Conciergerie offered a rare study in anomalies. With utter indifference on the part of the authorities a Duchess de Gramont and a pickpocket were sent to share the same pallet, a gentle nun was shut in side by side with a hardened criminal from the Salpêtrière, Madame Roland and a streetwalker were locked behind the same door. The constant vicious warfare among the criminal element was the most distressful feature for the decent women. Not a night passed without shrieks and screeches from some pair of disreputables clawing each other to pieces.

Upon this hellish landscape Madame Roland's cell stood out as an oasis of peace. Her appearance in the courtyard was a signal for good behavior to women who recognized no other authority on earth. Those viragoes were restrained by the very thought of displeasing Madame Roland! How different from the case of that vile creature, that disgrace to Louis XV and all his generation—that Du Barry woman, who was also among those present. As to her, the women in the Conciergerie demonstrated clearly that they considered themselves on an equal footing—despite her seductive affectations, despite the regal airs the haughty whore still gave herself.

The day of Madame Roland's trial, I found her in the corridor, waiting for the summons to the courtroom upstairs. She was dressed with an elegant simplicity: a white English-muslin gown, lace-trimmed and belted with black velvet. Her coiffure was meticulous; from under her hat, her beautiful hair floated about her shoulders. Smiling, composed, she used one hand to hold up her train, the other she extended to the throng of women who pressed close to kiss it. That tableau is beyond my powers of description. It had to be seen.

She replied to all those about her with affectionate kindness, with exhortations to faith and courage . . .*

Amid such scenes as these—and they were daily occurrences—the women of France lost not a whit of their delicious femininity. No sacrifice was too great to preserve the artistry of charm.

My section of the prison opened onto the womens' courtyard. The only spot where we could breathe fresh air was a narrow passage, separated from their courtyard by an iron railing—the bars of which, however, were not so closely spaced that a good Frenchman need despair.

This corridor was not only our favorite promenade, but our only one. We rushed for it as soon as the jailers unlocked the doors in the morning. The women, though released at the same hour, did not appear until somewhat later: the ritual of dressing exacted its inalienable tribute. The ladies appeared in a morning costume with all the coquetry of the casual, the négligé; an ensemble of which every component part was so prettily and tastefully arranged as to belie the fact that the wearer had spent the night on a pallet, most often on a heap of fetid straw. In general, the ladies of high rank who had been brought to the Conciergerie guarded the sacred flame of good taste and good manners to the very end.

I noticed that every woman who could adhered faithfully to the routine of three daily changes of costume. The ones who lacked the wardrobe made up for it by neatness and cleanliness. The womens' courtyard possessed a treasure, a fountain with running water, and I watched the poor women—who possessed probably only the single dress in which they had been arrested—busying themselves every morning at the fountain, washing, bleaching, drying. The first hour of the day was sacred to these ablutions; nothing could have distracted the ladies therefrom—not even a court order for immediate trial.

I am convinced that at this period no promenade in Paris could boast so decorative and elegant a group of ladies as that in the Conciergerie courtyard. At noon it seemed to be a garden bright with flowers, even

---

* *Her last words, uttered on the scaffold, were the famous "O Liberty, what crimes are committed in thy name!"*

though steel-bordered. France is probably the only nation in the world, and Frenchwomen the only women, capable of such delicious incongruity: creating there, in one of the most dismal, most hideous corners on earth, an ambiance of beauty, of charm, even of voluptuousness.

I preferred to talk with the ladies in the morning and to look at them at noon; and, of course, I responded to the mood of intimacy evoked by the twilight hours, although I limited it to such superficial dalliance as would not trouble my own or anyone else's already troubled heart.

Now, the evening offered opportunities not to be neglected: shadows lengthened, weary guards relaxed vigilance, most of the prisoners were off to bed. Those who remained were discreet. In that moment of peace which came as prelude to the horror of the night, there was good reason to bless the artisan who had constructed the iron railing for his lack of foresight. The passionate abandon of those men and women, whom I knew to be carrying death sentences in their pockets, I conceded to be a species of bravura for which I was not cut out.

Of greater appeal to me as a distraction were the alfresco luncheon parties frequently arranged by us with the ladies in the courtyard, when benches were drawn up on each side of the grating separating the sexes, and a feast was spread out between us. The topics of horror and tragedy were ignored as one might ignore the antics of some unruly child, and the gayest and wittiest repartee imaginable sparkled through the bars: conversations as stimulating, phrases as gracefully turned, allusions as subtle as could be hoped for in the most elegant salons of France. I do not exaggerate the tenor of these courtyard luncheons, but it should not be too surprising when one reflects that the company in the Conciergerie at that time represented perhaps the flower of France's talent, wit and distinction.

Somehow, however, with the passing months in the Conciergerie, and despite my efforts toward resignation, I seemed daily less able to endure it. I had lost, one by one, all my "old" friends—"old" to the extent that I had enjoyed their companionship as fellow prisoners for as long as a month or six weeks. I no longer took the trouble of cultivating new ones; I could no longer force myslf to the effort of forging bonds of friendship, only to have them severed by the guillotine's blade at week's end. Thus, although the Conciergerie was more crowded than ever, I found myself then, in a sense, alone.

To the other scenes of horror add the suicides, which were becoming daily more frequent; every inmate of a philosophical turn of mind was provided with laudanum tablets of so excellent a concoction as to guarantee a very smooth crossing to the other shore of the Styx. I had my supply in my pocket, although I had promised my wife not to swallow the dose until I had heard the death penalty pronounced. These tablets had been furnished us by a doctor, Doctor Guillotin, who, in serving us, displayed no reluctance at cheating his machine of its clientele. This poor man was a generous soul, a very philanthropist, and lacking in neither professional skill nor general erudition; it was the tragedy of his life to see his name attached to the infernal instrument.

Just beyond my quarters in the Conciergerie was a room originally used and designated as the "Little Pharmacy," but noteworthy at the time of my sojourn in the prison as having but recently served as cell to a prisoner of great renown, a distinction it owed to its double doors, a full five inches thick, steel-clad and garnished with three enormous locks. Of the two window slits through which daylight had formerly filtered, one had been hermetically sealed and the second almost totally closed; but in compensation for daylight the room boasted a wallpaper alive with republican emblems and slogans; one's eyes were dizzied by the words LIBERTY, EQUALITY, FRATERNITY, RIGHTS OF MAN, CONSTITUTION repeating themselves ad infinitum round and round the walls, the shibboleths of liberty incongruously punctuated by iron bars, by locks and bolts.

The wallpaper with its busy Revolutionary motifs, as Beugnot saw and described it, was described by another eyewitness as "hangings of paper nailed onto frames," tattered, decomposing from the dampness, the moisture beading and trickling down the walls. The Little Pharmacy was eleven and a half feet square, as Beugnot neglected to mention, and during the Queen's occupancy that narrow confine was further narrowed by a screen dividing it in two, from one side of which a pair of National Guardsmen stood twenty-four-hour watch. The cell's two windows opened, or had once opened, onto the women's courtyard, at approximately ground level. By the time Beugnot saw the cell, some few days after Marie Antoinette had vacated it, it is possible that the shabby furniture provided her had already been removed: a camp bed, a table, a basin, one or two cane chairs and a rusty nail on which she hung her watch, until that last of her personal possessions was taken from her too. Dismal, dark, dank, bare: it was in the Little Pharmacy that the Queen of France spent the last two and a half months of her life, from August

2 to October 16, 1793—termless, gloomy days little brighter than the endless black nights, the one distinguishable from the other for the Queen, as for Beugnot, only by the rasp of bolts, the clank of keys, the howling of dogs; endless days, nights, hours for thinking and remembering.

Did Marie Antoinette in the Conciergerie remember another famous female prisoner who had languished long months in that grim keep in 1786, and upon her own royal orders? Marie Antoinette could not have failed to remember the Countess de La Motte's Open Letter to the Queen of France, calling down this very curse upon her head:

Where were you, O evil and cruel Queen, while my tears drenched the cold stone floor of my prison cell? You were deceiving the ministers with your denial of having ever known me! You stood by and allowed me to be thrown into the Conciergerie, and in what company—a Valois among prostitutes!

At the moment I left my dungeon to go into the courtyard of the Palais to hear my dreadful sentence, I called down upon your head the most terrible curse I know—that you should one day endure like punishment. . . .

If only I can live to see that day!

The Countess de La Motte had missed seeing that day by two years, one month and twenty-three days.

In the event that Marie Antoinette had forgotten the Countess de La Motte and her imprecations, Public Prosecutor Fouquier-Tinville was to recall the Countess to the mind of the Queen within the last twenty-four hours of her life:

Q: Was it not at the Little Trianon that you knew the woman La Motte?
A: I have never seen her.
Q: Was she not your victim in the famous affair of the diamond necklace?
A: She cannot have been, since I did not know her.
Q: Then you persist in your system of denial?
A: I have no system of denial. It is the truth I have spoken and will persist in speaking . . .

"This room, the Little Pharmacy, recently signaled out for such distinction, for so unforeseen an occupancy," Beugnot concludes in his memoirs, "had been reassigned, by the time I saw it, to new 'guests' of the Republic, former representatives of the nation, delegates to the National Constituent Assembly."

Still later, to Danton, to Robespierre.

And in 1816, after the Revolution, after the Bourbon Restoration, another distinction for the Little Pharmacy—the erection of an altar; the Little Pharmacy was transformed, by order of Louis XVIII, into an oratory to commemorate the martyrdom of the prisoner Queen, his late sister-in-law. Louis XVIII paid her a second tribute: he had the beautiful Chapelle Expiatoire, the Chapel of Expiation, erected in memory of Marie Antoinette and Louis XVI at the corner of busy Boulevard Haussman, on the site of the old Madeleine Cemetery for victims of the guillotine. The laying of its cornerstone was the royalists' signal for the keening to begin: For every libel against Marie Antoinette during her lifetime, two eulogies were published in this period, twenty-odd years after her death (even including one by chief executioner Sanson). No prettier compliment could be paid the newly restored monarchy than to suggest that their late Queen might belong not only to history but to the martyrology—a literary canonization that turned the Queen from a Bourbon liability into a Bourbon asset.

(A Hapsburg asset as well. Until this time, "silence concerning the Queen of France was a fixed maxim in the house of Austria," according to Napoleon, who should have known whereof he spoke, having married into the family. "At the name of Marie Antoinette, they lowered their eyes and changed the subject . . . Such was the rule adopted by the entire Hapsburg family and recommended to Austrian envoys in foreign parts.")

The legend of the royal saint was substituted for the legend of the Revolution's whore; cloudbanks of hyperbole blotted out for almost two centuries the lineaments of the woman fogged in behind. The truth is somewhere between the two extremes and is far more poignant than either, with enough new evidence coming to light in every generation from state archives and ancestral châteaux to present an enduring challenge to honest researchers.

Carlyle set the pace for the 1830s with his threnody:

Beautiful Highborn that wert so foully hurled low! . . .
Oh, is there a man's heart that thinks, without pity, of those
long months and years of slow-wasting ignominy—of thy
birth, soft-cradled in imperial Schönbrunn, the winds of
heaven not to visit thy face too roughly, thy foot to light on
softness, thine eye on splendor; and then of thy death or hundred deaths, to which the guillotine and Fouquier-Tinville's
judgment bar were but the merciful end? . . . Far as the eye
reaches, a multitudinous sea of maniac heads; the air deaf
with their triumph yell . . . There is then no heart to say,
God pity thee? Oh, think not of these; think of HIM whom
thou worshipest, the Crucified, who also treading the wine
press alone, fronted sorrow still deeper; and triumphed over
it, and made it holy; and built of it a "Sanctuary of Sorrow,"
for thee and all the wretched! Thy path of thorns is nigh
ended. One long last look at the Tuileries where thy step
was once so light—where thy children shall not dwell. The
head is on the block; the ax rushes . . .

Beautiful Highborn that wert so foully hurled low! Thy
fault, in the French Revolution, was that thou wert the symbol of the sin and misery of a thousand years. . . . As poor
peasants, how happy, how worthy had ye two been! But by
evil destiny ye were made a King and Queen of; and so both
once more are become an astonishment and a byword to all
times.

It is an astonishment, as well, to find that canny Scotsman, the self-
constituted lifelong Archenemy of Humbug, taken in by the "poor peasants" bit, gulping the bait of that contrived rusticity, that studied informality, that deceptive simplicity of the "country life" as it was lived
in Trianon's lake-shore hamlet, presided over by Village Queen Marie
Antoinette in her marble-floored miniature dairy, her own fair hands at
Blanchette's gleaming udder or serving Brunette's foaming milk to her
guests in Sèvres bol-seins, "breast cups"—modeled by France's premier
sculptor from a cast of the bosom of the Queen of France—if such could
actually have been the purpose to which these baffling Sèvres souvenirs
were designed.

And twenty-five years after Carlyle there was Jules and Edmond Goncourt's Histoire de Marie-Antoinette, a rhapsody sweet to the ear of their

own sovereign, Napoleon III's Empress Eugénie, who had let it be known that she considered herself Marie Antoinette's historical soul mate.

Second Empire archivist Émile Campardon could take a hint. He searched out and retrieved from the records, after seventy-five years of government-office chaos, the original documents of the Bastille and the Parliament of Paris and published the first officially documented, if not impartial, history of the Necklace Trial, absolving the Queen from any complicity whatsoever in the old scandal.

When the secret Marie Antoinette–Maria Theresa, Count Mercy–Maria Theresa letters, released by the Vienna State Archives in 1866, were published as the five-volume Correspondance secrète, the brothers Goncourt refused to concede that they contained one single fact materially altering their original characterization of the Queen. The Goncourts sanctimoniously warned off any historian who so much as dared approach the shadowy region of the Queen's relations with Fersen, with an outraged "Let there be no further inquiry into this vicious calumny!" Count von Fersen's descendant, in his Swedish castle in the early 1900s, co-operated nobly, burning every letter of every packet addressed to his ancestor by the Queen of France; and generations of royalist-reactionary biographers joined in the conspiracy of silence.

The literary litany came to sound more and more like the Song of Solomon. The Goncourts psalmodized, "A radiant girl, on the threshold of life, running to the encounter with open arms and lilting heart . . . The most adorable, most womanly woman in all the Court of Versailles . . . In the places where she passed by, a melody lingered in the air." At the beginning of the twentieth century, Pierre de Nolhac, curator of the Versailles and Trianon palaces and official national biographer of Marie Antoinette, listened for the "dove . . . in the clefts of the rock, in the secret places of the stairs . . ." And scholar Funck-Brentano, musing, "She dreamed of life as a young girl dreams of it in the springtime," caught at the echoes of words by men fortunate enough to have glimpsed her in the radiant flesh: Edmund Burke's "She is like the perfume of spring," and Horace Walpole's "Hebes and Floras, Helens and Graces are tawdry as streetwalkers compared to her."

There was a third legend in the making: Marie Antoinette as a Queen of Hearts, still glamorous, with the power still to stir mens' minds and emotions, a phenomenon not confined to a set of scholarly vicarious lovers nor yet to the royalist-reactionary element, but extending to the

French nation as a whole—as Nancy Mitford discovered when a storm of protest followed the publication in the London Times of her article reporting on the Versailles exhibit of Marie Antoinette memorabilia in 1955, the bicentenary anniversary of the Queen's birth. Miss Mitford had written that, to her, Marie Antoinette was "one of the most irritating characters in history . . . frivolous without being funny, extravagant without being elegant," a woman whose "stupidity" was "monumental." Although the article ended on a conciliatory note—"When all hope was gone, she became an exemplary figure"—French reaction flashed swift and sharp as the guillotine blade. Hundreds of letters flooded the Times, deploring not only the brittle Mitford appraisal, but also, as if it had all happened only yesterday, "the fate of our dear Queen." If the Paris newspapers had speculated on what significance Marie Antoinette might hold for the mid-twentieth-century generations, the answer seemed to be that hers was an enduringly controversial figure, still very much of a live issue in the days of the Fourth Republic.

One explanation of the phenomenon may be that Marie Antoinette is intimately, inextricably bound up in the national guilt complex. Her death, serving no valid revolutionary reason, constituted the blood sacrifice for the nation. As Napoleon saw it, "There is something worse than regicide here." The Republic would have erected the expiatory chapel had Louis XVIII not done so; the national conscience had need of expression of expiation for its crime against Marie Antoinette, its thousands of crimes against thousands of victims sacrificed unnecessarily.

André Castelot, in his 1957 Queen of France, presents the most fully documented, most aseptically unemotional approach to the touchy subject any Frenchman has managed to date. Predictably, however, it was not a Frenchman but an Austrian, Stefan Zweig, who first—fifteen years before Castelot and therefore minus much of Castelot's recently discovered evidence—revealed the face of Marie Antoinette. Sympathetic but analytical and dispassionate, Zweig discovered "an average woman . . . a mediocrity . . . weak and reluctant material" out of which to weave a tragedy; for such a woman, "fate had no other whip than disaster." Remarkably, Marie Antoinette herself came to this realization, writing, "Adversity first makes us realize what we are"—remarkable words from a woman never given to introspection, who in the earlier years shied away from reflection as she did from ennui and boasted of the fact: "I am terrified of being bored!" Frivolous, shallow, superficial, it is the transfiguration of this woman in her moment of truth that makes of her story "an astonishment and a byword to all times."

If, hurrying too quickly up the ladder to the scaffold, she trod upon the toe of chief executioner Sanson, an incident still being argued (Zweig rejects it as "improbable, too good to be true," Castelot quotes it as gospel), and if she really said to him, "Pardon me, I did not mean to do it," then—as has been suggested, and by a Frenchman—she might have been addressing not only the executioner but all the thousands staring up at her from the great Place de la Révolution. It was an apology she might well have made to the entire French nation.

XXVII

Conclusions

H~ERE, THEN~," as Carlyle said, "our little labor ends. The necklace was, and is no more: the stones of it again 'circulate in commerce' . . . at this hour; and may give rise to what other histories we know not."

Hundreds of its stones may still "circulate in commerce," but the fate of some of the others is known—among them the twenty-two most fabulous brilliants of the fabulous necklace (over 140 carats' worth of them), the seventeen which comprised the choker circling the neck in a straight row at the top of the design; these, together with five other enormous gems, have been reunited in a simple setting, as a long chain, by the Duchess of Sutherland.

At any rate, so the Sutherland sautoir was catalogued in both the Marie Antoinette Bicentenary Exhibit at Versailles in 1955 and the Ageless Diamond Exhibit at Christie's in London in January 1959. It must be noted, however, that the diamond necklace, enduringly controversial, once again provoked controversy in 1959, when that noted English lady of letters, Victoria Sackville-West, wrote a letter to the London Times* citing a family tradition according to which not only the Duke of Sutherland but also the third Duke of Dorset—John Frederick Sackville, ambassador to Versailles from 1783 to 1789—had bought some of the neck-

---

* The text of this and other letters to the Times concerning the diamond necklace will be found in the Appendix.

584

lace diamonds, which were still at the Sackville seat, Knole, "having been reset into a tasseled diadem." In support of this claim Miss Sackville-West quotes a receipt made out to the Duke of Dorset for £975 "for a brilliant necklace," signed by one William Jones "for Mr. Jeffreys and self," and endorsed as paid in 1790. This was "the date when the necklace was sold by Monsieur de La Motte to Jeffreys, a jeweler-in Piccadilly," says Miss Sackville-West—mistakenly, as it happens (see pp. 366-67).

Mrs. Alfred Ezra of Poxwarren, Surrey, also claims to have diamonds emanating from the famous necklace—the six great gems described as "pendant brilliants" or "pear shapes" which, in the original Böhmer and Bassenge design, comprised the centers of the clusters and festoons and were listed by the crown jewelers as varying in weight between ten and twelve carats each. Mrs. Ezra's claim that the historic necklace was the provenance of her pear-shaped gems was substantiated by the catalogue of the Versailles exhibit, wherein the stones were so described.

On loan along with Mrs. Ezra's necklace and that of the Duchess of Sutherland at the Versailles exhibit in 1955 was a third, lent by Lucien Baszanger, jeweler, of Geneva. This, one of the pièces de résistance of the show, was executed not in diamonds but in crystal. It was the crown jewelers' own copy of the diamond necklace, which traveling-salesman Böhmer had carried on his rounds of the courts of Europe in his vain attempt to dispose of the blue-white elephant. This crystal replica was all that Monsieur Baszanger had inherited from his great-grandfather, Paul Bassenge. For the fact is that the firm of Böhmer and Bassenge, "crown jewelers by appointment to Her Majesty, Queen Marie Antoinette," had never collected any of the money due them for that "famous and world-famous," that history-making, that most talked-about, most written-about jewel of all recorded history, that 1,600,000-franc treasure of theirs (save for the paltry thirty thousand francs delivered by the Countess de La Motte to the Cardinal, and by him to the jewelers, as an "interest" or "on-account payment").

The Queen had promised Böhmer and Bassenge her protection in case of loss; or so they had understood it, writing to Baron de Breteuil in 1785: "Her Majesty, heeding the promptings of her just and generous heart, was so kind as personally to assure us that our necklace would be located and restored to us or, failing this, we would be indemnified for its full value . . ."

The Abbé Georgel, acting with the best of intentions, had assigned the jewelers the Cardinal's tremendous yearly revenues from the Abbey of St. Waast until such time as the full amount of the indebtedness should be liquidated, but the Revolutionary decree nationalizing Church properties came ahead of the liquidation, which had been calculated on an eight-year basis, and, in 1789, the firm of Böhmer and Bassenge was forced into bankruptcy. (They had sold their crown-jewelers brevet, but it could hardly have brought much of a premium at a time when the Crown was at its wobbliest.) Petition after petition by the former crown jewelers to the National Assembly to show just claim on the national treasury was rejected—eventually with intonations suggesting to Böhmer and Bassenge that they might be safer in emigration.

Long after the Revolution, the jewelers' legal heirs (as contradistinct from their natural heirs) brought suit for the amount owing on the purchase price of the diamond necklace against Princess Charlotte Louise de Rohan-Rochefort, the cousin whom the Cardinal had named as his heiress and who had succeeded to his estates in 1803. The case dragged on for years. At length the Paris Tribunal of the Seine in 1863 found in favor of the Rohan defendant, and in 1867 an appeal against that judgment was denied.

But on this point, too, there is controversy—this, too, aired in a letter to the London Times during the Ageless Diamond Exhibit in 1959: The Rohan family, wrote one of its descendants, Charles de Rohan, of Charmouth, Dorset, had paid off the cost of the necklace in installments "over a period of nearly one hundred years, the last payment being made in the early nineties of the last century." This, he added, had "brought no material benefit to the family beyond the satisfaction of meeting a debt of honor."

Only three of the supporting players in the necklace drama remain to be heard from.

Dapper Villette said his final piece in 1790, when his Mémoires historiques des intrigues de la cour was published in Venice, whither that onetime friend and amanuensis to the Countess de La Motte had hastily made his way upon his exile from France (after being booted—literally, if not unceremoniously—out of Paris, according to Cagliostro, who wrote in his own memoirs that Villette had been "led out of prison by a rope around his neck to the Paris city gates, where the public executioner, following the ancient ceremonial of banishment, delivered both *the traditional loaf of bread and the traditional boot heel implanted in the seat of his pants"). Villette himself wrote plaintively:*

Languishing far from my native land, persecuted, ruined, today a refugee in Venice, I have awaited the propitious moment to print this story, the true story as it actually happened, and a full confession of my sins, for which I ask pardon of God and man. I was the victim of a corrupt century, of a court steeped in intrigue; today, happily, despotism and arbitrary power have been eradicated, and the French nation has recovered its inherent rights.

What with his protestations of ardent republican sentiments and his subsequent revelations of amatory exploits to rival those of Casanova (a contemporary, a Venetian and a memoir writer too), it is surprising that after the overthrow of the monarchy in France Villette did not rush back to revolutionary Paris to cash in on his triple-crown reputation as victim of despotism, patriot and lover. But, with publication of his memoirs, the last had been heard from him; he had been lapped up, lost on Venice's liquid bosom.

In marked contrast to Villette's brief and loquacious post-Necklace-Case career was the subsequent history of the Count de La Motte, who lived far into the new century and made a career of silence.

For some reason which has never been clarified, Louis XVIII took it into his head, sometime in 1816, to commission the Count de La Motte to write his, the Count's, memoirs. Perhaps, his curiosity not yet satisfied by Madame de La Motte's series of revelations, the monarch wanted to see what else he could ferret out about his late sister-in-law's involvement in the diamond necklace business. Whatever the reason, he instituted a police search to discover the Count's whereabouts—and must have been surprised to find the widower a member of his own royal intelligence service; this appointment the Count de La Motte owed to an old comrade from Bar-sur-Aube, a friend of his (or, rather, of his wife's) salad days—Beugnot, a count himself now, who held successively the Restoration posts of director general of the national police, Marine Minister, Postmaster General and Minister of State. (Beugnot, in turn, owed his life to an uncle of his wife's, who had known someone who knew someone—Beugnot was never too sure who it had been—who in 1794 had wangled a transfer for him in the nick of time from the Conciergerie to *La Force*, which differed from the Conciergerie in that it was not directly under the eye and the floorboards of the Revolutionary Tribunal and was not a jumping-off place for the guillotine.)

In a report by Louis XVIII's police on Count de La Motte, a Commissioner Marlot wrote:

We were instructed to inform Monsieur de La Motte of the sovereign's wishes that he write his memoirs. But at the end of several months this original character advised us he would not complete the manuscript unless the King guaranteed him a life pension on the civil list. The King took offense at this impertinence and called off the project. Since that time Monsieur de La Motte has vegetated idly in the capital.

Later, it seems, the Count was struck by the ingenious idea that if this government balked at paying him to write his memoirs it might instead pay him not to write his memoirs, for in 1829, in the reign of Charles X, the same Commissioner of Police Marlot reported to his superior officer:

Monsieur de La Motte came to sound us out on the new Ministry's attitude with regard to continuing his pension, the traditional price for the wretch's silence. He confided to us that his memoirs contain some very virulent passages and, in particular, some curious revelations concerning the intimacy between the late Queen Marie Antoinette and the Duchess de Polignac, mother of the present Prime Minister. . . .

La Motte will give up publication if he is assured a pension of three to four hundred francs and shelter at the Hospice of Chaillot. In his state of decrepitude, the annuity should not have to be long continued. . . .

The pension was granted.

At such times as the Count de La Motte was not engaged in not writing memoirs, he turned for assistance to Count Beugnot, invariably high up in the councils of state and with a stock of sinecures for distribution among old friends: for La Motte, managership of the *Théâtre de la Porte St. Martin* at a salary of three thousand francs and, at another time, a prize plum of a post as supervisor of gambling houses in the Palais-Royal at equally handsome pay. Even La Motte's sister, Madame de Latour, a needy grass widow of the Revolution, was favored by Beugnot with appointment as postmistress of Bar-sur-Aube. (The reason prompting the emigration of Monsieur de Latour, whose name was unlikely to have been included on the republican blacklists as either aristocrat or plutocrat, remains one of the minor unsolved Revolutionary mysteries. Was it that astringent tongue of his wagging some irrepressible, wicked bon mot at the expense of the new revolutionary hierarchy at the local level? Or was it that the Revolution was the ill wind to blow him good—aloose from long-chafing matrimonial moorings, floating free of those damned La Motte in-laws and clear out of deadly dull, provincial Bar-sur-Aube, across no matter what frontier?)

Victor Hugo came across the Count de La Motte in Paris, plus royaliste que le roi in those days of the Restoration, an honored, sought-after guest in the royalist salons of the Old Regime nobility, with his elegant Versailles courtier's manners and impressive mien. Hugo, incorporating youthful reminiscences in Les Misérables, refers to him as "one of the cocks of the walk in the salon of the Baroness de T——, who lived far from the court in an exclusive, disdainful, penurious seclusion, greeting a few friends twice weekly at her widowed hearth for tea and for expression, in moans and groans, on the 'horrors of the age': on the Bonapartist faction, the Jacobinism of Louis XVIII, his prostitution of the Cordon Bleu to the bourgeoisie, his national charter"—the Constitutional Charter granted by Louis XVIII, which guaranteed freedom of the press, of speech and of religion (and which Count Beugnot had helped to draft). Behind his back, just out of earreach, Hugo says, this royalist society "whispered also about the Count de La Motte: 'Oh, you know who he is! He's the La Motte of the necklace business!'"

To young Hugo, La Motte appeared "an old man with nothing remarkable about him except his silent and sententious air, his perfectly polished manners, his sharp, expressionless features, his coat buttoned up to his cravat, and his long legs, always crossed, in loose pantaloons the color of burnt sienna—his face matching his pantaloons. His position as a celebrity around the tea tables of dowager duchesses he owed to the name of Valois, which he had tacked onto his own."

On November 6, 1831, the Journal de Paris published this announcement:

Monsieur Mustophragesis, Count de Valois, Knight of St. Louis and of the Crown, nobleman of Angoulême, has just died in Paris at an advanced age and in destitution.

The husband of the famous Madame de La Motte-Valois, he was generally known as "Necklace La Motte" . . .

And that should have been the end of it. But the mystery that had beclouded the Count's and the Countess's lives overhung their deaths, and the newspapers seemed reluctant to write off copy so picturesque, so romanesque as the La Mottes.

In May of 1844, all the Paris newssheets were printing a sensational story about the death of a mysterious "Countess Jeanne." A bishop returning from emigration, the story went, had introduced this mysterious lady into the home of one of the wealthiest noblemen of the city, a marquis, who, upon learning the lady's history, had assigned her a wing of his mansion, a pension and two servants to attend her. Before his death, the marquis recommended that his heir continue the favors. The unknown lady emerged only to attend Mass or to go about on her errands of mercy, when the poor pressed round to kiss her generous, jeweled hands. At length, besieged by the grandes dames of the Faubourg St. Germain, she opened her salon to guests, and those fortunate enough to be received by the "Countess Jeanne" (the only name she bore) reported a brilliant conversationalist with a store of fascinating ancien-régime anecdotes, an expert player at whist and reversi. After thirty years, death rent the veil of mystery. In the dead woman's room a heap of half-burned papers and documents was discovered; death had surprised her throwing her life's secrets to the flames. The amazing discovery proved to be genealogical charts and manuscripts of memoirs which could have belonged only to the Countess de La Motte.

In the mid-nineteenth century, the memoirs of a Baroness de Bodé appeared with a tale still more curious, concerning a Countess de Gachet, nee Valois, who had lived in the Crimea between 1820 and 1830. "I can see her still," Baroness de Bodé wrote, "no longer young, but a slim, trim figure, her white hair covered with a black velvet cap. She spoke a choice French with grace and animation. . . . She had known the famous Cagliostro, had an inexhaustible fund of stories of the court of Louis XVI, and gave me to understand that there had been a great mystery in her life." In her will the Countess de Gachet appointed the Baroness de Bodé's father as executor. Her Armenian servant related to the Bodés, said the Baroness, that the Countess, "taking ill, had spent the whole night sorting and burning great stacks of papers. She had given express orders to the household that her body not be touched after death, that she be buried just as they found her. But, in laying out the corpse, the old servant noticed two dreadful scars on her shoulder, marks that could have been made only by a red-hot branding iron."

One of the Countess de La Motte's biographers, Louis de Soudak, made a pilgrimage to the Crimea to check the Baroness de Bodé's tale and later wrote, in an article which appeared in the Paris Revue Bleue of September 16, 1899:

> In 1894 near Staroi-Krim, in the garden of an Armenian potter, I found the old man seated on a stone. In low tones and with measured gesture, the graybeard related as follows: "There used to be, in these parts, a Countess de Gachet, a former Queen of France [sic], who had stolen a necklace. I was a little fellow then, and she used to call me to her side and dazzle my child's eyes with a huge diamond so brilliant as to make me blink, which she dangled in the sunlight at the end of a golden chain. When she died and the servants undressed her to prepare her body for the coffin, two letters were found branded on her shoulders. . . ."
>
> It is strange that the name and story of the heroine of the Diamond Necklace Case should have reached the Crimea when that remote peninsula had few inhabitants save Tartars and illiterate Greek fishermen.
>
> One sunny morning I stopped near Yalta, under a great plane tree where Pushkin is reputed to have composed his finest verses. Seeing a Tartar pass by, I asked him what things of interest were to be seen in the district. Indicating the north by a gesture of his hand, he answered, "At Artek, a few versts in that direction, there is the house where a Madame de Gachet lived, a woman who had stolen a great necklace from the Queen of your country. When she died, two letters were seen burned into the flesh of her back . . ."
>
> The legend, it will be noted, is precise, and it is well known throughout the entire region.
>
> . . . Accompanied by an Armenian deacon, I walked through a cemetery so ancient that, on many of the tombs,

the inscriptions had disappeared. Thence I repaired to the
spot where the Countess's cottage stood. On the edge of a
lonely ravine, the small peasant's dwelling nestled in a bed
of verdure; behind the trees a great windmill spread its verte-
brated sails toward the sky. I reflected that the hapless exile
must often have wandered here, and that, far from France,
her poor heart must have suffered bitter rancor and poignant
regret.

In 1858, twenty-seven years after his death, the memoirs of the Count
de La Motte were finally edited and published by Louis Lacour. Composed as they were in La Motte's old age, forty years after the Necklace
Trial, the value of the personal recollections would be dubious even if
one granted the author's veracity. It is not even certain, however, that
his hand guided the pen. For whatever they are worth, his memoirs constitute the last of the eyewitness accounts which, together with the trial
briefs and the official court documents and records, comprise what
Carlyle called "one of the largest collections of falsehoods that exists in
print." Carlyle added that, unfortunately, this collection of lies, "after
all the narrating and history there has been on the subject, still forms
our chief means of getting at the truth of that transaction" and so it
must be "sifted, contrasted, rejected."

Granted. But even after this injunction has been scrupulously observed, not everyone comes to the same conclusion as does Carlyle; nor,
among those who do come to the same conclusion, is everyone as satisfied with it as he.

Abbé Georgel sums up with a sigh:

In retrospect, the only conclusion seems to be that the Queen was innocent; that she never received the necklace; that it was her bitter resentment against the Cardinal that was the main cause of that all too
famous case, which it would have been more prudent to prevent from
ever coming to public notice; that it was the snares and the infernal
machinations of Madame de La Motte which deceived the Cardinal,
susceptible as he was to deception because of his obsession to regain the
Queen's favor; that the implacable animosity of Baron de Breteuil misled the youthful King and Queen; that he extended their authority beyond the limits appropriate to their dignity. Not that I imply that the

case constitutes a blemish on their memory; the saintliness of their martyrdom ensures that their names will be uttered only with reverence by posterity. My only comment is that punishment from the throne should be through the law impartially administered, never out of the monarch's personal resentments.

The jigsaw puzzle of a thousand pieces may be said to be completed. A picture stands out, a definite design apparent. The Countess de La Motte's is the central figure; clear and clearly guilty, redhanded—with bags of diamonds in each—she is to be seen dictating to Villette, who sits at her bedside table flourishing a quill pen. And, of course, Prince de Rohan is featured in the puzzle picture, his cape a splash of cardinal red, his cardinal's biretta atop an ass's ears. And Mademoiselle d'Oliva's candy-box-pretty face peeps out from the greenery of the Grove of Venus. And Cagliostro is there too, off to one side, a cabalistic red herring, succeeding admirably in adding to the puzzle player's confusion.

Of the Queen there is no sign anywhere—unless the tip of a train that trails in one corner of the picture may be said to be hers?

Most puzzle players, ostensibly satisfied with their handiwork, call it completed. Some few others, perplexed, bemused, continue staring. Confronting them is a heap of oddly shaped, oddly colored puzzle pieces that will fit in nowhere, although they came in the original box.

Pieces such as the disappearance of the three prize pieces of state's evidence, the three prime exhibits for the prosecution: Exhibit A, the contract with the terms of purchase for the necklace, in the Cardinal's handwriting and with the signature, "Marie Antoinette de France," and the word "Approved," alongside every paragraph, declared forgeries by the state's handwriting experts and so designated and labeled by the Parliament's order; Exhibit B, Cardinal Rohan's memorandum of explanation, written in his own hand in the royal study on the day of the arrest, August 15, 1785; Exhibit C, Marie Antoinette's information to the Parliament, the document described by the court registrar as "comprising fifteen separate articles . . . consisting of seven pages, bound and laced with a narrow blue silk riband." These three exhibits Parliament had ordered to be registered and filed as Items 2, 3 and 4 in the dossier of the Diamond Necklace Trial. Today the file, marked "No. X2 B 1417" and stacked in two large cardboard boxes in the Archives de France, contains every official scrap of paper relative to the Necklace Trial—except Items 2, 3 and 4.

Why, and when, and by whom were these prime exhibits for the prosecution extracted from the files?

The secret correspondent of the Court of St. Petersburg, under date of January 21, 1792, reported to his Russian audience, "Although revision of the Diamond Necklace Trial is the main topic of conversation in Paris today, such a retrial is an impossibility in view of the fact that Baron de Breteuil, as I have just learned, has extracted the most important pieces of evidence from the records."

On the track of the necklace in this decade, historian Louis Hastier obtained access to Baron de Breteuil's library and papers through courtesy of that former Minister's heir and descendant, the first such investigation to be made. In the ancestral Château de Choisel, Hastier came upon charming mementos of the Queen, her set of gardening tools for Trianon flower beds—rake, hoe and spade, diminutive, doll's size instruments with exquisitely wrought mahogany handles—but not so much as a sheet of paper relative to the Diamond Necklace Case, not even the Goethe letters on the subject, which should have been well worth saving if only for the already famous author's autograph; the Breteuil files on the Necklace Case had been emptied clean as a hound's tooth.

Another refractory puzzle piece, obviously part of the Mademoiselle d'Oliva corner of the picture: her refusal to deviate from her original statement in the Bastille interrogations that she had been driven back to Paris from Versailles, that July evening in 1784, "in a court carriage." Oliva, according to Villette, was the only one in the whole case who never lied, and yet she continued to insist that it had been a court carriage. From the palace stables? On whose orders? Did Madame de La Motte have the privilege of ordering out the Queen's horses at all hours?

The leftover puzzle piece which has most perturbed and perplexed perfectionists, however, is the Queen's letter of May 19, 1786, to Count Mercy, in which she expresses her determination to "allow no mention whatsoever . . . of the midnight rendezvous, the [Versailles] terrace incident."

Alexandre Dumas père directed his novelist's inventive genius to the puzzle and, in Louis XVI, arrived at a plot to take care of many of the tantalizing odds and ends. His scenario has the Queen commission the Cardinal to negotiate on her behalf for the necklace, which she has coveted all along and now hopes to pay off secretly out of her privy purse. After receiving the necklace and keeping it several weeks, however, Marie Antoinette comes to the realization that she cannot, after all, negotiate the payments on her own, and so she renounces the jewel, delivering it back into the hands of Madame de La Motte to be restored by her to the Cardinal and by him to the jewelers—but Madame de La Motte, of course, seizes her opportunity to make off with the prize. Dumas obviously attached little significance to the fact that Public Prosecutor Fouquier-Tinville of the Revolutionary Tribunal had failed to locate a single witness to testify that Madame de La Motte had ever been seen in the Queen's apartments. Or perhaps Dumas was thinking of the rabbit warren of Versailles and the surreptitious coming and goings in that network of secret stairs, secret corridors and secret doors, that labyrinth of private apartments (Louis XV had built fifty tiny "private" rooms behind and around the state apartments, and Louis XVI, Madame Campan relates, had added more).

The Goncourts took offense at so much as being asked to play at the necklace puzzle, "one of the most painful duties devolving upon a biographer of the Queen. History," they wrote, "exacts the sacrifice that he stoop for a moment to consider the scandal, although he would prefer to bury under contemptuous silence the suspicions which are raised as an outrage to Her Majesty's memory."

The Goncourts' great contemporary, the historian Michelet, scorned the generally accepted solution of the puzzle picture, but for involute reasons of his own, directly opposed to theirs. To his jaundiced monarchophobe eye, the central figure was missing from the picture, the figure of the guilty Queen—not an overly surprising point of view, considering his rabid antiroyalist, anticlerical bias. It is by a most curious jugglery of the puzzle pieces that he arrives at his solution: he shows the Queen purchasing the necklace through Rohan's agency, signing the contract with her own hand and resorting to the irregular signature "Marie Antoinette de France" purposely—"to ensure against the possibility of the necklace's reverting to the Austrian crown jewels"!

Maître Labori, one of the brightest French legal lights of the nineteenth century and a specialist in historic trials, worked out another odd assemblage of puzzle pieces. While ardently defending the Queen as being innocent of any complicity in the necklace transaction proper, he did see and place her figure in the Grove of Venus scene alongside Oliva; he considered that the midnight Versailles rendezvous could never have been staged without the Queen's "high-spirited, mischievous connivance." To this theory Michelet, Hastier, Lacour and Georgel all subscribe, Georgel quoting the Cardinal as saying from the Bastille that he was positive he had spoken to Her Majesty in the bosquet, that his eyes and ears could not thus have deceived him.

The abbé, personally, plumped for a Cagliostro-cum-great-world-wide-conspiracy version of the puzzle, serving secret, sinister Masonic revolutionary purposes. But if Cagliostro, plotting the necklace affair at long range to discredit the monarchy, could have foreseen the morass of blunders into which the monarchs and their minister would flounder (blunders that would actually be responsible for the resultant scandal), then he was indeed a seer and a prophet.

Biographer de Soudak worked out the puzzle pieces to show a hard-pressed Cardinal as the central figure and guilty party, acquiring the necklace by subterfuge and chicanery and selling the diamonds to raise cash to pay off and silence his most clamorous creditors. This was the solution advanced by Marie Antoinette as early as September 19, 1786, in her letter to her brother, Emperor Joseph (calling the Cardinal "a vile and clumsy counterfeiter"), and by Louis XVI in his conversation with Madame Campan (calling him "a cheap swindler"). Certainly it was the theory which had gained the widest popular acceptance at the time, according to a newsletter from the Paris correspondent of the court of St. Petersburg:

Most people in Paris keep coming back to the theory that His Eminence, like so many reckless men of wealth, ruined himself by buying on credit with no thought of the inevitable consequences; in this instance, the Cardinal, unable to obtain the necklace on his signature alone, took advantage of the Countess de La Motte's forgery on the contract to dupe the jewelers.

Biographer Louis Lacour fitted the puzzle pieces into a pattern by which a capricious Marie Antoinette, covetous of the necklace from the day she first laid eyes on it, refused it only because the price was so high that she could not finance it from her own resources, and then regretted her refusal. The Cardinal came along and suggested that he might be able to deal for her on better terms than Böhmer and Bassenge had originally quoted. With his obsession for a return to royal favor, he was willing even to bear part of the cost himself, if necessary; he considered that the gratification of the Queen's passion for diamonds was his golden opportunity to restore himself to her good graces.

In accepting Prince de Rohan's offer [according to Lacour], the Queen discerned the means for bringing down the man she hated by his Achilles' heel of vanity and ambition. To reward a man's ardent services with treachery added a fillip to the sweetness of revenge. Yet another humiliation for haughty Rohan was to be effected by compromising him with a streetwalker, accidentally but conveniently at hand as the instrument of disgrace. Rohan's depravity amused the Queen; luring him on by a signal mark of her favor in the appointment for the midnight rendezvous, she staged the farce by which a prince of the Church and of the realm was inveigled into prostrating himself at the feet of a common whore whom he would mistake for his sovereign.

The Queen, however, having committed herself by the contract to meet the first payment of the necklace on a fixed date, soon realized that she could not manage it. To conceal that fact, she demanded a 200,000-franc reduction in the price in the hope that the jewelers would refuse and call off the whole deal. Imagine her shock and dismay when Böhmer and Bassenge agreed to the reduction and she was obliged to solicit another postponement! At this delay the jewelers panicked, and Rohan's enemy, Baron de Breteuil, a rancorous and evil man, upon being informed of the jewelers' laments rushed to the Queen and confronted her with a grim alternative: "Here is the situation in which you have involved yourself without the King's knowledge or approval. It takes on the aspect of a criminal offense. You will be lost unless you agree to throw the blame upon the Cardinal."

Lacour concludes, "The crisis permitted of no hesitation. Louis de Rohan was sacrificed."

Scholarly perspective, as may be seen, has become unfortunately distorted in the Necklace Case, especially as concerns the Queen, whose controversial character must supply the key to the enigma. The result, inevitably: an unscholarly bias among scholars.

Nor does the necklace affair permit of dispassionate commentators, politically speaking; causes apparently lost prove not to be totally lost after all, not wholly abandoned. The French royalist party, as late as the mid-twentieth century, could rally enough supporters to the Bourbon-

Orléans standard to disconcert the Fourth Republic, which did not permit the Count de Paris, the present pretender to the throne, to return to French soil until 1950, a bare ten years ago. As for the Fifth Republic's President de Gaulle, who has vastly augmented the executive powers at the expense of the legislative without providing (or revealing) any formula for a successful government, it has been said that he distrusts the masses and that the wistful gaze in his eyes may be in the direction of the Bourbon lilies.

The reverberations roused by the Necklace Case, the ostensibly dead issues of pro- and anticlericalism, pro- and antimonarchism have also been livened and complicated by latter-day fascist-Communist dialectics. If the case continues to be a controversial issue still good for an argument in these days of the Fifth Republic, it is because, as in the instance of our own American Civil War, it stirs up curious and ancient loyalties, antique resentments.

Thus it glitters across the centuries, an ignis fatuus to researchers and historians, with a glint of ideological significance to some; to others it is a mystery story with a solution generally accepted though far from acceptable to all—and with enough new evidence turned up every generation to keep it in the realm of perennial conjecture. The Diamond Necklace Case remains the best-kept secret of the eighteenth century, though it has stimulated a whole library of speculation and controversy, tantalizing the imagination, challenging the mind, generation upon generation.

?

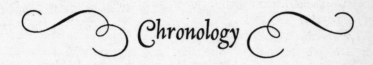

Chronology

1715	Death of Louis XIV Accession of Louis XV
1734	Birth of Prince Louis-René-Édouard de Rohan
1754	Birth of Louis-Auguste, the future Louis XVI (grandson of Louis XV; became Dauphin 1765)
1755	Birth of Marie Antoinette
1756	Birth of Jeanne de Saint-Rémy de Valois (future Countess de La Motte)
1770	Marriage of Marie Antoinette to the Dauphin Louis-Auguste
1772	Arrival of Prince de Rohan in Vienna as French ambassador to Austria
1774	Death of Louis XV Accession of Louis XVI Recall of Prince de Rohan from Vienna
1775	Recognition of Jeanne de Saint-Rémy de Valois's claims to honors of house of Valois; award of title "Mademoiselle de Valois" and crown pension

1777		Prince de Rohan appointed Grand Almoner of France
1778		Prince de Rohan named Cardinal Birth of Marie-Thérèse-Charlotte (Madame Royale), first child of Louis XVI and Marie Antoinette Completion of the diamond necklace; offered for the first time to Louis XVI by the crown jewelers
1780		Marriage of Jeanne de Valois to Marc Antoine Nicolas de La Motte Arrival of Count Cagliostro in France; meeting of Cagliostro and Cardinal Rohan
1783		Meeting of Countess de La Motte-Valois and Cardinal Rohan
1784		"Grove of Venus" scene
1785	JANUARY 29–FEBRUARY 1	Contract for purchase of the diamond necklace signed by Cardinal Rohan; delivery acknowledged by him
	MARCH 27	Birth of Louis Charles de France, second son of Louis XVI and Marie Antoinette, later Dauphin (on death of elder brother, 1789) and uncrowned Louis XVII
	AUGUST 15	Arrest of Cardinal Rohan
	AUGUST 18	Arrest of Countess de La Motte
	SEPTEMBER 19	Diamond Necklace Case referred by Louis XVI to Parliament of Paris for trial
1786	MAY 30	Hearing of prisoners before the Parliament
	MAY 31	Judgment pronounced
1787		Escape of Countess de La Motte from the Salpêtrière; her flight to England
1789	MAY–JUNE	Convocation of the States-General in Versailles; the Third Estate declares itself the National Assembly

1789		Publication of Countess de La Motte's memoirs (the first), in London
1789	JULY 14	Fall of the Bastille
	OCTOBER 5	March of the Womens' Army on Versailles; the royal family taken to the Tuileries Palace
	DECEMBER	Arrest of Count Cagliostro in the Papal States
1789		Publication of Countess de La Motte's memoirs (the second) in London
1791		Sentence pronounced upon Cagliostro by the Inquisition
1791	JUNE 20–25	Flight of the royal family; their capture at Varennes and return to the Tuileries
1791		Publication of Countess de La Motte's Story of My Life (first edition) in London
1791	AUGUST 23	Death of Countess de La Motte
1792	AUGUST 10	Attack on the Tuileries
	AUGUST 13	Imprisonment of the royal family in the Temple
	SEPTEMBER 21	Proclamation of the French Republic (the First) by the National Convention
1792		Publication of second edition of Countess de La Motte's Story of My Life in Paris
1793	JANUARY 21	Execution of Louis XVI
	OCTOBER 16	Execution of Marie Antoinette
1795		Death of Cagliostro reported Directory succeeds National Convention
1799		Consulate established
1803		Death of Cardinal Prince de Rohan
1804		Napoleon Bonaparte becomes Emperor of France (First Empire)

1814	Abdication of Napoleon; exile to Elba Restoration of Bourbon Monarchy—Louis XVIII, former Count de Provence, becomes King of France
1815	Return of Napoleon from Elba; the Hundred Days; Waterloo Second abdication of Napoleon; exile to St. Helena Second Restoration of Bourbon Monarchy (Louis XVIII)
1824	Charles X, former Count d'Artois, becomes King of France
1830	Louis Philippe (of the Orléans-Bourbon line, son of Philippe Égalité), becomes last "King of the French"
1831	Death of Count de La Motte
1848	Second Republic declared
1852	Napoleon III becomes Emperor (Second Empire)
1871	Third Republic declared

Appendix

(Page 38)

According to Madame Campan and others, Mademoiselle de Passy was the real culprit in an escapade for which many people blamed Marie Antoinette, on the occasion of the mourning reception held by the new King and Queen at the Château de la Muette following the death of Louis XV. Madame Campan writes in her memoirs (referring to the Boulainvilliers' daughter by her married name, Clermont-Tonnerre, although at the time of this incident the girl was still Mademoiselle de Passy):

All the ladies of the nobility, from the youngest to the oldest, came to offer condolences and pay homage to the new sovereign. Some of the dowdy old dowagers, their antique bonnets bobbing as they bowed low before the Queen, did appear grotesque, but Her Majesty maintained a proper mien of dignity and gravity. The Marquise de Clermont-Tonnerre was the lady in waiting who, stationed immediately behind Marie Antoinette and becoming weary and footsore after hours of standing, suddenly discovered a way to sink down out of sight on the parquet floor behind the wall of silk and satin formed by the panniers of the Queen and her ladies on the receiving line. There on the floor behind

603

them, the Marquise de Clermont-Tonnerre tugged at their skirts, pinched their legs and indulged in a thousand other antics, several times disrupting the Queen's composure. Her Majesty had to put her fan up to her face to hide the smiles she could not repress. And the "supreme court of dowager duchesses" pronounced against the young Queen that she welcomed only youth and showed disrespect to age, and that not a one of them would ever set foot in her court again. The epithet "*moqueuse*" [mocker], than which there was none more calculated to offend, attached itself to her name. A jingle appeared the very next day:

> Little Queen, have a care;
> If you behave with such an air,
> You'll be sent back over there!

And more than fifteen years afterward I was to hear elderly ladies, in the remotest corners of the provinces, still commenting on that con-dolence call at which Marie Antoinette broke out in rude laughter in the very faces of the sexagenarian ladies of her court.

(Page 74)

Baroness d'Oberkirch's description of the gala given by Marie Antoi-nette in honor of Grand Duke Paul and his wife:

Grétry's delicious opera *Zémire et Azor* was the production on the Trianon stage that night and was sung to perfection—which was not surprising, since it was under Her Majesty's supervision, she being a good musician, a student of Gluck. The little theater at Trianon is a jewel box—literally, too, for it has a diamond décor dazzling to the eye [a fact denied by Madame Campan, who insists it was strass, paste]. After the opera came a ballet, *The French Girl in the Harem*; the choreography was brilliant, the costuming splendid and the Queen's troupe of dancers more splendid still than the costuming. The court was in gala dress, Madame la Comtesse du Nord wearing in her coiffure a small jeweled hummingbird so scintillating one could not long focus on it without blinking as it fluttered its wings above a rose. From the theater the party moved to the dining rooms, where three tables were laid, a hundred covers each. And after supper the company was invited out into the gardens to witness the illuminations, which were magnificent. Trianon is indeed an enchanting spot, its groves perfumed with lilac, alive with nightingales; still, the landscape projects of private citizens have been more costly—the "*folie* Boutin," the "*folie* Saint-James" or the park of Brunoy, for example. Even so, the Queen has been accused of profligacy at Trianon. What a fuss over the construction of her Swiss Village there! Now, is that such an exorbitant fancy, I ask you, for a Queen of France? Ah, how vicious is envy, the secret source of most resentments . . .

(Page 135)

Madame Campan's memoirs give this view of the friendship between Marie Antoinette and the Duchess de Polignac:

The Queen often told me that I was the only one to whom she could confide her disillusionment in her chosen circle of close friends; that she was constrained to endure an unpleasant situation which she herself had brought about. Estrangement or open rupture in the case of an intimacy such as that with the Duchess de Polignac could only bring on still more serious complications. The Queen was suffering acute dissatisfaction, and her friendship with the Duchess de Polignac began to deteriorate. It was at this period that Her Majesty made the observation to me that when a sovereign raises up favorites in her court she raises up despots against herself. The ardor of such favorites, the Queen commented bitterly, while originally dedicated to service of their royal mistress' interest, is eventually diverted to service of their own. Interfering even in affairs of state, these favorites come to act independently, whereas the censure for their action falls upon the sovereign from whom they derived the power.

No Pompadour, no Du Barry had ever cost the French nation so dear as this favorite of a queen, this violet-eyed Duchess de Polignac. "Almost unexampled is the fact that in so short a time the royal favor should have brought such overwhelming advantages to one family," Count Mercy complained in a letter to Vienna.

The family managed to cling to these advantages throughout even revolution and emigration; the Prince de Polignac (father of Prince

Rainier of Monaco), head of the clan in this generation, still disposes of the fortune that stems from Marie Antoinette's prodigality to her dearest friend.

It is interesting that Madame Campan considered herself "the only one" to whom the Queen had confided on this subject. The Countess de La Motte was aware of the peculiar situation regarding the Polignacs, and she published it in her memoirs a quarter of a century before Madame Campan's appeared.

(*Page 198*)

August 8, 1960:

DEAR MRS. MOSSIKER:

Thank you very much for sending us the actual-size photostat of the design of the famous Queen's Necklace in connection with the publication of your book.

The director of our diamond department, Mr. Ray Haydon, has studied carefully the engraving and the information you furnished on earlier estimates of the weights of the diamonds. He concludes that the necklace could be duplicated today for $3,855,500.00. This would include the current 10% Federal Excise Tax.

Several factors were taken into consideration in reaching this estimate, and we believe they would interest you. We must assume, from your historical research, that the necklace contained the finest diamonds obtainable in the 18th Century. We must remember, however, that diamond cutting had not then reached its scientific zenith, nor did it until the 20th Century. The cutter of that time did not achieve the maximum brilliance demanded of today's diamonds. Also we must believe that the stones in the hands of an 18th Century jeweler were examined under a much lower power of magnification than is used today by reputable gem experts in pronouncing a diamond flawless. Thus if the diamonds in the "collier" were available on today's market they would not, aside from their historical value, command the same price as modern ones of the finest quality.

It is interesting to surmise, on the other hand, that anyone who ordered a jewel of this magnitude today would insist also that the diamonds be only the best that the world had to offer. It is on this premise that we have based our estimate of the cost to replace the necklace in our time.

Mr. Haydon's itemization of the number of diamonds and their approximate weights follows:

1 Pear Shaped Diamond	15 carats
5 Pear Shaped Diamonds (13 carats each)	65 carats
12 Pear Shaped Diamonds (6 carats each)	72 carats
1 Round Diamond	11 carats
14 Round Diamonds (10 carats each)	140 carats
3 Round Diamonds (5 carats each)	15 carats
8 Round Diamonds (3 carats each)	24 carats
603 Small Round Diamonds	2500 carats
647 Diamonds	2842 carats

You will notice that the total carat weight above exceeds by 42 carats the total mentioned in your source material, but we feel that the latter very possibly was given only as a round figure.

With kindest regards, we are,

Cordially yours,
LINZ BROS.

Joseph S. Linz
Vice President

(Page 283)

The reaction of the provincial gentry to the La Mottes' ostentatious behavior in the summer of 1785 is described in this passage from the unpublished souvenirs of the Vicomtesse de Loménie:

The main topic of conversation at the time was the splendor and opulence of the La Motte ménage.

Of course, the pair made a supreme effort to gain a foothold at the Château de Brienne, which was four leagues distant from Bar-sur-Aube. The husband came there twice without benefit of invitation and made so bold as to take his seat not only in the theater but later at the supper table. Monsieur de Brienne, however, dismissed him so summarily as to discourage his return.

Madame de La Motte was so insolent as to appear in public wearing a medallion with a miniature of the Queen, encircled with superb diamonds, which according to her was a gift from the Queen. The shrewd provincials in Champagne, however, were not so easily taken in. In that neighborhood, where she had been born, she had been known as a consummate liar from childhood on . . .

(Page 467)

The following poignant and charming note, renowned as the "Cher Coeur letter" and supposedly written by Marie Antoinette to the Duchess de Polignac in 1786, comes from the collection of Feuillet de Conches. Its authenticity, however, is suspect, as is that of all other Marie Antoinette letters collected by this exquisite nineteenth-century savant, who seems to have had an understandable obsession for rounding out his acquisitions of Revolutionary and pre-Revolutionary memorabilia. But even the more probable forgeries in his collection defy positive refutation, so impeccable is their execution not only in paper, script and individual literary styles but also in historical and biographical data, with which Feuillet was superlatively well acquainted.

Come weep with me, come and console your friend, dear Polignac. The judgment just pronounced by the Parliament is the most frightful insult. You will find me bathed in tears of sorrow and despair. Who can any longer be sure of anything in this world where malicious spirits take delight in shaking the very foundations of the throne? What ingratitude! . . . And yet, my triumph over my enemies shall take the form of redoubling my efforts for the national good. My enemies shall find it easier to wound me than to rouse my vengeance.

Come soon, dear heart.

MARIE ANTOINETTE

(Page 584)

The letters reproduced below, which appeared in the London Times in January 1959, were inspired by the display of the Duchess of Sutherland's sautoir at the Ageless Diamond exhibition at Christie's—a sautoir described by the Times's sale room correspondent as "part of the famous or, rather, notorious necklace which (though she was unaware of what was going on) helped to bring about the Queen's [Marie Antoinette's] downfall."

THE AGELESS DIAMOND

January 1:

To the Editor of The Times

Sir,— It would be interesting to know more of the history of the Duchess of Sutherland's diamond necklace, and its connexion with that which played so notorious a part in the tragedy of Marie Antoinette.

That famous ornament had 629 diamonds, of which seventeen of the largest were set in a string to encircle the neck; from this string depended one large and two smaller festoons (Carlyle's word), and falling below these again were broad ropes ending in four great tassels, all of diamonds. The contemporary drawing made for the jewellers, Böhmer et Bassenge, was reproduced as a steel engraving in the memoirs of the Abbé Georgel in 1817, and has been often republished, most recently in M. Louis Hastier's La Vérité sur l'Affaire du Collier (Paris, 1955).

The oral evidence and affidavits adduced at the trial leave no doubt that the conspirators La Motte and his wife broke up the necklace and sold the separate stones in small parcels anywhere they could find a market. But it may be that some of them are still identifiable. Your illustration in The Times of December 29 shows that the Duchess of Sutherland's necklace consists of twenty-two diamonds. Now, it so happens that La Motte in his disposition mentions having sold twenty-two stones from the "scallops" to Gray's, the jewellers in Bond Street, to make into a single string necklace. Reference to the engraving shows that each of the smaller festoons had just eleven stones, rather smaller than those in the string round the neck; and these are by no means unlike those in your picture. It is true that Mme. de La Motte in her memoirs says she sold a parcel of twenty-two stones, to a jeweller named Paris; but there is no mention of these having been set in one string, or brought to England. Is it a plausible guess that the diamonds in the possession of the Duchess of Sutherland are the ones that were bought by Gray?

I am, Sir, your obedient servant

DERMOT MORRAH

Oxford and Cambridge Club

January 3:

To the Editor of The Times

SIR,— In my book *Knole and the Sackvilles*, pp. 179-180 (Ernest Benn edition, 1958), there is quite a long passage about the affair of the diamond necklace, quoting from the dispatches of John Frederick Sackville, 3rd Duke of Dorset, Ambassador to the court of Louis XVI, 1783-1789.

I had always understood that some of the diamonds had been bought by the Duke of Dorset and some by the Duke of Sutherland, and that the Duke of Dorset's share was now at Knole, having been reset into a tasselled diadem.

Such, at any rate, was the family tradition, and it receives some evidential support in a receipt among the Knole archives: "Receiving of his Grace the Duke of Dorset nine hundred and seventy-five pounds for a brilliant necklace, £975. For Mr. Jeffreys and self, Wm. Jones." This receipt was endorsed "Paid 1790," the date when the necklace was sold by M. de La Motte to Jeffreys, a jeweller in Piccadilly.*

I regret that I have not got a copy of M. Louis Hastier's book, *La Vérité sur l'Affaire du Collier*, to verify the statements that M. de La Motte did indeed sell some of the diamonds to a Mr. Jeffreys, a jeweller in Piccadilly.

I remain, Sir, yours sincerely,

V. SACKVILLE-WEST

Sissinghurst Castle, Kent, Jan. 1

* According to the jeweler's affidavit presented at the Necklace Trial, the stones were sold to him by La Motte in 1785 (see pp. 366-67).

January 19:

To the Editor of The Times

Sir,— Whatever may have been the ultimate fate of the *"Collier de la Reine,"* it will interest your correspondents to know that the cost of the necklace was paid off in installments by the Rohan family over a period of nearly 100 years, the last payment being made in the early nineties of the last century.

It brought no material benefit to the family beyond the satisfaction of meeting a debt of honor.

Yours faithfully,

Charles de Rohan

Charmouth, Dorset

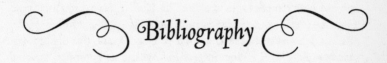

Bibliography

UNPUBLISHED DOCUMENTS

Bastille records (Archives de la Bastille), in the Bibliothèque de l'Arsenal, Paris.

Diplomatic representatives' reports and reports of French police agents in foreign countries, Archives des Affaires Étrangères, Paris.

Fleury, Joly de, chief prosecutor for the Crown: Dossier, papers, notes, résumés of the prosecution in the Diamond Necklace Trial, Bibliothèque Nationale, Paris.

Hardy, Simeon: Journal, "Mes loisirs, ou journal d'évènements tels qu'ils parviennent a ma connaissance," Bibliothèque Nationale, Paris.

"Le Procès du Collier," the official dossier of the entire Necklace Trial from the records of the Parliament of Paris—the depositions, interrogations and confrontations and the transcript of the minutes of the trial (May 31, 1786)—Archives de France, Paris. (Excerpts from the interrogation of the defendants have been published in Émile Campardon's *Marie Antoinette et le procès du Collier*, Paris, 1863.)

Target, Counselor at law (chief counsel to Cardinal Prince Louis de Rohan): Dossier, papers, notes relative to the Cardinal's defense in the Necklace Trial, Bibliothèque de la Ville de Paris.

PUBLISHED WORKS

LEGAL MÉMOIRES (TRIAL BRIEFS, DEFENSE PLEAS, PETITIONS)

BETTE D'ÉTIENVILLE, ed.: *Collection complète de tous les Mémoires qui ont paru dans la fameuse affaire du Collier.* Six vols., Paris, 1786. Of the several contemporary collections of legal mémoires of the various defendants in the Diamond Necklace Case, this one, though not complete, is the most interesting in that its compiler, an obvious publicity seeker, attempted to involve himself in the case as a defendant, publishing several mémoires of his own. A listing of the principal individually published mémoires of bona fide defendants follows. Most of them were written by the defendants' attorneys; all were published in 1786 and all but one of them in Paris.

BASSENGE, PAUL, and BÖHMER, CHARLES:

Mémoire des joailliers Böhmer et Bassenge, du Août 12, 1785.

CAGLIOSTRO, COUNT ALESSANDRO DI:

Lettre au peuple français. London, 1786.

Mémoire pour le Comte de Cagliostro contre Maître Chesnon fils et le Sieur de Launay.

Mémoire pour le Comte de Cagliostro, accusé, contre M. le Procureur-général, accusateur, en présence de M. le Cardinal de Rohan, de la Comtesse de La Motte et autres, co-accusés.

Requête au parlement, les chambres assemblées, pour le Comte de Cagliostro, signifiée à M. le Procureur-général, le 24 février, 1786.

Memorial for the Count de Cagliostro. London, 1786.

LA MOTTE-VALOIS, JEANNE DE SAINT-RÉMY DE:

Mémoire pour dame Jeanne de Saint-Rémy de Valois, épouse du Comte de La Motte.

Réponse pour la Comtesse de Valois-Lamotte au Mémoire du Comte Cagliostro.

Sommaire pour la Comtesse de Valois-Lamotte, accusée, contre M. le Procureur-général, accusateur, en présence de M. le Cardinal de Rohan et autres co-accusés. Paris, 1786.

OLIVA, MARIE NICOLE LEGUAY D':

Mémoire pour la demoiselle le Guay d'Oliva, fille mineure, émancipée d'âge, accusée, contre M. le Procureur-général.

Second mémoire et pièces justificatives pour Mademoiselle le Guay d'Oliva.

ROHAN, CARDINAL PRINCE LOUIS DE:

Mémoire pour Louis-René-Édouard de Rohan, cardinal, contre M. le Procureur-général, en présence de la dame de La Motte.

Pièces justificatives pour M. le Cardinal de Rohan, déclarations authentiques selon la forme anglaise.

Réflexions rapides pour M. le Cardinal de Rohan sur le sommaire de la dame de La Motte.

Requête au parlement, les chambres assemblées, par M. le Cardinal de Rohan.

VILLETTE, RÉTAUX DE:

Requête pour le sieur Marc-Antoine Rétaux de Villette, ancien gendarme, accusé, contre M. le Procureur-général.

PERSONAL MEMOIRS AND OTHER CONTEMPORARY BOOKS

ARNETH, ALFRED D', and FLAMMERMONT, JULES, eds.: Correspondance secrète du comte de Mercy-Argenteau avec l'empereur Joseph II et le prince de Kaunitz. Paris, 1889-91.

ARNETH, ALFRED D', and GEFFROY, A., eds.: Correspondance secrète entre Marie-Thérèse et le comte de Mercy-Argenteau. Paris, 1874.

BACHAUMONT: Mémoires secrets. Brussels, 1866.

BESENVAL, BARON PIERRE VICTOR DE: Mémoires de M. le baron de Besenval. Paris, 1805.

BEUGNOT, COUNT CLAUDE: Mémoires. Paris, 1866.

CAGLIOSTRO, COUNT ALESSANDRO DI: Open Letter to the French. London, 1786.

CAMPAN, MME JEANNE-LOUISE GENÊT: Mémoires sur la vie privée de Marie Antoinette. Paris, 1823.

CASANOVA, GIOVANNI JACOPO: Mémoires de Jacques Casanova de Seingalt. Paris, 1833-37.

CHARPENTIER: La Bastille Dévoilée. Paris, 1789.

Compte Rendu de ce qui s'est passé au parlement relativement à l'affaire de Monseigneur le cardinal de Rohan. Paris, 1786.

EDEN, WILLIAM, BARON AUCKLAND: Journals and Correspondence of William, Lord Auckland. London, 1860-62.

FLAMMERMONT, JULES: *Les correspondances des agents diplomatiques étrangers en France avant la révolution.* Paris, 1896.

GEORGEL, ABBÉ: *Mémoires pour servir à l'histoire des évènements de la fin du dix-huitième siècle.* Paris, 1817.

GLEICHEN, CHARLES-HENRI, BARON DE: *Souvenirs.* Paris, 1868.

GOETHE, JOHANN WOLFGANG VON: *Travels in Italy* (translated from the German). London, 1885.

Histoire véritable de Jeanne de Saint-Rémy. Villefranche, 1786.

Julie philosophe, ou le bon patriote. London.

Jugement rendu par le parlement de Paris sur l'affaire du Collier de diamants, avec le détail de ce qui s'est passé aux séances du parlement les 30 et 31 Mai, 1786, et les ordres du Roi après le jugement. Paris, 1786.

LABORDE, J. B. DE: *Lettres sur la Suisse en 1781.* Geneva, 1784.

LAMBALLE, MARIE-THÉRÈSE-LOUISE DE SAVOIE-CARIGNAN, PRINCESS DE: *Mémoires historiques de la Princesse de Lamballe.* Paris, 1801.

LA MOTTE, MARC ANTOINE NICOLAS: *Mémoires inédits du comte de La Motte-Valois* (ed., Louis Lacour). Paris, 1858.

LA MOTTE, JEANNE DE SAINT-RÉMY DE: *An Address to the Public Explaining the Motives Which Have Hitherto Delayed the Publication of the Memoirs of the Countess de La Motte* [believed to be authentic]. London, 1789.

————: *Detection, or A Scourge for Calonne.* London, 1789.

————: *Lettre à la reine de France.* Oxford, 1789. Published simultaneously in English under the title *An Open Letter from the Countess de Valois de La Motte to the Queen of France.*

————: *Mémoires justicatifs de la comtesse de La Motte-Valois,* first and second editions. Both, London, 1789.

————: *Memoirs of the Countess de Valois de La Motte.* Dublin, 1790.

————: *Supplique à la Nation et Requête a l'Assemblée nationale par Jeanne Saint Rémy de Valois, ci-devant Comtesse de La Motte,* en révision de son procès. 1790.

————: *Vie de Jeanne de Saint-Rémy de Valois* (referred to herein as *Story of My Life*). London, 1791; Paris, 1792.

LESCURE, M. DE, ed.: *Correspondance secrète inédite sur Louis XVI, Marie Antoinette, la cour et la ville, de 1777 à 1792* (based on manuscripts in the Imperial Library, St. Petersburg). Paris, 1866.

LÉVIS, GASTON, DUKE DE: *Souvenirs et Portraits.* Paris, 1815.

LUCHET, JEAN-PIERRE-LOUIS DE LA ROCHE DU MAINE, MARQUIS DE:

Mémoires authentiques pour servir à l'histoire du comte de Cagliostro, second edition. 1785.

MERCIER DE SAINT-LÉGER, BARTHÉLEMY: *Mercieriana, ou Notes inédites de Mercier de Saint-Léger* (ed., Maurice Tourneux). Paris, 1893.

——: *Notice raisonée des ouvrages, lettres, dissertations, etc.* (ed., Chênedollé). Brussels, 1853.

MÉTRA: *Correspondance secrète, politique et littéraire*. London, 1787-1788.

NOUGARET, M.: *Anecdotes du règne de Louis XVI*. Paris, 1791.

OBERKIRCH, HENRIETTE-LOUISE DE WALDNER-FREUNDSTEIN, BARONESS D': *Mémoires de la baronne d'Oberkirch*. Paris, 1853.

RECKE, CHARLOTTE ELISABETH CONSTANTIA VON DER: *Nachricht von des berüchtigen Cagliostro Aufenthalten in Mitau im Jahre 1779*. Berlin and Stettin, 1787.

Vie de Joseph Balsamo connu sous le nom de Comte Cagliostro (translated from the Italian, which was written by one of the judges at Cagliostro's Inquisition trial in 1790, and printed at the Apostolic Chamber, Rome). Paris, 1791.

VILLETTE, RÉTAUX DE: *Mémoires historiques des intrigues de la cour*. Venice, 1790.

CONTEMPORARY PAMPHLETS AND NEWSSHEETS

Addresse de la comtesse de La Motte-Valois a l'Assemblée nationale pour être déclarée citoyenne active [spurious]. London, 1790.

Le Capitaine Tempête à Jeanne de La Motte.

Confessions du Comte de C——. Cairo* and Paris, 1787.

Le Conte oriental

La Dernière pièce du fameux collier

Le Garde du Corps

La Lettre à l'occasion de la détention du cardinal

La Lettre de l'abbé G—— à la comtesse

Lettre de Mme de La Motte au François [sic] au sujet de son ami Calonne. Paris.

Lettre du Chevalier —— à un anglais, contenant le bulletin de ce qui s'est passé au parlement de Paris, etc. 1786.

* An obviously fictitious place of publication. Such designations were commonly used by the clandestine press of Paris.

Lettre d'un Garde-du-Roi pour servir de suite aux mémoires sur Cagliostro [attributed to L. P. Manuel]. London, 1786.

Les Lettres de Cachet presque ressuscitées, ou l'Enlèvement nocturne de Mme de la Mothe [sic].

Mémoires authentiques pour servir à l'histoire du comte de Cagliostro. Paris, 1786.

Observations de P. Tranquille sur le 1er mémoire de Mme la comtesse de La Motte. Mecca,* 1786.

Recueil de pièces authentiques et intéressantes pour servir d'éclaircissement à l'affaire du cardinal de Rohan. Strasbourg, 1786.

La Reine dévoilée, ou Supplément au mémoire de Mme la comtesse de Valois de La Motte. London, 1789.

Suite des Observations de Motus sur le mémoire de Mlle d'Oliva. Lima,* 1786.

CONTEMPORARY NEWSPAPERS

Courrier de l'Europe, French ed., London (an English edition was published also), Apr. 11 and Sept. 1, 1786, Aug. 26, 1791, and others.

Gazette d'Amsterdam, French ed., Amsterdam, Sept. 27, 1785, Mar. 31, 1786, and others.

Gazette de Hollande, French ed., September-December 1785; 1786.

Gazette de Leyden, French ed., Leyden, Nov. 9 and Dec. 9, 1785; April 14, June 28 and Sept. 25, 1786; and others, 1787.

Gazette d'Utrecht, French ed., Utrecht, Aug. 1, 1787, and others, 1785 and 1786.

Mercure de France, Paris, 1785 and 1786.

Le Moniteur, Paris, issues of 1791; No. 220, 1792; Oct. 6, 1795.

Morning Chronicle, London, Dec. 29, 1786, August 26, 1791, and others.

LATER WORKS

BELLEVAL, MARQUIS DE: Les Bâtards de la Maison de France. Paris, 1901.

BERRYER, M.: Souvenirs de M. Berryer, doyen des avocats de Paris, de 1774 à 1833. Paris, 1839.

---

* An obviously fictitious place of publication. Such designations were commonly used by the clandestine press of Paris.

BLANC, LOUIS: *Histoire de la Révolution Française*. Brussels.

BLAVATSKY, HELENA P.: *Isis Unveiled*. Rider, 1936.

BOLITHO, WILLIAM: *Twelve against the Gods*. William Heinemann, 1930.

CAMPARDON, ÉMILE: *Marie-Antoinette et le procès du collier*. Paris, 1863.

CAPEFIGUE, M.: *Les derniers jours de Trianon*. Paris, 1866.

CARLYLE, THOMAS: *Critical and Miscellaneous Essays*, collected and republished. London, 1889.

———: "The Diamond Necklace," *Frazer's Magazine*, London, 1837.

———: *The French Revolution*. Leipzig ed., 1851.

CASTELOT, ANDRÉ: *Marie-Antoinette*. Paris, 1958.   (British edition: *Queen of France*, Valentine, 1957.)

CHAIX D'EST-ANGE, GUSTAVE: *Marie-Antoinette et le procès du Collier*. Paris, 1889.

CHEVALIER, L.: *Histoire de Bar-sur-Aube*. Bar-sur-Aube, 1851.

COMBES, LOUIS: *Marie-Antoinette et l'Affaire du Collier*. Paris, 1876.

DUMAS, ALEXANDRE, PÈRE: *Louis XVI et la Révolution*. Paris, 1851.

———: *Joseph Balsamo* (*Mémoires d'un Médecin*). Paris, 1846-1848.

———: *Le Collier de la Reine*. Paris, 1849-1850.

———: *Ange Pitou*. Paris, 1851.

———: *La Comtesse de Charny*. Paris, 1852-1855.

FAY, BERNARD: *Revolution and Freemasonry, 1680-1800*. Boston, 1935.

———: *Franklin, Apostle of Modern Times*. Boston, 1929.

FLAMMERMONT, JULES: *Étude critique des Mémoires de Mme Campan*. Paris, 1886.

——— (ed.): *Correspondance du corps diplomatique*. Paris, 1896.

FUNCK-BRENTANO, FRANTZ: *L'Affaire du Collier*. Fifth ed., Paris, 1903.

GONCOURT, EDMOND and JULES DE: *Histoire de Marie-Antoinette*. Paris, 1884.

HASTIER, LOUIS: *La Vérité sur l'affaire du collier*. Paris, 1955.

J. F. G.: *Essais historiques sur la ville de Bar-sur-Aube*. Troyes, 1838.

KLEIN, C. G.: *Saverne et ses environs*. Strasbourg, 1849.

LABORI, FERNAND: "Le Procès du Collier," *Gazette des Tribunaux*, Paris, Nov. 26, 1888.

LEGIER-DESGRANGES, M.: *L'Évasion de Mme de La Motte*. Paris, 1949.

LENOTRE, THÉODORE GOSSELIN: *Paris Révolutionnaire*. Paris, 1894.

———: *Vieilles Maisons, Vieux Papiers*. Paris, 1900.

LOBET, J.: *Histoire du Bois de Boulogne*. Paris, 1856.

MICHELET, JULES: *Histoire de France*. Paris, 1868.

NOLHAC, PIERRE DE: *Marie-Antoinette, dauphine*. Paris, 1898.

——: *La reine Marie-Antoinette*. Paris, 1899.

SCHNUR, HARRY C.: *Mystic Rebels: Apollonius Tyaneus, Jan van Leyden, Sabbatai Zevi, Cagliostro*. London, 1949.

SOCARD, ÉMILE: *Table généalogique de la Maison de Valois Saint-Rémy*. Troyes, 1858.

SOUDAK, LOUIS DE: "Un procès à reviser," *Le Temps*, Paris, Apr. 1, 1902.

THÉVENOT, ARSÈNE: *Notice topographique, statistique et historique sur Fontette*. Bar-sur-Seine, 1884.

TOCQUEVILLE, ALEXIS DE: *L'Ancien Régime et la Révolution*. Paris, 1856.

TROWBRIDGE, W. R. H.: *Cagliostro*. London, 1910.

WILDING, PETER: *Adventurers in the Eighteenth Century*. London, 1938.

ZWEIG, STEFAN: *Marie Antoinette*. London, 1950.

Index

Adhémar, Count d', 362–3, 505

Aligre, Etienne-François, Marquis d', 324, 341–2, 344, 435, 448, 461–2

Angélique, 502, 503, 504, 507, 508, 509, 510–11, 538

Artois, Charles Philippe, Count d', 32, 116, 123, 160, 231, 270, 528

Artois, Countess d', 123, 160, 182

Artois, Hotel d', 124

Assembly, National (*later* Constituent Assembly), 525, 527, 564, 566–7, 579

Assumption Day, 268, 270–1, 286

Autichamps, Marquis d', 63, 65

Balsamo, Giuseppe *see* Cagliostro, Count di

Bar-sur-Aube, 50–1, 55–9, 62, 147–54, 238, 253, 260, 263–4, 280–1, 305–7, 312–13, 379, 380, 395–6, 479–80

Bassenge, Paul, 246, 259, 260, 377, 432, 585

Bastille, xiii, 277, 278, 289, 293–6, 304, 306–7, 309, 314, 339–41, 365, 429–30, 477, 525–6

Beaumarchais, Pierre Augustin Caron de, xiv, 171, 188, 264, 338

Beausire, Toussaint de, 348–9, 430

Beugnot (father), 53–4, 105, 106, 149

Beugnot, Jacques Claude, Count, 51–2, 104, 292–3, 328–9, 438, 566–7, 587–8

Beugnot, Count (grand-son), 52–3

Beugnot, Mme, 511, 512

Blin, 413–14

Blondel, Maître, 175, 356–7, 360, 474

Böhmer and Bassenge, 35–6, 194, 197–200, 208–9, 211–13, 217, 223–4, 227, 248, 250, 255, 267–8, 289, 334, 347, 373, 376, 394, 432–3, 458, 585–6

Böhmer, Charles, 162–3, 193, 201–4, 205, 206, 239–46, 256–9, 264–6, 272, 273, 373–4

Boulainvilliers, Marquis de, 16, 20–2, 26, 46, 48, 49, 88, 103–5, 111, 402

Boulainvilliers, Marquise de, 16, 17, 18–19, 20, 21, 23, 45, 48, 49, 50, 51, 60, 88–9, 102, 103

Braconiere, Antonio, 84–5

Breteuil, Louis Auguste Le Tonnelier, Baron de, 38, 69–70, 246, 247–51, 255, 258, 266, 267–8, 270, 271, 274–5, 276–7, 305, 310, 316, 339, 366, 432–3, 470, 491, 528, 594

Brienne, Count de, 281

Brienne, Countess de, 281, 282, 283

Briffault, Mme, 124, 125

Briffault, Rosalie, 124, 179, 224, 261, 264, 359, 372, 398–9, 418, 429–30

Brugnières, Inspector de, 225, 226, 303, 475

Brussels, 348–9

Cagliostro, Count Alessandro di, 65, 77–89, 93–9, 100–2, 144–5, 217, 221, 228–34, 237, 248, 301–5, 316, 350, 409–11, 426–9, 455–7, 459, 474–7, 547–56, 593, 596

Cagliostro, Countess di (Serafina Feliciani), 77–8, 80, 86, 94, 228, 303–4, 356, 372, 427–9, 548–9, 551

Calonne, Charles Alexandre, Count de, 120, 324, 507, 517–18, 519

Campan, M., 42, 160, 201–2, 542

621